FORGERY AND MEMORY AT THE END OF THE FIRST MILLENNIUM

Forgery and Memory at the End of the First Millennium

Levi Roach

PRINCETON UNIVERSITY PRESS

PRINCETON & OXFORD

Copyright © 2021 by Princeton University Press

Requests for permission to reproduce material from this work
should be sent to permissions@press.princeton.edu

Published by Princeton University Press
41 William Street, Princeton, New Jersey 08540
6 Oxford Street, Woodstock, Oxfordshire OX20 1TR

press.princeton.edu

ISBN 9780691181660
ISBN (e-book) 9780691217871

Library of Congress Control Number: 2020921533

British Library Cataloging-in-Publication Data is available

Editorial: Ben Tate and Josh Drake
Production Editorial: Natalie Baan
Jacket Design: Sara Pinsonault
Production: Danielle Amatucci
Publicity: Alyssa Sanford and Amy Stewart
Copyeditor: Francis Eaves

Jacket image: Pilgrim's completion stroke on Arnulf's monogram ©BayHStA

This book has been composed in Miller

Printed on acid-free paper. ∞

Printed in the United States of America

10 9 8 7 6 5 4 3 2 1

For Cathy

CONTENTS

List of Maps, Tables and Illustrations · ix
Acknowledgements · xiii
Note on Style and Citations · xv
Abbreviations · xvii
Preface · xxvii

INTRODUCTION   Forgery and Memory in an Age of Iron   1

CHAPTER 1   Forgery in the Chancery? Bishop Anno at Worms   21

CHAPTER 2   Forging Episcopal Identity: Pilgrim at Passau   61

CHAPTER 3   Forging Liberty: Abingdon and Æthelred   113

CHAPTER 4   Forging Exemption: Fleury from Abbo to William   153

CHAPTER 5   True Lies: Leo of Vercelli and the Struggle for
Piedmont   193

CONCLUSIONS   256

Bibliography · 273
General Index · 307
Index of Royal and Papal Charters · 323

MAPS, TABLES AND ILLUSTRATIONS

Maps

1. The bishopric of Worms, *c*. 970 — 22
2. Passau the Bavarian episcopate, *c*. 970 — 64
3. The bishopric of Vercelli and Ivrean march, *c*. 999 — 213

Tables

1. Constituent parts of a later tenth-century diploma (D O I 310) — 9–10
2. Pilgrim's preambles and their Carolingian model — 85
3. Opening protocol of the Gregory IV and Gregory V bulls for Fleury — 181
4. Details on abbatial election in the Gregory IV and Gregory V bulls for Fleury — 182

Illustrations

0.1 The Ottonian (Liudolfing) royal family — xxiii
0.2 The West Saxon royal family — xxiv
0.3 The West Frankish Carolingians — xxv
0.4 The Robertians and early Capetians — xxvi
1.1 Otto I confirms Anno's immunity — 25
1.2 Otto I confirms Richgowo in possession of tolls in Worms — 36
1.3 Otto II confirms Anno in possession of tolls and fiscal rights in Worms — 38
1.4 Latter part of the dating clause of Otto II's confirmation of Anno's toll and fiscal rights — 39
1.5 Otto II settles a dispute over forest rights in the Odenwald in favour of Worms — 43
1.6 a/b Opening *elongatae* of Otto II's Odenwald diploma and those of his earlier Magdeburg charter — 44
1.7 Diploma of Otto I in favour of Gumbert — 47
1.8 Otto II's lost diploma granting Mosbach to Worms (reproduced from a modern photo) — 50

2.1 The first diploma of Pilgrim of Passau   67

2.2 Pilgrim's Charlemagne forgery   84

2.3 Pilgrim's Louis the Pious forgery   87

2.4 a/b Pilgrim's Louis the Pious forgery and its imitative
copy (detail)   88

2.5 Passau Ötting forgery in the name of King Arnulf   90

2.6 Pilgrim's forged Arnulf immunity   92

2.7 a/b Pilgrim's completion stroke on Arnulf's monogram vs
that of an authentic diploma in his name   92

2.8 Closing eschatocol of Otto II's confirmation of Pilgrim's
possessions in the Wachau   96

2.9 a/b Monograms in Pilgrim's Kremsmünster diplomas,
as rendered in the Codex Lonsdorfianus   98

2.10 The first copy of Pilgrim's Niedernburg diploma   100

2.11 Otto II's grant of a residence in Regensburg to
Frederick of Salzburg   101

2.12 Closing eschatocol of Otto II's confirmation of Pilgrim's
immunity   102

2.13 The final (authorized) version of Pilgrim's
Niedernburg diploma   103

2.14 Otto II's grant of Ennsburg to Pilgrim   105

3.1 Æthelred restores liberty to Abingdon   115

3.2 Copy of a papal *rota* in the earlier version of the
Abingdon cartulary-chronicle   129

3.3 a/b Witness-lists of the Eadwig and Edgar *Orthodoxorum*
charters, as preserved in the earlier version of the
Abingdon cartulary-chronicle   132/133

3.4 Æthelred grants liberty to St Germans   137

3.5 Pershore *Orthodoxorum* charter   139

3.6 a/b Other alpha-omega chrismons of the tenth century   139

3.7 Eadred's purported confirmation of Downton and
Ebbesborne to the Old Minster, Winchester   149

4.1 Robert the Pious's diploma restoring Yèvre to Fleury   162

4.2 Script of Robert the Pious's Yèvre diploma   164

4.3 Alexander II's confirmation of Fleury's exemption   176

4.4 Earliest copy of Fleury's forged Gregory IV exemption   178

4.5 List of emperors in an eleventh-century Fleury manuscript   179

4.6 Script of the earliest copy of Fleury's forged Gregory IV
exemption   180

5.1 Erasure of Arduin's name within Warmund's 'Arduin dossier' 201

5.2 Autograph (?) cross of Adelheid's advocate 214

5.3 Example of gaps and insertions in the judicial notice
confirming Hugh of Tuscany's grant of Caresana 216

5.4 Bishop Peter's entries in the Vercelli martyrology-necrology
(probable entries highlighted) 220

5.5 Count Otto-William's donation of Orco 224

5.6 The dorse (reverse) of Arduin of Ivrea's diploma
for Tedevert 225

5.7 Earliest copy of Charles the Fat's notice for Vercelli 228

5.8 Early imitative copy of Otto III's concession of comital
rights to Vercelli 232

5.9 Arduin of Ivrea's grant of Desana to Cunibert 239

5.10 Arduin of Ivrea's grant to Alberic of Gassino 244

5.11 Bishop Leo's excommunication of Count Hubert 'the Red' 249

5.12 Twelfth-century copy of Henry II's two diplomas for Vercelli 251

5.13 Leo of Vercelli's own working draft of Henry II's diploma
of 1014 × 1017 (alongside other additions in his hand) 252

ACKNOWLEDGEMENTS

DESPITE ITS POPULAR image, academic study is rarely a solitary pursuit. And if, as the old adage runs, it takes a village to raise a child, then it takes a department to write a monograph. I have certainly been more than fortunate in my department. It was with the advice of colleagues in the Department of History at Exeter that I was able to secure the funding which enabled the research and writing behind this book; and ever since, they have been a constant source of sage counsel and constructive criticism. Particular thanks go to Sarah Hamilton, who read multiple drafts of the original funding application; Simon Barton, who showed an early interest in the project (but sadly did not live to see its completion); and Helen Birkett, who has patiently listened to my (often inchoate) thoughts on memory and ecclesiastical identity in the early and central Middle Ages for over four years now.

The research behind the book was made possible by generous funding from the Arts and Humanities Research Council (project grant: AH/P01495X/1). This not only covered a spell of leave from teaching duties in 2017–19, but also enabled numerous archival trips. It is a truism that serious work on medieval documentary traditions must be undertaken at the archival coalface, and I am fortunate to have been able to spend so much of the last three years there. I also owe a great debt to those archivists across Europe who have opened their doors to me, in person or electronically. Particular thanks go to Kathrin Kininger, who made the Haus-, Hof- und Staatsarchiv in Vienna feel like a home away from home; Timoty Leonardi of the Archivio Capitolare in Vercelli, who eased my entry into the Italian archival scene; Patrizia Carpo of the Archivio Storico (Archivio del Comune) in Vercelli, who let me run riot on her documents, at literally no notice; and Laura Tos of the Archivio Storico Castello di Masino, who went out of her way to have a rare diploma of Arduin photographed on my behalf. At a time when politicians in this country seem determined to burn bridges with our European neighbours, the generosity of these kind souls has been a constant and welcome reminder that a better future is possible.

Thanks also go to the many colleagues who have assisted in the research process, especially when—as was frequently the case—I stepped outside my traditional areas of expertise. Giacomo Vignodelli, Henry Parkes, Thomas Kohl, Ed Roberts, Justin Lake, Geoff Koziol, Sarah Greer, Megan Welton, Jürgen Dendorfer, Christolf Rolker, Björn Weiler, Rory Naismith, Ross Balzaretti, Florian Dirks, Dominik Waßenhoven, Guy Halsall, Susan Kelly, David Bachrach and Rutger Kramer all shared work-in-progress, thoughts or scans of hard-to-find publications. Simon Keynes, who first introduced me to the arcane world of charter criticism a decade and a half ago, helped secure images for reproduction during the difficult months of COVID-19 lockdown. Nick Vincent, David Bates and Ben Pohl assisted in my forays into French archival history and palaeography. And Bob Berkhofer generously shared his own thoughts on forgery on a number of occasions. I am similarly beholden to Fraser McNair for detailed comments on an early version of chapter 4. Even greater is my debt to Sarah Hamilton and Ed Roberts (both thanked a second time now), who read through the entire manuscript with great care and attention. Few know their way around the Latin West in the tenth century as well as Sarah and Ed, and the book is much the better for their input. Thanks are also due to Princeton University Press's two readers—who subsequently revealed themselves to be Geoff Koziol and Conrad Leyser—whose perspicacity helped turn a rather rough draft into a much more polished finished product. Finally, many friends and colleagues have provided more informal support, encouragement and discussion along the way (frequently over tea or beer). I should especially like to thank Helen Birkett (again), Danica Summerlin, Johanna Dale and Jennie England.

Throughout the process of writing and revising, the staff at Princeton University Press have been a model of professionalism. Ben Tate was a supportive and encouraging editor from the start, and accepted with good humour a manuscript with far more illustrations than he had anticipated. His colleagues, Josh Drake, Natalie Baan and Theresa Liu have guided it through to print in masterly fashion; and Francis Eaves's careful copyediting has caught more errors and inconsistencies than I would care to admit.

My greatest debt, however, is reflected in the dedication. My wife Catherine Flavelle has been a constant source of love, support and companionship for over a decade now. She was there when the project was first conceived; and she was there—minding our screaming four-month-old daughter—when the first full draft was completed. This book, my greatest academic labour of love to date, is for her.

Tiverton, The Feast of St Maurice, 2020

NOTE ON STYLE AND CITATIONS

BOOKS ON 'DIPLOMATIC'—the formal study of documentary traditions—are rarely page-turners. This is partly the nature of the subject. Much expertise is required to work with such texts, and it is understandable that diplomatists often fall into the habit of speaking to a few fellow cognoscenti. The result is works of lasting scholarly value, but rarely books one can commend to the student or interested general reader. In the following pages, I have done my best to take a different approach. While some of the material covered is (of necessity) highly technical, I have attempted to discuss it in a manner accessible—or at least comprehensible—to a non-specialist. This is not because I believe there is an untapped mass market for academic works on diplomatic (though my publishers will doubtless be delighted if this proves to be so). Rather, it is because I am convinced that the future of the subdiscipline depends on making our work less intimidating and arcane. I have always found working with charters fun; here I hope to share some of that enthusiasm.

For similar reasons, I have sought to streamline citations. All the most essential literature is cited (so far as it is known to me); however, preference is given to the most recent or relevant studies. Much of the literature cited is inevitably not in English, and I have not sought to hide this fact. However, in the interests of accessibility, I have cited translations where they exist. The only exceptions are cases where references have been removed from the translation (as with Heinrich Fichtenau's superb *Lebensordnungen*) or where I already happened to own working copies of the text in the original (as with Jan Assmann's *Kulturelles Gedächtnis*). Here, I have cited the translation alongside the original at the first point of reference, but thereafter have preferred the latter.

Abing	*Charters of Abingdon Abbey*, ed. S. E. Kelly, 2 pts, AS Charters 7–8 (Oxford, 2000–2001)
AC	Archivio Capitolare
AfD	*Archiv für Diplomatik*
ANS	*Anglo-Norman Studies*
AS	Archivio di Stato
ASC	*Anglo-Saxon Chronicle*
AS Charters	Anglo-Saxon Charters
ASE	*Anglo-Saxon England*
AfU	*Archiv für Urkundenforschung*
BA Facs.	*Facsimiles of Anglo-Saxon Charters*, ed. S. Keynes, AS Charters: Supplementary Series 1 (London, 1991)
Bark	*Charters of Barking Abbey*, ed. S. E. Kelly, AS Charters (Oxford, forthcoming)
BAV	Biblioteca Apostolica Vaticana
BayHStA	Bayerisches Hauptstaatsarchiv
BC	Biblioteca Capitolare
BCS	*Cartularium Saxonicum: A Collection of Charters Relating to Anglo-Saxon History*, ed. W. de G. Birch, 3 vols (London, 1885–93)
BEC	*Bibliothèque de l'École des chartes*
BL	London, British Library
BM Facs.	*Facsimiles of Ancient Charters in the British Museum*, ed. E. A. Bond et al., 4 vols (London, 1873–78)
BnF	Paris, Bibliothèque nationale de France
BSSS	Biblioteca della Società Storica Subalpina
BSV	*Bollettino Storico Vercellese*
Burt	*Charters of Burton Abbey*, ed. P. H. Sawyer, AS Charters 2 (Oxford, 1979)

CantCC	*Charters of Christ Church, Canterbury*, ed. N. Brooks and S. E. Kelly, 2 pts, AS Charters 17–18 (Oxford, 2013)
CCCC	Cambridge, Corpus Christi College
CCCM	Corpus Christianorum Continuatio Mediaevalis
CCM	Corpus Consuetudinum Monasticarum
CCSL	Corpus Christianorum Series Latina
CDL	*Codice diplomatico longobardo*
DA	*Deutsches Archiv für Erforschung des Mittelalters*
DBI	*Dizionario Biografico degli Italiani*
D(D) Ard	*Die Urkunden Heinrichs II. und Arduins*, ed. H. Bresslau, MGH: Diplomata regum et imperatorum Germaniae 3 (Hanover, 1900–1903)
D(D) Arn	*Die Urkunden Arnolfs*, ed. P. Kehr, MGH: Diplomata regum Germaniae ex stirpe Karolinorum 3 (Berlin, 1940)
D(D) Ber	*I diplomi di Berengario I*, ed. L. Schiaparelli, FSI 25 (Rome, 1903)
D(D) BerAd	*I diplomi di Ugo e di Lotario, di Berengario II e di Adalberto*, ed. L. Schiaparelli, FSI 38 (Rome, 1924)
D(D) H II	*Die Urkunden Heinrichs II. und Arduins*, ed. H. Bresslau, MGH: Diplomata regum et imperatorum Germaniae 3 (Hanover, 1900–1903)
D(D) H III	*Die Urkunden Heinrichs III.*, ed. H. Bresslau and P. Kehr, MGH: Diplomata regum et imperatorum Germaniae 5 (Berlin, 1931)
D(D) H IV	*Die Urkunden Heinrichs IV.*, ed. D. von Gladiss and A. Gawlik, MGH: Diplomata regum et imperatorum Germaniae 6 (Berlin/Weimar/Hanover, 1941–78)
D(D) HuLo	*I diplomi di Ugo e di Lotario, di Berengario II e di Adalberto*, ed. L. Schiaparelli, FSI 38 (Rome, 1924)
D(D) Kar	*Die Urkunden Pippins, Karlmanns und Karls des Großen*, ed. E. Mühlbacher, MGH: Diplomata Karolinorum 1 (Hanover, 1906)
D(D) K III	*Die Urkunden Karls III.*, ed. P. Kehr, MGH: Diplomata regum Germaniae ex stirpe Karolinorum 2 (Berlin, 1937)

D(D) K I	*Die Urkunden Konrads I., Heinrichs I. und Ottos I.*, ed. T. Sickel, MGH: Diplomata regum et imperatorum Germaniae 1 (Hanover, 1879–84)
D(D) K II	*Die Urkunden Konrads II.*, ed. H. Bresslau, MGH: Diplomata regum et imperatorum Germaniae 4 (Hanover, 1909)
D(D) Km	*Die Urkunden Ludwigs des Deutschen, Karlmanns und Ludwigs des Jüngeren*, ed. P. Kehr, MGH: Diplomata regum Germaniae ex stirpe Karolinorum 1 (Berlin, 1934)
D(D) L D	*Die Urkunden Ludwigs des Deutschen, Karlmanns und Ludwigs des Jüngeren*, ed. P. Kehr, MGH: Diplomata regum Germaniae ex stirpe Karolinorum 1 (Berlin, 1934)
D(D) L Fr	*Die Urkunden Ludwigs des Frommen*, ed. T. Kölzer, 3 pts, MGH: Diplomata Karolinorum 2 (Hanover, 2016)
D(D) L K	*Die Urkunden Zwentibolds und Ludwigs des Kindes*, ed. T. Schieffer, MGH: Diplomata Karolinorum 4 (Berlin, 1960)
D(D) Lo I	*Die Urkunden Lothars I. und Lothars II.*, ed. T. Schieffer, Diplomatum Karolinorum 3 (Berlin, 1966)
D(D) Mer	*Die Urkunden der Merowinger*, ed. T. Kölzer, 2 pts, MGH: Diplomata regum Francorum e stirpe Merovingica (Hanover, 2001)
D(D) O I	*Die Urkunden Konrads I., Heinrichs I. und Ottos I.*, ed. T. Sickel, MGH: Diplomata regum et imperatorum Germaniae 1 (Hanover, 1879–84)
D(D) O II	*Die Urkunden Otto des II.*, ed. T. Sickel, MGH: Diplomata regum et imperatorum Germaniae 2.i (Hanover, 1888)
D(D) O III	*Die Urkunden Otto des III.*, ed. T. Sickel, MGH: Diplomata regum et imperatorum Germaniae 2.ii (Hanover, 1893)
EHR	*English Historical Review*
EME	*Early Medieval Europe*
FMSt	*Frühmittelalterliche Studien*
FSI	Fonti per la storia d'Italia
GDB	*Great Domesday Book: Library Edition*, ed. A. Williams and R. W. H. Erskine, 6 vols (London, 1986–1992)
GLA	Generallandesarchiv

Glast	*Charters of Glastonbury*, ed. S. E. Kelly, AS Charters 15 (Oxford, 2012)
HHStA	Hof-, Haus- und Staatsarchiv
HMC	Historical Manuscripts Commission
HSJ	*Haskins Society Journal*
HStA	Hessisches Staatsarchiv
HZ	*Historische Zeitschrift*
JE, JK, JL	*Regesta Pontificum Romanorum ab condita ecclesia ad annum post Christum natum 1198*, ed. P. Jaffé, rev. S. Loewenfeld, F. Kaltenbrunner and P. Ewald, 2 pts (Leipzig, 1885–88)
JMH	*Journal of Medieval History*
KCD	*Codex Diplomaticus Aevi Saxonici*, ed. J. M. Kemble, 6 vols (London, 1839–48)
KUA	*Kaiserurkunden in Abbildungen*, ed. H. von Sybel and T. Sickel, 12 vols (Berlin, 1880–91)
LA	Landesarchiv
Malm	*Charters of Malmesbury Abbey*, ed. S. E. Kelly, AS Charters 11 (Oxford, 2005)
MGH:	Monumenta Germaniae Historica:
Dip. regum	Diplomata regum et imperatorum Germaniae
Epp.	Epistolae
Fontes iuris	Fontes iuris Germanici antiqui in usum scholarum
Leges nat. Germ.	Leges nationum Germanicarum
SS	Scriptores
SS rer. Germ.	Scriptores rerum Germanicarum in usum scholarum
SS rer. Germ. n.s.	Scriptores rerum Germanicarum: series nova
MIÖG	*Mitteilungen des Instituts für Österreichische Geschichtsforschung*
NA	*Neues Archiv der Gesellschaft für ältere deutsche Geschichtskunde*
North	*Charters of the Northern Houses*, ed. D. A. Woodman, AS Charters 16 (Oxford, 2012)
OS Facs.	*Facsimiles of Anglo-Saxon Manuscripts*, ed. W. B. Saunders, 3 vols, Ordnance Survey (Southampton, 1878–84)

Pet	*Charters of Peterborough Abbey*, ed. S. E. Kelly, AS Charters 14 (Oxford, 2009)
PL	Patrologia Cursus Completus. Series (Latina) Prima, ed. J.-P. Migne, 221 vols (Paris, 1844–64)
QFIAB	*Quellen und Forschungen aus italienischen Archiven und Bibliotheken*
RB	*Revue Bénédictine*
Recueil Charles III	*Recueil des actes de Charles III le Simple, roi de France, 893–923*, ed. F. Lot and P. Lauer (Paris, 1949)
Recueil Lothaire et Louis V	*Recueil des actes de Lothaire et Louis V, rois de France, 954–987*, ed. L. Halphen with F. Lot (Paris, 1908)
Recueil Philippe Ier	*Recueil des actes de Philippe Ier, roi de France (1059–1108)*, ed. M. Prou (Paris, 1908)
Recueil Saint-Benoît	*Recueil des chartes de l'abbey de Saint-Benoît-sur-Loire*, ed. M. Prou and A. Vidier, 2 vols (Paris, 1900–1907)
Roch	*Charters of Rochester*, ed. A. Campbell, AS Charters 1 (Oxford, 1973)
S	*Anglo-Saxon Charters: An Annotated List and Bibliography*, ed. P. H. Sawyer, rev. S. E. Kelly and R. Rushforth (https://esawyer.lib.cam.ac.uk)
SB Berlin	*Sitzungsberichte der Königlich Preußischen Akademie der Wissenschaften zu Berlin*
SB Wien	*Sitzungsberichte der Kaiserlichen Akademie der Wissenschaften in Wien: Philosophisch-Historische Klasse*
SC	Sources chrétiennes
Sel	*Charters of Selsey*, ed. S. E. Kelly, AS Charters 6 (Oxford, 1996)
Settimane	*Settimane di studio del Centro italiano di studi sull'alto medioevo*
Shaft	*Charters of Shaftesbury Abbey*, ed. S. E. Kelly, AS Charters 5 (Oxford, 1995)
Sherb	*Charters of Sherborne*, ed. M. A. O'Donovan, AS Charters 3 (Oxford, 1988)
StAlb	*Charters of St Albans*, ed. J. Crick, AS Charters 12 (Oxford, 2007)

SUB	*Salzburger Urkundenbuch*, ii, *Urkunden von 790–1199*, ed. W. Hauthaler (Salzburg, 1916)
TRHS	*Transactions of the Royal Historical Society*
WinchNM	*Charters of the New Minster, Winchester*, ed. S. Miller, AS Charters 9 (Oxford, 2001)
ZGO	*Zeitschrift für Geschichte des Oberreheins*
ZPUU	*Papsturkunden 896–1046*, ed. H. Zimmermann, 2 pts, rev. ed. (Vienna, 1988)
ZRG	*Zeitschrift des Savigny-Stiftung für Rechtsgeschichte*
GA	*Germanistische Abteilung*
KA	*Kanonistische Abteilung*

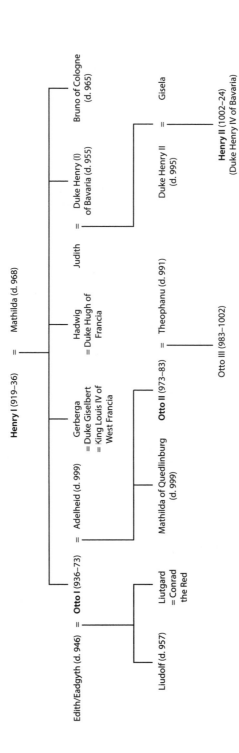

0.1 The Ottonian (Liudolfing) royal family

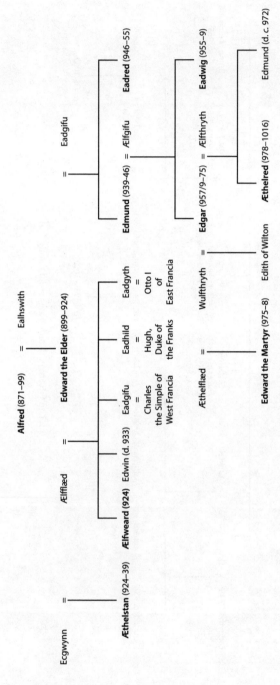

0.2 The West Saxon royal family

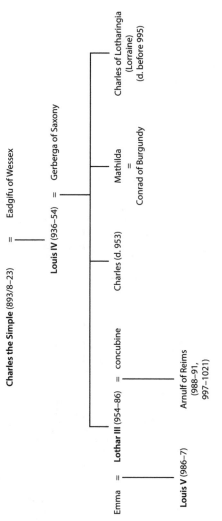

Charles the Simple (893/8–23)   =   Eadgifu of Wessex

Louis IV (936–54)   =   Gerberga of Saxony

Emma   =   Lothar III (954–86)   =   concubine

Charles (d. 953)

Mathilda
=
Conrad of Burgundy

Charles of Lotharingia
(Lorraine)
(d. before 995)

Louis V (986–7)

Arnulf of Reims
(988–91,
997–1021)

0.3 The West Frankish Carolingians

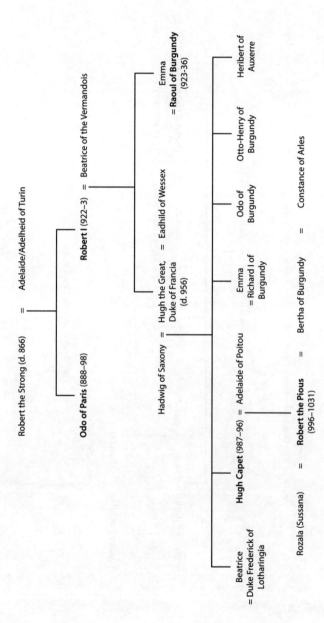

o.4 The Robertians and early Capetians

IN THE EARLY 970s, Pilgrim, the newly elected bishop of Passau in eastern Bavaria (971–91), began to survey the history of his see. The results were disheartening. Beyond a brace of privileges in the names of earlier monarchs, there was little to go on—certainly no indication of the exalted history Pilgrim had hoped to find. In his student days at Salzburg, he had read widely about the history of the region. It was probably there that he first encountered the *Life* of the fifth-century saint Severin (d. 482), detailing the experiences of the Mediterranean holy man during the turbulent decades which witnessed the eclipse of the Western Roman Empire; this work was also now available to Pilgrim at Passau. Wherever he may have come across it, Pilgrim's attention was now drawn to a fleeting reference in the *Life* to a pontiff (*pontifex*) called Constantius, who had been based at Lorch (in modern Upper Austria) in Severin's day. Lorch lay within Pilgrim's diocese, and this account suggested that there had been a bishopric in the area as early as the fifth century, long before the foundation of Passau or Salzburg, Pilgrim's neighbour and metropolitan to the south-west. That Lorch had indeed been an important early centre was borne out by physical remains of settlement there, including prominent antique walls and church buildings—remains Pilgrim knew at first hand. Perhaps most tantalizing of all, the Latin term used to designate this Constantius, *pontifex*, was an ambiguous one, equally applicable to a bishop or an archbishop (or even pope). In Pilgrim's eyes, Constantius soon became not just a lowly bishop, but a metropolitan charged with authority over all Noricum (as the region was known)—the first on record.[1]

Surveying this material, Pilgrim concluded that Salzburg's version of local history was partial and skewed, and that his own Passau (and its precursor at Lorch) had a much bigger part to play. Indeed, he became convinced that Passau was the lineal descendent of Lorch; and as such, the rightful regional archbishopric. An aside in a saint's *Life* and a few physical remains may seem like a slender basis on which to build such wide-ranging speculation. But this was all that Pilgrim had—and it was, in any case, hardly less plausible than many other versions of local history (Salzburg's included). These prospects were too good to ignore. Perhaps Pilgrim was an archbishop, after all!

The problem, of course, lay in convincing others of this. None of the surviving documents from Passau made reference to Lorch or a longer metropolitan past, nor was anything of the kind to be found at Salzburg. It was easy to explain some of these gaps. If external threats had forced the see's relocation

1. See further below, ch. 2.

from Lorch to Passau (as Pilgrim came to believe), then it was understandable that it should have lost many of its earliest records. Still, if Pilgrim was to be taken seriously, he would need more to show for his efforts than speculation and hearsay. Luckily for him, his early education had prepared him for the challenge. He was well acquainted with local history and knew at first hand the archives at Salzburg, where many fine examples of earlier documentary forms were to be found; he was also a deft hand at charter production, having written at least one such document in Salzburg's favour. Pilgrim now turned these skills against his old associates at the Salzach river metropolitan, producing a series of false privileges in the names of earlier popes, ranging from Symmachus (498–514) to Benedict (probably VII, 974–83), all of which served to demonstrate Passau's archiepiscopal past and direct descent from Lorch. To lend weight to these, Pilgrim also manufactured false diplomas in the names of the Carolingian rulers of the eighth and ninth centuries. The resulting texts amount to an impressive documentary edifice, a homage to Passau's purported metropolitan past. For Pilgrim, where there was a will, there truly was a way.

He was not alone in this attitude. Pilgrim's older contemporary Anno of Worms (950–78) had overseen a similarly ambitious set of forgeries in favour of his Rhineland see. Nor was forgery an exclusively 'German' phenomenon: in Vercelli, Bishop Leo (999–1026) was active in manipulating local documentary records, while the monks of Abingdon and Fleury oversaw equally ambitious campaigns of falsification in the tenth and eleventh centuries. And these figures represent but the tip of an iceberg.

What these individuals were doing was, on one level, nothing new. As Anthony Grafton notes, forgery is as old as textual authority—indeed older, if we do not restrict ourselves to the written record—and they were hardly the first to undertake such activity.[2] At another level, however, their actions *were* novel. As we shall see, the total haul of forgeries from the period between the Fall of Rome in the fifth century and Pilgrim's episcopate in the late tenth is remarkably small. Moreover, the earlier fakes that survive are, with a few notable exceptions—exceptions to which we shall return—more mundane and prosaic than those of Pilgrim and his contemporaries. Clearly something was afoot; more people were forging at greater length, and greater care was being taken in the preservation of the resulting texts. There was also a subtle but unmistakable shift in focus. Forgers of the tenth century do not simply claim legal rights, as their forebears had done; they also paint a history of the religious house in question. Here they were the heirs to the more prolific and adventurous falsifiers of the ninth century. Their products even stand out visually, preserving some of the earliest identified examples of imitative script from the Middle Ages.[3] All of this points toward a heightened sense of the

2. Grafton, *Forgers and Critics*, 8.
3. Crick, 'Insular History?', assembles the evidence from England.

past: scribes and readers were more keenly aware of the differences between present and past documentary forms, and were doing their best to bridge this gap. These developments are not limited to a single realm or region, but can be charted across western Europe.

This book is an attempt to make sense of these trends. After an Introduction surveying medieval forgery and its later tenth-century manifestations, we proceed roughly chronologically, taking Anno, Pilgrim, Abingdon, Fleury and Leo in turn. Each of these forgery complexes offers a starting point for considering wider issues of institutional memory and documentary culture. Though the prevalence of forgery in the Middle Ages has sometimes been taken as evidence of the childish naiveté of the period—as an indication that, in the words of one leading authority, the people of the era 'had no historical sense'[4]—here a different approach is taken. Far from revealing blind anachronism, it is suggested that forgery demonstrates a keen awareness of the contradictions within existing records and a desire to resolve these.[5] Forgery was (and is), in other words, a sign of historical sophistication of the highest order. Viewed in these terms, the story of forgery becomes a tale of innovation and experimentation, of the dynamic uses to which people of the tenth and eleventh centuries—and the Middle Ages more generally—put their historical records.

4. Clanchy, *Memory to Written Record*, 320. See similarly Stock, *Implications of Literacy*, 60–62, 455–521.

5. See similarly Crick, 'Insular History?', and 'Script'. Cf. C. S. Wood, *Forgery*, 125–27.

FORGERY AND MEMORY AT THE END OF
THE FIRST MILLENNIUM

Forgery and Memory
in an Age of Iron

FORGERY WAS NOT particular to Europe or the Middle Ages. It was known in ancient Greece and Rome, where authors such as Galen and Martial railed against literary impersonation; it was also rife in early Christian society, with many of the biblical apocrypha—not to mention a number of now-canonical texts—being products of forgery.[1] Nor was falsification new then. Some Old Testament books bear the hallmarks of forgery (most notably, Daniel); and evidence of textual falsification can be traced even further back, to the very origins of Eurasian civilization in the Nile, Tigris and Euphrates valleys.

These early fakes have much to teach the scholar of ancient and medieval forgery. Perhaps the oldest on record is a decree of the eighteenth-dynasty pharaoh Amenhotep III (c. 1391–c. 1353 BC) for his funerary temple in Thebes. This survives as an inscription exempting the temple from the normal demands of royal officers, save the local mayor of West Thebes. But while this may look perfectly pukka, there was no mayor of West Thebes in Amenhotep's reign; and the hieroglyphs themselves are formed in a manner not seen before the twenty-first dynasty (c. 1169–c. 945 BC), some three to four hundred years later. Evidently this was an attempt, probably around the turn of the first millennium BC, to claim special rights for a once-important centre.[2] A similar situation is reflected in the Cruciform Monument, found at the Ebabbar temple at Sippar (modern Tell Abu Habbah in Iraq) and now housed in the British Museum in London. This records the successes of the Akkadian ruler Maništušu (c. 2270–c. 2255 BC) and the gifts he made to the temple.[3] The

---

1. Speyer, *Literarische Fälschung*. On Graeco-Roman forgery, see further Peirano, *Rhetoric*; Higbie, *Collectors, Scholars, and Forgers*; and on early Christian forgery: Ehrman, *Forgery and Counterforgery*, and *Lost Christianities*, 9–89.

2. Murnane, 'Organization of Government', 219–20.

3. Rollston, 'Forging History', esp. 177–80.

inscription is written in the king's voice; however, the form it takes can be no earlier than the Old Babylonian period (*c.* 2000–*c.* 1600 BC), and probably belongs to the Neo-Babylonian period (*c.* 626–*c.* 539 BC), over a millennium and a half later.

A final early example is offered by the Famine Stele, located on Sehel Island in the Nile. This records a severe seven-year famine and drought which struck Egypt under the third-dynasty pharaoh Djoser, in the mid-third millennium BC. Disaster is reported to have been averted only when the pharaoh's leading adviser, Imhotep, suggested that Djoser appeal to Khnum, the god of the Nile based at Elephantine. This last roll of the dice succeeded and, as a consequence, Djoser granted the temple traditional pharaonic prerogatives in the region. Yet as in the previous cases, the story is too good to be true. As it survives, the Stele is clearly a product of the Ptolemaic period (*c.* 332–30 BC), over two millennia after its purported date. This was a time when myths and legends surrounding Imhotep—subsequently immortalized by Boris Karloff in the 1932 Hollywood blockbuster *The Mummy* (and more recently reprised by Arnold Vosloo in its 1999 remake)—were rife; it was also a time in which the priests of Elephantine lost many of their local rights to the temple of Isis at neighbouring Philae.[4] Once more, we are dealing with creative anachronism. The defining feature of these early fakes—and doubtless many others, since lost (or as yet unidentified)—is a desire to use the past to cement current claims. It is no coincidence that they should all belong to religious houses. In ancient Egypt and the Middle East, as in medieval Europe, the religious classes were specialists in literacy, some of the few capable of presenting and recording complex claims in written form. They also possessed a strong sense of corporate identity (like the later medieval clergy), which encouraged the creation of such false narratives.

Yet if the desire to deceive (and be deceived) is universal, the manner in which it is pursued is not. In the ancient Middle East, our best evidence comes (not surprisingly) from the epigraphic record, not least in the form of the monuments just mentioned. In ancient Greece and Rome, we begin to hear more of the falsification of ephemeral records, with forged wills figuring in the great codifications of Roman law by Theodosius (438) and Justinian (529 × 534). We can also observe the first vogue for authorial impersonation, reflecting the growing importance of named authors within the literary canon. Such literary falsification would later flourish among the Renaissance humanists of early modern Europe, who drew much of their inspiration from Classical antiquity. In the seventeenth and eighteenth centuries, meanwhile, the Grand Tour sparked a similar boom in epigraphic forgery, as continental dealers sought to meet the new demand for antiquities in north-western Europe.

4. Ibid. On Imhotep, see Wildung, *Egyptian Saints*; on the loss of rights: Hölbl, *Ptolemaic Empire*, 167–68.

The nineteenth and early twentieth century then saw a similar spike in counterfeit Greek, Middle Eastern and (above all) Egyptian texts and artefacts, as growing scholarly expertise, improved transportation and the development of European and American museum collections combined to inspire successive waves of Graeco- and Egyptomania. In more recent times, artwork and currency have garnered the lion's share of falsifiers' attention (and with it, the public eye); nevertheless, the antiquities market has also seen a significant uptick in false wares, particularly since the discovery of the Dead Sea Scrolls in the 1960s.[5]

In the European Middle Ages, the most common form of forgery—at least so far as our records reveal (an important caveat)—was the manufacture of false documents. Indeed, the period has, with some justification, been seen as a golden age of documentary forgery, a time before modern means of criticism, when the counterfeit was king. Numbers bear this out. Well over half of the surviving diplomas in the names of the Merovingian Frankish rulers of mainland Europe (c. 481–752) are products of forgery; a third of the charters of the Lombard rulers of northern Italy (568–774) are suspect; and over a third of the documents from pre-Conquest England have been tampered with in some way.[6] In almost all cases, these adjustments were made in the Middle Ages, sometimes within a lifetime or two of the documents' purported dates. Not surprisingly, forgers were particularly drawn to famous figures. Just as the creators of the Famine Stele latched onto the legendary Imhotep, so in the Middle Ages falsifiers saddled their productions on well-known and authoritative individuals, such as the Merovingian ruler Dagobert I (623–39), the Carolingian emperor Charlemagne (768–814) and the last monarch of Anglo-Saxon England's native line, Edward the Confessor (1042–66).[7]

Medieval Forgery and Modern Scholarship

As a general rule, the earlier one goes and the more famous the ruler, the higher the proportion of fakes. This was already known in the Middle Ages. But before the development of modern means of investigation—and before

---

5. Ancient Greece and Rome: Speyer, *Literarische Fälschung*, 111–49; Higbie, *Collectors, Scholars, and Forgers*; Peirano, *Rhetoric*; early modern Europe: Stephens and Havens, eds, *Literary Forgery*; Grafton, *Forgers and Critics*; Rowland, *Scarith*; the Grand Tour: Barron, 'Latin Inscriptions'; Egyptomania: Fiechter, *Egyptian Fakes*; various aspects of modern forgery: Rollston, 'Non-Provenanced Epigraphs'; Mihm, *Nation of Counterfeiters*; Lenain, *Art Forgery*; Keats, *Forged*; Davis, 'Caves of Dispute'.

6. Brühl, *Studien zu den merowingischen Königsurkunden*, and *Studien zu den langobardischen Königsurkunden*; Kölzer, *Merowingerstudien*; Sawyer, *Anglo-Saxon Charters*.

7. Brühl, *Studien zu den merowingischen Königsurkunden*; Hägermann, 'Urkundenfälschungen'. The specific interest in Dagbobert is being considered by Guy Halsall, who has kindly shared some of his preliminary thoughts with me.

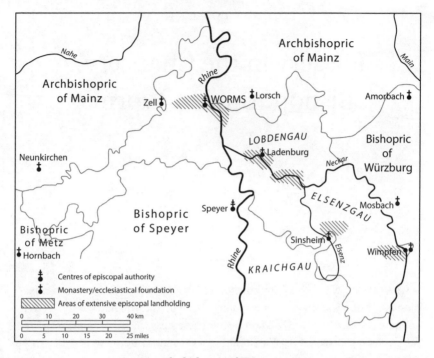

MAP 1. The bishopric of Worms, *c.* 970

these years.[3] Worms was similarly well placed on overland routes, straddling the Roman road west to Metz and Reims and lying near the start of the old *Bergstraße* (mountain road), which ran north–south along this section of the Rhine. Partly as a consequence, the surrounding region—the so-called Rhine-Main district (Rhein-Main-Gebiet)—was one of the royal heartlands, an area in which the Ottonian rulers spent more time than anywhere else save their East Saxon homelands.[4]

But for all these advantages, Worms was a decidedly small and poor bishopric. Its territory was tightly bounded by its neighbours at Mainz, Würzburg, and Speyer, forming a narrow, sickle-shaped strip running from southern Rheinland-Pfalz (Rhineland-Palatinate) through to northern Baden-Württemberg in modern Germany (Map 1). The only smaller see within the realm was the missionary bishopric of Merseburg, first established in 968 and dissolved barely a decade later (981) on account of its poverty.[5] Yet size was only half of the problem. Worms's neighbours were home to important imperial abbeys—Lorsch for Mainz, Weißenburg for Speyer and Fulda for Würzburg—which, if exploited judiciously, might bring additional wealth

3. McCormick, *Origins*, 653–69. See further Wickham, *Medieval Europe*, 121–40.

4. Müller-Mertens, *Reichsstruktur*.

5. Hehl, 'Merseburg'.

the advent of print, allowing findings to be disseminated swiftly (and comparatively inexpensively)—charter criticism was always an uphill battle.[8] The more that scholarly understanding of documentary traditions has developed, therefore, the higher estimations of forgery have become.

In fact, the formal study of medieval documents owes its existence to questions of forgery and authenticity. It was the claim of Daniel Papebroch (d. 1714), that no genuine document survived in the name of an early Merovingian king, which famously spurred the great French Maurist Jean Mabillon (d. 1707) to pen his pioneering treatise on the subject, *De re diplomatica* (On matters relating to charters; 1681). In this, Mabillon established the first serious criteria for judging medieval documents, many of which are used to this day. These were not, however, ivory tower debates. Mabillon's own sometime abbey of Saint-Denis possessed a large number of Merovingian charters (both forged and authentic) and Papebroch's attacks had implications for the centre's standing. Mabillon's work, for all its undoubted learning, was therefore not the act of dispassionate reasoning modern historians have often imagined; it was, first and foremost, a means of defending his own turf.[9]

Still, it was out of these and similar exchanges that the academic study of medieval documents ('diplomatic') was born, starting with Mabillon's own *De re diplomatica*—'On Diplomatic', as we might now call it. As a dedicated subject of study, however, diplomatic first came into its own with the professionalization of the historical profession in the second half of the nineteenth century. At this point, Theodor Sickel (d. 1908), Arthur Giry (d. 1899) and Carlo Cipolla (d. 1916)—to name but three of the most prominent practitioners—made an art of such criticism, turning diplomatic into its own distinctive subdiscipline, with chairs, schools and departments. The focus of these scholars' work was largely editorial, and the attitude taken towards forgery contemptuous; false texts were a problem to be overcome, not a matter of interest in their own right. Once identified, counterfeits could be safely relegated to well-deserved obscurity, often in an appendix to the edition in question. Yet as diplomatic developed in the later nineteenth and early twentieth century, opinions began to change. This was partly a product of the natural evolution of the discipline. As more and more documents came to be edited, scholars started to emphasize their role as interpreters as well as editors of these. Ascertaining forgery and authenticity was now just the first step; the next lay in appreciating what the texts had to say about their wider historical context.[10] Important impetus also came from pioneering studies of a number of particularly large and important forgery complexes, including those at Reichenau, Monte Cassino

---

8. On medieval charter criticism: Bougard and Morelle, 'Prévention'.
9. Brühl, 'Entwicklung'.
10. Ghignoli, 'Definizione dei principi'. See also Tessier, 'Leçon d'ouverture', esp. 262.

and Saint-Denis. These revealed just how subtle (and systematic) medieval forgers could be, and how important it was to study their work in isolation.[11]

As ever more forgeries came to be identified (and associated with known figures), their value as sources in their own right became clearer. Such texts may tell us little about their purported point of origin, but they reveal much about the context in which they were confected—about the concerns of the forgers and the threats faced by their communities. Forgery was, moreover, far too widespread to be dismissed as the reserve of one or two recalcitrant rogues; it was practised by many of medieval Europe's great and good, including leading bishops, abbots and intellectuals. This revelation posed the 'problem of medieval forgery': how was an age of faith also an age of falsification? This question famously drove T. F. Tout (d. 1929), one of England's pioneers of diplomatic, in his study of 'Mediæval Forgers and Forgery' (1919). Tout emphasized that medieval sensibilities were very different from modern ones, noting that 'it was almost the duty of the clerical class to forge'; by doing so, it served God and his earthly communities.[12] Similar themes were later taken up by Horst Fuhrmann (d. 2011), Christopher Brooke (d. 2015), and Giles Constable (1929–), in the mid- to later years of the twentieth century.[13] The central contention of their work, like that of Tout, was that medieval attitudes toward truth and fiction were different from our own. In an era in which divine providence was felt to guide historical events, the study of the past possessed a pronounced moral dimension; true history was that which accorded with God's plans, not necessarily that attested by prior documents. Medieval forgers may, therefore, have acted in the conviction that they were doing good. Most falsification was, on this view, pious fraud (or *pia fraus*), intended to enlighten, not to deceive.

There is much to be said for this approach. It reminds us that attitudes towards truth and falsehood are culturally conditioned; it also explains why manifestly God-fearing men were willing to forge, sometimes on epic scales. But lingering doubts remain. If forgery was acceptable in the Middle Ages, why was it so often condemned by contemporaries, from the ninth-century Frankish archbishop Hincmar of Reims (d. 882) to Pope Innocent III (d. 1216)? And if the ends really justified the means, why is no medieval forger known to have excused his work on these grounds?[14] The closest we come to a forger's own perspective is the remarks of the late antique theologian Salvian (d. *c.* 450), who when (rightly) accused of appropriating the name of the

11. Lechner, 'Schwäbische Urkundenfälschungen'; Caspar, *Petrus Diaconus*; Levillain, 'Études'.

12. Tout, 'Mediæval Forgers', 208.

13. Fuhrmann, *Einfluß und Verbreitung*, 64–136 (reprising material first published in 1963); Brooke, 'Approaches'; Constable, 'Forgery and Plagiarism'. See also Fuhrmann, 'Fälschungen'.

14. E. A. R. Brown, '*Falsitas*'; Koziol, *Politics of Memory*, 315–99.

apostle Timothy for his tract on avarice (*Ad ecclesiam*), responded that he had done so only to ensure that his teachings received the widest possible audience. Here we do indeed see elements of an 'ends justify the means' morality. But significantly, Salvian does not deny the accusation of deception. By his own admission, he used Timothy's name because it carried greater weight than his own. Salvian did not really think Timothy had written such words; he merely wished the apostle had.[15]

The key to cutting this Gordian knot lies in distinguishing motives from intentions.[16] Intentions are our immediate goals, while motives are our grounds for seeking these. Viewed in these terms, the *motives* of medieval forgers, like many of their antique and biblical forbears, may indeed have been pure (to restore what once was or should have been), but their *intentions* remained duplicitous (they wanted their documents to pass for the purportedly lost originals). Like Salvian, they did wish to deceive their contemporaries (and perhaps themselves); otherwise there would have been no point in the exercise. What good was a diploma in the name of Charlemagne, if no one thought it his? Why project present claims onto the past, if this did not fool anyone? The answer is obvious: they did, and it did.

Forgery, Rights and Charters in the Tenth and Eleventh Centuries

As Mabillon and Papebroch appreciated, we must understand how authentic documents were drawn up if we are to identify fakes. Forgeries were not produced in a vacuum; they are products of medieval documentary traditions, and typically offer hints as to the true context of their production. The difficulty lies in identifying the more subtle of these errors across the space of a millennium or more. In practice, this is best achieved by comparing suspect documents with authentic ones, and earlier texts with later ones from the house or region in question.

Since much hinges on these matters, it is worth setting out some of the general principles behind charter production. The focus here is on those documents issued in the names of rulers—what are known as royal charters or diplomas—from the tenth and eleventh centuries, though many of the same principles hold elsewhere (especially with regard to papal documents). Two matters concern us above all: who was responsible for these texts, and how they went about producing them. There has been considerable change in scholarly opinion on both fronts. Deeply influenced by the developing national

---

15. Salvian of Marseille, *Epistola* 9, ed. Lagarrigue, 120–32, with Ehrman, *Forgery and Counterforgery*, 94–96. See further P. Brown, *Through the Eye of a Needle*, 436–41.

16. Ehrman, *Forgery and Counterforgery*, 97–121. Ehrman's distinction is anticipated by E. A. R. Brown, '*Falsitas*', 103.

bureaucracies of the nineteenth century, early pioneers of diplomatic viewed charter production as a fundamentally top-down, bureaucratic affair: official documents were drawn up by a formal writing office (the chancery), operating in the name of the ruler. This was overseen by the chancellor—medieval middle management at its finest—and staffed by professional 'chancery scribes', whose chief responsibility lay in the production of public acts. Any individual responsible for more than two or three documents in a ruler's name was generally identified as a chancery scribe and presumed to be in more or less permanent royal employ. The assumption was, therefore, of a high degree of centralization: documents were produced by professionals operating under close administrative oversight.[17]

As even early diplomatists were aware, however, not all diplomas can be ascribed to a central writing office. Some were clearly drawn up locally, most often by the recipients of the grant in question. This was especially common in the case of important religious houses, which were well stocked with scribes, many of whom had experience of drafting and copying such texts. Yet recipient production presented—and continues to present—scholars with particular problems. By its nature, it tends to be limited to an individual house or region, leaving a similar archival footprint to forgery (which is also a localized affair, typically limited to a single centre). As a consequence, it can be hard to distinguish anomalies arising from authentic recipient production from those resulting from later local tampering. It is partly for this reason that nineteenth-century scholars were keen to downplay the role of the recipient in charter production—it presented major (at times insoluble) methodological challenges. Indeed, Sickel famously deemed only 'chancery-form' (*kanzleigemäß*) diplomas to be above reproach; all others stood under a cloud.[18]

Work over the last century has done much to challenge these presumptions.[19] It is now clear that medieval governance was more informal than nineteenth-century scholars imagined. And nowhere are changing attitudes clearer than in the case of the 'chancery' (now firmly in inverted commas). Though some established royal (and papal) scribes can be identified in the early to central Middle Ages, no more than a handful were in court employ at any time—and even these figures were more independent than traditional wisdom holds. Most combined duties at court with responsibilities elsewhere, often at local religious houses; and even those in regular royal service did not sever ties to friends and associates in other parts of the realm. Charter scribes were not, therefore, members of a formal government bureau, but rather

17. Bresslau, *Handbuch*, i, 41–43, 352–582; Giry, *Manuel de diplomatique*, 661–822.
18. Sickel, 'Beiträge zur Diplomatik VI.', 360–62.
19. Klewitz, 'Cancellaria'; Tessier, 'Originaux'; Bautier, 'Leçon d'ouverture'; Huschner, *Transalpine Kommunikation*, 18–94; Guyotjeannin, Pycke and Tock, *Diplomatique médiévale*, 223–27.

periodic associates of king and court. In this respect, 'chancery' and 'recipient' production are not alternatives, but either end of a sliding scale, with most documents falling somewhere between these poles. Typically, the person responsible for drawing up an act had a connection to *both* the issuer and recipient. And even when the recipients took the lead, they operated under royal fiat; the difference might be slight.

In terms of the mechanics, charters were normally drawn up shortly after the act of donation or confirmation they record.[20] The final text represents a fair copy of earlier working drafts. And normally, the same individual would be responsible for both draft and copy—in the technical language of diplomatic, he (or less often she) was draftsman and scribe. When the contents of a document were known in advance (as in the case of confirmations), the text might be largely drafted and copied before the transaction and simply approved and completed on this occasion. In such cases, earlier charters relevant to the rights in question would normally be brought to court alongside the new privilege, which would itself be modelled on these precedents, often repeating their terms verbatim. With new grants, draftsmen and scribes were freer in their choice of models, but naturally followed prevailing styles. (This is how we catch our forgers; because they do not belong to the documentary world they wish to evoke, they frequently fall into anachronism.) In any case, the final charter would be subject to formal presentation at court, either on the same occasion as the transaction or at a later date.[21] It was at this moment that it was sealed, authenticating its contents. In England, where royal charters bear witness-lists instead of seals, those present seem to have publicly signalled their assent at this point. Occasionally, a gap separated the grant and production of the requisite document. The final diploma would still be subject to approval and authentication at court, but this might take place months or even years after the transaction.

In terms of composition, scholars distinguish three distinct parts of a charter: the opening formulae (or protocol), main text (body) and closing formulae (eschatocol) (Table 1; see also Illustration 1.1 in the next chapter).[22] Each of these is, in turn, divided into subsections, not all of which are present in every document; the ordering of specific elements might also vary. The first part of the opening formulae is typically a chrismon (a symbolic invocation of Christ), often in the form of a cross or a stylized C. This is followed by a verbal invocation, along the lines of 'in the name of Our Lord' ('in nomine domini nostri'). Then comes the name and title of the issuing authority (superscription).

20. On charter production: Bresslau, *Handbuch*, ii, 62–193; Boüard, *Manuel de diplomatique*, i, 61–111; Tessier, *Diplomatique*, 102–14; Mersiowsky, *Urkunde*, 543–782. On England, see also Keynes, 'Church Councils'.

21. Keller, 'Zu den Siegeln', 424–33; Roach, *Kingship and Consent*, 77–103.

22. For the following: Fichtenau, 'Forschungen'; Guyotjeannin, Pycke and Tock, *Diplomatique médiévale*, 71–92.

Table 1. Constituent parts of a later tenth-century diploma (D O I 310)

Protocol	*(CHRISMON) In nomine sanctae et individuchuae trinitatis.*	Chrismon and verbal invocation
	Otto divina favente clementia imperator augustus.	Royal/imperial superscription
Main text/ body	*Dignum igitur censemus ut, quoniam exaltatio aecclesiarum salus regum vel imperatorum et stabilitas creditur esse regnorum, sublirnitas imperialis in eo quod sui est officii, studere non recuset, quin potius decreta antecessorum suorum, regum videlicet aut imperatorum, eisdem dei aecclesiis cultus amore concessa sua etiam auctoritate roboret et confirmet.*	Preamble
	Unde notum esse volumus omnium fidelium nostrorum tam praesentium etiam futurum industriae	Publication clause
	qualiter vir venerabilis Anno sanctae Uuormaciensis vel Uuangionensis aecclesiae episcopus nostrum adiit sublimitatem, ferens secum cartas seu praecepta regum vel imperatorum, Christianissimorum videlicet antecessorum nostrorum, in quibus continebatur; ipsam sedem cum aecclesiis cellulis vicis ac villis vel rebus omnibus illuc aspicientibus plenissima defensione et emunitatis eorum tucione semper fuisse munitam, petitique ut nos ob spem divinae remunerationis similia concederemus et confirmatione nostrae auctoritatis impertiremus.	Narrative section (*narratio*)
	Nos vero divino tacti amore pro statu et incolomitate regni vel imperii nostri, pro sanitate etiarn nostra dilectaeque coniugis nostrae Adelheidis filiique nostri carissimi Ottonis piç illius petitioni assensum praebuimus et in omnibus sicut petiit obedivimus, ita sane ut eadem Ucangionensis sedes vel aecclesia sub perpetua regiae vel imperatoriare eumnitatis defensione cum aecclesiis in Lobotonburg vel Uuinphina constructis consistat	Dispositio
	nullusque iudex publicus vel quislibet ex iudicaria potestate vel aliquis ex nostris sanctae dei aecclesiae fidelibus praesentibus scilicet et futuris	Prohibition clause
	in aecclesias vel parochias cellas aut loca vel agros seu reliquas possessiones praedictae sedis vel aeclesiae Uuangionensis in honore sanctorum apostolorum Petri et Pauli constructae quas hactenus iuste et rationabiliter possedisse visa est in quibuslibet pagis vel territoriis sitas vel quicquid ibidem tam a nobis quam ab antecessoribus nostris seu çeteris fidelibus quoquo modo propter divinum amorern collatum est vel quae deinceps in ius ipsius aecclesiae superna pietas addere vel amplificare voluerit, ad causas audiendas vel freda seu telonea exigenda aut mansiones vel paratas faciendas aut fideiussores tollendos aut ullas redibitiones inlititas requirendas aut ad homines ipsius aecclesiae tam ingenuos quam servos distringendos ingredi audeat vel quid exigere ullo umquam tempore praesumat, nec ab hominibus ipsius aecclesiae hostilis expeditio requiratur, nisi quando necessitas utilitati regum fuerit, simul cum suo episcopo pergant.	Appurtenances (with military exemption)

Continued on next page

Table 1. Continued

	Quiquid autem de rebus praefatae aecclesiae fiscus sperare poterat, totum nos pro nostrae mercedis incremento praedictae aecclesiae concedimus, ut perennibus terriporibus in perpetuos usus ipsius aecclesiae deoque ibi famulantium proficiat, quatinus, pro nostra dilecteque coniugis nostraeque prolis salute vel pro stabilitate regni vel imperii nostri illos iugiter exorare delectet.	Prayer clause (relatively unusual)
	Et ut haec emunitatis nostrae confirmatio rata et probabilis existat, volumus et firmiter iubemus et antecessorum nostrorum decreta sive statuta super eiusdem aecclesiae rebus nostra auctoritate probamus roboramus et confirmamus. Et ut hoc auctoritatis nostrae preceptum, firmum et stabile permaneat, cartam hanc conscribi et anuli nostri impressione signari issimus, quam et manu propria subtus firmavimus.	Corroboration clause
	Signum domni Ottonis (MONOGRAM) magni et invictissimi imperatoris augusti.	Subscription and royal/imperial monogram
Eschatocol	*Liudolfus cancellarius advivem Uuillihelmi archicappellani recognovi. (SEAL) (RECOGNITION SIGN)*	Chancery recognition (with seal and recognition sign)
	Data v kal. decemb. anno dominicae inearnationis DCCCCLXV, indictione VIIII, anno regni domini Ottonis XXXI, imperii vero IIII; actum Uualahuson; in dei nomine feliciter amen.	Dating clause

Together, these comprise the protocol, the first line of which is normally written in elongated letters (*litterae elongatae*). Thereafter comes the body. This sometimes opens with a preamble, reflecting on the (generally pious) motives of the donor. In almost all cases, there follows a publication clause, addressing the kingdom's great and good. Then we proceed to the donation proper, within which we find a narrative account of how the document came to be produced (a *narratio*); a legal statement of donation or confirmation (the *dispositio*); and a listing of any other associated rights (the appurtenances). A prohibition (or immunity) clause secures the new owner's rights against interference; sometimes this is followed by a sanction threatening those who infringe the document's terms with divine displeasure and/or monetary penalties. Finally, the main text is rounded off by a corroboration clause, in which the ruler asserts his desire to have the document authenticated. This prepares the way for the closing elements (eschatocol), which are separated from the body by a gap. Like the first line of the protocol, these are in elongated script, and their purpose is to authenticate the charter. They typically comprise a subscription by the ruler, formally consenting to the donation; a royal/imperial monogram, symbolically enacting this assent; and a recognition clause (or *recognitio*) in the name of the chancellor responsible for overseeing the act. The latter is sometimes accompanied by a recognition sign—the chancellor's equivalent to the royal monogram. Last but not least, at the very foot of the parchment— normally following a further gap—comes the dating clause (back in normal charter script), detailing where and when the document was issued. The seal is also found in this section, usually to the right of the subscription and recognition, though sometimes between these and the dating clause. (Note that hanging seals, attached to the bottom of the parchment by thread or a parchment strap, only become standard in later centuries.)

Most surviving charters, forged and authentic, concern lands and legal rights. And the rights most frequently claimed by religious houses are the institutional prerogatives of immunity, liberty and exemption. The medieval immunity was a descendent of a form of late Roman tax exemption. Originally, this granted the holder rights to dues otherwise owed to the monarch. But as taxation waned in the former Western Empire, immunity came to be defined by judicial independence—by the fact that the immunist did not have to answer to the local comital court and could receive the profits of justice on his or her lands. It also became closely associated with concepts of royal protection (*defensio*, *tuitio* or *mundeburdium*), the support offered by monarchs to certain prized individuals and, above all, religious centres. Indeed, this new form of immunity was an exclusively (and distinctively) ecclesiastical prerogative, a defining feature of sacred space and religious status.[23] Exemp-

---

23. Rosenwein, *Negotiating Space*, 25–96; Murray, 'Merovingian Immunity'. Further work on the subject is anticipated from Guy Halsall.

tion, on the other hand, was the ecclesiastical counterpart of immunity. Just as immunity removed a religious house from the interference of secular agents of the crown (particularly the count), so exemption took it—partially or fully— out of the control of its ecclesiastical superiors (generally the local diocesan bishop). In the seventh and eighth centuries, exemption was often granted by kings and bishops, but by the tenth it had become strongly associated with the pope. And just as immunity was often coupled with rights of royal lordship and influence, so exemption might involve a degree of dependence on Rome.[24] Liberty was less tangible, but no less important. It designates the character of a religious house. A centre was free if it was able to run its own affairs, above all when it came to choosing its own leader (abbot, prior or bishop). Liberty also incorporated ideas about integrity of landholding—the essential basis for such institutional independence.[25]

In practice, all three of these rights bled into one another.[26] Immunity and exemption were often a means of securing liberty, and grants and confirmations of both frequently mention the right of free abbatial election. Nor were immunity and exemption themselves hermetically sealed. The two are sometimes conferred in tandem; and popes might grant and confirm immunity (particularly in the tenth and eleventh centuries), just as kings might on occasion do with exemption. This overlap is reflected in contemporary linguistic usage, in which *immunitas* and *libertas* might be used for grants or confirmations of any (or all) of these rights. Still, it is useful to maintain a distinction between them, at least at a conceptual level. Liberty could exist without immunity or exemption, just as the latter two might be pursued independently. Moreover, none of these were themselves stable legal statuses; rather they represent constantly evolving socio-political relationships. What immunity, liberty and exemption constituted thus varied significantly across time and space. And in fact, one of the most common spurs to forgery was the need to update such texts to meet the legal and customary expectations of a later age.

Forgeries can be distinguished from authentic documents by the fact that they do not conform fully to contemporary conventions. The most common error here is anachronism, the transposing of ideas or formulation from later eras onto texts of earlier periods. If a charter includes turns of phrase not seen until decades or centuries after its purported date of issue, this is immediately suspicious; so too are grants or confirmations of rights we know to have later been under dispute. More subtle, but equally striking, is the reverse error, that of hyperarchaism. This is when forgers went *too far* in their efforts to mimic earlier documentary forms, applying older conventions to supposedly younger

24. Rennie, *Freedom*. See also Rosenwein, *Negotiating Space*, 35–36, 106–9, 171–83.
25. Tellenbach, *Libertas*.
26. Manganaro, 'Forme e lessico'.

documents. Where the original (or pseudo-original) single sheet charters survive, we can also apply palaeographical (script-historical) criteria. The key point is that script changes subtly but significantly over time, and it is a rare forger indeed who can imitate the writing of an earlier age with complete mastery.[27]

What is Forgery?

With these parameters established, we may turn to the thorny issue of defining forgery. Much ink has been spilt on this, so we may restrict ourselves to the essentials. Conceptions of forgery and falsity are culturally conditioned and defined by their antitheses: originality and authenticity. Where the original is not valued above the copy, there is little space for a concept of the fake; in such a world, any image or text which evokes the forms of the original may pass for it.[28] On the other hand, where the original is prized above the copy, forgery is often rife. Medieval documentary culture certainly qualifies here. Throughout the Middle Ages, original charters were accorded greater weight than copies. And considerable effort went into their authentication, by means of seals, subscriptions and monograms—devices all intended to prevent copies passing for originals. This is not to say that modern ideas about forgery and authenticity can be applied across the board, however. A helpful contrast is offered by the world of medieval art. Here the cult of the original had yet to establish itself, and forgery was indeed an alien concept; works of art were judged by the quality of their execution, not whether they had been produced by a specific artist or in a specific context.[29]

From a purely analytical standpoint, documentary forgery can be isolated easily enough: a document is forged if it claims to be something it is not. A diploma of the late tenth century pretending to be an original of Charlemagne is a fake; one of the same era claiming to be a copy of an earlier charter of Charlemagne is not (or at least, not necessarily). The question is, therefore, one of intentions (not motives): was the aim to deceive? A case in point is offered by the Donation of Constantine, perhaps the most famous forgery of the Middle Ages. In this, the late antique emperor Constantine I (306–37) is said to have conferred the entire Western Roman Empire on Pope Sylvester I (314–35) and his successors, including the Lateran Palace and many other specific (but still very extensive) rights in Rome and Italy. The anonymous eighth-century author of the Donation, who was inspired by the (largely fictional) late antique 'Acts of Sylvester' (*Actus Silvestri*), may well have believed that he was doing no more than recording the real actions of the historical Constantine I;

---

27. Crick, 'Historical Literacy', 169–70. See also T. J. Brown, 'Detection'.
28. Han, *Shanzai*.
29. Lenain, *Art Forgery*, 46–147. See also C. S. Wood, *Forgery*.

nevertheless, he must have known that the words he used were not those of the emperor. At the same time, he knew that they would command greater respect if others believed this to be so. This was forgery, pious or not.[30]

Theory may be clear, but reality is messy. If, as sometimes happens, a scribe produces an imitative copy of a text—one which closely reproduces the appearance of the original—is this forgery? By our criteria, the answer must be: only if intended to pass for the original. The problem is, how do we know? And how do we know that, even if not originally intended to deceive, it did not later pass for the original?[31] In practice there is, therefore, considerable middle ground between forged and authentic. The situation is further complicated by the tendency of copyists to update the documents they transmit. Much as we instinctively use modern registers to discuss the plays of Shakespeare, so medieval scribes often reverted to their own accustomed idioms when describing and transcribing earlier documents. An ancient formula might thus become a modern one, even if the contents are otherwise faithfully transmitted. These problems are particularly acute for documents from the earliest centuries of the Middle Ages. At most one royal diploma survives in its original format from Lombard Italy (568–774); the rest are all preserved in copies, often from much later. Some of these are quite faithful to their lost exemplars; but many show signs of updating, reflecting the legal, linguistic and cultural registers of subsequent centuries.[32] Is this forgery? As before, the answer must be: only if intended to deceive. The difficulty, however, lies in determining where harmless intervention stops and active deception starts. If the updating consciously improves the terms of the original, this is forgery; but since we do not have the originals for comparison, it is frequently hard to be sure. Moreover, even the most blatant forgeries tend to draw on authentic materials, preserving elements of (authentic) earlier texts. Forged and authentic are, therefore, rough-and-ready labels, which can obscure as much as they inform.

Once dated and localized, forgeries reveal a great deal about the context in which they were produced. The most common types of text forged in the Middle Ages were, as noted above, charters conveying or confirming legal rights, particularly of liberty, immunity and exemption—texts not dissimilar from the ancient epigraphic forgeries with which we began. Like those, they provide precious glimpses into how, when and why the rights of individual religious houses were contested. Moreover, because they are fictional, they give their authors freer rein than authentic texts, furnishing privileged access to

30. *Constitutum Constantini*, ed. Fuhrmann, with Goodson and Nelson, 'Roman Contexts'. Cf. Constable, 'Forgery and Plagiarism', 39; Hiatt, *Making of Medieval Forgeries*, 139–41, whose arguments do not entirely convince on this point.

31. Cf. Boüard, *Manuel de diplomatique*, i, 188–90.

32. Brühl, *Studien zu den langobardischen Königsurkunden*. See also Everett, *Literacy*, 186–87.

what Karl Leyser memorably called the 'ought world' of the age—a vision of the world as it should be, not as it is.[33] In this respect, it is important to bear in mind that charters of the tenth and eleventh centuries were more than legal texts (though they were this too). As Hagen Keller and Geoffrey Koziol have shown, they were powerful ideological tools, capable of shaping social and political realities.[34] This is why they were so highly valued; it is also why they were so often forged. In this context, it is important to appreciate that forgery itself is a deeply historical act. Each falsified document is an attempt to rewrite the past or plug gaps in an existing narrative. Counterfeit charters therefore not only tell us about contemporary concerns, but also shed light on attitudes towards the past. Scholars of early modern Europe have long noted that forgery and antiquarianism go hand in hand: as scholarly knowledge of (and interest in) the ancient world grew, so too did attempts to falsify its records. It has been less frequently appreciated that the same holds true of the ancient and medieval worlds; here, too, forgery is was often a sign of a heightened interest in the past.[35]

Pilgrim's era is of particular interest in this respect. Patrick Geary famously argued that the tenth and eleventh centuries saw a sea-change in attitudes toward the past in western Europe. These years saw new strategies of memorialization emerge, with a particular focus on local and institutional memory.[36] Geary's work is now complemented by that of Theo Riches, who notes that in these years many religious houses began to write their own narrative histories in the form of the 'deeds of bishops' (*gesta episcoporum*) genre. Such centres were starting to conceive of themselves as corporate entities, with collective pasts of their own.[37] For most major houses, we can trace a continuous history from the tenth or eleventh centuries, but only rarely can we take this back much further. It is not simply that there were no earlier records (though in some places, this was so); it is that earlier historical and archival undertakings took forms which did not encourage their later transmission and preservation. What we are seeing is, therefore, the formation of new kinds of institutional memory and identity which were to prove remarkably resilient. These processes are reflected in the upsurge in forgery noted in the Preface. In some regions, particularly in France, there are important ninth-century antecedents; but across the board, the tenth and eleventh centuries saw the spread and diversification of documentary falsification. Viewed in these terms, this period, famously branded an iron, leaden and dark age ('saeculum . . .

33. K. J. Leyser, 'Tenth-Century Condition', 4–5.

34. Keller, 'Hulderweis durch Privilegien'; Koziol, *Politics of Memory*.

35. Grafton, *Forgers and Critics*; Rowland, *Scarith*. Cf. Higbie, *Collectors, Scholars, and Forgers*.

36. Geary, *Phantoms*. For discussion and criticism: Morelle, 'Histoire et archives'. See also Southern, 'Sense of the Past', to somewhat similar effect.

37. Riches, 'Changing Political Horizons'. Cf. Sot, *Gesta episcoporum*.

ferreum ... plubeum, atque ... obscurum') by the great Counter-Reformation cardinal Cesare Baronio (d. 1607), emerges as an exciting and dynamic era.[38] To extend Baronio's own ferrous metaphor, it was in the crucible of these years that new identities and attitudes were forged, ones which would define the *Ancien Régime.*

Geary was alive to the potential of forgeries within this context, noting how at Saint-Denis, north of Paris, falsification was an important part of repackaging the Merovingian past in the 1060s. And Amy Remensnyder has similarly underlined the important memorial function of foundation charters—many of them forged—in the religious houses of southern France.[39] Still, forgery remains largely (and strangely) absent from the many studies of medieval memory, in which manuscripts and narrative histories loom large.[40] Such work provides a helpful framework for the present book. The essential point of departure is that memory is not simply an individual affair; it is a social phenomenon, reflecting wider socio-political trends. Especially important here are collective memories, which play a key part in group formation; these reflect (and inform) local, regional and national identities.[41] They are of particular salience in periods of rupture and innovation, when new pasts are developed in response to a changing present, processes famously dubbed 'the invention of tradition' by Eric Hobsbawm and Terence Ranger (with reference to the nineteenth century).[42] We are apparently observing something along these lines in the later tenth century, with forgery representing part of a wider set of initiatives aiming to recast local understandings of the past in the light of new challenges.

Particularly useful from the perspective of the present study is the work of the German couple Jan and Aleida Assmann. In his influential book of 1990, the former argued that collective memory can be subdivided into communicative and cultural memory (*kommunikatives* and *kulturellles Gedächtnis*). The former embodies lived oral tradition, stretching back two to three generations (or about eighty years); the latter, on the other hand, is constituted of distant origin myths and legends. Both are important, but it is cultural memory which typically defines group membership. If we were to take the example of the modern United States, the Bush (Sr) and Clinton presidencies belong firmly to the realm of communicative memory, while the Washington and Lincoln

38. Baronio, *Annales Ecclesiastici*, x, 647.

39. Geary, *Phantoms*, 107–13; Remensnyder, *Remembering Kings Past.*

40. Among others, see Goetz, 'Gegenwart der Vergangenheit'; Hen and Innes, eds, *Uses of the Past*; W. Pohl, *Werkstätte der Erinnerung*, and 'History in Fragments'; McKitterick, *History and Memory*; Ugé, *Creating the Monastic Past*; B. Pohl, *Dudo*; Rembold, 'History and (Selective) Memory'; Greer, Hicklin and Esders, eds, *Using and Not Using the Past.*

41. Fentress and Wickham, *Social Memory*; Wertsch, *Voices*; G. Cubitt, *History and Memory*, 118–74, 199–256.

42. Hobsbawm and Ranger, eds, *Invention of Tradition.*

eras have long since entered that of cultural memory. The former play comparatively little role in questions of national identity, whereas the latter are central to them. The Assmanns also identify a number of factors that go into creating and maintaining cultural memory. In literate societies, this is typically characterized by a recognizable (if often implicit) canon, excerpted from the larger body of the recorded past. To stick with the example of the United States, Washington and Lincoln belong to the country's active cultural memory (the Assmanns' canon), where they are kept alive by popular writings, sayings and cultural references. Other early presidents, however, such as James Monroe (d. 1831) and Martin Van Buren (d. 1862), are less frequently invoked; in Aleida Assmann's terms, they belong to the dormant archive (or 'storage cultural memory') of the nation, which must be activated if it is to play a part in questions of identity.[43] Viewed in these terms, forgery can certainly tell us much about the formation of cultural memory in the Middle Ages, especially within ecclesiastical institutions. To forge documents was to recreate the past, participating in a process of canonization; this is how certain iconic figures and moments came to dominate local and national memory.

Given this potential, it is perhaps surprising that there has not been more research into the memorial aspects of medieval forgery As noted, Geary and Remensnyder have undertaken pioneering work here. And more recently, Robert F. Berkhofer III and Constance Bouchard have added important detail, noting the deeply historicizing nature of forgery. Along similar lines, Alfred Hiatt has underlined the narrative qualities of false documents, particularly in the later Middle Ages.[44] Nevertheless, a connected story of the development of forgery, as reflected in attitudes towards institutional identity, remains to be told. Part of the problem lies the nature of forgery itself. It was undertaken locally, with a close eye to the history and interests of the religious house (or houses) in question. It therefore demands close contextual study of a kind which has discouraged generalization and synthesis. The most wide-ranging study to date—that of Hiatt—sensibly restricts itself to one country (England) and century (the fifteenth). Here, I have sought to range more widely, though similar limitations have had to be imposed.

The situation is further complicated by distinct national historiographical traditions, which begin to exert a strong pull on scholarship regarding these years. Because France, England and Germany can all trace a more (or less)

43. J. Assmann, *Das kulturelle Gedächtnis*, translated as *Cultural Memory and Early Civilization*. See also J. Assmann, *Religion and Cultural Memory*; A. Assmann, *Cultural Memory and Western Civilization*, esp. 119–34.

44. Berkhofer, *Day of Reckoning*, 40–48; Bouchard, *Rewriting Saints*, 22–37; Hiatt, *Making of Medieval Forgeries*. See also Ugé, *Creating the Monastic Past*, 149–53; Insley, 'Communities Past'; Maskarinec, 'Why Remember Ratchis?'. A monograph on the subject is anticipated from Berkhofer. For preliminary studies, see his 'Canterbury Forgeries', and 'Guerno the Forger'.

continuous history back to the tenth century, the history of these regions tends to be framed in terms of the birth and development of the medieval nation—and by proxy, the modern nation state. It is largely undertaken by historians of the country in question, with an eye to later developments, and connections and parallels are easily overlooked. Even in Italy, where no such simple continuity can be charted, the influence of national master-narratives is powerful; there, the tenth century is viewed in terms of the pre-history of the urban communes, which would dominate the politics of the peninsula well into (and beyond) the Renaissance.[45] These historiographical traditions strongly colour the way we view these years. The story of Italy is one of regions and cities, of the foundations of the later communes; that of England, one of kings, courts and administration, of the pre-history of the impressive Angevin state of the later twelfth century. France and Germany sit somewhere between these poles. In the former, the tenth century is an age of regional magnates and monastic reform, a period of royal weakness before the later ascent of the Capetians; in the latter, it is a time of surprising (but ultimately abortive) royal success, soon to be overtaken by the centripetal forces of the locality. By the late tenth century it is, therefore, hard to tell a connected tale at the best of times; that it has not been attempted for forgery is perfectly understandable.

This book is written in the belief that a more connected story can and should be told, even if it must be assembled from fragments. As Heinrich Fichtenau demonstrated, similar social practices and mentalities can be traced across the Latin West in these years, particularly in those regions which had once been part of the Carolingian empire. And much of the most exciting recent work spans national historiographical traditions in this fashion, revealing how subjects as diverse as ecclesiastical reform and queenship can benefit from a wider perspective.[46] In this respect, the differing historiographies sketched above can inform as much as they obscure. By engaging with studies of Italian urban history side by side with ones of English administration, French monastic reform and German regional history (*Landesgeschichte*), we may hope to achieve a more rounded picture of all regions.

Yet historiographical comparison is only truly meaningful when underpinned by detailed source criticism. And here charters (and forgeries) offer a promising point of entry, since they survive in substantial numbers from across these regions. The aim cannot, however, be to write a history of every falsified document of the later tenth century. Partly, this is a matter of pragmatism. By the final decades of the century, forgery was so widespread that

45. On France and Germany: Brühl, *Deutschland—Frankreich*, esp. 7–82; and on Italy: Wickham, *Sleepwalking*, esp. 8–11.

46. Fichtenau, *Lebensordnungen*, available in English (without footnotes) as *Living in the Tenth Century*. For subsequent studies in this vein: Hamilton, *Church and People*; MacLean, *Ottonian Queenship*.

anything approaching systematic treatment would be impossible. Nor, in any case, would it be desirable. The disparate nature of falsification means that comprehensive investigation risks getting lost in the detail: as examples are multiplied, it becomes harder to keep the big picture in focus. The attempt here, therefore, is to balance the benefits of the bird's and worm's eye view. Five forgery complexes—those of Worms, Passau, Abingdon, Fleury and Vercelli, mentioned in the Preface—are used to combine close contextual analysis with wider discussion and synthesis. Each case requires considerable contextualization, both historical and historiographical. But the result of taking them together is, I sincerely hope, greater than the sum of the constituent parts, a picture which allows for local variation alongside pan-European trends.

The case studies have been selected so as to span as much of the Latin West as possible, without overburdening an already heavily laden author (and critical apparatus). They take in all of the realms which had once been part of the Carolingian empire, as well as England, where the Carolingian legacy was strong (if indirect). East to west, they stretch from the Danube to the Loire (by way of the Rhine); north to south, they span the Thames Valley to the Piedmontese Sesia. They have also been chosen to take in different types of religious house, with two monasteries and three bishoprics represented. Finally, in each case forgery has been dated closely to the half century or so spanning the turn of the first millennium (c. 970–1020). This allows us to paint as detailed a picture as possible, one chronologically tight but geographically diverse (though, as we shall see, some of these dates have shifted under scrutiny). In most of these cases, forgery can also be associated with known individuals, enabling us to bring much ancillary evidence to bear.

What follows is thus an exercise in serial microhistory, the first—but hopefully not the last—attempt to study the documentary traditions of tenth- and eleventh-century Europe side by side. The overarching argument, to the extent that there is one, is that forgery tells us a great deal about changing attitudes towards past and present. In this respect, the later tenth century emerges as a significant turning-point: a time when mentalities changed alongside other elements of the socio-political order. Here, forgery speaks not of the blind anachronism earlier scholars saw as characteristic of the Middle Ages, but rather of a budding antiquarianism which would not have been out of place in *Quattrocento* Florence. Indeed, like later Renaissance counterfeits, these fakes were often intended for local consumption, giving voice to new regional and institutional identities. Karl Leyser once spoke of the 'ascent of Latin Europe' in these years, of how writers of the early eleventh century began to express a new-found confidence in the social and political order of the West.[47] The texts surveyed here flesh out Leyser's picture, illustrating how such processes played

---

47. K. J. Leyser, 'Ascent of Latin Europe'.

out on the ground. The forgers examined may be somewhat humbler than Leyser's historical narrators, but their voices are no less worthy of attention.

As an exercise in microhistory, this book makes no claim to comprehensiveness. In order to make the material manageable, I have focused on royal and papal documents at five centres, leaving local ('private') documentary traditions largely to one side. I likewise only touch on narrative history in passing. This is not because the subject is uninteresting or unimportant, but rather because it deserves treatment on its own terms. Points of contact between narrative history and forgery are, in any case, taken up in the Conclusions. Other absences weigh more heavily. Some will understandably baulk at my reticence regarding the Iberian Peninsula, a region rich in documentary records of these years (including forgeries), but regarding which I have little competence and no formal training. Others will, with equal justification, regret the absence of a female religious house among my examples. More still will find further matters wanting. All I can hope is that these dissatisfied readers will take my oversights as a challenge, and set about rectifying them. When they do, perhaps they will see further for being perched on these diminutive shoulders.

Forgery in the Chancery?
Bishop Anno at Worms

WHEN ANNO WAS appointed bishop of Worms in 950, it came as a mixed blessing. Anno was an ambitious young churchman, who had cut his teeth as abbot of the monastery of St Maurice in Magdeburg, the prize foundation (and future resting-place) of the East Frankish (German) ruler Otto I (936–73). As a bishopric, Worms came as a promotion, and Anno was one of a small but significant number of abbots to make the leap into the episcopate in these years. He was something of a prelate in the old mould in this regard. Until recently, it had been common to recruit bishops from the ranks of the realm's leading abbots. Under Otto, however, cathedral schools were now preferred, becoming the main training grounds for bishops –and the leading educational establishments full stop.[1]

If Anno was an old-school bishop, Worms itself was a decidedly old-fashioned kind of town. It had been an important administrative centre in the Roman Empire and later came to be a favoured residence of the great Frankish ruler Charlemagne (768–814). The royal palace fell victim to fire in 790, initiating something of a decline; but the city remained a significant regional centre.[2] These were not idle considerations. In an era in which antiquity was strongly equated with authority, a vaunted history was an essential part of episcopal identity. Yet age was not the only thing going for Worms. The bishopric overlooked the Rhine, that great ancient and medieval thoroughfare; and it also lay in the heart of the East Frankish wine district. This placed the city in an unusually good position to tap into the growing trade of

---

1. Fleckenstein, 'Königshof und Bischofsschule'; Vogtherr, *Reichsabteien*, 230–63. More generally: Barrow, *Clergy*, 181–87; Jaeger, *Envy of Angels*.

2. Kohl and Felten, 'Worms'; Brühl, *Palatium und civitas*, ii.1, 113–32; Classen, 'Bemerkungen'.

and lustre to the see. Worms had nothing of the sort. To make matters worse, Lorsch itself lay just 16.5 km (10 miles) east of the city, far closer to Worms than to Mainz. This made the abbey—one of the realm's wealthiest—a competitor rather than an ally. The greatest challenge, however, came from within the city of Worms itself. This was home to one of the kingdom's leading noble families, the future Salian dynasty, which vied with the bishop for local power and influence.

With problems came possibilities, however. Worms may not have been the most exalted post, but it offered plenty of potential. As diocesan bishop, Anno could expect to work alongside the archbishop of Mainz, one of the realm's leading prelates. And as noted, the city was in a good position to take advantage of the economic upturn of these years. Royal policies also played into Anno's hands. His bishopric lay on the road and river routes south from the Rhine-Main district to Swabia and thence to Italy, so Anno might expect to benefit from the king's growing interest in the Apennine peninsula. The kingdom of Italy had been something of a hot potato in recent years, passing from hand to hand with dizzying speed. Anyone with the requisite clout and connections might claim the throne—as had Hugh of Provence in 924. Otto I's interest in the region was piqued by Hugh's death in 947. And when Hugh's son Lothar passed away unexpectedly in late 950, he was ready to pounce.[6] Worms figured prominently in Otto's plans, and Anno's appointment at this juncture is no coincidence; a strategic see was being entrusted to a close royal associate. Indeed, it was in Worms that Otto appointed his eldest son Liudolf to the similarly strategic duchy of Swabia, probably on the same occasion as Anno's election. And while initial efforts to secure Italy proved abortive, the city came into its own in the 960s, when developments in the south once again invited East Frankish intervention. It was here that Otto I now had his second son, Otto (II), elected co-ruler in 961—Liudolf having died in 957, pursuing his own fortune in Italy—and it was here, too, that Otto would be received by his family upon returning north as emperor in 965.[7] Worms had gone from being a backwater to a showplace of empire in the space of less than two decades.

Anno knew how to make the most of these opportunities. He had received his education at St Maximin, just outside Trier, one of the kingdom's leading monasteries. St Maximin owed its influence to the popularity of the new brand of reformed monasticism it represented. This placed a premium on institutional independence and obedience to the Rule of Saint Benedict—the monastic regulations originally drawn up by Benedict of Nursia (d. 547) for his

---

6. Keller, 'Entscheidungssituationen'. The best English-language discussion remains Reuter, *Germany*, 166–74.

7. Friedmann, *Beziehungen*, 38; Rieckenberg, 'Königsstraße', 58 (and cf. ibid., 64–66); Keller, 'Reichsstruktur', 53.

monastery at Monte Cassino—as manifested above all in the right of monks to choose their own abbot. As important as its spiritual credentials, however, were the abbey's connections to regional and national elites. Otto I's father, Henry I (919–36), had helped initiate the monastery's reform in 934 alongside the local duke Giselbert (d. 939); and three years later the newly crowned Otto I chose to populate his foundation at Magdeburg with monks from the centre, foremost amongst these Anno.[8] Under Anno, the new monastery on the Elbe went from strength to strength, receiving thirteen royal grants in as many years (almost twice as many as any other religious house). Yet it is not just the number of privileges which impresses. Most of these documents were drafted by the monks of St Maurice, revealing the trust placed in Anno and the brothers.[9]

Anno's background now came in handy. He may have hailed from the Middle Rhine, and St Maximin held important rights in the region, so Anno came to Worms with a sense of the lay of the land.[10] As noted, the city hosted a number of important gatherings in Anno's early years. And as bishop, he was active at a number of key junctures in Otto I's reign, attending synods at Mainz (950), Augsburg (952) and Ingelheim (972), participating in the emperor's third Italian expedition (969–70), and securing the appointment of Giselher—a sometime Magdeburg student—as bishop of the new see of Merseburg in 971. Indeed, Anno maintained close contacts with his former associates at St Maurice, which in 968 had been raised to the status of an archbishopric, petitioning privileges for the centre and undertaking the translation of a valuable blood relic from Italy to the monastery in 971.[11]

Under Anno, Worms itself acquired a number of important rights. In 953, he received the final third on tolls at Ladenburg, an important market commanding the approaches to the lower Neckar, about 32 km (20 miles) upstream from the city (Map 1).[12] Three years later followed forest rights in Neunkirchen, just north-west of Anno's see, where since 937 the bishop had possessed a dependent church.[13] There is something of a lull thereafter. It has been suggested that Anno was involved in the uprising led by Conrad the Red—the local count of Worms—and Otto I's son Liudolf at this point (953–54). If so, this would explain the silence. Whatever the case, Anno was not sidelined for long. By November 965, he was in a position to obtain confirmation of the bishopric's immunity, in a document which extends these rights to dependent churches at Ladenburg and Wimpfen, to the south and

8. Nightingale, *Monasteries and Patrons*. More generally: Vanderputten, 'Monastic Reform'.

9. Uhlirz, *Geschichte*, 23–26, 77–84; Stengel, *Immunität*, 145–58, 163–66, 168–70.

10. Kölzer, *Studien*, 105–6.

11. Bude, *König und Bischof*, 274–78. Cf. Vincent, *Holy Blood*, 51–65, 146–47.

12. D O I 161.

13. D O I 178. Cf. D O I 10.

1.1 Otto I confirms Anno's immunity: Darmstadt, HStA A2 255/3, © HStA

east. This was an important act. As noted in the Introduction, immunity was closely tied to institutional identity. And such rights had been a particular concern at St Maximin, where the monks were keen to prevent domination by their secular and ecclesiastical neighbours (not least, the local archbishop of Trier). It may, therefore, be that the long arm of monastic reform is at work here. (Worms had not otherwise had these rights confirmed since the ninth century.) Thankfully, for our purposes, the charter survives as a single sheet, and this displays all the hallmarks of authenticity (Illustration 1.1). It is laid out according to contemporary conventions, with parchment wider than it is tall and elongated script in the first line and last lines. The seal is clearly authentic and takes the correct form for November 965; and to its right is the distinctive 'beehive' recognition sign, which is common in East Frankish diplomas until the late 960s.

This act also points toward a close bond between ruler, bishop and religious house. It opens with a preamble meditating upon the importance of confirming grants to churches, then proceeds to explain how Anno had approached the emperor with precepts of 'our most Christian predecessors'

('Christianissimorum videlicet antecessorum nostrorum') regarding the see's immunity. On account of these precedents, and in return for the canons' prayers for the realm and empire, as well as for Otto's wife Adelheid and son Otto (II), the emperor has now agreed to confirm these rights. The latter details are noteworthy. Requests for prayers for the emperor and realm were commonplace, but this is the only diploma of the period to mention Otto's wife and son in this connection. Recent events explain these unusual additions. A month and a half earlier, the emperor's younger brother, Bruno of Cologne (953–65), had died unexpectedly (11 October), and this was the first document issued since. Tragedy had evidently concentrated the imperial mind, and the canons' prayers are intended to ensure familial stability at a moment of uncertainty.[14] That Anno and Worms should be entrusted with this delicate task speaks of the trust placed in them.

The growth and development of episcopal power was not in the interests of all, however. As noted, Worms was home to one of the realm's most powerful noble families, the descendants of Conrad the Red (d. 955), who would later rise to royal dignity as the Salian dynasty. Conrad was one of the leading figures in Otto I's early years. The son of a Rhineland count, he remained staunchly loyal during the uprisings which wracked Otto's regime in the 940s and was rewarded with the duchy of Lotharingia in the lower Rhine, a strategic border region recently retaken from the rulers of West Francia (France).[15] In this capacity, Conrad went on to marry Liutgard, the king's eldest daughter. The Carolingian rulers of the eighth and ninth century had avoided matches between their daughters and local aristocrats, and this union—one of a number contracted by the new Ottonian (or Liudolfing) dynasty with the realm's leading magnates—served to underline Conrad's proximity to the king. Yet if elevation to ducal status and marriage into the royal family had expanded Conrad's horizons, the basis of his power remained firmly fixed in the Middle Rhine.[16] Worms was of particular significance. Here lay the family castle, probably erected in these years; and it was here, in the cathedral of St Peter, that the family mausoleum developed, starting with Conrad's own burial in 955, fondly recounted by Widukind of Corvey.[17] The castle was to prove a particular bone of contention. It was situated less than half a kilometre (a third of a mile) from the cathedral, posing a direct challenge to the bishop's authority. It may have been constructed atop the old royal residence, adding a numinous lustre to this up-and-coming aristocratic family. A sense of these tensions is provided by the later biography of Bishop Burchard of Worms (999–1025), which

14. D O I 310, Darmstadt, HStA, A2 255/3, with Wagner, 'Gebetsgedenken', 21.
15. MacLean, 'Shadow Kingdom', with further literature.
16. Werle, 'Titelherzogtum', 239–64; Scharzmaier, *Von Speyer nach Rom*, 20–37; Zotz, 'Adelsherrschaften'.
17. Widukind of Corey, *Res gestae Saxonicae*, III.47, ed. Lohmann and Husch, 128.

describes the stronghold as a den of thieves, responsible for 'many murders' ('homicidia multa') within the city.[18]

Upon his death, Conrad was succeeded by his capable son Otto (d. 1004), who went on to enjoy two stints as duke of Carinthia in south-eastern Bavaria, a promotion which saw the family return to ducal status (978–83, 995–1004). This was a matter of great importance to Otto, who continued to bear the ducal title even between these periods. As under Conrad, however, the family base remained firmly situated in the Middle Rhine. Even as duke of Carinthia, Otto is referred to as 'Otto of Worms' ('Uurmatcensis Otto'), a most singular form of address which underlines the degree to which the duke and his family were synonymous with the city.[19] As Anno began to extend his rights and holdings, this placed the bishop on a collision course with Conrad and Otto. In Anno's early years as bishop, there are few signs of strain; if anything, Conrad's burial in the cathedral may point toward continuing cooperation. But Worms was a small town, and the lid could not be kept on tensions forever.

When matters came to a head is hard to say, but pressure must have been mounting for some time. It is striking, for example, that Anno had a donation of Duke Conrad of 952 confirmed by the king, a move suggestive of a desire (or need) for additional security.[20] Yet if problems were brewing, they initially remained latent. As noted, Anno may have been involved in the rebellion of 953–54; and if so, he probably fought alongside Conrad, who also threw in his lot with the young prince Liudolf.[21] Conrad's death soon thereafter may have further encouraged cooperation. The duke was buried in pomp at Worms (on royal orders, according to Widukind), in an event which no doubt redounded to Anno's benefit. The situation was helped by the fact that Conrad's son, Otto, was only a child at the time—no older than eight and perhaps only five. Though Otto is accorded the title of 'count' from an early age, he can scarcely have been in a position to threaten Anno.

By the mid-960s, the situation was starting to change. Otto was now of age and determined to recreate the dominant position enjoyed by his father in the Middle Rhine. And as we might expect, there are signs that Anno was starting to feel the pinch. It is at this point that he—perhaps newly restored to royal favour—sought to have Worms's immunity confirmed (965), in the first confirmation of these rights in almost a century. The importance of this lies in the nature of immunity: this removed Anno and his successors from the jurisdiction of the local count—in this case none other than Otto of Worms. This was evidently a shot over Otto's bow, and the manner in which the diploma is

18. *Vita Burchardi*, chs 7, 9, ed. Boos, 107–8, 109–10, with Grünewald, 'Die Salier'.

19. D O II 279, Karlsruhe, GLA, A 47. It should, however, be noted that the diploma concerns rights in the Middle Rhine. See further Weinfurter, 'Herrschaftslegitimation'.

20. D O I 151.

21. Friedmann, *Beziehungen*, 41–42. See also Bude, *König und Bischoff*, 276–77.

framed betrays a distinctly anti-comital bent, as we shall see. And the text not only secures Anno's rights in Worms, but extends these to dependent churches at Ladenburg and Wimpfen, the linchpins of episcopal control and administration in the middle and eastern reaches of the diocese (in the latter case, in another region where Otto was apparently count). It is also in these years (967, to be precise)—and not in 952—that the diploma confirming Conrad's donation was produced. It was not uncommon for the production of royal charters to be delayed, sometimes even for a decade or two, but the timing is suggestive. It was in the late 960s, and not in the early 950s, that Anno was feeling under threat. Conrad was now long dead, as was his wife Liutgard (d. 953), who had petitioned the grant, so there was every reason to fear their son might claim an interest in such sometime patrimony.[22] The clearest signs of tension, however, emerge not from these authentic texts, but from a set of forgeries produced for the bishopric. It is to these that we must now turn.

The Making of a Forger

The combination of threat and opportunity faced by Anno always made forgery a likely resort. That tenth-century Worms should become almost synonymous with counterfeiting, however, was far from inevitable. The main texts comprised by the Worms forgeries have long been known. But new light is shed on the subject by a privilege of Louis the Pious of 814, which has only recently been the subject of scholarly scrutiny.

The diploma in question confirms Worms's immunity and grants its dependents partial exemption from military service—they are only to serve in cases of need, and then are to do so under direct episcopal oversight. The document only survives in copies of the central and later Middle Ages, and was long deemed authentic; however, Theo Kölzer, its recent editor, has now shown that it has been tampered with. As Kölzer notes, exemption from military service is not otherwise attested in the early years of Louis the Pious—and indeed, is not seen in these terms before the later ninth century. There are also signs that the original single sheet was not an authentic product of 814. Though this is no longer extant, when J. V. Armbruster consulted it in the seventeenth century, the imperial monogram—the symbolic representation of the emperor—followed (rather than preceded) Louis's name in his subscription at the foot of the text, an arrangement first found in documents of the later ninth century. He also reports that the seal wax was thick and white, again probably pointing to later production.[23] Still, much of the diploma's formulation

---

22. On the dating, see Stengel, *Immunität*, 339–40. Cf. Friedmann, *Beziehungen*, 39–40, for a different interpretation.

23. D L Fr 25. See *Urkunden Ludwigs des Frommen*, ed. Kölzer, 65–67. A study of the development of military exemption in the ninth and tenth centuries is a major

is acceptable for 814. It evidently draws on a genuine privilege of Louis the Pious, probably granting Worms immunity; all our forger seems to have done is to improve the terms by inserting a clause concerning military exemption. In this respect, his method of composition, subtly adjusting an authentic document, is reminiscent of that seen in the other Worms forgeries. Significantly, we know that this text must have been in circulation by autumn 965, since it forms the basis of Otto I's own confirmation of the see's immunity, which survives as an authentic original.[24]

The Louis the Pious counterfeit could, in principle, have been produced any time between the later ninth century and 965, but there is a strong case for associating it with Anno. As reported by Armbruster, its appearance conforms with documentary conventions of the 960s. More to the point, it is in Anno's episcopate that the immunity makes its first appearance—always a suspicious feature. It is also in the 960s that an obvious motive for forgery can be identified. Count Otto would have come of age in the early to middle years of this decade: as we have seen, a situation which threatened Anno's position in the city. A restatement of episcopal immunity—of Anno's freedom from comital oversight—would, therefore, have been most welcome. These years were also an obvious time for concerns about military service to surface. The rocky first half of Otto I's reign, which had seen repeated rebellions, placed those eligible for military service under considerable strain. And the almost permanent relocation of the court south of the Alps thereafter (961–65, 966–72) extended the distance and duration of this service even further. Bishoprics and monasteries contributed significantly to East Frankish military forces, and for a relatively poor see such as Worms, this must have posed a serious challenge. The situation was not helped by the bishopric's location, which ensured that Worms was disproportionately called upon to support the emperor's Italian ventures.[25] So just as the Swabian abbey of Reichenau—which lies on these same routes south—later responded to Frederick Barbarossa's Italian expeditions of the later twelfth century by claiming fictitious rights of exemption, Anno's first response upon Otto I's return north in 965 was to claim a reduction in military commitments on the basis of the Louis the Pious counterfeit.[26]

Yet imperial service is only part of the story here. The terms of the immunity reduce Worms's liability, but do not remove it entirely; in cases of national

---

desideratum. The earliest evidence comes from Corvey and Hamburg in the later ninth century; however, both archives are shot through with forgeries and require more careful handling than they have received to date. For some useful starting points, see Bachrach, 'Immunities', 23–30.

24. D O I 310, Darmstadt, HStA, A2 255/3.

25. Friedmann, *Beziehungen*, 51, 59. Cf. K.-F. Werner, 'Heeresorganisation'; Auer, 'Kriegsdienst'.

26. Dendorfer, 'Roncaglia', 111–14.

need ('quando necessitas utilitati regum fuerit')—potentially many situations—the see's dependents are still to serve. As important as exemption is the further stipulation that, if necessary, Anno's men are to serve directly under their bishop ('simul cum suo episcopo'). Normally, it would have been the count's resposibility to lead the local muster; this provision further removes Anno from Otto's oversight.[27]

The identification of the Louis the Pious counterfeit raises major questions about the other Worms forgeries. Believing the Louis the Pious privilege to be authentic, Johann Lechner, who first identified the complex, placed these in the episcopate of Anno's successor Hildibald (978–98). Theodor Sickel, however, had thought that these belonged to that of Anno (950–78); and the existence of another forgery of Anno's years opens the possibility of a more intimate association.[28]

A Master at Work: Hildibald B

If developments in the mid-960s presented Anno with a problem, his associations with the imperial court and the new Elbe River metropolitan at Magdeburg presented him with the solution. Already as abbot of St Maurice, Anno had overseen charter production in favour of the abbey; now he turned to similar means to protect his bishopric. Yet there was an important difference. As abbot of the ruler's prize foundation, Anno had been able to ask for almost anything; as bishop of a relatively obscure (if strategically significant) see, he could not. Anno would now have to appeal to precedent—and where precedent was not to be found, he would have to invent it. Thanks to his background, however, he possessed all the requisite skills. He knew his way around a charter, and may have known a thing or two about forgery, too. Already in 965 Anno had been mobilizing the written word to his aid, and in subsequent years he would do so ever more liberally.

That many of the earliest documents from the bishopric of Worms, none of which survives in its original format, had been tampered with was clear from an early date. It was not, however, until the brilliant forensic work of Johann Lechner (d. 1927) in the early twentieth century that the full scale and nature of counterfeiting at the centre was appreciated. Lechner made his discoveries while employed editing the charters of the Carolingian rulers, under Engelbert Mühlbacher (d. 1903) in Vienna. In this capacity, he

27. See further Bachrach, 'Immunities'.

28. Lechner, 'Die älteren Königsurkunden'; *Urkunden Konrads I., Heinrichs I. und Ottos I.*, ed. Sickel, 444, 533–34; *Urkunden Ottos II.*, ed. Sickel, 55. Cf. *Urkunden Ludwigs des Frommen*, ed. Kölzer, 67, shrewdly observing that 'our findings suggest a redating of the Worms forgeries, which would require further consideration in detail' ('unser Befund [legt] eine zeitliche Entzerrung der Wormser Fälschungen nahe, was erneuten Prüfung im Detail bedürfte').

had come into contact with a number of Worms counterfeits of the eighth and ninth centuries, texts he soon realized bore close similarities to charters of the tenth century. Lechner had recently made a splash with his pioneering treatment of the Reichenau forgery complex; Worms now promised similar prospects.[29]

In his discussion, Lechner proceeded from the deceptively simple observation that all tenth-century diplomas confirming earlier Worms forgeries were produced by the same individual, the draftsman-scribe known to scholars as Hildibald B. The latter was one of the most active scribes at court from 978 on; and, since the eighth- and ninth-century forgeries he confirms betray a number of stylistic similarities with Hildibald B's work, Lechner concluded that he was responsible for these. What is more, Lechner argued that the tenth-century confirmations were themselves clever counterfeits. The key point here is that the confirmations date from the 960s and early 970s, while Hildibald B is otherwise only known to have operated from 978 on. Like an elaborate set of Russian dolls, it would seem that this scribe confected a set of ancient privileges, then falsified more recent ones endorsing them, the result being a mix of true and false sufficiently complex to deceive all previous eyes. The forgeries were themselves to be placed in the mid-980s, at the peak of Hildibald B's career, and his motives to be sought in the recent return of Count Otto to the Middle Rhine. Otto had been stripped of his post as duke of Carinthia in 983 and was compensated with lands and rights in his traditional homelands. The bishop of Worms was thus facing a new threat, and Hildibald B rose to the occasion. His efforts were assisted by the fact that his immediate superior, the imperial chancellor, was none other than Hildibald, the local bishop of Worms. In fact, it was almost certainly Hildibald who had commissioned him. This was a case of forgery in the chancery, spearheaded by the imperial chancellor.[30]

There is an elegance to Lechner's case which is hard to deny. Theodor Sickel and his team, who had edited the diplomas of Otto I and Otto II, had judged all of Hildibald B's early diplomas for Worms—including those confirming earlier forgeries—to be authentic. But they had not known how deep falsification ran at the centre, nor were they aware of Hildibald B's forging proclivities. One of Sickel's more gifted students, Karl Uhlirz (d. 1914), sought to defend the old Sickelian line in an appendix to his contribution to the *Jahrbücher* series on Otto II. But his response smacks of wounded pride—Uhlirz had been part of Sickel's original editorial team—and has largely been ignored by subsequent scholarship. Indeed, Lechner soon published a reply; and, occasional doubts notwithstanding, his conclusions have been accepted ever

29. Lechner, 'Schwäbische Urkundenfälschungen'. See further Redlich, 'Lechner'; Lhotsky, *Geschichte*, 272–73.

30. Lechner, 'Die älteren Königsurkunden'.

since.[31] In the light of recent work on the Louis the Pious immunity, however, the question arises as to whether these texts can be so easily detached from Anno's episcopate, where Sickel and Uhlirz had originally placed them. Here we must dive into the detail.

As Lechner realized, Hildibald B's forgeries can be divided into three loosely related groups: those concerning the city of Worms itself; those relating to Lobdengau (the district around Ladenburg) and the Odenwald on the Neckar (a tributary of the Rhine); and those concerning Wimpfen, further upriver from Ladenburg. In what follows, each group will be considered in turn. But before doing so, it is worth summarizing their contents.

Group 1: Worms

1. D Kar 20 (——): **Pippin I** confirms the immunity of the church of Worms to **Bishop Erembert**.
2. D L D 74a (Frankfurt, 20 January 856): **Louis the German** grants **Bishop Samuel** of Worms mint, agricultural dues (*modius regis*), toll and other fiscal rights in the city.
3. D Arn 166 (Regensburg, 14 October 898): **Arnulf** grants **Bishop Hatto** of Worms mint, agricultural dues (*modius regis*), toll and other fiscal rights in the city.
4. D O I 84 (Frankfurt, 14 January 947): **Otto I** confirms **Bishop Richgowo** in possession of tolls in the city of Worms.
5. D O II 46 (Worms, 1 July 973): **Otto II** confirms **Bishop Anno** in possession of tolls and other fiscal rights in the city of Worms.

Group 2: Lobdengau and Odenwald

6. D Mer 30 (Mainz, 21 September 628): **Dagobert I** grants **Bishop Amandus** holdings and fiscal rights in Lobdengau and the Odenwald and extends immunity to these.
7. D Kar 257 (Valenciennes, July 798): **Charlemagne** confirms **Bishop Erembert** in possession of Ladenburg with fiscal rights in the Odenwald and Lobdengau, including immunity; and also grants the settlements of Edingen, Neckarshausen and Ilvesheim.
8. D L Fr 282 (Worms, 11 September 829): **Louis the Pious** and his son **Lothar** confirm **Bishop Folcwich** in possession of toll rights in Worms, Ladenburg and Wimpfen.

---

31. Uhlirz, *Jahrbücher*, i, 217–25, with Lechner, 'Zur Beurteilung'. For endorsement of Lechner's findings: Bresslau, Review of Lechner (with reservations); Stengel, *Immunität*, 199, 312–13; Böhmer, *Regesta imperii*, ii.2, no. 625. Note, however, Bresslau's later doubts: Bresslau, *Handbuch*, i, 87 n. 1. See also *Urkunden Ludwigs des Frommen*, ed. Kölzer, 703; Gilsdorf, *Favor of Friends*, 178–79; Kohl, 'Religious Exemption', all accepting Lechner *in toto*.

9. D L D 74b (Frankfurt, 20 January 856): **Louis the German** confirms **Bishop Samuel** in possession of Ladenburg with fiscal rights (including toll) there and in the Odenwald.

10. D O I 392 (Ravenna, 10 April 970): **Otto I** confirms **Bishop Anno's** right to forest income (*silvaticum*) in the Odenwald against the claims of Lorsch.

Group 3: Wimpfen

11. D L D 179 (Frankfurt, 20 August 856): **Louis the German** confirms **Bishop Samuel** in possession of immunity in and around Wimpfen.

12. D Arn 192 (Frankfurt, 7 August 897): **Arnulf** confirms Louis the German's grant of immunity at Wimpfen to **Bishop Thietlach**.

At the heart of the forgery complex lies the question of immunity—the subject of Anno's first forgery of 965—and its implications (above all, financial). The most important showplace was the city of Worms itself. It is here that episcopal authority was concentrated; it is here, too, that threats were greatest. The earliest diploma concerning episcopal rights in the city is in the name of Pippin I (751–68), the father of Charlemagne and founder of the famed Carolingian dynasty. This is framed as a confirmation of an even older privilege of the Merovingian ruler Dagobert—probably Dagobert I (623–39)—and there are similarities with the later Dagobert counterfeit concerning Ladenburg, as we shall see. The charter also draws on the forged Louis the Pious immunity of 814. It opens with a brief preamble, explaining that Pippin has deemed it right and good that he should conserve and confirm the grants of his predecessors to holy places. The king then proceeds to confirm immunity to Erembert on the terms previously granted by Dagobert. There is every reason to believe that a genuine diploma of Pippin lies behind this text, and probably one of immunity. (It is noteworthy, for example, that the older Latin *emunitas* is preferred to *immunitas*.) What identifies the charter as false, however, is a series of subtle anachronisms. The most obvious is the insertion of clauses adding toll rights to those of immunity. Tolls in the early Middle Ages came in three forms (broadly speaking): dues on goods crossing a frontier; dues on goods transported along major routes (rivers or roads); and dues on goods sold at market. In this case, the third is intended. As traditional regelian rights, tolls were analogous to immunity (which itself came with the profits of justice) and were of obvious importance in a trading town such as Worms. Immunity and tolls were, however, always granted separately in the eighth century; their combination here reflects the conventions of Anno's age, when the two were often transferred in tandem. Similarly significant is the manner in which episcopal estates are excluded from comital oversight, as the preference for prohibition formulae using the adjective *nullus* (no, not any) is also a later development.[32] Finally, signs of tampering can be seen in the text's efforts to locate these rights 'within the same city of Worms' ('in ipsa civitate Wormatiensi'), a turn of phrase found elsewhere in the complex.

Evidently tolls and comital oversight were points of contention, and these were to play a major part in the remaining forgeries. As noted, the importance of the latter lay in Worms's commercial prospects. As trade expanded, the city became important as a meeting point for merchants from north and south, a place where Italian, Frisian and Frankish traders rubbed shoulders. In a Carolingian context, the count was owed a third on all tolls and judicial fines (as the royal representative), even when the king had alienated the rest of these. By the mid- to later tenth century, however, grants of full toll, including the comital third, are found, as we see at Ladenburg in 953.[33] It may be this that Hildibald B had in mind: though no mention is made of the breakdown of incomes, the talk of 'all tolls' ('omne teoloneum') here could easily be construed as including the final comital third. If so, this was a creative misinterpretation of the original Carolingian formulation, one which sits well with the document's other anti-comital tendencies. Indeed, the privilege repeats the military exemption first found in the forged Louis the Pious immunity (and confirmed in 965), an exemption probably aimed at the local Salian count, as we have seen.[34]

The rest of the urban forgeries take a similar tack. The next, in the name of Louis the German (843–76), confirms Bishop Samuel in possession of mint rights, agricultural dues (the *modius regis*), complete toll (*omne theoloneum*) and other fiscal incomes within and without the city. Unlike the preceding Pippin text, Hildibald B has had to make do with a generic privilege of Louis the German here, from which he lifted the opening and closing sections (protocol and eschatocol). The rest of the diploma is his own creation, drawing elements from the Pippin privilege as well as from an authentic Louis the Pious and Lothar toll charter (of which more anon). It opens with a preamble reflecting on the benefits which accrue to those who confirm the pious grants of their predecessors, then has Louis confer mint and agricultural dues on Samuel before confirming his existing rights to tolls.[35] The focus of forgery has shifted subtly in the process. Already in the Pippin privilege, tolls were an essential part of immunity; now they take centre stage, and immunity is not mentioned at all. Similarly significant is the inclusion of minting rights—the right to strike coin and reap the profits of this. Carolingian rulers had been very reserved about granting out mint rights, but their Ottonian successors were far less so; once more, we seem to be seeing the ninth century through distinctly tenth-century spectacles. In fact, indications of renewed minting

32. Cf. Stengel, *Immunität*, 448.
33. Borchers, 'Untersuchungen'. See also Adam, *Zollwesen*.
34. D Kar 20. Cf. D Mer 30, D L Fr 25.
35. D L D 74a.

at Worms—dormant since *c.* 790—can be seen in the 960s, precisely when these counterfeits were probably being confected (as we shall see); and by the 970s there are signs of episcopal influence on the iconography of the resulting coins.[36]

Similar tendencies are visible in the Arnulf text, which confirms that of Louis the German. This opens with a briefer preamble, noting (again) the benefits to be gained from supporting the church, before proceeding to grant Bishop Hatto the same rights as secured by Samuel just over four decades previously. Here more use is made of an authentic exemplar (not least for the opening preamble), but Hildibald B's hand is revealed by the reference to the rights being 'within the city of Worms' ('infra Wormatiensem civitatem') and by the assertion that the confirmation extends to 'mint, toll and the *modius regis*' ('monetam, theoloneum, modium regis'), details lifted directly from the preceding Louis the German counterfeit.[37] The purpose of these charters is to provide cover for the Pippin fake, creating the impression of a longstanding tradition of episcopal rights in the city. Though it is likely that the bishopric had indeed received immunity in the Merovingian era, the main concern of the forgeries lies in the pertaining fiscal rights, above all to toll income. These details were almost certainly not in the original privileges. But the later counterfeits do more than just provide cover for the Pippin text. They also extend episcopal rights to the minting of coins, another royal prerogative frequently associated with immunity—and another valuable asset in the booming economy of the tenth-century Rhineland.

These claims are rounded off by privileges in the names of Otto I and Otto II, both of which survive as tenth-century single sheets (the others make their first appearance in the mid-twelfth-century Worms cartulary). Like the Louis the German and Arnulf texts, these are phrased as confirmations of toll rather than immunities. This may be because the bishopric's immunity had already been secured in 965. However, it also reflects Hildibald B's general interest in the financial (rather than judicial) implications of immunity. In any case, the Otto I privilege is based largely on an authentic Louis and Lothar charter, concerning tolls on Frisian merchants in the city.[38] Theodor Sickel, who edited the diploma in 1884, noted that though it is dated 947, the text is in a hand (that of Hildibald B) not seen before the 960s (or 978, if we follow Lechner). He therefore concluded that this was an imitative copy of an authentic earlier text (an *Abschrift in Diplomform*). As Lechner noted, however, it is hard to see this as an innocent 'copy'. The diploma was once sealed, and the surviving single sheet reveals a number of unusual signs of archaism—an

36. Heß, *Wormser Münzgeschichte*, 2–3. More generally: Kaiser, 'Münzprivilegien'; Kluge, *Deutsche Münzgeschichte*.

37. D Arn 166.

38. Cf. Lebecq, *Marchands et navigateurs*, i, 11–12, 27–28, 230–31, 239–40.

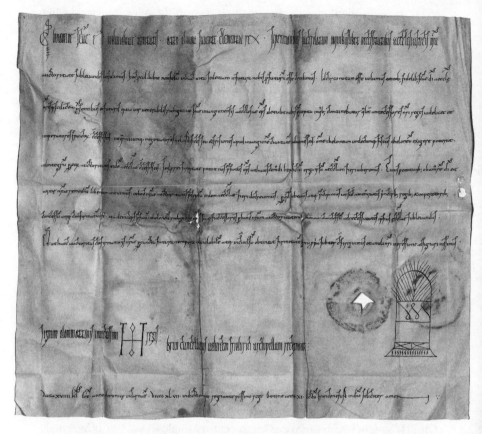

1.2 Otto I confirms Richgowo in possession of tolls in Worms: Darmstadt, HStA A 2
255/1, © HStA

indication, perhaps, that the scribe was trying to hide its true origins. Indeed,
though the hand is that of Hildibald B, the chrismon—the symbolic invocation
of Christ's name at the start—does not take his typical form, but rather evokes
those of the later Carolingian era (Illustration 1.2).[39] Similarly, Hildibald B has
constructed the closing eschatocol in a manner which harks back to an earlier
age, placing the royal subscription and chancery recognition on almost the same
line and including a 'beehive' recognition sign after this (all practices common till
the mid- to late 960s, but rare thereafter). Finally, the elongated capitals (*litterae
elongatae*) of the first line are shorter and more condensed than those we see
in most of Hildibald B's performances, perhaps also mimicking earlier forms.[40]

39. The diagnostic features are its modest size and use of 'wavy' horizontal (rather than
zig-zag) lines through the descender on C. See Eisenlohr, 'Invokations- und Rekognitionszeichen', with rich illustrative material.

40. D O I 84, Darmstadt, HStA, A 2 255/1. For diplomatic developments of these
years: Erben, *Kaiser- und Königsurkunden*, 116–88; Kölzer, 'Ottonisch-salische
Herrscherurkunde'; Rück, *Bildberichte*.

It is easy, therefore, to see why Lechner was inclined to condemn this diploma. Yet if this is a forgery, it makes a decidedly odd companion to the other fakes. For a start, it confirms the toll rights mentioned in the Pippin privilege, but passes over the additional fiscal rights of the Louis the German and Arnulf texts in silence. Moreover, its formulation is almost entirely lifted from the text of the Louis and Lothar toll charter, which Hildibald B also drew upon when formulating the Louis the German privilege. As we shall see, at some point the Louis and Lothar charter was itself 'improved' to make reference to Ladenburg and Wimpfen; but here it is quoted in its original (authentic) form. If this charter was intended to provide confirmation of Hildibald B's earlier counterfeits, it therefore does a pretty poor job. That said, the surviving single sheet is certainly not a product of 947, and probably belongs to the later 960s or (more likely) mid- to later 970s. Perhaps Otto I had publicly confirmed Worms's toll rights in 947, but production of the requisite diploma was delayed for two to three decades—an unusual, but by no means unprecedented, occurrence.[41] If so, Hildibald B may have worked from a draft text from this first occasion (what German scholars call a *Konzept*), which would explain the accurate dating clause and otherwise restrained terms (not to mention some of the odd archaisms). The most likely explanation, however, is that this is indeed a forgery, but one inspired by the terms of the authentic charter of Otto II concerning these rights. As we shall see, the latter refers to a prior privilege of the emperor's father, a detail taken over from its Louis and Lothar exemplar (where it refers to an act of Charlemagne). Since Worms possessed no such diploma of Otto I, Hildibald B may now have felt obliged to fill this gap. Whether he would have deemed the resulting product a forgery, however, is a good question. And it may once have borne an authentic seal, perhaps indicating a degree of acceptance at court.

Further light is shed by the final charter in the series, the Otto II diploma in question. This is dated 973 and framed as a confirmation of a privilege of his father, apparently the 947 text. As in the other cases, immunity is not the primary concern, but rather tolls, above all those on Frisian merchants in the city. As with the 947 privilege, the diploma is copied by Hildibald B, who is first attested outside Worms in 978. For Lechner, this suggested that this, like its purported Otto I model, was a product of these later years. He found signs of this in the imperial monogram at the foot of the text. As Sickel had already observed, this takes a form characteristic of Otto III's reign (983–1002), with the two o's of Otto (extending from the middle balcony) extremely small and rounded (Illustration 1.3). Sickel did not see this as grounds for suspicion, but did suggest that the present copy was produced in the 980s; Lechner went one step further, identifying it as an outright fake.[42] The fact that

41. The classic study remains Ficker, *Beiträge zur Urkundenlehre*.

42. D O II 46, Speyer, LA, F 7, 2, with Sickel, *Kaiserurkunden*, 52–53; Lechner, 'Zur Beurteilung'; Uhlirz, *Jahrbücher*, i, 222–23.

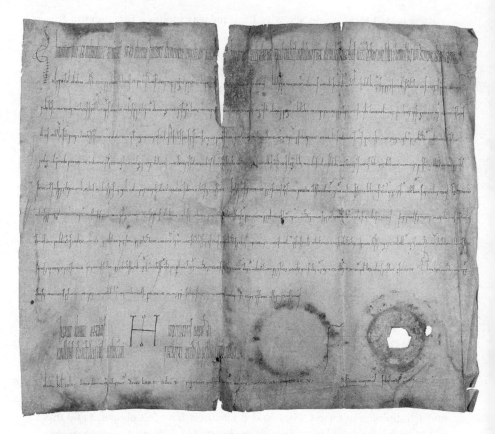

1.3 Otto II confirms Anno in possession of tolls and fiscal rights in Worms: Speyer, LA, F
7, 2, © LA Speyer

this diploma, unlike the 947 privilege, silently lifts details from the Louis the
German forgery—though not the concession of mint and agricultural dues
(*modius regis*)—does little to allay such concerns. Nevertheless, we should not
be too swift to condemn the charter. As we have seen, in 965 Anno used a false
immunity to obtain an authentic confirmation; he may now have attempted
the same with tolls.

   That this was indeed the case is suggested by another feature of the surviving single sheet, which has hitherto escaped notice. Close examination
of the original reveals that within the dating clause, the regnal and imperial
years of Otto I have been added later than the rest of the text, in slightly darker
ink and a larger hand (though conceivably still that of Hildibald B: Illustration
1.4). It was quite common for these details to be inserted later, since scribes
were often uncertain as to when the charter they were working on would be
formally sealed and issued; there was also frequently confusion about the correct regnal and imperial years. We would not, however, expect such uncertainty from a forger, who by definition knows what he intends to write before

1.4 Latter part of the dating clause of Otto II's confirmation of Anno's toll and fiscal rights: Speyer, LA, F 7, 2 © LA Speyer

he sets to work. This is not the only feature which speaks in favour of the diploma. If the monogram points toward later production, the hand itself tells a very different tale. As Lechner was aware, Hildibald B here uses a different abbreviation symbol from that of his later work, the closest parallel being in his privilege of 970 concerning episcopal rights in the Odenwald. Lechner was inclined to dismiss this, too, as a forgery of the mid-980s; and he interpreted the alternative abbreviation sign as an effort to hide Hildibald B's hand from prying eyes. Yet the 970 charter is certainly authentic, as we shall see, and this throws the 973 diploma into entirely different light. Rather than an elaborate deception, we are witnessing the natural evolution of Hildibald B's hand: in his early years he preferred one abbreviation sign, then came to adopt another in the later 970s. This conclusion finds support in what is likely to be Hildibald B's earliest work, a diploma of 966; here too, the less common abbreviation sign is used.

Given this, it is interesting to note that the 947 toll privilege uses the abbreviation sign associated with Hildibald B's later years. Might this actually have been drawn up after the 973 text? The fact that the latter mentions a precept of Otto I—apparently the 947 one—would seem to preclude this. And indeed, the editors of the 973 diploma presumed that it was modelled on the 947 charter. But both largely follow the earlier Louis and Lothar toll privilege, and detailed examination suggests a more complex relationship. On two points, the text of the Otto II diploma agrees with that of Otto I against their shared exemplar, potentially suggesting derivation. However, both of these are straightforward cases of modernizing formulation—replacing *fieri* (to be made) with *esse* (to be) in the publication clause and *eo quod* (because) with *qualiter* (how) in the narrative section—and so are hardly decisive. On the other hand, the 973 diploma refers to its exemplar as a 'precept of our lord and father of blessed memory' ('pręceptum domni genitoris nostri bonę memorię'), a line not found in the 947 privilege but present in the Louis and Lothar one, where it refers to a diploma of Charlemagne. Clearly the draftsman had this to hand when drawing up the 973 charter; and it is conceivable that it (rather than the 947 diploma) furnished the rest of the formulation. It may seem odd for a non-existent precept of Otto I to be invoked in a privilege of his son. But if the former had indeed been enacted in 947, there may have been every reason to maintain the pretence that it had, in fact, also been issued. (Certainly this would not be the only phantom diploma mentioned in these years.)[43] More likely is that this is simply an error. Hildibald B may have copied the turn of phrase unthinkingly from his exemplar, then found himself forced to forge an Otto I diploma in order to maintain the artifice. Whatever the solution, all indications are that the 973 charter is an authentic early example of Hildibald B's work. Like its 947 counterpart, this concerns rights claimed in earlier forgeries, but largely follows the more restrained terms of its authentic Louis and Lothar exemplar. The unusually advanced form of the imperial monogram is no major obstacle here. Hildibald B was the leading scribe at court when the new form was introduced in the 980s; it would seem that we are observing an early experiment, to which he later returned.

Further issues are presented by the fact that the 973 and 947 privileges seem to stand in contradiction to other evidence regarding these rights. As noted, both state that the bishop possessed full toll within the city, yet Anno's successor Hildibald first received the final (comital) third in 979. Here the problem may be more apparent than real. In both cases, the reference to 'full toll' ('omne teloneum') derives from the earlier Louis and Lothar charter, where it refers to the two-thirds at royal disposition; it may be that no more is intended here.[44] Slightly harder to explain is the reference to additional rights (such as *freda*) in the 973 privilege, since the comital share in these was apparently also first transferred to the bishop in 979. It is conceivable that here, too, the count's third was silently exempted in 973. Moreover, the rights conferred at this point are not mentioned by name in 979, so the latter grant may simply have built on the former, augmenting existing episcopal prerogatives. Certainly it would be dangerous to dismiss the 973 diploma, which survives as an acceptable single sheet, on the basis of the 979 privilege, which is only preserved in the twelfth-century Worms cartulary. The loss of the seal on the 973 diploma, like that of 947, means that we cannot categorically exclude tampering; nevertheless, the balance of probability is certainly in its favour.[45]

The next set of texts concerns the bishop's claim to comital, fiscal and forest rights in the Lobdengau (the district around Ladenburg) and the neighbouring Odenwald. As with the urban toll and immunity rights, the forger takes the history of these back into the Merovingian era. But whereas there

43. E.g. Kölzer, *Studien*, 69–72, and *Merowingerstudien* ii, 132. Note, however, the objections of Nightingale, *Monasteries and Patrons*, 228 n. 33.

44. D O II 199, with Borchers, 'Untersuchungen', 10, 34–35. See also Lechner, 'Die älteren Königsurkunden', 396–98.

45. Cf. Bresslau, *Handbuch*, ii, 620–21; Ewald, *Siegelkunde*, 228–29, on the process of removing and re-using seals, which often weakened them. For (possible) contemporary cases: Kölzer, *Studien*, 56–57; Kölzer and Ludwig, 'Diplom Ottos III.'.

he had started with Pippin confirming a Dagobert privilege, now Hildibald B goes one better and begins with Dagobert I himself. The diploma opens with a distinctive preamble, reflecting on the benefit to the king's soul, should he grant part of his inheritance to the holy places. At the advice of the mayor of the palace, Pippin, Arnulf of Metz and Hunibert of Cologne—so the diploma continues—Dagobert had agreed to grant Bishop Amandus of Worms Ladenburg with pertaining rights in the Lobdengau (above all, to market and toll) as well as forest income (*silvaticum*) in the Odenwald, extending immunity to all of these. As in the previous cases, Hildibald B had authentic material to work with, though probably a privilege of the lesser-known Dagobert III (711–15). If so, the change of ruler served not only to give the claims greater antiquity, but also to associate them with a king famed for his piety, not least at nearby Mainz. It may also reflect the frequent confusion of later observers (and modern scholars) over the three Dagoberts of the Merovingian era.[46] Interestingly, the Bishop Amandus in question is not otherwise attested in early sources from the region. His name may have been lifted from the original Dagobert III diploma. Alternatively, the seventh-century missionary saint of this name, who had been active around Maastricht, may have been conflated with other Worms traditions. Certainly by the early eleventh century an active cult of Amandus as episcopal founder can be identified at Worms, and this privilege speaks to these local traditions.[47] In any case, it is less the inherent implausibility of the transaction than the occasional lapse in formulation which betrays the forger. Thus the presence of an entrance prohibition for royal officers—a development of the later Merovingian period—reveals that the model post-dates Dagobert I's reign (hence the likelihood of a Dagobert III exemplar).[48] Moreover, the extension of immunity to specific holdings such as Ladenburg is not a feature of Merovingian diplomas, again reflecting later documentary practices. The resulting text is an attempt to secure Worms's claims in and around this strategic settlement, probably in response to encroachment from nearby Lorsch.

The next privilege buttresses these claims. This is the name of Charlemagne and dated 798, repeating and confirming the Dagobert donation while also granting the bishopric additional settlements (*villae*) at Edingen, Neckarhausen and Ilvesheim. Its formulation derives partly from the Dagobert text and partly from a lost privilege of Charlemagne, albeit one of the years 774–76, rather than 798.[49] This privilege is in turn confirmed by a diploma of Louis the Pious and his eldest son Lothar. Like the other pre-Ottonian texts, this

46. Wehrli, *Überlieferungen von Dagobert I.*, esp. 280–82, 305–7; Fouracre, 'Forgetting'.

47. Kohl and Felten, 'Worms', 104. On Amandus of Maastricht: Fletcher, *Conversion of Europe*, 147–54; I. N. Wood, *Missionary Life*, 38–42. Cf. Kölzer, *Merowingerstudien*, ii, 59, for a similar case.

48. D Mer 30. See *Urkunden der Merowinger*, ed. Kölzer, 82–83; Brühl, 'Die merowingische Immunität'. Cf. Murray, 'Merovingian Immunity'.

49. D Kar 257.

first survives in the mid-twelfth-century Worms cartulary. Unlike the others, however, it is substantially authentic, having furnished the model for the urban toll charters of 947 and 973. Yet at some stage the diploma has been adjusted to refer to Worms's tolls being located 'in the aforesaid city'—thus far the authentic text—'and also in the settlements of Ladenburg and Wimpfen' ('et in predicta civitate et in castellis Lobendunburg et Uuippina').⁵⁰ The effect of this change is to extend rights secured in Worms to the important market town at Ladenburg and to Wimpfen further upstream. Significantly, these additional details are reported in neither the 947 nor the 973 toll charters, which draw on the original text. Rights over Ladenburg are then confirmed in a privilege of Louis the German of 856. This is framed as a response to ongoing conflicts—perhaps a nod to the contested nature of these rights in later years. Again, material has been taken from an authentic early charter, but the detailed interest shown in the Lobdengau and Odenwald reveals the forger's interests.⁵¹ We know little about the history of Worms's rights in these areas, save that Anno had received the final third on tolls at Ladenburg in 953.⁵² This suggests existing interests, perhaps of some antiquity, but also indicates that these were more limited than the forgeries imply. Indeed, it is in 965 that we first hear of Worms's immunity extending to the Lobdengau.⁵³

Similar concerns lie at the heart of the final text in this set, which takes the story into the Ottonian period. This is in the name of Otto I, and was issued in Ravenna on 10 April 970, confirming Worms's right to forest income (*silvaticum*) in the Odenwald against the claims of Lorsch. Here the emperor explains how Anno had approached him on account of ongoing conflicts. Having re-read the precept of Dagobert, as well as subsequent privileges of Pippin, Charlemagne and Louis (the Pious)—the forgeries we have just met—Otto now saw fit to confirm Worms's rights, which are to be held under full immunity. As is the case with the other single sheets, the body of this charter has been written by Hildibald B (Illustration 1.5). And this, combined with the citation of the earlier fakes, led Lechner to conclude that it was a counterfeit of the 980s. The matter is complicated, however, by the presence of a second hand. As Sickel noted in his edition, the elongated script of the opening and closing lines does not take the forms characteristic of Hildibald B, but rather those of another figure. This otherwise unidentified individual supplied the same details in a charter for Magdeburg, issued just over two months earlier, also in northern Italy (Illustration 1.6).⁵⁴

50. D L Fr 282.
51. D L D 74b.
52. D O I 161.
53. D O I 310, Darmstadt, HStA, A2 255/3. See Büttner, 'Ladenburg am Neckar'; Schaab, 'Ladenburg'.
54. D O I 392, Darmstadt, HStA, A2 251/1; D O I 388b, Magdeburg, LA Sachsen-Anhalt, U 1, I 34b. Hand identity in the protocol is certain; whether this extends to the

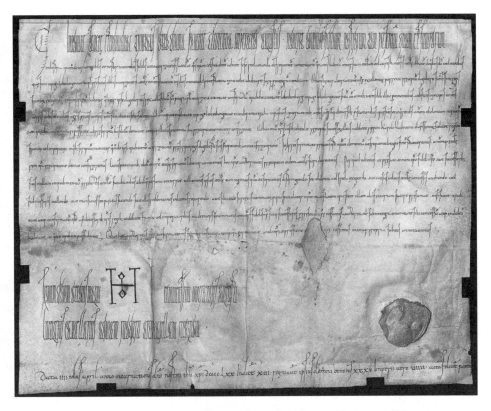

1.5 Otto II settles a dispute over forest rights in the Odenwald in favour of Worms: Darmstadt, HStA A2 251/1, © HStA

The presence of this second hand considerably complicates matters. Initially, Lechner argued that the main text of the Odenwald charter had been erased and rewritten by Hildibald B in the 980s, in which case these features can be readily explained: they are the relics of an earlier (authentic) version of the text. However, inspection of the original raises significant doubts here. For a start, there are no signs of erasure. The parchment is rough, but the patches of roughness do not coincide with areas of script, and no hints of earlier writing can be discerned. More to the point, the ink used throughout is of the same tint, indicating that the two hands worked together (or in very close succession), not decades apart.[55] With this, Lechner's case collapses. When confronted by Uhlirz about this, Lechner mooted the possibility that the

eschatocol, as Sickel suggests, is less so (though on balance more likely than not). In any case, this individual is not Hildibald B, as Huschner, *Transalpine Kommunikation*, 682 n. 258, asserts, but he may be right that D O I 388b is earlier than D O I 388a. See further Weinert, 'Offizielle Titulatur', 170–71; Klimm, 'Ottonische Diplome', 252.

55. Darmstadt, HStA, A2 251/1. See Lechner, 'Die älteren Königsurkunden', 374–75.

1.6 A/B Opening *elongatae* of Otto II's Odenwald diploma and those of his earlier Magdeburg charter: Darmstadt, HStA A2 251/1; Magdeburg, LA Sachsen-Anhalt U 1, I 34b, © HStA, LA Sachsen-Anhalt

Magdeburg text had itself not been drawn up in early 970. Yet his alternative solution—to push the production of both this and the Odenwald diploma into the 980s—creates more problems than it resolves.[56] It requires us to presume that transactions enacted within months of each other in northern Italy, for recipients on opposite sides of the realm, were then left over a decade before being completed with the involvement of the same (otherwise unattested!) hand. The chances of this are vanishingly small. In any case, the main text of the Magdeburg privilege is itself written by a well-known scribe, Liudolf H, who was present in northern Italy in early 970, but is not attested after 980; there can be no doubt that this diploma was indeed produced on the spot in Pavia in January of that year.[57] And since Anno petitioned this privilege, it would not be surprising if one of the scribes went on to operate in his favour a few months later.

Much hinges on this diploma. If it can be accepted, then many of the other Ottonian charters Lechner was inclined to impeach should be given the benefit of the doubt; if not, all early products of Hildibald B hang under a cloud. Given what has been said, it will come as no surprise that the text itself makes

56. Lechner, 'Zur Beurteilung', 103–8. Cf. Uhlirz, *Jahrbücher*, i, 220.

57. On this scribe, see most recently Hoffmann, 'Notare', 446–49.

a good impression. Nothing in its appearance or formulation speaks against placing it in 970 (save the presence of Hildibald B's hand, and here we must be wary of circular reasoning). And the rights claimed are less wide-ranging than has sometimes been presumed. Though mention is made of rights on either side of the Itter, the river which bisects the Odenwald, the terms do not contradict other sources regarding episcopal claims in the region.[58] Significantly, this diploma now cites the 'improved' version of the Louis and Lothar toll privilege, which the 947 toll charter had quoted in its original form. For this reason, the Ladenburg and Wimpfen counterfeits have been thought to post-date those concerning the city. Yet if so, the 947 privilege cannot be any later than 970—earlier than its palaeographical features suggest—while the 973 toll charter must also have ignored the interpolated version of the diploma (though its formulation is vaguer on this point). We should perhaps be wary of expecting too much consistency here. Hildibald B may have kept a copy of the original Louis and Lothar text to hand, to which he reverted—mistakenly or otherwise—when producing the 947 privilege. Alternatively, he may only have cited those details in need of confirmation, leaving to one side the Lobdengau rights already secured in 970.

In any case, the final set of counterfeits concerns Wimpfen, further upstream from Ladenburg on the Neckar. The bishop of Worms possessed a dependent house here, and one of Anno's major successes had been to have his immunity over this and Ladenburg confirmed in 965, on the basis of the suspect Louis the Pious privilege. The first of the relevant texts here is the interpolated Louis and Lothar toll privilege, discussed above, which links the bishopric's rights in Wimpfen to those at Ladenburg, associating both with those in the city of Worms. But while in the market towns of Worms and Ladenburg the main concern was tolls, at Wimpfen it was the judicial rights of immunity. This is clear from the second Wimpfen text, in the name of Louis the German. As previously, Hildibald B did not have a diploma of this king to hand, so resorted to lifting protocol and eschatocol, along with certain dispositive details, from the Louis the German privilege he had earlier confected for Ladenburg, merely adjusting the date. Specifically, Bishop Samuel is said to have complained of the difficulties he has encountered with royal tax collectors and counts ('regie potestatis procuratores et exactores atque comites'), on account of which the king conferred the generous immunity on the see. Samuel clearly ventriloquizes Anno's later concerns here, and it should be noted that Wimpfen probably lay in another of Otto of Worms's counties (Elsenzgau). The real novelty, however, lies in the charter's elaborate description of episcopal rights, carefully mapping out the boundaries of the immunity. If implemented, this would have extended Worms's judicial prerogatives well beyond its own properties, creating an island of episcopal jurisdiction on the Neckar. As Theodor Sickel noted, such territorial immunities (what German scholars call 'ban immunities', *Bannimmunitäten*) were a development of the later tenth century; and once more, we are observing concepts of Anno's own day finding their way into the forgeries.[59]

These rights then find partial confirmation in a privilege of Arnulf, dated 897. Here, too, Hildibald B did not have an authentic immunity of the king to work from, so was forced to take protocol and eschatocol from an authentic Arnulf precept in favour of Worms's dependent church at Neuhausen. The main text, however, largely draws on the earlier urban toll charter of Louis the German. Partly as a consequence, it lacks the detail of the preceding privilege, particularly with respect to the boundaries of the immunity; nevertheless, it is clearly intended as a confirmation of these rights.[60] No Ottonian charter rounds off this series, a situation which finds a partial parallel at Ladenburg, where only rights to forest income in the Odenwald had been subject to confirmation. It would seem that the 965 immunity, which already named Ladenburg and Wimpfen, sufficed in these cases.

Finally, beyond the three well-defined groups, a set of more miscellaneous texts has been associated with Hildibald B's forging activities. The first is a diploma of Conrad I (911–18), confirming earlier grants to the bishopric. There is nothing inherently suspicious about the act. But its terms, which speak of rights 'within and without the city of Worms' ('intra civitatem Wormatiam et extra'), loosely recall Hildibald B's formulation, raising the possibility that he reworked it at a later date. Since the diploma only survives in the Worms cartulary, certainty is impossible. However, it shares no material with the other identified forgeries, and seems unlikely to be an outright fake.[61] More important is a grant by Otto I to a certain Gumbert of estates in the Wormsgau, which had been confiscated in previous years. This is dated 966 and written in a hand which Sickel and Lechner identified as that of Hildibald B. However, the document differs in a number of respects from this scribe's other attested work. For a start, he has badly misjudged the spacing. After opening with three lines of close, evenly-spaced text, he has realized that far too much parchment remains and increased his line-gaps accordingly; he has also increased word-spacing and started to employ dramatically—almost comically—drawn-out ligatures, to eat up as much of the remaining sheet as possible. Even so, he has been left with far more parchment than he needs

59. D L D 179, with Sickel, 'Beiträge zur Diplomatik I.', 396–98. See further Stengel, *Immunität*, 589–98; and on comparable developments in France: Lemarignier, 'De l'immunité'; Mehu, *Paix et communautés*, 59–86, 133–93; Mazel, *Féodalités*, 146–48. More generally: Mazel, *L'évêque et le territoire*.

60. D Arn 192. Cf. D Arn 157, D L D 74a.

61. D K I 37, with Lechner, 'Die älteren Königsurkunden', 538–44; Weinert, 'Ofizielle Titulatur', 171–75; Brühl, *Deutschland–Frankreich*, 413 n. 8 (ironically unaware of Weinert's work). Cf. Goetz, 'Der letzte "Karolinger"?', who passes over the issue in silence.

1.7 Diploma of Otto I in favour of Gumbert: Darmstadt, HStA A 2 255/4, © HStA

for the seal and closing eschatocol, which follow after a long gap (Illustration 1.7). Here, too, he was unsure of himself: the imperial monogram is traced uncertainly, and the top right corner of this has been smudged: all signs of inexperience. The question is whether this is the work of the same accomplished hand we see in later years; and, if so, how we can explain these anomalies.[62]

To start with the first question, this does indeed seem to be Hildibald B's work. Though he has constructed the chrismon and opening elongated letters in different forms from those he would later employ, the consistent preference for 'cc' a, the form of ct ligature, and (above all) the distinctive looped

62. D O I 330, Darmstadt, HStA, A2 255/4. See *Urkunden Konrads I., Heinrichs I. und Ottos I.*, ed. Sickel, 444; Lechner, 'Die älteren Königsurkunden', 532–33; Uhlirz, *Jahr-bücher*, i, 221–22 (also citing the opinion of Wilhelm Erben).

descender on g all suggest hand identity. Similarly significant is the consistent preference for the abbreviation sign found in Hildibald B's other early work. In fact, we can observe hints of forms which would later be characteristic of this scribe. In the final dating clause, for example, the ascender of t just punctures the horizontal cross-stroke, as we often see in his mature work, while the elongated letters of the closing eschatocol much more closely resemble his later performances than those in the first line. Finally, there are a number of signs of archaism, which find interesting parallels in Hildibald B's other early performances. The presence of a beehive recognition sign is not especially unusual for 966, but certainly speaks of conservativism; the use of *et* (and) to introduce this—a relic of an era in which the symbol still possessed its original meaning as an abbreviation for *subscripsi* (I have subscribed)—is more so.[63] Likewise, in the imperial subscription Otto I is called 'most glorious' (*gloriossissimus*) rather than 'most victorious' (*invictissimus*) or 'most serene' (*serenissimus*), in line with ninth- rather than tenth-century conventions.

On the basis of these features, Lechner deemed this diploma suspect, suggesting that it was produced alongside Hildibald B's other forgeries in the mid-980s (by which time *gloriossisimus* had been reintroduced into the royal subscription). Yet there is no obvious motive for forgery. The diploma is not in favour of Worms—indeed the bishopric is not known ever to have possessed the estates in question. One might speculate that Gumbert was an associate of Anno or Hildibald, who subsequently granted these lands to the see (an arrangement which would, incidentally, explain how the cathedral came to possess the charter).[64] But if so, why forgery should be necessary, and why Hildibald B should manufacture a diploma in favour of a layman (rather than the cathedral itself), remains inexplicable. Since we know that Hildibald B had produced an authentic charter for Worms in 970, it is hardly a massive leap to imagine that he was doing so locally four years earlier. In fact, the uneven execution of this diploma—which stands in stark contrast with Hildibald B's other work—strongly suggests that it was a first effort.[65] This also explains the odd archaisms: as a local scribe with little prior experience of diploma production, Hildibald B may have thought these forms still current. One further consideration speaks in favour of the act. As Sickel noted, it and the next two diplomas of 966 bear the correct regnal dates, in contrast with other privileges of the time. Evidently most scribes had fallen into error, but as an outsider Hildibald B was in a good position to correct this. Once he had

63. Cf. Erben, *Kaiser- und Königsurkunden*, 163–64.
64. On Gumbert: Zotz, 'Adelsherrschaften', 351–52.
65. Bresslau, Review of Lechner, 546.

done so, the draftsmen of the next two diplomas—one of which survives as an original—were able to follow his lead.[66]

The final diploma which demands our attention is a grant to Worms of the imperial abbey at Mosbach. Mosbach lies on the eastern bank of the Neckar, between Ladenburg and Wimpfen, in precisely those regions where Anno had sought to secure the see's interests (Map 1). The editors of the charter in the late nineteenth century only had access to the copy preserved in the twelfth-century Worms cartulary, and they ascribed it to Hildibald B on the basis of formulation. Given the proposed draftsman (Hildibald B) and date (976), Lechner predictably condemned the text as a forgery, suggesting that the list of pertaining rights had been tampered with by Hildibald B at a later date. Yet unbeknownst to Lechner, the original had since been discovered, making its way into the collection of Marc Rosenberg. Here the archivist Peter Albert was able to consult it. The charter was already in bad condition, but Albert was satisfied that it was authentic, and promised a facsimile.[67] Sadly this never followed, and the charter itself went up (quite literally) in smoke, along with lion's share of the Rosenberg collection, when his Schapbach residence burned down in 1915. Thankfully, a photograph survives at the Generallandesarchiv in Karlsruhe—probably that made for Albert, who had begun his archival career at Karlsruhe—and this makes a good impression (Illustration 1.8).[68] It bears an authentic seal and shows no signs of tampering. The placement of the chancery recognition to the right (rather than immediately beneath) the imperial subscription is somewhat unusual for 976, but not unparalleled (and may, in any case, be put down to recipient influence).[69] Most importantly, the text was clearly written by Hildibald B, as the distinctive looped descenders on g (even in elongated forms), the preference for 'cc' a, the form of ę, and the formation of the ct and st ligatures all attest.[70] Interestingly, the forms used stand somewhere between those seen in this scribe's earliest works and his 'chancery' productions of the later 970s and 980s, precisely as we might expect of a text

66. D O I 331, Magdeburg, LA Sachsen-Anhalt, U 1, I 23; D O I 332, with Sickel, 'Beiträge zur Diplomatik VIII.', 164.

67. Albert, 'Die ältesten Nachrichten', 613–20. See further Lechner, 'Wormser Kaiserurkunde'; Albert, 'Noch einmal'.

68. D O II 143, Karlsruhe, GLA A 46a. On Albert: Leesch, *Die deutschen Archivare*, ii, 28; note that the remains of the Rosenberg collection also went to the Generallandesarchiv. Cf. Nienhaus, 'Schapbacher Schlössle'.

69. See, e.g., D O II 55, Trier, Stadtarchiv, Urk. D 4; D O II 123, Einsiedeln, Klosterarchiv, KAE A.BI.5; D O II 134, Munich, BayHStA, EU Salzburg 2; D O II 135, Munich, BayHStA, HU Passau 16; D O II 140, Magdeburg, LA Sachsen-Anhalt, U 1, I 44; D O II 142, Rheda, Fürstliches Archiv, H 2.

70. See also Erika Eisenlohr's judgement, cited in *Mosbacher Urkundenbuch*, ed. Krimm, 2–3 n. 1. For a modern facsimile: Rößling and Scharzmaier, *Unverrückbar für alle Zeiten*, 86–87.

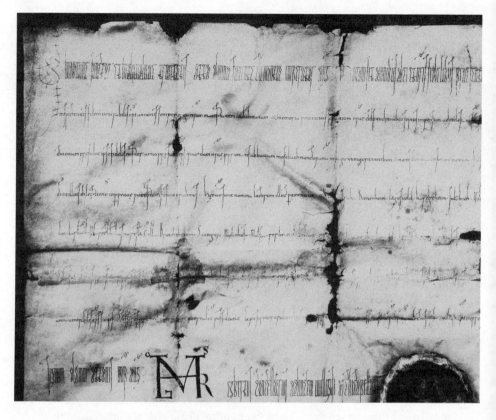

1.8 Otto II's lost diploma granting Mosbach to Worms (reproduced from a modern photo): Karlsruhe, GLA A 46a, © GLA Karlsruhe

of 976. In particular, he now adopts the abbreviation sign of his later years, but still employs a version of chrismon he had used earlier (but soon abandoned).

Finding the Forger

As we have seen, there has been some uncertainty about these texts, particularly those in the names of Otto I and Otto II. The latter were accepted as authentic by their editors in the 1870s and 1880s, but condemned by Lechner in 1901 and, following him, by most subsequent commentators. For Theodor Sickel and his team, it had been the presence of Hildibald B's hand which was decisive: this marked the diplomas out as products of a known chancery scribe—even if operating in a recipient capacity—and thus authentic. For Lechner, however, it was this which raised doubts. Because Hildibald B could only be found producing documents for recipients outside Worms after 978, Lechner concluded that all of his earlier texts must be dated to these later years—and must, therefore, be forgeries. Though differently applied, the principle behind these judgements was essentially the same: the famed dictum of Sickel that the strongest sign of authenticity comes when we find the same hand and formulation in documents of the same period for different recipients. For Sickel and his co-editors, Hildibald B's activities in the later 970s were sufficient to authenticate his earlier efforts; for Lechner, it was precisely these which raised suspicions.[71]

While Sickel's dictum remains a useful rule of thumb, models of charter production have changed considerably since 1901, as we have seen. Diplomatists have come to realize that though some scribes were employed at court over long periods of time, they did not belong to a formal institution (viz., 'the chancery') which they entered and left in the manner of a modern government bureau. Rather, many different individuals were involved in drafting and copying diplomas in a flexible manner. Anyone with the requisite skills might be called upon to do so; and those who were, usually were so more than once. Not all (or even most) of these were in permanent royal employ; and even those who were maintained local interests and connections.[72] Viewed in this light, there is nothing inherently suspicious about Hildibald B's activities: he was a local scribe gazetted into imperial service in the later 970s. Were his early efforts restricted to the confirmation of forged toll and immunity charters for his see, we might entertain Lechner's case. But they are not. He also produced authentic diplomas for Gumbert in 966 and concerning Mosbach in 976, neither of which bear any relationship to known fakes. Moreover, in the 970 Odenwald privilege he worked alongside another contemporary hand, making it all but certain that he was active at this point. And once we accept that he was involved in producing texts of 966, 970 and 976 in favour of Worms and its neighbours, it becomes all the more likely that the 947 and 973 toll charters belong to these years, too. The former may indeed be a forgery, but the latter is not, and their constrained terms continue to speak in their favour.

If placing the start of Hildibald B's activities in the mid-960s serves to rehabilitate some documents long deemed suspect, it also raises more forcefully the question of their relationship to the forged Louis the Pious immunity. As we have seen, this makes its first appearance in 965, only a year before Hildibald B's first recorded activity. Might it not be part of the same action? And if so, was it too the work of Hildibald B? Superficially, the case would not seem to be especially strong. As we have seen, the focus of the Louis the Pious forgery is military exemption, not tolls, and Hildibald B's diploma of 966 was almost certainly a first effort. Still, a number of interesting points of contact emerge. For a start, the terms of the military exemption betray a distinctly

71. *Urkunden Konrads I., Heinrichs I. und Ottos I.*, ed. Sickel, 444, 533–34; *Urkunden Otto des II.*, ed. Sickel, 55; Uhlirz, *Jahrbücher*, i, 217–25; Lechner, 'Zur Beurteilung'. For the principle: Sickel, 'Beiträge zur Diplomatik VI.', 360–62.

72. Huschner, 'Die ottonische Kanzlei'. See further above, 6–8.

anti-comital bent, much like Hildibald B's later productions for Worms and Wimpfen. More to the point, the Louis the Pious immunity extends the bishopric's rights to Ladenburg and Wimpfen, the other subjects of Hildibald B's later counterfeits (in the latter case, also concerning immunity). The approach taken by the forger is also similar. Wherever possible, Hildibald B drew on authentic texts, just as this individual did little more than add a few details to an otherwise genuine Louis the Pious privilege. Partly as a consequence, there are few signs of the forger's style here, which might allow for a more confident identification (though the same is true of many texts ascribed by Lechner to Hildibald B). Still, there may be hints of his involvement. The use of the slightly rarer verb *apsicere* (to belong) to designate the pertaining rights in the Louis immunity finds close parallels in the Arnulf Wimpfen immunity and an authentic later diploma of Hildibald B.[73] Likewise, the pronounced interest in the financial implications of immunity—particularly in tolls and the judicial exactions known as *freda*—is reminiscent of the later Worms forgeries, above all the Louis the German urban toll privilege, with which it also shares turns of phrase.[74] Most importantly, the Louis the Pious immunity was itself drawn upon at least twice within the series. We know that Hildibald B frequently recycled his own work—indeed, all the other texts he cites show signs of his tampering—so this may itself be grounds for suspicion.

A strong case can be made, therefore, for treating this diploma as part of the same complex, and perhaps even a product of the same forger. It was not uncommon for forgers to start small, reworking or interpolating one or two authentic texts, and this would explain the arc between the substantially authentic Louis the Pious, Pippin and Dagobert immunities and the more egregious privileges in the names of Louis the German and Arnulf.[75] If Hildibald B was indeed responsible for the Louis the Pious immunity, it may seem odd that he did not produce the diploma confirming it in 965, as he did in 970 for rights in the Odenwald and in 973 for urban tolls. Perhaps he was still learning the tricks of the trade (conceivably from an older confrère); certainly his first foray into diploma production in 966 was not a runaway

---

73. D L Fr 25: '**rebus** ibidem **aspicientibus**'; D Arn 192: '**rerum** atque locorum sancti Petri ad Wimpinam **aspicientium**'; D O III 109: 'cum omnibus **rebus** illuc rite **aspicientibus**'.

74. D L Fr 25: 'ergo iubemus, **ut nullus iudex publicus** neque quislibet **ex iudicaria potestate** . . . ad causas audiendas, **vel freda seu telonea** exigenda aut **mansiones** vel paratas faciendas aut fideiussores tollendos aut ullus redibitiones illicitas requirendas aut homines ipsius ecclesie **tam igenios quam et servos distringendas** ingredi audeat'; D L D 74a: 'hac nostra auctoritate concedimus interdicentes, **ut nullus iudex publicus** nec quisquam **ex iudiciaria potestate** in **mansionibus** ibi dandis **aut teloneo vel fredo** de familiis ecclesie uspiam poscendo aut homines eidem ęcclesię subditis **tam ingenuis quam etiam servis distringendis** aliquod ius habeat . . .' It should be noted that these are relatively common formulae, however: Stengel, *Immunität*, 632–39.

75. Cf. Kölzer, *Studien*, 53, 110.

success. In any case, the confirmation was written by Liudolf K, apparently working from a draft of Liudolf H, both figures associated with Anno's some-time abbey at Magdeburg.[76] These individuals were also in a sense recipient scribes, and the suspicion is that Anno was calling in a favour.

The final question which requires revisiting is that of Hildibald B's identity. As we shall see, in the 1960s Heinrich Fichtenau demonstrated that the career and activities of Pilgrim of Passau (971–91) overlapped to such an extent with those of the draftsman-scribe Willigis C that the two can be confidently iden-tified as one and the same. Fichtenau hinted that similar conclusions might hold of Hildibald B and Anno's successor Hildibald, whom Lechner thought had commissioned the Worms forgeries. Since then, Johannes Fried and Wolf-gang Huschner have adopted the identification, in the latter case as part of a wide-ranging argument that most draftsman-scribes of the era were lead-ing bishops.[77] The possibility of a connection should not be ignored. Though most of those responsible for diploma production were almost certainly not leading figures within the ecclesiastical hierarchy (*pace* Huschner),[78] prelates did occasionally operate as charter scribes. And under certain circumstances, this might extend to quite considerable duties, as in the case of Wibald of Stavelot (d. 1158), who was simultaneously abbot of Stavelot-Malmédy (and latterly Corvey) and a leading draftsman-scribe in the early to mid-twelfth century.[79] The problem, however, is that the connection between Hildibald B and Hildibald hangs on the presumption that the Worms forgeries were produced in the latter's episcopate—a presumption we have seen to be false. Without it, there is no a priori connection between the two. We are, therefore, better off leaving Hildibald B as one of the many anonymous charter scribes of the age, known only from script and formulation.

Form and Function

Since the pioneering work of Lechner, the Worms forgeries have been con-sidered a bold assertion of episcopal rights in the face of threat. In Lechner's own words, they constituted 'the foundation of the bishop's princely power' ('die Begründung der bischöflichen Fürstenmacht'). Moving the texts forward a decade or two would not seem to change this fundamentally. If anything, accepting most of the Ottonian toll and immunity privileges as authentic makes the ploy all the more ingenious: Anno had false precepts manufactured,

76. Stengel, *Immunität*, 168–70.

77. Fichtenau, 'Urkundenfälschungen', 178; Fried, *Weg in die Geschichte*, 571; Husch-ner, *Transalpine Kommunikation*, 168–74 (and cf. ibid., 175–81).

78. Hoffmann, 'Notare'; Merta, Review of Huschner. I hope the return to the subject elsewhere.

79. Hausmann, *Reichskanzlei und Hofkapelle*, 167–257. However, note the objections of Hoffmann, 'Briefbuch'.

on which basis he was able to secure genuine concessions. This certainly was part of the game. And, as we can see in the Odenwald, Anno's counterfeits could carry the day in the case of conflict. Still, the question remains as to whether the other forgeries, which are not cited in contemporary disputes, can be explained so easily.

In this respect, one of the most surprising features of these texts is how restrained they are. As Thomas Kohl notes, the forged Worms immunities do little more than extend episcopal rights to Ladenburg and Wimpfen; yet the extension is not strictly necessary. Unless otherwise specified, immunity covered all holdings of a religious house. That this was so at Worms is shown by the terms of the 965 immunity, which not only mentions dependent churches at Ladenburg and Wimpfen by name, but also emphasizes that the rights pertain to all 'the other holdings of that see' ('reliquas possessiones predicate sedis').[80] What advantage was to be achieved by forgery here? The answer lies partly in the ancillary rights, above all to tolls and mint at the valuable markets at Worms and Ladenburg. Though historians often speak of immunity as if it were a well-defined legal status, in practice it was remarkably protean. Depending on the church, region or era, it might encompass judicial independence, royal protection, religious liberty, fiscal rights, or a combination thereof.[81] At Worms, Hildibald B evidently sought to define these rights in such a way as to secure the see's financial interests, while insulating the bishop against comital influence. Yet even here, the forgeries largely serve to buttress existing claims. This is not entirely surprising. Antiquity was strongly associated with authority in the Middle Ages, and older texts might prevail where younger ones would not.[82] Perhaps most crucially, the counterfeits help frame established rights in manners more appropriate for a younger age. In defining the extent of Worms's immunity more precisely—a trend particularly pronounced in the Wimpfen diplomas—Hildibald B responds to the increasingly territorialized world of tenth- and eleventh-century power and justice (reflected not least by the rise of the ban immunity). His efforts also reflect wider trends within the institutional church, which saw bishops start to extend their authority further into the countryside.[83]

Still, the point remains that these documents do not so much claim what Anno lacks, as tease out the implications of what he has. The partial exception is the ambitious territorial immunity in the Louis the German Wimpfen diploma. But the details of this are left out of the Arnulf privilege confirming it, so can hardly be considered central to the forger's purpose. Indeed, we

80. D O III 310. See Kohl, 'Religious Exemption', 224–25, 228.

81. Manganaro, 'Forme e lessico'. See also Manganaro, *Stabilitas regni*, 235–320.

82. For the classic statements: Kern, 'Recht und Verfassung'; Clanchy, 'Remembering the Past'.

83. Innes, *State and Society*, 241–50; Mazel, *L'évêque et le territoire*. More generally: West, *Reframing*, 173–98.

may do better to think of these texts as an attempt to trace the history of the bishopric's rights, updating them as needs be. They are counterparts to the 965 immunity and its forged Louis the Pious exemplar: the latter had secured Worms's rights at Ladenburg and Wimpfen; the forgeries now supplied the backstory.

Much the same is true of the urban toll charters. Though some of these—particularly those in the names of Louis the German and Arnulf—include impressive lists of appurtenant rights, these made surprisingly little impression on the Otto I and II confirmations, which would furnish the basis for future privileges. The former, in particular, does no more than repeat the terms of the earlier (authentic) toll charter of Louis and Lothar. The Otto II diploma goes slightly further, as we have seen, but is still hardly brazen. If this was wishful thinking, Anno and his associates were decidedly unimaginative. In fact, here too the purpose probably lay less in claiming new rights than in explaining and justifying how existing ones came into episcopal hands. Worms had been granted toll by Louis and Lothar; the forgeries simply bridge the gap between this and the more extensive rights the see held in the mid-tenth century. The ambiguity inherent in the reference to 'all tolls' in the original grant left open the possibility of extending these into the final comital third, and the bishop did indeed acquire this in 979; whether this was the aim from the start, however, is far from clear (none of these texts are cited in the 979 grant).[84]

Most of the forgeries were, therefore, apparently not produced with litigation in mind. This is not to say that they were not intended to be credible evidence. The use of authentic exemplars reveals a desire for verisimilitude, and no doubt it was hoped that they would pass muster if required. Still, these undertakings are best understood as part of a broader antiquarian endeavour on the part of Anno and Hildibald B. As we have seen, the latter's earliest works—many of them authentic—reveal a number of interesting archaisms, which are best understood as the fruits of archival study. Hildibald B had evidently spent much time scrutinizing Worms's early muniments, and reverted accidentally to a number of older forms when he came to produce his own charters. Most of these features disappear during his later 'chancery' years, but he did play a part in reintroducing the tradition of summarizing earlier exemplars when confirming immunities, a compositional technique he had learned from earlier Worms texts.[85] This is not the only sign of historical interests at Worms in these years. Almost all the early originals from the bishopric bear endorsements—archival notes on the reverse, describing their contents.

---

84. D O II 199, later confirmed in D O III 12, Darmstadt, HStA, A2 255/5.

85. Stengel, *Immunität*, 202–3. Note that since D L Fr 282 must have been produced before 970, Hildibald B would have been acquainted with this approach by this point; certainly it also appears in D O I 84.

And though these are not in Hildibald B's hand, they are contemporary with it.[86] The importance of this lies in the nature of endorsement. Charters were endorsed as a means of organizing and categorizing an archive; it meant their contents could be easily identified without unfolding the parchment in question (being large and unwieldy, charters were stored folded).[87] These are, therefore, signs that the bishop and canons were taking stock.

Perhaps the most striking feature of the forgeries, however, is that none survives in its pseudo-original format (i.e., as forged in the 960s or 970s). In part, this is a function of the chequered history of the Worms archive, which suffered significant losses during the sack of the city in 1689 and again upon the see's dissolution in 1803. Still, other documents fared far better. Of forty authentic privileges in the names of the Ottonian rulers, fifteen survive as single sheets, giving a survival rate of just under 40%. Much the same is true of the smaller clutch of authentic Carolingian diplomas, three of seven of which survive as originals (just over 40%). Why, then, should all nine (or ten) of the forgeries have vanished? It can hardly be chance. Presuming a 40% survival rate, the random probability of such losses lies at about 1%—not quite impossible, but certainly improbable. It can also scarcely be neglect. Anno's investment in these texts is clear, and they remained important in later years, taking pride of place in the mid-twelfth-century cartulary, which opens with the Dagobert toll and immunity privilege. Three were also chosen for inspection by Emperor Sigismund (1411–37), revealing their relevance then.[88] It is conceivable that they were part of the same dossier, which went missing *en masse*; but why the closely related Ottonian privileges should have survived then becomes difficult to explain.

It is hard to resist the conclusion that many (perhaps all) of these never existed as pseudo-originals at all. In other words, Hildibald B may never have produced what he claimed to be the original documents, but rather satisfied himself with manufacturing copies of purportedly earlier texts. If so, their preservation would have been a matter of much less concern, particularly once the cartulary had been compiled in the twelfth century; there was little need to hold duplicate non-original copies.[89] The possible exception here is the Louis the Pious immunity, which clearly did exist as a single sheet, since Sigismund inspected this in 1415 and J. V. Armbruster consulted it for the Reichskammergericht (Imperial Chamber Court) in the early eighteenth century. But this is the text least firmly associated with Hildibald B, so we must be wary of generalizing on its basis. The fact that two other documents were also inspected

86. Hoffmann and Pokorny, *Dekret des Bischofs Burchard*, 14 n. 6.

87. Stengel and Semmelmann, 'Fuldensia, IV.', 121–43.

88. Hanover, Niedersächsische Landesbibliothek, HS XVIII 1020, fols 1v–2r; Böhmer, *Regesta Imperii*, xi, nos 1606–8.

89. Declerq, 'Originals and Cartularies', 164–65. See also Stengel and Semmelmann, 'Fuldensia IV.', 160–61.

by Sigismund may point to their existence as pseudo-originals in 1415. Inspection involved the production of an authenticated copy—what is known as a vidimus (in continental Europe) or an inspeximus (in Britain and Ireland)—and was typically reserved for single sheets which looked the part.[90] Still, forgeries and later copies were at times inspected, so we cannot be certain. Of the other documents, certainly, there is no hint in later years. Imitating earlier documentary forms could be a tricky business, as we shall see in later chapters, and Hildibald B may have deemed it better to err of the side of caution; better a plausible copy than a laughable pseudo-original. This was not necessarily a major concession. Copies did not possess the same probative value as originals, but they could still be brought forth at a court of law or confirmed by the ruler, as some of those under discussion later were.[91] Moreover, where other documents existed for the rights in question (as in most of these cases), copies could provide important ancillary evidence. In fact, two are attested by non-original copies of the early fourteenth century. These were intended for confirmation by Henry VII (1308–13) and remained behind in Italy following the emperor's sudden death from illness at Buonconvento, eventually making their way into the Archivio storico diocesano in Pisa.[92]

It is, therefore, hard to shake the impression that Anno's concern lay less in constructing an iron-clad documentary edifice, than in situating the bishopric's holdings within the wider history of the see. This was not a pure flight of fancy. Diplomas might lend weight to legal claims, but their success depended upon the willingness of local figures to accept their testimony.[93] For Anno to secure his rights, he had to convince others that these were his in the first place. Older interpretations thus confuse the means (counterfeit charters) with the motive (securing Anno's position). The resulting texts may be framed as legal instruments, but they are at least as much about memory and identity as about rights and regulations. They are the efforts of a relatively poor and weak bishopric to write the fruits of recent favour into the distant past. For these purposes, they look to those same semi-legendary figures who had done so much to shape the politics of the Middle Rhine: the great Merovingian Dagobert I; the first Carolingian, Pippin I; Pippin's son and grandson, Charlemagne and Louis the Pious; and the most important East Frankish rulers of the ninth century, Louis the German and Arnulf of Carinthia. The result is an almost textbook illustration of Jan Assmann's 'cultural memory', ending precisely three generations before the point of composition.

90. Bertrand, *Documenting the Everyday*, 83–91; Berenbeim, *Art of Documentation*, 160–85.

91. Kölzer, *Merowingerstudien*, ii, 109; Mersiowsky, *Urkunde*, 921–26, and 'Früh- bis spätmittelalterliche Kopien'.

92. D L D 179, D Arn 192.

93. Cf. Reuter, 'Mandate'.

Anno's inspiration may have come partly from his metropolitan neigh-bours. At Mainz and Trier, the archbishops of these years turned ever more eagerly to the past as a source of authority, forging charters and claim-ing ancient rights of precedence.[94] Similar impetus may have come from the material remains at Worms and Ladenburg. As at Mainz and Trier, the Roman ruins here spoke eloquently of Worms's past glories, glories only par-tially reflected in the see's surviving documents.[95] Most important, however, were almost certainly the lessons learned in Anno's school days at St Maximin. These involved tales not only of Trier's apostolic past, but also of St Maximin's claims to independence from the local archbishop. In fact, the Worms coun-terfeits closely resemble the famed St Maximin forgeries. The latter construct a continuous and independent history for the abbey, stretching back to the Carolingian and Merovingian era, an exercise made difficult by the complete destruction of the abbatial archive in 882. There may even be a connection between the two. Though the most recent study of the St Maximin forgeries dates the first round of these *c.* 1000, a more traditional dating to *c.* 950 or 953 × 963 remains possible (and perhaps preferable).[96]

So as Anno was ascending the episcopal throne in Worms, his old school-mates may have been launching their own ambitious campaign of forgery. This would not have been the only one within their circles. There are rea-sons to believe that under Giselher, whom Anno had put forward as bishop of Merseburg in 971 and who was transferred to Magdeburg in 981, documents were falsified to secure the rights of the new Elbe River metropolitan. What is more, the texts in question were confected by the draftsman-scribe known as Liudolf I, who was an associate of Hildibald B (perhaps even his tutor in charter production).[97]

Anno's Legacy: An Episcopal City

If the aims of Anno's forgeries were less tangible than is sometimes presumed, their delayed and uneven effects become less perplexing. For all the anti-comital posturing of the Worms forgeries, relations with the Salian counts remained broadly amicable. Members of the family continued to be buried at the cathedral well into the eleventh century, and at least two were entrusted to

94. Boshof, 'Köln, Mainz, Trier'.

95. Grünewald, 'Worms'. On Ladenburg: Schaab, 'Ladenburg'.

96. Kölzer, *Studien*, 29–74, 107–10; Wisplinghoff, Review of Kölzer; Nightingale, *Monasteries and Patrons*, 226–28, 230–31; Resmini, *Benediktinerabtei*, 198–203, 207, 517–18. However, note the response in Kölzer, Review of Resmini.

97. Huschner, *Transalpine Kommunikation*, 756–94, 971–72; Klimm, 'Ottonische Diplome', 243–52. If, as Huschner argues, Liudolf I first appears as a scribe under Otto II, then the traditional teacher–student relationship must be reversed (though cf. Hoffmann, 'Notare', 453–54). See also Uhlirz, *Geschichte*, 80–82.

the chapter for their education: Bruno of Carinthia, the future Pope Gregory V (996–99), and Conrad (II), the future emperor (1024–39).[98] The growth of the cathedral school was itself an important development of these years, attesting to the energy Anno and Hildibald brought to their duties.[99] Otherwise, the see's gains were gradual. As we have seen, Anno had his rights in the Oden-wald confirmed in 970, and Hildibald went on to receive the final third on tolls in the city in 979, perhaps aided by earlier forged and interpolated toll charters. The timing of the latter grant is significant. It comes shortly after Otto of Worms's first appointment to the duchy of Carinthia, when the power-ful Salian paterfamilias could afford to divest himself of rights in and around Worms. This was a compromise, in other words, and Otto himself intervened in the resulting diploma.

If Worms's rights extended slowly, they also did so steadily. After a shaky start in the 950s, we see a slow crescendo of privileges, culminating in ten diplomas under Otto III (983–1002) and thirteen under Henry II (1002–24). The latter's reign marked the high point of the centre's power and influence, during which the bishop—the learned and well-connected Burchard—finally acquired the Salian stronghold within the city along with comital rights in Lobdengau and the neighbouring Wingarteiba.[100] That Anno's forgeries should stand at the start of this process is no coincidence. In some cases, they furnished models for later confirmation; in others, they contributed more intangibly, by underlining the bishopric's local prestige and standing. Above all, they reflect the new-found confidence of the see, bursting onto the scene in the 960s. The forgeries' significance is, therefore, as much symbolic as pragmatic. Some were certainly responses to ongoing disputes, but all sprang from a broader interest in the past—an interest inspired by (and relevant to) a changing present.[101]

The Worms counterfeits are thus a symptom of change, a sign of the bishopric's growing ambitions and developing sense of corporate identity. In this respect, they were probably intended as much for a local as a national audience—for the canons of Worms, and perhaps also their lay and monastic neighbours (especially at Lorsch). By producing a more useful past, Anno and his associates served the present. This was not an attempt at a comprehensive history, however. It was a means of situating immediate concerns at Worms, Ladenburg and Wimpfen in relation with the past. And as ever with cultural memory, the focus was on those rights (immunity and tolls) and individuals

98. Schwarzmaier, *Von Speyer nach Rom*, 38–49; Wolfram, *Conrad II*, 19–23. See also Innes, *State and Society*, 243–44.

99. Staub, 'Domschulen', 282–86.

100. DD H II 20, 226, 227, 319. See Bönnen, 'Die Blütezeit'.

101. They are what Carlrichard Brühl might have termed 'confirmatory forgeries' ('fest-stellende Fälschungen'): 'Der ehrbare Fälscher'. See also Brühl, *Studien zu den merowing-ischen Königsurkunden*, 133.

(Dagobert, Louis the Pious, Louis the German, Arnulf) who were most con-
stitutive of local identity. In the Assmanns' terms, Hildibald B was involved in
a process of canonization, whereby the bishopric's undifferentiated past was
winnowed down to a few iconic moments. As Hildibald B put it, the resulting documents were designed to ensure that Worms's rights 'might remain
inviolable in future times' ('per future tempora inviolabilis permaneat').[102] He
would have been pleased to learn that they did.

102. D Arn 192. Cf. J. Assmann, *Das kulturelle Gedächtnis*, 103–29.

CHAPTER TWO

Forging Episcopal Identity: Pilgrim at Passau

IN 1854, THE YOUNG Berlin-educated historian Ernst Dümmler made an arresting discovery: most of the early documents concerning the bishopric of Passau had been forged. What is more, these forgeries could be associated with Bishop Pilgrim, who oversaw the Danube-river see between 971 and 991. This was a major scalp for the new brand of source criticism (*Quellenkritik*) practised by Dümmler and his associates; and it is no coincidence that two of the fathers of this movement, Leopold von Ranke (d. 1886) and Wilhelm Wattenbach (d. 1897), numbered among his teachers. It was also a disturbing revelation, at least for those in Catholic Bavaria. Pilgrim was a popular figure there, famed for his appearance in the Middle High German epic the *Nibelungenlied* (one of the main sources for Wagner's later *Ring* cycle). He had even been venerated as a saint—not the sort of man who was meant to be moonlighting as a counterfeiter.

Not surprisingly, Bavarian responses to Dümmler's findings were hostile. A stream of local historians, many of them professed Benedictine monks, took up pen to defend their saint from this northern upstart. Their fervour was fuelled by ongoing struggles (the *Kulturkampf*) between the Catholic church and the (Protestant) Prussian regime which was increasingly the driving force behind the new German state.[1] There was far more than historical accuracy at stake, and the resulting publications impress more in their unwavering conviction of Pilgrim's innocence than in their historical reasoning. Indeed, much as Catholic opposition to Prussia's Iron Chancellor soon faltered, so too this scholarly Charge of the Light Brigade was dispatched by an incisive riposte by Dümmler in the proceedings of the Prussian Academy of Sciences in Berlin

---

1. Cf. Bennette, *Fighting for the Soul*, esp. 122–56.

(a publication closely aligned with the Protestant corridors of power in the capital).[2]

Yet if Dümmler's discovery had caused consternation in Catholic Bavaria, it was to prove his making in Protestant Prussia. It was but the first of many coups, in a career crowned by the presidency of the Monumenta Germaniae Historica—then, as now, the most influential medieval history post in Germany. The Monumenta's own editorial undertakings were, in fact, to bring final confirmation of Dümmler's findings. When Theodor Sickel's Vienna-based team came to edit the later Ottonian diplomas in the 1880s and 1890s, one of its members, Karl Uhlirz—who would later defend the Ottonian toll privileges for Worms—noticed similarities between the hand of a number of the Passau forgeries and that of authentic Ottonian privileges for the see. He thus identified the forger as Willigis C, a draftsman-scribe active in the 970s, largely in favour of Passau.[3] Since then, few have doubted the essence of Dümmler's case, and work has focused on contextualizing these documents. A particularly important step came in 1964, when the Austrian diplomatist Heinrich Fichtenau (d. 2000)—then head of the Institute for Austrian Historical Research, which Sickel had once overseen—identified the forger with Bishop Pilgrim himself. Fichtenau's findings have found wide acceptance; and occasional doubts notwithstanding, much continues to speak in favour of the identification, as we shall see.[4]

We are, therefore, confronted by one of those rare situations in which we can not only date and locate the act of forgery, but also ascribe it to a known historical figure. We may hope to go one step further than we could at Worms, appreciating more fully the aims and intentions of our forger. But before we can do so, we must briefly survey Pilgrim's earliest years.

2. Dümmler, *Pilgrim von Passau*. For responses: Mittermüller, 'Bischof Piligrim'; Blumberg, 'Lorcher Fälschungen'; Ratzinger, 'Lorch und Passau. Neue Forschungen', and 'Lorch und Passau'; Widemann, 'Zur Lorcher Frage'; and for Dümmler's riposte: Dümmler: 'Über die Entstehung'. Significantly, the great Prussian church historian Albert Hauck endorsed these findings: *Kirchengeschichte Deutschlands*, 167 n. 4, 178–80 (only lightly revising the remarks of the first edition of 1893). Dümmler's own confessional perspective emerges from his obituary for Paul Scheffer-Boichhorst, whom he praised as 'though a Catholic, like his great teacher [Julius Ficker] nevertheless fully impartial in his works' ('obwohl Katholik doch wie sein großer Lehrer völlig unbefangen in seinen Arbeiten'): 'Nachruf Paul Scheffer-Boichhorst', 770.

3. Uhlirz, 'Urkundenfälschung'. See further Lehr, 'Pilgrim'.

4. Fichtenau, 'Urkundenfälschungen'. For doubts: Hoffmann, 'Notare', 436–37, with the response in Erkens, *Fälschungen*, 47*–8* n. 14.

Origins: Pilgrim before Passau

Pilgrim was born in the 930s or 940s into one of the leading families of Bavaria: the Sigehardinger clan (so named on account of their preference for the name Sigehard), which was dominant around Chiemsee and Salzburg, straddling the border between modern Austria and Bavaria (Map 2). This region had seen considerable upheaval in recent years. Under the later Carolingian rulers, Bavaria had been a royal heartland. However, the eclipse of that royal line with Louis the Child (900–911) and the sustained Hungarian attacks which accompanied this did considerable damage to church, state and society in the region. In response, Bavaria was reconstituted as a duchy led by a member of the local aristocracy, whose responsibility lay in protecting the local populus and mediating rule with the more northerly Ottonian rulers.[5]

In the *Life* of Godehard of Hildesheim (1022–38), who was educated alongside Pilgrim at Niederaltaich, we are informed that the future Passau bishop was a *nepos* of Archbishop Frederick of Salzburg (958–91).[6] The *Life* is a well-informed work, written around the time of Godehard's death (1038)—perhaps for a Niederaltaich audience—by Wolfhere, who had spent time there alongside Godehard and Pilgrim. What Wolfhere means by *nepos*, however, is far from clear. The term could designate any familial relation, near or distant; it could also be used more precisely to mean 'nephew'. That the latter is intended is suggested by the record of a transaction of *c.* 965, in which Frederick's brother, Count Sigehard of the Chiemgau (the region around the Chiemsee), appears alongside his wife (the donor) and two sons, Engilpreht and Pilgrim. Since it is scarcely likely that Frederick had two close relatives called Pilgrim, this is almost certainly the same figure as the bishop of the *Life*—and thus Frederick's nephew. It was common for episcopal uncles to promote the careers of their nephews, and Pilgrim stands in a venerable tradition, represented by such luminaries as Gregory of Tours (d. 594) and Hincmar of Laon (d. 879).[7]

Pilgrim was clearly destined for great things. Niederaltaich was one of the most venerable foundations in the region, which owed its origins to Bavaria's penultimate independent ruler, Duke Odilo (736–48). The church itself may have suffered in the earlier years of the tenth century, when the Hungarians raided Bavaria repeatedly. But we should be wary of exaggerating the resulting damage. Though the Hungarians loom large in modern scholarship on the abbey, no attacks on Niederaltaich are recorded. And our main source for the

---

5. Bührer-Thierry, *Évêques et pouvoir*. See also Wolfram, 'Bavaria'.

6. Wolfhere, *Vita Godehardi (prior)*, ch. 6, ed. Pertz, 172. See Coué, *Hagiographie*, 41–61, on the *Life*; and Störmer, 'Herkunft', on the family.

7. *Salzburger Urkundenbuch*, i, ed. Hauthaler, 178–80 (no. 14), with Fichtenau, 'Urkundenfälschungen', 158–60. See further Barrow, *Clergy*, 117–35, and 'Bishop in the Latin West'.

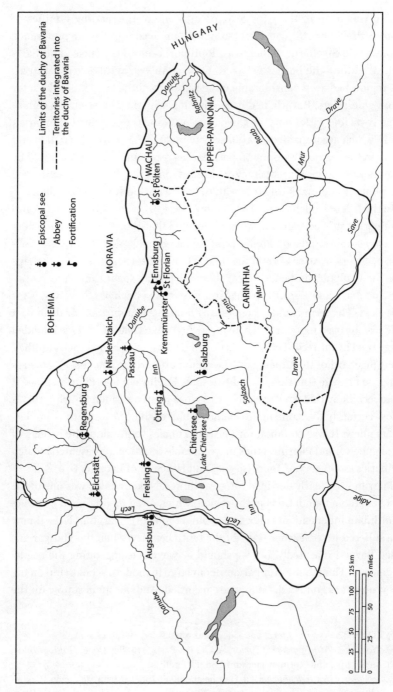

MAP 2. Passau the Bavarian episcopate, c 970

Legend:

Episcopal see
Abbey
Fortification

— Limits of the duchy of Bavaria
- - - Territories integrated into the duchy of Bavaria

HUNGARY

Danube
Rabnitz
UPPER-PANNONIA
Drave
Roab
Mur
WACHAU
St Pölten
Save
CARINTHIA
Ennsburg
St Florian
MORAVIA
Mur
Enns
Kremsmünster
BOHEMIA
Salzburg
Drave
Danube
Niederaltaich
Passau
Inn
Salzach
Regensburg
Ötting
Chiemsee
Lake Chiemsee
Eichstätt
Freising
Inn
Lech
Augsburg
Lech
Adige
Danube

0 25 50 75 100 125 km
0 25 50 75 miles

centre's decline, Wolfhere's later account of Godehard's *Life*—a by no means impartial source, as Godehard reformed the abbey—should be taken with a liberal pinch of salt. Certainly Niederaltaich remained an important local player. In fact, the abbey was well placed to benefit from royal and ducal politics at this juncture. Otto I's victory over the Hungarians in 955 had not only removed a major threat from the eastern frontier; it opened the way for missionary undertakings to Bavaria's Slavic and Hungarian neighbours.[8] These were rich prospects for a monastery founded by the great missionary Saint Pirmin.

Whatever his precise experiences, Pilgrim's stay at Niederaltaich was but one stop on the ecclesiastical *cursus honorum*. He had apparently not entered the abbey when he appeared alongside his father *c.* 965, yet by 971 he was already bishop—a rapid rise evidently enabled by his family connections. The support of his uncle was crucial here. According the *Life* of Godehard, it was Frederick who secured Pilgrim's episcopal throne. And Pilgrim's own recourse to Salzburg sources in later years reveals close contacts with the archbishopric, where he may also have received part of his education. Pilgrim's appointment was certainly not the only point of contact between him and his uncle in these years. Wolfhere mentions that Godehard had accompanied Frederick to Italy, where he was introduced to liturgical and scribal tasks—events we know to have transpired in 970.[9] Though nothing is said about Pilgrim in this connection, it is striking that the scribe identified by Karl Uhlirz as Willigis C makes his first appearance during this Italian sojourn, copying a privilege in favour of Salzburg. In future years, Willigis C would operate almost exclusively in favour of Passau, including producing a string of famous of forgeries.[10] This scribe was evidently a close associate of Pilgrim; and as noted, Fichtenau made a strong case for treating scribe and bishop as one and the same—a case which gains additional plausibility from other Passau texts of Pilgrim's episcopate, which reveal similar stylistic preferences. As Fichtenau put it, if Willigis C was not Pilgrim, then he 'followed him like his shadow', revealing all the attributes we would otherwise expect of the bishop.[11]

Presuming that Pilgrim is indeed Willigis C, we can expand on the brief remarks of the *Life* of Godehard. Pilgrim was not only promoted by his uncle, but also introduced to court by him, probably on the same Italian trip undertaken by Godehard. This was an important moment for the young churchman. As we saw in the last chapter, these years witnessed a move away from recruiting bishops from abbeys and towards taking them from cathedral chapters (often via the royal chapel). Pilgrim was at a potential disadvantage here; and by taking him to Italy, Frederick was able to give his nephew some of the contacts

---

8. Beumann, 'Laurentius und Mauritius'.

9. Wolfhere, *Vita Godehardi (prior)*, ch. 6, ed. Pertz, 172.

10. D O I 389, Vienna, HHStA, UR AUR 45. See Uhlirz, 'Urkundenfälschung'.

11. Fichtenau, 'Urkundenfälschungen', 175. See also Erkens, *Fälschungen*, 47*–48* n. 14.

he might otherwise have lacked. During this trip, Pilgrim had the chance to rub shoulders with the kingdom's great and good, including other up-and-coming clerics. Especially valuable was the introduction to charter production. This was not only a useful skill, which Pilgrim would later turn to his advantage; it also offered further opportunities to hobnob.

From Pilgrim's one surviving diploma of this trip—not necessarily the only one he produced—we can reconstruct some of the resulting contacts. The document in question concerns a grant of a number of estates in the Carinthian march, the largely Slavic lands in eastern Bavaria, near the Hungarian frontier. It was petitioned by Duke Henry 'the Quarrelsome' of Bavaria (d. 995)—Bavarian dukes typically intervening in donations within their duchy—and Empress Adelheid (d. 999), Otto I's second wife, who was a close associate of the duke (and an important political force in her own right).[12] The charter also reveals something about Pilgrim's schooling in charter production (Illustration 2.1). Issued at Pavia in early 970, its closing eschatocol is supplied by the draftsman-scribe known as 'Italian C' ('Italiener C'). Though this is the only time the two figures are known to have worked together, Pilgrim's scribal practices reveal many reminiscences of Italian C, particularly in the manner he forms his chrismon and recognition sign. This marks him out as part of a small but distinctive group of scribes, all of whom directly or indirectly owe their forms to Liudolf F (Italian C's teacher), an influential draftsman-scribe active from 956 onwards.[13]

What other effects his time in Italy had on Pilgrim can only be a matter of speculation. Here he will have encountered a much more literate and Latinate culture than that north of the Alps. Written testimony played a major role in local litigation, and it is tempting to suggest that Pilgrim first became fully aware of the potential of the written word here.[14] This was not the only difference between Pilgrim's Bavaria and the Apennine peninsula. Italy's highly developed urban culture, in which bishops played key roles as city representatives, must also have made an impression on the young churchman; so too would the encounter with Romance speech, in the form of early proto-Italian. The diploma Pilgrim produced bears marks of these experiences. Not only does its script—his distinctive diplomatic minuscule—reveal signs of Italian influence (not least in the preference for v over u at the start of words), but within the text, Pilgrim carefully distinguishes the Slavic and German names for the estates in question (Nidrinhof, within what is now tellingly known as

12. On intervention practices: Gilsdorf, *Favor of Friends*; Görich, 'Mathilde—Edgith—Adelheid'.

13. Uhlirz, 'Urkundenfälschung', 180–82. See also Huschner, *Transalpine Kommunikation*, 511–12, 547, 615–16.

14. Cf. Bougard, '"*Falsum falsorum*"'; Sennis, 'Documentary Practices'.

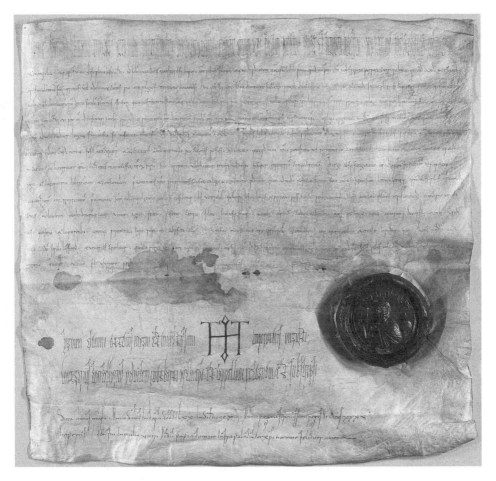

2.1 The first diploma of Pilgrim of Passau: Vienna, HHStA UR AUR 45, © HHStA

Deutschlandsberg). In part, this was a pragmatic move, reflecting the bilingual culture of the Carinthian march. Nevertheless, it is also one of the earlier uses of the term *theotisca* (more commonly, *theodiscus*) for the German vernacular by a charter scribe from north of the Alps. The term was much more common in Italy, where it designated speakers of Germanic tongues; it may be that Pilgrim picked it up there.[15]

In Italy, Pilgrim will also have become better acquainted with Otto's missionary plans. It was at synods in Rome (962) and Ravenna (967, 968) that the emperor had recently achieved his goal of raising the monastery of

15. Thomas, 'Die Deutschen', esp. 33. More generally: Roberts and Tinti, 'Signalling Language Choice'.

St Maurice, Magdeburg, to metropolitan status, and entrusting this and its suffragans with the mission to the Elbe Slavs. And it was from Italy, too, that the new archbishopric received much of its initial support, including a large number of privileges.[16] In fact, less than two weeks before Pilgrim put quill to parchment, Anno of Worms had intervened on behalf of the see in the Magdeburg diploma we encountered in the last chapter. It is, therefore, quite likely that Pilgrim met Hildibald B, who just over a month later would draw up the emperor's settlement of a dispute between Worms and Lorsch. Pilgrim may also have met Bishop Anno, who used this trip to acquire a prestigious blood relic—perhaps that discovered in Mantua in the early ninth century—for his former monastery, which he then brought to Magdeburg on Pentecost Monday (5 June) of the following year.[17]

Pilgrim's early associations with Italy and Salzburg are important from another angle. In late October 969, probably soon after his arrival in Lombardy, Frederick had been granted the abbey of Chiemsee (Herrenchiemsee), which lay within his familial heartlands. This monastery had first been granted to Salzburg by Arnulf of Carinthia (887–99) in the late ninth century, but was apparently lost in the intervening years, since the diploma is framed as a new grant. Significantly, a Salzburg forgery survives concerning Chiemsee, in the name of Louis the Child. And there are grounds to believe that it was confected in order to achieve (or consolidate) the 969 grant (which does not mention it by name). This is not the only forgery with which Frederick can be associated. It was also around this time that the 'Salzburg magna carta', an ambitious (false) confirmation of the archbishop's holdings in the name of Arnulf, was produced (a conclusion suggested not least by the absence of Chiemsee from the otherwise comprehensive list of episcopal holdings).[18] The significance of this lies in the Pilgrim connection. Neither document seems to have been produced as evidence in Italy at this point—indeed, it would be 977 before the latter was confirmed—but it is likely that Pilgrim was aware of their existence. And if so, he presumably also knew the nature of their genesis. In any case, it was soon after Frederick's return north that the archbishop arranged for his nephew's elevation.

16. Huschner, *Transalpine Kommunikation*, 624–794.

17. Friedmann, *Beziehungen*, 50. For the ninth-century discovery: *Annales regni Francorum*, s.a. 804, ed. Kurze, 119; and on the relic: Vincent, *Holy Blood*, 51–65, 146–47.

18. D L K 85; D Arn 184, Vienna, HHStA, UR AUR 18. On the latter: Koller, 'König Arnolfs großes Privileg'; Gänser, 'Diplom König Ludwigs', 20–21. Note, however, that the main text of D O II 165 (Vienna, HHStA, UR AUR 47) confirming D Arn 184 is clearly not a palimpsest, as Koller claims (it is written throughout in the same ink) and 977 thus remains a firm *terminus ante quem* for forgery. Cf. Brühl, *Deutschland—Frankreich*, 199–200, who accepts Otto II's privilege as authentic, albeit without reference to the doubts of Koller and Gänser.

The Missionary Moment: Pilgrim at Passau

Pilgrim came to Passau with all the advantages he might have desired. A member of one of the most powerful local families and the nephew of the archbishop, he was also personally acquainted with the region's duke. Yet this did not make his task easy. Passau may have been larger than Worms, but it faced similar challenges. The see had benefited from royal generosity during the reigns of the Bavarian-based rulers Arnulf and Louis the Child. But since then, times had been tough. As the most south-easterly bishopric within the duchy, Passau had been on the front line during the Hungarian wars. Bishop Richard (899–902) was one of the leaders of the force which caught the retreating Hungarians unawares in 900; and episcopal forces were almost certainly among those defeated at the catastrophic Battle of Bratislava (Preßburg) in 907, at which the Bavarian duke Luitpold fell alongside much of the native aristocracy and episcopate (including the archbishop of Salzburg and bishops of Freising and Brixen). Further raids on (or through) Bavaria in 909 and 910 did little to help the situation, and it would be the 930s before a degree of calm was to prevail. Later accounts held these conflicts responsible for considerable losses on the part of the church. And while such tales are probably exaggerated, there can be no doubt that real damage was done.[19]

The accession of the Ottonians did little to help the situation. Their victories over the Hungarians in 932 and 955 were welcome, but the focus of royal authority now shifted decisively northwards, and with it a crucial source of patronage. The local Luitpolding dukes offered a partial alternative; however, they were often at loggerheads with the Ottonians, and in little position to offer serious assistance. Only with the appointment of Otto I's brother, Henry, as duke in 947 did the situation start to improve; and it would be the early eleventh century before Bavaria returned to the centre stage of national politics.[20] If Bavaria at large suffered from benign neglect, this was doubly true of Passau, the region's youngest and most remote bishopric. The see's fate is reflected in the *Indiculus loricatorum* (c. 980), a list of troops (perhaps reinforcements) due to Otto II in Italy. Though many problems attach to the interpretation of this text, a rough order of precedence emerges, with wealthy bishoprics such as Mainz and Cologne owing one hundred heavily armoured troops, and poorer ones such as Brixen owing twenty (or fewer). Alone of the Bavarian bishoprics, Passau is not mentioned at all. Perhaps, like the Saxon sees, it was exempted on account of its frontier status; but if so, the heavy demands on Salzburg and Regensburg (both also

---

19. Boshof, 'Reorganisation'. See also Holzfurtner, 'Destructio monasteriorum'.
20. Bührer-Thierry, *Évêques et pouvoir*, esp. 23–52. Cf. Weinfurter, 'Kaiser Heinrich II.'.

frontier bishoprics) are hard to explain.[21] It would seem that Passau was simply too poor.

Yet if Passau faced similar pressures to Worms, it possessed one significant advantage: it was not hemmed in by its neighbours. When Pilgrim ascended his throne in 971, there were no diocesan structures to his immediate north (Bohemia), north-east (Moravia) and east (Hungary). He might, therefore, hope to tap into the missionary politics of these years—a politics he knew only too well. The period following Otto I's victory over the Magyars (955) and imperial coronation (962) had seen concerted efforts here. A key role was accorded to Magdeburg in the north-east, which was entrusted with the mission to the Elbe Slavs (in modern eastern Germany), including oversight of the newly founded bishoprics of Merseburg, Meißen and Zeitz, as well as the slightly older foundations at Brandenburg and Havelberg. Such changes in diocesan structure were anything but straightforward. First efforts to raise Magdeburg are visible in 955, but it was to be another thirteen years before Otto was in a position to realize his ambitions.[22] The problem, as contemporaries noted (often with chagrin), was that in promoting St Maurice and creating new suffragans for it, the emperor was infringing upon the rights of existing sees and provinces. Particularly affected were Halberstadt, in whose diocese the new bishopric Merseburg lay, and the archbishopric of Mainz, whose province this had been. In the latter case, Otto may have sweetened the deal by promising future influence over Bohemia, a promise fulfilled with the foundation of the bishopric of Prague, under Mainz's oversight (c. 974). For the former, the setback would rankle for years to come, creating major problems for the fledgling bishopric of Merseburg.[23]

These developments clearly demonstrated the potential of the mission. Yet in fixing responsibilities in the north and north-east, they raised questions about what would happen in the south. East Saxony had long been the point of contact with the Elbe Slavs and Poles, so it was natural that the Saxons should take the lead here. It was Bavaria, however, which traditionally looked to Bohemia, Moravia (now under Bohemian control) and Hungary; similar missionary moves might be expected in these regions. Certainly there was a longstanding local missionary tradition, stretching back to Bavaria's own christianization by Rupert, Pirmin and Boniface—figures keenly remembered in Salzburg, Regensburg and Passau. The latter two sees, in particular, may have hoped their time had come. Bohemia, already partially christianized, could easily be integrated into an extended Regensburg; Moravia, meanwhile, was the natural place for Passau to look. Hungary lay further afield, but promised less competition—and potentially

---

21. *Idiculus loricatorum*, ed. Uhlirz, *Jahrbücher*, i, 247–48. See further Auer, 'Kriegsdienst', i, 372–82, noting the possible exemption of the Saxons on account of their frontier duties at 376.

22. Beumann, 'Laurentius und Mauritius'. See further Althoff, 'Magdeburg'.

23. Beumann, 'Entschädigungen'; Hehl, 'Merseburg'.

even greater gains. A successful campaign of christianization might do more than merely justify the extension of existing diocesan boundaries. As the case of Magdeburg revealed, there was a chance of promotion to metropolitan rank. For Pilgrim, educated at Niederaltaich and acquainted with the rich library and archival materials at Salzburg, this potential must have been obvious. The former had been founded by the missionary Pirmin and was dedicated to Maurice, the patron saint of Magdeburg (and thus one of the standard-bearers of eastern mission). At the latter, meanwhile, the ideal of mission lay at the very heart of archiepiscopal identity, as developed in the eighth and ninth centuries and expressed in the dramatic narrative account of the 'Conversion of the Bavarians and Carinthians' (*Conversio Bagoariorum et Carantanorum*), composed *c*. 870.[24]

Pilgrim thus came to Passau prepared. Yet if he hoped to find evidence of the see's past greatness, he was sorely disappointed. There were many material signs of Passau's antiquity, but the textual trail was decidedly slim: a few royal diplomas, and a larger number of local tradition notices (i.e., records of transactions); a copy of the *Life* of Severin (d. 482), who had lived in the region in the fifth century; and not much else besides. If he was to tap in to the emperor's missionary plans, Pilgrim would need to have more to show than this. It was in this context that, as noted in the Preface, the bishop's mind turned back to one of those few accounts he had, that of the early sixth-century *Life* of Severin, a copy of which had been given to Passau by the auxiliary bishop (*chorepiscopus*) Madalwin in 903.[25] Here Pilgrim could read that a pontiff (*pontifex*) called Constantius had once been based at Lorch, on the outskirts of modern Enns in the south-east of his diocese. This was precisely what Pilgrim had been looking for: a sign that the origins of the local church went back further than had been appreciated—right back, in fact, to the earliest days of Christianity within the region. This evidence accorded well with the material remains at Lorch, which included a late antique church dedicated to Laurence (who, alongside Maurice, was the other standard-bearer of the eastern mission).[26] Pilgrim knew only too well that the intervening years had been hard on the region. Already in Constantius's day, Noricum was facing the brunt of the barbarian migrations which had accompanied Rome's fall; and in more recent years, it had suffered at the hands of the Avars and Hungarians. It was easy to imagine circumstances under which a prelate of Lorch might have been forced to relocate further upriver to the safety of Passau. Pilgrim may not even have been the first to make the connection. In some of the copies of the proceedings of the synod of Ingelheim (948), his predecessor Adalbert (946–70)

24. *Conversio Bagoarium et Carantanorum*, ed. Lošek, with Airlie, 'True Teachers'; I. N. Wood, *Missionary Life*, 145–86.

25. Erkens, 'Die ältesten Passauer Bischofsurkunden', 504–7 (no. II). For words of caution: Resl, 'Was bleibt'.

26. Eugippius, *Vita Severini*, ch. 30, ed. Regerat, 256–58. See Erkens, 'Ursprünge'; Igl, *Basilika*.

attests as 'bishop of Lorch'; and the mid-twelfth-century chronicle compiled by the enigmatic Annalista Saxo—who largely reproduces earlier material—likewise refers to Adalbert as bishop of Lorch in 961.[27]

But if Lorch had indeed been established this early, surely it was more than a mere bishopric? The term used for Constantius, *pontifex*, may have suggested as much. This could be used to describe any senior figure within the church (including the pope), and was as appropriate for an archbishop as a bishop. This connection—tenuous though it may have been—was too good to ignore. Lorch lay on the main routes between Bavaria, Bohemia and Hungary and was an ideal staging post for any future missionary undertakings Pilgrim may have envisaged.[28] By embracing Lorch's legacy, Pilgrim had much to win. His case would have been further strengthened by the late antique account of the demise of Saint Florian, which, thanks to the local popularity of the saint, may also have been known to Pilgrim. In this, Lorch plays the role of provincial capital, the natural place for a metropolitan seat.[29] Here Pilgrim certainly did go beyond his predecessor. He identified Passau not only with an earlier bishopric at Lorch, but with a metropolitan past there. The result was one of the most famous forgery complexes of the Middle Ages: a set of false papal privileges and imperial diplomas tracing Passau's history back to this alleged antique (archiepiscopal) past.

The Passau Forgeries, I: The Papal Bulls

As was already clear to Dümmler, the heart of the forgery complex lies in a series of papal privileges (or bulls), spanning the pontificates of Symmachus (498–514) to Benedict (VI or VII, 973–74 or 974–83). As previously, it helps to list these:

1. JK 767: **Pope Symmachus** (498–514) grants **Archbishop Theodore** of Lorch (?c. 500) the pallium on account of his archiepiscopal dignity and metropolitan standing in the province of Pannonia.
2. JE 2566: **Pope Eugenius** (II, 824–27) informs the bishops of Moravia and Pannonia that he has named **Archbishop Urolf** of Lorch (= Passau) (804–6) his vicar and metropolitan over the region.
3. JL 3602: **Pope Leo** (VII, 936–39) grants **Archbishop Gerhard** of Lorch (= Passau) (931–46) the pallium and specifies when he can wear it.
4. JL 3614: **Pope Leo** (VII, 936–39) informs the magnates of East Francia, including bishops Egilolf of Salzburg (935–39), Isingrim of

27. *Konzilien Deutschlands*, ed. Hehl, 135–63 (no. 13), at 158; Annalista Saxo, *Chronicon*, s.a. 961, ed. Naß, 194. On the compositional technique of the latter: Naß, *Reichschronik*. Cf. Erkens, 'Ursprünge', 424–25.
28. Cf. Bowlus, *Franks, Moravians, and Magyars*, 59.
29. *Passio S. Floriani*, ch. 2, ed. Krusch, 68.

Regensburg (930–40), Lantbert of Freising (938–56) and Wisund of Säben (938–56), of his decisions on various pastoral matters raised by **Archbishop Gerhard** of Lorch (= Passau) (931–46).

5. JL 3644: **Pope Agapit** (II, 946–55) raises **Gerhard** of Lorch (= Passau) (931–46) to metropolitan status after examining a series of authentic privileges he has presented, alongside other documents in the papal archive.

6. JL 3771: **Pope Benedict** (VI or VII, 973–74 or 974–83) informs various prelates that, after inspecting the documents produced by **Pilgrim** of Lorch (= Passau) (971–91), he has named the archbishop his vicar, granted him the pallium and freed his diocese from subjugation to Salzburg.

7. **Pilgrim** informs **Pope Benedict** (VI or VII, 973–74 or 974–83) of his missionary work amongst the Hungarians and requests permission to ordain bishops for the region and that the pallium be granted to him (as it had his forbears).

All of these concern Lorch and its standing, serving to associate this ancient (metropolitan) centre with the newer bishopric (or more rightly, archbishopric) at Passau. And most take the form of pallium privileges. The pallium was the most important symbol of metropolitan status. It was (and is) a band of white wool which encircles the wearer's shoulders, falling in strips down the front and back, often embroidered with crosses. The pallium had to be obtained in person from the pope, and was in origin a sign of special favour. When the Italian missionary Augustine (d. 604) was sent to convert the English in the late sixth century, he was granted the vestment; and in the ensuing years, it came to be closely associated with archiepiscopal standing—at Augustine's Canterbury and elsewhere. Pilgrim was well aware of this. As we shall see, he had read Bede's account of the conversion of the English, in which Augustine's missionary efforts are recorded. Moreover, historical writing in Salzburg made much of that see's early pallium privileges, not least in the *Conversio* (another text Pilgrim seems to have known).[30] It was, therefore, only natural that Pilgrim should dress Passau's claims in a pallial guise.

Pilgrim was fortunate—for fortune it certainly was—in his choice of pope for the first of these texts, since Symmachus happens to be the first pope for whom an authentic pallium privilege survives. Still, in Symmachus's day such grants were restricted to a small circle of recipients (above all, Arles), and there can be little doubt that what we are dealing with is a much later creation. For a start, the text's formulation shows influence from the *Liber diurnus*, the formulae collection first brought together at the papal court in the later

---

30. *Conversio Bagoarium et Carantanorum*, ch. 9, ed. Lošek, 116–18. On Pilgrim's likely knowledge of this work: Fichtenau, 'Urkundenfälschungen', 164 n. 29; Resl, 'Ethnic History', 93–94; Erkens, *Fälschungen*, 83* n. 199. More generally: Schoenig, *Bonds of Wool*.

seventh and eighth centuries (680 × 790) and subsequently used through to the eleventh. More to the point, it is directly modelled on a pallium privilege of Eugenius II (824–27) for Salzburg. The Eugenius bull was itself the first to employ a distinctive new version of the pallium formula (beginning 'Si pastores ovium'), and the appearance of such formulation here points to the ninth-century pedigree of our text.[31] Why Pilgrim should choose Symmachus for the start of his series is not entirely clear. The obvious option would have been a direct contemporary of Severin's Constantius; and in picking Symmachus, Pilgrim has been forced to invent an otherwise unknown 'Archbishop Theodore of Lorch' as the recipient. Perhaps his sources for the early papacy were simply too patchy. Equally, Symmachus may have appealed as a foundational figure. It had been in the wake of Symmachus's schism-plagued pontificate that papal biographies were first written down in Rome; and one of the main purposes of the resulting serial biographies of popes (the *Liber pontificalis* or 'Book of Pontiffs') was to underline the justice of his case.[32] He was, therefore, a well-known figure. There were also more specific grounds for Pilgrim to turn to Symmachus. The *Life* of Severin is dedicated to the Roman deacon Paschasius, who had been an active supporter of Laurence (498–506), Symmachus's rival for the papal throne.[33] By making the latter into a patron of Lorch, Pilgrim was able to defuse a potential problem, presenting the Norican archbishopric a loyal papal subject from the start. In choosing Theodore as the first bishop, Pilgrim was channelling a rather different precedent. Through Bede's *Ecclesiastical History of the English People*, Pilgrim knew of the achievements of Theodore of Tarsus (668–90), who had overseen the institution of diocesan structures and ecclesiastical discipline among the English; here he was conjuring up a Passau equivalent.

The resulting document—the only one to claim a pre-ninth-century pedigree—serves to underline the antiquity of Lorch's (and hence Passau's) claims. The text itself is relatively short and closely follows its ninth-century exemplar. The only changes are to the greeting and the addition of a few details regarding the symbolism and function of the pallium. Here Pilgrim, ventriloquizing Symmachus, notes that the vestment is to be 'a sign of the cross, through which you know that you should have compassion for your brothers and should be crucified in spirit on account of enticements of this world'

31. JK 767 (ed. Erkens, *Fälschungen*, no. 1; ed. Lehr, 'Pilgrim', no. 1). Cf. JE 2558 (*SUB*, no. 7b), with Hacke, 'Palliumverleihungen', 11–13. The latter echoes *Liber diurnus* V 47 (= C 46 = A 41), ed. Foerster, 106, 204–5, 307–8. On 'Si pastores ovium': Knibbs, *Ansgar* 141–45. On Erkens's recent edition of the Passau forgeries, see Schütte, 'Bemerkungen'. In light of Schütte's remarks, I also cite the older (and in certain respects better) edition by Lehr.

32. Demacopoulos, *Invention of Peter*, 102–16.

33. C. Leyser, *Authority and Asceticism*, 108–12. I am grateful to Conrad Leyser for pointing this out.

('signum . . . crucis, per quod scito te et fratribus debere compati ac mundiali-bus enlecebris in affectu crucifigi'). This is an important addition, and Roman Michałowski suggests that it concerns martyrdom, the highest calling of mis-sionary life. Yet the focus is less on crucifixion than upon the spiritual and symbolic significance of the cross (and thus pallium). Indeed, Pilgrim does not say that the bishop is to suffer alongside his brothers (as Michałowski claims), but rather that he should show compassion for them (the secondary mean-ing of the deponent verb *compati*).[34] Towards the end of this excursus on the pallium, Pilgrim also inserts a comment to the effect that the recipient should reflect upon the fact that this is 'a burden rather than an honour' ('oneris quam honoris'), a calque on a line from another Salzburg bull (of 798), which is echoed elsewhere in the series.[35] Otherwise, where Pilgrim has adjusted the details of the recipient, he has taken the opportunity to assert that Lorch is being raised to metropolitan status over all Pannonia—the Roman province incorporating much of medieval Hungary, which had traditionally been Salz-burg's missionary field. Lorch itself lay in the Roman province of Noricum, as Pilgrim knew full well; the sleight of hand serves to extend the remit of his prospective province considerably.[36]

The next text is in the name of Pope Eugenius II (824–27), about whom Pilgrim knew from the exemplar for his Symmachus bull. Perhaps to avoid suspicion, he does not draw on that text here, but rather on another which Salzburg had received from Leo III in 798 (a phrase of which had already been echoed in the first forgery). He evidently did not know the name of Passau's bishop in the 820s, as Urolf, who is here addressed as archbishop(!), had only overseen the see in the early years of the century (804–6).[37] In any case, the resulting privilege is much more ambitious than the first. Pilgrim sticks less closely to his model, which only furnishes the sentence regarding the grant of the pallium, and instead lets his imagination run freely. As a result, this is not so much a pallium privilege in the traditional sense, as a letter to the bishops and magnates of Passau's eastern neighbours in Pannonia, Moravia and the land of the Avars (*Avaria*). Specifically, Eugenius informs these figures that he has appointed Urolf as his vicar and metropolitan over them, granting him the pallium—here the phrase from the Leo bull—and requesting their sup-port for Urolf's missionary endeavours.[38] It is at this point that we start to

34. Michałowski, *Gniezno Summit*, 64–66. What Michałowski's interpretation misses is that the dative *fratribus* cannot be in apposition to the accusative *te*. Cf. Schoenig, *Bonds of Wool*, 266–67, who renders the phrase accurately.

35. Cf. JE 2498 (*SUB*, no. 2a): 'Officum sacerdotalis adsumere . . . plus est oneris quam honoris'.

36. Cf. Wolfram, *Salzburg*, 68–73.

37. Boshof, *Regesten*, i, nos 80–87.

38. JE 2566 (ed. Erkens, *Fälschungen*, no. 3; ed. Lehr, 'Pilgrim', no. 2). Cf. JE 2498 (*SUB*, no. 2a).

see Pilgrim apply his learning. Pilgrim was evidently aware of earlier missionary undertakings by Passau and Salzburg in Moravia—a region incorporating much of modern Slovakia and the eastern Czech Republic[39]—and the resulting tensions. In fact, one of the suffragan bishops of Passau is addressed as 'Methodius of Speculiiuliensi'. Although the see in question has not been identified, the individual is clearly modelled upon (if not identical with) the later Greek missionary of this name, whose use of the Slavic vernacular and efforts to win the people of Moravia for the eastern (Byzantine) rite would prove so controversial in the second half of the century.[40] The reference to Slavic dukes named 'Tutund' and Moimir reveals a similar tendency to conflate information about various earlier figures. The former is a corruption of *tudun*, the title of a high office-holder among the Avars (here mistaken for a proper name), while Moimir was a prominent Moravian leader in the 830s and 840s.[41] The letter also shows an interest in the region's more distant past, remarking on how Moravia had once boasted seven bishoprics under the oversight of Lorch. Urolf's new responsibilities are thus cast as a return to an idealized former state, preparing the ground for Pilgrim's similar claims. Indeed, it is on account of these prior responsibilities— so runs the letter—that Eugenius has seen fit to entrust Urolf with the mission to the regions of the Huns (i.e., Avars) which are known as 'Avaria', to Moravia and also to Pannonia, granting him the pallium. There he is to be not only archbishop, but also papal vicar ('nostrum apostolicam vicem'), acting in Eugenius's stead. In this guise, he is to convert and minister to the people, driving out diabolic beliefs, restoring the church and founding new bishoprics.

This is all most impressive. Passau had been involved in earlier missionary undertakings, including those to the Moravians, but the terms of the privilege unmistakably echo the concerns of Pilgrim's day. Particularly striking is the mention of vicarial rights—the right, that is, to act as papal representative. This was a hot topic in later tenth-century Germany. In response to the competition for status and prestige between the Rhineland metropolitans at Cologne, Mainz and Trier, the papal vicariate had become a much coveted status. The ultimate model was furnished by the eighth-century English missionary Saint Boniface (d. 754), who had used papal support, including vicarial status, to effect major changes in diocesan and provincial structures east of the Rhine.[42] What being the pope's vicar actually meant in practice, however, was often far from clear (hence, in part, its desirability). In fact, just as (or

39. Wolfram, *Salzburg*, 87–100. For dissenting views: Bowlus, *Franks, Moravians, and Magyars*; Eggers, '"Moravia" oder "Großmähren"?', and 'Slawenmission Passaus', with further literature.

40. Fletcher, *Conversion of Europe*, 327–68; McCormick, *Origins*, 181–97, 765–68.

41. W. Pohl, *The Avars*, 361–63; Goldberg, *Struggle for Empire*, 138–40.

42. I. N. Wood, *Missionary Life*, 57–78, 145–67. See also Fletcher, *Conversion of Europe*, 204–13; Fuhrmann, 'Studien'.

just after) Pilgrim set to work on his forgeries, Willigis, the new archbishop of Mainz (975–1011)—Boniface's own foundation—secured a new, wider-ranging form of vicarial privilege, one which allowed for the foundation of new bishoprics. Whether Pilgrim knew of this—and if so, how—is unclear, but certainly he was responding to similar stimuli.[43]

The remaining bulls are all dated to the early to mid-tenth century. The next, in the name of Leo VII (936–39), is more like the first, taking the form of a pallium privilege for Gerhard of Lorch (= Passau, 931–46). As in the Symmachus bull, Pilgrim follows his exemplars closely here, in this case two Salzburg pallium privileges of the ninth century, for Liupram (836–39) and Adalwin (859–73). He has again risked a degree of anachronism, by placing ninth-century formulation into the tenth, perhaps in an effort to hide the true origins of these texts. He has also made a few important textual interventions.[44] To the occasions on which Gerhard can wear the pallium, he has added the consecration of the chrism—the holy oil used for baptism and ordination—as well as the attendance synods, consecration of bishops and priests and gatherings of new converts. These were not traditional pallium days, though consecration and ordination do appear in other privileges of the later tenth century (particularly for East Frankish recipients). They clearly reflect the missionary concerns of the would-be metropolitan, providing for the wearing of this symbolic vestment on precisely those occasions of baptism, ordination and preaching to neophytes which would have defined the mission. Less noteworthy, perhaps, is the replacement of the feast days of Salzburg's patron saints by those of Stephen and Laurence, the patrons of Passau and Lorch.[45] Still, the resulting elision is characteristic of Pilgrim's work, which seeks to identify modern Passau with ancient Lorch, and Stephen with Laurence.

More interesting is a second purported privilege of Leo VII. This is framed as a letter to bishops Egilolf of Salzburg(!) (935–39), Isingrim of Regensburg (930–40), Lantbert of Freising (938–57) and Wisund of Säben(-Brixen) (938–56), informing them of the pope's responses to a series of queries brought forward by Archbishop(!) Gerhard of Lorch. Pilgrim was on firmer ground here, and the text reveals none of the chronological inconsistencies of the earlier privileges. Echoes of two bulls of Leo III (795–816) for Salzburg can be discerned; but like the Eugenius privilege, this is largely a work of imagination. Here, however, the contents are pastoral and canonical in nature, taking the form of answers to a series of questions about penance, liturgical practice and

43. JL 3784 (ZPUU 237), with Beumann, *Theutonum nova metropolis*, 88–110. See also Johrendt, *Papsttum*, 184–92; Roberts, 'Construire', 21–24.

44. JL 3602 (ZPUU 70; ed. Erkens, *Fälschungen*, no. 5; ed. Lehr, 'Pilgrim', no. 3). Cf. JE 2580 (*SUB*, no. 13), JE 2681 (*SUB*, no. 19). See most recently Schoenig, *Bonds of Wool*, 261–62.

45. Cf. Johrendt, *Papsttum*, 73 n. 88, who overlooks the local context of Laurence's cult here.

marriage regulations—common concerns in the mission field. The role of auxiliary bishops (*chorepiscopi*) is also touched upon, a matter which had been much debated in the ninth century and also had important missionary implications. After these initial exchanges, however, the privilege suddenly changes tack. The subject matter shifts, as Gerhard's Bavarian counterparts are now informed that Leo has appointed the prelate his vicar in those regions recently visited by pagan incursions, calling upon them to assist Gerhard in restoring the church there. Finally, a further address—against all internal textual logic— is appended to Duke Eberhard of Bavaria (937–38), to the effect that he, too, should offer the Lorch metropolitan every support.[46]

The resulting text makes a Janus-like impression. The bulk of material is canonical and pastoral, reading like a vademecum for the prospective missionary bishop. Pilgrim's model here was the famed exchange between Augustine of Canterbury and Gregory the Great, preserved in Bede's *Ecclesiastical History* (a work cited elsewhere in the series).[47] The opening address to the bishops, however, and the final call for their obedience—including the mention of vicarial rights—is reminiscent of the bull of 12 February 962 announcing the initial decision to raise Magdeburg to metropolitan status. This was directed to all the peoples of Otto I's realm ('cuncto clero et populo in Saxonia, Gallia, Germania, Bauuaria'), and as such would have been widely known; what is more, it closes by demanding the support of the archbishops of Mainz, Trier, Cologne, Salzburg and Hamburg(-Bremen).[48] Whatever the precise model, this splicing together of different textual types is without parallel in the corpus of authentic papal privileges. Partly on account of these features, doubts have sometimes been raised as to whether this was a product of the same forger as the other documents. But shared sources and a common interest in metropolitan and missionary prerogatives place Pilgrim's authorship beyond doubt.[49]

Finally, one further privilege survives in favour of Gerhard, who seems to have been Pilgrim's predecessor of choice where these rights are concerned. This is in the name of Agapit II (946–55), taking us into the middle years of the century. Unlike the previous texts, it is presented as a response to controversies between Gerhard and his neighbours at Salzburg. Up to this point, Salzburg's archiepiscopal status had been consistently (and deliberately) ignored, even reducing Archbishop Egilolf to the status of a mere bishop in order to maintain the fiction of Passau's traditional pre-eminence. As Pilgrim neared his own day, however, he could no longer deny the existence of a metropolitan

46. JL 3614 (ZPUU 87; ed. Erkens, *Fälschungen*, no. 7; ed. Lehr, 'Pilgrim', no. 4). Cf. JE 2503 (*SUB*, no. 2d), JE 2495 (*SUB*, no. 2c), which furnish elements of the protocol and eschatocol.

47. Bede, *Historia ecclesiastica*, I.27, ed. Colgrave and Mynors, 78–102. Cf. Schütte, 'Bemerkungen', 61.

48. JL 3690 (ZPUU 154). See Beumann, *Theutonum nova metropolis*, 95–96.

49. See most recently Erkens, *Fälschungen*, 70* n. 132.

neighbour, and this bull is an attempt to defuse the problem. It recounts how Abbot Hadamar of Fulda had brought forward a petition from Gerhard relating to ongoing conflicts between himself and Archbishop Herold of Salzburg (939–55).[50] These had broken out because both men enjoyed pallium rights within the same province. Agapit informs Gerhard that he possesses written records of which churches receive the pallium, and both these and the 'authentic privileges' ('privilegia authentica') brought forward by Hadamar had demonstrated that Lorch was indeed a longstanding metropolitan and archiepiscopal see. He goes on to explain that he found privileges within the papal archive confirming Gerhard's version of events, namely that Lorch had from earliest times been charged with oversight of Upper and Lower Pannonia. However, on account of the damage done by the Huns—a reference which could be to the late antique Huns or later Avars or Hungarians ('Hun' being a generic term for steppe peoples in this period)—its prelates had been forced to relocate, renouncing their metropolitan status. Only in more recent times was Salzburg made the archiepiscopal seat of Bavaria, under Arno—a detail Pilgrim would have known from his Salzburg sources, though one strangely at odds with his earlier Leo VII privilege—as is likewise shown by papal records ('testatur annosa memorialis sacri scrinii hystoria'). Now that there was once again calm on the eastern frontier, however, Agapit has seen fit to restore Lorch (and hence Gerhard) to its former glory, in accordance with the pronouncements of his own predecessor Leo (clearly an allusion to the two prior privileges for Gerhard). Finally, Agapit notes that since there can only be one metropolitan per province, he has divided Noricum, granting Herold western Pannonia and Gerhard and his successors eastern Pannonia, that is, the regions of the Avars, Moravians and Slavs. There Gerhard is to acquire converts to Christ through baptism and to act as papal vicar, preaching and establishing bishoprics. If, however, Herold or any of his successors seek to block this, they are to forfeit their rights and be incorporated into the newly restored province of Lorch.

This is perhaps the most important of our texts. It is designed to counter any objections from Salzburg by declaring the entire affair a fait accompli. Every effort is made to enhance the authority of the bull, which alone within the series closes with a sanction, declaring those who infringe its terms anathema, damned by apostolic sentence like Ananias and Sapphira—who fell miraculously dead upon lying to the Holy Spirit (Acts V:1–11)—and eternally crucified alongside such blasphemers.[51] Yet it is not just the explicit endorsement of Passau's claims which is striking. The privilege also serves to authenticate the earlier bulls, mentioning those of Leo by name and declaring that these were found to be in accordance with earlier records in Rome. Moreover,

---

50. JL 3644 (ZPUU 116; ed. Erkens, *Fälschungen*, no. 2; ed. Lehr, 'Pilgrim', no. 5).
51. Cf. Rosé, 'Judas, Dathan'.

by threatening Salzburg with a 'return' to episcopal status, it tries to discourage attempts to question these pronouncements. Pilgrim shows an impressive command of recent history here. The conflict described is fictional, but Gerhard and Herold were indeed contemporaries, and the choice of the latter is telling. Herold had sided with Otto I's son Liudolf during the rebellion of 953–54, in which the rebels were accused of conspiring with the Hungarians against royal authority. When finally captured by Duke Henry—Otto I's brother—in 955, Herold had been blinded and removed from his post. This was an extreme (and controversial) punishment, which reflects the hostility felt towards Herold within the Liudolfing family.[52] By mentioning Herold, Pilgrim was able to draw attention to one of the darkest hours of Salzburg's recent history. Similarly noteworthy is the mention of Hadamar of Fulda. Like many abbots of this monastery, Hadamar was in regular contact with the pope, travelling to Rome in winter 947–48 and again in summer 955 (in the latter case, on royal duties). He was, therefore, a plausible interlocutor for an 'archbishop' of Passau.[53]

To round off the series, Pilgrim takes the story into his own episcopate. Here he mocked up a bull of a 'Pope Benedict' (either VI or VII, 973–74 or 974–83), addressed to all the archbishops of East Francia, as well as Emperor Otto II, Otto's relative (*nepos*) Duke Henry II of Bavaria (955–76, 985–95) and the other leading ecclesiastics and magnates of Gaul ('Gallia', i.e., Lotharingia) and Germany ('Germania'). It explains how Pilgrim had presented documents demonstrating Passau's traditional metropolitan status, stretching back to the days of Symmachus. This had been lost following the barbarian ravages of previous ages, now put to an end by the glorious victory of the most victorious Augustus (i.e., Otto I), father of the present emperor—a clear allusion to the battle of the Lechfeld (955).[54] Since peace and tranquillity reign, Benedict has seen fit to restore the archbishopric of Lorch, that it might minister to the Hungarians, Moravians and other Slavic provinces. He has also freed the centre from the oversight of Salzburg, which had exploited Lorch's previous mishaps in order to secure its subjugation. The pope now sets the borders of the two provinces, in accordance with the earlier privilege of Agapit (II); and establishes that seniority should go to the archbishop who has been consecrated first, in accordance with the regulations set out by Gregory I (590–604)—a reference to regulations originally intended for the early English church, as recorded by Bede (though also echoed in an earlier Salzburg bull).[55] He further ordains that neither archbishop should invade

52. Bührer-Thierry, *Évêques et pouvoir*, 199–205.

53. Hussong, 'Studien', 251–54, 257–61.

54. JL 3771 (ZPUU 223; ed. Erkens, *Fälschungen*, no. 9; ed. Lehr, 'Pilgrim', no. 7).

55. Bede, *Historia ecclesiastica*, I.29, ed. Colgrave and Mynors, 104–6. Cf. JE 2503 (*SUB*, no. 2d).

the other's diocese, before finally granting Pilgrim the pallium 'according to the ancient custom of that same church of his [viz. Lorch/Passau]' ('secundum antiquum eiusdem ęcclesię suę usum') and according him vicarial status in the regions of 'Avaria', Moravia and lower Pannonia, including permission to ordain priests and bishops as well as to found bishoprics.

As with the Agapit bull, this privilege seeks to silence naysayers. According to it, Pope Benedict has already endorsed Pilgrim's view. And in doing so, he has done little more than uphold his predecessor's decisions, themselves grounded in ancient custom. To strengthen this impression, the bull is accompanied by perhaps the most unusual text of the series: a letter of Pilgrim to Pope Benedict, requesting the pallium in the first place. This first informs the pope of Pilgrim's recent missionary successes among the Hungarians. Then, drawing attention to the earlier history of the church within the region, as well as Passau's role therein—disrupted by the Hungarian invasions—it requests a return to this prior position. To demonstrate his suitability for the task, Pilgrim includes a confession of faith, itself largely lifted from well-known canonical sources, before closing with a final entreaty.[56] Although Dümmler thought this letter genuine, it can scarcely be any more authentic than the response—or the other documents in the dossier.[57] What it does, like the other recent forgeries, is create the impression of an ongoing dialogue between the (arch)bishops of Passau-Lorch and the pope.

The general drift of the bulls should by now be clear. They focus on archiepiscopal and vicarial rights, above all those to wear the pallium and to establish bishoprics (and ordain their bishops). To achieve this, they focus on two periods: the distant past, starting with the pontificate of Symmachus; and the more recent present, providing an immediate precedent for Passau's 'return' to metropolitan standing. There can be no doubt that these texts reflect Pilgrim's hopes in their purest form. Many are freely composed, and even those closely modelled on Salzburg texts suggest a creative (and often idiosyncratic) view of local history. Although they only survive in copies of the twelfth century or later, they do so in close proximity to one another, and clearly constitute a set. They also share a common focus, sources and—most crucially—means of expression, demonstrating beyond doubt that they are the product of a single mind—that of Pilgrim.[58] But if the bulls present Pilgrim's hopes at their most unbridled, they can only be fully appreciated alongside the diplomas he produced, both forged and authentic.

56. *Fälschungen*, ed. Erkens, no. 9; 'Pilgrim', ed. Lehr, no. 6. Cf. *Concilios visigóticos*, ed. Vives, 346–54.

57. As already noted by Mittermüller, 'Bischof Piligrim', 343–47.

58. Cf. Resl, 'Ethnic History', 95–96.

The Passau Forgeries, II: The Diplomas

The fact that the false bulls end by bringing the story into Pilgrim's pontificate already suggests his involvement. Secure evidence of this, however, comes from the diplomas in Pilgrim's favour. As Dümmler noted, a number of these refer to him as 'bishop of Lorch'. And Dümmler drew a connection between this title and the forged bulls, which present Pilgrim and his predecessors as the successors to earlier (arch)bishops of Lorch. Although the silence of Pilgrim's diplomas on the subject of metropolitan status disturbed some early commentators—Pilgrim is always 'bishop' here—this is hardly surprising. At home in Passau, Pilgrim could speak freely of his plans; at court, greater circumspection was doubtless required. The decisive proof of a connection, however, first came from Karl Uhlirz, who noted that all of the surviving diplomas styling Pilgrim 'bishop of Lorch' are in the same hand. What is more, this hand can be found in a number of forged Carolingian diplomas for Passau, one of which speaks of an earlier 'archbishop of Lorch', who had been forced to abandon his see for Passau—precisely the scenario envisaged by the bulls. Uhlirz concluded that these documents were all the work of the same figure, an association strengthened by Waldemar Lehr, who identified significant formulaic similarities between the bulls and diplomas.[59]

Yet for all their importance in dating the bulls, Pilgrim's forged diplomas themselves have rarely received much attention. They tend to be dismissed as subsidiary texts—'flanking measures' ('flankierrende Maßnahmen'), as the most recent commentator puts it.[60] Yet precisely because they survive in their (pseudo-)original format, these promise further insights into Pilgrim's aims, interests and modus operandi. We must proceed carefully here. Unlike the bulls—or, for that matter, the Worms forgeries of the previous chapter—these do not constitute a coherent series. Rather, we are dealing with occasional texts, probably forged over many years, with only loose and indirect links to each other—and to Pilgrim's other counterfeits.

The earliest of the false diplomas is in the name of Charlemagne and dated 789. This confirms Bishop Walderich (of Passau) in possession of the abbey of Kremsmünster, which had been granted to the see by Duke Tassilo III (745–87, d. 796). Tassilo was the last independent ruler of Bavaria, whose name was later blackened by his Carolingian overlords. He had founded Kremsmünster in 777, and the diploma is modelled on an authentic confirmation of its holdings of 791, which had made its way into Pilgrim's hands as Kremsmünster's later lord. The key difference between the forgery and its exemplar is that in the former, the abbot of Kremsmünster, the appropriately named Fater, has been replaced as recipient by Bishop Walderich, creating the impression that

---

59. Uhlirz, 'Urkundenfälschung'; Lehr, 'Pilgrim', 8–18, 25.
60. Erkens, *Fälschungen*, 67*. See similarly Lehr, 'Pilgrim', 8.

the abbey is a longstanding episcopal holding.[61] In fact, Kremsmünster had passed from ducal into royal hands following the fall of Tassilo, and as late as the reign of Arnulf (887–99) it remained independent of the bishop. At some point in the intervening years, however—perhaps in the aftermath of the Hungarian raids, though conceivably under other circumstances—it came under Passau's control. There were evidently still questions about its status in Pilgrim's day, since in 975 Otto II issued a diploma confirming its donation to the see. Interestingly, this latter document, which only survives in later copies, is preserved in two distinct versions, both of which can be ascribed to Willigis C (i.e., Pilgrim). It is rare to have two texts of the same transaction, and the best explanation is that a first version was rejected at court and that Pilgrim was forced to produce a revised text, which was then duly approved. This was not the only time the bishop would have had to revise his work, as we shall see, and the main difference between the diplomas lies in their description of the abbey's early history. In the first, Otto II refers to how Pilgrim had produced documents demonstrating 'how our ancestors of pious record, the emperors Louis [the Pious?] and Arnulf' ('qualiter pię recordationis antecessores nostri Hludovicus et Arolfus imperatores') had granted the monastery to Passau; yet in the second, we are simply informed of the precedent of 'our ancestors of pious memory' ('pię memorię antecessores nostri').[62] One suspects that Pilgrim was asked for evidence that Louis and Arnulf had granted the monastery to Passau and came up short. In any case, neither version mentions a diploma of Charlemagne, so the forgery probably post-dates the confirmation. Indeed, its existence may reflect the lessons learned at this point: unsupported claims were unlikely to find favour.

The surviving single sheet of the Charlemagne forgery is certainly in the hand of Willigis C, who—as already noted—had also been responsible for Otto II's confirmation of these rights. Pilgrim's script can be recognized by the form of a; the distinctive flourishes on c, e and t in elongated script; the preference for v over u, especially at the start of words (where the left diagonal stroke is longer and more horizontal than the right one); the looped descenders on g, somewhat reminiscent of those of Hildibald B; and the distinctive chrismon, adopted from Italian C (Illustration 2.2).[63] Indeed, Pilgrim has made little effort to conceal his native diplomatic minuscule—a script first developed in the second half of the ninth century—nor has he sought to render the chrismon and opening line in plausibly eighth-century fashion. Still, he has not entirely ignored his exemplar. The royal monogram makes a good impression,

---

61. D Kar 247. Cf. D Kar 169.

62. D O II 111a/b, with Fichtenau, *Urkundenwesen*, 128–29. On the abbey: Pösinger, 'Rechtsstellung', 67–72, 77–79.

63. Munich, BayHStA, HU Passau 1. On Pilgrim's hand: Uhlirz, 'Urkundenfälschung', 183–86.

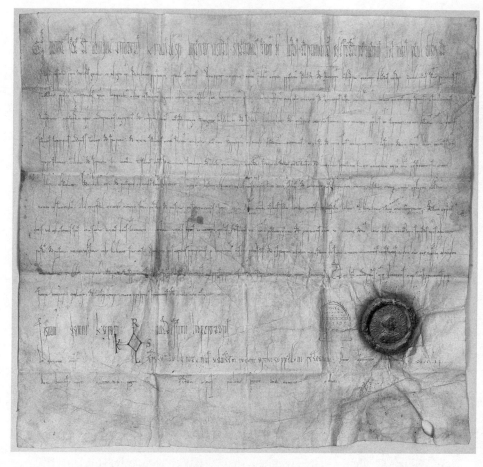

2.2 Pilgrim's Charlemagne forgery: Munich, BayHStA, HU Passau 1, © BayHStA

even if it is positioned after Charlemagne's name in tenth-century fashion.
And the inclusion of a recognition sign—albeit in early tenth-century 'beehive'
form—similarly shows an awareness of Carolingian documentary norms. The
seal itself is modelled on one of Charles the Fat (876–87) rather than Charlemagne. This may have been a conscious decision, the former's diplomas being
more numerous in Bavaria. But it is probably just an error, perhaps occasioned
by the loss of the seal on Pilgrim's model. (Like modern undergraduates,
tenth-century observers often struggled to distinguish the many Charleses
and Louises of the Carolingian dynasty.)[64] Formulation tells a similar tale.

64. Richer of Saint-Remi tellingly remarks that 'since the names Charles and Louis
are frequently presented both here [in the *Historiae*] and there [in Hincmar's work], the
skilled reader will distinguish between like-named kings on account of the time period
of the author' ('Unde cum hic atque illic sepe Karoli, sepe Ludouici notę offeruntur, pro

Table 2. Pilgrim's preambles and their Carolingian model

D K Gr 169 (Pilgrim's exemplar)	D K Gr 247 (his forgery)	D O I 423 (one of his other charters)[1]
Si peticionibus sacerdotum vel servorum dei, in quo nostris auribus fuerint prolatę, libenter obaudimus et eas in dei nomine ad effectum perducimus, regiam consuetudinem exercimus et hoc nobis ad mercedem vel stabilitatem regni nostri pertinere confidimus. Igitur notum sit omnibus fidelibus nostris presentibus et futuris . . .	Si petitiones servorum dei **iustas et rationabiles** ad effectum perducimus, hoc nobis **procul dubio** et ad capessenda regni caelestis gaudia et ad regni nostri stabilitatem **profuturum liquido credimus. Quapropter comperiat omnium fidelium nostrorum** presentium scilicet et futurorum **industria** . . .	Si petitiones servorum dei **iustas et rationabiles** ad effetum a perducimus, hoc nobis **procul dubio** ad aeternę remunerationis premia capessenda **profuturum liquido credimus. Quapropter conperiat omnium fidelium** sanctae dei aecclesiae **nostrorum**que presentium scilicet et futurorum **industria** . . .

[1] These formulae are subsequently copied in DD O II 27, 138.

While elements of this are taken from the authentic Kremsmünster diploma of 791, Pilgrim has adjusted these forms to suit his own tastes and needs. The opening preamble, for example, is Carolingian in origin, but in its present form is closer to that used by Pilgrim in his own authentic diplomas. The same is true of the immediately following publication formula (Table 2). The list of estates is largely copied from the exemplar, but Pilgrim has taken the liberty of adding a few names, presumably concerning Kremsmünster's subsequent acquisitions. Finally, he also inserts a further confirmation of these grants, before moving on to the closing eschatocol. Here the imperial subscription takes elements from its authentic model, but Pilgrim has not been able to resist updating Charlemagne's title to suit the expectations of his day, replacing the superlative 'most glorious' with 'most invincible'. The dating clause, on the other hand, seems to have been lifted from another charter entirely.

Clearly the function of this privilege is to provide a secure basis for episcopal control of Kremsmünster, confirming the monastery's holdings in the process. To achieve this, Pilgrim partially contradicts the tale told by his bulls. Walderich is simply *presul* (prelate, bishop) here; what is more, he is said to oversee 'the sacred church of Passau' ('sancta Patauiensis aecclesia')—there is thus no whiff of Lorch or metropolitan status. This may be because Pilgrim's archiepiscopal ambitions had already failed. Alternatively, he may not have

tempore auctorum prudens lector reges ęquivocos pernotabit'): *Historiae*, prol., ed. Hoffmann, 35. See similarly Aimoin, *Gesta Francorum*, prol., PL 139, col. 628. More generally: Geary, *Phantoms*, 147–53.

wanted his possession of Kremsmünster yoked to his other efforts. Still, there may be a connection of sorts with Pilgrim's missionary plans. Kremsmünster lies to the south and east of Passau—within the Slavic lands, as the forgery itself states—along precisely those routes which linked the see to Hungary (Map 2). The abbey had originally been founded to assist with the conversion of the Carinthians; if Pilgrim was to take a lead in the mission, this would have been an ideal staging post.[65]

The next of the counterfeit diplomas chronologically is in the name of Louis the Pious (dated 28 June 823). This confirms Passau's possession of a list of lands granted to the bishopric following the conquest of the Avars (in the 790s), including Litaha (near the modern Leitha) and Zeiselmauer with the march associated with the latter. This is clearly modelled on an authentic privilege, perhaps of 823. And a shorter version, more closely approximating the original, survives in a mid-thirteenth-century copy. Significantly, the latter text makes no mention of Litaha or Zeiselmauer, so these additions seem to have been the grounds for forgery. As in the previous case, the purpose was to claim strategic estates along the Danube, the main thoroughfare between Passau and Hungary (Zeiselmauer lies just downstream from modern Vienna). The forged text itself survives in two near identical single sheet copies, only one of which bears a seal. For reasons which are not entirely clear, the first was deemed unsatisfactory and replaced with a second, whose seal was probably lifted from the first (Illustration 2.3). In any case, the first (now without a seal) is certainly in Pilgrim's hand. The second shows signs of his influence, but its script is imitative—there is a palpable instability to the hand—and it may belong to a slightly later context (Illustration 2.4).[66] As in the Charlemagne charter, little effort has been taken to hide the scribe's tenth-century habits, both in script and layout. Still, Pilgrim had access to an early ninth-century model, either the lost original or the diploma issued by Louis the German for Salzburg in 837, which he consulted when producing his Arnulf immunity. Indeed, the monogram is largely correct and precedes the emperor's name in ninth-century fashion (unlike that in the Charlemagne counterfeit). And the subscription, though on two lines (as we would expect in the later tenth century, but not the ninth), echoes that of the 837 Louis the German diploma.[67] Pilgrim has apparently misjudged the space available—though not nearly as badly as Hildibald B in his first effort—and the last three lines of text

65. Fletcher, *Conversion of Europe*, 344. Cf. Bowlus, *Franks, Moravians, and Magyars*, 230–32.

66. D L Fr 225 (II), Munich, BayHStA, HU Passau 2/2 and 2/1. See *Urkunden Ludwigs des Frommen*, ed. Kölzer, 554–55, 556–57; Erkens, 'Ludwig des Frommen Urkunde'. Cf. Crick, 'Historical Literacy', 169–70, on script imitation.

67. Munich, BayHStA, HU Passau 2/2. Cf. Vienna, HHStA, UR AUR 7 (=D L D 22). Another conceivable inspiration is D L D 7 (*KUA*, i, no. 9), though Pilgrim is not known to have used this text elsewhere.

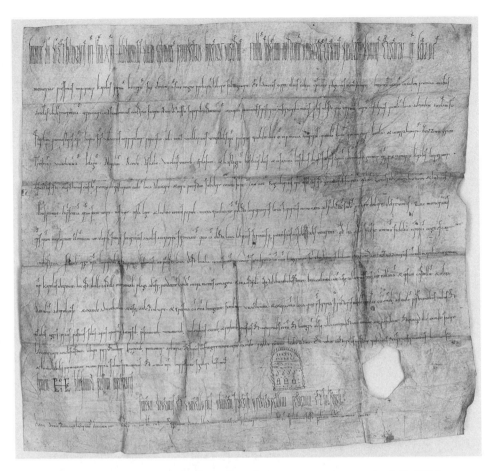

2.3 Pilgrim's Louis the Pious forgery: Munich, BayHStA, HU Passau 2/2, © BayHStA

show a degree of bunching. This probably explains the decision to produce a second (otherwise identical) copy. The seal itself is a counterfeit, modelled on that of Louis the German—perhaps another case of confusing like-named Carolingians, and certainly a further indication that the Salzburg privilege of 837 set the tone. In any case, Litaha was first granted to the bishopric by Louis the German, while no record survives as to Zeiselmauer's acquisition.[68]

Pilgrim's interest here evidently lay in strengthening his position at these sites, an effort doubtless helped by associating them with established holdings elsewhere. As previously, no attempt has been made to include the 'legend of Lorch'; Reginhard is addressed as 'bishop' ('episcopus') and his see is named as Passau ('Patauia'). Still, there may be hints of Pilgrim's historical and missionary interests. He has inserted a reference to the devastation and poverty

---

68. D L D 9. On the probable location of this estate: Klebel, 'Ostgrenze', 374.

2.4 A/B Pilgrim's Louis the Pious forgery and its imitative copy (detail): Munich, BayHStA, HU Passau 2/2 and 2/1, © BayHStA

of the see being the grounds for the grant, details in keeping with his version of early Lorch-Passau history. Likewise, he has inserted a spiritual sanction threatening those who contravene the text's terms with answering for themselves at the Day of Judgement—a feature uncommon in diplomas of the early ninth century, but far less out of place in Pilgrim's tenth.[69] Similarities in formulation between the list of estates in these single sheets and that in a ducal notice of 991 may indicate that one of them was produced before the duke on

69. Cf. Studtmann, 'Pönformel', 291–302; Bautier, 'La chancellerie', 57–59.

this occasion, but the textual relationship is (sadly) far from certain.[70] Finally, Zeiselmauer, like Lorch, boasted Roman ruins, which may explain Pilgrim's interest; if he had wanted to demonstrate Passau's antiquity, possessing this centre was a step in the right direction.[71]

Two further forged Passau diplomas concern the abbey of Ötting (modern Altötting), upriver from Passau on the Inns. This had been founded by the late Carolingian ruler Carloman of Bavaria (876–80), who was later buried there, and had previously been an important royal palace. Like Kremsmünster, Ötting came into the hands of the bishop of Passau, probably in the early tenth century. And as in the former case, there was now a desire to project this state of affairs into the more distant past. The first of the two texts, in the name of Arnulf of Carinthia, has been subtly adjusted from its model to describe the abbey—which is the recipient—as 'belonging by perpetual right to the see of Passau' ('ad sedem Patauiensis ecclesię iure perpetuo pertnentis'), while the second, in the name of Louis the Child, confirms Bishop Burchard of Passau's possession of the abbey.[72] Only the former survives as a single sheet, but the two are clearly related. And there has been some uncertainty as to their relationship with the other Passau forgeries. Uhlirz assigned the Arnulf diploma to a different hand from that from that of Willigis C, but left open the possibility that it was produced alongside the other counterfeits.[73] In 1960, Theodor Schieffer argued that Willigis C had indeed been responsible for drafting—and perhaps also copying—both this and the Louis the Child forgery, though he said nothing about the hand of it (the original of which he had apparently not consulted). On this basis, Heinrich Fichtenau went on to assign full responsibility for both texts to Pilgrim; and such was (and is) the authority of Schieffer and Fichtenau, that all subsequent commentators have followed them, presuming Pilgrim's involvement.[74]

Unfortunately, examination of the Arnulf pseudo-original confirms the initial judgement of Uhlirz. There are some resemblances of Pilgrim's script, but also many important differences, including the absence of flourishes on c, e, and t in elongated forms; the differently formed loop on g; the consistent use of an alternative abbreviation sign; and the generally more stiff and upright aspect (Illustration 2.5). Such variations cannot be attributed to the scribe's exemplar (as Schieffer suggested), since none of them are found in Pilgrim's other Arnulf forgery (of which more anon). Indeed, while there the bishop made a small but

70. Fichtenau, *Urkundenwesen*, 107, 128; Erkens, 'Ludwig des Frommen Urkunde', 94–95.

71. Cf. Genser, *Der österreichische Donaulimes*, 376–96.

72. D Arn 161, D L K 84. Cf. Mühlbacher, 'Zwei weitere Passauer Fälschungen'.

73. Uhlirz, 'Urkundenfälschung', 189. See also *Urkunden Arnolfs*, ed. Kehr, 244.

74. *Urkunden Zwentibolds und Ludwigs des Kindes*, ed. Schieffer, 228–29; Fichtenau, *Urkundenwesen*, 129–30. For endorsement: Boshof, 'Reorganisation', 77; Brunner, *Herzogtümer und Marken*, 95; Erkens, *Fälschungen*, 61*–62* (esp. n. 92). Previously Fichtenau had (correctly) placed the Arnulf diploma in the eleventh century, apparently on Kehr's authority: 'Urkundenfälschungen', 178 n. 182.

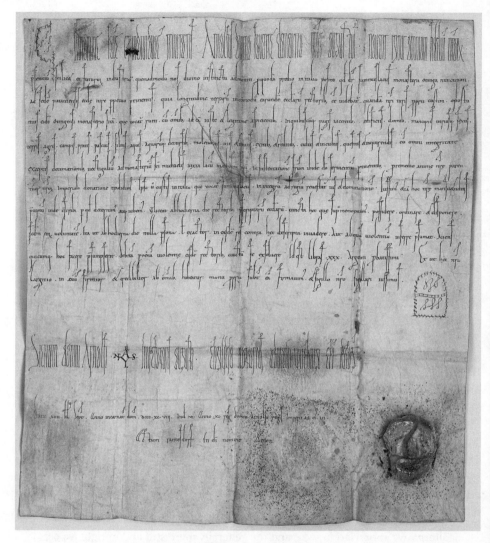

2.5 Passau Ötting forgery in the name of King Arnulf: Munich, BayHStA,
DU Passau 1, © BayHStA

significant error in rendering Arnulf's monogram, here it is copied correctly—a
further sign that we are dealing with different forgers.[75] Yet it is not just the hand
which speaks against Pilgrim's involvement; so too does formulation. Neither
the Arnulf privilege nor the Louis the Child text reveals formulaic links with the
bishop's other known productions (certain thematic similarities notwithstanding). There can, in short, be no question of Pilgrim having drafted or copied
these. In fact, as Paul Fridolin Kehr noted, the hand of the Arnulf text is more

75. Munich, BayHStA, DU Passau 1. See Mersiowsky, *Urkunde*, 214 n. 783, on the
monogram.

advanced than that of Willigis C. And this, combined with the vertical (or 'portrait') layout—which first starts to win out under Henry II (1002–24)—points more naturally toward production in the eleventh (or very late tenth) century. The same is suggested by the presence of a secular sanction threatening monetary fines, a feature which first becomes common north of the Alps in the later 990s, under Italian influence.[76] In this respect, it is tempting to place the counterfeits in the pontificate of Pilgrim's successor, Christian (991–1013). In 993, Christian received confirmation of Kremsmünster, Mattsee (another local house, which since 877 had been in Kremsmünster's hands) and Ötting, along with the estate of Reut, and this may have occasioned the forgery. Certainly Christian was not above falsification. A charter dated only one week after this confirmation and written in the same hand (conceivably that of Christian himself) has had a false seal appended to it. And the surviving single sheet of the Kremsmünster, Mattsee and Ötting confirmation itself reveals signs of erasure and rewriting in the final lines—tampering probably undertaken by Christian.[77]

The last of the forged diplomas is perhaps the most important. This takes the form of an immunity of Arnulf, dated Regensburg 9 September 898. The text draws on an authentic diploma of Arnulf's years (perhaps an immunity). And the surviving pseudo-original—one of the largest single sheets to survive from the Passau archive—reveals that Pilgrim has attempted to copy a number of features of his model, including the form of the opening elongated script (particularly in the name Arnulf), the imperial monogram and the single-line subscription and recognition (Illustration 2.6). However, unlike the later forger of the Ötting privilege, he has mistakenly formed the completion stroke in Arnulf's monogram as a 'v' rather than a horizontal line. The completion stroke (*Vollziehungsstrich*) is the final element of the royal/imperial monogram, whose presence is necessary for the text's validity (much like the seal). Sometimes this was appended by the ruler himself, and an important innovation of Arnulf's reign was that the older v form was replaced with a simple horizontal line—a convention still current in Pilgrim's day (Illustration 2.7). Pilgrim has thus fallen into hyperarchaism, inspired by earlier Carolingian models; he has tried too hard.[78] Beyond the lost Arnulf exemplar, the text shows clear signs of influence from privileges of Louis the German for Salzburg and Charles the Fat for Passau.[79]

76. Studtmann, 'Pönformel', 309–10; Uhlirz, 'Rechtsfragen'.

77. D O III 112, Munich, BayHStA, HU Passau 21; D O III 115, Munich, BayHStA, HU Passau 22, with Uhlirz, *Jahrbücher*, ii, 474–76. Note, however, that this is not the same hand as that of the Arnulf forgery.

78. D Arn 163, Munich, BayHStA, HU Passau 11. See Mersiowsky, *Urkunde*, 213–14 (= Mersiowsky, 'Carta edita', 356–57); Erben, *Kaiser- und Königsurkunden*, 151–52. Interestingly, one modern scholar has also been seduced into hypercorrection by Pilgrim here: Schneidmüller, *Karolingische Tradition*, 96.

79. D L D 22, Vienna, HHStA, UR AUR 7; D K III 134; D K III 135, Munich, BayHStA, HU Passau 6.

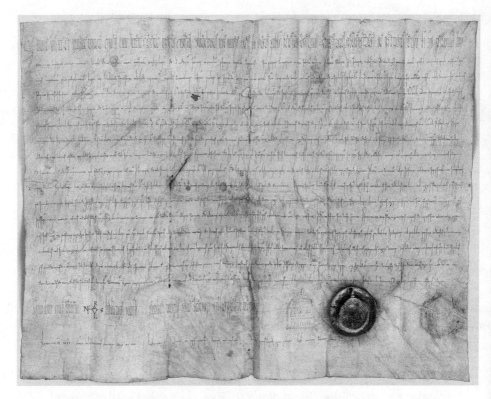

2.6 Pilgrim's forged Arnulf immunity: Munich, BayHStA, HU Passau 11, © BayHStA

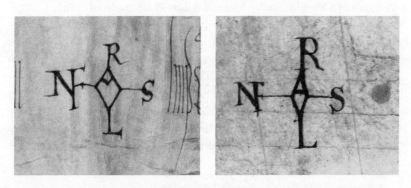

2.7 A/B Pilgrim's completion stroke on Arnulf's monogram vs that of an authentic diploma in his name: Munich, BayHStA, HU Passau 11; Münster, LA Nordrhein-Westfalen, Fürstabtei Corvei, Urkunde 24 (reproduced from *KUA*, vii, no. 23), © BayHStA

Unlike the other counterfeit diplomas, the focus here is indeed on Lorch. In fact, one of Pilgrim's main additions to his models is a lengthy narrative excursus on how, over a century before the confirmation, 'the sometime archbishop of the sacred church of Lorch' ('quondam sanctae Lauriacensis aecclesię archiepiscopus'), Vivulo, had been forced to abandon his see 'after the destruction and the miserable barbarian devastation' ('post excidium et miserabilem barbaricam devastationem'), seeking succour from Odilo of Bavaria (Tassilo's father), who set him up at the church of St Stephen the Protomartyr (in Passau). There is no doubt here that Vivulo had been reduced to episcopal status upon his transfer, and that this state of affairs continued to prevail in Arnulf's day. Still, the manner in which these events are framed suggests that the draftsman (again, Pilgrim) was angling for restitution. By placing the movement from Lorch to Passau in the mid-eighth century, he manages to associate this event not only with the first securely attested bishop of Passau (Vivulo), but also with the ducal family which had been responsible for the foundation of Niederaltaich and (perhaps more importantly) Kremsmünster. In fact, the diploma claims to have been issued in response to privileges of Odilo and Tassilo, brought forward by Bishop Wiching; and it goes on to confirm all prior donations to the see. With this, Pilgrim may have hoped to cover his tracks, much as he had done with the Agapit II privilege. The documents confirmed are not listed by name, so it may be that he had yet to produce them (or at least some of them). Either way, the effect is the same: a blank cheque to adapt and improve Passau's past. What is more, Pilgrim manages to associate this purported ducal largesse with the legend of Lorch; it was on account of the see's tribulations that it had been favoured by the Bavarian dukes. The inconsistencies in his story have not been entirely ironed out, and the bull presenting Urolf as 'archbishop' in the early ninth century sits awkwardly alongside this. Still, there is no mistaking the fact that Pilgrim's two worlds were starting to come together, and the impressive dimensions of the single sheet speak of the document's significance. Pilgrim is cautious here, as we might expect, and the diploma's claims to immunity could be maintained without those to metropolitan status. Nevertheless, there is an unmistakable bridge between the undertakings.

The forged diplomas are, therefore, far more than flanking measures. Unlike the bulls, many survive in pseudo-original format (a fact which may itself be significant), and these make a good impression. Though a long way from fooling a trained modern eye, most passed muster till the late nineteenth century; and by the standards of their day, they were far from inept. Their aims vary, but generally relate to Passau's territorial integrity, particularly in the eastern reaches of the diocese. As such, they come across as more pragmatic and down-to-earth than the bulls. Yet there are connections between the endeavours, as we have seen. In the Arnulf immunity, territorial integrity is associated with the bishopric's historic move up the Danube. And the estates and churches secured almost all lie along this river, on precisely those routes between Passau and Hungary so important for Pilgrim's missionary plans.

Pilgrim's Privileges: The Authentic Texts

Pilgrim was not, however, simply a forger. He was first introduced to charter production by his uncle in Italy, where he produced at least one authentic diploma for Salzburg; and throughout his episcopate, he drafted and copied imperial privileges for his see. So far as we can tell, Passau had not received any diplomas since the early years of Louis the Child—the last ruler to spend any amount of time in Bavaria—and these texts herald a sudden rise in standing, a rise in which the well-connected Pilgrim was evidently instrumental.[80] The majority survive as single sheet originals, and some mention Lorch, providing further insights into the bishop's intentions and ambitions in these years.

The first two were issued at Nierstein on the Rhine on 18 October 972, probably just after Pilgrim had attended an important synod at Ingelheim, some 40 km (25 miles) downriver.[81] These are a pair of near-identical privileges of Otto I and his son (and co-emperor) Otto II, issued at the request of Duke Henry of Bavaria and Bishop Theoderic of Metz (the latter only named in the Otto I text). They confirm Passau's possession of vineyards and a mountain in the Wachau, a region of Lower Austria straddling the Danube, just over half way between modern Linz and Vienna (Map 2). The rights lie on those same routes as Kremsmünster and Zeiselmauer; and the diplomas thus complement Pilgrim's more questionable efforts to secure his holdings. In fact, there may be hints of missionary interests here. Pilgrim is accorded the potentially significant title 'pontiff of the sacred church of Lorch' ('sanctae Lauriacensis aecclecię pontifex') in both; and the confirmation is said to be made 'for our Lord and the sacred martyrs Stephen and Laurence' ('domino nostro et sanctis martiribus Stephano atque Laurentio'), the patrons of Passau and Lorch.[82] As in the bulls, the attempt is to associate Passau and Lorch, Stephen and Laurence, and the choice of the more ambiguous title 'pontiff' (*pontifex*) is telling. Pilgrim's immediate inspiration for associating the centres may have been the joint archbishopric of Hamburg-Bremen, which had been entrusted with the mission to Scandinavia. There were also precedents nearer to home, as the Bavarian see of Brixen often went by the older designation Säben. Whether Pilgrim had entirely thought through the consequences of his identification with Lorch—whether this was an early bid for metropolitan status, that is—is unclear. But certainly the thought process had begun.

---

80. Boshof, 'Reorganisation', 72–79. See also Scharer, 'Bishops', 14–15.

81. Though Pilgrim is not recorded as present, our only source for attendance of the synod is a later forgery: *Konzilien Deutschlands*, ed. Hehl, 324–31 (no. 34). (Note that Theoderic of Metz is recorded as present.)

82. D O I 423, Munich, BayHStA, HU Passau 13; D O II 27, Munich, BayHStA, HU Passau 14. Cf. Zibermayr, *Noricum*, 393–95, whose efforts to dismiss all documents bearing the Lorch title before 977 as forged or interpolated is little more than a *petitio principii* (see Fichtenau, 'Urkundenfälschungen', 166 n. 35).

Pilgrim must have been aware that the mention of Laurence, Lorch's patron, was likely to go down well at court. Alongside Maurice, the latter was a figure central to the eastern mission. It had been on Laurence's feast day (10 August) that Otto I achieved victory at the Lechfeld. And according to later reports, the king had promised to found a bishopric in honour of the saint on this occasion, a promise fulfilled at Merseburg, one of Magdeburg's missionary suffragans.[83] Evidently Pilgrim was keen to make an impression, and the decision to seek diplomas from both the ageing emperor and his son may itself be significant; he was seeking maximum security.[84] In fact, there are a number of signs of haste in the production of the second of these, suggesting that it have been something of an afterthought. Thus Pilgrim initially omitted part of the royal style in the first line, then had to complete this over erasure, squeezing in the final adjective *aug[ustus]* to do so. He also had to correct a number of minor slips (including something like *nepos neposter* for *nepos noster*, 'our nephew'); and it may be that the absence of Theoderic of Metz as petitioner is a further error, occasioned by the reworking of the intervention clause (though it is conceivable that Theoderic's involvement was simply limited to the initial confirmation by Otto I). Even in its completed form, the diploma erroneously refers to Duke Henry II of Bavaria as Otto II's nephew (*nepos*) rather than cousin, a reference carelessly carried over from the first charter (and perhaps repeated in Pilgrim's Benedict bull, where scholars have presumed *nepos* to be used in the generic sense). More interestingly, the placement of the place-name Nierstein to the right of the seal in the final dating clause clearly indicates that Pilgrim was working from a pre-sealed parchment (what German scholars term a *Blankett*: Illustration 2.8). This was, in other words, originally something of a blank cheque, which Pilgrim wrote up in Otto II's name. Only the most trusted recipients were accorded such freedom, and this speaks of Pilgrim's standing. Evidently the new bishop enjoyed considerable favour at court, and this would not be the last *Blankett* he received.

The next diploma is dated Worms 27 June 973. By this point, Otto II had succeeded his father—indeed, this was Otto's first major assembly as independent ruler. As such, it was an important opportunity for the emperor to forge contacts with the great and good of the realm. One of the most important figures here was Duke Henry II of Bavaria, who as Otto's elder cousin had his own residual claim to the throne. It is therefore significant that the charter Pilgrim produced grants Duke Henry Bamberg, a strategic fortification in the Bavarian Nordgau, at which Henry's own son and presumptive heir (another Henry) had probably just been born. This is the only charter Pilgrim produced for another recipient during his episcopate, and his involvement suggests close ties to the ducal court. Pilgrim had met Duke Henry in Italy in 970, and the

83. Beumann, 'Laurentius und Mauritius'; Hehl, 'Merseburg'.
84. On Otto II's charter production: Schieffer, 'Otto II. und sein Vater'.

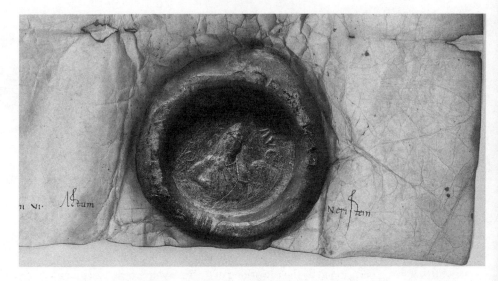

2.8 Closing eschatocol of Otto II's confirmation of Pilgrim's possessions in the Wachau: Munich, BayHStA, HU Passau 14, © BayHStA

duke was among those who had intervened in his favour in the previous year; here he was returning the favour. Still, we should be wary of inferring too much, as Pilgrim was apparently acting as something of a stopgap. The diploma's text reveals none of his stylistic traits and it would seem that it had been composed by another figure, then left to be copied out by Pilgrim (completed diplomas being fair copies of working drafts, as we have seen).[85]

Thereafter, Pilgrim seems to have remained at court, since in early September he received his own reward at Erfurt, when the emperor confirmed the bishop's possession of land in Regensburg. This had first been received by Pilgrim's predecessor, Adalbert, from Duke Henry I. The confirmation is now petitioned by the latter's son, the same Duke Henry (II) whose diploma Pilgrim had produced two months previously. This too was a significant act. Regensburg was the traditional Bavarian capital, and these lands were intended to ease the bishop's attendance at the ducal court.[86] The text itself follows the formulation of the first privilege of Otto I for Pilgrim closely—so

85. D O II 44, Bamberg, StA, Bamberger Urkunden 8. A facsimile is available in Schneidmüller, 'Einzigartig geliebte Stadt', 33. See further Pfeiffer, 'Bamberg-Urkunde', 19–21, who, on the basis of formulaic links with D O I 431 (issued to Judith of Bavaria in April 973), argues that both were drafted by Willigis C. Yet neither of these documents shows similarities with Pilgrim's other identified works, and the traditional attribution to Willigis B (who copied the latter) remains more convincing: Uhlirz, 'Urkundenfälschung', 192. For the possibility that Duke Henry's son was born in Bamberg: Geldner, 'Geburtsort'; and on the wider political constellations: Welton and Greer, 'Establishing Just Rule'.

86. Brühl, 'Hauptstadtproblem', 90–4.

much so, in fact, that he has retained the erroneous reference to Duke Henry as the emperor's nephew. Some of these slips point towards haste; others are indicative of Pilgrim's inexperience. He had only produced a small number of charters to date, and perhaps only drafted one (in Italy he was under the tutelage of Italian C). In any case, the references to Laurence and Lorch are both taken over from the previous year's exemplar. These may point to a continuing interest in such matters; but this could equally be a matter of thoughtless replication (as we see in the address of Duke Henry). Interestingly, there are also signs of adjustment to the dating clause, reflecting Pilgrim's uncertainty regarding the incarnation, regnal and imperial years—features also visible in his first two diplomas for Passau.[87]

More interesting is the next privilege, confirming Passau's possession of Kremsmünster at Allstedt in Saxony in June 975. This only survives in later copies, but from these it is clear that there were once two different versions of the text. As we have seen, the likely explanation is that the more elaborate one represents Pilgrim's first effort, brought to court at Erfurt some two weeks before the second was finally approved (they bear different dating clauses). When the first charter did not find favour, perhaps on account of its more extravagant claims, Pilgrim was forced to redraft, the result being a shorter privilege issued at Allstedt (21 June).[88] These are not the only differences between the texts. As has long been noted, the compilers of the Passau cartularies of the twelfth and thirteenth centuries went to considerable efforts to reproduce the visual features of their exemplars, particularly in the royal monograms. And none was more faithful here than the main copyist of the Codex Lonsdorfianus, the most comprehensive of these, compiled during the episcopate of Otto of Lonsdorf (1254–65).[89] Significantly, here the horizontal completion stroke is missing from the monogram of the first of these charters, suggesting that it was either never completed or this element was later erased. It is also noteworthy that the resulting (incomplete) monogram takes the form common before 975, while that of the revised version—also accurately rendered in the Codex, with full completion stroke—is of the newer type, integrating the imperial title (*imperator*) into the composition (Illustration 2.9). Evidently Pilgrim was behind the curve where diplomatic developments were concerned, but by later June was able to make good this deficit.[90] Despite Kremsmünster's potential significance

87. D O II 59, Munich, BayHStA, HU Passau 15. On dating issues: Uhlirz, 'Urkundenfälschung', 196.

88. D O II 111a/b, with Sickel, 'Erläuterungen', 136–37.

89. Cf. Berenbeim, *Art of Documentation*, 44–69; Atsma and Vézin, 'Originaux et copies'.

90. Munich, BayHStA, HL Passau 3, fol. 54r. The earlier two cartularies present the monogram as completed, albeit taking the older form: Munich, BayHStA, HL Passau 7, fol. 19r; Munich, BayHStA, HL Passau 2, fol. 50r. For the monogram of the revised version: Munich, BayHStA, HL Passau 3, fol. 55r; Munich, BayHStA, HL Passau 7, fol. 27v;

2.9 A/B Monograms in Pilgrim's Kremsmünster diplomas,
as rendered in the Codex Lonsdorfianus: Munich,
BayHStA, HL Passau 3, fols 54r, 55r, © BayHStA

for the mission, no mention is made of Laurence or Lorch in either text. This is often interpreted as a sign of Pilgrim's waning archiepiscopal ambitions.[91] This may be inferring too much, but there certainly are signs that the bishop's strategies were starting to shift. Since 973, Pilgrim's leading patron, Duke Henry, had led a major rebellion. Forced to choose between duke and emperor, Pilgrim plumped for the latter, as did most of the Bavarian episcopate. In return, he might now expect a reward for his loyalty, and Kremsmünster was the ideal choice. Though already in Passau's hands, the abbey had once been independent, and Henry had a residual interest as local duke (the Bavarian duke traditionally enjoying quasi-regelian rights over the church).

The renewal of Duke Henry's rebellion in 976 offers the immediate context for a further flurry of privileges in Passau's favour. As previously, Pilgrim stood by the emperor. This time, he paid a higher price. His church suffered significant material damage, in response to which Otto II showed Pilgrim further generosity. As found in the standard scholarly edition, the first diploma Pilgrim received in this connection was issued from the imperial camp in Regensburg, the day after this city had been taken (22 July 976). This confirms Passau's immunity, extending this to the cell of St Florian, just southwest of Lorch, and to the monastery of St Pölten, about 100 km (60 miles) further east, along the same strategic routes as the Wachau, Zeiselmauer and Kremsmünster (Map 2). The text is modelled largely on an immunity of Louis the German for Salzburg—that same text Pilgrim had drawn on briefly elsewhere—and only takes a few elements from that of Charles the Fat for Passau (the more obvious choice).[92] Significantly, it also mentions Kremsmünster as a dependent house of the bishopric. The result is most impressive: nearly

Munich, BayHStA, HL Passau 2, fol. 58v. On Otto II's new title monogram: Rück, *Bildberichte*, 22–23, 111–13; Bude, *König und Bischof*, 423–43 (though the latter's interpretation is not entirely convincing).

91. E.g., Fichtenau, 'Urkundenfälschungen', 169.

92. D O II 135, Munich, BayHStA, HU Passau 16. Cf. D L D 22, D K III 134. See Stengel, *Immunität*, 310–11.

twice the size of an ordinary privilege—and close in dimensions to the (forged) Arnulf immunity—it underlines the imperial favour enjoyed by Pilgrim. As in the previous year, however, there is no whiff of Lorch or Laurence.

On the same occasion, Pilgrim received the nunnery of Niedernburg, which lay within the city of Passau. This was another foundation of Duke Odilo or his son Tassilo, and the donation effectively gave the bishop undivided control of the city. The relevant diploma survives in two versions, much like the earlier Kremsmünster privilege. This time, both survive as single sheets, allowing closer scrutiny. The first of these reveals numerous signs of haste: many spelling errors have gone uncorrected, including *rationabines* for *rationabiles* in the preamble and *sillatam* for *sigillatam* in the corroboration clause (something like 'rationable' for 'rational' and 'silled' for 'sealed' in modern English); Pilgrim addresses the emperor's nephew, Otto, as duke of Swabia rather than duke of Bavaria (his new office, in which guise he intervenes); the chancery recognition has been placed above the emperor's subscription, flying in the face of all convention; the essential word *data* ('granted') is missing from the dating clause; no space has been left for the date itself(!) here, whereas unfilled blanks have been left for the indiction and regnal year; and, finally, the parchment has been folded before the ink on the final line had time to dry, leaving a tell-tale smudge (Illustration 2.10). These are not the only oddities. The recognition follows almost directly on from the main text (rather than being placed on a distinct line of its own), and the completion stroke in the monogram was originally drawn, but has since been erased.[93] The best explanation of these anomalies is that the diploma was drawn up by Pilgrim, but then rejected at court, much as his first Kremsmünster privilege had been. As a consequence, it has not been subjected to a final proof-reading, and the completion stroke has been removed to reflect its informal status (an important indication, incidentally, that this element was not always completed by the ruler).[94] Given this, the presence of an authentic seal—generally the mark of a completed diploma—is striking. This indicates that Pilgrim was once again working from a *Blankett*, a blank parchment already bearing a seal. Indeed, since wax dries more slowly than ink, the seal must have been in place before the final (smudged) line of text, a conclusion which sits well with the unusual placement of the recognition, which was presumably occasioned by the need to avoid the seal. There is little in the original text which might have caused offence at court—in fact, the final version is more wide-ranging—so

93. D O II 136a, Munich, BayHStA, HU Passau 17/2. Interestingly, the later copyist of the Codex Lonsdorfianus, the main Passau cartulary, silently corrected *rationabines* and *sillatam*; he has also accurately rendered the monogram, leaving out the completion stroke, and kept the gaps in the dating clause: Munich, BayHStA, HL Passau 7, fol. 51r.

94. Traditional wisdom holds otherwise, e.g., Erben, *Kaiser- und Königsurkunden*, 149–52. For doubts: Bautier, 'La chancellerie', 38, 47; Stieldorf, 'Magie', 23 (with n. 85). See further Morelle, 'Main du roi'; Mersiowsky, *Urkunde*, 693–701. For a somewhat comparable case, in which the completion stroke was never finished: Welton and Greer, 'Establishing Just Rule'.

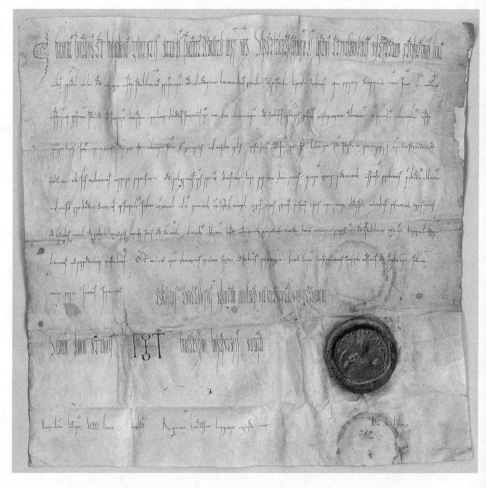

2.10 The first copy of Pilgrim's Niedernburg diploma: Munich, BayHStA,
HU Passau 17/2, © BayHStA

the decision to have it recast presumably stems from these errors, errors which
extend to the use (again) of the older form of imperial monogram (a further
indication, perhaps, that Pilgrim was pressed for time).

Why was Pilgrim in such a hurry? The answer is to be sought in the events
of the previous day, as Fichtenau noted.[95] On 21 July, just after imperial troops
had stormed Regensburg, Frederick of Salzburg had been rewarded for his loyalty with a residence in the city (akin to Pilgrim's). This grant is recorded in a
most unusual charter, which seems to have been produced by one of Fredrick's
own clerics.[96] Thanks to his forged bulls, we know that Pilgrim was deeply

95. Fichtenau, 'Urkundenfälschung', 175–76. See also Sickel, 'Erläuterungen', 138–39.
96. D O II 134, Munich, BayHStA, EU Salzburg 2. The inference that this was a recipient scribe is mine.

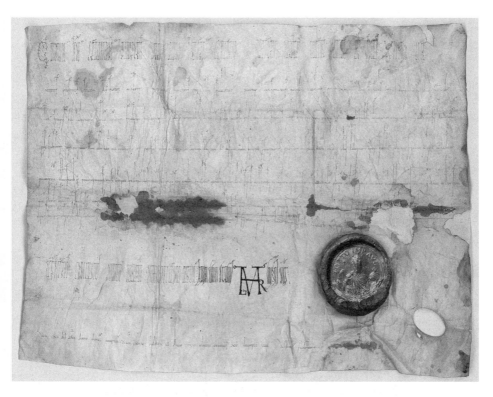

2.11 Otto II's grant of a residence in Regensburg to Frederick of Salzburg: Munich, BayHStA, EU Salzburg 2, © BayHStA

jealous of his uncle's standing. Here it would appear that we are dealing with a case of keeping up with the ecclesiastical Joneses: since Frederick had just been rewarded, it was imperative that Pilgrim be so too. The final Niedernburg diploma was issued the next day, on the same occasion as the immunity just mentioned (which precedes it in the standard edition). The presumption has been that the first (abortive) version also belongs to 22 July. However, since the dating clause of this diploma was never completed, it seems more likely to belong to the previous day, in the immediate aftermath of Frederick's privilege. Drafting and copying diplomas took considerable time and effort, particularly for a relatively inexperienced scribe, and Pilgrim produced at least three (and possibly four) other charters on the 22nd. The appearance of the first version of the Niedernburg diploma also speaks in favour of production on the 21st. In Frederick's privilege, the recognition and imperial subscription have been reversed (Illustration 2.11), with the latter added in darker ink by a different hand; it is hard to resist the conclusion that Pilgrim had this in front of him—or at least fresh in memory—when he proceeded to make precisely the same error the first time around.

2.12 Closing eschatocol of Otto II's confirmation of Pilgrim's immunity: Munich, BayHStA, HU Passau 16, © BayHStA

One therefore imagines that Pilgrim set to work as soon as he got wind of Frederick's privilege, perhaps in the late morning or early afternoon of the 21st. This would explain the presence of the older monogram, which has given way to the correct (newer) one in all of Pilgrim's productions of the following day. Having initially got this detail wrong (in haste?), he had now learned his lesson. In any case, Pilgrim's sense of urgency is not limited to the original Niedernburg draft. In the later immunity, he has corrected a number of misspellings and forgotten an abbreviation sign in *atq* (for *atque*, 'and'). He has also written *curricula* in the corroboration clause as *currica*, rendering the phrase meaningless, and has left insufficient space for the closing eschatocol, forcing him to place the imperial subscription and the recognition on the same line (Illustration 2.12)—precisely the arrangement he had sought to avoid in his first attempt at the Niedernburg charter (and the arrangement also found in the Salzburg privilege).[97]

In any case, on the following day, an improved version of the Niedernburg donation was indeed authorized. Pilgrim has not modelled this on his first effort, either visually or formulaically. But it does provide hints as to why the initial version had not been accepted. Now Otto is more appropriately addressed as duke of Bavaria; there are fewer copying errors (and those present have been corrected); the details of a number of pertaining rights have been included; and the emperor's monogram takes the correct form. Here, too, Pilgrim has been given a pre-sealed parchment (or *Blankett*), as revealed by his efforts to avoid the seal in the penultimate line of text (Illustration 2.13). Pilgrim has also taken the opportunity to elaborate on his first effort, including a lengthy narrative account of recent damage done to Passau and the Bavarian realm by Henry's rebellion.[98]

A toll charter for the bishopric and nunnery survives in the Passau cartularies, which may also have been produced on this occasion. If so, it was

97. Munich, BayHStA, HU Passau 16.
98. D O II 136b, Munich, BayHStA, HU Passau 17/1.

2.13 The final (authorized) version of Pilgrim's Niedernburg diploma: Munich, BayHStA, HU Passau 17/1, © BayHStA

apparently not authorized, since the final dating clause is incomplete (much as we see in the first version of the Niedernburg charter).[99] A second toll privilege of this date, conceding Pilgrim a portion (a third?) of tolls in the city to assist in the 'reconstruction of the destroyed church of the sacred protomartyr of Christ, Stephen' ('ob restaurationem destructae aecclesiae sancti Stephani protomartyris Christi'), survives as an original. This may represent the revised version of the first. If so, its terms have been significantly toned down. Interestingly, this latter text also reveals signs of haste, in the form of a number of small slips, most notably the omission of *cartam* (charter) in the original corroboration clause, a detail added later, apparently by Pilgrim himself.[100] Alone among the charters issued on this occasion, this addresses Pilgrim as 'pontiff [*pontifex*] of Lorch'. The title may not, however, be quite as isolated as it appears. In the final version of the Niedernburg charter, the grant is made out 'to the same church of Passau of the sacred protomartyr Stephen' ('eidem Patauiensi aecclesiae sancti Stephani protomartyris'), details which stand on an erasure. While it is impossible to discern the original text, it is tempting to posit a reference to Laurence and Lorch. If so, these details were probably removed out of deference to—or at the insistence of—Archbishop Frederick, who had received a grant on the previous day and was probably still present at court.[101]

99. D O II 137, with Sickel, 'Erläuterungen', 139–40.
100. D O II 138, Munich, BayHStA, HU Passau 18. The editor (Sickel) identifies a different hand here, following Uhlirz ('Urkundenfälschung', 191); but the ductus is clearly that of Willigis C, bearing comparison with that seen in Munich, BayHStA, HU Passau 19 (= D O II 167b), where *cartam* is also a later addition.
101. Munich, BayHStA, HU Passau 17/1.

Certainly when Pilgrim next appears at court, Lorch was very much
on his mind. Summer 977 had seen Otto II invade Bohemia, where Duke
Henry had sought shelter after the previous year's reverses. In the emper-
or's absence, however, rebellion was renewed by a swiftly returning Henry.
Given its strategic location on the Bohemian–Bavarian frontier, Passau
became a showplace for the resulting conflict. Initially, the city was taken
by Henry and the rebels. But by 1 October, it was back in imperial hands,
following a fierce siege. It was just after this, on 5 October, that Pilgrim
received his next (and final) grant. Now he received the Ennsburg, an
important fortification at or near Enns in modern Upper Austria (Map
2). This had been part of earlier defensive measures against the Hungarians, and is now granted along with ten *mansi* (the *mansus* being the land
required to support a single peasant family) at neighbouring Lorch.[102] As
in a number of other cases, two versions of this diploma survive: one sealed
and approved, preserved as an original single sheet; and a longer text,
which only survives in later cartulary copies. As previously, it would seem
that the latter was a first attempt, which failed to find favour. Both make
reference to Lorch and its earlier history, but the differences are instructive.
The longer text includes more detail regarding the history of the rights in
question, presenting the earlier Henrician dukes—whose living representative was now awaiting trial—in particularly negative terms. It also speaks of
Passau having recently been destroyed 'to the foundation' ('funditus') at the
emperor's orders. In contrast, the sealed text refers more diplomatically to
how the emperor's troops, 'driven by necessity' ('necessitate impulsi'), had
wreaked havoc on the city. Most crucially, the finalized version lacks a long
excursus on the bishopric's earlier history, which presents this as 'mother
church [archbishopric?] and episcopal seat before the fall and destruction
of the Bavarian realm' ('ante discidium et desolationem regni Bauvariorum
mater ecclesia et episcopalis cathedra'); in its stead, we find a lapidary aside
to the effect that Lorch lies 'where indeed in ancient times the first episcopal seat was held' ('ubi antiquis etiam temporibus prima sedes episcopalis
habebatur').[103] Elements of Pilgrim's version of local history thus found
acceptance, but there was significant reticence regarding his more exalted
claims. As in the previous cases, reworking seems to have taken some time.
The first version anticipated being issued at Regensburg, where the imperial court was to be found on the morning of 5 October; but the final text
was issued at Etterzhausen, about 10 km (6 miles) north-west of the city, on
the same day. Otto was evidently marching north, and the sealed text must

102. For the possibility that the Ennsburg was at Lorch itself: Igl, *Basilika*, 93–95.

103. D O II 167a/b, Munich, BayHStA, HU Passau 19. See further Erkens, *Fälschungen*,
53*–56*; Uhlirz, 'Excurse', 549–50. On the connotations of *mater ecclesia*: Mazel, *L'évêque
et le territoire*, 44; Ewig, 'Kathedralpatrozinien', 316.

2.14 Otto II's grant of Ennsburg to Pilgrim: Munich, BayHStA, HU Passau 19,
© BayHStA

have been produced in the afternoon or evening, by which time the emperor
had reached Etterzhausen.[104] Though the final privilege is a consummate
calligraphic performance, there are a number of small slips, suggesting that
Pilgrim was again pressed for time, doubtless because his first attempt had
been rebuffed. Indeed, as previously, he has had to resort to placing the ruler's subscription and chancery recognition on the same line (though in the
correct order, at least) and has again forgotten *cartam* in the corroboration
clause, this time inserting it just above the line in the same ink (Illustration
2.14). Interestingly, Salzburg had received a wide-ranging confirmation of
its own immunity and holdings just four days before this, right after Passau
had been retaken. No other diplomas survive for the intervening days, and
it is tempting to suggest that Pilgrim's (wounded?) pride was once more in
play. This would explain the ambitious terms of the privilege, particularly
in its initial version. In fact, the Salzburg diploma derives much of its formulation from that see's false Arnulf immunity (the 'Salzburg magna carta'
mentioned above), a text Pilgrim may have known at first hand—and known

104. That the emperor began the day in Regensburg is revealed by D O II 166.

to be counterfeit.[105] Having seen his uncle pull the wool over the emperor's eyes, was Pilgrim not tempted to do the same?

With this, the flow of privileges in favour of Passau stops. In the following years, Pilgrim was busy rebuilding his church and city and strengthening episcopal authority in the region. He next sought out royal favour in the early years of Otto III's reign. There was cause for concern at this point. In order to shore up the child king's regency, Otto III's mother and grandmother, Theophanu and Adelheid, had concluded a compromise with Henry of Bavaria, allowing the latter to return to his ducal post in exchange for his support. For Pilgrim, who had backed Otto III's father in the 970s and benefited from Henry's fall, this was an awkward moment. His reappearance at court is, therefore, only too understandable. The diploma Pilgrim now received is not especially spectacular—it grants him rights to revenue from tenants (*coloni*) on the see's estates in the eastern march— but it sends an important message: the bishop of Passau was still a force to be reckoned with. The text itself touches on many of Pilgrim's favourite themes, evocatively painting the depredations Passau suffered from 'barbarians' in recent times. And though the hand is not that of Willigis C, it was probably produced by another Passau cleric, who had taken inspiration from Pilgrim's earlier works.[106] There is, however, no mention of Laurence or Lorch. This has been seen as symptomatic of Pilgrim's waning interest in these matters; he started his episcopate ambitiously, but went out with a whimper, not with a bang. Yet it is questionable whether we can make so much of a single document, particularly one not drafted or copied by Pilgrim himself. Pilgrim clearly valued the Lorch title, but he had only ever used it intermittently: it appears in all three of his earliest diplomas, but these closely follow a single model; thereafter it had been no more than a periodic presence.

If we cannot chart a simple waxing and waning of Pilgrim's plans, his diplomas do allow us to trace the contours of his activities more closely. He showed an active interest in Passau's holdings throughout his episcopate, above all those in the exposed regions to the south and east—precisely those regions with the greatest missionary potential. Perhaps more importantly, there are clear signs of competition with his uncle at Salzburg, a competition which seems to have driven Pilgrim to many of his more ambitious claims.

105. D O II 165, Vienna, HHStA, UR AUR 47. Interestingly, the main text is produced by an otherwise unknown hand (apparently a local Salzburg cleric) on what also looks to have been a *Blankett*. See further n. 18 above.

106. D O III 21, Munich, BayHStA, HU Passau 20. On *coloni*, see Wickham, *Framing*, 562–64; Rio, *Slavery after Rome*, 192–93, 196–97.

Sources and Sentiments: Forgery and
Memory in Ottonian Passau

As at Worms, the big question raised by Pilgrim's activities is that of intent and function. Dümmler thought that the bulls were meant for the pope, a conclusion informed by his belief that Pilgrim's letter was indeed sent to Benedict. From this perspective, they were designed to initiate a papally sponsored restoration of Passau-Lorch. Dümmler was followed by most early commentators, but there are significant obstacles to this interpretation.[107] For a start, Pilgrim's bulls are unlikely ever to have looked the part. Until the early eleventh century, papal privileges were produced on papyrus, a fragile writing material vanishingly rare north of the Alps. Even at well-connected Saint-Denis, earlier (authentic) papyri had to be recycled for the purpose of forgery in the 1060s.[108] Since Pilgrim was dependent on Salzburg exemplars (themselves probably in the form of parchment copies), he certainly had nothing of the sort to hand. Yet papyrus was only half the problem. It is equally unlikely that Pilgrim could have mimicked the distinctive curial script employed by the papal chancery.[109] Whatever Pilgrim produced were, therefore, a far cry from credible originals. Perhaps he planned to excuse his texts as copies of lost originals; and the second false Agapit privilege, with its reference to similar texts in the papal archives, may have been intended to provide the requisite cover.[110] But even as copies, Pilgrim's bulls are problematic. They lack the customary dating by indication and pontifical year, and the naming of scribe and *referendarius* (a role within the papal chancery); and in many the closing *bene vale(ete)* is also absent—all features present in his Salzburg exemplars. As an experienced draftsman-scribe, who had learned his trade south of the Alps, Pilgrim can hardly have passed over these details in ignorance. Why, then, the apparent carelessness?

The simple answer, of course, is that they were never intended for the pope at all. Indeed, in the light of these considerations, most recent commentators have preferred to identify Pilgrim's audience nearer to home, at the imperial court.[111] It was Otto I—not the pope—who had driven Magdeburg's elevation

107. Dümmler, *Pilgrim von Passau*, 54–56; Hauck, *Kirchengeschichte Deutschlands*, 179–80; Uhlirz, *Jahrbücher*, i, 96–98; Lehr, 'Pilgrim', 28–29. See also Lhotsky, *Quellenkunde*, 168. For a recent return to this perspective: Schoenig, *Bonds of Wool*, 196, 209–10.

108. Brühl, *Studien zu den merowingischen Königsurkunden*, 137–201; Atsma and Vézin, 'Les faux sur papyrus'; Lemay, 'Diplomatic Mischief'. Further work on the subject is to be anticipated from Bob Berkhofer. On the distribution of papyrus, see further McCormick, *Origins*, 704–8.

109. Rabikauskas, *Römische Kuriale*. See also Vezin, 'Écritures imitées', 63–64.

110. It was common to make copies of bulls, in part because of their fragility: Mersiowsky, *Urkunde*, 923–25.

111. Fichtenau, 'Urkundenfälschungen', 170; Erkens, *Fälschungen*, 91*–95*, and 'Vom Handwerk'.

to metropolitan status; it made sense for Pilgrim to look to Otto's son to do the same for Passau. But while an imperial audience is certainly more plausible than a papal one, it is not without problems. The emperor in question was no newcomer to the scene. Otto II had been co-ruler for over a decade and co-emperor since 967. What is more, he had spent most his recent years in Italy (967–72). Otto would, in other words, have had a very good idea what a real bull looked like; and if not, he would have had no shortage of friends who did.[112] There were also significant obstacles to Pilgrim achieving his aims at the imperial court. As we have seen, it was his uncle Frederick who had introduced Pilgrim to court circles, and Frederick was hardly going to roll over now for his nephew. Perhaps Pilgrim was a blind optimist. But if so, this left little mark elsewhere in his career. There is, therefore, also good reason to doubt that Pilgrim would have risked approaching the emperor (an emperor who was not above rejecting Pilgrim's demands, as we have seen). The restricted circulation of the bulls suggests as much. None of these survives in its tenth-century format, and few made their way into the Codex Lonsdorfianus, the great thirteenth-century Passau cartulary. Evidently they were treated differently—and stored separately—from the cathedral's main muniments.

The one place where we do see signs of Pilgrim's efforts is at Salzburg. Here a privilege survives in the name of a 'Pope Benedict' (again, either VI or VII), addressing Frederick and the Bavarian episcopate. This ordains that, in accordance with previous privileges, Frederick is now to be Benedict's vicar 'in all of Noricum [= Bavaria] and also in all of Pannonia, both Upper and Lower' ('tota Norica provincia et in tota Pannonia superiori scilicet et inferiori'). It goes on to confirm Frederick's position as sole pallium-bearer within the province, who alone is to undertake the consecration of bishops and other metropolitan functions.[113] This text is clearly a response to Pilgrim's false Agapit and Benedict bulls, reasserting Salzburg's rights in diametrically opposed terms. What is more, there is every reason to believe that this, too, is a forgery. Frederick's predecessors had not received vicarial status on these terms, and the intention was evidently to nullify Pilgrim's claims. The message could not be clearer: anything Pilgrim can do, Frederick can do better. Had Pilgrim presented his texts to his uncle—and if so, why?

Here it is worth bearing in mind that Pilgrim's bulls were probably intended less as proofs in the modern legal sense than as part of a wider strategy of negotiation. As Fichtenau notes, they represent a maximal case, one perhaps intended to elicit concessions elsewhere (an extension of Pilgrim's

112. On contacts with (and knowledge of) Italy, see Huschner, *Transalpine Kommunikation*, esp. 290–332.
113. JL 3767 (ZPUU 224). See Beumann, *Theutonum nova metropolis*, 89–97, 103–4; Schoenig, *Bonds of Wool*, 215–16.

diocese into Hungary or Moravia, under Salzburg's aegis?).[114] And if Frederick seems to have been in little mood for compromise, the silence of his bull on the subject of Moravia may point to some middle ground (after all, Moravia was in Passau's traditional sphere of influence). The impression, certainly, is of an ongoing debate, and it has even been suggested that this was little more than a game of friendly one-upmanship, a familial in-joke of sorts.[115] That would go too far. But there can be no doubt that Frederick was part of the intended audience. To modern eyes, Pilgrim's actions may look like rank ingratitude here: scarcely had he landed on the episcopal throne than he turned on the uncle who had secured his promotion. But it is worth bearing in mind that in the Middle Ages (as in the modern world) familial bonds were a source of tension as well as support, and Pilgrim would not have been the first clerical nephew to turn against an avuncular patron (one thinks of Hincmar of Laon).[116]

Presuming an audience closer to home also throws Pilgrim's use of Salzburg exemplars into a fresh light. This was not simply a matter of necessity. Although Pilgrim had no Passau bulls to work from, even where he had local texts, he seems to have preferred Salzburg models (as, for example, in his Arnulf immunity). This preference for Salzburg sources is symptomatic of the competitive sentiment we saw in Pilgrim's first (botched) Niedernburg charter; it reveals a desire to claim for Passau all those rights enjoyed at Salzburg. Here the very fact that Pilgrim had so many texts rejected at court is significant. We should not imagine this as a stuffy, bureaucratic affair. The court was a place of competition, and winning support for your version of rights (and local history) was the highest success, as Geoffrey Koziol notes in a similar (West Frankish) context.[117] Pilgrim was evidently engaged in tug-of-war with his uncle, and risk was part of the game. What surprises is not so much that he lost, as that he tried at all—and that he kept the records of his failures. Was this because the reverses rankled? Or was Pilgrim storing the alternative texts for a rainy day? Either way, the gains were worth the risk.

Pilgrim's version of local history was, in a sense, no more fictitious than the historical records kept at the Salzach River metropolitan. As we have seen, Pilgrim may have been aware of his uncle's forging proclivities. And he almost certainly knew the main narrative of Salzburg's history, the *Conversio Bagoariorum et Carantanorum*, a text so tendentious that its leading modern authority characterizes it as 'lying with the truth'.[118] Pilgrim's forgeries did the reverse (at least in his eyes)—they told the truth with lies. This is not the only

---

114. Fichtenau, 'Urkundenfälschungen', 170–71.
115. Brunner, *Herzogtümer und Marken*, 93.
116. Cf. Barrow, *Clergy*, 130–31.
117. Koziol, *Politics of Memory*, 315–99.
118. Wolfram, 'Einleitenung'. See also Fletcher, *Conversion of Europe*, 344–50.

similarity. The *Conversio* is a deeply legalistic text, which quotes and excerpts charters at length. Pilgrim's bulls, with their long historical digressions, perform an analogous exercise in reverse. At Salzburg, documents were cast in a narrative guise; at Passau, narrative was cloaked in documentary form. Interestingly, all of the Salzburg bulls used by Pilgrim were copied together in a late ninth- or early tenth-century parchment role (or *rotulus*). This is almost certainly the form in which Pilgrim consulted these, copies of which he may have brought with him to Passau. Here, too, Pilgrim's forgeries—which cannot ever have looked the part—seem to have taken their cue from what he had seen at Salzburg.[119] Indeed, this may be why he was so unconcerned with the appearance of his bulls: Pilgrim knew the Salzburg texts as copies, so saw no problem in presenting his own in the same manner.

Certainly a local Bavarian context makes better sense of the oddities of these texts, which seem less intended to fool inquisitive eyes—Frederick clearly saw straight through them—than to preach to the proverbial converted. Already Heinrich Büttner noted that the texts have the whiff of a learned exercise to them, and Karl Brunner evocatively called them a 'novel in charters' ('Roman in Urkunden').[120] We should not, however, overlook their contemporary resonances. The choice to frame these texts in the names of earlier popes and rulers indicates a desire to deceive, and an awareness that successful deception would add an authority to Pilgrim's claims which they otherwise sorely lacked. Still, in the absence of evidence that they were put into practice, we must be equally wary of inferring intention. If intended for anyone beyond Pilgrim—and their late and restricted transmission allows for the possibility that they were a largely personal endeavour—the bulls were designed for consumption at Salzburg and at Passau. Here they were a means of positioning the bishop and his canons further up the local pecking order. The focus on the pallium and vicarial status suggests as much. These are largely iconic rights, but all the more potent for this fact. This is not to say that Pilgrim did not wish to be archbishop, nor that he did not entertain the possibility of becoming one. Rather, it is to suggest that doing so would have constituted but the most successful end of an enterprise whose primary focus lay elsewhere: in constructing a more appropriate (and more glorious) past for his bishopric.

Accepting that Pilgrim was less concerned with *Realpolitik* also allows us to explain other anomalies.[121] The inconsistency with which he employed the Lorch title has long troubled scholars, leading to alternative datings of

119. Vienna, HHStA, UR AUR 15, with Fichtenau, *Urkundenwesen*, 97; Wolfram, *Salzburg*, 294–95.

120. Büttner, 'Erzbischof Willigis', 14 (with n. 51); Brunner, *Herzogtümer und Marken*, 91 (and cf. ibid., 95, comparing the forgeries to 'a good crime novel' ['einen guten Kriminalroman']).

121. Cf. Marckhgott, 'Bischof Pilgrim', for a very different take.

the forged bulls 973–74 and 977.[122] Yet this may be less a sign of inconsistent effort (or mixed success) than an indication of a periodic (but sustained) interest in Passau's past. It also allows for the possibility that Pilgrim's efforts did not fail—at least not entirely. Most accounts presume an early interest in Lorch, focusing on the years 973–74 or 977, giving way to later disinterest. Yet as we have seen, the only evidence that Pilgrim dropped these claims is the silence of the bishop's 985 privilege on the subject, and this document is not even in his hand. In fact, while Pilgrim may never have become archbishop, when narratives of Passau's early history came to be written in the central and later Middle Ages, his bulls played an important role therein. Thereafter, they continued to inform local memory and identity up to the eighteenth century. If Pilgrim failed to change contemporary perceptions, he met considerably greater success with posterity.[123] Even in the missionary field, Passau's fortunes may not have been as dismal as is often presumed. While we know little about the progress of the Hungarian mission, when King Vajk I (997–1038) finally converted in the early eleventh century, he adopted the baptismal name of Passau's patron, Stephen, to whom he dedicated the new archbishopric of Gran (Esztergom). It is not too much of a stretch to presume that Pilgrim and Christian had a part to play here.[124]

As noted, Pilgrim's forged diplomas show rather less immediate interest in these matters. This may be an indication of his uncertainty regarding his missionary plans. Unlike the bulls, the diplomas certainly were meant to be read outside Passau (as in a number of cases they were), and Pilgrim may have feared (quite reasonably) that too overt a reference to an archbishop of Lorch would not help his cause. The transmission of these texts is also different from that of the bulls: while few of the latter made it into the Codex Lonsdorfianus, most of the diplomas did, and many survive as single sheets as well. But while they certainly have a more official air, it also remains unclear whether the diplomas were intended primarily for the imperial court. Certainly none is quoted in the authentic privileges for Pilgrim, even though he was responsible for both sets of texts. And most simply strengthen existing episcopal claims, rather like the Worms forgeries discussed in the previous chapter. One imagines, therefore, that Pilgrim had varied audiences in mind here too: the duke and emperor, if needs must; but above all the cathedral canons of Passau and their neighbours and local competitors at such sites as Salzburg and Kremsmünster. In fact, at the latter house they attracted a response. Here the monks reworked a privilege of Charlemagne to strengthen their claims to

---

122. See, e.g., Zibermayr, *Noricum*, 346–48, 381–401 (977); Fichtenau, 'Urkundenfälschungen', 168–69 (973/4); Erkens, *Fälschungen*, 75*–76* (before 975/6, probably at the start of his pontificate). Cf. Büttner, 'Erzbischof Willigis', 12 (974/5).

123. Erkens, 'Rezeption', and 'Geschichtsbild und Rechtsstreit'. See also Arnold, 'Episcopal Authority', 73–78.

124. Wolfram, 'Bavaria', 307. See also Zibermayr, *Noricum*, 381–83.

independence, probably around this time.[125] Once again, we are privy to an ongoing debate, albeit one which Passau was winning.

So even at their most pragmatic, Pilgrim's texts look more like attempts at persuasion than legal deception. The bishop must have been aware that the documents he produced were false, and he went to considerable efforts to make them look the part. Still, his business was consolidation, not expansion. Like Anno, Pilgrim was providing evidence for rights he and his church had enjoyed, but for which he lacked documentation. Though his forgeries extend into more recent years (at least in the case of the false bulls), as at Worms the ultimate focus is historical: recent texts are used to buttress the earlier ones, and the diplomas are all placed at a safe remove. Moreover, as at the Middle Rhine bishopric, the rulers chosen for the latter are telling: the semi-legendary Charlemagne, the reform-minded Louis the Pious and the bellicose Arnulf, all of whom had done much for Passau. Yet Pilgrim's activities reveal an imaginative side entirely lacking at Worms. This is probably in part a matter of personality; Anno and Pilgrim were evidently very different people, with very different aims and ambitions. But it also points to the different contexts in which they operated. For Anno, at a strictly defined bishopric within long-christianized territory, there was little hope for territorial expansion; improvement, if it was to come, would be achieved through exploiting local resources more intensively. Pilgrim, on other hand, lived in the Ottonian 'Wild East' (as Herwig Wolfram dubbed it); his forgeries breathe the air of the frontier.[126] They express hopes and dreams which, like those of the later American gold rush, often proved impractical, but were no less potent for this.[127] As Fichtenau put it five decades ago, 'there is always something timeless about great ideas' ('große Gedanken haben stets etwas zeitloses in sich'); Pilgrim would have agreed.[128]

125. D Kar 169, with Wolfram, *Salzburg*, 356–72.

126. Cf. Wolfram, 'Bavaria'.

127. For a judicious application of the 'frontier thesis' to medieval central Europe: Berend, *At the Gate of Christendom*.

128. Fichtenau, *Urkundenwesen*, 133.

CHAPTER THREE

Forging Liberty: Abingdon and Æthelred

WHEN ABBOT WULFGAR of Abingdon (990–1016) set out for the synod of Winchester in spring 993, he had every reason for optimism. Recent years had been hard on his abbey, but change was in the air. Wulfgar's own appointment suggested as much. The last time Abingdon's abbacy had been vacant, in 985, the king—Æthelred II (978–1016), known to posterity as 'the Unready'—had sold this to the brother of a friend. That five years later he should be willing to allow the monks to elect one of their own was an important step in the right direction. Similarly promising were the bridges the king had begun to build with Abingdon's patrons. Foremost among these was the queen mother, Ælfthryth (d. *c.* 1001), who had long been a champion of the abbey. She had fallen from favour in 984, shortly before the king's unwelcome intervention at Abingdon; her return to court in the early 990s offered the prospect of renewed prosperity and security.[1]

Wulfgar may not have known what was planned for the gathering, but here too the signs were hopeful. The synod was scheduled to take place at Pentecost (Whitsun), one of the three great Christian festivals, celebrating the moment when the Holy Spirit descended upon the apostles and prepared them for the mission. This was a time for pious acts, new starts and new resolves. It was also a feast symbolic of the monastic vocation. As the first gathering of Christ's disciples following his death (Acts 2:1–31), Pentecost celebrated the apostolic life on which monks modelled themselves.[2] To hold a synod then was to celebrate the monastic life. The choice of location was equally encouraging. Winchester was not only one of the kingdom's three great cities (alongside York and London); it was the former seat of Bishop Æthelwold (963–84),

---

1. For this and the following: Roach, *Æthelred*, 100–152.
2. Cf. Beach, *Trauma of Monastic Reform*, 33–34.

Abingdon's founder and a leading figure in England's recent monastic reform movement. It had been at Winchester that Æthelred's father, the reform-minded Edgar (957/9–75), had famously entrusted Æthelwold with drawing up a set of monastic customs to be observed throughout the realm (c. 970). To return here was to return to the origins of English reformed monasticism, of which Abingdon was a shining example.

But however high Wulfgar's hopes, they were almost certainly exceeded. We do not possess a detailed account of the ensuing synod, but a diploma issued shortly thereafter gives a sense of what transpired. According to this, Æthelred publicly admitted to wrongdoing, including the previous sale of Abingdon's abbacy, and committed to amending this. Specifically, he restored the abbey's liberty—the brothers' institutional independence, not least in their choice of abbot—apologizing for his earlier infringement of this. He also pointed the finger firmly at those who had led him astray: namely Wulfgar of Ramsbury, the local diocesan bishop, and Ælfric, the ealdorman of nearby Hampshire (the ealdorman being the English equivalent of a continental duke or count). It was the latter whose brother, Eadwine, had been made abbot in 985, in exchange for an appropriate sum. The resulting privilege, which survives to this day in the British Library, is a sight to behold. By some way the largest authentic single sheet to survive from the pre-Conquest period, it exceeds even the copies of 1215 Magna Carta in size. And while the latter are scrappy, workmanlike affairs, with small lettering spilling across the crowded page (a testament to the bureaucratic mind-set of a later age), this is a feast for the eyes (Illustration 3.1). It opens with a distinctive alpha-omega chrismon, representing Christ's dual nature as first and last (A and Ω being the initial and final letters of the Greek alphabet). This is followed by a long but generously spaced text, in which the names of key players, including King Æthelred and the Blessed Virgin (Abingdon's patron), are highlighted by the use of darker ink and rustic capitals (a display script). Finally, in the witness-list recording those present on this occasion—which itself is far longer than those of most Anglo-Saxon charters—the crosses next to the names of many of these figures have been added not by the main scribe (as was customary), but rather drawn by the witnesses themselves. This most novel act of state was thus authenticated in an equally novel manner.[3]

What its appearance suggests, this document's contents confirm: it is Æthelred's most important privilege to date. After a long preamble meditating on the Fall of Man—Adam's ejection from Eden, which had first brought

---

3. S 876 (*Abing* 124), BL, Cotton Augustus ii. 38. For a facsimile: *BM Facs.*, iii, 36; and for discussion: Keynes, 'Church Councils', 112–16; Roach, 'Tale of Two Charters', 235–44. The diploma's dimensions are 485 × 610 mm, which compare favourably with those of the four surviving engrossments of 1215 Magna Carta: 310 × 505 mm, 514 × 343 mm, 451 × 454 mm, and 354 × 405 mm. See further Vincent, *Magna Carta*, 206–13.

3.1 Æthelred restores liberty to Abingdon: BL, Cotton Augustus ii. 38, © BL

sin into the world—and the subsequent redemption of mankind through Mary's immaculate conception, it explains how the king had come to reflect on the recent misfortunes suffered by his nation. Here Æthelred clearly has in mind the viking raids, which had been plaguing English coasts since the late 980s; he may also be alluding to the murrain (livestock plague) of 986. The king then notes that all these misfortunes had begun upon the death of his adviser Æthelwold (1 August 984) and concludes that they have transpired in part on account of his own (earlier) youthful errors, and in part on account of the detestable greed of others, who ought to have counselled him better. Now Æthelred promises to amend these wrongs, starting by restoring Abingdon's liberty. Here he admits to previously selling the centre's abbacy to Eadwine—an event we know to have transpired in 985—at the instigation of Bishop Wulfgar (of Ramsbury) and Ealdorman Ælfric (of Hampshire). This not only contravened the monks' right to elect their own abbot; it also made Æthelred guilty of simony: of trading in ecclesiastical office. The latter was not simply a sin; it was a heresy, much like the Arian and Sabellian heresies of late antiquity, which had been condemned in the charter's opening preamble. In this respect, Æthelred contrasts his present actions with his past errors: whereas once he acted out of desire for base profit, now he seeks only the prayers and masses of the monks. The diploma finally gives a potted history of the abbey's liberty, noting that this was first granted by Pope Leo (III, 795–816) and Coenwulf of Mercia (796–821), and had been confirmed by Æthelred's predecessors, Kings Eadred (946–55), Eadwig (955–59) and Edgar (957/9–75).

This was a triumph for Wulfgar, and in the coming years he and other reform-minded figures—not least, the queen mother Ælfthryth—were to be at the forefront of national politics. This period saw a steady stream of privileges to houses which had suffered previously—Abingdon having been far from alone in its fate—including two for the bishopric of Rochester, one for the Old Minster at Winchester and one more for Abingdon itself. If the 980s had seen Æthelred turn against the legacy of Æthelwold and the reformers, the 990s saw him re-embrace this. In this respect, these restitutions are the tip of the iceberg. The decade witnessed many efforts to court divine grace, from founding monasteries to promoting new saints' cults, including that of the king's murdered half-brother, King Edward the Martyr (975–78). At Abingdon, there was a similar sense of bustle. Buoyed by the success of the Winchester synod, the local monks, under Wulfgar's watchful gaze, embarked on one of the most ambitious forgery campaigns England had ever seen. The resulting documents are companion pieces to the 993 privilege, serving to trace the history of Abingdon's liberty and endowment.[4]

Taking Liberties: Æthelred, Abingdon and Monastic Reform

At the heart of Wulfgar's complaints in 993 lay the subject of liberty, a freedom the monks were meant to enjoy, but which they had been rudely denied in 984–85. The ultimate basis for this was the regulations on monastic life drawn up by Benedict of Nursia in the mid-sixth century (the so-called Benedictine Rule). Though originally intended for Benedict's foundation at Monte Cassino, by the ninth century the Rule had achieved a degree of pre-eminence within the monasteries of mainland Europe, becoming *the* yardstick by which to measure monastic life—at least within discerning circles.[5] The Rule was slower to make its influence felt in England. Though known from the earliest years of Anglo-Saxon monasticism, it would take the reforming efforts of the mid-tenth century to establish it in a similar position.

The Benedictine reform came at an important juncture in English history. The first half of the tenth century had seen the southern kingdom of Wessex expand rapidly at the expense of its Scandinavian-ruled neighbours to the north and east. The result was the formation of the first coherent kingdom of

---

4. The following draws on Roach, 'Privilege of Liberty'.
5. de Jong, 'Carolingian Monasticism'; Kramer, 'Monasticism'.

the English, encompassing most of the modern nation. Edgar's reign was an essential part of this process. It saw earlier conquests consolidated by a series of important administrative undertakings. Here the religious and political went hand in glove. Monastic reform, actively supported by Edgar, offered a blueprint and rationale for centralization and standardization: just as there was only one realm, so there was to be only one form of monastic observance.[6] One of the reformers' main concerns was naturally adherence to the Rule, and monastic liberty took on particular salience. Monks were meant to be free to choose their own leaders, a right designed to ensure the abbot's holiness and suitability (as Benedict himself made clear). The fear was that externally appointed abbots would be beholden to their patrons, as Eadwine proved to be at Abingdon.

If the theory was clear, practice was often more complicated. External involvement in abbatial appointment was common, even in reforming circles, and might be in the interest of all concerned: a powerful patron offered much-needed protection and material support.[7] Still, such arrangements posed dangers, and reformers were chary about them, except where used to improve standards. It is clear that Æthelred's intervention at Abingdon in 985 did not fall into this category, and it soon attracted criticism. As mentioned above, the monastery had been at the forefront of the reforming initiatives of earlier years. To strike at Abingdon was to strike at the very foundations of English Benedictinism. Reform had involved the expulsion of the previous inmates from many houses—individuals invariably dubbed 'clerics' by reformers—and their replacement with professed Benedictines. Although the degree of change is probably exaggerated by our accounts (which come exclusively from the pens of reformers), there can be no doubt that a very different political and ecclesiastical landscape emerged, one at once more moralized and more monastic. Æthelwold and Abingdon were key participants in this process. It was with monks from Abingdon that Æthelwold had repopulated his newly monasticized cathedral at the Old Minster, Winchester, in 964; and it was Æthelwold's death in 984 which had precipitated Æthelred's change of tack.[8]

Part and parcel of this movement was a major shift in landholding in and around newly founded (or refounded) monasteries, with immense wealth being acquired by the monks in a short span of time. Not surprisingly, this proved controversial, particularly in regions which saw considerable monastic endowment. And much of the rich literary production of the reformers speaks of a need to justify their interventions. Important early evidence here is furnished by the New Minster refoundation charter, a document produced in 966

---

6. Molyneaux, *Formation*, esp. 187–94. Cf. Noble, 'Monastic Ideal'.

7. S. Wood, *Proprietary Church*. See also Rosé, 'Interactions'.

8. C. Cubitt, 'Tenth-Century Benedictine Reform'. See also A. Hudson, 'Æthelwold's Circle'; Atherton, *Making of England*, 225–37.

to celebrate the reform of this monastery two years previously (at the same time its local neighbour, the Old Minster). Though framed as a royal diploma, this is actually a programmatic tract on monastic life and the nature of reform. Produced by the local brothers and presented as a codex, rather than a single sheet of parchment, it is written throughout in gilded letters. The codex itself opens with an imposing frontispiece, in which Edgar, flanked by the Virgin Mary (as at Abingdon, the abbey's patron) and Saint Peter, presents the charter to Christ enthroned on high. This is one of the finest early examples of the Winchester School of artwork, a style closely associated with the reform.[9]

The ensuing text sends a similar message. This tells of the New Minster's recent refoundation, instigated by Æthelwold and Edgar. Here the king, ventriloquized by the monks, describes (and justifies) the expulsion of the previous inmates, before going on to establish how the new brothers are to live there thereafter. Particularly important is the opening preamble (or proem, as Anglo-Saxonists frequently call this element), which reflects on the origins of sin and Fall of Man, likening these to the fate of monasticism in England (and the New Minster), which has fallen from earlier heights. Æthelwold's intervention thus becomes an act of purification, and there are clear thematic similarities to Æthelred's later diploma of 993.[10] There is also a strongly historical element to royal intervention: reform is a matter of restoration, not creation, marking a return to a prior state of grace. Given the immediate context, the charter reads both as justification and call to arms. The main accusation against the earlier 'clerics' is their worldliness, a worldliness symbolized by their dependence on external (lay) patrons. By contrast, Æthelwold, Edgar and Ælfthryth now remove the monks from these entanglements, allowing them to live in accordance with the Rule, including the right to elect their own abbot (explicitly underlined). This is an extraordinary document, which takes us as close as we are likely to get to the reformers' own perspective on their work. Indeed, close parallels emerge with the writings of Æthelwold, and a strong case has been made for the bishop's authorship of the text.[11]

Whether Æthelwold's approach was as hard-nosed in practice as his rhetoric suggests is a moot point. But there can be no doubt that he conceived of his interventions as a sharp break with the past. Central to the endeavour was thus a rhetoric of reform, which contrasted the worldliness (and slovenliness) of the earlier secular canons with the purity of their Benedictine predecessors and successors. For all this, reform never completely removed monks from secular life—nor was this the intention. By taking a back-to-basics approach

9. Deshman, 'Benedictus Monarcha'.

10. S 745 (WinchNM 23), BL, Cotton Vespasian A.viii., with Barrow, 'Ideology'. For a facsimile of the frontispiece: Breay and Story, eds, *Anglo-Saxon Kingdoms*, 286–87 (no. 112).

11. Lapidge, 'Æthelwold', 189–90, with further literature.

to communal life, it was hoped that the quality of prayer and ministry under-taken by the brothers would be improved. Paradoxically, it was only by remov-ing them from worldly constraints that the reformers could enable monks to perform their worldly functions properly.[12] It is for this reason that liberty was so important. In practice, however, such freedom was often in the eye of the beholder. Æthelwold himself had been appointed to Abingdon by King Eadred (946–55), not elected by the monks; and he went on to designate his own successor, Osgar, in a manner reminiscent of practice at Cluny, one of the leading centres of reform on the continent.[13] Reformed monasteries were, therefore, not so much 'free' in an absolute sense, as subject to a particular type of regime. Still, ideals mattered, and the fact that the reformers saw the world in such Manichean terms is significant: houses were either Benedictine or secular, free or not. Liberty was a shorthand for all that was good about reformed monasticism; its absence, symptomatic of the ills of an earlier age.

Against this background, Æthelred's intervention at Abingdon was a direct assault on the legacy of Æthelwold, Edgar and Ælfthryth. Those advising the young monarch, including Ælfric of Hampshire, doubtless saw matters dif-ferently. To them, this was a matter of restoring balance: not so much a rejec-tion of monasticism (or even reform) *tout court*, as the cutting down to size of a puffed-up monastic neighbour. As already noted, our sources come almost entirely from the circles of reform. But even these make it clear that Æthel-wold faced stiff opposition, not least from the clerics he evicted or forcibly 'reformed'. According to the bishop's later *Life* (997 × 1002), Æthelwold was subject to an attempted poisoning while at the Old Minster. And though this is something of a trope—Benedict of Nursia was said to have been poisoned, and the account directly echoes that of the poisoning of Martin of Tours (another foundational figure in the history of western monasticism)—there can be no doubt that the tensions were real.[14] Indeed, factionalism was endemic within medieval monasteries (reformed or not), and it is conceivable that Eadwine, the abbot appointed in 985, was a survivor from the pre-reform era, a relic of Abingdon's secular past come back to haunt Æthelwold's successors.[15] Yet dis-gruntled clerics were only part of the problem. Since reform was framed as an act of restoration, the introduction of Benedictine monks went hand in hand with an ambitious politics of territorial restitution. At Abingdon as elsewhere, estates and rights were now claimed as traditional ecclesiastical holdings, lost in the previous years, and lay neighbours were bought out or dispossessed. However firmly the reformers may have believed in the justice of their cause,

12. Tinti, 'Benedictine Reform'. See also Riedel, 'Praising God Together'.

13. Wulfstan Cantor, *Vita S. Æthelwoldi*, chs 11, 21, ed. Lapidge and Winterbottom, 18–22, 36. On Cluniac practice: Rosé, 'Un cas problématique'.

14. Wulfstan Cantor, *Vita S. Æthelwoldi*, ch. 19, ed. Lapidge and Winterbottom, 34 (cf. ibid., 35 n. 3).

15. Cf. Patzold, *Konflikte im Kloster*.

to others, such as Ealdorman Ælfric, this must have seemed like little more than a cynical land grab. Still, in throwing his weight behind the dissatisfied, Æthelred was making a highly political decision, effectively reversing the policies of his father and mother. His actions were eerily reminiscent of the 'anti-monastic' reaction which had followed his father's death in 975. This had seen local landholders exploit temporary political instability to retake lands from their monastic neighbours.[16]

For those of a Benedictine persuasion—most at Abingdon and Winchester, and many at court too—Eadwine's abbacy offered an object lesson in the importance of ecclesiastical liberty. These rights had been transgressed in 985, and the result was substantial losses. Eadwine's abbacy was later recalled as a low point in the abbey's history, and there are signs that he used his position to enrich friends and family (his nephew Ælfgar, for example, reportedly received monastic lands in these years). As important as these pragmatic considerations, however, was the symbolic blow Æthelred's intervention represented. As already noted, following Edgar's death lay potentates had staked claims to monastic lands; now, it seemed that reformed monasticism itself was on the out. This is revealed not only by the fate of Abingdon. A number of other prominent reformed centres suffered, including the Old Minster at Winchester, Æthelwold's old see, and Glastonbury, where Æthelwold had first been introduced to monastic life. The precarious position of the monastic party is also illustrated by the shrinking number of abbots attesting royal charters. Unlike their continental counterparts—but like private charters elsewhere in Europe—Anglo-Saxon diplomas bear witness-lists recording those present at the time of their production. These lists are arranged hierarchically, reflecting attendance (and prominence) at court. A reduction in abbatial attestations therefore represents a very real decline in monastic power and influence.[17] It was also in these years, however, that the viking raids which were to characterize Æthelred's reign began in earnest. Watchet was sacked in 988, and a larger force arrived in 991, inflicting a decisive defeat on the East Saxon levy at Maldon. The reform-minded would not have needed to look long for the cause. Æthelwold and the reformers had associated the material well-being of the realm with the piety of its ruler (and monks), a line of logic embraced by Edgar, who in 962 had responded to a bout of plague by calling upon his nation to mend its errant ways.[18] To those raised on such lessons—which, for all his wavering, included Æthelred—it must have been clear that two and two did indeed make four. The king had sown the wind; now he would reap the whirlwind.

16. Roach, Æthelred, 64–68.

17. Keynes, Atlas of Attestations, table LXI.

18. 'Edgar's Establishment of Monasteries', ed. Whitelock, Councils and Synods, 143–54 (no. 33); IV Eg prol., ed. Liebermann, Gesetze, i, 206–7.

Documenting Liberty: Æthelred,
Abingdon and Monastic Freedom

If reform had made liberty topical, discussions were initially restricted to broad, normative statements. The subject was addressed at length in the Rule, which stipulates that monks should be free to choose a leader from their midst, either unanimously or according to the judgement of those of 'sound counsel'. Only if the brothers were to choose an inappropriate candidate is external involvement permitted—and then simply to reassert higher standards.[19] These strictures were known widely within English monastic circles. Many manuscripts of the Rule survive from these years and the text was also translated into the vernacular, apparently by Æthelwold himself.[20] Benedict's stipulations on monastic liberty are also echoed in the *Regularis concordia*, a supplement of sorts to the Rule, composed by Æthelwold and dedicated to the additional customs (largely liturgical) to be observed within English monasteries. This latter work was promulgated at the famous council at Winchester (*c.* 970)—not coincidentally, the scene of Æthelred's later contrition—which had crowned Edgar's reforming efforts.[21] Finally, the Rule's teachings are adumbrated in the New Minster charter of 966.

But just as important is where monastic liberty is not mentioned: in diplomas for reformed houses. With the exception of the New Minster charter—itself a locally produced narrative-cum-customary, rather than a traditional single sheet—we find no mention of such matters within the diplomatic corpus. This stands in stark contrast to the continent. Here documents confirming rights of immunity and royal protection had been issued since at least the seventh century. And as the reforming movements of the ninth and tenth centuries began to find traction, rights of free abbatial election were often appended to these. The resulting texts are sometimes called liberties (*libertates*, a term with strong ecclesiastical undertones) and were highly prized.[22] And as we saw at Worms and Passau, it was customary for religious houses to seek serial confirmation of these rights, the result being chains of closely associated—and often verbally linked—immunities (or liberties). In England, however, where the break with the documentary traditions of Roman antiquity was starker than on mainland Europe, concepts of religious freedom developed very differently. Here early grants to the church enjoyed a special status. Known as bookland (Old English: *bocland*)—literally 'land owned by

19. *Regula Benedicti*, ch. 64.1–2, ed. Neufville with de Vogüé, 648.

20. *Die angelsächsischen Prosabearbeitungen*, ed. Schröer, with Gretsch, *Intellectual Foundations*, 226–60. See further Gretsch, 'Æthelwold's Translation' and 'Corpus Christi College 57'.

21. *Regularis concordia*, chs. 9–10, ed. Symons and Spath, 74–76.

22. Stengel, *Immunität*, esp. 427–37, 527–28, 532; Mayer, *Fürsten und Staat*, 39–49. See also Rosenwein, *Negotiating Space*.

charter (i.e., the book)'—they were exempt from certain secular burdens and stood outside customary inheritance practices.[23] The important difference is that this quality pertained to the land, not to the religious house, and we never see liberty linked to judicial immunity (a concept alien to pre-Conquest law). As documentary traditions evolved, it became progressively more common for laymen to hold land by charter. Bookland thus ceased to be an ecclesiastical prerogative and became little more than a privileged form of tenure. The resulting charters might still be called 'liberties', but the term carried few of the implications it did elsewhere. This was a shorthand for a specific set of tenurial rights, not the freedom of the church so powerfully championed by continental reformers.[24]

The continental-style immunity (and chartered liberty) therefore posed a conceptual challenge to tenth-century English observers. The reformers must have been aware of this. They derived much of their inspiration from the continent, and many had spent time there, at such centres as Fleury and St Peter's, Ghent—both abbeys with long and proud traditions of liberty and immunity.[25] Yet they had no equivalent in England. This problem may have been more apparent than real, at least initially. In the early years of the reform, King Edgar was a staunch supporter of the movement; and as such, a reliable guarantor of monastic liberty (a role accorded to him in the *Regularis concordia*). The problem came when kingship showed its darker face in the 980s; now firmer commitments were required. In fact, the first mention of liberty in an authentic single sheet comes in the Abingdon diploma of 993, with which we began. A few purportedly earlier charters mention the subject, but none of these survives in its original format, and almost all conform to a single documentary type: the *Orthodoxorum* charter. It is to this that we must now turn, if we are to appreciate developments in and around Abingdon more fully.

Discrimen veri ac falsi: *The* Orthodoxorum *Charters Revisited*

The *Orthodoxorum* charters are set of diplomas in favour of Abingdon and associated houses, confirming longstanding rights of liberty. As has long been noted, they are closely related, with the majority of formulation shared across the series. Most of this material is also found in the Abingdon charter of 993. Given this, the early texts—most of which survive in later copies—have long been considered suspect, probably forged on the basis of the 993 original. However, Susan Kelly has mounted a spirited defence of these documents,

23. Crick, 'Pristina *libertas*', 58–67; Lambert, *Law and Order*, 310–22.
24. Cf. Tellenbach, *Libertas*.
25. Wormald, 'Æthelwold'; Nightingale, 'Oswald'.

and her arguments have garnered notable support.[26] Much hinges on the issue, so we must give it some space, before returning to wider questions about Abingdon's experiences in these years.

First, it is worth summarizing their content:

1. S 658 (959): **King Eadwig** grants **Abingdon** the right to elect its abbot freely following the death of Æthelwold and confirms the ancient liberty acquired from Pope Leo III and Coenwulf of Mercia and later secured by Eadred, along with the community's estates (both recent acquisitions and older holdings).

2. S 673 ('958' for 959): **King Edgar** restores **Abingdon** estates at Ginge, Goosey, Longworth and 'Earmundesleah' (Bessels Leigh) and confirms the ancient liberty acquired from Pope Leo III and Coenwulf and later secured by Eadred, along with the community's estates (both recent acquisitions and older holdings), and annuls those charters for lands wrongly taken from the foundation in the meantime.

3. S 786 (972): **King Edgar** grants **Pershore** the right to elect its abbot freely following the death of Foldbriht, confirms the ancient liberty granted by Coenwulf through the petition of Ealdorman Beornoth, and restores a collection of estates, annulling those charters for lands wrongly taken from the foundation in the meantime.

4. S 788 (972): **King Edgar** grants the community at **Worcester** the right to elect its abbot freely after the death of N.[= *nomen* (name), representing an individual of unknown name], confirms the ancient liberty granted by Coenwulf through the petition of Ealdorman Beornoth, and restores a number of estates, annulling those charters for lands wrongly taken from the foundation in the meantime.

5. S 812 (959 × 975, perhaps 971 × 975): **King Edgar** grants **Romsey** the right to elect its abbess freely following the death of Merewyn, confirms the liberty granted by previous kings (details unspecified), and secures the estates granted by himself as well as previous rulers and benefactors.

6. S 876 (Winchester, 4 June 993; Gillingham, 17 July 993): **King Æthelred** expresses regret for having infringed upon the liberty of **Abingdon** after the death of Æthelwold; restores this liberty, including the right to elect the next abbot freely; confirms that same ancient liberty once granted by Pope Leo III and Coenwulf, and later secured by Eadred, Eadwig and Edgar, along with landed estates (both recent acquisitions and older holdings); and annuls those charters wrongly issued in earlier years for seized estates.

26. *Charters of Abingdon*, ed. Kelly, lxxxiv–cxv. For support, see Insley, 'Where did All the Charters Go?', 116–17; C. Cubitt, 'Bishops and Councils', 163 with n. 56 (though note the subsequent change of heart: Cubitt, 'Politics of Remorse', 181 n. 12).

As the most cursory glance reveals, the largest number of these texts concern Abingdon, and it is clear that the documentary form originates here: the (purportedly) earliest ones concern the monastery, and the only certainly authentic one—the 993 privilege—is also in its favour. Of the remaining texts, that in the name of Worcester is obviously a later fake—the scribe did not even know the name of the bishop in 972 (the saintly Oswald!)—while those in favour of Pershore (972) and Romsey (*c*. 971? × 975) may have some claim to authenticity. Still, the crux of the matter lies with the first two Abingdon texts: if these can be accepted, the later ones probably can too; if not, doubt falls upon the entire series.

The main difficulty is that in form and formulation these documents look more like diplomas of the 990s and early 1000s than of the late 950s.[27] To start with the seemingly banal, they are far longer than any other mid-tenth-century charters. Eadwig's authentic diplomas average two to three hundred words of text, and almost never exceed four hundred. By contrast, the first two *Orthodoxorum* charters run to 633 and 704 words apiece. They find themselves in far better company in Æthelred's reign. The obvious point of comparison is the 993 privilege, which boasts an impressive 1,298 words. But this was not a one-off. The charter confirming liberty to the bishopric of Cornwall (at St Germans) in the following year runs to 656 words; three restitutions of the mid- to later 990s for Rochester and the Old Minster, Winchester, run to 573, 639 and 745 words; a further restitution to Abingdon *c*. 999 comprises 837 words; a diploma for Shaftesbury of 1001 boasts 626 words; a confirmation for Burton in 1004 extends to 752 words; a privilege for St Albans of 1005 contains 625 words; and so on.[28] While only two of these documents are preserved in their original format—Anglo-Saxon diplomas surviving at much lower rates than their continental counterparts—the trend is unmistakable and, most importantly, observable across archives.

One of the main reasons for the greater length of the *Orthodoxorum* texts is the narrative excurses they contain regarding the history of the rights in question. This feature, too, is uncommon in documents of the 950s or 960s, but frequent in texts of Æthelred's reign.[29] Other considerations point in the same direction. The Edgar *Orthodoxorum* privilege contains a stern warning against those who might bring forth future claims on the basis of 'false' charters (either forgeries or superseded diplomas), details rare in documents of the mid-tenth century, but again common in Æthelred's reign.[30] Perhaps

27. The best treatment remains Keynes, *Diplomas*, 98–102.

28. S 880 (KCD 686), S 885 (*Roch* 31), S 891 (KCD 698), S 893 (*Roch* 32), S 937 (*Abing* 129), S 899 (*Shaft* 29), S 906 (*Burt* 28), S 912 (*StAlb* 11). The first of these is Exeter, D.C., 2070; for facsimiles: *OS Facs.*, ii, Exeter 8; Breay and Story, eds, *Anglo-Saxon Kingdoms*, 302–3 (no. 120).

29. Keynes, *Diplomas*, 200–202. See also Stafford, 'Royal Government', 62–70.

30. Keynes, 'Church Councils', 103–4.

the most decisive evidence, however, comes from formulation. The first two *Orthodoxorum* privileges contain much phraseology which is acceptable for the middle years of the century (as we might expect), but also include a few elements more properly belonging to the 990s. For a start, their preamble includes an allusion to how God formed Adam of 'fourfold material' ('quadriformi . . . materia'), a distinctive turn of phrase first attested in 961 and 962— two years after these charters are said to have been issued—and then found in privileges for Abingdon and St Germans in 993 and 994.[31] More telling, perhaps, is the sanction threatening eternal damnation to those who might undermine the grant. This represents a development of a common formula of the 960s (though not, it should be noted, of the 950s). And in this precise form, it is first attested in the same Abingdon and St Germans texts of 993 and 994; it is then found in lightly adjusted form in a further document of 998. All three of these diplomas survive as authentic originals, proving beyond doubt that such formulation belongs to these years.[32] Finally, the *Orthodoxorum* charters contain the same phrase introducing their witness-lists as the Abingdon and St Germans diplomas of 993 and 994. The importance of these connections can scarcely be overstated. In the absence of a large corpus of originals, criticism of Anglo-Saxon charters depends heavily upon formulation, with pride of place going to examples attested in undoubted originals or (failing that) in otherwise unsuspicious texts from multiple archives. In this case, we are dealing with turns of phrase only found in the *Orthodoxorum* series before the later tenth century, then attested in authentic single sheets of 993, 994 and 998, all from different archives. When we add to this the fact that the earlier *Orthodoxorum* privileges are all confirmations of liberty—a documentary type itself not seen before the 990s—the suspicion grows that we are dealing with later confections.

But the greatest objection to these documents lies less in this or that formula, than in the degree of intertextual borrowing they display. Occasional variations aside, the *Orthodoxorum* charters are almost carbon copies, with well over 95% of text shared across the series. Since they claim to be distinct grants, made by three different rulers over the course of thirty-four years (for four different houses) this is most suspicious. It is even more so in light of the distinctive nature of the Anglo-Saxon royal diploma. English charters display much more formulaic variety than their continental counterparts; preambles and sanctions are occasionally lifted from earlier texts, but otherwise variation

31. S 690 (*Abing* 87), S 703 (ed. Hart and Syme, 'Earliest Suffolk Charter'), S 876 (*Abing* 124), S 880 (KCD 686). The first of these is BL, Cotton Augustus ii. 39; for facsimiles: *BM Facs.*, iii. 23; Bishop, *English Caroline*, pl. IX (no. 11) (partial).

32. S 876 (*Abing* 124), BL, Cotton Augustus ii. 38; S 880 (KCD 686), Exeter, D.C., 2070; S 892 (ed. Napier and Stevenson, *Crawford Collection*, no. 8), Oxford, Bodleian Library, Eng. hist. a. 2, no. vi. For a facsimile of the latter: *BA Facs.*, 13.

is the order of the day—the aim is to riff on a theme, not to copy verbatim.[33] This is partly a product of the unique history of the diploma in England, where it had been imported with Christianity in the course of the seventh century. It also reflects the absence of a tradition of serial confirmation akin to that of the continental immunity.[34] So while intertextual borrowing is sometimes a sign of authenticity elsewhere, in England it is often the reverse. This is particularly so when, as here, the charters in question span many years and recipients. Where we would expect variation, we are presented with monotonous repetition.

The only point of comparison here is the 'Second Decimation' charters of the West Saxon king Æthelwulf (839–58), offering a tenth of royal land within his realm in 854. Yet there the context readily explains the unusual form of these grants: this was a prominent display of piety before the king's departure to Rome, and the resulting documents are not so much distinct donations as engrossments (authentic copies) of a single legal act. The same grant was being made multiple times on the same occasion; that it should take the same form is hardly surprising.[35] In contrast, the *Orthodoxorum* charters claim to concern confirmations of liberty to at least three different religious houses over the course of over three decades. That they should still take exactly the same form, not only in preamble and sanction, but also in the core dispositive ('granting') sections, is most suspicious. But while extensive borrowing is not otherwise found in authentic documents of the era, it goes without saying that it is a common feature (and indeed symptom) of forgery. Genuine draftsmen sought to vary their expression, while forgers tried to stick as closely as possible to their models. In this respect, the variations speak strongly against the earliest charters of this type. The 993 privilege possesses much unique and appropriate detail pertaining to the context of its production, yet the others are notably devoid of this; it looks as if someone has taken the Æthelred diploma, then shorn it of the specifics.[36]

This does not exhaust the problems of the earliest *Orthodoxorum* privileges. Their witness-lists are far more closely related than we would expect of documents issued on separate occasions, having the names of over three quarters of the thegns—the thegn being a nobleman below comital rank—in

33. Snook, *Anglo-Saxon Chancery*. See also Woodman, "'Æthelstan A'".

34. I leave aside the different (and later) tradition of writ-confirmation: Sharpe, 'Use of Writs'.

35. Keynes, 'West Saxon Charters', 1019–22; Nelson, 'England and the Continent', 14–21; *Charters of Malmesbury*, ed. Kelly, 66–79. Another potential case of verbatim repetition is offered by S 862 (*Malm* 32) and S 931b (*Bark* 10), of 986 and 1013. But the texts in question are much shorter than the *Orthodoxorum* privileges and the parallels less striking; the status of the latter is also not above question. Rather different is the case of S 674 (*Pet* 13) and S 679 (*North* 3), which were almost certainly produced by the same individual, on the same occasion.

36. Cf. Ehrman, *Forgery and Counterforgery*, 158–60, 174, 445.

common. What is more, the list of the second of these, in Edgar's name, clearly derives from that of a diploma of 960 from the Abingdon archive, which itself survives as an authentic original.[37] It would seem that the latter provided the model for the Edgar privilege, whose list then furnished the basis for that of the Eadwig charter—precisely the reverse order to that in which they were purportedly issued. These are, in other words, not witnesses to real gatherings of 959, but lightly adjusted records of one of 960. This may explain why the attestations of the Eadwig privilege include Archbishop Oda of Canterbury, who we know to have died in 958. Though no authentic diploma of 959 includes the archbishop's name, a later forger—even an unusually able one— might be forgiven such an oversight.[38] This approach to composition explains one of the few significant textual variations within the series. Only the Edgar and Æthelred diplomas speak of the command of the 'One Enthroned on High' in the opening phrase of the preamble ('Altitroni moderatoris imperio triuia-tim instruimur'), while the rest refer to receiving the admonition of orthodox men ('Ortodoxorum uigoris ecclesiastici monitu creberrime instruimur'). The former was apparently the original form, taken over into the Edgar diploma, but then adjusted for the Eadwig text, which is followed in all subsequent iterations. (Much the same holds true for the reference to 'false' diplomas of earlier kings, which is found in the Æthelred and Edgar texts, but not their Eadwig equivalent.)

There is, therefore, a strong a priori case against the earliest *Orthodoxo-rum* privileges. In various manners these prefigure the documentary traditions of the 990s, when the one undoubted original of the type was produced. The only evidence for such formulation before then comes from within the series itself, and arguments in their favour rapidly become circular. The fact that the second of the resulting privileges, in Edgar's name, not only secures Abingdon's liberty, but also restores estates at Ginge, Goosey, Longworth and Bessels Leigh (all—until 1974—in the county of Berkshire), fits this profile. As we shall see, the lands in question spawned a large number of forgeries, probably of Æthelred's reign. Any document purporting to secure them en masse must be treated with utmost caution.

Reconstructing Lost Single Sheets: The Abingdon Cartulary-Chronicle

It is, however, not only textual considerations which point towards later production; the preservation of these charters does so, too. Here a bit of background is necessary. Both the Eadwig and Edgar *Orthodoxorum* diplomas first

---

37. S 673 (*Abing* 86), BL, Cotton Augustus ii. 40. Cf. *Charters of Abingdon*, ed. Kelly, xcix–c.

38. Though Oda's subscription is only found in the later version of the cartulary-chronicle, the scribe of this clearly went back to the original, so there is no reason to doubt its presence. Cf. *Charters of Abingdon*, ed. Kelly, xcv–xcvi.

survive in the Abingdon cartulary-chronicle, a work which combines charters with narrative material relating to the abbey's early history (a popular genre in post-Conquest England). The chronicle exists in two different versions, each represented by a unique witness: an earlier one, preserved in a manuscript of the second half of the twelfth century (probably the mid- to later 1160s); and a revised one of the early thirteenth century, which includes a number of additional documents and further historical details (many of the latter fantastic). The author of the second version clearly went back to the original documents, since he often offers fuller versions of their texts (the earlier scribe typically omits vernacular boundary clauses and much of the witness-list). And because of this, his testimony has been preferred by most modern scholars and editors.[39] Less attention has, therefore, been given to the earlier version, despite its greater antiquity; and as a consequence, important features of this have been overlooked.

The manuscript in question is written throughout in a clear, mid- to late twelfth-century hand. Most of the text is in a form of early protogothic minuscule, though the scribe has employed red ink (rubrication) or majuscule forms (generally rustic capitals)—sometimes both—to highlight certain elements within the text.[40] The distribution of the latter forms is significant. Within his copies of charters, these are found where we might expect display script in the original single sheets: in the names of saints, important players in the transaction (donor and/or recipient) and the estates granted. This is clearly a conscious policy, since elsewhere rubrication and majuscules are reserved for chapter headings and initials.[41] Evidently our scribe has sought to preserve features of the originals before him, and in later sections he similarly reproduces two papal *rotae* and *bene valete* monograms—the distinctive subscription signs used by papal scribes from the 1050s on (Illustration 3.2).[42] Where we can check his work, he has been a quite faithful copyist. In his copies of the five diplomas also preserved as original single sheets, he has employed display script twenty-nine times, of which at least twenty-five can be found in his exemplars. (If we add two originals attested by Robert Talbot's sixteenth-century transcriptions, this becomes twenty-six of thirty-two.) The four (or six) exceptions concern words often highlighted in other documents—twice he has introduced display script for the name of King Eadwig, once he has done so for the recipient Ælfwine, and once for the Blessed Virgin—so we are

39. BL, Cotton Claudius C.ix; BL, Cotton Claudius B.vi. See further *Historia ecclesie Abbendonensis*, ed. Hudson, i, clxxvii–cxc; *Charters of Abingdon*, ed. Kelly, liv–lvi.

40. J. Hudson, 'Abbey of Abingdon', 185. On such practices: Bertrand, *Documenting the Everyday*, 203–6.

41. *Historia ecclesie Abbendonensis*, ed. Hudson, clxxxi. For exceptions: BL, Cotton Claudius C.ix, fols 109r, 120v, 143v.

42. BL, Cotton Claudius C.ix, fols 170v, 171v, with Berenbeim, *Art of Documentation*, 57–58.

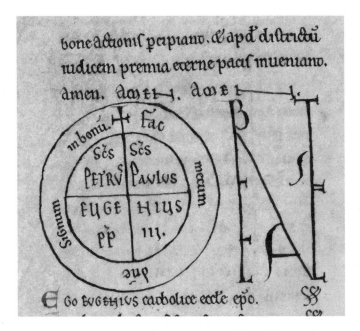

3.2 Copy of a papal *rota* in the earlier version of the Abingdon cartulary-
chronicle: BL, Cotton Claudius C.ix, fol. 171v, © BL

probably dealing with straightforward slips.[43] He also occasionally overlooks
such forms in his exemplars; again, it would seem, by accident. (By contrast,
the copyist of the early thirteenth-century version of the cartulary-chronicle—
who in other respects is more faithful to his models—has introduced his own
script hierarchy.)

This observation provides important insights into how an Abingdon scribe
of the 1160s navigated the pre-Conquest documents at his disposal. He evidently felt free to drop elements of these—particularly the vernacular boundary clauses and long witness-lists—but in other respects accorded them considerable authority, seeking to maintain their original features. The result is
reminiscent of the less strict cases of script imitation discussed by Julia Crick:
the scribe seeks not so much to reproduce the original single sheets in facsimile form, as to give a subtle nod to their form and appearance.[44] In keeping
these features, he has also given us precious clues as to how these texts originally appeared—clues which may, in turn, inform our criticism. The significant

43. For these purposes, I have compared BL, Cotton Claudius C.ix, fols 109r–v, 115r–v,
115v–16r, 116v–117r, 117r, 119v–120r, 121v, 124r–125v, with CCCC 111, pp. 171–73; BL, Cotton Augustus ii. 33; BL, Cotton Augustus ii. 41; BL, Cotton Augustus ii. 43; CCCC 111,
pp. 161–62; BL, Cotton Augustus ii. 39; CCCC 111, pp. 167–68; and BL, Cotton Augustus
ii. 38, respectively.

44. Crick, 'Historical Literacy', 164, 171–72.

point here is that display script had not always been a feature of Anglo-Saxon diplomas. It first appears in the later years of Æthelstan's reign (924–39), particularly in the work of the draftsman-scribe known as Æthelstan C; and it only became widespread in Edgar's reign, thanks to the work of another influential draftsman-scribe, Edgar A.[45] Even then, majuscule forms remained limited to important details in the main text.[46] Further developments are next seen in Æthelred's reign, when individual names in the witness-list—often those of donor, recipient or other significant players—start to be singled out for similar treatment. The first surviving example of this is the 993 Abingdon privilege, in which the names of the king, archbishop of Canterbury and abbot of Abingdon are all highlighted thus. As in so many other regards, its example is followed by the St Germans diploma of the following year, in which Æthelred's name is rendered in impressive gilded square capitals (see below, Illustration 3.4).[47] Thereafter, this becomes a frequent (though by no means universal) feature of witness-lists, with further examples from 996, 1002, 1007 and 1009.[48] The trend then strengthens as we move into the mid- to later years of the eleventh century, when the use of display script becomes a standard feature in witness-lists.

How, then, are these developments reflected in the charters preserved exclusively in the cartulary-chronicle? Among those texts generally deemed authentic, the use of display script reassuringly mirrors that seen in originals, with occasional employment in the main text in the 940s and early 950s giving way to heavier (and more consistent) use thereafter, including cases in the witness-list from the 990s on. Yet if we turn to those charters of questionable authenticity, we see considerably greater variation. In copies of diplomas in the names of the Mercian rulers Æthelbald (716–57) and Coenwulf

45. The earliest examples I can find are S 447 (*CantCC* 107), BL, Cotton Augustus ii. 23; and S 449 (BCS 734), BL, Cotton Charters viii. 22, both of 939. The latter is not by Æthelstan C, but an associate: Keynes, *Diplomas*, 24, 43. For facsimiles: *BM Facs.*, iii, 9, 8.

46. A possible exception is the anomalous 'Alliterative Charters', produced under the auspices of Coenwald of Worcester in the 940s and 950s. In Robert Talbot's copy of the lost original of S 544 (*Abing* 43), Coenwald's name is rendered 'KOENÞALD monachus' in the witness-list: CCCC 111, p. 144. Talbot was generally a reliable copyist, so there is every reason to trust his text. Our one other early modern facsimile of an alliterative charter lacks this feature, however, so this may have been a one-off: S 550 (BCS 882), BL, Cotton Charters viii. 6.

47. S 876 (*Abing* 124), BL, Cotton Claudius ii. 38; S 880 (KCD 686), Exeter, D.C., 2070.

48. S 878 (*Burt* 27), Stafford, William Salt Library, 84/4/41; S 905 (*CantCC* 139), BL, Stowe Charter 35; S 916 (*St Alb* 12), Oxford, Bodleian Library, Eng. hist. a. 2, no. vii; S 922 (*Burt* 32), Stafford, William Salt Library, 84/5/41. For facsimiles: *BA Facs.*, 12; *OS Facs.*, iii, 36; *BA Facs.*, 16, 17. Judging by the copy in the late twelfth-century Eynsham cartulary, we can add the Eynsham foudation charter (S 911) of 1005 to the list: Oxford, Christ Church, MS 341, fol. 9r (where King Æthelred's name is in majuscules in the witness-list). Cf. Thompson, *Anglo-Saxon Royal Diplomas*, 38–40, noting the tendency, but overlooking a number of key examples.

(796–821), for example, the names of Abbot Cuma, Abingdon, Mary and Peter are all highlighted, as we would expect of documents of the mid- to later tenth century. And indeed, these texts were probably forged in these years, as we shall see.[49] Likewise, in three purported charters of 931—eight years before the first securely attested use of display script—the names of Æthelstan, Mary, Abingdon and the estates granted are highlighted, in one case in the witness-list.[50] This suggests production in the second half of the tenth century, probably in the 990s or later, a conclusion which sits well with the fact that two of the texts draw their witness-list from another (authentic) diploma, which first entered the Abingdon archive between 984 and 990.[51] A similar case is presented by a diploma of Eadred of 955, granting Ginge, Goosey, Longworth and Cumnor (all in the historic county of Berkshire) to Æthelwold. In this, the names of the estates and all major players are highlighted, including those of Eadred and Æthelwold in the witness-list. Again, this points toward later production, probably no earlier than the 990s; and it provides confirmation of the most recent editor's view that the formulation belongs to the second half of the tenth century.[52] Finally, the copy of a diploma in the name of Edgar concerning Bedwyn (Wiltshire) has Æthelwold's name highlighted in the witness-list. The presumption once more must be that this is a product of the 990s or later, a conclusion which sits well with the fact that the text takes elements of its formulation from the Edgar *Orthodoroxorum* privilege.[53]

The importance of establishing these developments lies in the fact that the copies of the Eadwig and Edgar *Orthodoxorum* privileges both make considerable use of display script, including for the names of Eadwig, Edgar and Æthelwold in the witness-list (Illustration 3.3). If these features were indeed present in the originals—and there is every reason to believe they were (they are found in the copies of both)—it is a further indication that their proper context is to be sought in the later years of the tenth century at the earliest, not the 950s.[54] To suggest otherwise is not only to insist that Abingdon was some three to four decades in advance of its neighbours when it came to diplomatic developments; it is also to insist that these precocious features were restricted to documents which are suspect on other grounds.

49. BL, Cotton Claudius C.ix, fols 106r–107v, containing S 93 (*Abing* 5) and S 183 (*Abing* 9).

50. BL, Cotton Claudius C.ix, fols 109v–110r, containing S 409 (*Abing* 25), S 408 (*Abing* 27), S 410 (*Abing* 26).

51. *Charters of Abingdon*, ed. Kelly, 109, 113–14. The witness-list stems from S 1604 (*Abing* 24).

52. BL, Cotton Claudius C.ix, fol. 111r–v. The charter is S 567 (*Abing* 51). See *Charters of Abingdon*, ed. Kelly, 213–14.

53. BL, Cotton Claudius C.ix, fol. 118r–v. The charter is S 756 (*Abing* 108). See *Charters of Abingdon*, ed. Kelly, 427–28.

54. BL, Cotton Claudius C.ix, fols 112v–113v, 117v–118r.

3.3 A (ABOVE) AND B (RIGHT). Witness-lists of the Eadwig and Edgar *Orthodoxorum* charters, as preserved in the earlier version of the Abingdon cartulary-chronicle: BL, Cotton Claudius C.ix, fols 113v, 118r, © BL

Libertas ecclesiae *between Edgar and Æthelred*

As noted, the density of early *Orthodoxorum* privileges for Abingdon, combined with the existence of the 993 original, means that we can confidently ascribe the origins of the series to the abbey.[55] And while we must allow for the possibility that we are dealing with authentic recipient production, a number of features speak against the proposition: not only formulaic links with authentic texts of the 990s, but also visual features otherwise restricted to known forgeries within the cartulary-chronicle which preserves them.

As important as such formal considerations, however, are broader issues surrounding the growth and development of the ecclesiastical liberty as a

55. See similarly Stokes, 'King Edgar's Charter', 57–58.

crucietur. Anno dnice incarnatio
nis. dcccc. lviii. indictione. ii. scripta e.
hui munificentie singrapha. his aliisq;
testib; consentientib; quorum inferi[us]
nomina secdm unicuiq; dignitatem
utriq; ordinis decusatim do disponen
te taraxantur. Ego Eadgar brito
tannie anglorum monarchus. hoc tau
mate agie crucis roboraui. Ego Dunstan
dorobnensis eccle archiepc eidem regi be
niuolentiam consensi. Ego Oscytelus
eboracensis basilice pmas insignis. hoc
donum regale confirmaui. Ego Osulf
⁊ Ego Brichælni. ⁊ Ego Odulf. ⁊ Ego
Alfwold. ⁊ Ego Ælfstanus. ⁊ Ego Dani
el epi canonica subscptione manu ppa
hilariter subscpsimus. ⁘ Ego Eadiua
eidem regis aua. hanc largitione firma
ui. Ego æthelwold abbas abbendo
nensis cenobii. hoc sintagma timphans
dictaui. Ego Alfwoldus abbas. ⁊ Ego
Aldred abbas consensimus. Ego Alfer
dux. ⁊ Ego Alpheah dux annuimus.

documentary form. As noted, monastic liberty was not an established feature
of the documentary landscape of tenth-century England, and the only texts
to discuss such matters before Æthelred's reign are broad, normative works—
works analogous (and often supplementary) to the Rule. Kelly was aware of
this fact and, in an attempt to make the *Orthodoxorum* charters look less
exceptional, she drew attention to two other early charters which concern the
subject: a privilege for Muchelney of 964, and another for Tavistock of 981.[56] If
authentic, these would indeed cast the *Orthodoxorum* charters in better light.
Yet both are deeply problematic texts.

56. *Charters of Abingdon*, ed. Kelly, xci–xciii.

The former only survives in the thirteenth-century Muchelney cartulary. What raises doubts here is not simply the unusually early mention of
liberty, but the fact that the privilege specifically forbids the interference of
the local diocesan bishop in the process of electing the abbot.[57] Muchelney
had been overseen by a bishop—either Ælfwold of Sherborne or Ælfwold of
Crediton—in the 960s, and this may have made episcopal interference topical. But the stipulation is unique within the pre-Conquest corpus. If mentioned at all within the context of abbatial election, the local bishop (or king)
is *always* accorded a degree of influence, as we see in the Rule and *Regularis
concordia*—not to mention a number of charters derivative of these.[58] There
is, moreover, no evidence that Muchelney had been reformed by 964, and liturgical sources suggest that Benedictine practices were only being introduced in
the late tenth or early eleventh century, around the time that an authentic
diploma of Æthelred speaks of the regular life at the centre.[59]

The terms of Muchelney's liberty thus breathe the air of post-Conquest
litigation. In the later eleventh and twelfth centuries, conflicts between monks
and bishops were rife, as monastic communities sought to frame their rights
in ever more exclusionary terms.[60] At Muchelney, there is ample evidence of
strain between abbot and bishop. In the late eleventh century (*c.* 1080), the
brothers had to secure the support of Abbot Thurstan of Glastonbury (*c.* 1077–
96) to fend off encroachment by Bishop Giso of Wells (1060–88). Thurstan
was able to produce charters demonstrating that Muchelney and its western
neighbours at Athelney—against whom Giso had also raised claims—were
under his protection; and with this, the matter was laid to rest.[61] Just over
a century later, however, the plan of Bishop Savaric (1192–1215) to relocate
his seat from Bath to Glastonbury threatened to deprive the monks of their
northerly protectors. And while this, too, came to naught, it did not prevent

57. S 729 (ed. Bates, *Two Cartularies*, no. 3). The cartulary is BL, Add. 56488, where
this text is at fols 9v–10r. Note that within the witness-list Ælfwold is a later addition. It was
not uncommon for recipients to be omitted in witness-lists, so the insertion is probably a
later hypercorrection. See further Keynes, 'Conspectus', 63–64 and 76, who designates the
charter 'problematic', but does not expand on the judgement.

58. *Regularis concordia*, chs 9–10, ed. Symons and Spath, 74–76, echoed in S 904 (KCD
707), and S 911 (KCD 714). See also *Ælfric's Letter to the Monks at Eynsham*, ed. Jones,
212; *Charters of St Albans*, ed. Crick, 58–63, 116–17, 122. For contemporary comparanda:
Herkommer, *Untersuchungen*, 8–43.

59. Billett, "'Old Books of Glastonbury'", esp. 332–34. Æthelred's diploma is S 884 (ed.
Bates, *Two Cartularies*, no. 4), Taunton, Somerset Record Office, DD/SAS PR 502. For
facsimiles: *BA Facs.*, 11; John, 'Return of the Vikings', 200. It was apparently copied by the
same scribe as the Muchelney Breviary (presumably a monk of Muchelney), as Billet notes
(citing Michael Gullick's opinion).

60. The classic study remains Knowles, 'Growth of Exemption'.

61. William of Malmesbury, *De antiquitate Glastonie ecclesie*, ch. 76, ed. Scott, 154–56,
with Keynes, 'Giso', 248; Cowdrey, *Lanfranc*, 125–26.

the bishop from appropriating Ilminster from Muchelney, which he restored to the abbot as a prebend (a dependent holding), curtailing the centre's independence considerably.[62] Under these circumstances, it is easy to imagine why the brothers might have wished to invent or improve an earlier text securing freedom from the influence of the local bishop. That this was the main point of interest here is revealed by a marginal addition to the charter's rubrics in the cartulary: this turns the original heading 'charter of confirmation of King Edgar' into 'charter of confirmation of King Edgar regarding the election of an abbot' ('carta confirmationis edgari regis **pro electione abbatis**').[63] Diplomas had saved the day when Thurstan intervened c. 1080; the monks presumably hoped they now would do so again.

With the Muchelney charter removed, the *Orthodoxorum* charters start to look distinctly isolated. They become even more so when we turn to the one other purportedly early privilege of this type, the Tavistock diploma of 981. This is the only pre-Conquest charter to survive from the abbey, and it does so in the form of two Edwardian inspeximuses. The inspeximus—or vidimus, as it is known on the continent—was the medieval precursor to the modern notarized copy. It involved bringing a document forth to be examined at court (*inspeximus* literally means 'we have seen/inspected'), then receiving a new sealed and authenticated copy in return. Until recently, these inspeximuses were known only from exchequer enrolments—copies made by the body charged with oversight of royal finance, that is—but an independent witness to the first of them has now come to light, providing a firmer basis for discussion.[64] From this, it is clear that a pre-Conquest charter underlies the text, since a number of transcription errors have been occasioned by its unfamiliar letter forms. The witness-list is plausible for 981, and the formulation bears the hallmarks of the complex 'hermeneutic style' of Latin employed by the tenth-century reformers (but deplored by post-Conquest commentators such as William of Malmesbury).[65]

But the mere fact of its origins lying before 1066 does not mean that this is an authentic text of 981. And indeed, a number of serious problems attach to it. For a start, the diploma is said to have been issued because 'certain others' ('caeteri') had infringed upon the abbey's liberty, at a time when the king was too young and helpless to prevent them. Yet in 981 Æthelred was no older than fifteen (and perhaps only eleven), still firmly under the tutelage of his

---

62. HMC, *Calendar*, ed. Bird, i, 48; *Bath and Wells, 1061–1205*, ed. Ramsey, no. 240. Cf. Ramsey, 'Savaric'.

63. BL, Add. 56488, fol. 9v.

64. S 838 (KCD 629). To the copies listed in the Sawyer catalogue should be added Exeter, Devon Heritage Centre, W1258M/D84/1–10, which was discovered by Todd Gray and has been transcribed by Julia Crick, to whom I owe the following observations. More generally: Vincent, 'Charters of King Henry II'.

65. Cf. Lapidge, 'Hermeneutic Style'.

guardians and de facto regents. Whether he would have been in a position to respond to his earlier impotence is, therefore, more than questionable. More to the point, in the 990s, Æthelred would frame his earlier actions as a product of youthful error, in the Abingdon privilege as elsewhere. And the manner in which events at Tavistock are depicted, with a strong emphasis on the king's 'infantile age' ('infantili . . . aetate') and the actions of those (unnamed) 'others' who took advantage of this, bear remarkable similarities to these later texts (including the Abingdon diploma). It is hard to resist the conclusion that such ideas (and formulation) belong to that period.[66] In this respect, the sanction employed is closely related to that of the *Orthodoxorum* series, which is not otherwise seen before the 990s. And the listing of the abbey's estates without relevant boundary clauses is unusual, perhaps pointing to later attempts to improve the text. All indications are, therefore, that the Tavistock diploma belongs no earlier than the mid- to later years of Æthelred's reign (perhaps with even later adjustments). The monastery itself was sacked by vikings in 997, and the suspicion is that the brothers lost most of their early records, possibly including an original foundation charter of 981.[67] The surviving text was presumably forged to make good this loss.

Elsewhere, too, the 990s saw considerable interest in the subject of liberty. The year after the production of the Abingdon privilege, Æthelred granted similar rights to Bishop Ealdred of Cornwall, in a document whose scribe was evidently acquainted with the former text (not least, in the form of its alpha and omega chrismon: Illustration 3.4).[68] This is then joined by a diploma issued upon the reform of Sherborne in 998—an act which saw the cathedral chapter become monastic, much as the Old Minster had in 964. The latter secures the centre's freedom and establishes how future bishops should be appointed, couching this in terms which go well beyond the generic rights pertaining to bookland (in fact, no lands are 'booked' at all). Once more, the subject is liberty.[69] Four years later, Æthelred confirmed the holdings of his mother's foundation at Wherwell, including the nuns' right to elect their own abbess (in agreement with the local metropolitan); and a similar privilege was probably issued for her foundation at Amesbury too.[70] Finally, in 1005 Æthelred confirmed the foundation of Eynsham in another striking document, in which he allows the founder Æthelmær to oversee affairs there 'in the guise of father' ('patris uice'). After the latter's death, however, the monks are to be free to elect a leader from among their ranks, unless a sufficiently

66. Keynes, *Diplomas*, 180 n. 101; Stafford, 'Royal Government', 44–45. Cf. *Charters of Abingdon*, ed. Kelly, xci–xciii; Holdsworth, 'Tavistock Abbey'.

67. *The Anglo-Saxon Chronicle MS C*, s.a. 997, ed. O'Brien O'Keeffe, 88.

68. S 880 (KCD 686), Exeter, D.C., 2070.

69. S 895 (*Sherb* 11).

70. S 904 (KCD 707); Finberg, *Early Charters of Wessex*, 103–4.

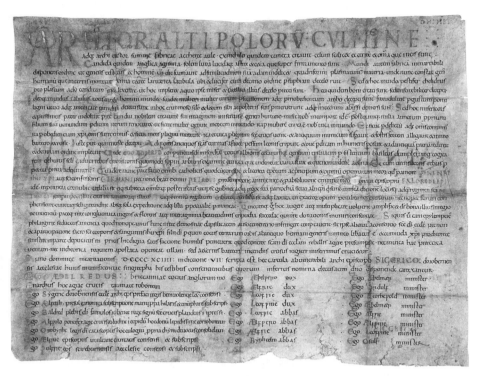

3.4 Æthelred grants liberty to St Germans: Exeter, D.C. 2070, © Dean and Chapter, Exeter Cathedral

worthy candidate is not to be found (an allusion to the *Regularis concordia*, itself echoing the Rule).[71]

There is, therefore, ample evidence for an interest in ecclesiastical liberty in the 990s and early 1000s. Though only the Abingdon and St Germans privileges survive in their original format, the others come from a range of houses and reveal points of contact with many other authentic texts of these years. This is crucial. Before this point, our evidence for ecclesiastical liberty is almost entirely limited to a single documentary type (the *Orthodoxorum* charter); now we find the kind of colourful variety we would expect if such rights were being routinely granted and claimed. Moreover, there are good historical grounds for positing such a development. As we have seen, in the 980s the king had shown himself to be an unreliable guarantor of religious (and above all, monastic) freedoms; it was only natural that firmer promises should now be demanded. Liberty therefore became the watchword of Æthelred's mature years. And not surprisingly, many of the centres which received these grants can be associated with Ælfthryth, Æthelwold and the monastic reform.

71. S 911 (KCD 714). Cf. *Ælfric's Letter to the Monks at Eynsham*, ed. Jones, 212.

Dating Forgery: Abbot Wulfgar and the 990s

Forgeries are notoriously difficult to date, particularly when they only survive in later copies. Nevertheless, there are good grounds for thinking that the two earliest *Orthodoxorum* privileges are products of the 990s or very early 1000s. As we have seen, their formulation reveals influences from authentic documents of these years, and their focus on liberty sits well alongside other charters of the period. Definitive evidence of their early existence, however, comes from a rather different direction—namely, the three remaining charters of this type.

Of the non-Abingdon diplomas, the Worcester one is an obvious post-Conquest fake, while the Romsey text lacks witness-list and dating clause, providing us with little information as to its gestation. The Pershore privilege, however, is a different kettle of fish. This survives as a single sheet. Written throughout in a late square miniscule hand, without any obvious signs of anachronism, this must have been produced before the end of Æthelred's reign, and in all probability before his last decade on the throne.[72] By script alone, it could be an authentic product of 972. But formulaic links with other documents of the 990s (as outlined above) suggest later production, as do a number unusual features within the single sheet itself (Illustration 3.5). Thus the chrismon takes the form of an alpha and omega, which is rare before the 990s, but then found in quick succession the Abingdon and St Germans texts of 993 and 994.[73] The manner in which this is formed is also significant: unlike the one earlier example, here Ω is placed beneath A on a separate line, precisely as we see in 993 (and also, in adjusted form, in 994: Illustration 3.6).[74] There are further anomalies. The scribe has misjudged the space available and been forced to place the witness-list on the reverse (or dorse), an arrangement not otherwise seen in authentic texts of the period. Similarly worrying are the many erasures and adjustments to the main text, particularly in the boundary clauses.[75] These suggest that the diploma continued to be tinkered with after its initial production—another feature which finds no immediate parallel among the sixty-eight or so authentic originals produced between the accession of Æthelstan (924) and death of William the Conqueror (1086).

The terms of the Pershore charter are similarly troubling. It concerns a massive 320 hides—the hide being the English equivalent to the *mansus*:

72. BL, Cotton Augustus ii. 6, with Stokes, 'King Edgar's Charter', 34–36. A facsimile can be found in *BM Facs.*, iii, 30. See also Dumville, 'Beowulf Come Lately'.

73. Cf. Thompson, *Anglo-Saxon Royal Diplomas*, 32–36.

74. S 736 (BCS 1165), Dorchester, Dorset Record Office, D 124, 1. For a fasimile: *OS Facs.*, ii, Earl of Ilchester 1.

75. See further Stokes, 'King Edgar's Charter', 57–67, 72–73; Roach, 'Privilege of Liberty'.

3.5 Pershore *Orthodoxorum* charter: BL, Cotton Augustus ii. 6, © BL

3.6 A/B Other alpha-omega chrismons of the tenth century: BL, Cotton
Augustus ii. 38 (reproduced from *BM Facs.*, iii, 36); Dorchester, Dorset Record
Office, D 124, 1 (reproduced from *OS Facs.*, ii, Earl of Ilchester 1), © BL

the land required to support a single peasant family—scattered across multiple estates. This is far more generous than any authentic diploma of Edgar, securing the abbey's entire endowment in one go. In this respect, the diploma conforms to a type, the *pancarte* (or *pancarta*), not seen in England before the mid-eleventh century (and then under exceptional circumstances).[76] The safest conclusion, therefore, is that this is indeed a forgery, based on the Abingdon texts in the names of Eadwig and Edgar (and, ultimately, the 993 privilege). We know that Pershore enjoyed close contacts with Abingdon, since its first abbot had hailed from the centre. It is easy to imagine collaboration between the houses, perhaps even extending to Abingdon forging documents to order. Pershore itself was burned down in 1002, an event which may have led to substantial material and archival losses; it is tempting see this diploma as a convenient means of securing the abbey's endowment in the aftermath.[77]

If the Pershore privilege was indeed produced no later than the early years of the eleventh century, then it goes without saying that its Abingdon exemplars must have been in existence by then. This allows us to place them with some confidence in the abbacy of Wulfgar, who had first obtained confirmation of Abingdon's liberty in 993 and would go on to outlive Æthelred by just five months. Wulfgar was one of a set of religiously minded individuals who played a major part in the politics of the 990s.[78] Within this context, the *Orthodoxorum* forgeries were intended to lend weight to Wulfgar's claims, securing the gains he had made in 993. Æthelred's restitution invited such treatment. As we have seen, this mentions how Eadred, Eadwig and Edgar had confirmed the monks' liberty, on the basis of texts of Leo III and Coenwulf; yet none of these earlier documents had survived. The loss of the Leo and Coenwulf charters might perhaps be excused, but the absence of the Eadwig and Edgar diplomas was more troubling. The obvious solution, however, lay in the 993 privilege itself. Shorn of the specifics, this could be repackaged as liberties of Eadwig and Edgar. Æthelred's diploma had asserted a long and proud history for Abingdon's liberty; the *Orthodoxorum* forgeries now fill in the gaps.

This was not the only act of forgery at Abingdon in these years. Wulfgar proved to be something of a second Æthelwold here, leading a spirited campaign to restore lands and rights he believed belonged to the monks. An early victory is represented by the 993 privilege. A second came *c.* 999, with a second restitution, compensating the brothers for lands which Æthelred had received during his half-brother's reign (975–78). A third restitution may then have followed in 1008.[79] Yet royal intervention was only one means of fighting the monks' corner. Further signs of Wulfgar's activities emerge from an

76. Keynes, 'Giso', 236–38.
77. Cf. Tinti, *Sustaining Belief*, 162–63.
78. Roach, *Æthelred*, 133–85. See similarly Abels, *Aethelred the Unready*, 61–71.
79. S 937 (*Abing* 129), S 918 (*Abing* 135).

examination of the Abingdon archive. As Susan Kelly notes, many of the abbey's purportedly early charters reveal signs of tenth-century formulation. And she concluded, reasonably enough, that these are pre-Conquest forgeries. Kelly placed most of the fakes (tentatively) in the abbacy of Æthelwold (955–63); but a stronger case can now be made for that of Wulfgar (990–1016). Not only do many of the resulting texts reveal close affinities with authentic documents of Æthelred's reign, but the historical context is a better fit. It is Wulfgar who was confronted with major obstacles to the abbey's territorial integrity, and it is he who can be associated with other counterfeits.[80] Indeed, many of these forgeries betray similar interests to the *Orthodoxorum* texts, and a number show signs of their influence.

To start with the clearest case, two counterfeits concerning the abbey's core endowment survive in the name of Coenwulf of Mercia, dated 811 and 821. These are evidently meant to be foundational texts. Of the two, the first is the more important, concerning a massive 310 hides at Abingdon, as well as smaller holdings at Longworth, Sunningwell, Eaton, Dry Sandford (probably), Denchworth, Goosey, Culham, Ginge, Leckhampstead (all traditionally Berkshire, save Culham in Oxfordshire) and three further unidentified sites. The second then repeats and extends the latter grants, covering land at Culham, Cumnor, Bessels Leigh ('Earmundelæh'), Eaton, Sunningwell, Dry Sandford (probably), Ginge, Denchworth and Goosey (again, all traditionally Berkshire, save Culham). As we have seen, Coenwulf was feted as Abingdon's earliest benefactor in Æthelred's 993 diploma and its *Orthodoxorum* siblings; here too, he appears in the guise of a founder. But this is not the only point of contact. In textual terms, these documents draw strongly on early Mercian models, probably of Coenwulf's reign, as revealed by the straightforward syntax and the distinctive exemption from duties of hospitality. Nevertheless, they also betray certain tenth-century features. Particularly revealing is the emphasis on Mary as the monastery's patron. The cult of the Blessed Virgin was very popular among the tenth-century reformers, and Abingdon's dedication to her may well date to these years. Certainly the *Orthodoxorum* charters make much of Mary, not only as the mother of Christ (a role emphasized in the opening preamble), but also in her guise as the centre's patron. Moreover, like the Edgar *Orthodoxorum* charters for Abingdon and Pershore, the Coenwulf diplomas take the form of *pancartes*—that is, diplomas concerning multiple transactions or estates. Most crucially, the sanction of the second of these, which threatens those who do not obey its terms with being removed from the company of the church of God and participation in the body and blood of Christ (i.e., with excommunication), directly echoes that of the *Orthodoxorum* series. Finally, it is worth noting that, as preserved in the earlier version of the Abingdon cartulary-chronicle, the names of Mary and Peter have been

---

80. See Keynes, 'Church Councils', 112 n. 349, for similar remarks.

highlighted in the main text, suggesting that the original single sheet belonged to the second half of the tenth century (not the earlier ninth).[81]

These are not the only similarities between these texts and the *Orthodoxorum* charters. The first Coenwulf privilege concerns the abbey's core endowment, including those holdings at Goosey and Ginge mentioned in the Edgar *Orthodoxorum* privilege; and the second adds to these the estate at Bessels Leigh, also 'restored' in the Edgar diploma. The status of these lands was clearly in question in the later tenth century, and three further charters survive for them, all of similarly questionable authenticity.[82] The first is in the name of the eighth-century ruler Æthelbald, whose reign had laid the foundations of Mercia's later ascendancy. Even more than that of the Coenwulf diplomas, this text's formulation belongs to the late tenth or early eleventh centuries. The most obviously anachronistic feature is the use of first (rather than third) person subscriptions within the witness-list. Moreover, here Æthelbald is styled 'monarch of the English [Angles?] of Britain' ('Brittannie Anglorum monarchus'), an unusual title, which directly echoes that of Æthelred in the 993 privilege (and those of Eadwig and Edgar in its *Orthodoxorum* derivatives).[83] The second Ginge diploma, which also concerns Goosey and two other holdings, is in the name of Eadred. This is framed as a restitution, issued after Æthelwold had recited various ancient charters to the king. As it stands, it is clearly a forgery, probably intended to authenticate the other early counterfeits in a manner analogous to Pilgrim's Agapit bull. Indeed, despite its purported date (955), the diploma is modelled on a charter of Eadred's successor, Eadwig (955–59), which is itself a forgery of the late tenth or early eleventh century. Its sanction, meanwhile, is an elaboration of that employed by the influential draftsman-scribe Edgar A in the early 960s. Yet the reference here to malefactors being 'inspired by demonic love of money' ('demonica instinctus philargiria') and removed 'from participating in the body and blood of Christ' ('a participatione sacrosancti corporis et sanguinis Domini nostri Iesu Christi') clearly derives

---

81. S 166 (*Abing* 8), S 183 (*Abing* 9), with *Charters of Abingdon*, ed. Kelly, 40–41, 44; Edwards, *Charters*, 185–92. For the influence of the *Orthodoxorum* sanction on the second (not noted by Kelly), see S 183 (*Abing* 9): 'Siquis autem prescriptis statutis noluerit obedire, sciat se alienum **esse a consortio sancte Dei ecclesie et a participatione corporis et sanguinis Domini nostri Iesu Christi** per auctoritatem beati Petri apostoli, nisi digne emendauerit quod contra Dei ecclesiam fecisset.'; S 876 (*Abing* 124): 'Si quis uero tam epylempticus phylargirie seductus . . . sit ipse alienatus **a consortio sanctae Dei aecclesie necnon et a participatione sacrosancti corporis et sanguinis Domini nostri Iesu Christi** . . ' (emphasis added). These details are not to be found in the standard Edgar A sanction, which furnishes the model for the latter. On the cult of the Blessed Virgin: Clayton, *Cult of the Virgin Mary*, esp. 122–41.

82. See Thacker, 'Æthelwold and Abingdon', 51.

83. S 93 (*Abing* 5), with *Charters of Abingdon*, ed. Kelly, 25, 27. The same style can also be found in S 690 (*Abing* 87) of 961, which survives in its original format: BL, Cotton Augustus ii. 39. See Chaplais, 'Royal Anglo-Saxon "Chancery"', 49–50.

from that of the *Orthodoxorum* series (itself an elaboration of the Edgar A type). Significantly, the second turn of phrase is the same one found in the second Coenwulf privilege.[84] All indications are, therefore, of production in the later tenth or early eleventh century; and this is one of those diplomas which, as copied in the earlier version cartulary-chronicle, has display script in the attestations. Finally, the third Ginge diploma is in Eadwig's name, purporting to grant the estate (on its own) to the abbey. This has stronger claims to authenticity. Nevertheless, the presence of an Edgar A-style sanction sits awkwardly with a date of 956—the latter scribe having begun operation in 959, perhaps after an early career at Edgar's Mercian court—and the fact that it concerns Ginge is itself troubling. Perhaps tellingly, it borrows its opening formulae from the text of the important reforming council of Clofesho of 747 (a subtle nod to the supposed Mercian origins of these rights), elements of which also reappear in a suspect diploma of Edgar for Cumnor.[85]

These diplomas are, in turn, associated with further forgeries. As we have seen, the first Coenwulf text mentions holdings at Longworth (historically Berkshire, now Oxfordshire), whose reversion is also promised in the Eadred counterfeit. The latter was intended as an ersatz (re)foundation charter, and the estates in question were evidently of particular concern. Thanks to another (apparently authentic) diploma, preserved in the revised (thirteenth-century) version of the cartulary-chronicle, we know that Longworth was actually granted to a layman in 958, and only came into monastic hands later.[86] The Coenwulf privilege also concerns ten hides at Eaton (historically Berkshire, now Oxfordshire). According to a note in the later version of the cartulary-chronicle, this pertained to the Cumnor estate in Edgar's day—the latter being another part of Abingdon's core endowment, mentioned in the second Coenwulf diploma and the Eadred restitution—but had since been 'completely taken away' ('omnino ablata').[87] (Interestingly, it does not feature among the centre's holdings in Domesday Book.) A further diploma concerning Cumnor is, however, preserved in both versions of the cartulary-chronicle. This bears the date 968 and shares its formulation with three other Abingdon privileges of this year. Direct grants to religious houses are often suspect—forgers being most likely to manufacture direct claims—and they are particularly so in England, where the peculiar nature of bookland tenure meant that laymen could pass estates to religious houses simply by handing over the diploma

84. S 567 (*Abing* 51). Cf. S 605 (*Abing* 52), S 876 (*Abing* 124). See further *Charters of Abingdon*, ed. Kelly, 213–14, 219–20.

85. S 583 (*Abing* 58). Cf. *Charters of Abingdon*, ed. Kelly, 248–49, whose assessment is somewhat more optimistic. On the draftsman-scribe Edgar A, see most recently Keynes, 'Edgar, *rex admirabilis*', 14–16.

86. S 654 (*Abing* 80). That this is preserved in the revised version of the chronicle is significant: Keynes, *Diplomas*, 11–13.

87. *Historia ecclesie Abbendonensis*, B178, ed. Hudson, i, 331 (with n. 228).

in question. We should expect to see many charters for laymen, even in an ecclesiastical archive; where we do not, it is often suspicious.[88] The replication of so much formulation across three different diplomas is also troubling, as is the fact that the same formulation is found in an obvious fake in the name of Æthelstan (924–39).[89] And as presented in the earlier version of the cartulary-chronicle, the latter text bears display script in the witness-list, pointing towards production no earlier than the 990s. The same is true of the transcript of one of the others taken by Robert Talbot in the sixteenth century, strengthening the impression that these are later confections.[90] According to a thirteenth-century memorandum, Cumnor was one of seven outlying manors which traditionally furnished supplies to the abbey.[91] There can be little doubt that the 968 privilege was intended to secure a key estate. Significantly, its opening preamble draws on the same acts of the council of Clofesho of 747 as the Eadwig Ginge diploma (and the four other texts with which it shares its formulation). The council in question had condemned lay usurpation of church lands under the Mercian ruler Æthelbald, launching an ambitious set of reforming initiatives; to the later monks of Abingdon, who looked keenly to past glories, the appeal of this precedent must have been obvious.[92]

A final site of interest at this point was Denchworth. A holding there is mentioned in both of the Coenwulf privileges, the first of which grants the estate along with neighbouring Goosey to the abbey, lands together comprising thirty hides. Domesday Book records two estates at South Denchworth (historically Berkshire, now Oxfordshire), assessed at six and seven hides in 1066; and these, combined with the abbey's seventeen hides at Goosey, neatly give a total of thirty, as recorded in the Coenwulf privilege. But these had not always constituted a single holding, nor had they always been in monastic hands. Two further diplomas survive regarding the grant of a five-hide estate at Denchworth to the prominent local magnate Wulfric Cufing (who may have been a patron of the abbey).[93] This indicates that at least some of these lands were in lay ownership in the mid-tenth century. And another text records a grant of two hides at Denchworth in 965, which together with Wulfric's five conveniently gives the seven hides at Denchworth incorporated into the abbey's Goosey estate at the time of the Domesday survey. Like the Edgar Cumnor privilege, however, the latter text is problematic, sharing its

88. Keynes, *Diplomas*, 6–13 (and cf. ibid., 33–34).

89. S 757 (*Abing* 111). The three other diplomas of 968 are S 758 (*Abing* 110), S 759 (*Abing* 112), S 760 (*Abing* 113), while the Æthelstan text is S 409 (*Abing* 25).

90. CCCC 111, p. 168. On Talbot's transcriptions: *Charters of Abingdon*, ed. Kelly, lxiii–lxiv.

91. *Two Cartularies of Abingdon*, ed. Slade and Lambrick, no. C405.

92. Cf. Keynes, 'Reconstruction'.

93. *GDB* 59r, 60v, 62r; S 529 (*Abing* 41), S 657 (*Abing* 81). See *Charters of Abingdon*, ed. Kelly, clxxiv–clxxxv, esp. clxxvi–clxxvii.

formulation with two charters of the same date in favour of Abingdon; and their shared witness-list derives from an authentic diploma of 970 in favour of a local deacon, raising further doubts.[94] The same formulation also appears in a purported diploma of Edward the Martyr (975–78), which still bears the original (impossible) date of 965.[95] It is hard to shake the impression that these are all rather artificial constructions. Finally, one of these other diplomas concerns a massive fifty hides at Marcham, for which an authentic diploma of the West Saxon king Ecgberht (802–39) has been reworked, probably in the later tenth or early eleventh century.[96] Here the efforts were only partially successful; as of 1066, Abingdon possessed just twenty hides there.

The result of the preceding analysis is to revise estimations of forgery at Wulfgar's Abingdon considerably upwards. The evidence is strongest in the case of the *Orthodoxorum* texts, which must have been in existence by the early eleventh century. But the connections between these and the other charters are strong. They all concern similar subjects, with most estates finding mention in more than one text; and we can work outwards from the Edgar *Orthodoxorum* privilege (the only one of the series to mention land as well as liberty) to the Coenwulf diplomas, and then on to the Ginge, Denchworth and Marcham counterfeits. More importantly, there are close formulaic links between these texts. The second Coenwulf privilege echoes the sanction of the *Orthodoxorum* series, which has also influenced the Eadred restitution of 955; the Æthelbald Ginge privilege likewise reveals influence from the *Orthodoxorum* texts in the royal subscription; and the Eadwig Ginge charter employs a preamble closely related to that found in the Edgar Cumnor text (both ultimately derived from the acts of the synod of Clofesho), which is itself identical to that of three other forgeries (including one for Marcham, for which we have an 'improved' Ecgberht diploma). There is also a thematic unity to the texts, which look back fondly to the distant Mercian and West Saxon past, as well as the more recent Edgarian present.

In the absence of the (pseudo-)original single sheets, we cannot be certain whether all of these were produced by the same individual or at the same time. Nevertheless, it is clear that many are related, and probably quite intimately so. The aim is to strengthen Abingdon's claims, wherever possible associating these with the abbey's initial growth and endowment in the eighth and ninth centuries. The monks were thus able to cast lay claimants to these properties as usurpers—a tried and tested approach within ecclesiastical circles. Yet the monks did not simply satisfy themselves with ancient texts. As at Worms

94. S 733 (*Abing* 104). The other diplomas are S 732 (*Abing* 103), S 734 (*Abing* 102). The witness-list comes from S 778 (*Abing* 114). Cf. *Charters of Abingdon*, ed. Kelly, 412–14, for a more generous assessment.

95. S 829 (*Abing* 116).

96. S 278 (*Abing* 11). See *Charters of Abingdon*, ed. Kelly, 51–54; Edwards, *Charters*, 193–95.

and Passau, they furnished more modern privileges to take the story into recent years. In almost all of these cases, the most recent charter is in favour of Æthelwold, the abbey's (re-)founder. These are thus also a paean to the golden age of reform of the 960s and 970s. In this respect, they were produced at a time of considerable uncertainty. It was Æthelwold's death in 984 which had precipitated Abingdon's difficulties, and the holy man's cult was being actively promoted in the second half of the 990s, starting with the ceremonial translation of his bodily remains on 10 September 996. The forgeries represent further efforts to consolidate the great abbot's legacy.[97]

Diplomas were accorded considerable authority in Anglo-Saxon law courts, and the monks of Abingdon clearly hoped to benefit from their privileges.[98] The 'anti-monastic reaction' of Edward the Martyr's reign and Æthelred's new direction of the 980s had placed the abbey under considerable strain, and some gains had almost certainly been lost (perhaps including Eaton). Yet it is hard to imagine that all or even most of these estates were actually contested. In most cases, they constitute part of the abbey's core endowment, and many fulfilled important administrative functions.[99] One suspects, therefore, that the majority of forgeries are prophylactic, intended to strengthen the brothers' hand. The resulting documents present the estates in question as Abingdon's oldest and most venerable; they thus become part of the very fabric of monastic life. It was this that really mattered: creating a viable backstory for the monastic endowment.

Forgery and Authenticity in Æthelredian England

If Wulfgar's Abingdon was indeed forging documents on an industrial scale, it was not alone. At Canterbury, a number of diplomas were fabricated in the name of Offa of Mercia (757–96) in the later tenth and eleventh centuries; at Glastonbury, a charter was confected in the name of Baldred (c. 681), probably in the later tenth century; at Westminster, a pseudo-original of Edgar was mocked up, restoring lands supposedly granted by Offa at Tyburn; at Selsey, the canons possessed a counterfeit in the name of the early eighth-century king Nunna, perhaps produced at Canterbury in these years (conceivably in connection with a forged foundation charter); at Worcester, a privilege of Wulfhere of Mercia (658–75) was falsified at this point; at Rochester, diplomas were feigned in the names of Edgar and Ecgberht; and at the Old Minster, Winchester, diplomas were confected in the names of Edward the Elder,

---

97. On the early development of the cult, see the editors' introduction to Wulfstan Cantor, *Vita S. Æthelwoldi*, ed. Lapidge and Winterbottom, cxii–cxliii. See also Browett, 'Cult of St Æthelwold'.

98. Cf. Wormald, 'Charters'.

99. Cf. Lambrick, 'Abingdon Abbey'; Thacker, 'Æthelwold and Abingdon'.

Æthelstan and Eadred. And this is to limit ourselves to centres for which single sheet pseudo-originals survive.[100]

A number of these cases bear comparison with that of Abingdon. At Rochester, for example, one of the estates the cathedral sought to secure in the later tenth century was Bromley. Though now a bustling south-east London borough, Bromley then lay in Kent, on the overland routes between Rochester and the growing Thames River metropolis. When the cathedral first obtained the estate is unclear, but by the early to mid-980s the bishop and canons evidently had an interest. These rights were contested, however, and matters took a turn for the worse when Bishop Ælfstan (964–94/5) fell foul of the king, under circumstances similar to those at Abingdon after 985. The result was considerable losses, including Bromley, which Æthelred now gave to a Kentish associate named Æthelsige. The king must have known what he was doing, as the grant comes in the context of a wider set of disputes between bishop and crown (perhaps set off by this transaction). These led to Rochester being ravaged by royal forces in 986 and Ælfstan disappearing entirely from diploma witness-lists for four years.[101]

Whatever the original basis for the bishopric's claim to Bromley, it was evidently not up to the challenge. The local canons therefore set about rectifying the situation. The result was a diploma in Edgar's name granting Bromley directly to Rochester—precisely the sort of direct grant to a religious house which is so suspicious. The supposed date of this act (955) is impossible—Edgar's reign south of the Thames having begun in 959—and the script is clearly later than the mid-tenth century (and imitative). Notwithstanding these shortfalls, the text seems to have had the desired effect. When, at Easter 998, Æthelred was prevailed upon to restore Bromley to Rochester—much as he had Abingdon's liberty five years earlier—the resulting diploma follows the distinctive variant version of the estate's bounds given in the Edgar charter.[102] This was not the only forging activity at Rochester. Around this time, the canons also confected a charter concerning Snodland, which was claimed by a local noble family. And though there is no hint of royal impropriety here, there may be in another case. The endorsement to the Bromley diploma refers to this as 'the other charter for that same place' ('et est alia charta similis huic'), suggesting the existence of a second single sheet, either for Bromley or for nearby

100. Crick, 'Script', provides an excellent survey. See further *Charters of Christ Church*, ed. Brooks and Kelly, 109–12, 273–74, 388–89, 393–94, 415–17; Crick, 'St Albans, Westminster', 76–79; *Charters of Glastonbury*, ed. Kelly, 221–25; *Charters of Selsey*, ed. Kelly, 26 (and cf. ibid., 6–10); Keynes, 'Church of Rochester', esp. 333–36; Wormald, 'Æthelwold', 187, 201–2 n. 106.

101. Keynes, 'Church of Rochester', 323–25, 334–36, 343–47.

102. S 671 (*Roch* 29), BL, Cotton Charters viii. 33. The later restitution is S 893 (*Roch* 32).

Fawkham (which was also contested).[103] Whatever this diploma's contents, the suspicion is that it, too, was a fake, concocted under similar circumstances.

We can see analogous trends at the Old Minster in Winchester. As Æthelwold's onetime see, this had been among the houses to suffer in the later 980s. Here the main recorded loss was a massive one hundred hides at Downton and Ebbesbourne (in Wiltshire), which Æthelred restored in 997. As at Rochester, we know the fate of part of this estate in the meantime, since a diploma of 986 records that five hides at Ebbesbourne were granted to a royal retainer named Ælfgar. The latter is almost certainly the son of the Ealdorman Ælfric who had bought the abbacy of Abingdon for his brother Eadwine in 985. And it comes as no surprise that Ælfgar was also recalled as a despoiler of Abingdon, where his uncle (the abbot) is said to have ceded him rights. There is clearly a connection between these events; and in the year that Æthelred first voiced his contrition for the sale of Abingdon's abbacy (993), Ælfgar is reported to have been blinded, presumably on account of his prior misdemeanours.[104] We are thus dealing with a close-knit group of associates, who profiteered at the expense of the monks in the later 980s. And at the Old Minster, too, the response of choice was forgery. Here a single sheet survives in the name of Eadred, confirming Winchester's possession of precisely those lands restored in 997. Though this displays none of the historical inconsistencies of Rochester's Bromley forgery (it is dated 948 and bears a plausible witness-list), its script stands out even more starkly. The charter is written throughout in a distinctive—and not entirely unskilful—imitation of Insular minuscule (with half-uncial features), the script used in southern England until the later ninth century. In this precise form, the writing is at least a century too early for its date (Illustration 3.7).[105] This document bears similarities to another Winchester counterfeit, in the name of Edward the Elder (899–924). The latter confirms the beneficial hidation of Chilcomb—a tax-break, effectively—in exchange for the lease of one hundred hides at Downton and seventy hides at Beddington (in Surrey). The focus here is Chilcomb, but in describing Downton as a lease, the diploma also underlines the see's possession of that estate. Significantly, the hand of this charter also imitates early Insular script, albeit of an even more archaic nature. Considering the nature of script imitation, which seeks to hide the scribe's native forms, it is hard to be certain whether these documents are the work of the same individual. But given the common interest in Downton and the shared misapprehensions about earlier tenth-century script, it is likely that we are indeed dealing with the same forger.[106]

103. BL, Cotton Charters viii. 33, with Keynes, 'Church of Rochester', 335. For a facsimile: *BM Facs.*, iii. 26.

104. *Anglo-Saxon Chronicle MS C*, s.a. 993, ed. O'Brien O'Keeffe, 86–87.

105. S 540 (BCS 862), BL, Cotton Charters viii. 11. For a facsimile: *BM Facs.*, iii, 14.

106. S 376 (BCS 620), BL, Harley Charter 43 C 1. For a facsimile: *BM Facs.*, iv, 10. See further Crick, 'Script', 11–16; Wormald, 'Æthelwold', 187, 202 n. 107.

3.7 Eadred's purported confirmation of Downton and Ebbesborne to the Old Minster, Winchester: BL, Cotton Charters viii. 11, © BL

These are not, in any case, the only counterfeits concerning the estate. Near identical texts survive in the names of Cenwalh (642–45, 648–74) and Ecgberht (802–39) for Downton; and though these do not survive as single sheets, they may well belong to a similar context.[107]

Evidently these texts were fabricated to assist the monks of the Old Minster in the face of recent losses. Versions of these claims also appear in the textually linked *Sinthama* charters. The latter is an unusual set of documents, which Alex Rumble argues once constituted a cartulary-like composition, compiled at Winchester in the late tenth or early eleventh century. The texts are not diplomas in the traditional sense—or certainly not authentic ones—but rather renditions of earlier traditions (many of them of questionable authenticity), intended to be read as a set. In this respect, they mention both Downton and Chilcomb prominently, and it is tempting to posit a connection here. External threats to monastic endowment naturally encouraged a heightened interest in local documentary traditions; at Winchester this may have found expression in both forgery and a proto-cartulary.[108] In any case, the same hand as that of the Downton and Chilcomb charters may lie behind a further imitative single

107. S 229 (BCS 27), S 275 (BCS 391), with Edwards, *Charters*, 131–32, 148; Wormald, 'Æthelwold', 187. Cf. S 393 (BCS 690).

108. *Property and Piety in Early Medieval Winchester*, ed. Rumble, 17, 98–104. See ibid., no. v, for a critical edition.

sheet in the name of Æthelstan, granting the Old Minster Taunton, another estate which figures in the *Sinthama* texts.[109]

The connection between forgery and royal caprice is less clear elsewhere, but not to be ignored. In the second half of the tenth century (probably), the monks of Glastonbury forged a diploma concerning Pennard (in Somerset) in the name of Baldred (*c.* 681), an otherwise obscure south-west Midlands ruler. Like the Rochester and Winchester single sheets, this is in an imitative hand; however, in this case there is little ancillary evidence, making dating difficult. Palaeographically, a late tenth- or early eleventh-century origin is likely (if not certain).[110] Given this, it may be significant that Glastonbury was another of the houses to suffer in the 980s. William of Malmesbury preserves a tale about how Æthelred assisted a certain Ælfwold in his (abortive) attempts to despoil the abbey, while a letter survives from a 'Pope John' (probably XV, 985–96) to an 'Ealdorman Ælfric' (probably of Hampshire), urging the latter to restore what he has taken from the centre.[111] Again, we have hints of tensions, occasioned by some of the same individuals. And while in neither case do we know whether Pennard was involved, the possibility should not be ignored—nor should that of other cases like it. Indeed, many attacks on monastic holdings must have gone unrecorded, and it is conceivable that some (perhaps much) of the forgery elsewhere can be associated with similar developments (certainly Westminster and Worcester both belonged to the same circles of reform).

Nor was forgery limited to those houses for which pseudo-originals survive. Though it is harder to date forgeries preserved in later copies, we have seen that Abingdon was very active in this regard; and we would doubtless know much more, had the abbey's muniments not suffered so heavily during the Dissolution. The same is true of Glastonbury, whose once-great archive only survives in fragments (thankfully including the precious Pennard charter). For at least one other monastic house we can detect signs of forgery on some scale. At some point in the later tenth or early eleventh centuries the monks of St Albans concocted documents in the name of their purported founder, the Mercian king Offa, concerning certain core monastic estates and liberty. The stipulations for abbatial election in these documents echo those of the Rule and *Regularis concordia*. And, like the many of the liberties of Æthelred's reign (but not those of the post-Conquest period), these explicitly allow for episcopal oversight of such matters. Given the later history of St Albans, which hotly contested its freedom with the bishop of Lincoln in the twelfth century, it is scarcely credible that these provisions were produced after the Conquest.

109. S 443 (BCS 727), BL, Cotton Charters viii. 17, with Wormald, 'Æthelwold', 187, 202 n. 107. For a facsimile: *BM Facs.*, iii, 6. Cf. S 825 (BCS 1149).

110. S 236 (*Glast* 3), Longleat, Marquess of Bath, Muniment 10564. See Crick, 'Insular History?', 538. For facsimiles: ibid., 539; *OS Facs.*, ii, Marquess of Bath 1.

111. William of Malmesbury, *Vita S. Dunstani*, II.25, ed. Winterbottom and Thomson, 280–82; JL 3752 (ZPUU 282).

And the obvious context for forgery is offered by the later years of Æthelred's reign, when the recently reformed centre enjoyed considerable favour.[112] In fact, these documents are probably related to an authentic grant of Æthelred of 1007, which is itself framed as a restitution of lands originally donated by Offa.[113] Finally, it is to these years, too, that we should probably date the Pershore *Orthodoxorum* charter and the Tavistock privilege of 981, adding further to our tally of monastic forgery.

It is noteworthy that a number of the resulting documents are foundation charters. It is in these years, too, that this documentary type—another continental import—first becomes common in England. That the liberty and foundation charter should emerge in tandem is no coincidence: it was at the moment of foundation (or refoundation) that the need was greatest to lay out how the monks or canons of a house were to live; and it was convenient for those claiming such rights to present them as being integral to communal life from day one.[114] In both cases, the development of a new documentary form acted as a spur to forgers. Those who had obtained these rights were keen to cloak them in an air of suitable antiquity, while those who had not sought to furnish precedents for their acquisition. The resulting boom in falsification may explain further documentary trends of these years. Starting in the 980s, diplomas frequently refer to the dangers posed by earlier or 'false' texts.[115] It would seem that as forgery spread, so too did anxieties about it. While not on quite the same scale, the disruption caused by the 'anti-monastic reaction' of the 970s and the king's 'youthful indiscretions' of the 980s had an effect akin to that of the Norman Conquest three generations later. In the face of tenurial uncertainty—the rupture and alienation of which Richard Southern spoke so eloquently—religious houses took solace in the past, a past which itself lent weight to present claims.[116]

At the same time, there was more to forgery than royal politics. At Rochester, the canons falsified texts concerning Snodland, as we have seen; at the Old Minster, only one of three surviving pseudo-originals relates to estates lost at royal hands; at Canterbury, forgery was largely a response to local struggles (perhaps compounded by a degree of royal apathy); and at Abingdon, counterfeiting went well beyond making good recent losses. Æthelred's youthful

---

112. S 136 (*St Alb* 1), S 136a (*St Alb* 2), with *Charters of St Albans*, ed. Crick, 58–74, 116–17, 122. More generally: Knowles, 'Growth of Exemption', 213–18.

113. S 916 (*St Alb* 12), Oxford, Bodleian Library, Eng. hist. a. 2, no. vii.

114. Keynes, 'Charter for Eynsham', 456–59. Cf. Vincent, 'Charters of King Henry II'.

115. E.g., S 856 (KCD 648), S 860 (KCD 650), S 861 (KCD 655), S 872 (*Sel* 21), 881 (KCD 687), S 883 (*Abing* 125), S 891 (KCD 698), S 896 (*Abing* 128), S 901 (*Abing* 132), S 902 (*Abing* 131), S 926 (*Roch* 33), S 927 (*Abing* 136), S 937 (*Abing* 129), with Keynes, 'Church Councils', 103–4. See also Crick, 'Script', 21–23.

116. Southern, 'Sense of the Past'. See further O'Brien, 'Forgery'; Savill, 'Prelude to Forgery'.

exuberance may have been an important impetus, but it was certainly not the only one. Of similar significance were developing literate mentalities. As Michael Clanchy famously argued, growing reliance on written proof often inspired forgery, a conclusion which holds as true for our tenth century as it does for his twelfth and thirteenth.[117] Along similar lines, the emergence of new documentary forms often demanded that estate histories and institutional memories be adapted accordingly. Yet perhaps the most important single factor—the yeast which brought this heady brew to ferment—was the attitudes towards the past developed within the circles of reform. In conjuring up an earlier 'Golden Age' of English monasticism, Æthelwold and his associates had encouraged a new brand of antiquarianism—and with it a new fad for forgery. That this should reach its high point in the 990s, and not the 960s or 970s, makes perfect sense. In the Middle Ages, as in more recent times, it was often left to a second generation of administrators to consolidate and record the efforts of charismatic reformers.[118] Our documents are a natural accompaniment to the development of the cults of the great reformers Æthelwold (d. 984, translated 996), Oswald (d. 992, translated 1002) and Dunstan (d. 988), all initiated in the space of a decade around the turn of the year 1000; they, too, are part of their legacy.

Such activity certainly was new. Though we must reckon with considerable losses, before these years we only know of forgery at Canterbury (and possibly Rochester)—and then on a limited scale.[119] Yet as important as its prevalence is the manner in which forgery was practised. In many cases, imitative script was employed, suggesting a heightened sense of anachronism. As Julia Crick notes, to imitate script is to appreciate the difference between past and present documentary forms. In this respect, these are our earliest examples of script imitation from England, complementing similar evidence from the continent.[120] Formulation tells a similar tale. The first two Abingdon privileges in the name of Coenwulf, for example, are closely modelled on authentic Mercian texts. Just as the scribes of the Bromley and Downton diplomas adjusted their hands to mimic earlier forms, so the draftsman (or -men) of these documents stepped outside his usual habits, drawing consciously on older traditions. What we are observing, therefore, is not simply a monastic land grab (though it is this too), but a creative re-imagining of Abingdon's past. The results would prove as fascinating as they would be enduring. These origin legends, now dressed in documentary guise, went on to provide firm foundations for central medieval chroniclers, at Abingdon as elsewhere.

117. Clanchy, *Memory to Written Record*, 318–28. See also Crick, 'Script', 21–26.

118. Cf. d'Avray, *Religious Rationalities*, 80–84.

119. Brooks, *Early History*, 191–97. For a possible case of ninth-century forgery at Rochester: S 266 (*Roch* 11), BL, Cotton Charters vi. 4. Given the proximity of the sees, the it cannot be ruled out that the text was produced at Canterbury.

120. Crick, 'Script', and 'Insular History?'.

CHAPTER FOUR

Forging Exemption: Fleury from Abbo to William

WHEN ABBO, the well-connected abbot of Fleury (Saint-Benoît-sur-Loire) in the Orléanais, sought out papal protection in the mid-990s, he was breaking with centuries of tradition, for Fleury was a royal monastery with close links to the Carolingians, the traditional ruling dynasty of West Francia (France). It was to kings that the monks looked for support, as an impressive run of immunities attests.[1] At times, they had added papal to royal support, but this was a matter of augmenting existing aid, not replacing it. Abbo now had something different in mind. As the terms of the bull he solicited from Gregory V (996–99) reveal, he was out to remove the monastery almost entirely from these established networks of patronage and association. Saint-Benoît would henceforth be an exempt house, answering only to Rome and the pope.

This was a dramatic decision, and it was not one Abbo took lightly. It was occasioned by his difficulties with the local bishop of Orléans, Arnulf (970–c. 1003). The latter hailed from a powerful local family, having followed his uncle Ermentheus (c. 950–70) onto the throne in one of those familial successions so characteristic of the early to central medieval episcopate. Arnulf was also a close associate of the king, Hugh Capet (987–96), and as such posed a double threat. Neither at court nor in the countryside could Abbo count on support. This is why he turned to the pope. What he sought was papal exemption. This often served similar purposes to royal immunity, securing abbatial lands and the brothers' rights of institutional independence; but it was particularly well suited to Abbo's needs, also addressing issues of ecclesiastical obedience and hierarchy. Just as Anno had found immunity the best means

---

1. *Recueil Charles III*, no. 34; *Recueil Lothaire et Louis V*, nos. 27, 28, 34, 70; *Recueil Fleury*, no. 69. See further Koziol, *Politics of Memory*, 291–93, raising the possibility of a lost immunity of Raoul of Burgundy.

of fending off the local count of Worms, so exemption offered Abbo the ideal solution to his problems with Arnulf.

In this showdown between abbot and bishop, we see the fault lines of the tenth- and eleventh-century French realm. The background is offered by a recent regime change. On 21 May 987, the last Carolingian king of West Francia, Louis V (986–87), had died of a hunting injury—the characteristic fate of his family, which had seen off at least two of Louis's predecessors. Since the young monarch had no direct heirs, the leading magnates of the nascent French realm were left with a difficult choice. In dynastic terms, the strongest candidate was Louis's paternal uncle, Charles of Lotharingia (alias Charles of Lorraine: see Illustration 0.3). However, Charles was an unpopular figure west of the Rhine, having been a thorn in the side of Louis's father, Lothar III (954–86). He was also duke of Lower Lotharingia in neighbouring East Francia (Germany) and thus beholden to another monarch. Some held Charles's loyalty in doubt; others reportedly objected to his marriage to a low-born woman; many more seem to have simply disliked him. But whatever the rationale, Charles was now passed over and the crown went to the only other serious contender, Duke Hugh of Francia (known to posterity as Hugh Capet). In recent years, Hugh had been the leading figure within the northern heartlands of the West Frankish realm. His chances were helped by his presence on the spot immediately following Louis's passing. Before the ill-fated hunting trip, Louis had called an assembly at Senlis to consider allegations of infidelity against Archbishop Adalbero of Reims (969–89). And as the magnates started to gather—some only just apprised of Louis's death—Hugh was able to seize the initiative, ensuring that the succession would take place on his terms.

Writing shortly after these events (991 × 996), Richer of Reims reports that the king had wished to be buried alongside his father at Saint-Remi, but was now interred at Compiègne, the prize foundation of his great-great-great-grandfather Charles the Bald (840–77). The grounds were that Compiègne was considerably nearer.[2] These remarks are sometimes put down to partisanship—Richer being a monk of Saint-Remi—but the rushed burial is not the only sign of haste. Hugh was quick to intervene in favour of Adalbero at the planned assembly, now relocated to Compiègne for the funeral, making sure that the archbishop was cleared of all charges (against the dead king's desires). Adalbero, in turn, backed Hugh's election a week or so later, now back at Senlis. Senlis lay within the sphere of influence of Hugh's family, the Robertians; and according to Richer, the newly elected king was consecrated at Noyon less than a week later (1 June). Unlike Compiègne—or, for that matter, Saint-Remi—Noyon was not a traditional royal site; indeed it was not even a metropolitan see (though Archbishop Adalbero did preside). The impression,

---

2. Richer of Saint-Remi, *Historiae*, IV.5, ed. Hoffmann, 234–35. On the dating: Hoffmann, 'Historien Richers', 447–55.

therefore, is one of improvisation. Even if we disregard Richer's testimony, as some are inclined to do, and place the inauguration somewhat later, Hugh was on the throne by early July. All indications are of a swift *coup de main*.[3] (By way of comparison, Henry II of Germany was only consecrated five months after Otto III's death in 1002, and even Conrad II had to wait seven and a half weeks in 1024.)

Though not a Carolingian, Hugh was descended from kings: from the Robertian Odo (888–98), who had held fort against the vikings in the late ninth century, when the infant Charles the Simple (898–922) was deemed too young to rule; and from Odo's younger brother, Robert I (922–23), who had deposed Charles in the early 920s, only to die before securing his rule. He was also the son of Hadwig, the sister of Otto I, and was thus royal on both sides of the family.[4] More importantly, Hugh enjoyed a dominant position between the Seine and the Loire, bordering on the royal heartlands.[5] This meant that the duke was a known entity at a time when the distinctions between the France and Germany began to harden; it also meant that he was poised to strike when the opportunity arose. Not surprisingly, Hugh was opposed by Charles of Lotharingia, and it would be the middle years of his son's reign before the new Capetian dynasty (as it came to be known) could sit comfortably on the throne.

Matters were further complicated by the weakened state of the realm. The effective control of the late Carolingians had been limited to what was known as Francia, a compact region between the Seine and the Meuse. Elsewhere, they depended heavily on the support of lay and (especially) ecclesiastical associates. One of the most important of these was the archbishop of Reims, who since the late ninth century had claimed the right to consecrate a new monarch. Stationed on the Vesle, a sub-tributary of the Oise, running down into the Seine, Reims overlooked the strategic border region of Lotharingia between the French and German realms. Duke Hugh had mixed relations with the last two Carolingian rulers, and his chances were considerably enhanced by the difficulties the kings had encountered with Adalbero of Reims, who was (as noted above) facing charges of infidelity in May 987. Adalbero hailed from a prominent noble family in Upper Lotharingia and had opposed Lothar's and Louis's efforts to retake the region (which had passed into East Frankish hands in the 920s).[6] The candidature of Charles was not in the archbishop's interests, and Adalbero was among the first to throw in his lot with Hugh. (It

---

3. Richer of Saint-Remi, *Historiae*, IV.11–12, ed. Hoffmann, 237–40. See further Lemarignier, 'Autour de la date'; Bautier, 'L'avènement d'Hughes Capet'; Brühl, *Deutschland-Frankreich*, 589, 594–96. As will be clear, I incline to the view of Lemarignier.

4. Cf. K. J. Leyser, '987'.

5. Sassier, *Hugues Capet*, 122–75. Hugh Capet's influence may, however, be overestimated by Sassier; certainly he never reached the same heights as his father.

6. Bur, 'Adalbéron'. Cf. MacLean, 'Shadow Kingdom'.

was he who spoke decisively in Hugh's favour at the Senlis election.) This was crucial. If Noyon was an unorthodox place of coronation, the involvement of the archbishop of Reims gave this event a much-needed seal of approval.

Yet consecration was just the first step. As the fate of Hugh's ancestors showed, it would take considerable effort—not to mention much good fortune—if he was to make the leap to royal status permanent. It is for this reason that Hugh, scarcely on the throne, sought to have his son, the future Robert the Pious (996–1031), crowned. Here Hugh faced stiff opposition, since many—including Adalbero—preferred to adopt a 'wait and see' policy towards the new dynasty. But Hugh was eventually able to prevail, using a planned expedition to the south as grounds. And so at Christmas 987, Robert was duly consecrated by Adalbero. This took place at Orléans, the birthplace of the young prince and the closest thing to a Robertian capital. Here Hugh's writ ran unfettered, supported and sustained by the local bishop, Arnulf—the same Arnulf who would trouble Abbo so.[7] In fact, if Adalbero was the public face of Hugh's accession, Arnulf of Orléans was its other chief architect. It was to Arnulf's hands that Hugh entrusted Charles of Lotharingia when the latter was captured in 991; and it was Arnulf who would lead the charge for Hugh at the controversial council of Saint-Basle-de-Verzy (17–18 June 991), when the king sought to depose Adalbero's contumacious successor (another Arnulf).[8]

Yet if Hugh had powerful allies in Adalbero and Arnulf, he had equally dangerous enemies—and not just in Lotharingia. Among these were probably Seguin, the archbishop of Sens (977–99). Sens lay 110 km (68 miles) upriver from Paris on the Yonne, another of the many affluents of the Seine. It often competed with Reims for royal favour and prestige, as symbolized by the right to consecrate a new king.[9] It was Walther of Sens (887–923) who had anointed Hugh's ancestors in the late ninth and early tenth centuries, while their Carolingian counterparts were all crowned by archbishops of Reims. But since Adalbero now backed the Robertians, these roles were reversed, and Seguin may initially have sympathized with Charles. Other magnates' interests were equally ill served by Hugh's accession. Foremost here were Albert of Vermandois and Odo of Blois (the latter a former associate of Hugh). It was with the assistance of these two that Charles invaded northern France in 988, taking the strategic fortification at Laon. This was no laughing matter. Laon holds a commanding position north-west of Reims, towering over the surrounding countryside and controlling traffic along the Ardon, a sub-tributary of the Oise (and thus of the Seine). Yet its importance was more than strategic. It was at Laon that Charles's grandfather, Louis IV (936–54), had been crowned king in

7. Bautier, 'De Robert le Fort'. Cf. Bautier, 'L'hérésie d'Orléans'.

8. Lake, 'Arnulf of Orléans'. See also Riché, 'Arnoul, évêque d'Orléans'.

9. Roberts, 'Flodoard', 223–30. See also Roberts, 'Construire', 21–24; Depreux, 'Saint Remi'; McNair, 'A Post-Carolingian Voice'.

936 with the support of Hugh's father, Hugh the Great (d. 956), re-establishing the Carolingian dynasty following the fourteen-year interregnum of Robert I (922–23) and Raoul of Burgundy (923–36).[10] This was thus a site redolent of Carolingian legitimacy and of Robertian fidelity. To set up camp here was to make a statement. Further gains were not forthcoming, however.

It was at this point, in mid-January 989, that Adalbero died. For Hugh, the timing could not have been worse. Reims was not only the kingdom's most important bishopric; it formed a natural bridge between Charles's base in Lower Lotharingia and the royal heartlands north and east of the Seine. It was imperative that Hugh find a replacement who could wield the same kind of authority as Adalbero, ideally with the same tact. The obvious candidate was the archbishop's learned secretary, Gerbert, who had done much to place the school of Reims on the map in recent years (Hugh had sent his own son Robert to study there). But for all his undoubted skill, Gerbert had earned enmity as well as adulation during his time at Reims. Another candidate was therefore preferred: Lothar III's illegitimate son Arnulf (Arnulf being the Carolingian dynasty's name of choice for bastard offspring). This was a high-risk option. It had the potential to isolate Charles from his few remaining friends and supporters, but risked leaving Reims vulnerable when Hugh needed it most. The king was well aware of the danger, yet decided to take the plunge. By way of security, however, he demanded a written oath of fidelity from Arnulf, a matter which would later come back to haunt the archbishop.[11] If Hugh hoped this would do the trick, he was sorely disappointed. By summer, Arnulf had indeed turned coat, allowing his uncle Charles to take Reims and leaving the Île-de-France dangerously exposed.

Hugh now moved swiftly, the result being a stalemate lasting much of the next two years. It was only thanks to another act of deception—that of Bishop Adalbero of Laon (977–1030/1), the deceased archbishop's nephew and namesake—in early spring 991 that Hugh was able to get the upper hand. The younger Adalbero had been acting as intermediary between the two sides and now used this position to seize Charles and Arnulf, handing them over to Hugh. The former was imprisoned at Orléans, under the watchful eye of the local bishop Arnulf.[12] The latter, meanwhile, was dragged before the synod of Saint-Basle (17–18 June) to face charges of oath-breaking. This was a show trial. Hugh had already sought papal dispensation for Arnulf's deposition. And while this had not been forthcoming, he was not going to let the opportunity slip. So long as Charles was alive and Arnulf in office, Hugh could not sit comfortably on the throne; they had to go. The presidency of Seguin of Sens, who had now accommodated himself to the new regime, gave the ensuing

---

10. Flodoard, *Annales*, s.a. 936, ed. Lauer, 63–64.
11. Richer of Saint-Remi, *Historiae*, IV.28–29, ed. Hoffmann, 250–51.
12. Adémar of Chabannes, *Chronicon*, III.30, ed. Bourgain, 150.

council a veneer of impartiality. But the remaining bishops were avowed supporters of Hugh, and there could be little doubt as to the result. The king and his son (and co-ruler) Robert had called the council and remained nearby during the deliberations; their imprimatur is clear throughout.

The case for the prosecution was led by none other than Arnulf of Orléans. And if our main account of these events, written some years later by Gerbert (Adalbero's old secretary and now Archbishop Arnulf's replacement at Reims), is to be trusted (a big 'if'), Bishop Arnulf was followed by most of the other bishops in attendance. Some expressed uncertainties as to the competence of an ecclesiastical council over secular affairs (the charge being infidelity); others were concerned about the legality of the written oath of fidelity exacted from Archbishop Arnulf in the first place. But none took up his case in uncertain terms. When the bishop of Orléans spoke again, Arnulf urged the defence to make its case. At this point, Abbo of Fleury spoke up. He was backed by two others, a fellow abbot called Romnulf and a scholar (*scolasticus*) of Auxerre called John. That some defence should be made was clear; the form it would take was not. Significantly, none of the bishops present joined them. And though Richer speaks of 'many' ('plures') who were sympathetic to the cause, there was evidently a degree of reticence.[13] Abbo and his associates were breaking ranks. His abbey lay within the Robertian heartlands, in Arnulf's diocese of Orléans; and it was a royal monastery, whose immunity Hugh had recently confirmed. Abbo might, therefore, have been expected to toe the line. Yet as the nature of Abbo's intervention reveals, he was not so much a partisan of Charles—all indications are that he and Fleury accepted the new dynasty—as a proponent of papal authority. Abbo's problem lay in matters of procedure. Archbishop Arnulf should have been restored to Reims before facing summons; the pope should then have been informed; and the final decision should have been left to a general synod under papal oversight (rather than a local one, such as the Saint-Basle council). What made Abbo and his associates uncomfortable were the wide-ranging powers being claimed by the French episcopate, powers which they believed rightly belonged to the bishop of Rome.

Abbo was speaking with conviction, and the works he penned in subsequent years present a similarly Romano-centric view of the Latin church. But he was also representing a view of the episcopate amenable to his own monastery. As noted, Abbo had much to fear from unbridled episcopal power, and it is significant that he was backed by at least one other abbot. It is also

13. Gerbert of Aurillac, *Acta synodi Remensis ad Sanctum Basolum*, chs 1–23, ed. Hehl, *Konzilien Deutschlands*, 391–417 (no. 44A); Richer of Saint-Remi, *Historiae*, IV.67, ed. Hoffmann, 277–78. On the events: Riché, *Gerbert d'Aurillac*, 126–40; Huth, 'Erzbischof Arnulf von Reims'; and on our accounts: Glenn, *Politics and History*, 276–84; Lake, *Richer of Saint-Rémi*, 130–42, 204–8.

no coincidence that, in upholding papal prerogatives, Abbo was challenging Arnulf of Orléans. He and Arnulf had a fraught relationship, and it was to evade interference from the bishop of Orléans that the monks of Fleury would resort to forgery in later years. The result was a set of false papal privileges, intended to remove Saint-Benoît from the control of the local diocesan bishop. To understand how and why, we must turn from national to local affairs, appreciating the delicate balance of secular and ecclesiastical power within the Orléanais.

Abbo, Arnulf and Fleury

By the time of the Saint-Basle synod, Abbo was a well-known figure. Like Gerbert of Aurillac—alongside Bishop Arnulf, Abbo's main opponent there—the Fleuriac abbot came from modest origins, earning promotion on account of his learning. He had entered Fleury as a youth and received most of his formal education there, with stints at Reims and Paris for further studies. Such a peripatetic life was becoming increasingly common among intellectual luminaries, and Gerbert enjoyed a similarly varied ecclesiastical *cursus honorum*. But while the latter spent much of his later life between schools and sees, Abbo made Fleury his base, as befitted a reformed monk, always returning there after sojourns elsewhere. At Saint-Benoît, he soon rose to the respectable post of schoolmaster, garnering a reputation for his abilities as scholar and teacher. Schoolmasters frequently rose to higher dignities; and when the abbatial office became vacant in 985, Abbo seems to have harboured realistic hopes of promotion. Initially, these were foiled, as a certain Oylbold was elected in his stead. Abbo's decision to accept an invitation to teach at Ramsey in the English fenlands—one of the many new monastic foundations of Edgar's reign—at this point was almost certainly a response to this disappointment.[14] He would not, however, have to wait long for a second chance. By 987, Abbo had been recalled by Oylbold, who may have been ailing. Certainly early in the following year Oylbold was dead and Abbo elected abbot in his place—though not without opposition, as his biographer notes.[15]

This was a critical moment for Fleury. The monastery was among France's largest and most influential, a position it owed in no small part to the presence of the relics of Benedict of Nursia (d. 547), the father of western monasticism. These had been transferred to the Loire valley from Benedict's abandoned foundation at Monte Cassino in the later seventh century; now they made Saint-Benoît a natural point of interest for reformers, who were keen to channel Benedict's legacy. The most famous of those to make their way there was Odo of Cluny (927–42), who reportedly reformed the centre in the

14. Mostert, 'Le séjour d'Abbon'.
15. Aimoin, *Vita Abbonis*, ch. 7, ed. Bautier and Labory, 58–60.

930s (an event which may, however, have left less of a mark than Odo's biographer would have us believe).[16] It was to Saint-Benoît, too, that many of the English reformers turned, including Oswald of York, Ramsey's founder, and Osgar, Æthelwold's successor at Abingdon. Its position on the north bank of the Loire, straddling the major river and overland routes between Le Mans, Tours, Paris and Auxerre, meant that the monastery also had an important part to play in regional and national politics. Here it was in the unique (and challenging) positon of being a traditional royal monastery within the Robertian heartlands. Already in the 930s there are signs of competing interests in the centre. And Fleury's reform by Odo, instigated by Hugh the Great (Hugh Capet's father), may have been an attempt to bring it into the Robertian fold. This would explain why the newly restored Archbishop Hugh of Reims (925–31, 940–46)—who was backed by Duke Hugh—sought out Odo's co-abbot and successor, Archembald of Fleury, to reform Saint-Remi in the mid-940s.[17] Yet if intended to secure Robertian influence, these efforts were no more than partially effective. Both Lothar III and Louis V confirmed the abbey's prized immunity—in the latter case, in one of only two surviving acts of the king—and the late Carolingians continue to loom large in Aimoin's contemporary continuation of Adrevald's *Miracles of Saint Benedict*, an account of the miraculous interventions of the abbey's patron.[18] Evidently the abbot and monks still sought out—and received—royal patronage.

The accession of Hugh in 987 placed Saint-Benoît in an awkward position. As a royal monastery, it naturally looked to the king for succour; however, it had not been among Hugh's backers to date. This explains the ambivalent position the early Capetians adopted towards the centre. Hugh confirmed Fleury's immunity in 987, as his Carolingian predecessors had before him; but Robert did not, and there are signs of strain.[19] These were partly a product of local power constellations. As we have seen, Arnulf of Orléans was one of Hugh's leading supporters, and he continued to enjoy good relations with Hugh's son Robert. Arnulf was also a figure of considerable local standing, having succeeded his uncle to the episcopal throne. The problem here was one of proximity. Arnulf's seat at Orléans lay just 40 km (25 miles)—less than a day's travel—downstream from Fleury, far too close for comfort. This was

16. John of Salerno, *Vita S. Odonis*, III.8, PL 133, cols 80–81. See Nightingale, 'Oswald'; Rosé, *Construire*, 304–24.

17. Flodoard, *Historia Remensis ecclesiae*, IV.32, ed. Stratmann, 424, with Roberts, 'Narratives of Reform'.

18. *Recueil Lothaire et Louis V*, nos 27, 28, 34, 70; *Miracula S. Benedicti*, ed. Certain. See Koziol, *Politics of Memory*, 291–93.

19. *Recueil Fleury*, no. 69. See Koziol, 'Conquest of Burgundy', 205–6 (with n. 106). The only securely attested diploma of Robert for the abbey, sadly no longer extant, concerns the monastery's holdings around Pithiviers, for which his father had also issued a diploma: *Recueil Philippe Ier*, no. 55 (mentioning the Robert *deperditum*).

a time when bishops across western Europe began to extend their influence beyond their urban seats, and Arnulf was no exception. His ninth-century predecessor Theodulf (c. 798–818) had doubled as bishop and abbot; now Arnulf sought to channel this example, much to the monks' dismay. Hugh's dependence on Arnulf only served to fan the flames.

Similarly important were transformations in the nature and function of royal authority at this juncture. As rulers receded somewhat from the picture, bishops sought to use their formal powers of oversight to increase influence over their monastic neighbours, particularly those (like Fleury) which had previously been independent. Abbots, for their part, were keen to escape such interference. These processes can be observed in the Orléanais.[20] Smaller monasteries, such as Micy on the outskirts of modern Orléans, were already under effective episcopal control; it must have seemed like a matter of time until Fleury followed suit. Under Oylbold, there had already been problems. According to Aimoin, Arnulf was a fundamentally good bishop, but had it in for the monks of Saint-Benoît. The reason was that they only deferred to royal authority—at this point, still that of the late Carolingians—and would not submit to episcopal control. In order to teach them a lesson, one day Arnulf instructed his men to overrun abbatial vineyards on the outskirts of the city, preventing the brothers from harvesting their grapes. Wary of challenging Arnulf on his turf, the monks decided to invoke saintly assistance—a common tactic within monastic circles. Specifically, they placed the remains of Maurus and Frongentius, two of the community's lesser-known saints, into the reliquary of Saint Benedict. They then brought this out with them to harvest the grapes on following day. When asked whose remains they had in tow, the brothers boldly asserted that they were those of Benedict, out to defend his vines. This act of pious deception worked, and Arnulf and his men withdrew in the face of superior spiritual firepower.[21]

With the accession of Hugh, however, Arnulf's position strengthened; and with the death of Oylbold and contested election of Abbo, that of the monks weakened. It therefore comes as little surprise that the first event of Abbo's abbacy, as reported by his biographer (the same Aimoin), was an ambush at the hands of Arnulf's men, while en route to Saint-Martin in Tours—a journey which involved passing by (or through) Orléans. As previously, the abbot and monks were not in a position to fight fire with fire. Abbo reportedly refused to judge the malefactors; but the Lord still exercised justice (so says Aimoin), bringing about their untimely demise. Thanks to Abbo's own writings, we know that matters were not left entirely in the hands of the Almighty. Both Seguin of Sens (the local metropolitan, and no particular friend of the

20. Head, *Hagiography*, 211–55.

21. *Miracula S. Benedicti*, II.9, ed. Certain, 123–25. See further Barthélemy, *Chevaliers et miracles*, 138–53.

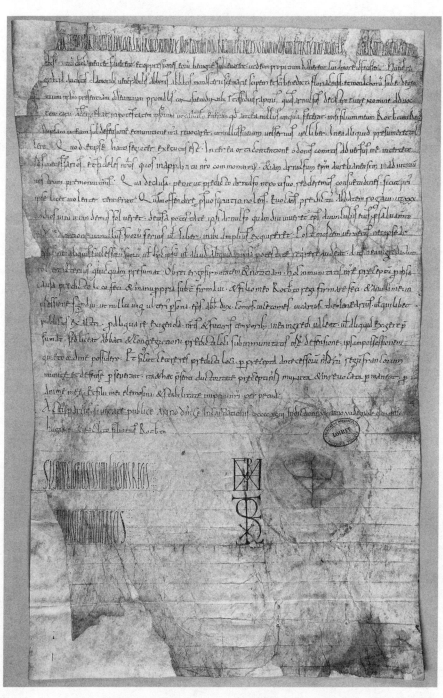

4.1 Robert the Pious's diploma restoring Yèvre to Fleury: Orléans, Archives
départementales du Loiret, H 37, © Archives départementales du Loiret

Capetians) and Odo of Chartres (Abbo's northern neighbour) excommunicated the abbot's attackers, apparently to little avail.[22]

Further details of Abbo's relationship with Arnulf emerge from a diploma
of 993 in favour of Fleury. In this, King Hugh attempts to settle a dispute over
of Yèvre-la-Ville, an estate about 40 km (25 miles) north of the abbey. The
bishop's nephew, confusingly another Arnulf, had laid claim to local payments
at Yèvre from his fortification just to the north (Yèvre-la-Châtel)—wrongly,
in the eyes of the monks. The latter did as the inmates of any self-respecting
royal monastery would, and appealed to the king. But Hugh's response was
equivocal. He acknowledged the brothers' rights, yet in recognition of Bishop
Arnulf's service in ongoing conflicts with Odo of Blois (d. 996), sought compromise. Fleury's claim to Yèvre-la-Ville would be upheld, but Arnulf would
continue to receive a set income during his uncle's lifetime. This is a most
singular act which, unusually for Fleury (and fortunately for us), survives as an
authentic original, allowing closer scrutiny (Illustration 4.1). It is laid out like
a standard late Carolingian diploma, with parchment taller than it is wide and
impressive elongated script in the first and last lines. But its contents break
all the rules of West Frankish diplomatic. It is framed as a formal statement
of royal authority, yet after the opening preamble all semblance of objectivity
is dropped, and the remaining text reads more like the informal third-person
transaction notices which were gaining popularity in France in these years.
Here the conflict is described in the past tense and presented emphatically
from Fleury's standpoint: Arnulf's exactions are wanton and unjust, the
monks' rights are acknowledged, and even the compromise is excused by reference to Hugh's recent difficulties with Odo of Blois. This strongly suggests that
the local brothers were responsible for this text, a conclusion which sits well
with its rather unusual script. The scribe is clearly unaccustomed to such work
and has struggled to adjust his native book hand to the longer ascenders and
descenders demanded of diplomatic minuscule (a script slowly abandoned in
French diplomas as we move into the eleventh century). A number of odd
archaisms (open a; the ligatures on ro, rt and nt) similarly suggest a copyist
new to his task, attempting to mimic earlier forms (Illustration 4.2). There can
be little doubt that we are hearing voice of Saint-Benoît here.[23]

Hugh was trying to have his cake and eat it, and the monks were putting the best spin on an awkward compromise. The king valued (and needed)
Arnulf's support, for all that Fleury's well-being should have been his concern. The situation was further complicated by Hugh's dispute with Odo of
Blois, in which Arnulf of Orléans was one of his main backers (as the diploma

---

22. Aimoin, *Vita Abbonis*, ch. 8, ed. Bautier and Labory, 62–64. Cf. Abbo, *Liber apologeticus*, PL 139, col. 469.

23. *Recueil Fleury*, no. 70, Orléans, Archives départementales du Loiret, H 37, with
Guyotjeannin, 'Diplôme de Hugues Capet'. See also Guyotjeannin, 'Surinterprétation'.

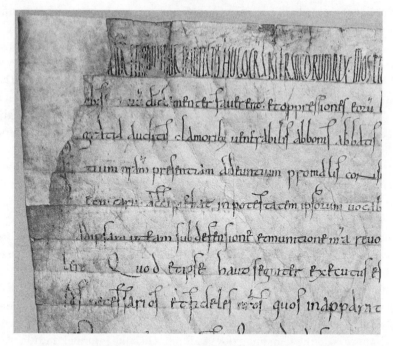

4.2 Script of Robert the Pious's Yèvre diploma: Orléans, Archives
départementales du Loiret, H 37, © Archives départementales du Loiret

emphasizes). It is hard not to read the resulting text, whose preamble underlines the royal responsibility to respond with clemency to petitions of churches
suffering oppression, and whose narrative excursus makes much of the 'evil
customs' ('malae consuetudines') and 'incessant plundering' ('assiduae rapi-
nae') the brothers have suffered, as rhetorical compensation for the restrained
terms of Hugh's concession. This was not, however, entirely empty rhetoric.
By framing Arnulf of Yèvre's actions in terms of violence, the monks of Fleury
responded to the changing landscape of later tenth- and eleventh-century law
and order. In these years, lordly power bulked ever larger, as new power structures crystallized out of the old Carolingian order—developments traditionally
framed in terms of a 'Feudal Revolution' or transformation (in French, *mutation féodale*). As part of this process, lordship and property-holding became
more closely aligned. In response, litigants turned to accusations of violence
as a means of bypassing the fraught world of claim and counterclaim. It was
easier to prove physical threat than ancient ownership, especially when the
boundaries of local jurisdiction were fluid and increasingly defined by landholding; disputes about land and income thus became ones about violence.[24]

24. McHaffie, 'Law and Violence'. On 'Feudal Revolution', see below, Conclusions,
269–72.

The latter months of 993 saw further disruption between monastery and bishopric. A tract on the dating of Advent (the elaborate liturgical celebrations leading up to Christmas) reports that problems emerged when the canons of Orléans visited Fleury to celebrate the feast of the reburial of Benedict's relics (4 December)—a deeply symbolic festival for the community. The difficulties arose from the fact that the canons had begun Advent on Sunday 26 November and were expecting to observe the liturgical celebrations for the second week of the season, whereas the monks (more properly, in the author's eyes) had only started Advent the previous day. The differences soon became apparent. As the monks were still within eight days (the octave) of the commencement of Advent, Fleury custom dictated that they should start the day with the mass for Advent Sunday. Upon realizing this, the canons began to mutter and accuse the brothers of neglect. Eventually, the matter had to be brought before a church council, where the monks, 'armed with the authority of the fathers' ('patrum auctoritate armati'), were able to prevail.[25]

Given the fragmentary nature of the Fleury archive, which was sacked in the French Wars of Religion (1562) and widely dispersed thereafter, these isolated incidents must stand for a wider set of conflicts and tensions. The Yèvre charter, the oldest to survive from the abbey intact, bears a late tenth- or early eleventh-century endorsement 'Abbo 31' ('Abbo XXXI'). This suggests that it was once one of at least thirty other documents of Abbo's abbacy, giving some sense of the scale of losses.[26] Partial compensation is offered by Abbo's own actions and writings, which we can follow in some detail. As we have seen, he intervened strongly in favour of papal authority at Saint-Basle (991), in terms which speak of a desire to fend off episcopal encroachment. And this was but the first of a series of high-profile interventions. The next came at a synod at Saint-Denis, just north of Paris, in 993 or 994. Here the bishops railed against the possession of tithes by laymen and monks, who were not in a position to undertake pastoral care (the original raison d'être for these exactions). Such concerns were common in these years and, as before, Abbo was quick to leap to the defence of the monastic party. This time his intervention was cut short: news of the bishops' aims quickly spread to the monks and laymen in attendance, leading to a riot and the forced adjournment of the synod.[27] The resulting turmoil may have prevented Abbo's worst fears from materializing, but his opponents were swift to jump on the opportunity, painting the abbot as a fomenter of discord. In response, Abbo took up quill, writing a justificatory

25. Bern of Reichenau(?), *Ratio generalis de initio adventus Domini*, ed. Parkes. As Parkes notes, the author was probably Thierry of Amorbach. See also Blume, *Bern von Reichenau*, 63–68; Parkes, *Making of Liturgy*, 185–87, 202–3.

26. Orléans, Archives départementales du Loiret, H 37, with Guyotjeannin, "*Penuria scriptorum*", 17.

27. Aimoin, *Vita Abbonis*, ch. 9, ed. Bautier and Labory, 70–74, with Constable, *Monastic Tithes*, 79–85. More generally: Eldevik, *Episcopal Power*.

treatise for Kings Hugh and Robert: his *Liber apologeticus* (Book of defence). Here Abbo ranges widely, framing his disputation as part of a broader reflection on church and society. Still, there is no mistaking the purpose. Abbo notes the unjustified claims which have been made against him and the many attacks, physical and verbal, he has suffered. He also takes the opportunity to present his ideal society, one in which the three orders (of each gender)— laymen, clerics and monks—live in harmony, with the last of these atop the moral-spiritual pyramid, backed by firm but fair royal authority. Finally, in a closing exhortation, Abbo encourages the kings to call councils to consider the pressing issues of the age, including the nature of the Holy Spirit, heresies about the end of time and the correct date for the start of Advent (a matter which, as we have seen, had placed him at odds with Arnulf's canons).[28] In doing so, Abbo deftly sidesteps the thorny question of tithes, encouraging Hugh and Robert to look at the 'big picture'.

Nor did Abbo leave matters there. In the following years, he drew up a collection of canon (i.e., ecclesiastical) law for Hugh and Robert (his *Collectio canonum*). We know he had been gathering canonical and patristic texts for some time—at the Saint-Basle council, Abbo and his associates deployed the Pseudo-Isidorian decretals to good effect—but recent controversies now encouraged him to put these into a more formal guise. The opening address makes the purpose clear: having brought these materials together for his own defence, the abbot thought it worth sending them to the kings, so that 'the senate of monks [might] be ever safe' ('monachorum senatum semper salvum esse'). This was, in other words, not a general reference work, but a specific tool of defence. As in the *Apologeticus*, the subjects touched upon range widely—and go well beyond the strictly monastic—but recurring themes are the independence of the clerical and (above all) monastic orders. In later years, Abbo would come back to the subject, producing a streamlined and augmented canon law collection for a fellow abbot (probably Gauzbert of Saint-Julien, Tours). The message of both works is clear. As the 'most pious defenders' ('piissimi defensores') of the monks (so the preface to the *Collectio*), it behoved Hugh and Robert to uphold the independence of the monasteries within their domains.[29]

These works are traditionally read as signs that Abbo was starting to gain traction at court,[30] but this is far from clear. That the abbot wrote to kings does not mean that they listened. In certain respects, political developments in the mid-990s did play into Abbo's hands. At some point before 995, Charles

28. Abbo, *Liber apologeticus*, PL 139, cols 461–72. See Mostert, *Political Theology*, 48–51, 87–107; Riché, *Abbon*, 146–60; Dachowski, *First among Abbots*, 133–43.

29. Abbo, *Collectio canonum*, pref., PL 139, cols 473–74, with Roumy, 'Remarques'. See also Abbo, *Epistola* 14, PL 139, cols 440–60.

30. E.g., Mostert, *Political Theology*, 55; Riché, *Abbon*, 161–63; Winandy, 'Äbte und Bischöfe', 345–46.

of Lotharingia passed away, removing the main threat to Hugh and Robert (and reducing their dependence on Arnulf, the duke's gaoler).[31] Similarly significant was Hugh's own death (23 × 25 October 996) and Robert's subsequent marriage to Bertha, the widow of Odo of Blois. This involved a rejigging of Capetian alliances, with Robert swapping his father's Flemish pact—cemented by his first marriage to Rozala (Susana)—for one with the house of Blois to the west. This had obvious implications for the Orléanais. One of the main reasons for compromise over Yèvre had been the support Arnulf accorded Hugh against Odo; with Blois now falling into line, Abbo might hope for a change of tune. Still, the concrete evidence for Abbo's growing influence is remarkably elusive. Beyond a letter of Gerbert of Aurillac to Constantine of Micy, indicating that the monastic and lay party had indeed prevailed in the aftermath of the Saint-Denis council—a fact which may owe as much to the interests of Hugh and Robert's lay supporters (not to mention the monks of Saint-Denis) as to Abbo's principled stand—this evidence consists entirely of the abbot's own writings.[32] And these show few signs of wider reception. The *Collectio canonum* and *Liber apologeticus* each survive in a single manuscript (in the latter case, copied at Saint-Benoît), and neither is cited outside monastic circles. So while Abbo evocatively addresses Hugh and Robert as 'benevolent to our [i.e., the monastic] order' ('in nostrum ordinem benevolos'), it is hard not to feel that he is protesting too much. Like Hincmar of Reims in the later ninth century, Abbo was a parchment tiger, taking up pen precisely because his voice would not otherwise be heard.[33]

Certainly it was not all smooth sailing in these years. If Robert's marriage to Bertha had eased the local situation in the Orléanais, it created fresh problems elsewhere. As the king soon discovered, the new pope, Gregory V, was no more inclined to allow Robert's match—which fell within prohibited degrees of relation (i.e., was incestuous)—than his predecessor had been to accept the deposition of Archbishop Arnulf. For a long-time champion of papal authority such as Abbo, this made reconciliation difficult, if not impossible.

Between a Rock and a Hard Place: Abbo at Court and Curia

Faced with royal apathy and episcopal rapacity, Abbo did as a growing number of abbots would, and turned to Rome. This was not an entirely new approach. As the symbolic head of the Latin church, the bishop of Rome had long been accustomed to confirm the rights of local abbeys. And since conflicts between abbots and bishops were as old as the monastic order, these frequently find

---

31. Lot, *Les derniers Carolingiens*, 277–82.

32. Gerbert of Aurillac, *Epistola* 190, ed. Riché and Callu, 498–500.

33. Cf. Patzold, 'Konsens und Konkurrenz', 77–88.

mention in the resulting documents. Already Gregory the Great (590–604), a sometime monk, had intervened in favour of monasteries, and the later *Liber diurnus*—the book of form charters used in the papal chancery—contains formulae for the exemption and protection of such centres.[34]

The monks of Fleury were aware of the potential here. In 878, they had received a privilege from John VIII, one of the most active early popes in this regard. More recently, they had become reacquainted with papal protection through the services of Odo of Cluny. Cluny had well-established links to Rome, and one of the immediate effects of Odo's reform had been a papal privilege for the abbey, petitioned (and perhaps also drafted) by the reform-minded abbot. This not only confirmed Fleury's liberty, on terms similar to earlier privileges of Charles the Bald, and secured its landed endowment; it also includes elements of exemption, decreeing that such monastic rights should fall under the dominion of 'neither bishop nor canon, nor any abbot nor layman' ('aut episcopo aut canonico vel alicui abbati sive laico homini').[35] Here was a model worthy of emulation. Yet if these texts alerted Abbo to the prospect of papal protection, they also reminded him of its limitations. Odo's bull had not stopped Arnulf of Orléans's intrusions, nor had it prevented the bishop from supporting his homonymous nephew's claims to Yèvre (a centre explicitly mentioned in this text). Indeed, for all its generous terms—which go well beyond most of the period—Odo's privilege was frustratingly vague on the nature of the abbot's relationship with Rome and the local diocesan bishop. The precedent may have been encouraging, but there was much work to be done.

It is in this context that we must place the forged and authentic papal privileges for Fleury. If Hugh and Robert would not support Abbo, he and his monks would have to look elsewhere. Abbo had already championed the papacy's cause in 991. And if the pope had not immediately got wind of this, by 995 he certainly had. At this point, if not somewhat earlier, Gerbert of Aurillac had begun circulating his account of the Saint-Basle council, in which Abbo figures prominently. This soon attracted a response from the pope's legate north of the Alps, Leo of SS Bonifacio ed Alessio. The latter was an abbot himself, who had overseen the new (and distinctly reform-minded) monastery on the Aventine since 981. Starting in 992, Leo became the pope's representative of choice regarding conflicts over Reims. In this connection, Leo organized councils at Aachen (March/April 992) and Ingelheim (March 993), from which Hugh's bishops—at the king's request—remained distant. Pressure began to

34. *Liber diurnus*, V 32 (=C 29=A 24), V 86 (=C 71=A 66), ed. Foerster, 93–94, 164–67, 193–94, 286–87, 378–82 (note that the loss of a sheet of parchment in C means that C 71 does not survive). See further Rennie, *Freedom*.

35. JE 3182 (*Recueil Fleury*, no. 29; *Konzilien*, ed. Hartmann, Schröder and Schmitz, 142–44), JL 3606 (ZPUU 83), with Rosé, 'Odon de Cluny', 249–51, 265; Kortüm, *Zur päpstlichen Urkundensprache*, 259–61. See further Rosé, *Construire*, 384–403.

mount, however, and in early June 995 Gerbert appeared to defend himself at a third council at Mouzon. A month later (1 July 995), probably at Reims, these discussions were continued. Now Leo gained the important concession that a definitive settlement would be put off to a general council overseen by the pope—an event which, however, never materialized.[36] The ins and outs of these debates need not detain us; their importance lies in the fact that Leo and John XV will soon have learned of Abbo's activities in this connection. What is more, Leo and Abbo seem to have met, probably at the last of these councils. The two were fighting the same corner, and Abbo would later recall Leo's eloquence in a letter to the Roman abbot.[37]

Abbo's connections to the papacy were growing stronger by the day, and the opportunity to meet a leading papal adviser at Reims may have provided the final impetus he needed to make the fateful decision to turn to Rome. It was now clear that Abbo could expect no more than equivocal support from Hugh and Robert. And soon after the Reims council, he departed south. Abbo's biographer, Aimoin, describes the trip in detail. As he notes, Abbo's objective was to have the privileges of his church confirmed and renewed by the pope. Yet what Abbo experienced would shock him to the core. He did not encounter the sort of pope he ought to have on the throne of Saint Peter (so writes Aimoin); rather he found a man desirous of wealth and venal in all actions, who refused to lift a finger without an appropriate payment.[38] For a champion of papal primacy, this was a bitter pill, and Abbo later wrote of his experiences to Leo. He expressed profound disappointment that he had not seen the Roman abbot during his visit. He also spoke pointedly of how he 'found the Roman church deprived of a worthy shepherd' ('Romanam ecclesiam digno viduam pastore . . . offendi'), an ambiguous turn of phrase which has given rise to differing interpretations of Abbo's movements. Pierre Riché takes this as a reference to the papal vacancy between John XV (d. March 996) and Gregory V (consecrated 3 May 996), positing a second trip (of three) to Rome at this point—one unmentioned by Aimoin. In the light of Aimoin's own remarks, however, Abbo is may simply be expressing his disapproval of John, who was not in any way worthy of his post.[39] Whatever the correct interpretation, Abbo's first (and possibly also second) trip was an abject failure. Aimoin is quick to pin the blame on John. But there may be more to Abbo's experiences than meets the eye. Given the nature of the privilege he later secured from Gregory V, it is likely that Abbo requested wider-ranging rights than had previously been conferred on Fleury. He may, therefore, have run into

36. *Konzilien Deutschlands*, ed. Hehl, 470–72, 485–516 (nos 45, 48–50).

37. Abbo, *Epistola* 15, PL 139, col. 459.

38. Aimoin, *Vita Abbonis*, ch. 11, ed. Bautier and Labory, 88.

39. Abbo, *Epistola* 15, PL 139, cols 459–60, with Riché, *Abbon*, 203–5. See also Lot, *Études*, 266–79.

difficulties when queried about these precedents, much as Pilgrim had concerning Kremsmünster. Certainly, when Abbo next came to Rome, he was looking for a more ambitious privilege than those Saint-Benoît had hitherto received.

The changing political situation meant that Abbo soon found himself back in the Eternal City. John XV died in March 996, just as the young Otto III arrived in northern Italy. The future emperor then arranged for the appointment of his cousin Bruno to the papal throne. A scion of the Salian family we met in the first chapter, Bruno had been educated at the cathedral school of Worms and became the first non-Roman pope in living memory. Partly in response, he also became one of the first popes to take on a new (suitably Roman) pontifical name: Gregory (V).[40] For Robert, who had been at loggerheads with John over the deposition of Arnulf of Reims (the Jarndyce vs Jarndyce case of late tenth-century France), a new pope raised hopes of new priorities—and with these, of reconciliation. It was in this connection that he now sought out Abbo. Abbo was an obvious choice for mediator. As a known supporter of the papacy (and Archbishop Arnulf), his voice might be heard where others would not. Robert may also have had his prospective match with Bertha in mind. This too was a delicate matter, since Robert was related to Bertha spiritually and by blood: he was the godfather to one of the children from her first marriage, and the two shared great-grandparents in the form of Henry I and Mathilda of East Francia. Gerbert later reports that Leo of SS Bonifacio ed Alessio secured Arnulf of Reims's release in exchange for papal acknowledgement of this match; it is often presumed that Abbo was entrusted with a similar proposal at this point.[41]

Whatever Abbo may have made of the king's motives, he must have relished the chance to try his hand in Rome again. Change was in the air there. As noted, a new pope had ascended the throne of Saint Peter. And from Abbo's perspective, Gregory's choice pontifical name was most promising, suggesting an affinity for the pope's great sixth-century namesake (one of Abbo's own favourite authorities). Gregory then used his first council in late May to confirm his commitment to Arnulf of Reims's cause. In his letter to Abbot Leo around this time, Abbo expressed his approval of the new pontiff, 'composed entirely of virtues and wisdom' ('totum virtutibus et sapientia compositum').[42] The precise date of Abbo's second (or third) trip to Italy poses problems, however. The finer points need not concern us, but the matter is of some importance for ascertaining his (and Robert's) intentions. The difficulty lies in the fact that the privilege Abbo eventually received from Gregory V is dated

40. Cf. Scholz, *Politik—Selbstverständnis*, 416–21.

41. Gerbert, *Epistola* 181, ed. Riché and Callu, 456–64 at 458. See further Theis, *Robert le Pieux*, 79–87, 101–3.

42. Abbo, *Epistola* 15, PL 139, col. 460.

13 November 997, yet Aimoin clearly describes this being issued in Spoleto, where the pope was only to be found in autumn 996. As a general rule, Germanophone scholars, well versed in the pope's movements, have preferred to trust Aimoin over the exemption bull, while their Francophone counterparts, better schooled in the politics of the French court, have done the reverse.[43] If Abbo's business was indeed negotiating Robert's marriage, a later date is certainly preferable. Hugh Capet, who had opposed this match, was still alive in early autumn 996 (d. 23 × 25 October 996). And though we know that Robert and Bertha tested the waters before Hugh's death, asking Gerbert's thoughts on the subject, Bertha's first husband had only died on 12 March, leaving a very short space of time for Robert to have decided to wed Bertha (early spring), canvassed opinions at court (late spring/early summer), then entrusted Abbo (secretly?) with taking this request to the newly appointed Gregory V (mid- to late summer).[44]

These difficulties are, however, removed if we acknowledge that Abbo's voyage need not have had anything to do with Robert's marriage. Writing about a decade later, Aimoin is silent on the subject—diplomatically so, according to modern scholarship—and our only other source, a later letter of Gerbert, states that Abbot Leo (not Abbo) secured Arnulf's release in exchange for Gregory's acceptance of the king's union.[45] We know that Abbo was involved in the negotiations over Reims, since he wrote about this (and about Robert's resulting anger) to Gregory V upon his return; yet he, too, says nothing about the king's marriage in this connection.[46] In fact, the only source to mention Abbo in relation to Robert's second union, Helgaud's *Life* of the king, states that the abbot firmly opposed this. In the absence of other evidence, we would do well to take Helgaud at his word.[47]

If Karl Ferdinand Werner is correct, a set of additions to a Fleury copy of Bede's *Ecclesiastical History*—a work with much to say on the subject of incest—may confirm this reading. These include Isidore of Seville's remarks on consanguinity and a set of papal decrees on the matter. Unfortunately for Werner, the texts in question—which he only knew through a nineteenth-century library catalogue—are in the same ninth-century hand as the main text of the manuscript. What is more, they constitute a well-known eighth-century letter

43. Aimoin, *Vita Abbonis*, ch. 11, ed. Bautier and Labory, 88–92. See Lot, *Études*, 271–77; Uhlirz, *Jahrbücher*, ii, 518–25; Tessier, Review of Ramackers, 298–99.

44. Richer of Saint-Remi, *Historiae*, IV.108–9, ed. Hoffmann, 306–8. These constitute a set of late, notice-like additions to the autograph manuscript: Bamberg, Staatsbibliothek MS Hist. 5, fol. 57v.

45. Gerbert, *Epistola* 181, ed. Riché and Callu, 458. On Aimoin's 'diplomatic silence': Mostert, *Political Theology*, 59. See similarly Winandy, 'Äbte und Bischöfe', 352.

46. Abbo, *Epistola* 1, PL 139, col. 419.

47. Helgaud of Fleury, *Epitoma vite Robertii pii*, ch. 17, ed. Bautier and Labory, 92–96, with Hamilton, 'New Model'.

on incest, which is frequently transmitted alongside the *Ecclesiastical History* (the pope 'Gregory the younger' here being Gregory II [715–31], not Gregory V [996–99]).[48] While an immediate connection with Abbo is thus rendered improbable, the manuscript was available for consultation at Fleury in his day. And if the ex-schoolmaster had looked this way, it would only have confirmed his doubts.

There is, therefore, no obstacle to placing Abbo's journey in mid- to late 996, and much to be said in its favour. It is only at this point that his surprise at not encountering the pope in Rome—reported by Aimoin—can be understood, since Gregory was driven from the city in early autumn of the year. It is also only then that the dispute over Reims, which had begun to cool by late 997, was still a pressing concern. One further consideration speaks in favour of an early date. Thanks to a letter to Herveus, a sometime student of Abbo who became treasurer at Saint-Martin, Tours, we know that the canons of Tours had requested Abbo's intervention with the pope in an ongoing dispute with their local archbishop. Abbo's initial response had been equivocal. But a papal privilege for the canons survives from 29 September 996, only shortly before the Fleuriac abbot's arrival in Rome. As it is presently preserved, this text is a forgery of the late eleventh century, but there is every reason to believe that a genuine privilege of 996 lies behind it. The dating clause is correct for early autumn 996, and in 1075 Archbishop Radulf sent the original to the local abbot of Marmoutier, Bartholomew, because he could not decipher its 'Roman letters' ('Romana litterae'), a clear allusion to the distinctive curial script employed by the papal chancery (but rarely mastered elsewhere).[49] This indicates that these matters were being debated in mid-996, just as Abbo was preparing to depart. If the abbot of Fleury had indeed raised the matter with Gregory (or Abbot Leo)—perhaps by letter—this may explain why Archembald, the archbishop of Tours, went on to bless Robert's controversial marriage.

The only remaining problem is the correct date of Abbo's own bull. Here we would do well to follow Marco Mostert in positing a delay between when Abbo received formal approval for his abbey's exemption (perhaps including discussion of its terms) in autumn 996, and when he received a completed privilege to this effect in autumn 997.[50] A year may seem an unusually long gestation period for such a text, but finds ample parallels in royal and imperial documents of the period. It also resembles the later experiences of the monks of Corbie, who had their exemption confirmed by Leo IX (1049–54) at

48. Bern, Burgerbibliothek, Cod. 49, fols 248v–250v, with K.-F. Werner, 'Vorbilder', 211–12. On the letter, see Ubl, *Inzestverbot*, 241–44, with further literature.

49. JL 3870 (ZPUU 332). Bartholomew's letter is transcribed in Mabillon, *De re diplomatica*, 640. On script: Rabikauskas, *Römische Kuriale*, esp. 2–3; on questions of authenticity: Frank, *Klosterbischöfe*, 68–81; Gasnault, 'Étude', 39; and on the wider context: Farmer, *Communities of Saint Martin*, 37–62.

50. Mostert, 'Urkundenfälschungen', 305–6.

the famous council of Reims in early October 1049, but would have to wait till mid-April of the following year to receive a sealed bull to this effect.[51] Indeed, as Abbo himself seems to have been entrusted with drawing up the resulting privilege, it may be that he needed to consult his sources back in Fleury before completing it (the text cites a number of his favoured canonical authorities). Certainly Abbo was determined to make his case stick, and the final exemption is nothing short of a tract on monastic independence. Whether he came to Rome with an ambitious forged bull of Gregory IV (827–44) in order to elicit this, however, remains to be seen.

Establishing Exemption: Abbo's Privilege and its Afterlife

As reported by Aimoin, the high point of Abbo's journey came when he obtained Gregory V's approval for a new 'privilege of apostolic authority' ('privilegium . . . apostolicę auctoritatis'). This is clearly the confirmation sought on the first trip, and the biographer emphasizes that this was obtained without any money passing hands ('solum nullum pecunię . . . lucrum'), in pointed contrast to John XV's behaviour. Aimoin then outlines the salient features of the document: namely, that Bishop Arnulf of Orléans was to have no access to the abbey, unless invited; and that no bishop should be able to ban the celebration of the divine office there, even if all Gaul (i.e., France) should be placed under papal anathema. Evidently these rights were still controversial, since Aimoin goes on to justify them, providing precedents from the writings of Gregory the Great 'lest someone should consider that they [Gregory V and Abbo] . . . in doing this expressed a sentiment contrary to the rules of the sacred fathers' ('ne quis eos . . . existimet in hoc facto contraria regulis sanctorum sensisse patrum').[52]

A privilege along these lines survives for Fleury. And since first published by Christian Pfister in 1885, it has been clear that this was the subject of Aimoin's remarks. The text itself is addressed to all the bishops and faithful of France ('Gallia', the term preferred within ecclesiastical circles). It explains that the pope was told by Abbo about the foundation of his monastery, as well as the subsequent translation of Benedict's relicts to there and Emperor Charles's (the Bald, 843–77) later privilege for it. Gregory goes on to report that, at Abbo's request and with the consent of the bishops present, he has now seen fit to confirm the holdings of the monastery along with its immunity; to grant the abbot first place amongst all the abbots of France ('primus inter abbates Gallie'); to forbid all archbishops, bishops and clerics from entering the abbey or exercising priestly functions there, without the express

51. JL 4212 (PL 143, 641–42), with Morelle, 'Moines de Corbie', 201–4.
52. Aimoin, *Vita Abbonis*, ch. 12, ed. Bautier and Labory, 92–98.

permission of the abbot; and to confirm the monks' right of free abbatial election. This alone would be noteworthy, but Gregory continues, ordering the correct consecration of monks to priestly orders by the local bishop, who is not to require their subjection in exchange (it was common to elicit oaths of obedience on this occasion); decreeing that the abbot is only to be judged by a full provincial synod or the pope himself, and then is to have the right of appeal to Rome; ordaining that the abbot is to have the power of binding and loosing within the monastic precinct; instructing that those monks who have been promoted to clerical status are not to remain in the monastery or to exercise sacerdotal functions there; allowing for monks excommunicated on account of any pressing fault ('exigente culpa', a favoured turn of phrase of Gregory the Great) to receive communion at specific locations in the diocese; conceding that, even under interdict, masses may be celebrated at the abbey; and, finally, stipulating that the centre may accept monks from other monasteries and dismiss those not living according to the Rule.[53] This is a truly extraordinary text, and it is instructive to compare its contents with Aimoin's summary. As we have seen, the latter states that Bishop Arnulf was forbidden from entering the monastery, confirming what we might otherwise have inferred: that for all its general terms, the privilege was drawn up with one person in mind—the bishop of Orléans.

As noted above, there was a long tradition of popes confirming the holdings and independence of monasteries, in France as elsewhere. And Fleury had benefited from such favour, receiving early exemptions from John VIII (872–82) and Leo VII (936–39). But nothing like this had been seen before, at Fleury or elsewhere.[54] It removed Abbo and his successors almost entirely from episcopal oversight, allowing bishops to enter the monastic precinct and undertake duties there only with the abbot's express permission. In case of conflict, moreover, it ensures that the abbot can only be judged by a full provincial synod, and even then has the right of recourse to Rome. This considerably weakens the bishop's means of correction and coercion, and it is striking that the abbot is accorded the characteristically episcopal powers of binding and loosing within cloister walls. The result is a monastic island in a sea (or, indeed, see) of episcopal oversight. Similarly important is the freedom from excommunication and interdict (interdict being a ban on religious celebrations—the equivalent of excommunication for a region or realm). This speaks to Abbo's specific concerns in the later 990s. Abbo had been excommunicated by his opponents following the Saint-Denis synod—wrongly, in his eyes—and by autumn 997 France itself stood under threat of interdict, thanks

53. JL 3872 (ZPUU 335), first edited in Pfister, *Études*, lvii–lix. Cf. Gregory the Great, *Registrum epistularum*, e.g., VIII.14, IX.108, XI.24, ed. Norberg, 532, 660, 895, for Gregory's frequent recourse to 'exigente culpa'.

54. Johrendt, *Papsttum*, 118–32. See further Lemarignier, 'L'exemption'; Cowdrey, *Cluniacs*, 3–43; Falkenstein, *La papauté*, 1–61; Rennie, *Freedom*, 88–149 (highlighting, inter alia, John VIII's important role); B. Pohl, 'Problem of Cluniac Exemption'.

to ongoing struggles over Reims and Robert's marriage. (This is, incidentally, one of our earliest references to interdict.)[55] Less tangible, but no less significant, is the concession of abbatial primacy, rights which for a status-conscious prelate such as Abbo were far from trivial. More standard is the general confirmation of abbatial holdings, though in the light of recent conflicts with Arnulf of Yèvre, there may be an edge to this too. Perhaps the most distinctive element of the privilege is the right to accept monks from other houses and dismiss those failing to live up to standards. These details are taken from the bull issued upon Fleury's reform by Odo in 938, which had evidently impressed Abbo so, and they echo earlier privileges for Déols and Cluny, issued at Odo's behest. These measures place the abbey in a strong position vis-à-vis its neighbours, allowing the abbot to accept new recruits—a monk normally required his abbot's permission to move houses—and to prune those unsuitable for regular life.

Given what has been said, it is scarcely surprising that doubts have been expressed about this document; it seems to ventriloquize Abbo's deepest desires. Maurice Prou and Alexandre Vidier, who edited it along with the other Fleury charters in the early twentieth century, deemed the bull suspect on account of its extravagant terms, which were (to their minds) not in keeping with contemporary canon law norms. They also noted similarities with a later bull of Alexander II in favour of the abbey (dated 1072), which survives in its original format (Illustration 4.3). This led them to conclude that Abbo's privilege—along with two other closely related documents—was forged on the basis of the Alexander text. Yet, as Ferdinand Lot observed soon thereafter, the privilege must have been in existence in some form before 1072 (indeed, before 1022), since Aimoin mentions it. Lot therefore took a kinder view of the text, concluding that it was substantially authentic. Initial doubts proved hard to shift, however, and in 1958 Johannes Ramackers renewed the assault. Ramackers noted that the bull's stipulations concerning clerical ordination are absent in the confirmation of 1072, suggesting that these were later additions to an otherwise authentic text. Finally, in the 1980s, Mogens Rathsack went one step further, arguing that the entire privilege was one of a series of elaborate fakes produced by Abbo c. 998. Rathsack's interpretation was then followed by Harald Zimmermann, in his monumental edition of the tenth- and eleventh-century papal charters.[56] In more recent years, the more generous approach of Lot has prevailed. Marco Mostert has shown that the privilege is indeed Abbo's work, but far from being a later forgery (as Rathsack insisted)

55. Cf. Keygnaert, 'L'excommunication collective'.

56. Recueil Saint-Benoît, ed. Prou and Vidier, i, 185 n. 1; Lot, Études, 272–75; Papsturkunden, ed. Ramackers, 46–48; Rathsack, Fuldaer Fälschungen, 313–31 (reprising the arguments of the 1980 Danish original); Papsturkunden, ed. Zimmermann, 655–56. Alexander II's bull is JL 4708 (Recueil Fleury, no. 83), which survives as Orléans, Archives départementales du Loiret, H 29.

4.3 Alexander II's confirmation of Fleury's exemption: Orléans, Archives départementales du Loiret, H 29, © Archives départementales du Loiret

constitutes an authentic recipient product. This explains the recourse to formulation from earlier privileges in favour of Fleury; it also explains the use of so many of Abbo's favoured sources. What is more, since the use of these sources extends to those sections on ordination suspected by Ramackers, the entire text may be considered an authentic product of the later 990s.[57] Subsequent work on papal diplomatic has added weight to Mostert's conclusions. We now know that that recipient production—viewed so suspiciously

57. Mostert, 'Urkundenfälschungen'.

by Rathsack—was the norm in these years (even if the final text was normally copied out by papal scribes).[58] And it has been noted that the exalted rights claimed for Fleury find close parallels in the bull issued for Cluny in the following year. This may have been the first exemption of this nature, but it would not be the last.[59]

If Abbo's privilege is authentic, there can be no doubt that it keeps company with forgeries. As Prou and Vidier noted, it shares almost all of its formulation with a bull in the name of Gregory IV (827–44), and much of this also appears in a privilege of Benedict VII (974–83).[60] Neither of these texts can be accepted as is. For a start, in both, innovations of the later 990s are transposed onto earlier years. More to the point, between these privileges lie the authentic Fleury bulls of 878 and 938, neither of which shows any awareness of such rights or precedents. Yet if the fact of forgery is well established, its dating has proven trickier. As with most of the Fleury muniments, the Gregory IV and Benedict VII bulls only survive in later copies, most notably in the seventeenth-century copy of the (lost) cartulary of La Réole, a dependent priory of Fleury. Prou and Vidier were keen to place them after the Alexander II bull, as we have seen; but since Abbo's privilege is almost certainly authentic, we must entertain the possibility of an earlier date. In fact, on one key point the Alexander exemption agrees with the forgeries against Abbo's text, suggesting that they (or at least one of them) furnished the model in 1072. This, combined with borrowings from the authentic Leo VII privilege, allow us to narrow the date range to 938 × 1072, and in all probability 997 × 1072 (i.e., between the authentic Gregory V and Alexander II privileges).

This dating receives partial confirmation in the earliest witness to the Gregory IV privilege, copied onto spare leaves at the back of a Fleury manuscript (Illustration 4.4). Prou and Vidier were unaware of this, but Mostert drew attention to its existence in 1988. Based on similarities with a Fleury copy of Abbo's own abbreviated version of the *Liber pontificalis* (Book of pontiffs, the serial biography of popes), he was inclined to place the addition in the first third of the eleventh century, further tightening the possible timeframe for production.[61] Unfortunately, the dating of the *Liber pontificalis* manuscript is itself less secure than Mostert thought. This is traditionally placed in the imperial reign of Conrad II (1027–39), on the basis of its list of Roman emperors, which ends with Conrad. Yet all this proves is that the manuscript's exemplar is no younger than Conrad II's reign—or indeed the start of Henry

---

58. Kortüm, *Zur päpstlichen Urkundensprache*. See also Jarrett, 'Archbishop Ató'; J. Werner, *Papsturkunden*.

59. Cowdrey, *Cluniacs*, 3–43.

60. JE 2570 (*Recueil Fleury*, no. 18), JL 3803 (ZPUU 258).

61. Leiden, University Library, Voss. lat. Q 15, fol. 57r–v, with Mostert, 'Urkundenfälschungen', 299 (with n. 6). Cf. Mostert, *Library of Fleury*, 98 (entry BF 333), placing the manuscript more conservatively in the first half of the eleventh century.

4.4 Earliest copy of Fleury's forged Gregory IV exemption: Leiden, University Library, Voss. lat. Q 15, fol. 57r, © University Library, Leiden

4.5 List of emperors in an eleventh-century Fleury manuscript: Leiden, University Library, Voss. lat. F 96 I, fol. 24v, © University Library, Leiden

III's (1046). In fact, a second (coeval) hand has added Henry III to the list (Illustration 4.5), pointing more naturally to an origin in the middle years of the century (Henry's imperial reign being 1046–56).[62] In any case, the hand of the copy of the Gregory IV privilege is more advanced than that of the list (at least to these eyes), suggesting production in the second half of the century, and probably the third quarter. Particularly noteworthy features include the script's angularity and compression—only partially dictated by considerations of space—and the clear feet on the minims of m, all signs of the slow shift from Caroline to (Proto-)Gothic (Illustration 4.6).[63] This conclusion finds confirmation in other Fleury manuscripts of the period. Thus the script of the bull is clearly younger than that of the copy of Aimoin of Fleury's *Gesta Francorum* in the same codex (which itself can be no earlier than the late 990s); it is also younger than the three hands of the unique copy of Helgaud's *Life* of Robert the Pious, one of which is almost certainly authorial (1033 × 1041). The same is true of the two hands (one of which, again, is probably autograph)

62. Leiden, University Library, Voss. lat. F 96 I, fol. 24v, with Lieftinck, *Manuscrits datés*, no. 216.

63. Cf. Kwakkel, 'Biting, Kissing'.

4.6 Script of the earliest copy of Fleury's forged Gregory IV exemption: Leiden, University Library, Voss. lat. Q 15, fol. 57r, © University Library, Leiden

of the earliest copy of the *Life* of Gauzlin, produced in the following decade (1041×1044).[64] Some allowance must be made for the fact that the latter manuscripts are presentation pieces, and naturally more conservative in script. Greater similarity emerges with a poem concerning the death of an 'Abbot Rainald' (perhaps Rainier, d. 1060), inserted in the margins of one of the early copies of Abbo's grammatical treatise (*Quaestiones grammaticales*). Yet even here the hand of the bull looks somewhat younger, and a dating to the later 1060s or early 1070s seems reasonable (if not certain).[65]

The fact that the forged Gregory IV privilege is textually almost identical to the authentic Gregory V one would normally indicate that it was produced on this basis, but Mostert ingeniously argues the reverse. He suggests that the forgery was produced in the immediate run-up to Abbo's second Italian voyage (if not, in fact, some years earlier), with the intention of eliciting the

64. Leiden, University Library, Voss. lat. Q 15, fols 14r–55v; Vatican, BAV, Reg. lat. 566, fols 3r–22v; Vatican, BAV, Reg. lat. 592, fols 54r–75r.

65. Vatican, BAV, Reg. lat. 596, fol. 10v, with Dümmler, 'Aus Handschriften', 634–36. I am grateful to Ben Pohl and Lisa Fagin Davis for discussion here.

Table 3. Opening protocol of the Gregory IV and Gregory V bulls for Fleury

JE 2570 (*Recueil Fleury*, no. 18)	JL 3872 (ZPUU 335)
Igitur **cum propter multiplices ecclesię Dei cura, Gallicanam adeuntes regionem, ad gloriosum devenissemus imperatorum HLUDOVICUM, inter alia** suggessit auctoritati nostrę **idem serenissimus Augustus et** venerabilis **partium vestrarum** abba nomine Boso, ex cęnobio quod nominatur Floriacus, in **pago Aurelianensi,** quod idem monasterium quidam religiosus abba, Leodebodus nomine, monachis extruxerit in honorem Dei et sanctę genetricis MARIĘ nencon et beati principis apostolorum Petri quodque revelatione divina per monachos eiusdem loci ad Capuana provincia corpus illuc sancti Benedicti fuerit allatum ibique reverenter humatum, sicut manifestissima constat historia; nam propter stabilimentum monasticę religionis, pię memorię imperator Carolus, **pater eius,** per praeceptum suae auctoritatis eidem loco multa contulit et ab aliis collata testamento firmavit.	Igitur suggessit auctoritati nostre venerabilis abba nomine Abbo, ex cęnobio quod vocatur Floriacus, quod idem monasterium quidam religiosus abba, Leodebodus nomine, monachis extruxerit in honorem Dei et sanctę genetricis Marie necnon et beati principis apostolorum Petri quodque revelatione divina per monachos eiusdem loci ad Capuana provincia corpus illuc sancti Benedicti fuerit allatum ibique reverenter humatum, sicut manifestissima constat historia. Nam propter stabilimentum monastice religionis pie memorię imperator Carolus per praeceptum sue auctoritatis eidem loco multa contulit et ab aliis collata testamento firmavit

Gregory V bull.[66] And Mostert has been followed here by all subsequent scholarship.[67] But while such actions were common enough—one recalls Anno of Worms's immunity of 965—Mostert's arguments face a number of significant difficulties. For a start, the Gregory V bull makes no mention of a Gregory IV exemplar, as we might expect had this furnished the model. More to the point, there are a few small but significant discrepancies between the two texts, all of which suggest that the latter derives from the former, not vice-versa. It is worth considering these in detail.

The first concerns the opening preamble and historical excursus. Here the Gregory V text speaks of an earlier precept of an 'Emperor Charles' (= the Bald)—a reference lifted from the bull's John VIII exemplar—but the Gregory IV bull has been adjusted to refer to a privilege of Louis the Pious, followed by a more general allusion to an earlier precept of Louis's father, another 'Emperor Charles' (= Charlemagne, 768–814) (Table 3). Mostert argues that

66. Mostert, 'Urkundenfälschungen'. See also Mostert, 'Forgery and Trust', 53.

67. Head, *Hagiography*, 247; Jakobs, 'Zu den Fuldaer Papsturkunden', 36 n. 15; Rosenwein, *Negotiating Space*, 171; Riché, *Abbon*, 221–22; Dachowski, *First among Abbots*, 180; Morelle, 'Que peut-on savoir', 132–33; Rennie, *Freedom*, 124–25; Winandy, 'Äbte und Bischöfe', 347–48, 354.

Table 4. Details on abbatial election in the Gregory IV and Gregory V bulls for Fleury

JE 2570 (*Recueil Fleury*, no. 18)	JL 3872 (ZPUU 335)
Abba vero, qui ordinandus ibi est, cum electione fratrum, propter vitę meritum et honestatem morum et non propter turpia lucra seu par pecuniam eligatur, **et absque ulla calumnia a quocunque episcopo, prout sibi placuerit, benedicatur.**	Abba vero, qui ordinandus ibi est, cum electione fratrum, propter vite meritum et honestatem morum et non propter turpia lucra seu par pecuniam eligatur.

the forger of the Gregory IV bull (to his mind, Abbo) has simply confused the two Charleses here—a common enough mistake, as we have seen. But this is clearly not the case. Rather, he has realized that he cannot have an imperial diploma of Charles the Bald confirmed in 829, forty-six years before that emperor's coronation in Rome, so has had to improvise. Since a Louis the Pious diploma exists for Fleury, which itself mentions an earlier precept of his father (another 'Emperor Charles'), this offered the obvious solution. The forger could change the initial focus from Charles to Louis, then re-use the original reference to a precept of an 'Emperor Charles' to refer to Charlemagne.[68] In any case, the final Gregory V text follows that of the John VIII bull (their shared model) here, so must have had this—and not the Gregory IV counterfeit—as its immediate exemplar.

More significant is another divergence. In Pseudo-Gregory IV, the pope not only ordains that the abbot should be elected by the brothers on account of his merits and honest ways, rather than for filthy lucre or riches (thus far the Gregory V text); he also goes on to state that thereafter the abbot-elect 'should be consecrated without any calumny by whichever bishop he wishes' ('absque ulla calumpnia a quocunque episcopo, prout sibi placuerit, benedicatur') (Table 4). This addition considerably extends Fleury's rights, removing one of the few remaining elements of episcopal oversight. Again, the Gregory IV privilege can scarcely have been the model for the Gregory V one, since these details are lacking there. In fact, the first authentic papal privilege to confer such rights is that of Gregory V for Odilo of Cluny in 998, which itself builds on Abbo's exemption of 997. These prerogatives were later extended in John XIX's confirmation of Cluny's exemption in 1024, which also allows the abbot free choice of bishop to perform ordinations within the abbey. Elsewhere, however, such grants remained a rarity, at least until the second half of the century.[69] If these details had indeed been in Abbo's exemplar, it is hard

68. Mostert, 'Urkundenfälschungen', 300–301. For a convenient side-by-side comparison of the texts: ibid., 309–18. The Louis the Pious diploma is D L Fr 142, which is modelled on an immunity for Saint-Aignan (D L Fr 31), whence the reference to a prior privilege of Charlemagne.

69. JL 3896 (ZPUU 351), JL 4065 (ZPUU 558). See Cowdrey, *Cluniacs*, 32–36; Pohl and Vanderputten, 'Fécamp'. More generally: B. Pohl, 'Problem of Cluniac Exemption'.

to imagine why he would have left them out—and doubly so, if he had been responsible for their presence in the first place. Moreover, there is no evidence that abbatial consecration was a concern in Abbo's day. Unlike the other subjects covered in Pseudo-Gregory IV (and the authentic Gregory V), this finds no mention in Abbo's canon law collections or the *Liber apologeticus*. These details are, however, found in the Alexander II confirmation of 1072, suggesting that the Gregory IV text furnished the model here.

One final consideration points away from Abbo's involvement in the Gregory IV privilege. As Mostert already noted, this cites an extract from the *Register* of Gregory the Great—one of Abbo's favourite sources—in a different version from that in the Gregory V privilege. The readings of the latter accord with those in the copy of Gregory's *Register* that Abbo is known to have used, now preserved in two related manuscripts at the Bibliothèque nationale de France. Mostert argued that Abbo originally used a different text for his forgery (perhaps one with him while visiting the pope in Italy?), then reverted to his favoured version when he came to finalize the terms of the privilege back at Fleury. But a more natural reading is that we are dealing with two different individuals (albeit both based at Fleury), each with his own textual preferences.[70] We may even be able to identify the later forger's source. Pseudo-Gregory IV's rendering of letter XIII.11 in the *Register* (to the 'senators', priests and abbots of the Franks) shares this rare variant with a ninth-century fragment of the work which was indeed at Fleury. Sadly, the relevant section of the manuscript is now illegible, but according to the late nineteenth-century transcription by Albert Starzer it contained the same reading.[71] Since whichever text was used must have been present at Fleury by the eleventh century, this does not preclude Abbo's involvement (in fact, we know he had recourse to other versions of the *Register* upon occasion); but the impression once more is of distance between the abbot and forger.[72] Indeed, Mostert's main argument in favour of Abbo's authorship of the Gregory IV bull—its extensive recourse to Abbo's favoured sources—only takes us so far; all of the relevant sections are to be found in the authentic Gregory V privilege, which presumably furnished the forger's model.

Where, then, should we place Pseudo-Gregory IV's genesis? It clearly post-dates 997; it probably also post-dates 998, when Odilo's exemption was issued. Given the differences between it and Abbo's bull, and given the novelty Aimoin ascribes to the latter, a date after Abbo's abbacy seems preferable.

70. Mostert, 'Urkundenfälschungen', 305–6. The manuscripts in question are BnF lat. 2278 and 11674: Mostert, *Political Thought*, 71–75; Saenger, *Space between Words*, 158–59.

71. Vatican, BAV, Reg. lat. 598, fol. 68v; *Registrum Gregorii*, XIII.11, ed. Hartmann, 378 (cf.. ibid., xiv, noting that it was Starzer who undertook the transcription). See also Mostert, 'Urkundenfälschungen', 306 n. 113. Note that this is letter XIII.9 in Norberg's edition.

72. Cf. Roumy, 'Remarques', 322–23.

In this respect, the most likely contexts are offered by the abbacy of Abbo's immediate successor Gauzlin (1005–30) or the run-up to Alexander II's confirmation in 1072. Certainly Fleury's difficulties with the local bishop did not end with deaths of Arnulf of Orléans (*c.* 1002) and Abbo (1004). As we have seen, Abbo's privilege was still controversial when Aimoin wrote (1005×1022, probably towards the start of this period). And though Gauzlin's years witnessed some improvement in the abbey's standing, the monks continued to struggle for influence at court. Indeed, Andrew's *Life* of Gauzlin ascribes this upturn largely to the abbot's own initiative; and King Robert is strangely peripheral to the account—a fact all the more striking since another Fleuriac monk, Helgaud, had just written a *Life* of the king. Even in Helgaud's work, the signs of Robert's favour for Saint-Benoît are slim pickings in comparison with those adduced for other centres, such as Saint-Aignan (in Orléans). This impression of benign neglect finds confirmation in the diplomatic record: Robert is only known to have issued one diploma for the centre (no longer extant, but probably from Gauzlin's abbacy), and did not confirm its prized immunity.[73]

A few years after Arnulf's death, his successor Fulk (*c.* 1002–8×13) attempted to ride, almost literally, roughshod over the abbey's rights, arriving in Fleury uninvited on the feast day of Benedict (11 July, probably 1007). This contravened the terms of Abbo's privilege, and the choice of date is telling—it was a strike against the monks on the very feast which was meant to symbolize their independence. Fulk came with a considerable following, ready for trouble; but after facing stiff resistance, he withdrew. The matter was then taken up at a synod overseen by Leotheric of Sens (999–1032), Fulk's metropolitan, and attended by King Robert and the papal legate Peter. As we might expect, the monks produced and read aloud their privilege (the Gregory V bull); but Fulk's supporters, including Leotheric, refused to acknowledge its testimony, threatening to put the document to flames. The result was a stalemate, which even the intervention of Pope John XVIII (1003–9) could not break. Interestingly, it is possible that the monks of Fleury were already active improving local documentation in this connection. The letters of John XVIII to Leotheric complaining about the latter's behaviour survive uniquely in Andrew's *Life* of Gauzlin. And here the address of Leotheric as 'pseudo-archbishop' ('pseudoarchiepiscopus') is most suspect. This is the language of local polemic, not papal correspondence.[74]

Like the Saint-Basle and Saint-Denis synods, this was part of a wider set of monastic-episcopal conflicts, and the learned Fulbert of Chartres—something of a latter-day Gerbert—now took up the bishops' cause.[75] For Fleury, the

73. Andrew of Fleury, *Vita Gauzlini*, ed. Bautier and Labory; Helgaud of Fleury, *Epitoma vite Robertii pii*, chs 15, 24, ed. Bautier and Labory, 88, 116–18. See further Morelle, 'Que peut-on savoir', 131–36; Koziol, 'Conquest of Burgundy', 206 n. 106.

74. Andrew of Fleury, *Vita Gauzlini*, ch. 18, ed. Bautier and Labory, 50–58; JL 3958–61 (ZPUU 438–41), with Hoffmann, *Mönchskönig*, 102–3.

75. Fulbert of Chartres, *Epistolae* 7, 8, 26, ed. Behrends, 16–20, 48–50.

situation first eased after the death of Fulk (1008 × 1013), which was followed
by a lengthy conflict over the episcopal succession in Orléans. Even so, respite
was partial and temporary; and during Odolric's later episcopate (c. 1022–36)
troubles flared up again, with Yèvre once more a flashpoint. The testamentary
value—indeed, very existence—of Abbo's privilege was therefore under threat,
and it is conceivable that the Gregory IV bull was forged in response. Two privileges might succeed where one had failed; and a second provided a degree of
insurance, should the first be destroyed. Still, there are reasons to doubt that
Pseudo-Gregory IV was confected so early. External abbatial consecration, the
major concern of the forger (but not of Abbo), is not mentioned in this connection; rather, the point of contention remained the abbot's right to exclude
the bishop from the monastic precinct. Moreover, Andrew, who reports these
events at first hand, clearly speaks in the singular of the monks' privilege (as a
'decretum' and 'scriptum'). Indeed, Fulk and Leotheric's threat to destroy this
only makes sense if the monks' claims hung by a thin documentary thread.

More likely, therefore, is an origin under Abbot William (1067–80), in prepa-
ration for the confirmation obtained from Alexander II. It is at this point that we
have our first secure evidence of the bull's existence; and it is in these years that
the form it takes makes best sense. As monastic exemption started to take on
more formal guises—a process well under way by the second half of the eleventh
century—the existence of a demonstrable tradition of exemption came to be its
defining feature. An exempt house was one which had always been exempt.[76]
In this respect, exemption was much like other rights of preferential treatment
within the church, which were thought to exist since time immemorial. In fact,
the experiences of Abbot William bear comparison with those Lanfranc of Canterbury (1070–89) in these years. The latter sought to have his claims to primacy
within the British Isles confirmèd in the early 1070s. Yet despite the archbishop's
good relations with the pope, the absence of an established primatial tradition
proved fatal to the endeavour.[77] It is this kind of documentary evidence that the
Gregory IV privilege furnishes to Saint-Benoît, much as the famous Canterbury
forgeries soon would to Lanfranc and his successors.

It is also in the second half of the eleventh century that French monasteries began to look more actively to Rome. Inspired by Leo IX's presence at
the council of Reims in autumn 1049—the first papal presence in France in
almost two centuries—more and more abbots sought out the protection of the
bishop of Rome, using forged and authentic texts to secure this.[78] It is in these
years, too, that the Cluniac tradition of external abbatial consecration began
to spread, partly through such channels, finding emulation at Fruttuaria,

76. Falkenstein, La papauté, 96, 105–6, 221–25.

77. Cowdrey, Lanfranc, 101–2. See further Berkhofer, 'Canterbury Forgeries'.

78. Bouchard, 'Forging Papal Authority', 1–4; Berkhofer, Day of Reckoning, 42–48. See
also Große, 'Ubi papa'.

Fécamp, Marmoutier and elsewhere. Finally, it is in the later eleventh century that monastic canon law collections began circulating more widely, led by the *Collection in 74 Titles*, a work drawn up (probably) in a northern French monastic milieu and preserved, among other places, in the famed Saint-Denis dossier, a set of texts (largely forged) which betray remarkably similar interests to the Fleury bulls. Significantly, the *74 Titles* is the only canon law collection to reveal signs of influence from Abbo's canonical works. When French monks came to defend their rights, they knew where to turn.[79]

That our earliest copy of the Gregory IV privilege comes from these years reinforces the case for later production, as does the fact that it was interpolated at La Réole, probably in the early 1080s (as we shall see). Whether the second forgery, in the name of Benedict VII, belongs in the same context is harder to say. This document has received less attention, partly because it shares less material with its Gregory IV and Gregory V counterparts. Whereas the latter two are almost identical, both ultimately modelled on the earlier privilege of John VIII for Fleury, the opening of the Benedict VII bull is taken from Odo's exemption of 938, with material from Pseudo-Gregory IV only inserted later. The result is analogous, with most of the same rights covered, albeit in more streamlined fashion (the details on monastic excommunicants and interdict have been dropped; likewise there is less on the consecration of monks to priestly orders). That it was the Gregory IV forgery, not its Gregory V exemplar, which furnished the model is revealed by fact that the abbot is accorded the key right of external consecration (in identical terms).[80] But since Pseudo-Benedict VII goes no further than Pseudo-Gregory IV, it is tempting to place it in a similar context, perhaps as part of the same forgery action. If so, excommunication and consecration to priestly orders were now less of a concern, while abbatial consecration had become more of one.

A later date is also suggested by interpolations in both texts, as transmitted in the La Réole cartulary. Here, both bulls extend Fleury's exemption to three dependent houses: Perrecy, Sacierges and La Réole. Thanks to independent witnesses to the Gregory IV privilege, Prou and Vidier were able to identify the section in question as a La Réole addition (a further counterfeiting of a Fleury forgery), a conclusion now confirmed by the readings of the earliest manuscript (identified by Mostert). In the case of the Benedict VII privilege, where we do not possess such independent controls, Prou and Vidier accepted the cartulary text as is, as have all subsequent editors. Yet since this extends Fleury's exemption to the same three priories, in almost identical terms, a strong case can be made for treating this, too, as a local addition. Certainly the clause in question looks like an intrusion: it interrupts the natural flow of thought and

---

79. Rolker, 'Collection'. See also Roumy, 'Remarques', 314–15; Rolker, 'Monastic Canon Law'.

80. JL 3803 (ZPUU 258).

is sandwiched between phrases lifted directly from Pseudo-Gregory IV. It is easy to see why the monks of La Réole might have made these adjustments. Priories did not automatically enjoy the same rights as their mother houses (though they sometimes claimed as much), and these improvements were necessary if La Réole was to guard against local episcopal encroachment. The obvious context for interpolation is offered by the 1080s, as Laurent Morelle notes, when the local bishop of Bazas threatened to appropriate the centre.[81] The forgeries had evidently made their way to La Réole by this point, and it may be that they were adjusted soon after arrival.

We are, therefore, dealing with two counterfeits, probably of the third quarter of the eleventh century. Unfortunately, this is a period when our sources run dry for Saint-Benoît. After Gauzlin's abbacy, the literary flourishing at the abbey comes to something of a halt—and with it, our main source of information. Only in the early twelfth century does Hugh of Fleury (d. after 1118) shine further light, and he is too late to be of assistance here. Yet it is precisely this paucity of evidence which makes the testimony of the bulls so valuable. They reveal that problems with the bishop continued long after Gauzlin's day. They also demonstrate how the points of contention shifted: abbatial consecration had evidently become more important, and interdict and excommunication less so. Above all, they reflect new attitudes toward exemption. As already noted, the forgeries serve to turn Abbo's newly won rights into a venerable tradition of exemption, and one of the most important innovations of Pseudo-Benedict VII is to frame itself as a confirmation of 'the privileges that our predecessors granted' ('privilegia [quae] nostri antecessores concesserunt'). The bull thus authenticates the earlier Gregory IV counterfeit, creating the impression of a long line of papal exemptions. The choice of these two popes is probably not coincidental. In Gregory IV and Benedict VII, the monks were able to invoke the names of Abbo's favourite authority (Gregory the Great) and the monastery's patron (Benedict of Nursia).

Such efforts bear similarities to those of many other French monasteries in these years. At some point in the late tenth or early eleventh century, the monks of Saint-Vaast in Arras forged an exemption in the name of Pope Stephen II (752–57). Like their Fleuriac brethren, they hoped to avoid encroachment from the local bishop of Cambrai; and to achieve this, they used one of the same letters of Gregory the Great as had Abbo.[82] Closer to home, the monks of Micy produced an imposing set of false Merovingian and Carolingian

81. Bordeaux, Archives départmentales de la Gironde, La Réole II, 6, fols 30r–31v, 47v–48v, with Morelle, 'Que peut-on savoir', 115. As the seventeenth-century copyist of the cartulary notes, these were to be found at fols 44v–46v, 69v–71r of the (lost) original. See further Berland, 'La place', 35–37; and on the rights of priories and mother houses: Falkenstein, *La papauté*, 126–28.

82. JE 2328 (*Cartulaire*, ed. van Drival, 22–25), with Lemarignier, 'L'exemption', 332–40; Vanderputten, *Reform*, 56–57.

diplomas, starting (probably) in the second half of the eleventh century. Again, the aim was to secure the abbey's institutional independence, which had long been threatened by the bishop.[83] Better known are the forging activities of the monks of Saint-Denis, which look very much like those of Fleury writ large. Here the result was an impressive combination of forged royal and papal privileges, all underlining the abbey's independence from the bishop of Paris. And similar efforts on a smaller scale can be discerned at a host of other houses, including Corbie, Fécamp and, perhaps, Montier-en-Der (to name but a few of the best studied).[84]

Primacy and Precedents: Fleury from Abbo to William (997–1072)

The main purpose of the Fleury privileges is thus clear: to remove Saint-Benoît and its abbot from the oversight of his diocesan bishop at Orléans. As such, they bear comparison not only with the many forged French bulls of the eleventh century, but also the Abingdon counterfeits of the last chapter. In both cases, the independence of a monastic house was under threat, and in both the response was to mobilize the past in the cause of the present. These similarities should not be chalked down to coincidence alone. Not only were the houses responding to similar pressures; as we have seen, they were in close contact. It was to Fleury that Æthelwold had threatened to retire in the 950s, before being offered Abingdon to reform; it was here that his chosen successor as abbot, Osgar, received his monastic training; and it was Fleury customs which set the tone for the *Regularis concordia*, the monastic customs drawn up by Æthelwold for his English brethren. And these are part of a much wider set of connections, which encompassed Oswald of York and the first abbot of Oswald's foundation at Ramsey, Germanus.[85]

Nor were such channels one-way. Abbo spent two years in England, not coincidentally at Oswald's Ramsey (985–87), and remained in close contact with his English associates thereafter. Abbo's stay coincided with Æthelred's 'youthful indiscretions', which saw the king despoil many monastic centres, and the Fleuriac schoolmaster must have known of this. At Abingdon, the abbey's troubles followed the death of the Fleury-trained Osgar, while Glastonbury's travails would have been known to Abbo through Archbishop Dunstan,

83. Head, *Hagiography*, 216–17; Brühl, 'Clovis', 222–25 (reprised in Brühl, *Studien zu den merowingischen Königsurkunden*, 52–56); *Urkunden der Merowinger*, ed. Kölzer, 4–5; *Urkunden Ludwigs des Frommen*, ed. Kölzer, 905. As the latter works make clear, Head placed at least some of the forgeries too early.

84. Levillain, 'Études', esp. 259–88; Große, 'Frühe Papsturkunden'; Morelle, 'Moines de Corbie'; Pohl and Vanderputten, 'Fécamp'; Bouchard, 'Forging Papal Authority'. However, see also Falkenstein, 'Weitere Fälschungen', contesting Bouchard's findings.

85. Nightingale, 'Oswald'. See also Donnat, 'Recherches'.

the centre's sometime abbot. Indeed, Abbo seems to have been especially close to Dunstan, who had told him the tale of the martyrdom of Edmund of East Anglia (later written up by Abbo). And Ælfstan of Rochester, whose diocese was ravaged by Æthelred in 986—and whose canons responded with forgery— was reportedly present on this occasion (985×987).[86] When confronted by episcopal intransigence and royal apathy, the similarities would not, therefore, have been lost on Abbo. It has long been noted that Abbo's idealized views of kingship may owe something to Edgar's patronage of the English reformers. It has less often been appreciated that he would have learned of this at a time when Edgar's own legacy stood in the balance.[87]

Abbo and the later Fleury forgers may, therefore, have been aware of how Wulfgar and others had mobilized the past in the 990s. But while in England forgery seems to have been the main response to these challenges, at Fleury it was part of a larger project, one which finds its fullest expression in the literary and canonical works of these years. Abbo's bull capped off almost a decade's efforts, while the later forgeries in the names of Gregory IV and Benedict VII extend these endeavours in new directions. Certainly the monks were under no illusions as to what a distant pope might achieve. Their previous privileges had availed them little against the two Arnulfs, and the Reims affair had under- lined just how hard it was for the pope to assert himself outside Rome. It is for this reason that Aimoin goes out of his way to justify the terms of Abbo's bull; it is for this reason, too, that later forgers sought to buttress it. In its defence, Aimoin draws on five key letters of Gregory the Great, which would them- selves form the basis of most later monastic canon law. These same authorities had been cited in Abbo's second canon law collection (his *Letter 14*) and were evidently favoured points of reference at Saint-Benoît (two are also included in the chapter on abbatial election in his *Collectio canonum*). The most impor- tant of these is Gregory's letter to Marinianus of Ravenna, impressing upon the bishop the importance of monastic quietude and independence; this is quoted in Abbo's authentic bull and the Saint-Vaast forgery, and would go on to be the touchstone for much later regulation on exemption.[88]

The monks had good reason to be concerned. This was a period in which bishops were extending their influence into the countryside; it was also a time when legal rights were being defined more precisely. There was, therefore, a real danger that loose episcopal oversight might give way to something more intrusive, as was happening at Micy. Still, what Abbo and William claimed

86. Abbo, *Passio S. Eadmundi*, prol., ed. Winterbottom, 67, with Keynes, 'Church of Rochester', 331–33.

87. Cf. Dachowski, 'English Roots'; Gransden, 'Abbo', 47–56.

88. Aimoin, *Vita Abbonis*, ch. 12, ed. Bautier and Labory, 92–98; Abbo, *Epistola 14*, PL 139, cols 444–46, and *Collectio canonum*, ch. 15, PL 139, cols 484–86. See further Rennie, '*Quam sit necessarium*', 330–39 (though note that the *Collectio* here only cites two of these letters and not, as Rennie states, all five); Rolker, 'Monastic Canon Law', 626–29.

went beyond the purely pragmatic. The rights they secured include primacy among the abbeys of France, a position owed to Benedict's role as 'legislator and lord of the monks' ('monachorum legislator et dominus'). Just as Benedict had been first among monastic instructors, so Saint-Benoît was to be first among abbeys. There are echoes here of Pilgrim's interest in hierarchy and standing, and the phrase in question develops the vaguer statement of Odo's bull of 938 that Fleury was 'like a head or foremost one' ('quasi caput ac principium') within the monastic order.[89]

Interestingly, abbatial primacy was not a major concern elsewhere in France, where monasteries tended to be more worried about the judicial implications of episcopal influence (also an issue at Saint-Benoît). Closer parallels emerge east of the Rhine, where bishops and abbots alike were engaged in a veritable arms race for such titles and honours.[90] It may be that Abbo, who had studied at the frontier archbishopric of Reims and whose monastery had overseen the reform of Saint-Remi, owed his interest in such matters to these Lotharingian connections. Certainly the archbishops of Reims, in part inspired by their Trier neighbours, were keen to claim a similar brand of episcopal primacy. Further inspiration may have come from the late antique list of Roman provinces known as the *Notitia Galliarum*, a copy of which was to be found in Fleury, where it was consulted by Aimoin. It was this list that the ninth-century forger-compilers of the canon law collection known as Pseudo-Isidore had used to develop the concept of primacy in the first place (the primate being a figure between archbishop and pope). And the Pseudo-Isidorian collection was itself gaining traction in these years, perhaps informing Abbo's views on papal authority.[91] Whatever Abbo's precise source, he may, in turn, have furnished the model for the eccentric Aquitanian monk Adémar of Chabannes, whose forgeries made such a stir in the 1020s. Adémar may have met Abbo in his youth and had certainly been responsible for copying the unique witness of the *Collectio canonum*. It is, therefore, noteworthy that Adémar later claimed a similar brand of abbatial primacy for Saint-Martial in Limoges, including exemption from interdict (another precocious reference to this new form of collective excommunication).[92] This is not the only sign of distinctive

89. JL 3872 (ZPUU 335), JL 3606 (ZPUU 83).

90. Johrendt, *Papsttum*, 131–32, 176–77, 193–94, 238–40.

91. Roberts, *Flodoard*, 63–70. On Aimoin's use of the *Notitia*: K.-F. Werner, 'Vorbilder', 203–4 n. 38; on Abbo's knowledge of Pseudo-Isidore: Mostert, *Political Theology*, 74 n. 42; and on Pseudo-Isidore: Fuhrmann, *Einfluß und Verbreitung*, esp. 237–585; Roberts, 'Bishops on the Move'. Further work on the use and dissemination of Pseudo-Isidore is to be anticipated from Ed Roberts.

92. Landes, *Relics*, 85–86, 109–10, 123, 131–32, 197–281, 362–65; Trumbore Jones, 'Discovering', 89–90. The canon law manuscript is BnF lat. 2400. Fleury was also in prayer confraternity with Saint-Martial: BnF lat. 5 (II), fol. 219v. See further Vezin, 'Manuscrits témoins'; Bellarbre, 'Adémar de Chabannes'.

interests in Abbo's bull. Alongside the characteristically West Frankish concern to remove Fleury from the disciplinary oversight of the bishop, echoed in the Saint-Vaast and Saint-Denis forgeries, we find measures to limit the bishop's ability to celebrate mass and perform consecrations—measures which, again, find their closest analogues east of the Rhine.

The impression is, therefore, that are we dealing not only with an increasingly assertive episcopate, but also a more sensitive and self-aware monastic order. It was episcopal–monastic relations that been at stake at the Saint-Basle and Saint-Denis councils; it was these, too, that motivated Fulk and Gauzlin in later years. As Adalbero of Laon's famous diatribe against the monks of Cluny reveals, this was a time in which the monastic and episcopal orders began to drift apart, at least on an ideological plane.[93] As bishops began to extend their influence beyond their urban bases, monks responded by defining their institutional independence in ever more exclusionary forms. The Fleury forgeries are intimately associated with these processes. Like Abbo's writings, they claim a key role for the monastic order, and foremost within this for the monks of Fleury, who as Benedict of Nursia's guardians and successors were the natural leaders of their professed brethren. They also model Abbo's office in quasi-episcopal terms, granting him many episcopal prerogatives within cloister walls and conferring on Fleury a form of primacy otherwise largely limited to episcopal circles.

Though Abbo's privilege was framed as a new grant—a weakness for which the later forgeries seek to compensate—it was already deeply historical in outlook. The opening sections, lifted from the John VIII privilege, speak movingly of the abbey's ancient foundation and the translation of Benedict's relics, 'as attested in historical accounts' ('sicut manifestissima constat historia')—presumably a reference to Adrevald's later ninth-century *Miracles*, which were continued by Aimoin and Andrew in these years. The text then goes on to note the generosity of Emperor Charles (the Bald), before explaining the decision to grant Abbo this 'privilege of our authority' ('privilegium nostre auctoritatis'). The forgeries take up and develop this approach. In particular, Pseudo-Gregory IV makes much of Louis the Pious's generosity, which the forger knew from the emperor's diploma of 818 for the abbey.

Abbo's privilege and the later counterfeits also complement other Fleuriac works of these years. It has long been noted that similar views of kingship underpin Abbo's account of the passion of Saint Edmund and his later writings for Hugh and Robert; these, in turn, bear similarities to the presentation of Louis the Pious and Charles the Bald in the forged and authentic bulls. Rather less attention has been given in this connection to Abbo's abbreviated version of the *Liber pontificalis*, the serial biography of popes. Yet for a leading

---

93. Adalbero of Laon, *Carmen ad Robertem regem*, ed. Carozzi, with Iogna-Prat, 'Entre anges et hommes'.

advocate of papal authority, this was at least as important; and, like the forgeries, it serves to underline the centrality of Saint Peter's successors in Rome.[94] Connections can also be traced outside Abbo's oeuvre. Aimoin's account of the 'Deeds of the Franks' (*Gesta Francorum*), written in the mid- to later 990s, is similarly notable for its focus on kings and kingship. It too is a mirror of princes, probably intended for Robert. However, its incomplete nature suggests that the *Gesta* was abandoned at some point, perhaps in 995 when Abbo gave up his hopes for royal assistance.[95] Still, a lively interest in kings was maintained at Fleury, as reflected in Helgaud's *Life* of Robert (1033 × 1041), the first biographical treatment of a Frankish king since the days of Charles the Fat. This unusual attachment to king and court is traditionally interpreted in terms of Fleury's status: as one of the few remaining royal monasteries, Saint-Benoît remained wedded to older ideals of kingship.[96] This is certainly part of the story. Yet one cannot help but wonder whether, like Abbo, these writers were not interested in kings precisely because they could no longer be counted upon. Viewed in these terms, they are also monuments to a bygone age.

Confronted by new challenges in the tenth and eleventh centuries, the monks of Fleury therefore turned their literary skill and historical acumen towards recasting the history of the kingdom and their monastery. On the one hand, they extended Adrevald's narrative of the miracles enacted by Benedict up to their own day, underlining the long (and continuing) tradition of saintly patronage and protection at the abbey. On the other, they crafted idealized portraits of kings past and present, models they hoped would inspire emulation (even if they feared otherwise). Yet as kings proved increasingly fickle—at once too powerful to be ignored, yet too weak or unwilling to stand up to the bishop of Orléans—the monks turned ever more to Rome and the papacy. The pope had the singular advantage of being authoritative enough to demand respect, yet distant enough (for the time being) to preclude meddling.[97] This turn to Rome is reflected in miniature in Abbo's privilege of 997, which makes much of past royal protection, but now looks to Gregory V to perform these functions. In doing so, Abbo was channelling the example of Odo half a century earlier, and the forgeries represent an important further step. Together, they not only enshrine and extend Fleury's rights, but project these into the past, creating a long and venerable tradition of exemption. A monastery which had only been in periodic contact with the pope now became a bastion of papal authority and influence in the Orléanais.

94. Abbo, *Epitome de XCI Romanorum pontificum vitiis*, PL 139, cols 535–70, with Sot, 'Pratique et usages', 213–15.

95. Aimoin, *Gesta Francorum*, PL 139, cols 627–798, with K. F. Werner, 'Vorbilder'; Lake, 'Rewriting Merovingian History'.

96. Head, *Hagiography*, 270–82; Paxton, '*Abbas* and *rex*'. See also Koziol, 'Conquest of Burgundy', 205–6.

97. Cf. Trumbore Jones, 'Power of an Absent Pope'.

CHAPTER FIVE

True Lies: Leo of Vercelli and the Struggle for Piedmont

ON 18 MARCH 997, Vercelli, a sleepy city in north-western Italy, became the talk of the realm. The occasion was the death of Peter, the local bishop, at the hands of the margrave of Ivrea and his men. Violence against an anointed prelate was rare enough. But what made this truly shocking was the manner in which it was enacted. Peter was killed in the cathedral of S. Eusebio—on consecrated ground, that is—and his remains were then burnt, in an act of conscious desecration. This was not just another violent act in an aggressive age; it was sacrilege of the highest order. And much like England's later experience of murder in the cathedral, the resonances would be felt for years to come.[1]

To understand why, we must place these events in context. Peter's death was a dramatic flashpoint in a wider set of struggles for power and influence between bishop and margrave. These have their origins in the transformations the region had undergone since the eclipse of Carolingian rule. As in much of the Latin-speaking West, the tenth century was a period of transition in northern Italy. While the Carolingians clung on doggedly in France and the Ottonians established themselves in Germany, the Italian realm experienced a series of pronounced power vacuums, which served to suck in neighbouring rulers and magnates (not to mention Hungarian raiders). The first of these northern potentates was Louis of Provence (887–928, 900–905 in Italy), who was invited south in 900 in opposition to the local king Berengar I (887/98–924). After some initial success, Louis's ambitions met a sticky end, when he was blinded at Berengar's behest (hence his later moniker: Louis the Blind). But this did not discourage other would-be lords of Lombardy. Less than two decades later, Rudolf I (912–37), the ruler of Burgundy, to the north-east of

---

1. On the phenomenon of episcopal murder: Kaiser, '"Mord im Dom"'; Fryde and Reitz, eds, *Bischofsmord im Mittelalter*.

Louis's Provence, accepted a similar invitation. And though his reign proved abortive, too, Rudolf was replaced by another northern potentate in the person of Hugh of Arles (924–47), thitherto Louis's right-hand man in Provence. The significance of this dizzying array of regime changes lies in the role the Ivrean march (roughly, modern Piedmont and western Liguria) came to play. It was here that Vercelli was to be found; it was here, too, that the Mont Cenis and Great and Little St Bernard passes emerged into the Po basin, controlling access between Italy and its north-western neighbours.[2] To control the march was to control Italy—and Italy was a considerable prize. The region was also excellent hunting country, with a high concentration of fiscal lands.[3]

The Anscarid lords of the march, which stretched from Ossola, northeast of Novara, to central Liguria in the south, played an important part in the developments outlined above. They hailed from Burgundy and were well placed to make the most of the complex transalpine politics of the era. The first of them, Anscar (d. 902), had been appointed by Guy of Spoleto (889–94), Berengar I's sometime rival for the crown. Upon Anscar's death, his son Adalbert I (d. 929) inherited the post. Initially, Adalbert threw in his lot with Berengar, whose authority was now unopposed, receiving the king's daughter Gisela in marriage in return. Relations soured following Gisela's death, however, and Adalbert went on to be one of the king-makers in the early 920s, when his compatriot Rudolf was invited south to contest the realm. Adalbert was rubbing shoulders with royalty, and his ambitions find expression in his choice of name for his eldest son: Berengar, after the king. When this Berengar took over the march in the final years of the decade, he swiftly established himself as one of the leading figures in Hugh of Arles's regime, marrying the Provençal monarch's niece Willa, herself a member of the influential Bosonid clan.

In the end, Italy proved too small for both Hugh and Berengar. The former was set on removing the old guard of magnates who had until then dominated the political scene, while the latter was a leading exponent of this group (with royal ambitions of his own). Berengar revolted in the early 940s and was forced into exile at Otto I's court north of the Alps. Hugh then took the opportunity to divide the Ivrean march, which had so often been the key to Italy. What had been an office encompassing all of Piedmont and much of Liguria was now divided between Arduin (Glaber) of Turin in the west and Aleram and Otbert in the south and east, three of the many new men who owed their rise to Hugh. Upon Berengar's return in the later 940s, he was able to secure his old position in and around Ivrea, Vercelli and Novara in the north; but Arduin, Aleram and Otbert remained in place to his south and west, and the new Ivrean march was less than half the size of its predecessor. Upon the death of Hugh's own son and heir, Lothar (947–50), Berengar took the crown for himself, ruling

2. Cf. Winckler, *Alpen im Frühmittelalter*, 130–33; Brühl, *Fodrum*, i, 429–30.
3. Settia, 'Nelle foreste del re'. See also Panero, *Signoria*, 9–13.

alongside his son Adalbert (950–62). But a decade later they lost out to the East Frankish ruler Otto I (936–73, 961–73 in Italy), in another of those characteristically Italian regime changes. While these events did much to change the balance of power within the wider realm, in subalpine Piedmont stability reigned. From the moment of his return, Berengar had apparently been the power behind Hugh's throne; as such, he had little reason to upset Arduin, Aleram and Otbert. Thereafter Otto I had even less, so Hugh's policy of divide and rule was judiciously maintained.[4]

It was into this scene that another Arduin now stepped. Following Otto's conquest, the newly reduced Ivrean march passed to Berengar's younger sons, Guy and Corrado Conone. Unlike their elder brother Adalbert (d. 972 × 975), these two had not been anointed king and were able to accommodate themselves to the new regime, salvaging something of their position. The family itself remained on the out, however. In retribution for their father's (and brother's) actions, Guy and Corrado were stripped of holdings outside Piedmont; and, following the latter's death (987/9 × 997), the family slipped into obscurity. The result was a vacancy in the Ivrean march, which the new Arduin filled. This figure is first attested as margrave in 997, as the individual responsible for Bishop Peter's death, and his succession can probably be placed in the early to middle years of the decade. Despite efforts to associate this Arduin with the like-named Torinese count and margrave, Arduin Glaber, there is no evidence of a familial relationship—and good reason to look elsewhere. The new margrave probably hailed from Milan, where his father Dado is attested as count; he may also have enjoyed ties to Pombia in north-eastern Piedmont.[5] The eclipse of the Anscarids had long been on the cards, so Dado and Arduin may have been angling for the succession for some time; it has even been suggested that Arduin was appointed directly by the Ottonian court.[6] However, as his succession came in the midst of a prolonged imperial absence—between Otto II's death in late 983 and Otto III's arrival in spring 996, Italy only saw a brief (and uneventful) visit by the latter's regent Theophanu (d. 991)—local considerations were probably paramount.

Whatever the circumstances, Arduin's rise would have been welcome north of the Alps. Theophanu, who ruled on behalf of her son till her own death in mid-June 991, had little interest in the continued prominence of the Anscarids; and Adelheid (d. 999), the king's grandmother, who then took over, had even less reason to mourn their passing. The latter had been married to Hugh's son (and co-ruler) Lothar and was besieged by Berengar in the early 950s. There was thus no love lost between the two, and the claims of Adelheid's son

4. Sergi, *Confini*, 56–229; Vignodelli, 'La competizione'. The best English-language survey remains Sergi, 'Kingdom of Italy'. See also now Houghton, 'Hugh, Lothar and Berengar'.

5. Andenna, 'Grandi patrimoni', 216–17.

6. Sergi, 'Arduino', 16, 18. See similarly Sergi, 'Kingdom of Italy', 364.

and grandson to the Italian throne depended upon her position as Lothar's rightful heir; they presuppose Berengar's illegitimacy.[7] Yet if Arduin's rise initially worked in favour of the young Otto III and his regents, it created tensions locally. Newcomers to high office often faced a frosty reception, and Arduin was no exception. Indeed, he was not the only one who sought to benefit from the eclipse of the traditional margravial family. As the other leading office-holders in the region, the bishops of Ivrea, Novara and Vercelli harboured similar ambitions. In Vercelli, in particular, the bishop had been the dominant force for some time. The foundations for his power and influence had been laid by the long episcopate of the reform-minded Atto (924–57/8) in the first half of the century. One of the leading political and intellectual figures of the era, Atto was a supporter of Berengar of Ivrea (II), as befitted one of the foremost prelates of the march.[8] He and his clergy had reaped dividends for their loyalty, receiving valuable rights in Hugh and Lothar's later years, when Berengar was increasingly influential at court. Atto did not live to see Otto's accession, the prospect of which had concerned him so. The sympathies of his successor Ingo (957/8–74) are less clear, but may also have lain with Berengar. Ingo had been appointed before Otto's arrival and was the beneficiary of a (lost) diploma of Berengar and Adalbert. In later years, Bishop Leo would claim that Ingo had been responsible for the loss of important episcopal holdings at Santhià, Cavaglià and Alice. The latter two went to a Count Aimo (probably of Lomello) shortly after Otto I's conquest, and it is tempting to posit a connection: this may have been a move to reward a faithful retainer and punish a prelate whose loyalty had proven suspect.[9] But whatever the bishop's initial feelings, Ingo soon accommodated himself to the new regime, much as Guy and Corrado Conone had done.

With Peter, bishop from the later 970s till his dramatic demise in 997, the situation began to improve. We do not know if Peter was a local candidate or an imperial appointment, but he certainly enjoyed good relations with the court. Soon after his accession, he proved his loyalty by participating in Otto II's southern Italian campaign of 982. Here he showed particular mettle, being captured following the disastrous battle of Crotone (Capo Colonna) against Abū l-Qāsim (970–82), the Kalbid emir of Sicily. These events are recorded in the *Annals* of St Gall, a southern Swabian monastery which, thanks to its location at the entrance of the mid-Alpine passes, enjoyed close ties with the Italian peninsula. These *Annals* also report that, after his capture, Peter endured a lengthy period of incarceration in Alexandria on the Nile Delta (Egypt being

7. MacLean, *Ottonian Queenship*, 95–126. See also Jestice, *Imperial Ladies*, 49–59.

8. Vignodelli, *Il filo a piombo*, and 'Politics, Prophecy and Satire'. However, see Houghton, 'Hugh, Lothar and Berengar', 71–72, now suggesting greater circumspection. On the chronology of Atto's episcopate: Vignodelli, 'I palinsesti'.

9. Della Chiesa, *S. R. E. cardinalium, archiepiscoporum*, 141; D O III 383; D O I 251.

the base of Abū l-Qāsim's Fatimid overlords). Further detail is furnished by the *Life* of the Bolognese saint Bononio (d. 1026), who spent a number of years as a hermit near Cairo. While in Egypt, Bononio saw Peter's plight and assisted in his release. In reward, the Piedmontese bishop appointed the itinerant holy man abbot of Lucedio, a dependent monastery within his diocese. The length of Peter's incarceration is unknown, but by 990 at the latest he was back in Vercelli.[10]

At this point, it becomes harder to trace developments. This much, how-ever, is clear: the new margrave and Peter were on a collision course. The former wanted to recreate the old Anscarid march, while the latter wished to reinforce his control over Vercelli and its hinterland, a control endangered by his recent absence. Politically active bishops were often more vulnerable to violence in the earlier Middle Ages, and Peter is a case in point.[11] The situation was complicated by divisions within the cathedral of Vercelli itself, which pitted the canons (soon to be supported by Arduin) against the bishop. The causes here are equally obscure, but probably lie in recent developments. The canons would have enjoyed greater freedom during Peter's absence and may have taken unkindly to his return. Tensions must have been mounting for some time, but we only catch sight of them when they spill over into violence in early 997. The timing is suggestive. The mid-990s had seen Otto III come of age, and spring and summer 996 witnessed the emperor's first visit to the Italian peninsula. It was also probably around this time that Corrado Conone died, leaving the Ivrean march vacant. At least one of Corrado's estates, Caresana, now passed to the canons at Vercelli; and there are signs that the bishop had an interest in the family's collapse elsewhere, too (Leo would later claim many episcopal holdings as quondam donations of Berengar and Adalbert). Arduin, for his part, seized or inherited Corrado's margravial title—and with it, pre-sumably, a residual claim to many of these estates.

Political instability was not limited to Piedmont, however. Otto III's first Italian sojourn witnessed efforts to assert imperial authority in the peninsula which were as bold as they were ill-conceived. Scarcely across the Alps, Otto had sided with Venice against bishops John of Belluno and Rozo of Treviso in a conflict over local rights in the Veneto. In Ravenna, the traditional staging post to Rome, he then oversaw a court judgement against the local count of Rimini, Rudolf.[12] Finally, en route to Rome, Otto appointed his own cousin Bruno of Carinthia (the son of Otto of Worms, whom we met in Chapter 1) as pope, following the unexpected death of John XV (985–96). The latter

10. *Annales Sangallenses maiores*, s.a. 982, ed. Zingg, 180; *Vita S. Bononii*, ch. 7, ed. Schwartz and Hofmeister, 1028. See further Pauler, *Regnum Italiae*, 31–32.

11. Cf. Fouracre, 'Why Were so Many Bishops Killed?'.

12. John the Deacon, *Istoria Veneticorum*, IV.34–39, ed. Berto, 180–82; D O III 194. On Ravenna's role in the royal itinerary: Alvermann, *Königsherrschaft*, 156–57.

move was especially problematic. Bruno was the first non-Roman pope in living memory, and the decision to impose an outsider on the city was bound to ruffle feathers. To ease his entry into the local scene, Bruno adopted the suitably papal designation Gregory, becoming the fifth pontiff of this name. He then went on to channel the example of his late sixth-century namesake, Gregory the Great (590–604), overseeing an ambitious set of efforts to restore traditional church rights in and around the city. It was from Gregory that Otto received imperial consecration at Ascension (21 May), and thereafter the two jointly oversaw a church council. At this, they accepted the submission of the Roman city prefect Crescentius (Crescenzio), whose family had dominated the papacy in recent years and whose nose was (understandably) out of joint about Gregory's appointment. It was also at this council that the emperor and pope began considering the difficulties churches were experiencing in maintaining their landed claims, issues which would be a hallmark of their respective reigns.[13] Shortly thereafter, Otto headed back north.

In Ivrea, none of the questions raised by the eclipse of the Anscarids had been answered. So far as we can tell, the emperor did not visit the region—in fact, no Ottonian ruler is known to have done so[14]—nor is there any sign of contact between him and the bishop or margrave. Perhaps Peter and Arduin were too preoccupied with their own struggles to seek out Otto; certainly within months of the emperor's departure, trouble was brewing. In Rome, Crescentius drove out Pope Gregory and appointed John Philagathos, Otto's returning envoy to Constantinople, in his stead.[15] In Vercelli, meanwhile, violence broke out. As we have seen, Peter had sought to consolidate his position since his return, in part by securing traditional Anscarid lands; Arduin, for his part, was keen to claw back as much of this as possible.[16] At least as important was another conflict, that between Peter and his canons. This may originally have been a response to the bishop's return, but now came to focus on control of the estate of Caresana (itself a sometime margravial holding), just south of the city on the Sesia. This had recently passed from Corrado to the canons, and was confirmed there by Otto in late 997. But Peter and his successors claimed it as their own, presumably on the grounds that what belonged to the chapter belonged to the bishop.

Otto's first priority upon his return to Italy in the winter of 997–98—affairs on his eastern frontier having kept him occupied in spring and summer—was

13. *Annales Hildesheimenses*, s.a. 996, ed. Waitz, 27; D O III 201. For the former in its manuscript context: BnF lat. 6114, fol. 36r. See further Scholz, *Politik—Selbstverständnis*, 332–64; Moehs, *Gregorius V*.

14. Brühl, *Fodrum*, i, 404–7, 462–68; Alvermann, *Königsherrschaft*, 189–90 (and cf. ibid., 225).

15. Leo of Synada, *Correspondence*, Letters 6, 11, 12, ed. Vinson, 8–10, 14–22, with Holmes, *Basil II*, 508–9; Kaldellis, *Streams of Gold*, 135–36.

16. Sergi, *Confini*, 163–64. See also Panero, *Signoria*, 48–49.

naturally Rome. Vercelli and Ivrea may have been strategically important, but they lacked the lustre of the imperial capital. The situation in Rome was also clearer. Here Crescentius had opposed Otto and Gregory in 996; there was little doubt who was now in the right (at least from an imperial perspective). In Piedmont, however, conflicts were rooted in local struggles. Both Peter and Arduin could cast themselves as the injured party; both could also claim prominent allies.[17] For Otto and his advisers, new to the Italian scene, discretion was indeed the better part of valour here.

First indications of a heightened interest in the north-west can be detected in late summer 998, when the emperor, having restored Gregory, travelled north to Pavia, the traditional Italian capital. Here, in the monastery of S. Pietro in Ciel d'Oro, just off the modern Viale Giacomo Matteotti to the north-west of the city centre, he held an important assembly, at which a set of ordinances on ecclesiastical landholding was promulgated (perhaps alongside decrees on servile dependents and the observance of religious festivals). The focus of the ordinances was two typically Italian forms of tenure, the *libellus* and *emphyteusis*. Both involved the contractual lease of land, the former for twenty-nine years and the latter (generally) for three lifetimes. These were popular within ecclesiastical circles, since churches were not meant to give land away; such arrangements allowed the fiction of stable landholding to be maintained in the face of pressures to exchange and alienate. The problem came, however, when leases were up for renewal. As elsewhere in Europe, there was a strong tendency for such temporary forms of tenure to become permanent, with recipients treating leased lands as their own patrimony. In response, the emperor now ordained that leases should only last as long as the bishop or abbot who enacted them; his successor should then be free to reclaim the lands or renegotiate the terms under which they were let.[18] This was intended to counteract the de facto heritability of leases and to guard against venal prelates, who might grant church property to friends and family.

The S. Pietro ordinances were informed by the emperor's recent experiences. While in Rome, Otto had intervened decisively in favour of Farfa, an imperial abbey some 54 km (33 miles) north-east of the city. Farfa had suffered substantial losses in recent years, partly on account of such leases, and one of the main lines of transmission for the ordinances runs through the Sabinese monastery.[19] In the months immediately preceding the assembly, the emperor had similarly assisted in S. Pietro's attempts to claw back lands from its tenant vassals; and shortly therafter, he would do likewise at Bobbio, where Gerbert of Aurillac—the centre's onetime abbot, now an imperial adviser—had a vested

17. Lucioni, 'Re Arduino', 45–54.

18. *Konzilien Deutschlands*, ed. Hehl, 562–64 (no. 58A). See further Bougard, 'Actes privés'.

19. Cf. Manganaro, 'Protezione regia', 118–41.

interest in redressing past wrongs.[20] The situation in Vercelli and Piedmont, where religious houses had suffered similarly, cannot have been far from mind either. In fact, it has been suggested that Leo, Peter's eventual successor to the episcopal throne, was responsible for drafting these ordinances. And while the philological arguments are far from watertight, the future bishop's involvement in the deliberations is likely.[21] More immediately important, however, must have been the input of Gerbert, through whose hands the decrees are said to have been promulgated ('promulgata per manus Gerberti') and whose own abbey at Bobbio benefited from imperial favour at this juncture. Since losing out to Arnulf at Reims, Gerbert had sought out the Ottonian court. He had previously served the emperor's father, Otto II, being rewarded with Bobbio in the 970s; now he was promoted to the archbishopric of Ravenna, the second most important cisalpine see (after Rome). As later events reveal, Gerbert had little time for Arduin, and one suspects that he and Otto already had the Ivrean margrave in their crosshairs.

It may be at this same S. Pietro gathering that the leading bishops of the realm wrote to the pope about these matters. They complained in the strongest possible terms about Arduin's depredations, depredations which, they noted, continued unabated despite the excommunication placed upon him. This letter survives as part of a set of early eleventh-century additions to an Ivrea manuscript. Thanks to these, we know that Warmund, the local bishop (c. 969–c. 1006), had also suffered at Arduin's hands. And the additions speak to Warmund's immediate needs. As they appear in the manuscript, they comprise a record of episcopal deliberations on Arduin's excommunication (no. 1); an excommunication formula (no. 2); the excommunication used on Arduin, reportedly by Warmund (no. 3); another excommunication rite, furnishing more detailed instructions for the presiding bishop (no. 4); a rite for reconciling excommunicants (no. 5); a letter threatening Arduin with anathema, sent by Warmund and a group of bishops (no. 6); a text announcing Arduin's final excommunication by the pope (no. 7); a letter of Gregory V to Arduin, threatening him with excommunication (no. 8); our present letter recounting an episcopal synod regarding Arduin's actions, sent to Gregory V (no. 9); and a record of Arduin's penance, as imposed upon him at Easter 999 (no. 10). These are not in chronological order, but all focus on the application of excommunication—a uniquely episcopal prerogative—and its implications, matters of direct pertinence to the Arduin affair. They also bear the marks of these

20. D O III 281, Milan, AS, Museo diplomatico, cart. 10, prot. 193/320; D O III 303.

21. H. Bloch, 'Beiträge', 67–68; L. M. Hartmann, *Geschichte Italiens*, 156 n. 16; Schramm, *Kaiser, Rom und renovatio*, i, 128–29. Cf. Fuhrmann, 'Konstantinische Schenkung', 134–35 n. 195; Kortüm, '*Gerbertus*', 54–58.

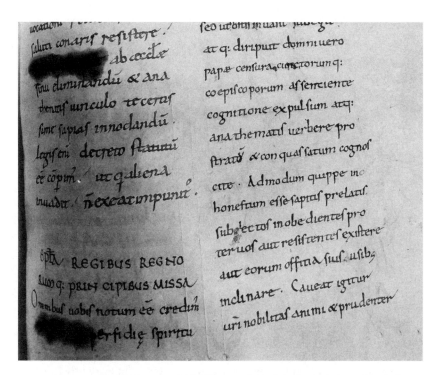

5.1 Erasure of Arduin's name within Warmund's 'Arduin dossier': Ivrea, BC, Cod. LXXXVII (54), fol. 112r (photo by author)

struggles, as the margrave's name has been erased at a number of points in the formulae and letters (Illustration 5.1).[22]

It is not long after this that we start seeing more proactive measures against Arduin. At some point following the Pavia assembly, Pope Gregory responded to the bishops' letter with an epistle of his own to the margrave (also preserved in the Ivrea manuscript), instructing Arduin to desist from his attacks on the local bishopric and make good the damage by Easter or face anathema.[23] While this reveals a distinct hardening of stance, Gregory's approach remains remarkably restrained. Arduin had already been excommunicated by the northern Italian bishops, yet there is no hint of this here; Gregory merely threatens him with a fresh anathema should Arduin not now acquiesce. Evidently there were lingering uncertainties about the rights and

22. Ivrea, BC, Cod. LXXXVII (54), fols 108v–114v, with *Konzilien Deutschlands*, ed. Hehl, 561. For the letter: *Konzilien Deutschlands*, ed. Hehl, 565–66 (no. 58B), with Wolter, *Synoden im Reichsgebiet*, 161. On excommunication rites: Hamilton, 'Interpreting Diversity', noting, inter alia, their tendency to survive as additions to manuscripts; and on manuscript production in Ivrea: Ferrari, 'Libri e testi', esp. 528, 530–31.

23. Ivrea, BC, Cod. LXXXVII (54), fol. 112v; *Konzilien Deutschlands*, ed. Hehl, 582 (no. 60A), with Wolter, *Synoden im Reichsgebiet*, 165.

wrongs of the case, uncertainties perhaps felt by the emperor, who according to the bishops' original letter had been hesitant to take action without papal endorsement. Similarly striking is the silence on the subject of Vercelli. Though Ivrea had apparently also suffered at Arduin's hands, we might expect some acknowledgement of Peter's fate, which had first kicked off the affair. Here, however, it is important to remember that the letter is preserved within an Ivrea dossier; a Vercelli equivalent would doubtless look very different.

Papal monition did not, in any case, change Arduin's tune, and the conflict now entered its end phase. Pressure mounted following the appointment of Gerbert as Gregory V's successor in early February 999. As noted, Gerbert was no friend of Arduin, and at his first synod as Sylvester II (Easter 999), he finally brought the margrave to heel. According to the surviving record (again, uniquely preserved in the Ivrea manuscript), the margrave now confessed his sins—doubtless under duress—and was sentenced to public penance. This was a significant choice of punishment. Penance was a religious sanction, and Arduin was being treated as a sinner rather than a criminal. Public penance was also closely associated with—indeed, sometimes indistinguishable from—excommunication, the sanction imposed on the margrave by the local bishops. In theory, what distinguished 'public' from other forms of penance was that it was for sins which threatened the wider social order. As practised in antiquity, this removed the penitent permanently from secular life; evidently this was now the intention. According to the sentence, Arduin was to lay down his arms (the symbols of his secular vocation); to eat no flesh (another crucial element of aristocratic life) and to kiss neither man nor woman (i.e., give them the 'kiss of peace' in greeting); to wear to no linen clothing and never stay more than two nights at the same place (unless ill); not to take part in communion, except at the end of his life; and not to seek retribution against those who had sworn oaths against him. The only alternative was to become a monk, itself a distinctly penitential vocation.[24]

Bella diplomatica: *Leo in Court and Country*

It is at this point that the situation in Vercelli starts to come into sharper focus. Just as Sylvester II's appointment ushered in a new era in Rome, so the appointment of Leo (999–1026) to the episcopal seat of S. Eusebio opened a new chapter in Vercelli's history. Leo had hitherto been a court chaplain and belonged to a tight-knit group of churchmen at the heart of Otto III's regime. Though little is known about his background, Leo hailed from Italy and starts

24. Ivrea, BC, Cod. LXXXVII (54), fol. 114r–v; *Konzilien Deutschlands*, ed. Hehl, 582–83 (no. 60B), with Hamilton, *Practice of Penance*, 1–2, 173; Dessì, 'Double conversion'. On late antique penitential traditions: Meens, *Penance*, 15–25; and on episcopal justice in these years: Hamilton, 'Inquiring into Adultery'.

to make an impression on our sources in 996, when the emperor first sought to establish his authority in the region. He is probably the 'Archdeacon Leo of the sacred imperial palace' ('Leo archidiaconus sacri imperii palatii') who represented Otto at a court judgement in Farfa's favour in April 998; he is certainly the individual responsible for a series of distinctively court-focused poems (reminiscent of Gerbert's), starting at this point.[25] Leo's immediate predecessor, the otherwise obscure Adalbert, had died on 4 June 998, after an episcopate of less than a year. The date of Leo's own accession, however, is a matter of some speculation. Traditionally, it is placed in summer 998, in the immediate aftermath of Adalbert's passing.[26] But since Leo does not appear as bishop until early May 999, there are grounds for doubt. There had been a lengthy vacancy between Peter's death (18 March 997) and Adalbert's accession (early to mid-998), since on 31 December 997 the canons had to ask Bishop Raginfred of Bergamo (996–1012)—a quondam Vercelli archdeacon— to petition a diploma in their favour.[27] The same may have been true in summer 998, when Arduin was still on the loose and the situation in the march far from settled. In fact, as late as March 999, an archdeacon named Giselbert, who later stood accused of being one of Arduin's chief allies, can be seen making donations to the cathedral chapter; it seems unlikely that Leo had made his influence felt yet.[28] Similarly significant is the manner in which Leo makes his entrance in May 999. His arrival is met with two lengthy diplomas, then two more in autumn 1000; it is hard to imagine he had already been quietly in post for over a year before this.

The first of these privileges, issued in Rome on 7 May 999—less than a month after the Easter synod at which Arduin had been sentenced (and at which Leo may have been appointed)—is a confirmation of the bishopric's holdings. It was common for bishops to seek confirmation of their rights upon their appointment or the accession of a new ruler; and since Peter had not done this in 996, it was only natural that the well-connected Leo should do so now. The situation in the Ivrean march remained precarious—in fact, we do not know whether Leo had yet set foot there—and the new bishop needed all the help he could get. In this respect, what Leo received was far from a standard confirmation. The diploma not only secures Vercelli's landed holdings on highly beneficial terms; it also confirms its rights to toll and *districtus*—the

25. *Placiti*, ed. Manaresi, no. 236, with Bougard, 'Rationalité et irrationalité', 102, 116; *Die lateinischen Dichter*, v.1–2, ed. Strecker and Fickermann, 476–89. Cf. Görich, *Otto III.*, 219, for the alternative identification of the former with Leo of SS Bonifacio ed Alessio. More generally: Dormeier, 'Un vescovo'; Gandino, 'Orizzonti politici', 74–81; Witt, *Two Latin Cultures*, 96–100.

26. E.g. Dormeier, 'Un vescovo', 46; Panero, *Signoria*, 53; Bedina, 'Leone', 479.

27. D O III 264, Vercelli, AC, Diplomi, II Cartella, 7, with Vignodelli, 'Prima di Leone', 70.

28. *Carte dello Archivio Capitolare*, ed. Arnoldi et al., no. 23.

latter being public jurisdiction over a specific area (often a city and its hinterland)—in Vercelli and its environs. These are framed as a confirmation of established rights, originally granted by the Lombard king Liutprand (712–44) and Frankish emperor Charles (the Fat, 881–87 in Italy), among others.

Rights of jurisdiction (*districtus*) had not been granted in this fashion before the last decade of the ninth century (and such concessions only became common in the early tenth), but this evidently troubled our draftsman little. Indeed, he makes much of Charles the Fat, whose privileges in favour of Liutward—the emperor's archchancellor and leading adviser in the 880s—become the basis for Leo's most exalted claims.[29] In this respect, reference is made not only to 'precepts' ('precepta') of the emperor (note the plural), but also to 'letters in the church of Saint Eusebius [i.e., S. Eusebio, the main cathedral in Vercelli], written above the altar of Saint John the Baptist' ('litere in ecclesia sancti Eusebii . . . super altare sancti Iohannis baptiste scripte'), the latter suggesting an inscription of some sort. After this initial list of rights, a series of new donations follows. These start with 'all the estates of Arduin, the son of Dado, who was named a public enemy because he killed Bishop Peter of Vercelli and was not afraid to burn his body' ('omnia predia Ardoini filii Daidonis, quia hostis publicus adiudicatus episcopum Petrum Vercellensem interfecit et interfectum incendere non expavit'): one of the few contemporary descriptions of these events. The text then continues with the estates of Arduin's followers and of all those 'who devastated the church of Saint Eusebius with arms' ('qui cum armis ecclesiam sancti Eusebii vastaverunt'). Whether the two groups in question are synonymous is not explicitly stated, though context suggests as much. Indeed, the entire dispositive ('granting') section of the diploma is sprawling, with new donations interspersed between confirmations, themselves based upon a myriad of purportedly earlier texts.[30] The confusion is only heightened by Leo's elevated Latin style and tendency to vary between verbs of confirmation, donation and restitution. But this much is certain: the bishop was making a maximal case for his see. In the wake of Arduin's fall, Leo was claiming not only a large number of (supposedly) ancient rights, but also the entire landed wealth of the margrave and his closest allies. Particularly significant here are the signs that Arduin had found support within episcopal circles. Among those dispossessed are unfree tenants (*servi*) of the see, a subdeacon of the nearby church of S. Agatha (Santhià), an archdeacon of Vercelli itself (Giselbert) and also an archpriest of the see (Cunibert). Similarly noteworthy is the fact that the diploma refers again to a precept of an Emperor Charles (the Fat) towards the end, now listing among the rights there conferred the monastery of S. Michele

29. On Liutward: Gandino, 'Orizzonti politici', 66–74; Panero, *Signoria*, 23–44; MacLean, *Kingship and Politics*, 178–91.

30. D O III 323.

in Lucedio; it then confirms S. Michele's possessions, including the estate of 'Quadradula', reportedly granted to the abbey by Emperor Lothar (I, 840–55).

This is a most unusual privilege. The detail furnished is extraordinary, even for Italy, where levels of literacy and legal expertise were high. More striking yet is the tone, which condemns the attacks of Arduin and his supporters in the strongest terms while making much of Vercelli's own glorious past. Charles the Fat plays a key role, as the source of the bishopric's most prized rights. The diploma also underlines the connection between Leo and Vercelli's late antique founder, the saintly Eusebius (d. c. 371), who is apostrophized throughout (grants and confirmations are made directly to the saint rather than to the bishopric). In doing so, the draftsman (Leo himself, as we shall see) emphasizes the antiquity of the see of Vercelli, which was greater even than that of Milan, its metropolitan (and occasional competitor) to the east. The connection with Eusebius may run even deeper. Leo would later cast himself as a bastion of orthodoxy within the Ivrean march, standing firm amidst the heretical forces of Arduin. The precedent of Leo's fourth-century forebear Eusebius, whose role in fighting the Arian heresy is underlined in his surviving *Life* (a work written in Vercelli, probably a century or two earlier), was, therefore, most à propos. Here Leo was following in the footsteps of his more recent predecessor, Atto, whose tract *De pressuris ecclesiasticis* (On the pressures of the church) Leo had personally annotated. Atto conceived of his office in distinctly Eusebian terms, even writing a sermon on the late antique episcopal founder; Leo evidently felt similarly.[31]

Vercelli had not seen anything like this, even under Liutward. At every turn, the diploma serves to secure the see's interests. Even the sanction, which threatens malefactors with a fine of one thousand pounds, stands out. This is ten times the normal sum, such elevated sanctions being reserved for particularly favoured centres. This, combined with a number of other exceptional features—the absence of an opening preamble (an increasingly common feature, especially in Italy), the extremely long body, the oddly personal corroboration clause—make the charter as striking diplomatically as it is rhetorically. Close parallels emerge with other diplomas of these years for Vercelli, including one which survives as a working draft copied and annotated by Bishop Leo (itself squeezed into the free space at the end of a Vercelli manuscript: below, Illustration 5.13). And these, in turn, reveal strong similarities with

---

31. Atto of Vercelli, *Sermo* XVI, PL 134, cols 853–55, with Meens, 'Mirror of Eusebius'. See also Vignodelli, *Il filo a piombo*, 260, and 'Prima di Leone', 64; and cf. Everett, 'Narrating'. For Leo's annotation of Atto's *De pressuris ecclesiasticis*: Vatican, BAV, Vat. lat. 4322, fol. 95r, with Gavinelli, Review of *Leone di Vercelli*, 489. More generally: Gavinelli, 'Leone'. In invoking the bishopric's late antique founder, Atto and Leo were participating in a broader trend: Miller, *Bishop's Palace*, 132–33.

other writings of Leo. The conclusion seems inescapable: the bishop himself was responsible for this text.[32]

On the same occasion, a second charter was issued in favour of Leo. This is, if anything, more extraordinary than the first. Produced at the request of Margrave Hugh of Tuscany (d. 1001), Pope Sylvester II (d. 1003) and the Italian chancellor (and future archbishop of Cologne) Heribert (d. 1021), it grants Leo comital rights in the city of Vercelli and at nearby Santhià (S. Agatha). As in France and (in particular) Germany, bishops in late tenth- and early eleventh-century Italy began to accumulate comital rights in addition to the more localized powers of *districtus* they had enjoyed since the turn of the century.[33] As in other regions, however, such grants were restricted to the most powerful and favoured sees and prelates. And this is, in fact, one of the first concessions of this nature. In granting Leo these rights, the emperor carved a hole in the heart of the Ivrean march, cutting off the counties of Novara and Ossola in the north and east from that of Ivrea itself in the west (Map 3).[34] The similarities between this diploma and the first are clear. Here, too, the preamble is dispensed with and we move straight from invocation and royal superscription to publication clause and main dispositive section; and here, too, the latter is sprawling, full of asides and contextual detail. Though not named, Arduin is an unspoken presence throughout. It is he who had possessed comital authority over these regions, and the grant is said to be enacted in honour of God and reverence of Eusebius, who (like Leo) had stood firm against the heresiarchs. That it is Arduin and his followers who now pose the threat is made clear by the prohibition clause, which not only includes a standard statement to the effect that that 'no duke, margrave . . . [or] count' ('nullus dux nullus marchio . . . nullus comes') is to interfere with the grant, but adds 'and especially no margrave of Ivrea' ('nec etiam Yporiensis marchio')! Leo knew exactly where the threat lay.

It is presumably this immediacy which inspired the bishop to include a blessing-curse in addition to the more standard sanction (which itself threatens the higher sum of a thousand pounds): those who seek to preserve the precept are to be blessed by the Holy Trinity, while those who undermine it are to be cursed and damned among the heretics (Leo's second recourse to the language of heresy and orthodoxy). These latter details were judged to be later interpolations by the text's late nineteenth-century editors. But they are present in the earliest copy, from the first half of the eleventh century, and conform well to Leo's stylistic preferences, so should be given the benefit of the doubt. Indeed, blessing-sanctions may not have been a standard feature

---

32. H. Bloch, 'Beiträge', 62–71. On the corroboration clause, see also Erben, *Rombilder*, 85.

33. See Sergi, 'Poteri temporali', with further literature.

34. For the distribution of comital rights, see Sergi, *Confini*, 153–82.

of imperial diplomas, but they were common enough in the local ('private') charter traditions with which Leo would have been acquainted (not least at Vercelli).[35] Even more than the previous privilege, this is a sign of the new bishop's favour. And there is an unmistakably personal tone to the transaction, which is said to have been undertaken 'so that, insofar as the church of God remains free and unharmed, our [i.e. Otto III's] empire prospers, our bands of soldiers triumph, the power of the people of Rome grows and the commonwealth is restored, we shall be worthy of living honourably in this world, and of flying up more honourably from the prison of this life to rule most honourably with the Lord' ('ut libere et securę permanente dei ecclesia prosperetur nostrum imperium, triumphet corona nostrę militię, propagetur potentia populi Romani et restituatur res publica, ut in huius mundi hospitio honeste vivere, de huius vitę carcere honestius avolare et cum domino honestissime mereamur regnare'). Clearly success in battle, the restoration of the church and well-being of the empire were intimately associated—and all part of a broader effort to secure the eternal soul of the emperor.[36]

On their own, these two diplomas would warrant note. Yet after a lull of a year and a half, they are followed by two similarly striking texts of early November 1000 (once again, issued in Rome). The first of these grants the fortified town of Santhià (S. Agatha), 20 km (13 miles) north-west of Vercelli, along with rights of jurisdiction (*districtus*) stretching five miles around it. At least one of Arduin's supporters hailed from Santhià, a strategic site on the main routes between Vercelli and Ivrea, and the purpose of the grant is clear. But as in the previous privileges, there is more than one transaction going on. After the initial donation, the diploma proceeds to transfer a series of further rights to the bishopric (again, personified by Eusebius). These include the lands of Arduin (once more), to which are now added the holdings of the margrave's son Ardicin, who had refused to appear in court to face justice in Pavia (the first we hear of this). The diploma also restores forest rights in Lucedio and Rovasenda and confirms episcopal control over the abbey of Lucedio, explaining that these rights had been alienated by Bishop Ingo. This is thus a confirmation and extension of the previous year's privileges, and the additional historical detail serves to underscore Leo's claims. The town of Santhià lay at the heart of the county of that name, and its donation amounts to little more than a reiteration of the prior year's comital grant (the town and *districtus* of five miles together evidently constituting the county). This may suggest that Leo was struggling to assert his rights, a fact which would explain why Arduin's estates are now listed in full—though with the important proviso that any additional lands he should possess elsewhere ('et omnia predia . . .

---

35. See, e.g., the charter of donation of Empress Adelheid of 995, reprised in *Placiti*, ed. Maneresi, no. 226, Vercelli, AC, II Cartella, 1. More generally: Bougard, 'Jugement divin'.

36. D O III 324. See further Gandino, 'Orrizonti politici', 79–81.

ubicunque iacent') are also to go to the see. Finally, the diploma declares that the semi-free dependents (*coloni*) of the bishopric should remain in servitude. This, too, may be a response to recent difficulties, since slaves (*servi*) of the see had been mentioned among Arduin's earlier associates. It also echoes a set of ordinances about unfree dependents issued by the emperor, perhaps at the S. Pietro gathering two years earlier.[37] In any case, the same personal animus is on show, with Arduin addressed as 'cursed' ('maledictus') and Ardicin's lands said to have been 'rightly' ('iuste') confiscated.

The second of this pair of diplomas then grants and confirms further regelian rights, including control of all gold mined within the bishopric's two counties, and further estates in Lucedio. Here Arduin starts to recede from the picture, though it does not take much to imagine who the draftsman—again, Leo himself—has in mind when he speaks of any who, 'driven by diabolical spirit' ('diabolico ductus spiritu'), might infringe its terms. And as previously, the rights conferred are most valuable. Lucedio had long been a point of interest (and dispute), as we shall see, while the upper reaches of the Po were an important source of gold in the Middle Ages.[38] Taken together, these diplomas are most impressive. They bear witness to a degree of favour and concern only otherwise seen at Farfa and, perhaps, Ravenna—and then in far more pedestrian form. It is not just the rights conceded which are important here; it is the manner in which they are framed. When not listing claims, Leo's diplomas are packed with verbal pyrotechnics, as befits one of the great Latin stylists of the age: his opponents are 'heresiarchs', 'damned' or 'driven by diabolical spirit'; his supporters, on the other hand, are (quite literally) on the side of the angels. Such sentiments are most unusual in imperial diplomas.[39] They reveal the strength of the bishop's convictions; they also reveal the severity of his situation. These were Leo's parchment weapons in the struggle for Piedmont.

Yet it is precisely these features which have inspired doubts. Already Ferdinando Gabotto (d. 1918) had expressed concerns about these diplomas; and, in 1944, the great Italian diplomatist Cesare Manaresi (d. 1959) led an all-out assault. Manaresi did not deny a connection with Leo, but argued that they were part of a concerted campaign of falsification, launched by the bishop between July 1024 and June 1025, upon the accession of Conrad II (1024–39).[40] Manaresi's doubts stemmed in no small part from Leo's involvement. He noted that such sustained recipient production was without immediate parallel or precedent; further suspicions were raised by the diplomas' generous terms. But above all, it was the reference to a county of Santhià in the

---

37. D O III 383. Cf. *Constituiones*, ed. Weiland, 47–48 (nos. 21–22). Leo's interest in the subject is also reflected in his manuscript annotations: Gavinelli, 'Leone', 260–61.

38. D O III 384. Cf. Menant, 'Pour une histoire', esp. 783.

39. See Fichtenau, 'Rhetorische Elemente', 133, 135–36.

40. Manaresi, 'Alle origini', 285–313. Cf. Gabotto, 'Diplomi regi', esp. 18–22.

second text which troubled Manaresi, since the county is otherwise first attested in Conrad's reign, at which point it became more common for rulers to grant out comital rights in this fashion. According to Manaresi, Leo's third diploma gives the lie to his second here, by referring more accurately to a fortified settlement ('castellum')—not county—of this name; only two and a half decades later would the castle develop into a fully fledged comital jurisdiction. Manaresi also argued that the concession of regelian rights in the fourth diploma would have been superfluous had Leo really enjoyed comital authority over Vercelli and Santhià. Finally, he objected in principle to the presence of multiple diplomas (two pairs, in this case) for the same recipient on the same date, a feature he deemed symptomatic of forgery. Manaresi's case is powerfully presented and internally consistent, but requires the dismissal of a swathe of otherwise acceptable texts. Few have, therefore, been willing to go quite so far. Still, lingering doubts surround these texts, doubts reiterated in the recent consideration by Francesco Panero, who sees the series as heavily reworked (if not forged outright) at the start of Conrad's reign.[41]

There are parallels with the *Orthodoxorum* series here. As there, we are confronted with a set of unusually generous privileges, in favour of a single centre and produced by the recipients in a manner which finds few parallels elsewhere. And as in that case, the texts only survive in later copies—mostly in notarial transcripts of the later Middle Ages—further complicating matters. Still, there are important differences, which make a more positive judgement appropriate here. For a start, Leo's texts are not entirely isolated. They display strong links with a fifth and final diploma of early 1001 in favour of Vercelli, which even Manaresi was willing to accept as authentic.[42] More to the point, similarities can be found between the corroboration clauses of these texts and that of the famous grant of eight counties to Sylvester II in 1001. Though this, too, is only preserved in later copies, it is almost certainly authentic, and was probably drafted by Sylvester himself (though perhaps with Leo's input).[43] Since Leo's diplomas were all issued in Rome, in one case at Sylvester's intervention, this connection lends weight to all of these texts. In fact, it may be that Leo was involved alongside Gerbert in drafting the latter diploma. And while the concession of the counties of Vercelli and Santhià may be one of the earliest grants of this nature, it finds close parallels in the document confirming of Ravenna's rights—which include a number of comital jurisdictions—a few months later. Unlike Leo's texts, this survives as an authentic original.[44] So

41. Panero, *Signoria*, 13–105. For expressions of uncertainty: Settia, 'Nelle foreste del re', 376 n. 82; D'Acunto, *Nostrum Italicum regnum*, 17; Vignodelli, 'Prima di Leone', 53.

42. D O III 388.

43. D O III 389, with Kortüm, '*Gerbertus*', 52–62; Scholz, *Politik—Selbstverständnis*, 372–78. See also Gandino, 'Ruolo dei linguaggi', esp. 188.

44. D O III 330, Bologna, AS, S. Cristina, Camaldolesi, 15/2876. Cf. D O III 341. For a reproduction of the former: Rabotti, 'Dai vertici dei poteri', 137.

whereas the *Orthodoxorum* charters suspiciously prefigure later documentary forms, Leo's charters find their closest associations with authentic documents of the later 990s and early 1000s. They are unusual, but in manners which speak in their favour.

Other considerations point in a similar direction. Since Manaresi wrote, estimations of recipient influence on diploma production have been revised significantly upwards. As a local draftsman-scribe, Leo now finds himself in good company with Hildibald B, Pilgrim of Passau, Sylvester II and Abbo of Fleury—to name only those considered in the present book. Moreover, recipient production was especially common in the highly literate world of northern Italy, with a peak in Otto III's later years. Here Leo's Vercelli stands alongside S. Ambrogio in Milan, Bobbio and S. Pietro in Ciel d'Oro.[45] There is, therefore, nothing suspicious about Leo's activity—quite the reverse. Nor was he even the first bishop of Vercelli to act in this guise. There are reasons to believe that Atto, whose actions prefigure those of Leo in many ways, had been responsible for the text of the diploma of Hugh and Lothar in favour of the cathedral canons in 945.[46] Interestingly, Leo's recourse to the language of diabolical inspiration may have its origins here, since the sanction of Atto's diploma speaks similarly of malefactors being 'instigated by the devil' ('instigante diabolo').

The case of Santhià is more complex, but also capable of sustaining different readings. The later tenth century was a period of considerable (and growing) fluidity where comital rights were concerned. This instability was in part a consequence of the move towards fortified and nucleated settlements (what Italian scholars call *incastellamento*), of which Santhià is a prime example. As we have seen, the fortified town of this name came with considerable judicial rights—a *districtus* of five miles (larger, that is, than that of most episcopal sees)—and may, therefore, have warranted designation as a county, even though it had not been one previously.[47] More to the point, perhaps, had Leo forged these documents in 1024/5, we would expect consistency here, not variation. The growing fluidity of comital jurisdiction also explains the final grant of regelian rights. Counties were increasingly bundles of loosely associated prerogatives, rather than offices in the traditional sense, so it is by no means

45. Kehr, *Urkunden*, 80–81. Cf. ibid., 67–68.

46. D HuLo 81, Vercelli, AC, Diplomi, I Cartella, 8, with Vignodelli, 'Prima di Leone', 64–5. Note, however, that Atto was clearly not the (otherwise unknown) scribe, as the hand differs markedly from that of the bishop's autograph subscription in Vercelli, AC, Diplomi, I Cartella, 9. Cf. Schiaparelli, 'Diplomi di Ugo e di Lotario', 72.

47. Sergi, *Confini*, 160–62. Cf. Pauler, *Regnum Italiae*, 40–42, for the alternative suggestion that the castle and county were distinct entities. This struggles in the face of Santhià's substantial *districtus*, which runs almost half-way to Vercelli and scarcely leaves sufficient space for a distinct county of this name. On comital rights: Violante, 'Marchesi'; Castagnetti, 'Feudalizzazione', esp. 731–35; and on *incastellamento* in the Vercellese: Adrizio, 'Origini dell'incastellamento', esp. 107–10.

certain that control over gold mining came with the original grant of Vercelli and Santhià (particularly since the latter had grown organically out of the fortification there). Finally, it scarcely needs saying that the production of two diplomas for the same recipient on the same occasion is nothing suspicious. As even Manaresi had to admit, many similar cases can be adduced; and in any case, the transactions in favour of Leo are sufficiently different to justify the decision to divide them between distinct diplomas.

The other main objections to these texts arise from the fact that they contradict the history of the estates and rights in question, as presented in other sources. As we shall see, in a number of cases this is true. Similarly troubling is the fact that many of these claims derive from a diploma of Charles the Fat, which has itself been reworked, probably by Leo. Still, we must be wary of hypercriticism. As we saw at Worms, forgeries can be employed to elicit authentic privileges; it may be that Leo was doing the same. In fact, the bishop was probably making a virtue of necessity. Vercelli had been sacked by the Hungarians in 899 and the resulting archival losses were apparently substantial. Only two charters survive from before this, in the names of Aripert II (701–12) and Charles the Fat, both of which show signs of reworking, probably around this time.[48] By inserting historical asides into new grants and confirmations, Leo might hope to make good this deficit.

The question must ultimately be whether Leo is more likely to have produced such ambitious and politically charged documents in the late 990s, at the height of his powers and in the heat of the moment, or many years later, long after Arduin's death, upon the accession of a monarch with whom he had little prior contact. The answer should be obvious. It is only in the context of Otto III's later years that the unusual form of these documents can be understood; it is also only then that Leo's lies and omissions can themselves be comprehended. The bishop was fighting for survival, and these texts were an essential part of the strategy.

False Truths: Leo's Diplomas and the Struggle for Piedmont

Accepting these diplomas as genuine does not, however, mean accepting all the claims therein. As Manaresi noted, they are in many respects deeply mendacious texts. The real problems attach not to the status of Santhià, but to that of various other rights, as presented therein.

Particularly revealing is a comparison of the privileges Leo received from Otto III with those produced following Henry II's imperial coronation in

---

48. Ferraris, *Le chiese 'stazionali'*, 2–5. The charters are *CDL*, iii.1, ed. Brühl, no. 8, and D K III 54. See further Brühl, *Studien zu den langobardischen Königsurkunden*, esp. 85–86.

early 1014. A number of interesting inconsistencies emerge here. Estates recently confiscated from a certain Count Richard in Henry II's diploma for Leo (1014 × 1017) appear as established episcopal holdings in the bishop's first confirmation from Otto III; likewise, lands forfeited by Richard's brother (or half-brother) Hubert 'the Red' ('rufus') to Pavia in 1014 are found in Leo's first confirmation.[49] Vercelli may have lost control of some of these rights in the meantime. But one suspects that Leo also downplayed the scale of the original confiscations in 999, presenting lands forfeited to Vercelli then—and later reforfeited *c.* 1014—as longstanding episcopal rights. He had good grounds for doing so. Confiscated lands were more easily contested than estalished holdings, and Leo may have hoped to bypass future claims from Richard and Hubert (or their relatives). The sleight of hand also suited Leo's wider arguments. One of his central claims was that Arduin and his associates were despoilers of church property (above all, that of Vercelli); by presenting their lands as quondam episcopal rights, he furnished the requisite proof.

Greater difficulties are presented by the history of Caresana, some 15 km (9 miles) south-east of Vercelli, overlooking the Sesia (a local tributary of the Po: Map 3). This is among the estates confirmed in the first diploma of 7 May 999, in which it is said to have been granted to the see by Berengar of Ivrea and his son Adalbert (i.e., 950 × 962). Yet we lack a diploma to this effect, and the holding had been the subject of a number of other transactions in the intervening years. The first was a bequest to the chapter (note: not the bishopric) by Berengar's youngest son, Corrado Conone. This was made in 987 and intended to take effect upon the margrave's death, perhaps some years later. There are, however, signs of competing interests in these rights. Corrado's donation is followed by similar ones by Empress Adelheid (995) and Margrave Hugh of Tuscany (996), in the former case petitioned all the way from Frankfurt, some 700 km (430 miles) to the north. Both of the latter documents were themselves subject to further confirmation at court, with Adelheid's only surviving in the resulting (incomplete) judicial notice. And all of these charters (save Adelheid's first grant) survive in their original format, so there cannot be any question of tampering.[50]

The grounds for this sudden slew of documents are to be sought in the origins of the estate and the circumstances surrounding its donation. Caresana was fiscal land and Corrado's bequest, made during Otto III's minority, was clearly felt to lack the requisite authority. Leo's later confirmation claims

49. D O III 323, DD H II 321, 322, with Keller, *Adelsherrschaft*, 278, 280–81; Andenna, 'Grandi patrimoni', 217 n. 61.

50. *Carte dello Archivio Capitolare*, ed. Arnoldi et al., nos 16, 17, 18, 19, Vercelli, AC, Diplomi, II Cartella, nos. 6, 1, 2, 4. The best editions of the two judgements are now *Placiti*, ed. Manaresi, no. 226; and Vignodelli, 'Prima di Leone', 74–77, respectively. See further Vignodelli, 'Prima di Leone', 66–67; Panero, *Signoria*, 51–52; Manaresi, 'Tre donazioni'; Groneuer, *Caresana*, 1–19.

MAP 3. The bishopric of Vercelli and Ivrean march, *c.* 999

the estate to have been a donation of Berengar and Adalbert, so it may be that Corrado had claimed Caresana back from the bishopric in the intervening years and was now merely restoring it (though, as we shall see, Leo was not above inventing such claims). That questions should arise in the mid-990s is, in any case, significant. It was at this point that Otto III came of age; it was also then that Corrado probably died. (The margrave is not securely attested after 989, and his successor Arduin first appears in early 997.) Further questions may have been raised by Corrado's status as Berengar II's son. Berengar was considered a usurper at the Ottonian court, where the legitimate line of succession was held to pass through Adelheid (as the widow of Lothar) to her (second) husband Otto I and thence to their son and latterly grandson (Otto II and Otto III). This had implications for Berengar's offspring. Soon after Otto I's conquest of Italy, Corrado and his brother Guy had their holdings in the counties of Modena, Bologna, Reggio and Bergamo confiscated.[51] Initially, they kept their rights in the Ivrean march; but after Corrado's death, the prospect of further forfeitures surely loomed. As a quondam fiscal estate inherited from a usurper, Caresana may not, in other words, have been Corrado's to give

51. DD O I 260, 272. See further MacLean, *Ottonian Queenship*, 105–25.

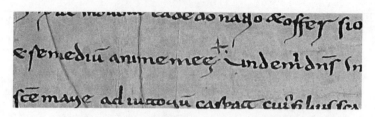

5.2 Autograph(?) cross of Adelheid's advocate: Vercelli, AC, Diplomi, II
Cartella, no. 1, © Biblioteca e Archivio Capitolare, Vercelli

in the first place. This explains why the canons had Adelheid repeat the donation. Here she acted not only as a representative of the Ottonian dynasty, but
also as the direct heir to Hugh and Lothar. Why Margrave Hugh should have
repeated the grant is less clear. He had been one of the bastions of imperial
authority in Italy in recent years, so was perhaps adding his weight to that of
the dowager queen. More importantly, Hugh himself was a grandson of King
Hugh, so may have had a residual claim of his own to the lands. In fact, the
judicial notice confirming Adelheid's donation lacks the closing signatures of a
judge and other judicial notables, the most likely explanation being that news
of Hugh's claim arrived just as proceedings were coming to a close. That the
canons still kept the resulting charter is a sign of the importance they invested
in their case. Interestingly, the surviving single sheet bears a cross in a hand
and ink different from that of the main text, precisely where Adelheid is said
to have endorsed it (Illustration 5.2). The queen was not present on this occasion, so this cannot be her own hand; but it is not too far-fetched to imagine
that it was added by her advocate (i.e., legal representative), Peter, whose presence is mentioned. In any case, Hugh himself enjoyed ties to the bishopric of
Vercelli, and it was around this time that the Tuscan margrave appointed the
saintly Bononio, abbot of Lucedio, to oversee his monastery of S. Michele in
Marturi. There the abbot would remain till Hugh's death.

Despite these variations, and despite the fact that none of these grants
mentions the others, all three agree that Caresana went to the canons in the
early to mid-990s, and none mentions any prior connection to the bishopric.
Yet the flurry itself indicates that the canons' rights were far from secure, and
it is telling that Adelheid's and Hugh's grants were both almost immediately
subject to confirmation at a court. The resulting judgements are not products
of litigation per se, since no one is reported to have contested the chapter's
rights. Rather, they take the form of what scholars call *ostensio cartae* ('presentation of the charter') cases. These were increasingly popular in the tenth
and early eleventh centuries. They involved bringing a document forward for
formal confirmation at a court of law and receiving a judicial notice repeating
its contents and affirming its validity. Sometimes this was a way of settling
an ongoing dispute quietly; more often, it was a means of pre-empting future

claims. Almost always, it was a cipher for deeper conflicts.[52] As the various donations themselves indicate, there were differing traditions regarding Caresana, a situation perhaps complicated by Arduin's own position as Corrado's successor to the march (and with it, presumably, to rights over pertaining fiscal lands). It is, therefore, scarcely surprising that the canons sought maximum security. In fact, it may be these concerns which inspired them to seek a general confirmation of their rights upon Otto III's return to Italy in December 997, a document which explicitly names Caresana and, like the others considered here, survives as an authentic original. That these matters were indeed at the forefront of the canons' minds is further suggested by the intervention of Bishop Raginfred of Bergamo in their favour. Until recently, the latter had been the local archdeacon, in which guise he had played a central role in Adelheid's concession of Caresana in 996; now he was securing his legacy.[53]

Even more revealing is the judicial notice endorsing Margrave Hugh's grant. The original, preserved in the Archivio Capitolare in Vercelli, was not known to the text's earlier editors, and has only recently been saved from obscurity by Giacomo Vignodelli. As Vignodelli notes, the single sheet presents a number of significant and unusual features. In particular, the scribe has left gaps at six points within the text. In three of them, the gap precedes the designation 'archpriest' ('archipresbiter'); and in each of these another hand has subsequently added the name 'Giselbert' ('Giselbertus'). In the other three, the space precedes the title 'advocate' ('auocatus')—the advocate here being the lay legal representative of a church. These gaps immediately follow those left for Giselbert—the archpriest and advocate always being mentioned in tandem—but no name has been supplied here, so the lacunae remain (Illustration 5.3). These omissions cannot be put down to ignorance, since both figures are said to have been present on the occasion of the judgement ('ueniens presentia [Giselbertus] archipresbiter canonice baxilice Sancti Euxebii una cum . . . eius et ipsius canonice auocatus'). And we know that the scribe was operating on the spot, since a number of those mentioned go on to append their autograph signatures (including the judge Alberic).[54]

The best explanation for these omissions and revisions is to be sought in the identities of the archpriest and advocate in question. Only one archpriest is recorded for Vercelli in these years, a certain Cunibert, and he was a figure of considerable standing. In Adelheid's original donation of Caresana (November 995), we find him listed alongside Archdeacon Raginfred receiving

52. Bougard, La justice, 307–31; Wickham, 'Justice'; Keller and Ast, 'Ostensio cartae'; Vallerani, 'Scritture'; Costambeys, 'Disputes', esp. 133–41. See also Bougard, 'Diplômes et notices'.

53. D O III 264, Vercelli, AC, Diplomi, II Cartella, 7. Cf. Placiti, ed. Manaresi, no. 226, Vercelli, AC, Diplomi, II Cartella, 1.

54. Vercelli, AC, Diplomi, II Cartella, 4, with Vignodelli, 'Prima di Leone', 68–70 (discussion), 74–77 (edition).

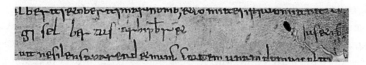

5.3 Example of gaps and insertions in the judicial notice confirming Hugh of Tuscany's grant of Caresana: Vercelli, AC, Diplomi, II Cartella, no. 4, © Biblioteca e Archivio Capitolare, Vercelli

the grant on behalf of the canons. Evidently these two were the representatives of the chapter house. Archpriest was a role akin to that of the later dean (i.e., the head of the chapter), and Cunibert is also addressed as 'provost' ('prepositus').[55] This is clearly the same figure as the 'Archpriest Cunibert' whose lands would be forfeited to Leo on account of his support for Arduin; and a Cunibert later appears as chancellor for Arduin, when the margrave made his bid for the Italian crown in the early eleventh century. Given this career trajectory, it is easy to imagine why Cunibert's presence might have been problematic at this juncture. At some point between November 995 and 7 May 999—and in all probability between 18 April 996 (the date of the court judgement confirming Adelheid's grant) and 18 March 997 (Peter's death)— the archpriest had jumped ships, abandoning Peter for the margrave (or perhaps, rather, was joined by Arduin in his opposition to the bishop). In all likelihood, this notice records the tipping point. If Cunibert had only recently fallen foul of the bishop (who, unlike in April, was not present), it is easy to see why the scribe, operating on 4 September 996, might have been wary of acknowledging his involvement. The notice was intended to ward off episcopal claims, and the archpriest's presence was a distraction best passed over in judicious silence. Perhaps most tantalizing of all, the Giselbert who now filled in for Cunibert may have been responsible for the addition of his own name. The hand in question is clearly distinct from that of the main text, as Vignodelli notes. And it reveals an uncertainty and instability we would not expect from an experienced scribe, but might well imagine of a cleric principally occupied with other duties (see above, Illustration 5.3). In any case, it is in the same ink, indicating that these adjustments were made on the same occasion

Something similar is presumably true of the missing advocate. In Adelheid's judicial notice, a judge by the name of Liuprand is recorded as the canons' advocate. Much like Cunibert, this figure seems to have been an associate of Arduin, since a Liuprand appears among those whose lands were forfeited to Leo in May 999. There he is said to be a relative of Archdeacon Giselbert,

55. *Placiti*, ed. Manaresi, no. 226 (= *Carte dello Archivio Capitolare*, ed. Arnoldi et al., no. 17). The office of archpriest is defined in a Vercelli copy of the *Collectio Anselmo dedicata*, where it is placed immediately below that of archdeacon: Vercelli, BC, Cod. XV, fols 183v–184r, with Landau, *Officium*, 13–15, 50–51.

almost certainly the same Giselbert who now filled in for Cunibert. This may also be the 'Judge Liuprand' ('Liuprand iudex') who appears alongside a son-in-law Bruning and his own (unnamed) children in the lengthier confiscation charter issued by Henry II for Leo (*c.* 1014 × 1017). The situation is complicated, however, by the existence of a second judge of this name, recorded as the deceased(!) father of Archdeacon Giselbert in March 999.[56] But since the two Liuprands are almost certainly related, it makes little difference which was intended. Either way, we are dealing with a relative of the archdeacon, who is himself reported to have made off with episcopal lands (perhaps Caresana) and joined forces with Arduin in later years. Liuprand thus belonged to the same circles as Cunibert, and presumably his loyalties had been similarly compromised. If so, the decision to insert Giselbert's name into the spaces originally intended for Cunibert is all the more noteworthy. The canons were starting to turn against Peter, but the archdeacon had apparently kept his powder dry. It was only a matter of time till tensions boiled over, however, and by the following year Giselbert had indeed joined the cause. In fact, Caresana may have been the spark which lit the fuse.[57]

This estate was, therefore, at the heart of conflicts in and around Vercelli, and in presenting it as an episcopal holding, Leo was wading right into the midst of these. He was also exploiting the ambiguities of local landholding. The big question here was that of the distinction between episcopal and canonical lands. The move towards the establishment of distinct cathedral chapter houses, which received decisive impetus from the 'Aachen rule' of 816, went hand in hand with the allocation of different lands and rights to the bishop and canons. In essence, the bishopric was now separated into two distinct (but related) institutions: the bishopric proper and the chapter. Chapters were, however, often more independent in name than in fact, and it would be the twelfth century before their position was legally formalized. In the intervening years, they led something of a shadowy existence, frequently mentioned and sometimes quite prominent, but often still under considerable episcopal oversight (mitigated or not). As a consequence, canonical rights and possessions could and did pass into episcopal hands, and conflict was common.[58]

In Vercelli, the origins of the chapter are obscure. It may have existed in latent form in the ninth century, but the first clear signs of its presence come under the reform-minded Atto, when we start seeing regular grants to the canons. Even so, the chapter's constitution and composition remain unclear,

56. D O III 323, D H II 322, *Carte dello Archivio Capitolare*, ed. Arnoldi et al., no. 23. See Keller, *Adelsherrschaft*, 285 nn. 183–84; Brunhofer, *Arduin von Ivrea*, 297–300.

57. Brunhofer, *Arduin von Ivrea*, 115–19. See also Rust, 'A guerra', 212–20 (though note that Bishop Peter's involvement in the earlier court judgements is not as clear as Rust implies).

58. Miller, *Bishop's Palace*, 80–85, 222–23; Kurdziel, 'Au prisme des faux'. Cf. Schieffer, 'Kanoniker'.

a situation complicated by the existence of two episcopal churches within the city, the larger S. Eusebio outside the walls and the smaller S. Maria Maggiore within them. With the exception of the grants of Hugh and Lothar of 943 and 945, only Eusebius is ever mentioned in documents for the chapter. It would seem that the canons of S. Maria were silently subsumed into the same corporate body as their extramural colleagues, together constituting the 'canons of the church of Vercelli' ('canonici Vercellensis ecclesiae') or 'canons of Saint Eusebius' ('canonici sancti Eusebii'), as they are addressed in diplomas of these years.[59] (Indeed, even in Hugh and Lothar's charters, the groups are joint recipients.) The waters are further muddied by the fact that donations to both the chapter and the bishopric might be made out to Eusebius, their shared patron. Under these circumstances, it is easy to see how the bishop might claim rights originally intended for the canons, cynically or otherwise. In fact, a degree of continuing episcopal oversight is implied by Atto's own grant to the canons in 945, which describes them as 'living under our direction' ('sub nostro regimine degentes').[60]

Leo was evidently grouping together as many of the 'lands of Saint Eusebius' as he could, and placing them all under his own direct control. The final grant of Caresana by Margrave Hugh only speaks of the estate going to the 'bishopric' ('episcopio'), an ambiguity which may have encouraged such treatment—and may have inspired the ensuing court judgement, which specifies that the lands in question are indeed for the canons. By such a *coup de main*, Leo might hope to collapse episcopal and canonical rights. All indications are that he was successful, at least where Caresana is concerned: all confirmations of the eleventh century list the centre among the bishop's holdings. The chapter's rights were not forgotten, however. In 1040, Leo's successor Arderic (1026/7–44) promised the estate's return, should the canons commit to living a regular life (i.e., in common, according to a rule). The estate may even have briefly passed into their hands, though it is still listed among the bishop's holdings in Henry III's confirmation of 1054, and the first clear indications of canonical control come in the following century. Certainly Caresana remained a subject of lively debate, as revealed by the later insertion of a manicule pointing to the phrase concerning its donation in Arderic's charter.[61] This document may reveal further features of these disputes. When cathedral chapters were constituted in the ninth and tenth centuries, the process was generally associated with the institution of communal life according to a set of norms

59. D HuLo 73, Vercelli, AC, Diplomi, I Cartella, 6; D HuLo 81, Vercelli, AC, Diplomi, I Cartella, no. 8. Cf. D O III 264, Vercelli, AC, Diplomi, II Cartella, 7. See further Ciccopiedi, *Diocesi e riforme*, 66–68; Dormeier, 'Capitolo', 40–55. Note, too, the diploma of Berengar granting Regio (i.e., Orco) for the support of the canons ('ad usum et substentationem canonicorum') in 913: D Ber 87.

60. *Carte dello Archivio Capitolare*, ed. Arnoldi et al., no. 9, Vercelli, AC, Diplomi, I Cartella, 9.

61. Ibid., no. 48, Vercelli, AC, Diplomi, III Cartella, 7.

(frequently the 'Aachen rule'). Arderic's remarks suggest that communal life had broken down by the mid-eleventh century, at least in episcopal eyes, and such a breakdown could well have served as a justification for episcopal intervention (if it was not, in fact, a consequence of this). Given Leo's own reformist bent, it may well be that issues of regular life and clerical marriage—hot topics in later years—were already at stake in the later 990s. Atto had already railed against clerical marriage in the 930s and 940s; and Leo may also have been influenced by more 'northern' attitudes, since married priests were much less common in Otto III's Germany.[62]

These conflicts are further reflected in local liturgical commemoration. Uniquely, Bishop Peter was entered two—and perhaps originally three—times into the chapter's necrology-martyrology, a copy of the martyrology of Hraban Maur (d. 856) into which local names have been added in later hands, starting in the 1030s (Illustration 5.4). Here, Peter's name and a note of his death were first added in the right-hand margin of the manuscript under the date 18 March ('XV kal. apr.'); second, a more exalted entry was apparently produced in the left-hand margin, under the same date but in a special box created for this purpose; finally, this second entry was erased (baring the now-empty box) and a third produced immediately above it, now beside 17 March ('XVI kal. apr.'). Evidently Peter died on the eighteenth, but uncertainty over how he should be commemorated led to his name being dislocated from this date, an error now perpetuated in most modern scholarship. The probable cause of controversy is revealed by the nature of the final entry, which reads '† Peter, venerable bishop of this church, died, through whose intervention Caresana was given to the canons by the kings' ('† Obiit petrus venerabilis huius ecclesię epissopus, cuius interventu Caresiana a regibus data est canonicis'). While it is impossible to make out the erased entry (even under ultraviolet light), it presumably gave a different version of events, one in which Caresana either did not figure or was celebrated as an episcopal (rather than canonical) possession. That the final text should reflect the canons' interests is only natural; this was, after all, *their* book. This is not the only sign of interest in such matters. Hugh of Tuscany is also commemorated, being described as the one 'who gave Caresana to the canons of Saint Eusebius for the remedy of his soul' ('qui dedit pro animae suae remedio Carisanam canonicis sancti Eusebii').[63] Clearly it was on account of this intervention that the margrave warranted their prayers. In the end, Caresana did indeed pass to the canons, with three quarters going to S. Eusebio and one quarter to S. Maria Maggiore. The first signs of their possession come in 1102, however, and the situation only comes fully to light in the 1140s, when Bishop Gisulf (1131–51) oversaw an ambitious reconstitution

---

62. Atto of Vercelli, *Epistola* IX, PL 134, cols 115–19. Cf. Stone, 'Spiritual Heirs'.

63. Vercelli, BC, Cod. LXII, fols 187v [188v], 212v [213v], with Dormeier, 'Capitolo', 47–51.

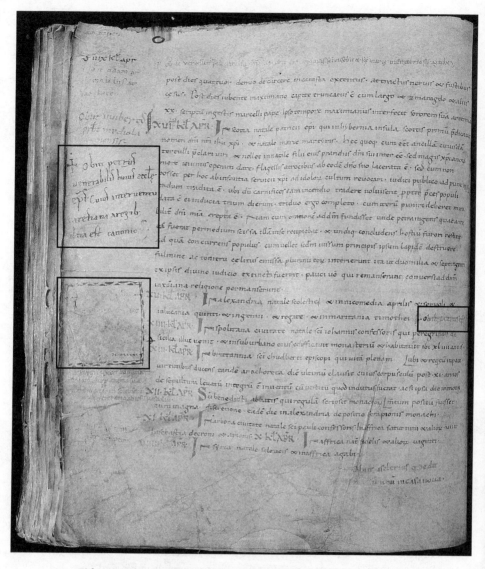

5.4 Bishop Peter's entries in the Vercelli martyrology-necrology (probable entries highlighted): Vercelli, BC, Cod. LXII, fol. 187v [188v], © Biblioteca e Archivio Capitolare, Vercelli

of canonical life in the city. This involved the first formal division between S. Eusebio and S. Maria and the reimposition of regular discipline.[64]

64. *Carte dello Archivio Capitolare*, ed. Arnoldi et al., nos 48, 65, 127, 128. Cf. D H III 328. In addition to the literature already cited: Ferraris, 'Vita comune'; Minghetti Rondoni, 'Rinnovamento spirituale'.

We can discern similar trends where rights over the rivers Sesia and Cervo are concerned. These tributaries of the Po meet just north of Vercelli, before running through the city and down into the Lombard plain (Map 3). Rights over them are mentioned as episcopal holdings in Leo's diplomas, and thereafter can be found in all confirmations of the eleventh century. But as with Caresana, the Cervo and Sesia originally belonged to the canons. In this case, they had been granted by Hugh and Lothar in 945, in the diploma probably drafted by Atto.[65] We know that they had not been lost in subsequent years, since they are listed alongside Caresana among the canons' possessions in Otto III's confirmation of December 997—a text which, as we have seen, was probably designed to ward off episcopal encroachment. And both of these diplomas survive in their original format. In presenting the Cervo and Sesia as episcopal rights, Leo was once again stepping on the canons' toes.

While these are the only places where we can be confident that Leo was twisting facts, scholars have identified a number of other possible cases. The most problematic perhaps is that of Andorno, north of Biella in the see of Ivrea (Map 3). This had been in the hands of Count Aimo (962) and latterly those of Aimo's son Manfred (988), yet is mentioned in Leo's diplomas of 999 and 1000 as an established episcopal holding. Andorno was associated with another (perhaps dependent) estate at Molinaria, which likewise finds mention in Leo's diplomas of 999 and 1000. And these are in turn associated with smaller holdings at Alice and Cavaglià, granted to Aimo in 962 and confirmed to his son in 988, but now claimed for Leo. In Manfred's confirmation, the two are listed alongside six further estates, four of which are also mentioned in Leo's first diploma of May 999.[66] The impression is, therefore, that a substantial part of the comital family's patrimony passed to the bishopric at some point in the later tenth century. In his confirmation of 1000, Leo claims that Alice and Cavaglià had originally been lost by Bishop Ingo by means of a 'diabolical exchange' ('cambium diabolicum'). And while we must be wary of such statements, a plausible context for their loss is offered by Otto I's conquest of the Italian realm, in the wake of which Aimo first received these estates (as we have seen). In fact, a charter of exchange concerning Alice has recently been recovered in Ingo's name, confirming at least part of Leo's story.[67] It would seem that Aimo's family had risen under imperial patronage and was later eclipsed when this was withdrawn. Certainly by the mid- to later 990s, a new family seems to have been entrusted with Lomello, while the snubbed Manfred may have been among Arduin's early supporters.

---

65. D HuLo 81, Vercelli, AC, Diplomi, I Cartella, 8.

66. D O I 251, D O III 50, with Brunhofer, *Arduin von Ivrea*, 111–13; Sergi, *Confini*, 183–84; Panero, *Signoria*, 49–50, 61–62; D'Acunto, *Nostrum Italicum regnum*, 71–73.

67. Vignodelli, 'I palinsesti', 12–13, 22–23.

The history of Canava, just to the north of the river Orco—another tributary of the Po (Map 3)—is somewhat comparable. In Leo's confirmation of
999, this is said to have been granted to the see by an Emperor Louis (?the
Blind, 900–905 in Italy), but only now restored. An earlier diploma of this
description does not, however, survive. What is more, the estate had been
confirmed as a holding of the nunnery of S. Maria del Senatore in Pavia by
Berengar and Adalbert in 951.[68] It is possible that we are dealing with another
opportunistic land grab by Leo. But since we do not know the history of the
estate between 951 and 999, we should perhaps give the bishop the benefit of
the doubt. In fact, there is no mention of Canava in the next confirmation of
the nunnery's rights in 1054, a document which clearly draws on earlier (lost)
confirmations of Otto I and Otto III.[69]

More serious issues attach to Monte, just south of the Po, 40 km (25 miles)
downstream from Vercelli (Map 3). This had been granted to the monastery
of S. Ambrogio in Milan by Hugh and Lothar and was confirmed there by
Otto I during his first (abortive) invasion of Italy in 951, in a document which
survives in its original format. It is one of a number of Piedmontese rights
acquired by S. Ambrogio, and we know that the monks continued to possess
Monte in later years, since Hugh and Lothar's grant was confirmed in early
997. This is followed by a general confirmation of the monastery's holdings
(probably in early 998), in which the estate is also mentioned. Like the Otto
I confirmation, both of these survive in their original format.[70] The problem
here is that an estate of this name is apparently conferred on Leo in the second
diploma of 1000. Since Monte lies considerably closer to Vercelli than Milan,
it is easy to see why Leo may have had an interest. Nevertheless, there are
no signs of tension between Vercelli and S. Ambrogio, which might explain
such a move. More to the point, there are no indications that Vercelli ever
held Monte. It may therefore be that we are dealing with two different estates.
Monte, meaning 'mount', was a common designation, particularly in the hilly
landscape of subalpine Piedmont. But it is rarely used as a place-name on
its own, precisely on account of its ubiquity (much as 'Mount' is a rare top-
onym in English). In Leo's case, it may be that the 'Monte' of 1000 is actually
a short form for the 'Mount Cisidola' ('mons Cisidola')—perhaps Coggiola to
the north-east of modern Biella (Map 3)—mentioned in the first diploma for

68. D BerAd 3.

69. D H III 317, with Bresslau, 'Exkurse', 395 n. 2.

70. D HuLo 64; D O I 138, Milan, AS, Museo diplomatico, cart. 6, prot. 57/196; D O III
236, Milan, AS, Museo diplomatico, cart. 10, prot. 188/316; D O III 266, Milan, AS, Museo
diplomatico, cart. 10, prot. 186/314. On the latter, see Huschner, 'Original, Abschrift', 54 n.
25, though note that the diploma shows every sign of having once been sealed (*pace* Huschner); and this, combined with the autograph *Vollziehung*, suggest that this may indeed
have been an authorized text. On S. Ambrogio's interests in Piedmont: Minghetti Rondoni,
'L'espansione territoriale'.

the see. Certainly in the charter of 1000 'Monte' appears in proximity with rights mentioned alongside 'Cisidola' in the first. That we are indeed dealing with a Mount Cisidola, rather than separate estates of Monte (mons) and Cisidola, in the first privilege (as some have suggested) is indicated by Conrad II's later confirmation for the see—based ultimately on this text—where this is described as 'the small estate of Cisidola on the mountain/hill' ('Cisidulam curticellam in monte').[71] There is, therefore, no particular reason to suspect foul play, and Monte was confirmed in S. Ambrogio's hands by Henry II in 1005, without any signs of opposition.[72]

Similar inconsistencies can be found in the history of Orco (modern Cortereggio) and pertaining forest rights in the Chy valley (Map 3), mentioned in the reworked Charles the Fat diploma and also in Leo's first confirmation of May 999. In the former, the estate goes by the alternative name Regio (whence the modern designation). Yet Regio itself was first granted to the see by Berengar I in 913, a quarter century after Charles's demise.[73] The problems multiply as we move into Leo's episcopate. Just four years after Orco had been confirmed in Vercelli's hands, the estate was granted by Arduin—now risen to the kingship, thanks to the power vacuum left by Otto III's unexpected death in early 1002—to a deacon of Ivrea named Tedevert. This has raised doubts about the reality of Vercelli's possession, doubts deepened by a charter of 1019 of Count Otto-William of Burgundy (d. 1026), recording the donation of a number of estates, including Orco, to the new abbey of Fruttuaria, a document which survives as an apparent original (Illustration 5.5). There can be no doubt that, like Caresana, Orco was the subject of competing claims. Nonetheless, there is little reason to suspect Leo of outright falsehood here. Orco lies within the diocese of Ivrea, in an area in which many of Arduin's followers were to be found. This is why Leo was interested in the estate (it is in this region that Canava is also to be found); this is also why Arduin wished to contest the bishop's claims. In this respect, it is significant that Fruttuaria, to which Otto-William donates the estate in 1019, was a foundation of Arduin's associates. These forays into Ivrean territory may explain the later remark in the *Chronicle of Novalesa* (c. 1050), a well-informed (if eccentric) local source, that Leo sought to take over the see of Ivrea and monastery of Breme in these years.[74]

In any case, Henry II's first diploma for Leo, issued in 1007, confirms Orco alongside a few other estates. This can only be understood in the light of Arduin's grant of 1003, to which it responds; and it was presumably Henry's

71. DD O III 384, 323, D K II 147. Cf. Brunhofer, *Arduin von Ivrea*, 93–94 n. 186; Panero, *Signoria*, 63, 96. Cisidola has also been identified with Cossila on the northern outskirts of modern Biella: Sergi, *Confini*, 158–59 n. 48.

72. D H II 95, Milan, AS, Museo diplomatico, cart. 11, prot. 20/363.

73. D Ber 87.

74. *Chronicon Novaliciense*, V.36, ed. Alessio, 298–300. See also E. A. Clark, 'Chronicle of Novalese', 217–18; and cf. Geary, *Phantoms*, 115–23.

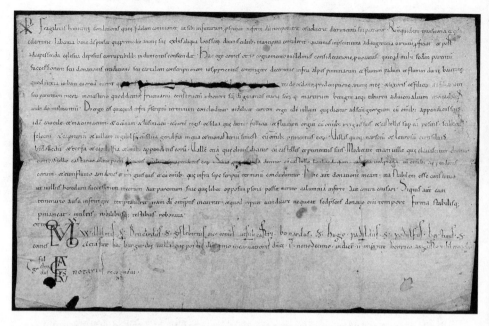

5.5 Count Otto-William's donation of Orco: Turin, AS, Materie ecclesiastiche, Abbazia di S. Benigno, mazzo 1, 6, © AS Turin

privilege which gave rise to Otto-William's donation. Henry's charter is framed as a confirmation of an earlier privilege of Charles the Fat. Yet it does not simply follow the terms of the surviving (reworked) diploma of this ruler, which we have already met in passing; it also includes details from a suspect notice in Charles's name (of which more anon). The suspicion in both cases is that Leo has doctored these texts so as to provide the necessary cover. If so, his efforts were rewarded. Arduin's diploma for Tedevert survives as a damaged single sheet, which doubled as a book cover in the later Middle Ages (it is this which has caused the cropping of its left margin). Thanks to this colourful afterlife, we know that the charter passed into the hands of the cathedral, since the book is described as a possession of S. Eusebio (Illustration 5.6). While we cannot know precisely when this happened, the mid- to later years of Leo's episcopate seem likely.[75]

Finally, questions have been raised as to Leo's claims to the monastery of Lucedio and its dependent estate at 'Quadradula/Quadratula', apparently at a site near modern Brusasco, just south of the Po between Vercelli and Turin

75. D Ard 8, Turin, AS, Museo storico I, 1; Poupardin, *Le royaume de Bourgogne*, Appendix 7, 420–29, Turin, AS, Materie ecclesiastiche, Abbazia di S. Benigno, mazzo 1, 6; D H II 132. For a facsimile of the second: Penco, 'Le "Consuetudines Fructuarienses"', 151. The last survives in an imitative copy of the twelfth century: Vercelli, AC, Diplomi, III Cartella, 3. See further Panero, *Signoria*, 32–33.

5.6 The dorse (reverse) of Arduin of Ivrea's diploma for Tedevert: Turin, AS,
Museo storico I, 1, © AS Turin

(Map 3).[76] The difficulty here lies in the status of the abbey of S. Michele di
Lucedio itself. Diplomas in the name of Lothar I (840–55) and Berengar I
grant and confirm the centre to the bishop of Novara, Leo's neighbour to the
north-east. On this basis, Luigi Schiaparelli concluded that all Vercelli documents concerning Lucedio before Arderic's episcopate are forgeries. He was
predictably followed by Manaresi, who saw Lucedio's presence in Leo's documents as a further sign of the bishop's forging proclivities.[77] That some of the
Vercelli texts have been improved is quite likely, but they cannot be dismissed
so swiftly. Lucedio lay within Vercelli's diocese—indeed, the city of Vercelli
lies between the abbey and Novara—and had evidently once belonged to the
bishopric, as a lightly reworked (but fundamentally authentic) diploma of

76. For the localization: Settia, 'Assetto', 245.

77. D Lo I 41, D Ber 64, with Schiaparelli, 'Diplomi di Berengario I', 142–43; Manaresi,
'Alle origini', 295.

Aripert II (701–12) attests.[78] There are, furthermore, signs that Lucedio had been under episcopal influence for some time before Leo's episcopate. As we have seen, the *Life* of Bononio, probably drawn up at Lucedio at the behest of Leo's successor Arderic, records that the saintly hermit was appointed abbot by Bishop Peter. And the impression of episcopal influence is reinforced by the *Life* of William of Volpiano (1031×c. 1035), which reports that the future reformer had left S. Michele as a youth because he was unwilling to swear allegiance to the local bishop of Vercelli (again, Peter).[79] In fact, it is Novara's texts, not Vercelli's, which have probably been more drastically manipulated. To maintain his case in favour of Novara, Schiaparelli had to dismiss a fundamentally acceptable judicial notice of 900, conferring Lucedio on Vercelli. It would appear that the monastery had passed back into the hands of the local bishop then, and that the purported confirmation for Novara of 905 was itself confected in order to challenge this.[80]

There are, therefore, grounds to doubt some of Leo's territorial claims. In at least two cases, he presented canonical rights as episcopal ones. And in many others, he was economical with the truth. The association of these claims with prior privileges of Charles the Fat further complicates matters. Only two texts in Charles's name survive for Vercelli: a diploma, which like those of Leo survives in later medieval copies; and a notice, which is preserved in copies of Leo's episcopate. The former reveals a late ninth-century substratum, but has clearly been revised, almost certainly by Leo himself. The bishop's interventions are partly stylistic, serving to underline the connection between Vercelli and Eusebius; they also serve to turn donations into restitutions at a number of points, emphasizing the antiquity of the see's rights. Most crucially, Leo has added to the estates originally conferred. The additions include Caresena, which as we have seen did not pass to Vercelli until after 987 (and then, to the canons), and Orco (here called Regio). The notice in Charles the Fat's name provides further detail about the latter. It speaks of a 'Regio within the walls', evidently an urban holding of some description. Leo's intervention here may have been to associate the name of this urban holding with an entirely different (rural) estate (Orco). Indeed, Leo has Charles refer to the rights in question as 'our large estate which is called Regio by earlier people' ('cortem nostram magnam que dicitur Regio antiquo . . . vulgo'), a clear admission that it no longer goes by this designation.[81] Similarly problematic is the inclusion

78. *CDL*, iii.1, ed. Brühl, no. 8, with Brühl, *Studien zu den langobardischen Königsurkunden*, 77–86; Cancian, *L'abbazia di S. Genuario*, 1–21.

79. *Vita S. Bononii*, ch. 10, ed. Schwartz and Hofmeister, 1029; Raoul Glaber, *Vita Willelmi abbatis*, ch. 4, ed. Bulst, 260–62.

80. *Placiti*, ed. Manaresi, no. II. See Gabotto, 'Contrasto'.

81. D K III 54. Cf. D H II 132, with Manaresi, 'Alle origini', 292, 294–95. However, note that in Beregnar I's (apparently authentic) diploma of 913 this estate is already addressed as 'which was once called the estate of Regio' ('qui olim Curtis Regia dicebatur'): D Ber 87.

of Formigliana in the diploma. In Leo's confirmation of 999, this is listed as an episcopal holding; but there it is said to have been granted by Berengar and Adalbert, over half a century after Charles's reign. Finally, the presence of Trecate (Trecade), 9.5 km (6 miles) east of Novara, has raised doubts, since this was in Novara's possession in the early tenth century. It apparently later found its way into the hands of Corrado Conone, perhaps as a fiscal estate, and in a now-lost donation of 989 the margrave gave it to the archbishop of Milan. Be that as it may, by 1014 Trecate had been restored in Novara, in a charter framed as a response to Arduin's depredations; thereafter, it is a well-attested Novarese holding.[82] Yet the very absence of a demonstrable connection with Vercelli speaks in favour of this detail. We would expect Leo (or any other interpolator) to have manufactured claims to contested (or recently acquired) rights, not ones in which Vercelli had little immediate interest.

More problematic is the notice in the name of Charles the Fat. As we have seen, Leo's first diploma refers to both precepts of Charles (in the plural) and 'letters written above the altar of Saint John the Baptist' ('litere . . . super altare sancti Iohannis baptiste scripte'). It is almost certainly the latter which the notice records. This is first copied on multiple lines at the start of a manuscript of the *Anselmo dedicata* (a northern Italian canon law collection) in an elegant uncial hand of the early eleventh century, apparently in an attempt to render the monumentality of the original (Illustration 5.7).[83] Its contents align even more closely with Leo's territorial claims than those of the reworked diploma. Three of the same estates are mentioned: Regio (here referred to as 'within the walls'), Romagnano and Formigliana. But the notice also includes additional rights, including the abbey of Aruna in north-eastern Piedmont, the fortified settlement of Victimulli, sets of estates at Canava and Cavaglià and Andorno and Colubino (respectively), the church of S. Salvatore, and the abbey of S. Michele di Lucedio with the pertaining estate at 'Quadradula'. As has long been noted, these contents are most misleading. To start with the obvious, the abbey of Aruna (modern Arona on Lake Maggiore: Map 3) was not founded until the later 960s and can scarcely have been conferred on Vercelli by Charles the Fat.[84] Similarly worrying is the presence of Lucedio, since this did not return to Vercelli's hands before 900, as we have seen. The history of the other rights is less well known, but Andorno and Cavaglià were in the hands of Aimo and Manfred in the second half of the tenth century, while Canava was at least briefly held by the nuns of S. Maria del Senatore in Pavia. In fact, the overlap between this notice and the first diploma for Leo in

82. *Carte dello Archivio Capitolare di Santa Maria*, ed. Gabotto et al., no. 28, D H II 320. Cf. Calco, *Mediolanensis historiae*, 119, mentioning Corrado's donation of 989.

83. Vercelli, BC, Cod. XV, fol. 1v; Böhmer, *Regesta Imperii*, i.1, no. 1635; Cipolla, 'Di un diploma perduto'. Another copy, in an early eleventh-century Caroline minuscule hand, can be found in Vercelli, BC, Cod. CXXXIV, fol. 254r. Cf. Vezin, 'Écritures imitées', 58–61.

84. Lucioni, 'Arona'.

5.7 Earliest copy of Charles the Fat's notice for Vercelli: Vercelli, BC, Cod. XV, fol. 1v, © Biblioteca e Archivio Capitolare, Vercelli

May 999 is striking, with all but one of the holdings in the former making their way into the latter. This strongly suggests production (or at least reworking) around this time, precisely when the earliest copies were made. Still, this was not just a brazen land grab. With the exception of Romagnano—the one estate not mentioned in the diploma of 999—these holdings all went on to become established episcopal rights, mentioned not only in the first confirmation for Arderic in 1027 (which closely follows Leo's texts) but also the second in his favour (which shows greater independence). Moreover, in at least some of these cases (such as Andorno and Cavaglià) traditions regarding earlier episcopal ownership may be authentic.

Finally, Francesco Panero has raised doubts about those rights that are mentioned in Leo's privileges and Arderic's first confirmation, but dropped in Arderic's second (and then absent in Henry III's on this basis).[85] He sees the latter texts as an independent control on the former—an 'interpretive key' ('chiave interpretativa'), as he puts it—giving the lie to their more egregious claims. From this perspective, those rights found only in Leo's texts and their

85. DD K II 84, 147, D H III 328, with Panero *Signoria*, 13–18, 84–97. See also Panero, 'Consolidamento', 424–40. Note that D K II 147 may have been a draft, in which case arguing from silence becomes dangerous.

direct derivatives are to be treated as suspect. We must certainly be alive to the possibility of tampering, but in none of the cases identified by Panero is this clear cut. His strongest arguments concern Cerreto, 'Vulpara' and Casanova, mentioned in Leo's first diploma but absent from Arderic's second. The first two of these may be the same as the 'castle of Cerreto and Vulparia' confiscated from Hubert the Red and transferred to Pavia in 1014. Panero sees herein a serious contradiction: if Vercelli had held these rights, they can scarcely have been Hubert's to forfeit—let alone Pavia's to receive. Yet as at Orco, we must be wary of being too prescriptive. It is easy to imagine circumstances under which Leo's rights had been seized by Hubert, who was one of Arduin's most prominent followers; and if so, there need be no contradiction with the later grant. Certainly Cerreto seems to have been a hotbed of anti-episcopal sentiment. Not only was it a holding of Hubert in 1014, but it had been the site of Archdeacon Giselbert's donation to the chapter in March 999. It is also significant that Leo himself drafted the later diploma for Pavia; he was presumably involved precisely because this touched upon Vercelli's interests.[86]

Panero similarly suggests that problems may attach to the concession of judicial rights (*districtus*) in S. Evasio, as found in Leo's first diploma, since these were only later conferred on the bishopric by Henry IV. Yet the donation of 1070 is clearly distinct from the earlier confirmation, as Panero acknowledges; it concerns property at (Casale) S. Evasio, not *districtus*, and was presumably intended to supplement existing episcopal prerogatives.[87] Matters are murkier with the monastery of Aruna, mentioned in Leo's diplomas (and the doubtful Charles the Fat notice), but dropped in Conrad II's first confirmation and, following it, all later texts. Clearly the abbey soon passed from Vercelli's hands—if, indeed, it had ever been there in the first place. But whether this proves that the centre is an interpolation in Leo's diplomas of 999 and 1000, as Panero insists, is far from clear.[88] In fact, as at Trecate, the very absence of demonstrable episcopal interest in the centre points in the opposite direction.

So while there are ample signs that Leo touched up the documentary records at Vercelli, we must be wary of treating inconsistencies alone as signs of forgery.[89] Then as now, there was many a slip 'twixt cup and lip, and it is easy to imagine circumstances under which Leo (or his neighbours) struggled to make good their claims, as recorded in otherwise authentic texts. In this respect, his diplomas are best read as a wish-list. They present the bishop's maximal demands, not his precise holdings. By simplifying estate histories, Leo pulled a similar trick to Æthelwold and the English reformers, presenting

---

86. D H II 321, with H. Bloch, 'Beiträge', 62–71, 73. Cf. *Carte dello Archivio Capitolare*, ed. Arnoldi et al., no. 23.

87. D H IV 320. Cf. Panero, *Signoria*, 104 n. 99, 109, and 'Consolidamento', 436 n. 78, 441 n. 91.

88. Panero, *Signoria*, 60.

89. Cf. Guyotjeannin, 'Pouvoirs publics', 20–21, for similar remarks.

newly acquired rights as longstanding ones while manufacturing claims to others he hoped to secure. In the literate and litigious world of northern Italy, such documents were powerful tools. However, they did not necessarily take immediate effect. It would be Henry II's later years before Leo's position was secure, and it may have taken until then for him to make many of his claims stick.[90] But make them stick he did. The majority of estates for which we have conflicting reports in Leo's episcopate are found in Arderic's second confirmation (c. 1030) and Henry III's on this basis (1054).[91] At least here, Leo's wishes came true.

The one remaining problem concerns the later judgement of the cardinal and papal legate Hugh of S. Lorenzo. Hugh was charged with deciding a dispute between the canons and bishop in 1146. This focused on the local port, those rights over the Sesia which had been conceded to the canons in 945 but then claimed by Leo in 999. The impetus for conflict came from the reconstitution of communal life among the canons by Bishop Gisulf, a process which involved for the first time dividing the community of S. Eusebio from its smaller intramural counterpart at S. Maria. This naturally raised questions about the respective rights of the houses, and the resulting sifting of documents led to a number of challenges, including this one. The important thing from our present perspective is that Cardinal Hugh found in favour of the canons and against the bishop, on the basis of those diplomas of Hugh and Lothar and Otto III already mentioned—both of which were recopied around this time—as well as another (apparently lost) privilege of Otto III's time as king (i.e., before Ascension 996), all of which he deemed of utmost authority ('firmissa dedimus auctoritatem'). In contrast, Hugh found the bishop's documents 'of no force' ('nihil vigoris') in this matter, because they were 'false on account of the impression of seals and the alteration of the letters' ('falsa propter sigillorum impressionem ac literrarum mutationem'): that is, they bore suspect seals and showed signs of tampering. Since Leo's confirmation of 999 is the first document to mention episcopal rights over the Sesia (and Cervo), it has been suggested that this and the confirmation of 1000 are intended.[92] Certainly these were two of the main texts to mention episcopal rights over the river. But in the absence of the surviving single sheets, we can neither be certain that they were intended (these rights are also found in the later confirmations of Conrad II and Henry III), nor that Hugh's judgement was correct. Medieval charter criticism was not as rudimentary as some believe, but it was far from a fine art. And in this case, the same texts were deemed authentic by those who copied them in the second quarter of the fourteenth century,

90. See similarly Settia, 'Nelle foreste del re', 404–5.
91. D K II 147, D H III 328.
92. *Carte dello Archivio Capitolare*, ed. Arnoldi et al., no. 130, Vercelli, AC, Diplomi, III Cartella, 8, with Panero, *Signoria*, 57–58; Gabotto, 'Diplomi regi', 18–22. For the wider context: Ferraris, 'Vita comune'; Minghetti Rondoni, 'Rinnovamento spirituale'; Alberzoni, 'Vercelli e il papato', 88–93.

professional communal notaries with little reason to favour the bishop.[93] Given the indications that Leo liked tinkering with his own compositions, it may be that herein lay the problem. Formal imperial diplomas were not normally subject to updating and adjustment. But as a recipient draftsman who held the emperor's ear, Leo may have felt empowered to behave differently. Certainly the one charter of his to survive in a contemporary copy (in his own hand!) was an evolving text, with many additions and improvements. Leo's 'original' diplomas may therefore have looked something like the northern French *pancartes* of these years: documents covering multiple estates and/or transactions, which on account of their composite nature were frequently subject to adjustment in line with the later needs and interests of the recipient.[94]

Given these uncertainties, surprisingly little attention has been given to the preservation of these charters. The initial confirmation of May 999 and the grant of Santhià in the following year first survive in the mid-fourteenth-century cartulary of the Commune of Vercelli (the *Liber Biscioni*); but the donation of comital rights in Vercelli and Santhià (999) and the grant of additional regelian rights (1000) are preserved in earlier single sheet copies. In the former case, the copy comes from the first half of the eleventh century, not long after the initial grant (conceivably even in Leo's episcopate). Not only does this demonstrate the early existence of the charter, but crucially, the scribe has shown considerable care in reproducing the appearance of the lost original. The result is an imitative copy in the full sense of the term (what French scholars would call a *copie figurée*). The opening protocol and closing eschatocol are correctly laid out and rendered in the impressive elongated script reserved for such elements (in fact, the former ends short of the right-hand margin, presumably because the exemplar was narrower); the imperial monogram is carefully copied; and the main text is in the elegant diplomatic minuscule characteristic of contemporary diplomas (Illustration 5.8). Were it not for the absence of a seal and the presence of a second charter, copied immediately beneath the first (also in imitative form), this could easily pass for the original. In this respect, a number of features suggest that this text derives from an authentic document of spring 999. Particularly noteworthy is the use of majuscules (specifically uncials) for Eusebius's name in the main text, as well as for a number of details in the dating clause (the nones of May, the emperor's name and final 'amen'). The use of such display script—typically square capitals or uncials—in the body of diplomas was an innovation of Otto III's reign, first popularized following the emperor's long sojourn in Rome in spring 998. Similarly significant is the form of the imperial monogram. This shows every sign of having been completed—unusually for rulers of the period, Otto III often undertook this duty himself—and takes the form of the new title monogram

93. Ferraris, 'Il "cerchio magico"', 23–33.

94. Cf. Parisse, 'Écriture et réécriture'. In a strict sense, Leo's diplomas are indeed *pancartae*.

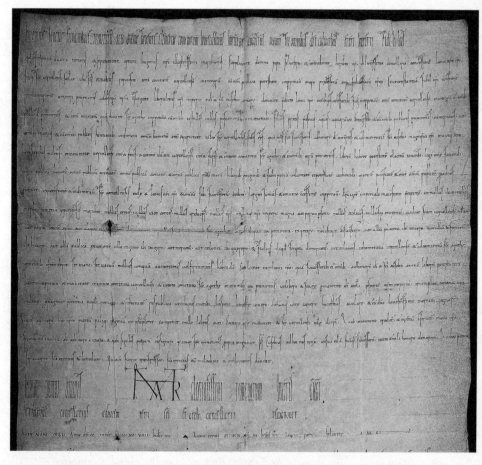

5.8 Early imitative copy of Otto III's concession of comital rights to Vercelli: Vercelli, AC, Diplomi, II Cartella, no. 9, © Biblioteca e Archivio Capitolare, Vercelli

introduced following the emperor's consecration in Rome at Ascension 996. This owes much to the imperial title monogram of Otto II's later years (the one Pilgrim so often failed to produce); however, an A has now been added in the lower quadrant, a detail found, significantly, in our copy. Finally, the imperial subscription bears the rarer epithet 'most glorious' ('gloriosissimus'), which had been reintroduced by Hildibald B in the 980s; it also adds 'of the Romans' ('Romanorum') to the title, as is periodically observed from 997 on, particularly in recipient productions.[95]

95. Vercelli, AC, Diplomi, II Cartella, 9. On the introduction of majuscule forms: Erben, *Kaiser- und Königsurkunden*, 133–34; Huschner, *Transalpine Kommunikation*, 358–60; on imperial monograms: Rück, *Bildberichte*, 22–24, 111–19; and on subcriptions: Kehr, *Urkunden*, 137–43. That local scribes frequently (and generally faithfully) reproduced such

The earliest copies of the other charters are somewhat less revealing, but also not without interest. While none of these is imitative in the same sense, they too render elements of their exemplars (as was common in Italy), particularly in the closing eschatocol.[96] And again, the forms given speak in favour of the texts. Thus the grant of additional regelian rights in 1000 survives in a single sheet copy of the later twelfth or thirteenth century. Here the scribe has accurately copied the traditional C-formed chrismon at the start of the charter and the new imperial title monogram—including tell-tale A in the lower quadrant—towards the end.[97] The remaining two diplomas are first preserved in the great Biscioni cartulary of the Commune, produced in the second quarter of the fourteenth century. Yet even here, we are only at a slight remove from the originals. The copyists of the cartulary showed considerable interest in royal and imperial monograms; and again, the forms given are acceptable for May 999 and November 1000.[98] Textual considerations reinforce these conclusions. The first confirmation of 999 bears the same 'most glorious' epithet as the comital grant of this occasion, as does the final concession of regalian rights, while the donation of Santhià has 'most invincible' ('invictissimus') here, a common Italian alternative. Rarer is the introduction of the emperor's ordinal (*tercius*) into the second of these; but again this is far from unprecedented, especially in Italian recipient products of these years.[99]

Yet if no archforger, Leo certainly exploited the opportunity of producing his own diplomas to cast Vercelli in the best possible light. In the tumultuous politics of the late ninth century, the see had been sacked at least once, resulting in substantial archival losses. Where elsewhere forgery was used to plug such gaps, Leo resorted to more subtle means of documentary manipulation: he improved one of the few surviving diplomas for his see (in the name of Charles the Fat), while furnishing his own texts with numerous historical asides, which helped anchor his claims in the bishopric's longer history.

Leo, Arduin and the Politics of the Early Eleventh Century

In pursuing an aggressive policy of territorial restitution, Leo was not on his own. Otto III's brief reign in Italy witnessed concentrated efforts to reassert imperial and ecclesiastical authority in the peninsula. The resulting

---

elements is revealed by the mid-twelfth-century copy of Otto III and Hugh and Lothar's diplomas, which we can check against the originals: Vercelli, AC, Diplomi, II Cartella, 8.

96. On Italian copying practices: Ghignoli, '"*Die Geschichte*"'; De Angelis, 'Tradizione in copia'; Huschner, 'Originale, imitierende Kopien, Fälschungen'.

97. Vercelli, AC, Diplomi, III Cartella, 1.

98. Vercelli, Archivio del Comune, *Biscioni* I, fols 60r–61r, 216r–217r, 223r–224r.

99. Kehr, *Urkunden*, 142.

undertakings saw the emperor join forces with a number of reform-minded prelates, including Gregory V, Gerbert of Aurillac (alias Sylvester II), Hugh of Farfa and Leo of SS Bonifacio ed Alessio (the latter a close associate of Abbo of Fleury)—not to mention Leo himself.[100]

In Rome, imperial intervention focused on Gregory V and Sylvester II. As newcomers to the scene, both popes struggled to gain traction. In response, they (and the emperor) positioned themselves as the restorers of tradition and orthodoxy. This approach finds its clearest expression in Otto's famed privilege for Sylvester of 1001, in which the emperor presents his and (above all) the pope's efforts as a cleansing of the Augean stables, a necessary return of the papacy and Rome to their former glory.[101] Such convictions also underpinned Gregory and Sylvester's actions in these years, as attested by the many church councils they convened (often with the emperor). And a similar note is struck by Leo's own poem on Gregory and Otto (*Versus de Gregorio papa et Ottone augusto*) which he copied into a canon law manuscript, perhaps intended for presentation to the emperor. Here Leo praises the two men, underscoring in suitably alliterative terms Gregory's efforts to purge the world, aided and abetted by imperial authority ('Sub caeseris potentia, purgat papa saecula').[102]

These efforts went hand in hand with reforming initiatives elsewhere. In the neighbouring Sabina, Otto supported Hugh of Farfa's territorial claims, as witnessed by a dramatic series of diplomas and court judgements over the years 998–99. These are complemented by the abbey's own reform under Cluniac oversight in autumn 999.[103] Nonantola, an important imperial abbey to the north, was likewise removed from the oversight of the turncoat John Philagathos in spring 997 and handed over to Leo of SS Bonifacio ed Alessio to reform, actions justified by the need to secure the abbey's territorial integrity.[104] And Otto also intervened at the Cluniac-influenced S. Pietro in Ciel d'Oro in spring 998, restoring lands which had wrongly been alienated in previous years (the *terra vassalorum*)—actions which prefigure the S. Pietro ordinances of later in the year.[105] Shortly after the S. Pietro assembly, the emperor issued an analogous privilege for Gerbert of Aurillac's sometime abbey of Bobbio. Petitioned, and perhaps also drafted, by Gerbert, this

100. Görich, *Otto III.*, 209–63; D'Acunto, *Nostrum Italicum regnum*, 139–58.

101. D O III 389, with Kortüm, '*Gerbertus*', 52–62; Gandino, 'Ruolo dei linguaggi'.

102. Bamberg, Staatsbibliothek, Msc. Can. 1, fol. 13v, with Dormeier, 'Un vescovo', 47–49. See also Mayr-Harting, *Ottonian Book Illumination*, ii, 49–53.

103. DD O III 276, 277, 282, 329, 331, 332, 340, *Placiti*, ed. Manaresi, nos. 236, 254. See further Boynton, *Shaping a Monastic Identity*; Manganaro, 'Protezione regia'; Vallerani, 'Scritture', 117–27.

104. D O III 237.

105. D O III 281, Milan, AS, Museo diplomatico, cart. 10, prot. 193/320.

condemns and restores recent alienations of monastic land.[106] Finally, at the archbishopric of Ravenna, John (983–98), Gerbert (998–99) and Leo (999–1001)—the last perhaps the onetime abbot of SS Bonifacio ed Alessio (and latterly Nonantola)—enjoyed a similar brand of imperial assistance.[107]

Leo's actions were, therefore, part of a broader set of initiatives to reassert what Otto III and his advisers felt to be the correct order of things within the Italian church and realm. In the Ivrean march, these soon bore fruit. Between Arduin's condemnation at Easter 999 and the emperor's death in early 1002, nothing more is heard of the margrave, and all indications are that Arduin was on the back foot. A circular letter announcing Arduin's excommunication, preserved in the Ivrea manuscript mentioned a number of times already, envisages this being received outside the Italian realm (perhaps in Burgundy); evidently flight was a serious consideration.[108] There are also signs that Arduin's followers were starting to feel the pinch. Noteworthy here is the appearance of the margrave's brother, Guibert, at a court judgement overseen by Otto III in mid-October 1001. Guibert had evidently sought reconciliation, and now appears alongside Arduin's old nemesis Warmund of Ivrea.[109] Even more telling are the actions of William of Volpiano and his brothers. As we have seen, William had been educated at Lucedio, but sought greener pastures to avoid swearing obedience to Bishop Peter. He was evidently no friend of episcopal authority, and according to the abbot's biographer, Raoul Glaber, William later described Leo as 'this most cruel lion' ('hic crudelissimus leo')—a clever pun on the bishop's name, which means 'lion' in Latin—and 'completely without God' ('totus . . . sine Deo').[110]

Interestingly, William and his brothers, the 'sons of Robert of Volpiano' ('filii Roberti de Volpiano'), are later mentioned among Arduin's supporters in Henry II's confiscation charter for Leo (c. 1014 × 1017).[111] Given this, the foundation of Fruttuaria, William's only house on Italian soil (and Arduin's future resting place), takes on particular salience.[112] Glaber reports that when William visited Vercelli—events we can date to late 999 or early 1000—he was

106. D O III 303. I intend to pursue the arguments in favour of Gerbert's authorship elsewhere.

107. D O III 330, Bologna, AS, S. Cristina, Camaldolesi, 15/2876; D O III 341. A number of further privileges were available to the early modern antiquarian Girolamo Rossi (alias Hieronymus Rubeus, d. 1607): *Historiarvm Ravennatvm libri decem*, 812, with Rabotti, 'Dai vertici dei poteri', 138–41.

108. Ivrea, BC, Cod. LXXXVII (54), fol. 112r–v; *Konzilien Deutschlands*, ed. Hehl, 584 (no. 60C).

109. *Placiti*, ed. Manaresi, no. 266, Milan, AS, Museo diplomatico, cart. 11, prot. 3/346½. See Brunhofer, *Arduin von Ivrea*, 153–54.

110. Raoul Glaber, *Vita Willelmi abbatis*, ch. 11, ed. Bulst, 284–86.

111. D H II 322.

112. Lucioni, 'Da Warmondo a Ogerio', 150–53; Kaminsky, 'Zur Gründung von Fruttuaria', 242–45.

(perhaps symbolically) struck down by illness in S. Eusebio. His three brothers then took him back to convalesce at the family estate of Volpiano, overlooking the Orco. Upon William's recovery, they implored him to found a monastery there. And two of the brothers, Godfrey and Nithard, swore that they would renounce the profession of arms ('saecularem ... militiam') and take up religious life, donating their possessions to the cause. Monastic conversion was an increasingly popular form of piety in these years, but the timing is suggestive.[113] Spring 999 had seen Arduin's fall, followed by the first raft of diplomas in favour of Vercelli; the following year saw this sealed with the second set, including the forfeiture of Arduin's son Ardicin. The emperor also threw his weight behind the other local bishops of the Ivrean march. For the first time, Warmund now received judicial authority (*districtus*) over Ivrea and its hinterland, removing the very heart of Arduin's march from margravial oversight. Meanwhile, Peter of Novara (993–1032), another important imperial associate, had his possession of *districtus* over the local city confirmed.[114] This was a difficult time for Arduin's sympathizers, and it seems that William's brothers jumped before they were pushed. In founding a monastery, they pursued a well-established strategy to maintain family patrimony in the face of threat. It was one thing to dispossess a rebel magnate; it was quite another to despoil a church.

In Piedmont as elsewhere, Otto's interventions therefore met with resistance as well as approbation, a resistance only exacerbated by the emperor's death on 23 January 1002. This was the moment for which Arduin and his associates, including the Volpiano brothers, had been waiting.[115] Their cause was helped by the fact that the emperor's passing was unanticipated. Otto was only twenty-one at the time, and there was every reason to believe that a long and fruitful reign awaited him (his grandfather had lived to over sixty, and even his father had made it to twenty-eight). More to the point, Otto was still unmarried and without a legitimate heir. The result was a pronounced power vacuum, felt especially acutely south of the Alps. Here the reigns of the three Ottos had brought a stability not seen since the ninth century. This was achieved largely by smooth dynastic succession. Otto II had been crowned before his father even set foot on Italian soil in 961, and Otto III was consecrated just before news of his father's untimely death had arrived on Christmas Day 983. There had also been considerable Italian involvement in both successions. Otto II was crowned co-emperor on Italian soil in 967, formally inaugurating his rule in the region; he also celebrated his marriage to the Greek princess Theophanu there. And when it came time to designate

113. Raoul Glaber, *Vita Willelmi abbatis*, ch. 9, ed. Bulst, 276–78. Cf. Dessì, 'Double conversion'.

114. DD O III 376, 374. See Lucioni, 'Da Warmondo a Ogerio', 126–34.

115. Arnaldi, 'Arduino'; Brunhofer, *Arduin von Ivrea*, 172–96.

his own son and heir, Otto II had the three-year-old Otto III elected in Italy (at Ravenna), then consecrated at Aachen with the involvement of Archbishop John of Ravenna.[116]

This fragile stability was now shattered. North of the Alps, a protracted succession dispute emerged, as various magnates jostled for the vacant throne. In Italy, Arduin and his allies struck while the iron was hot. On 15 February, scarcely three weeks after Otto's passing—perhaps before his body had even left Italian soil—a small group gathered in the church of S. Michele in Pavia for Arduin's consecration.[117] Much like Henry II's coronation in Mainz later in the year (7 June 1002), this was intended to create a fait accompli. And like that event, it met with considerable success, at least initially.[118] Five days later, Arduin was in a position to issue his first diploma, for the monastery of S. Salvatore, to the west of the city. This was a confirmation of a privilege of Otto III. As such, it provided a welcome opportunity to present Arduin as the late emperor's legitimate successor. Yet the diploma does more than merely reaffirm the status quo. Among the possessions confirmed to the Pavian monastery is the dependent abbey of S. Maria in Pomposa, just south of the Po Delta on the Romagnan coast. Though mentioned in Otto III's privilege of 1000 for S. Salvatore, this had subsequently been conferred on the archbishopric of Ravenna by court judgement. The case in question had been witnessed by a wide cross-section of the kingdom's great and good—including Leo, who in the resulting judicial notice is addressed as 'most prudent bishop' ('prudentissimus episcopus') and, more unusually, 'logothete of the sacred palace' ('logotheta sacri palatii'). The latter is a Byzantine title, designating a leading financial officer at the Constantinopolitan court; here it underlines Leo's standing in imperial circles. More importantly, both pope and emperor went on to subscribe the notice, the latter bearing the similarly programmatic title 'servant of the apostles' ('servus apostolorum'). Otto III evidently had an active interest in S. Maria, where he spent considerable time in his later years; and Archbishop Frederick of Ravenna (1001–4) subsequently exchanged the centre with the emperor—that is, he allowed it to become an imperial abbey—in return for public rights over his other lands. Arduin was therefore not just confirming S. Salvatore's holdings, but silently undoing his predecessor's most recent interventions in the process.[119] This was change dressed up as stasis.

116. Huschner, 'Erzbischof Johannes von Ravenna', esp. 1–5.

117. John the Deacon, *Istoria Veneticorum*, IV.64, ed. Berto, 202; Thietmar of Merseburg, *Chronicon*, IV.54, ed. Holtzmann, 192–95. The date and location are supplied by the king-list preserved in a manuscript of the first half of the eleventh century, probably from Novalesa: Milan, Biblioteca Ambrosiana, O 55 sup., fol. 79r. See *Monumenta Novaliciensia*, ed. Cipolla, 409–16.

118. Cf. Weinfurter, *Heinrich II.*, 36–58.

119. D Ard 1, Milan, AS, Museo diplomatico, cart. 11, prot. 8/351. Cf. D O III 375, Milan, AS, Museo diplomatico, cart. 10, prot. 214/340; *Placiti*, ed. Manaresi, no. 263, revised and

As it became clear that a successor was not immediately forthcoming north of the Alps, Arduin's position strengthened. The uncertainty of these years finds expression in Leo's poem on the death of Otto and succession of Henry (*Versus de Ottone et Heinrico*), which praises the former's accomplishments, while urging the latter to intervene promptly south of the Alps.[120] It is important to distinguish this phase of Arduin's career from earlier conflicts in and around Piedmont. His support base was now wider and more varied; the stakes were also higher. Still, within the Ivrean march the situation remained much the same, with Arduin and his allies facing off against Bishops Leo, Warmund and Peter. The difference was that the boot was on the other foot. This is clear from Arduin's first diploma. Not only does this undo a number of Otto III's most recent actions; Cunibert, the archpriest so visibly absent from the record of the Caresana judgement in autumn 996, appears as his chancellor. This figure was to prove a firm ally of Arduin and would be rewarded for his service in the following year with the grant of Desana, an estate some 7.5 km (4.5 miles) south-west of Vercelli. Desana lies on one of the main routes between the city and the Po, and its transfer effectively cut Leo off from the rest of the realm. In this respect, it is not merely the estate itself that goes to Cunibert, but also all public jurisdiction (*districtus*) over it. If Leo could punch holes in Arduin's march, Arduin was showing that he could do the same to the bishop's county (Illustration 5.9).[121] Cunibert may even have briefly been (anti-) bishop of Vercelli in Leo's stead, as a bishop of this name is recorded in the see's martyrology-necrology—a source which, as we have seen, presents the canons' perspective (though the individual in question may simply be the later bishop of Turin of this name).[122] Similarly revealing is Arduin's choice of archchancellor: Peter of Como. Although Peter had performed this role under Otto III, he did not belong to the inner circle of associates around the emperor; and, unlike Leo and Gerbert, Peter had not received any noteworthy rewards for his service. This was all to change now. From Arduin, Peter and his canons received three privileges in quick succession, issued shortly after that for S. Salvatore. Interestingly, one of these reveals signs of Leo's distinctive Latin style, suggesting that, like the S. Salvatore text, it goes back to an earlier (in this case, lost) diploma of

---

improved in Volpini, 'Placiti', 345–51 (no. 16); D O III 416; D O III 419, Modena, AS, Casa e Stato, Membranacei, cassetta 1 n. 21. This is an 'accession act' in the sense of Koziol, *Politics of Memory*, 63–95. On Leo's and Otto III's titles: Huschner, *Transalpine Kommunikation*, 270–72, 386–98.

120. *Die lateinischen Dichter*, v.1–2, ed. Strecker and Fickermann, 480–3, with Bornscheuer, *Miseriae regum*, 169–83.

121. D Ard 6, Masino, Archivio Storico Castello di Masino, mazzo 43, 703. Cf. Brunhofer, *Arduin von Ivrea*, 176–77.

122. Vercelli, BC, Cod. LXII, fol. 190v [189v]. See further Ferraris, *Le chiese 'stazionali'*, 227 n. 353; Dormeier, 'Capitolo', 29–30.

5.9 Arduin of Ivrea's grant of Desana to Cunibert: Masino, Archivio Storico Castello di Masino, mazzo 43, 703, © Archivio Storico Castello di Masino

Otto III, which Leo had drafted. If so, the message could not have been clearer: Leo's words were being turned against him and his associates.[123]

Another early supporter was Tedevert, a deacon in Arduin's home town of Ivrea. We know little about this individual, but his presence at the Italian

123. DD Ard 2, 3, 4. For Leo's draftsmanship underlying the latter: Bresslau, 'Exkurse', 77–78 n. 5. More generally: Huschner, 'Piacenza—Como', 30–36.

monarch's court is suggestive of divisions within the local clergy of Ivrea similar to those observed at Vercelli. Significantly, Tedevert was rewarded by Arduin with Orco. As we have seen, this diploma bears witness to Arduin's efforts to wrest this estate from Leo; it also points to his ultimate failure, since it led a later life as a book cover in the cathedral library at Vercelli.[124] Noteworthy, too, is the support Arduin lent to the monastic foundation of Fruttuaria in modern S. Benigno Canavese, 20 km (12.5 miles) north-east of Turin on the Volpiano family lands. This too was a strategic site, overlooking the Orco river valley, where the royal estate and forest of that name were to be found. It also controlled one of the main points of access between the Alps and the Po, into which the Orco empties, straddling the routes between Turin and Ivrea in an area where Leo had active interests. As we have seen, plans for the foundation had been laid in the final years of Otto III's reign, when William's brothers found themselves out on a limb. In order to shield the endeavour, they had first passed their patrimony to an archdeacon of Turin. The latter then endowed the abbey, details emphasized in Fruttuaria's foundation charter, a complex and composite document, drawn up some years later by the recipients (probably Abbot William himself).[125]

If Arduin's accession initially eased the situation, by the time Fruttuaria was starting to take shape, questions were once again being asked. Already in January 1003, Henry II had sent Otto of Worms south to stabilize the situation in Italy. And while this first foray failed, in spring 1004 the East Frankish monarch himself appeared. Henry faced a difficult situation. His position north of the Alps remained precarious—a situation not helped by his autocratic ruling style—and he did not have the time to travel south to Rome for imperial consecration, as was customary. Forced to improvise, Henry staked his claim to the Italian realm by the same means as Arduin two years previously, being crowned king in S. Michele in Pavia on Sunday 14 May. This allowed Henry to erase the traces of Arduin's kingship, ritually undoing the margrave's earlier inauguration.[126] Almost as soon as he had achieved this, however, Henry hightailed it back north. That he was indeed seeking to efface Arduin's reign is revealed by a brace of diplomas issued at Locarno, in the south of modern Switzerland, as he crossed the Alps. These are in favour of Eberhard, the new bishop of Como (and perhaps the later bishop of Bamberg of this name), whom Henry had appointed in Peter's stead. Neither text mentions Arduin or Peter, even though the latter was probably still alive and well (as we shall see), and even though the first is an almost verbatim repetition of one of Arduin's grants. In fact, Henry confirms precisely that privilege for Como which had

124. D Ard 8, Turin, AS, Museo storico I, 1.

125. The text is edited in Bulst, *Untersuchungen*, Appendix 1, 220–48. See ibid., 115–56; Lucioni, 'L'abbazia'; S. Wood, *Proprietary Church*, 840–42. The original charter was stolen in the 1970s; a facsimile can be found in the rear flap of Bulst's *Untersuchungen* as well as its Italian translation (*Ricerche*).

126. Roach, 'Ottonians and Italy', 359–60.

been based on a (lost) diploma of Leo. If Arduin had made the bishop of Vercelli eat his words, Henry now reclaimed these for the imperial cause.[127]

But all did not go Henry's way. The people of Pavia, many of whom sympathized with Arduin, rose up on the day of his consecration, besieging Henry in the nearby imperial palace. Henry was only able to regain control by force, putting much of the city to flame. The next day, he began his northward progress, leaving as many questions as he had answered. Still, Henry's appearance had a lasting impact on Arduin's standing. Only three of the Piedmontese monarch's diplomas were issued after this point, two in 1005 and one in 1011, and the last of these may in fact be an early modern forgery. The two clearly authentic texts both concern rights in the Ivrean march, suggesting that Arduin's effective control was now limited to the region. If accepted, the third, in favour of S. Siro, would extend this as far as Pavia, where Henry had faced such fierce opposition and where there are signs of Arduin's presence in late 1008 or early 1009.[128] In any case, the impression is that Arduin was on the retreat. The dating clauses of private charters indicate a degree of continued acceptance in some regions; but here too the Ivrean monarch was swimming against the tide.[129] A similar tale is told by judicial notices, another important index of public authority: only one of these was issued in Arduin's name, in 1004.[130] (In contrast, Otto III's six-year reign had witnessed over forty.) In general, uncertainty reigned. Few still looked to Arduin, but it remained to be seen how effective Henry would prove.

If the battle of Italy was over, the battle of Piedmont was about to begin. The first diploma Arduin issued after Henry's consecration is especially revealing here. This was produced in Vercelli and is dated 28 January 1005. There has, however, been some question as to whether this text, which is only preserved in an early modern transcript, belongs to 1005. The problem is that Peter still subscribes as archchancellor, yet his successor at Como, Eberhard, had appeared in Henry II's diplomas of the previous summer. Presuming that Eberhard only succeeded Peter upon the latter's death, this must have been produced in early 1004, not 1005 (an easy scribal error: *mv* for *miiii* or *miv*). An earlier date also seems to be suggested by Arduin's next privilege. This bears the date 27 February 1004 and, unusually, makes no reference at all to an archchancellor, presumably because Peter had recently died and was yet to be

127. D H II 74, with Bresslau, 'Exkurse', 77–78 n. 5. Cf. D Ard 4, with Huschner, *Transalpine Kommunikation*, 831–34.

128. DD Ard 9, 10, *Il conte Umberto I*, ed. Carutti, no. 6, with Holtzmann, 'Urkunden König Arduins', 473–77; Pivano, *Stato e chiesa*, 258–59; Brühl, *Deutschland—Frankreich*, 651 n. 185. For signs of Arduin's presence in 1008/9, see the private charter of Count Palatine Otto (of Lomello) for the bishopric of Pavia, edited in Cappelletti, *Chiese d'Italia*, 420–21. (I was unable to consult the more recent critical edition in Bucchi de Giuli, 'Carte del vescovo di Pavia', no. 9.)

129. See Brunhofer, *Arduin von Ivrea*, 203–52, who is somewhat more optimistic.

130. *Placiti*, ed. Manaresi, no. 269, with Wickham, 'Justice', 194–95.

replaced. Yet there are problems with the dating of this text, too. It claims to
be produced in Arduin's fourth regnal year, which began on 15 February 1005,
despite bearing the incarnational date 1004. Perhaps the draftsman simply
miscalculated one of these (he would not have been the first to do so); we may,
alternatively, be dealing with a miscopying, either of three for four (*iii* for *iiii*
or *iv*) or 1004 for 1005 (*miv* or *miiii* for *mv*)—finished diplomas generally
being fair copies of working drafts. Most likely, however, is that the draftsman
was operating according to the Florentine calendar, in which the New Year
begins on the feast of the Annunciation (25 March). If so, his 27 February 1004
would be our 27 February 1005.[131]

Certainty is impossible, but a strong case can be made for accepting both
charters at face value. All elements of the former point to early 1005, and at
least one element of the latter does too (and both, if we work from the presumption of Florentine dating). Moreover, there need be no contradiction
in Eberhard appearing before Peter's demise. In Henry's eyes, Arduin was
a usurper, so it was only natural that his archchancellor should be deposed.
Indeed, Peter of Como would not have been the only bishop to lose his post for
backing the wrong horse; Peter of Asti was removed from his seat by Henry II,
as Arnulf of Milan reports, and Odelric of Cremona and Andrew of Lodi may
have faced a similar fate.[132]

If the first of these diplomas can indeed be placed in early 1005, then it
reveals that Arduin was still in control of Vercelli at this point (which, since
Henry had not ventured into Piedmont, is entirely plausible). Of greater interest are the contents of the privilege. Though only preserved in an early modern
transcript, there can be no doubt as to its authenticity, since it went on to
furnish the model for a diploma of Conrad II in favour of S. Dionigi in Milan
(which does survive as an original). The privilege itself is in favour of Fruttuaria and its focus is on the freedoms the monastery—which, as it makes clear,
has yet to be constructed—should enjoy. Specifically, it asserts that S. Benigno
is to be 'perpetually removed from all clerical and lay power' ('seclusa omnium
clericorum laicorumque potestate perpetuo') in order to prevent any 'simo-
niac heresy' ('simoniaca haeresis')—the first mention of the latter in an Italian
(or German) diploma. It then goes on to define this liberty as encompassing
not only the immunity granted to many religious houses, but also what what
we might more properly call exemption: neither lay *nor* ecclesiastical office
holders are to have influence over the centre, be it in (secular) business *or*

131. DD Ard 9, 10. The latter survives as Turin, AS, Materie politiche per rapporto
all'estero, Diplomi imperiali, mazzo 1.1, 5.2, while the diplomas of Henry II for Como are
DD H II 74, 75. See Holtzmann, 'Urkunden König Arduins', 457–59; Pivano, *Stato e chiesa*,
259–60; Brühl, *Deutschland—Frankreich*, 651 n. 185. On Florentine dating: Bresslau,
Handbuch, ii, 423–31, 435 (with n. 2); Giry, *Manuel de diplomatique*, 112–29.

132. Arnulf, *Gesta episcoporum Mediolanensium*, I.18, ed. Bethmann and Wattenbach,
11. See further Brunhofer, *Arduin von Ivrea*, 201–2.

in (ecclesiastical) matters of ordination ('aliquibus rebus vel ordinationibus'). What this means in practice is left somewhat vague. On the subject of abbatial succession, however, there is clarity. This is to be undertaken without interference, and the abbot-elect is to receive his staff—like the bishop's, a symbol of his office—from the previous abbot, if the latter is still alive (clearly the preferred scenario); if not, it is to be taken from the main altar.[133] These details are unique, reflecting a keen desire to prevent dependency on the local bishop, who would normally have overseen such matters. In fact, the diploma goes on to say that the new abbot is then 'to be consecrated without any objection by an external bishop' ('sine ullius contradiction ab externo consecretur episcopo'), an unusual turn of phrase which suggests free choice of presiding prelate.

We know that William was deeply concerned about episcopal interference, since he had refused to swear obedience to Peter of Vercelli in his youth. And this was one of many moves to secure his new foundation's institutional independence. The decision to have the abbey endowed by an archdeacon of Turin, whose see stopped just short of the centre, may have been designed in part to preclude meddling from the diocesan bishop at Ivrea. And at some point in 1005 or 1006, William obtained formal written acknowledgement of the monastery's exemption from Bishop Warmund. Though this does not survive, the text went on to furnish the basis for a string of papal exemptions, starting in December 1006. Finally, these concerns are reflected in the later customs of Fruttuaria, which report that the centre's first abbot had been consecrated 'in another realm by an unknown bishop' ('in extero regno ab ignoto episcopo').[134] Evidently William was seeking to protect his monastery from its episcopal neighbours, above all Warmund and his successors.[135]

These measures reflect growing concerns about the rituals of entry into ecclesiastical office, concerns which in amplified form would contribute to the Investiture Contest of the later eleventh century.[136] They also represent the fruits of William's experiences north of the Alps. As we saw in the last chapter, the tenth and eleventh centuries were a transformative time in relations between monks and bishops in France. And many of William's concerns find close parallels at Fleury, whose monks resorted to forgery to secure similar rights. His immediate model, however, probably lay closer to home. William had been introduced to reformed monasticism by Maiolus of Cluny (954–94),

133. D Ard 9. Cf. D K II 58, Milan, AS, Museo diplomatico, cart. 14, prot. 150/488.

134. JL 3950 (ZPUU 429); *Consuetudines Fructuarienses-Sanblasianae*, ed. Spatling and Dinter, i, 15. That it was Warmund who granted the exemption is suggested by JL 4007 (ZPUU 495). On the former, which was probably drafted by the recipients: Kortüm, *Zur päpstlichen Urkundensprache*, 186–88.

135. Lucioni, 'L'abbazia'.

136. Mayer, *Fürsten und Staat*, 58–62, 65–79; Depreux, 'Investitures'. More generally: West, *Reframing*, 199–227; Schieffer, *Entstehung des päpstlichen Investiturverbotes*.

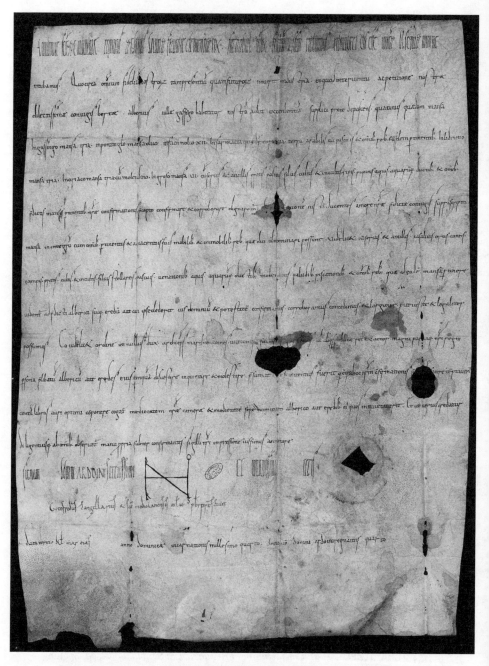

5.10 Arduin of Ivrea's grant to Alberic of Gassino: Turin, AS, Materie politiche per rapporto all'estero, Diplomi imperiali, mazzo 1.1, 5.2, © AS Turin

soon after his departure from Lucedio. And though his monastery at Saint-Bénigne was not formally subordinated to Cluny, William continued to work closely with Maiolus and Odilo (994–1049) in later years. In fact, he and Odilo had jointly reformed Farfa in autumn 999, just before William's arrival in Piedmont and the decision to found Fruttuaria. It was in these years that Odilo first received the right of external consecration for Cluny (in April 998), in a bull loosely modelled on Abbo's; presumably this document now set the tone.[137]

If issuing a diploma in Vercelli was a show of strength, it was to be one of Arduin's last. Within weeks, things were starting to unravel. In Arduin's next (and probably last) diploma, issued in late February, Peter of Como has disappeared, apparently having died in the interim. But his is not the only absence. In the place of Cunibert, we now encounter the otherwise obscure Gotefred as chancellor. While Peter and Cunibert may have happened to die in the same two months, the suspicion is that Arduin's support was starting to falter (a fact which would explain why Peter had yet to be replaced). Indeed, Cunibert's absence is especially striking, since the diploma is in favour of Alberic of Gassino, who had been present at the court judgement over Caresana in autumn 996. The overriding impression is of disorder, an impression only strengthened by the appearance of the surviving single sheet (Illustration 5.10). This is laid out like a traditional diploma, with elongated script in the first and last lines. Yet it lacks an opening chrismon and the scribe is evidently unaccustomed to such work. He has done his best to increase the ascenders and descenders on his letters, but the result is simply a stilted book hand, not the true diplomatic minuscule used for such documents. These are not the only irregularities. The individual responsible for the closing eschatocol—a second hand—was even more uncomfortable with these forms. Though he has managed to produce the requisite elongated letters for the royal subscription, it was evidently a struggle, and he immediately reverts to his native minuscule for the chancery recognition (against all convention). Interestingly, this hand may be that of the new chancellor, Gotefred, whose name appears here. If so, his inexperience could not be clearer. Similarly striking is the omission of a place of issue in the dating clause, which sadly denies us the opportunity of locating Arduin. The diploma mirrors Arduin's own position at this point: it desperately seeks to project royal dignity, yet fails at almost every hurdle.[138]

That the scales were indeed beginning to tip is revealed by the fact that William now sought out Henry II's support for his foundation at Fruttuaria.

137. JL 3896 (ZPUU 351). On William and Cluny, see esp. Bulst, *Untersuchungen*, 186–205.

138. D Ard 10, Turin, AS, Materie politiche per rapporto all'estero, Diplomi imperiali, mazzo 1.1, 5.2. That not all of Arduin's diplomas were such lacklustre affairs is revealed by two of his earlier texts: D Ard 7, Lucca, AS, 22-08-1002—S. Giustina; D Ard 8, Turin, AS, Museo storico I, 1, of which the latter is the more assured production.

At some point after Henry's return north, the king sent a letter to Warmund of Ivrea, Gezo of Turin, Arnulf of Milan and Guy of Pavia, as well as a number of leading lay magnates, asking them to lend support to the abbey. This letter can only be reconstructed on the basis of the remarks of the early modern Piedmontese antiquarian Francesco Agostino Della Chiesa (d. 1662), but there is every reason to trust his report. And since the letter presupposes an earlier entreaty, William must have sought out Henry's patronage almost as soon as the abbot had received his diploma from Arduin.[139] That the winds of change were indeed blowing through the march is confirmed in the following year, when Henry followed up his letter with a diploma for the centre. The latter was issued from Aachen in late August, indicating that, even from Lower Lotharingia, Henry now commanded greater authority in Piedmont than Arduin. From William's perspective, this was pragmatism rather than betrayal. Henry was now in the ascendant, and the German king's support would be paramount for the abbey's survival. Indeed, William continued to enjoy good relations with Arduin, who would later retire to the monastery. Ironically, the more precarious the Italian monarch's position became, the more the abbey came to fulfil its original function of providing cover to those exposed by his ventures.

The differences between Henry's and Arduin's privileges for Fruttuaria are instructive. Like Arduin, Henry took the abbey into his protection and extended immunity to it. But here for the first time we are informed that the Volpiano brothers had initially passed their lands to the Torinese archdeacon Gunthard, who oversaw the conveyance to the abbey (a tale later repeated in the centre's foundation charter). This act is traditionally seen as a strategy to ward off claims from William's monastery at Saint-Bénigne, where Godfrey and Nithard had retired. The danger was that the Dijon mother house might claim Fruttuaria as a dependency, since it had been founded on the lands of its monks. Another motive may have been to preclude meddling from Fruttuaria's diocesan bishop, Warmund of Ivrea, as we have seen. Yet given the context in which the story first appears, just as important must have been the threat of confiscation. This had already been suffered by many of Arduin's supporters—probably more than Leo's early diplomas admit—and was extended to ever more by Henry II, including the Volpiano brothers. In this respect, the efforts of William and his kinsmen resemble a sophisticated modern money-laundering operation. By first passing their lands to Gunthard (the shell company in this scheme), they created maximum distance between themselves and the new foundation. This is not the only difference between the privileges. While Arduin removed the abbey almost entirely from episcopal oversight, there is no whiff of this here; all Henry concedes is immunity and

---

139. Della Chiesa, *S. R. E. cardinalium, archiepiscoporum*, 83, with Lucioni, 'L'abbazia', 267–68; Bulst, *Untersuchungen*, 137 n. 102a. On Della Chiesa: Stump, 'Della Chiesa, Francesco Agostino'.

protection, not exemption.[140] In fact, only in 1023 did he go any further, and then under the weight of papal precedent. Benedict VIII (1012–24) had confirmed the house's exemption, on the basis of Warmund's earlier pact; Henry simply acknowledged and endorsed this.[141]

When it comes to the wider situation in Piedmont at this point, we are largely in the dark. William's actions reveal a subtle but significant shift in prevailing winds, and this must have been as true in Vercelli as it was in the Orco valley (if not more so). Leo probably spent the three years after Henry's departure reconstructing his position, a process marked by the retaking of Vercelli (in 1005 or 1006) and securing Orco and other key estates (1007), the latter in a document that the bishop (or his representatives) travelled all the way to Regensburg to obtain. As we have seen, the privilege in question is a response to Arduin's machinations, which had included granting Orco to Tedevert, and Leo frames his text—for which, again, he was personally responsible—as a confirmation of an earlier donation of Charles the Fat.[142] Otherwise, the bishop's silence in these years is itself significant. In 1002, Leo had forcefully called for royal intervention in Italy, and he would do so again when threatened in 1014–16. Between these dates, he apparently had little cause for concern. It is in these years that Arduin was probably besieged in the fortress of Sparone, on the north bank of the Orco at the foot of the Alps, some 37 km (23 miles) upstream from Fruttuaria.[143] Though only reported *en passant* in the *Chronicle of Novalesa*—a confused but local source, drawing on memories of the monks' time at Breme in the Lomellina—this scene would become a favourite of nineteenth-century scholars within the newly formed Italian state. Even the otherwise reserved Ferdinando Gabotto, a leading pioneer of Piedmontese history and its documentary records, could not resist waxing lyrical about the 'heroic resistance' ('eroica resistenza') offered by Arduin there, recalling the youthful shiver he felt upon first sighting the remains of the fortress. For a nation only recently reacquainted with monarchy, the last 'national' king before Vittorio Emanuele II (1861–78) held a special fascination.[144]

After 1007, Henry and his associates held the whip hand, but they failed to land a decisive blow. That matters were far from settled is revealed by the events surrounding the king's second Italian expedition (December 1013–May 1014).

140. D H II 120, Turin, AS, Materie ecclesiastiche, Abbazia di S. Benigno, mazzo 1, 1. For a facsimile: Penco, 'Le "Consuetudines Fructuarienses"', 145.

141. D H II 494. Cf. D H II 305, JL 3950 (ZPUU 429). The privilege of Benedict VIII does not survive, but is also mentioned in a confirmation of John XIX (1024–31): JL 4083a (ZPUU 575). These rights were then confirmed by Conrad II: D K II 70.

142. D H II 132.

143. *Chronicon Novaliciense*, Appendix ch. 16, ed. Alessio, 346–48, with Dormeier, 'Un vescovo', 59–60.

144. Gabotto, 'Un millennio', 26–27. On Gabotto, who also published on the Risorgimento: Fagioli Vercellone, 'Gabotto, Ferdinando'.

During this, support initially rallied around Henry, with S. Salvatore in Pavia and S. Salvatore in Lucca now seeking out his favour. And though, as previously, Henry did not appear in person in Piedmont, the northern monarch buttressed his supporters' position there, confirming and extending judicial and market rights to Peter of Novara, Leo's chief ally since Warmund's death (*c.* 1006).[145] Thietmar reports that Arduin now offered to drop his claims in exchange for a return to his former comital (margravial?) status, but it is hard to know how seriously to take the story.[146] In any case, Henry was no more inclined to tarry in the south than he had been ten years earlier; and shortly after being crowned emperor in Rome on the first Sunday of Lent (14 February 1014), he set off north to Pavia. After a short sojourn there, he headed east to Verona and thence over the Alps. By mid-June, Henry was back in his native Germany, celebrating Pentecost at the bishopric he had recently founded in Bamberg.

If Henry's arrival had bolstered his allies' position, his departure put wind in the sails of their opponents. Already that summer, Arduin and his associates struck at Novara, Como, Vercelli and Pavia, forcing Leo and his episcopal colleagues to take flight. In response, Henry issued a set of diplomas in favour of these sees, condemning the actions of Arduin's allies, confiscating their lands and restoring lost properties.[147] Despite this, matters remained in the balance. Well into 1015, Arduin was on the loose; and even after he retired from the political scene, taking up the religious life at Fruttuaria in the face of his imminent demise, the situation remained unstable. In the Vercellese, two of Arduin's supporters, Count Hubert and Margrave Olderic-Manfred of Turin, continued to defy Leo's authority from the strategic settlement at Santhià, which the former had occupied during the upheaval of the previous years. Faced with this new threat, Leo wrote repeatedly to Henry. Yet, as his increasingly frantic letters reveal, the support proffered was at best lukewarm.[148] This response in part reflects Henry's wider attitudes; for Henry, unlike his predecessors, the Apennine peninsula held little allure.[149] It also speaks of his shifting position in these years. As Henry's authority became more widely accepted within the Italian realm, he was less beholden to his old allies—and had every reason to build bridges with prior enemies, starting with Hubert and Olderic-Manfred. The latter two had not claimed the throne, and enjoyed considerable support in certain circles, so Henry was largely happy to leave them and Leo to sort matters out for themselves. In response, Leo now excommunicated Hubert,

145. D H II 306. See Houghton, 'Reconsidering', 10–11.

146. Thietmar of Merseburg, *Chronicon*, VI.93, ed. Holtzmann, 384–87.

147. DD H II 320, 321. See also D H II 336; D H II 337, Halle, Universitäts- und Landesbibliothek Sachsen-Anhalt, Morbio VIII, 3.

148. Leo of Vercelli, *Epistolae* 1–4, ed. H. Bloch, 'Beiträge', 16–23.

149. Weinfurter, *Heinrich II.*, 232–33, 249. See similarly Fried, *Weg in die Geschichte*, 624–29.

5.11 Bishop Leo's excommunication of Count Hubert 'the Red': Vercelli, BC, Cod.
XXXVIII, fol. 279v, © Biblioteca e Archivio Capitolare, Vercelli

much as the northern Italian bishops had Arduin a decade a half earlier. And
much like that act, we owe our knowledge of this to an addition to a local
manuscript, this time undertaken by Leo himself (Illustration 5.11). Evidently
the bishop of Vercelli was feeling the pinch, and it is interesting to note that he
addresses Hubert as 'heresiarch and new worshipper of devils' ('hersiarcham
et novum demonicolam'), a turn of phrase reminiscent of his earlier addresses
of Arduin. Here the pen of religious reproach met the sword of canonical cen-
sure; if Henry would not act, Leo would.[150]

150. Vercelli, BC, Cod. XXXVIII, fol. 279v, with Gavinelli, 'Leone', 249 n. 56. I follow
Gavinelli in associating this excommunication with struggles over Santhià in 1016, rather
than Harry Bresslau's dating of 1019: Hirsch, Pabst and Bresslau, *Jahrbücher*, iii, 371.

In the end, Leo and his associates emerged victorious. But it was only after they had done so (*c.* 1016 × 1017) that Henry issued his most impressive privilege for the bishop of Vercelli. Based on an earlier text, apparently of 1014, this confers on Leo all the holdings of Arduin's supporters within the bishop's sphere of influence. It repeats much material from Leo's earlier charters of 999–1000, but the focus is now exclusively upon confiscation, and many new names are added to the original list of forfeitees (among these, the Volpiano brothers). In this respect, Henry's diploma reflects the growth of Arduin's support in the intervening years—and perhaps also the growth of Leo's ambitions. Predictably, this document, too, has been branded a forgery. Yet the differences between it and Leo's earlier texts speak strongly in its favour. We would expect consistency from a later forger, not such organic growth.[151] In the absence of an original, we cannot exclude the possibility that what survives is an unauthorized version, rather like those preserved by Pilgrim at Passau. But the twelfth-century copy made at the cathedral goes some way towards making good this deficiency. Here the precept is presented on a single sheet, beneath a copy of Henry II's earlier confirmation for the see. In both cases, the scribe has reproduced elements of the lost originals, particularly in the closing eschatocol. Among other features, he carefully renders Henry's monograms. And the forms given differ in manners which speak in favour of both texts: the first bears the ruler's royal monogram, as is correct for 1007, while the latter displays the distinctive new imperial monogram introduced in early 1014 (Illustration 5.12).[152]

Significantly, a contemporary copy of the latter charter survives in a Vercelli manuscript, where it has been entered upside-down in the remaining space at the end of a copy of Isidore of Seville's *Etymologies* (Illustration 5.13). The hand in question can be identified as that of Leo, elsewhere responsible for the bishop's distinctive 'Nota Leo' (Leo's note) annotations (found at a number of other points in this manuscript, as well as others from Vercelli) and the excommunication of Count Hubert. He has used the other spaces on the same spare sheet to insert copies of his letters to Henry II of 1014–16, along with a poetic obituary for Bishop Peter, reinforcing the connection between the texts and bishop. Leo has also undertaken a number of adjustments to the diploma's wording, indicating that this is a working draft. And since almost all of these corrections find their way into the final version of the privilege, as preserved in the twelfth-century copy, this too cannot be any earlier than the later months of 1016 (the earliest possible date for Leo's final letters). The importance of this lies in the fact that the diploma bears the date 1014 and the place of issue Sohlingen (in southern Saxony), where the emperor was to be

151. D H II 322. For the most recent doubts: Panero, *Signoria*, 80–84.

152. Vercelli, AC, Diplomi, III Cartella, 3. For an overview of Henry's monograms: Rück, *Bildberichte*, 122–25.

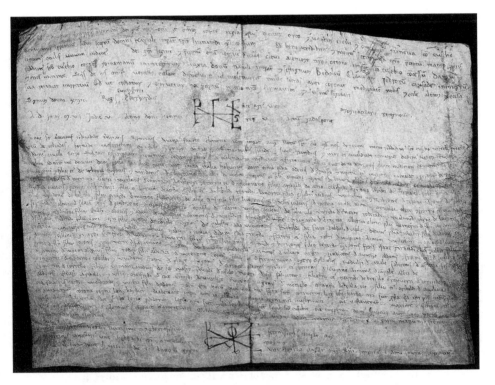

5.12 Twelfth-century copy of Henry II's two diplomas for Vercelli: Vercelli, AC, Diplomi, III Cartella, no. 3, © Biblioteca e Archivio Capitolare, Vercelli

found in autumn 1014.[153] For those suspicious of the text, this contradiction is the surest sign of tampering—we are not dealing with an authentic product of 1014, but a fiction of the years following 1016. There are, however, enough authentic documents of Henry's reign with problematic dating clauses to urge caution. In all likelihood, we are dealing with an updated version of a (lost) original of 1014, either undertaken at Henry's behest or (perhaps more likely) on Leo's own initiative, a situation which would readily explain these eccentricities. In Leo's third letter to Henry, he speaks of how his enemies had made fun of him because he could not obtain a new privilege for his rights; it may be that this is the charter 'sealed in either lead or even gold' ('sin plumbo, saltem auro sigillatum') which he then requested.[154]

Whatever the solution to these problems, there can be little doubt that Vercelli received a grant to this effect, probably in the later months of 1014, since similar privileges were produced for Peter of Novara and Syrus of Pavia at this

153. Vercelli, BC, Cod. CII, fol. 149v, with H. Bloch, 'Beiträge', 45–59. See further Gabotto, 'Diplomi regi', 37–45 (for doubts); and Ferraris, *La chiese 'stazionali'*, 238–39 n. 406; Gavinelli, 'Leone', 242, 248–49 (confirming Bloch's findings).

154. Leo of Vercelli, *Epistola* 3, ed. Bloch, 'Beiträge', 21–22.

5.13 Leo of Vercelli's own working draft of Henry II's diploma of 1014×1017 (alongside other additions in his hand): Vercelli, BC, Cod. CII, fol. 149v, © Biblioteca e Archivio Capitolare, Vercelli

point. Interestingly Syrus's text, which bears exactly the same date and place of issue, shows signs of Leo's distinctive draftsmanship. Evidently the bishop of Vercelli was present on this occasion—and presumably not just to produce a diploma for his Pavian colleague![155] So while Henry may have been hesitant to put boots on the ground, he was happy enough to throw his judicial weight behind his allies. And it is significant that these charters are followed by further forfeitures for Como in the following year. If Henry had not furnished Leo with such a privilege, it would have been completely out of step with his actions elsewhere (not to mention quite a snub).[156]

The revised text of Leo's charter is, therefore, certainly in the spirit, if not necessarily to the letter, of Henry's original. Much like the diplomas of 999 and 1000, it is hard to imagine when other than in the heat of the moment this might have been produced. Leo needed help in the years between 1014 and 1016, not a decade later. His diplomas may all pursue the same overarching

155. DD H II 320, 321. On the latter: H. Bloch, 'Beiträge', 62–71, 73.

156. D H II 336; D H II 337, Halle, Universitäts- und Landesbibliothek Sachsen-Anhalt, Morbio VIII, 3.

goal of consolidating episcopal authority, but they are anything but a 'unified project' ('progetto unitario'), as some have imagined.[157] Rather, they vary significantly, reflecting the difficulties and challenges he faced across a long and eventful episcopate.

Leo's Legacy: Vercelli between Bishop and Commune

In the end, Leo's victory in late 1016 proved permanent. We hear little from him in the remaining years of Henry's reign. And where the pugnacious (and loquacious) bishop of Vercelli is concerned, no news certainly is good news. When Henry died and a new king and dynasty emerged in the person of Conrad II, Leo was quick to garner his support, perhaps obtaining a lost privilege in 1025. This would then become the basis for all future confirmations for the see. The bishop of Vercelli, already a force to be reckoned with in the tenth century, now emerged as the unchallenged lord of the city.

Leo's struggles are traditionally viewed against the backdrop of the communal movement, which swept northern Italy in the later eleventh and twelfth centuries. Feeding off local socio-political tensions between bishops and their vassals, this produced the complex mosaic of semi-independent city states which would characterize Italian politics well into the modern era. Within this master narrative, Arduin's attacks on Peter and Leo become the first of a series of urban risings, a precursor to the wider unrest which wracked cities such as Milan, Cremona and Pavia in later years of the eleventh century.[158] Yet there are significant obstacles to this interpretation. For a start, the revolts at Cremona and (in particular) Milan were led by episcopal vassals, above all those of the second order (the sub-vassals or *valvassores*). But none of our sources identify these figures as Arduin's main supporters. True, the letter announcing the margrave's excommunication in 999 reports that Arduin had turned military followers ('secundi milites') against their episcopal lords. But the turn of phrase is rarely read in context. Within the letter, this is embedded in a long list of Arduin's crimes; it is scarcely intended as a characterization of his entire support base. In any case, the focus is on the sin of perjury ('periurii crimen') Arduin has forced these men to commit, not social tensions between them and their episcopal lords. The fact that Arduin had turned sworn men against their lords revealed the depths of his perfidy.[159]

---

157. The phrase is that of Panero, *Signoria*, 85. See similarly Manaresi, 'Alle origini', 309–11.

158. Arnaldi, 'Arduino'; Keller, *Adelsherrschaft*, 270–91; Sergi, 'Arduino'; Lucioni, 'Re Arduino', 43–44; Immonen, 'Saint as a Mediator', 77, 83, 90. See also Menant, *Campagnes lombardes*, 580–601; Keller, 'Das Edictum de beneficiis'. For criticisms: Panero, *Signoria*, 52; Brunhofer, *Arduin von Ivrea*; and for a fresh perspective: Houghton, 'Vocabulary of Groups'.

159. Ivrea, BC, Cod. LXXXVII (54), fol. 112r; *Konzilien Deutschlands*, ed. Hehl, 584 (no. 60C).

All the indications are that Arduin was pulled into an internal struggle between Peter (and latterly Leo) and the cathedral chapter, a situation exacerbated by ongoing tensions between the bishop and margrave. What was at stake was not so much the status of episcopal vassals, as the constitution of the cathedral community and the broader balance of power in the Ivrean march. The closest parallels are therefore not with Cremona and Milan in later years, but with Bergamo, Asti and Parma in the early eleventh century. At the first of these, in north-central Lombardy, the canons received confirmation of their rights (above all, to the local market) from Henry II in 1013, in a diploma explicitly issued in response to depredations by Bishop Raginfred—the same Vercellese archdeacon we met earlier—and other (unnamed) malefactors ('quę de territoriis rebus canonicę suę a Reginfredo episcopo aliisque malis hominibus passi fuerant'). In order to secure this, the canons had concocted an earlier donation in the name of Bishop Adalbert (891-935), giving their claims a spurious patina of pedigree. At Asti, in south-eastern Piedmont, the canons similarly resorted to forgery following the appointment of Bishop Alric (1008-36), the brother of the local margrave of Turin (the same Olderic-Manfred who tormented Leo). Here the texts were intended to shield the chapter from the advances of a well-connected incoming prelate. Finally, at Parma in Emilia the canons contested the bishop's judicial oversight (*districtus*) over the city, falsifying at least two imperial diplomas for this purpose.[160] This was thus an era of intra-ecclesiastical conflict every bit as much as of 'feudal' quarrels between bishops and their military entourages. In this respect, there are few signs of tension between bishop and vassals in Vercelli in later years, but there is ample evidence of continuing episcopal–canonical strain, stretching well into the twelfth century (as Bishop Gisulf's experiences reveal). The bishop's position had always been strong, but was left considerably enhanced by Leo's episcopate, much to the dismay of others. Even in the twelfth century, a commune only emerged haltingly, under considerable episcopal influence—and, at times, opposition.[161] The bishop also remained a bastion of imperial influence, standing beside Henry IV in the Investiture Contest and Frederick Barbarossa in his interminable conflicts with the Lombard League.

From our present perspective, the interest of Leo's experiences lies in the light they shed on the use and abuse of charters within the Italian realm.[162] As we have seen, the bishop of Vercelli was anything but an innocent bystander

160. Bergamo: *Pergamene degli archivi di Bergamo*, i, ed. Cortesi and Pretesi, no. 46, with Kurdziel, 'Au prisme des faux', 251–56; Asti: Fissore, 'Antiche falsificazioni', 5–86 (with an edition of the relevant documents at 78–86); Parma: D Km 24; *Codice diplomatico parmense*, i, ed. Benassi, no. 13; D K III 115; D O II 257, with Guyotjeannin, 'Pouvoirs publics', 20–25. More generally: Kurdziel, 'Au prisme des faux', 265–70.

161. Grillo, 'Il comune di Vercelli'. See also Wickham, *Sleepwalking*, esp. 170–71, 188–89.

162. Cf. Sennis, 'Documentary Practices'.

here. He adjusted a diploma of Charles the Fat to suit his purposes and probably forged a notice in the emperor's name, too. Even in Leo's authentic texts,
he played fast and loose with the truth, presenting recent acquisitions (and
canonical holdings) as longstanding episcopal rights. But while some scholars
see these falsehoods and inconsistencies as grounds for suspicion, in almost
every case they speak in favour of our texts (at least in a strict diplomatic
sense). Leo's diplomas are genuine, even if their content is often tendentious.
They provide a welcome reminder that modern scholarly judgements of forgery and authenticity are analytical, not moral, ones. Just as counterfeits can
tell the truth, so authentic texts are often deeply deceitful. Leo was not the first
bishop to exploit the power of the written word in this fashion, nor would he
be the last. In fact, his close ally, Peter of Novara, had lands 'restored' which
had probably never belonged to his see, and one suspects the same is true of
many of Otto III's supporters.[163]

Modern distinctions between forgery and authenticity thus only take us so
far. Even when authentic, diplomas are not neutral sources; they tell tales.[164] In
Leo's case, they provide *his* version of events, furnishing precious insights into
the challenges he faced and the means by which he sought to surmount these.
Leo created a documentary edifice that would serve his successors well. But
even in literate Italy, Leo could only expect these to do so much. It would take
almost two decades of conflict, much of it armed, before he could sit comfortably on his throne. And Leo's final success was due as much to deft politick-
ing as it was to his documentary interventions. The charters he produced are,
therefore, not so different from the others we have been considering. They
were part of wider strategies of persuasion, a means of rewriting the past to
serve the needs of the present. Some of them may have been intended to ward
off external threat, but none are cited in court, and their primary audience
probably lay closer to home. It was difficulties within the chapter house which
had sparked Peter's death, and these continued to dog Leo's later episcopate.
It is to friends and supporters, not hostile enemies, that his diplomas appeal.
They help to compensate for earlier documentary losses, while insulating the
bishop from challenges by his local nemeses. As Leo's poems and manuscript
annotations amply attest, he possessed a reformer's zeal—a zeal which more
than once moved documentary mountains.

163. Brunhofer, *Arduin von Ivrea*, 103. Cf. W. Brown, 'Charters as Weapons'.
164. Cf. Foot, 'Reading Anglo-Saxon Charters'.

Conclusions

AS WE HAVE seen, forgery took many forms in western Europe around the year 1000. It often started small, with the adjustment or improvement of a single text. But like any good story, it soon grew in the telling. Anno may have begun by having an authentic immunity of Louis the Pious judiciously improved, but he ended up with a string of counterfeits, covering all of Worms's most important claims. At each step, one false text demanded another, till almost every early record from the house had been reworked in one way or another. His example was followed by Pilgrim less than a decade later, whose missionary ambitions demanded a similarly elaborate set of false bulls, themselves buttressed by a forged Arnulf immunity. Still, it was not always forgery which stood at the start of the process. In Vercelli, it may have been the terms of Leo's authentic charters—which claimed that the bishopric owed its most valuable rights to Charles the Fat—that inspired him to adjust a diploma of that ruler. Likewise at Abingdon, it was Æthelred's authentic privilege of 993 which spawned the false *Orthodoxorum* texts and their derivatives. But however the process started, the result was forgery complexes, sets of reworked and improved charters in which only the most critical and discerning eye can tell true from false.

These efforts look remarkably similar to the earliest Eurasian forgeries, surveyed in the Introduction. Like the producers of the Amenhotep III decree, Cruciform Monument and Famine Stele, our forgers sought to secure preferential treatment for their institutions, either in the form of landed perquisites or (more often) general exemptions. But whether it was judicial independence, estates and revenues or simply prestige that they sought, in all cases this involved an active and creative engagement with the past. It is important to emphasize this, because it has often been suggested that such behaviour reflects a kind of childish naïveté. Since the people of the Middle Ages could not distinguish past from present, so the argument runs, they naturally projected present rights and property arrangements onto earlier years.¹ But while much of the forging activity surveyed here did involve postulating a longer history for more modern rights, it is hard to see the resulting texts as either childish or naïve. Their authors modelled these on authentic documents, often quite closely, and adjusted their script and formulation to evoke such forms. The results may look obviously anachronistic to a trained modern eye, but they did not in the tenth and eleventh centuries. Most passed muster well into the nineteenth century, and a few continue to have their defenders. So if our forgers were guilty of transposing present concerns onto the past, it was not because they were incapable of telling the difference between the two. Quite the reverse: they appreciated earlier documents on account of their alterity and antiquity—it was this which gave them authority.

Here the forgers of the tenth and eleventh centuries behaved much like the authors of narrative history; they were acutely aware of, yet keen to reduce, the gulf between past and present.² This is not the only similarity between the endeavours. Traditionally, forged charters have been seen as highly legalistic texts, whose value derived from their juridical status; like the counterfeit coin of the modern era, they might carry all before them. There may be an element of truth to this.³ Charters were frequently invoked in disputes, particularly in Italy, and forgery could improve one's chances at court, as we see in Anno's conflicts with Lorsch. Nevertheless, in most cases we have little or no evidence of these texts being invoked in a judicial context; and in many, there are reasons to doubt they ever were. In part, this reflects the informality of early and high medieval law and justice. Even at its most powerful and efficient, central authority was but one player here, and the written word but one factor.⁴ Yet there is more to this. As a raft of studies has shown, charters were not merely—nor even sometimes primarily—judicial texts; they also performed important social functions. Even in the heyday of medieval forgery, the 'long'

1. See, e.g., Tout, 'Mediæval Forgers', 216 ('mediæval man . . . was was almost altogether lacking in the rudiments of a historic sense'); Burke, *Renaissance Sense*, 13 ('[t]he Pseudo-Isidor and the Donation of Constantine were written by men without a sense of anachronism'); Lowenthal, *Past is a Foreign Country*, 152 ('faking along with liking the marks of time first became widespread with the Renaissance'), 232 ('[i]n the Middle Ages history was a unified Christian drama with no scope for or interest in differences between past and present'); Clanchy, *Memory to Written Record*, 320 ('[f]orgery was necessary because contemporaries had no historical sense'). See also Eisenstein, *Printing Revolution*, 118–22; C. S. Wood, *Forgery*; Lowenthal, *Past is a Foreign Country—Revisited*, 257, 360–61.

2. Goetz, 'Gegenwart der Vergangenheit'.

3. Stieldorf, 'Magie', 28–29; Mersiowsky, *Urkunde*, 740–41.

4. Among others: Geary, *Living with the Dead*; Bougard, *La justice*; Althoff, *Spielregeln*; Keller, 'Idee der Gerechtigkeit'; Patzold, *Konflikte im Kloster*; Barthélemy, *Chevaliers et miracles*; White, *Feuding and Peace-Making*; Wormald, 'Charters'; Rio, *Legal Practice*; Roach, *Kingship and Consent*, 122–46; Costambeys, 'Disputes'.

twelfth century, many counterfeits were not invoked at courts of law, as the rich documentary evidence from England reveals.[5] Either their authors were remarkably ignorant of their trade, or their purpose lay elsewhere.

It is here that the analogy with historical writing becomes especially helpful. As many have noted, charters are not distinct from narrative texts. They often bear sections recounting the events which gave rise to their production; and when they do not, they present an implicit narrative ('X petitioned and received Y rights from Z'). Diplomas and bulls are therefore not simply storehouses of fact, but partisan texts, a conclusion which holds doubly true of forgeries, documents which by their nature seek to persuade. Indeed, if diplomatists have come to appreciate the narrative quality of their texts more keenly, students of historical writing now emphasize the argumentative—and sometimes downright legalistic—nature of their works. The narrators of medieval history wrote to persuade and contest, not just to recount, and claims to lands and legal rights are frequently embedded in their accounts.[6] Narrative history and documentary forgery were thus often different means of achieving similar results. That there was no simple divide is revealed by the cartulary-chronicle, that distinctive blend of local history and documentary record which, like much else considered here, owes its origins to the tenth century. It was Folcuin of Saint-Bertin who apparently first came up with the idea of joining the house chronicle and charter collection in the 960s, and this approach to local memorialization soon gained popularity, not least in post-Conquest England.[7] Under these circumstances, it is scarcely surprising that forger and historian were frequently one and the same. Thietmar of Merseburg (d. 1018), for example, was responsible for counterfeit charters alongside his famous chronicle, works best read as a diptych, distinct but related parts of a programme to secure the rights and revenues of his recently restored bishopric.[8] Likewise the typically sober canon Flodoard (d. 966) was apparently behind a number of additions to the documents transmitted in his monumental history of Reims.[9] Nor was this an exclusively tenth- and eleventh-century phenomenon. Suger of Saint-Denis (d. 1151) cut his teeth confecting a diploma in the name of Robert the Pious; and as abbot, he would be responsible for further false privileges of Charlemagne and Louis the Pious.[10] And around the same time, more comprehensive campaigns were being launched by Peter the

5. Vincent, 'Use and Abuse'.

6. Althoff, '*Causa scribendi*'; McKitterick, *History and Memory*, 60–155. For words of caution: Lake, 'Authorial Intention'.

7. Morelle, 'Diplomatic Culture'. Cf. Roberts, *Flodoard*, 104–44; Gransden, *Historical Writing*, 270–86.

8. Lippelt, *Thietmar von Merseburg*, 89–115. See also Huschner, 'Hoch- und spätmittelalterliche Fälschungen', 117–22, and 'Echt, gefälscht oder verloren?'

9. Roberts, *Flodoard*, 122–27.

10. Grant, *Abbot Suger*, 80–81, 119–20, 240. See also Morelle, 'Suger et les archives'.

Deacon (d. after 1159) at Monte Cassino, who produced countless counterfeits while continuing the local house chronicle and compiling the abbey's massive cartulary (the 'Register of Peter the Deacon'); and Osbert de Clare (d. in or after 1158) at Westminster, who was responsible some of England's most notorious fakes, in addition to numerous hagiographical works.[11]

As Matthew Kempshall reminds us, there was good Classical precedent for such actions. Medieval historians modelled themselves on the antique rhetor, whose primary purpose was to pursue plaints in court. It is, therefore, perfectly natural that legal documents should make their way into the resulting narratives, just as that rhetorical flourishes are to be found in charters (one thinks, for example, of Leo of Vercelli's texts). Forgery might even be seen as an extension of the Classical tradition of rhetorical fiction (*fictio*), which allowed rhetors (and, by extension, historians) a degree of literary licence in making their case.[12] Forged charters were thus less proofs, in the modern sense, than parts of an argument—and often not the only ones.[13] At some level, they had to look the part, but they did not need to be perfect. They were intended as much (if not more) for those favourable to the house as for hostile enemies.[14] In this respect, it is hardly surprising that they tend to focus on the most iconic rights: immunity, liberty and exemption. What was at stake was not just the legal status of the house in question; it was its local, regional and national standing. It is for this reason that the most common response to forgery was not criticism, but counterforgery. It was easier to forge an alternative version of the past than to deny the validity of an existing one; it was also often more persuasive. Close similarities emerge with the fractious world of early Christianity, in which religious communities of various descriptions falsified texts to defend their doctrinal stances.[15]

Forgery in the tenth and eleventh centuries was, therefore, as much about memory and identity as property and rights. This is not to say that counterfeit charters did not serve practical purposes, any less than the partisan narratives to which they bear such similarities. In fact, any attempt to distinguish strictly between memorial and legal functions is doomed to failure. Partly, this is because local memory informed legal proceedings: if you could convince your neighbours and tenants that you traditionally held certain rights, your chances at court would be much better. But it is also because material wealth

11. Peter the Deacon: Caspar, *Petrus Diaconus*; Hoffmann, 'Chronik und Urkunde'; H. Bloch, *Monte Cassino*, 941–1049; Osbert de Clare: Chaplais, 'Original Charters'; Crick, 'St Albans, Westminster'; England, 'Crown-Wearing Abbeys', 81–103.

12. Kempshall, *Rhetoric*.

13. See similarly Kölzer, '*Cui bono?*'.

14. Härtel, 'Fälschungen', 34. See also Kölzer, *Merowingerstudien*, ii, 59, on forgeries as a part of local tradition.

15. Speyer, *Literarische Fälschung*, 278–85, 295–303; Ehrman, *Forgery and Counterforgery*.

was an essential element of institutional identity. In these years, a respectable religious house was a wealthy one. To consolidate one's endowment therefore was to shore up corporate identity, attitudes whose roots, as Peter Brown has shown, are to be sought in the rapid endowment of the church in late antiquity.[16]

It is in this wider sense that forgery was about memory and identity. It encompassed, but also transcended, property rights. Previous analyses are thus not so much wrong as partial. They prioritize the judicial implications of texts whose function was first and foremost social. Appreciating this not only allows for a more rounded view of the phenomenon, but also enables us understand developments in the practice of forgery better. If, as we have seen, the falsifying of documents attests to an active and developed (or developing) sense of the past, then it becomes an important barometer of this. Some societies certainly are more past-oriented than others; and what kind of past is valued (and why) varies significantly across time and space.[17] No one acquainted with *Quattrocento* humanism will wish to deny the heightened sense of anachronism developed within learned circles (especially in Italy) at this point, any more than those who work on eleventh- and twelfth-century England will wish to overlook the new historicism fostered by the Conquest and its aftermath.[18] Such moments must, however, be seen as the high-water marks of an ever fluctuating ocean. They do not constitute the origins of a true 'sense of the past' or the birth of an appreciation of anachronism (as is often claimed), but rather represent moments when these were suddenly more pronounced.

In modelling medieval (and modern) attitudes toward the past, we would do well to follow the lead of Alexandra Walsham. Walsham argues that the reforming movements of medieval and early modern Europe—whose origins are similarly contentious—should be seen in terms of waves: attitudes and approaches changed over time, but changes were rarely linear, and there was no single point of origin or destination.[19] The same is true of forgery and a sense of the past ('Renaissance' or otherwise). All societies have some appreciation of the alterity of the past, even if all are not equally attuned to this— or interested in the same elements thereof. In this respect, the later tenth century provides a useful case study of a moment of heightened interest in such matters. It is, however, certainly not the only one. The developments traced here are foreshadowed in the ninth century, as we shall see, and would

16. P. Brown, *Through the Eye of a Needle*. See also I. N. Wood, 'Entrusting Western Europe'.

17. J. Assmann, *Das kulturelle Gedächtnies*, esp. 31–34, 66–86. See also Lowenthal, *Past is a Foreign Country*.

18. Grafton, *Forgers and Critics*; Ginzburg, *History, Rhetoric, and Proof*, 54–70; Southern, 'Sense of the Past'.

19. Walsham, 'Migrations of the Holy'.

continue across the eleventh and twelfth. Indeed, Richard Southern's twelfth-century English forgers and chroniclers are in many respects the lineal descendants of Abbot Wulfgar and his associates, just as Peter the Deacon, Suger and the Reichenau forgers are those of Anno, Leo and the monks of Fleury.

There need be no contradiction in asserting a highly developed medieval (and particularly tenth-century) sense of the past, and a new-found Renaissance antiquarianism.[20] What was new in the fifteenth and sixteenth centuries was less the sudden appreciation of the past's alterity—though in certain circles, this may be so—than the focus on its specifically Classical elements. Forgers of the tenth and eleventh centuries had sought authority and legitimacy above all in the Christian world of late antiquity and the early Middle Ages—in the founders and early benefactors of their churches and realms (Dagobert, Charlemagne, Louis the Pious). Their Renaissance counterparts, by contrast, such as Giovanni Nanni (alias Annius of Viterbo, d. 1502) and Jerónimo Román de la Higuera (d. 1611), looked more actively to pagan antiquity. The latter is a particularly interesting case in point. Higuera is famous as the author of an elaborate set of false chronicles recounting Spain's early history. In framing his work as a universal chronicle and emphasizing the apostolic origins of Spanish Catholicism, he operated much like a medieval forger (or, for that matter, historian). Yet in the person of Flavius Dexter, the first of Higuera's four invented narrators of Iberian history, he showed an interest in the pre-Christian past far greater than that of most medieval falsifiers. The novelty of Higuera's approach is further reflected in his deft deployment of epigraphic evidence—something all but unknown in the Middle Ages. So if Higuera, like Nanni, is in some respects one of the last of the medieval forgers, his interests and modus operandi look forward to the new historical science of the Enlightenment.[21]

Forgery thus speaks of an interest in the past, and its subjects reveal much about the types of past which are valued. The focus here has, of necessity, been on five case studies. But in all the regions considered, we have seen further signs of falsification, be it at Saint-Denis on the Seine, at Salzburg in Bavaria, at St Maximin outside Trier, at Bergamo in the Alpine foothills, or at St Albans off Watling Street. In almost all of these centres, moreover, forgery was a new phenomenon in the tenth and eleventh centuries. Whether at Magdeburg or Glastonbury, across Europe monks and clerics were busy improving their written records. It has been insufficiently emphasized that the tenth century (and in particular its second half) is the first period in which such activity can be

20. See similarly F. Clark, 'Forgery, Misattribution', painting 'a picture of profound if silent continuity' (93).

21. Grafton, *Defenders of the Text*, 75–103; Olds, *Forging the Past*. Cf. Grafton, *What Was History?*.

charted across the core regions of the Latin West.[22] It is then that we find the
first forgeries in the names of the Lombard kings; it is then, too, that counterfeit Carolingian diplomas start being manufactured in significant numbers.[23]
This may, in part, be a trick of the sources. Few archives boast an uninter-
rupted history across the early and central Middle Ages, and many earlier
counterfeits must have fallen victim to the vagaries of transmission. But this
can only be part of the story. Substantial numbers of original documents do
survive from the eighth and ninth centuries, yet forgeries remain rare. Moreover, the very fact that the false documents of the tenth and eleventh centuries
have survived so well is significant; these spoke to later institutional needs in
a manner their precursors failed to do.

These years therefore represent an important moment in the history of
European forgery. They may not mark its origin or high point—the former is
obscure, the latter probably belongs to the twelfth century—but they were an
essential step along the way. This is not, however, to ignore earlier evidence.
The ninth century, in particular, has been heralded as one of the great ages
of forgery, and not without reason.[24] This was the time of Pseudo-Isidore,
the most ambitious (and successful) counterfeiter of canon law of the Middle
Ages; of the Le Mans forgeries, one of the most intricate forgery complexes
of medieval France; and of Hincmar of Reims, literary impresario and forger
extraordinaire (as his contemporaries knew only too well).[25] It is also the
period which saw some of the first forgeries in the names of Merovingian rulers, with a particular concentration in the second half of the century at centres such as Saint-Denis, Saint-Maur-des-Fossés and Corbie.[26] Most of this
forging activity is to be found in West Francia and the Lotharingian Middle
Kingdom (a matter to which we shall return), but it is not restricted to these.
In north Saxon Bremen, Ansgar and Rimbert rewrote the history of their see
with a creativity worthy of Pseudo-Isidore, in terms which would fool scholars well into the twenty-first century; and in Mercian-controlled Kent, Archbishop Wulfred (805-32) was equally active on behalf of his see.[27]

22. See Crick, 'Script'; Dufour, 'État et comparaison', esp. 208–9; Jakobs, 'Sammlung',
all attesting to the spread of forgery in the tenth and early eleventh centuries.

23. Brühl, *Studien zu den langobardischen Königsurkunden*, 86, 116–17, 139, 145, 158–
60, 170; Mersiowsky, *Urkunde*, 740–41.

24. Levison, 'Politik in Jenseitsvisionen', 236. See similarly Bouchard, *Rewriting Saints*,
63–86.

25. In addition to the works already cited: Knibbs, 'Ebo'; Ubl and Ziemann, eds, *Fälschung*; Goffart, *Le Mans Forgeries*; W. Hartmann, 'Fälschungsverdacht'. See also Hampe,
'Zum Streite Hincmars'.

26. Brühl, *Studien zu den merowingischen Königsurkunden*, esp. 137–259; Kölzer,
Merowingerstudien, i, 97–110, 137–43.

27. Knibbs, *Ansgar*; Brooks, *Early History*, 191–97.

Still, the number of centres involved in forgery at this point remains comparatively small, for all the resulting noise. Furthermore, the focus of much of this work is different from what we later see. Geoffrey Koziol notes that forgery in these years was an expression of power; to forge was to assert authority, and there was no greater victory than to have an obvious fake taken for authentic.[28] This is reflected in the subjects chosen by forgers. They tended to confect not ancient or foundational texts, but contemporary records. Ansgar (847–65) and Rimbert (865–88) reworked charters of Louis the Pious (816–40), Gregory IV (827–44) and Nicholas I (858–67); Ebbo of Reims (816–35, 840–41) concocted a bull in the name of Gregory IV (827–44); and Ebbo's chief adversary, Hincmar (845–82), stood accused (probably rightly) of interpolating a bull of Benedict III (855–58). Even Pseudo-Isidore spoke largely to immediate political needs, for all the antiquarian learning on display; and, in contrast with the texts we have been considering, his false decretals reveal almost nothing about their place of origin (which remains a matter of speculation). These were not historical and memorial endeavours in the sense we have been considering.

This is not, however, to deny all similarity. Ansgar and Rimbert were deeply interested in institutional history, and the latter contributed significantly to the form this would take at Bremen in his *Life* of Ansgar. If they did not look further back, it was because their see was itself a recent creation. Hincmar, for his part, was similarly concerned about his province's past, even if he rarely expressed this in forged charters; and Reims owes much of its later prominence to Hincmar's historical and archival undertakings.[29] But perhaps the most significant case from our present perspective is that of Le Mans, one of the first centres to forge Merovingian (and, for that matter, Carolingian) diplomas on any scale. Although the Le Mans forgeries, produced (probably) in the second quarter of the ninth century, were a charged political affair, focusing on control of the monastery of Saint-Calais, the arguments deployed by their author display a strongly historicizing character. Indeed, the resulting texts comprise not only charters, but also narratives of the episcopate of Alderic (832–57) and his predecessors, into which these are inserted (the *Gesta Aldrici* and *Actus pontificum Cenomennis*).[30] Here we certainly do see the kinds of institutional interest so prevalent in the later tenth century. Between these years, what we seem to be observing is an extension and intensification of these trends. Just as the tenth- and eleventh-century flowering of the 'deeds of bishops' (*gesta episcoporum*) genre owes much to Carolingian antecedents (including the Le Mans *Actus*), so the distinctive brand of institutionally

28. Koziol, *Politics of Memory*, 315–99.

29. Schneider, *Erzbischof Hinkmar*.

30. *Actus pontificum Cenomannis* and *Gesta Aldrici*, ed. Weidemann, with Goffart, *Le Mans Forgeries*, esp. 155–68; Bouchard, *Rewriting Saints*, 66–77; Mazel, *L'évêque et le territoire*, 43–44, 63–72, 140–42, 150–51.

focused forgery we have been surveying represents a development of existing practices, particularly west of the Rhine.[31] Falsification remained political, but more houses were now involved, and such efforts were increasingly directed towards local institutional identities, to which they gave voice.

This is not the only sign of change. As Julia Crick notes, the second half of the tenth century sees some of the first examples of imitative script, in England as elsewhere. She argues that this new-found visual (and manual) appreciation of anachronism was not merely functional, but bears witness to deeper-seated antiquarian interests, ones not so far removed from those of the Renaissance *savants* beloved of modern scholars of forgery.[32] The evidence we have considered confirms and extends these findings. At Worms and Passau, where a substantial body of single sheets survives, we can observe similar efforts to mimic earlier forms; where they do not, as at Fleury, Abingdon and Vercelli, formulation tells a similar tale. At all centres, forgers did not simply impose contemporary styles and attitudes on the past; they modelled their works closely (if not entirely successfully) on older texts. What the deeper causes of this heightened historicism were is, of course, the million pound question. In part, we are probably dealing with organic growth. As more and more religious houses began to show an interest in institutional history (and express this through forgery), others will soon have followed suit. This makes sense of the geographic spread just observed, starting from an initial focus on the traditional Frankish heartlands, then moving out to (and beyond) the Carolingian frontiers. We can see this process at work at Passau on the empire's eastern march. Here Pilgrim's forgeries cannot be understood without reference to the archival and historical traditions of neighbouring Salzburg, including the latter's numerous counterfeits. Salzburg began forging, Passau soon followed suit.

Similarly important were the development of literate mentalities and of documentary practices. This may come as a surprise to some readers, as an earlier generation of scholars diagnosed a significant retreat in literacy in the tenth century, caused by the eclipse of the Carolingian order and attendant socio-political turmoil. According to this perspective, this was a 'time poor in sources' ('quellenarme Zeit'), in which ritual and symbolic communication compensated for the lack of literacy. In Germany, such changes were thought to be typified by the transition from the hyper-literate Carolingians, who regularly communicated to their subjects by means of written ordinances (capitularies), to the Ottonians, who scarcely ever used the medium.[33] In

---

31. Riches, 'Changing Political Horizons'. See also Koziol, 'Future of History'.

32. Crick, 'Script'. See also Vezin, 'Écritures imitées', 62–65; Brühl, *Studien zu den merowingischen Königsurkunden*, 250–59; Kölzer, *Merowingerstudien*, i, 124–25, 134–35. Cf. Grafton, *Forgers and Critics*, 99–123; Ginzburg, *History, Rhetoric, and Proof*, 54–70; C. S. Wood, *Forgery*, esp. 109–84.

33. K. J. Leyser, 'Ritual'; Althoff, *Ottonen*, 230–33. Cf. Schmid, 'Unerforschte Quellen'.

France, they were identified in the 'documentary anarchy' ('anarchie documentaire') of these years, which saw the demise of many traditional types of written instrument and the emergence of new ones.[34] It is, however, now clear that such characterizations are wide of the mark. The Ottonian rulers may not have issued many new ordinances, but older decrees continued to circulate within their domains—in fact, some Carolingian capitularies were more accessible in the tenth century than they had ever been in the eighth or ninth.[35] Likewise, in France developments are now seen in terms of a diversification of the written word: older documentary types were giving way to newer ones, but the value of writing itself was rarely in question—indeed, in most regions we have more charters than ever before.[36] Elsewhere, different trajectories can be traced, but none suggests a widespread retreat in literacy. In northern Italy—as, for that matter, in Catalonia and Spain— recourse to written documentation remained regular; the only real change was the growing popularity of new types of judicial notice (particularly the *ostensio cartae*), which led to the written word being instrumentalized in new (often more self-conscious) fashions.[37] In England, moreover, there can be little doubt that literacy was on the rise, encouraged by the demands of a newly assertive royal government, but also sustained by local lay initiatives and the Benedictine reform, which rejuvenated intellectual life across the kingdom.[38]

A strong case can, therefore, be made for treating these years as ones of continuing (and perhaps even growing) recourse to the written word. More important than the simple numbers is how such documents were used. Here it is significant that many parts of Europe saw the development of new documentary forms. In France, the sudden vogue for informal third-person notices has long attracted comment in this connection; equally important from the standpoint of the present study is the gradual formalization of the ecclesiastical exemption. In England, on the other hand, the introduction of the chartered liberty and foundation diploma had important implications, not least at Abingdon. Greater stability can be observed in Germany and northern Italy, though the evolution of the 'ban immunity' and increasing delegation of comital rights raised similar issues. The significance of these developments

34. Boüard, *Manuel de diplomatique*, ii, 137–49. See similarly Tessier, *Diplomatique*, 208–10.

35. Patzold, 'Capitularies'. Cf. Bachrach, 'Written Word'.

36. Guyotjeannin, '"*Penuria scriptorum*"'; Heideicker, '30 June 1047'.

37. Bougard, '"*Falsum falsorum*"'; Vallerani, 'Scritture'; Sennis, 'Documentary Practices'; Costambeys, 'Archives'. On Catalonia: Zimmermann, *Écrire et lire*; Kosto, *Making Agreements*, 268–94; Bowman, *Shifting Landmarks*, 33–54, 141–64; and on Spain: Barrett, 'Written and the World'; Davies, *Windows on Justice*.

38. Keynes, 'Royal Government'; Lowe, 'Lay Literacy'; Insley, 'Lay Documentary Practice'.

lies in the fact that new documentary forms demanded adjustments to earlier records, by means of either subtle improvement or outright forgery. As ideas about liberty, immunity and exemption evolved, so too did the expectations of earlier documents conferring these.

Another important factor was the reforming efforts of these years. As Jan Assmann notes, movements of renewal and restoration are frequently associated with a heightened sense of the past.[39] This was certainly so in the tenth century, when monastic reform was frequently framed as a return to an idealized (and often largely invented) prelapsarian state. Among the centres considered, the connection between forgery and reform is especially clear at Abingdon and Fleury, as we might expect. At the former, the eighth- and ninth-century Mercian past became the basis for the monks' claims to land and liberty; at the latter, the possession of Benedict's relics, translated from Monte Cassino in the eighth century, became an essential part of the abbey's case for wide-ranging rights of exemption (rights which themselves enjoyed a purportedly ninth-century pedigree). But the influence of these movements can also be observed beyond cloister walls. Bishop Anno was a monk by training, and his interest in Worms's immunity owes much to his earlier experiences at St Maximin and St Maurice—both reformed houses (and known centres of forgery). Leo of Vercelli and Pilgrim of Passau were exposed to such ideas more indirectly, the former through the court of Otto III, where many leading reformers (including at times Abbo) were to be found, and the latter through his early education at Niederaltaich, where he rubbed shoulders with the likes of Godehard.

As the latter two cases illustrate, however, reform can only be part of the story. Not surprisingly, the three bishoprics considered reveal less interest in the past as an idealized golden age; for them, it is more often a point of reference for present rights and status. The key issues within episcopal circles tended to be ones of rank and standing, vis-à-vis either secular office holders (as at Worms and Vercelli), or their ecclesiastical neighbours (as at Passau). Ultimately, the forgeries produced at these centres are about the bishop's (and sometimes chapter's) place in local society. As such, they reflect wider developments in episcopal office and ecclesiastical hierarchy. This was an important time for both. As Steffen Patzold has shown, the ninth century witnessed much earnest discussion about what it meant to be a bishop. The resulting texts (and ideals)—disseminated from those Frankish heartlands in which institutional forgery first flourished—laid the foundations for what Timothy Reuter called the tenth-century 'Europe of bishops', an era in which a keen sense of episcopal identity combined with the relative autonomy of bishoprics to make

39. J. Assmann, *Das kulturelle Gedächtnis*, 32–33, 181, 225–27. See also J. Assmann, *Religion and Cultural Memory*, 117–21.

prelates key players in local society and national politics.[40] If the characteristically Carolingian interpenetration of church and state had encouraged (and at times demanded) royal involvement in ecclesiastical matters in the eighth and ninth centuries, in the tenth we start to see significant movement in the opposite direction: bishops were now drawn more firmly into the secular sphere. These trends are visible at many of the centres we have been considering. At Worms, Anno and his successors established the bishop as lord of the city (and its booming trade); at Vercelli, Leo secured secular powers in order to ward off threats from the local margrave (and his clerical allies); and at Passau, Pilgrim took aim at his uncle, Archbishop Frederick, by claiming himself to be the true local metropolitan.

But just as forgery was not simply a tale of abbots and reform, so too it is about more than bishops and episcopal office. Here it is important to remember that religious communities possessed their own corporate identities. Theo Riches has argued that the flourishing of the *gesta episcoporum* genre reflects a growing perception of the bishopric as an 'imagined community', a distinct entity, with its own distinctive history.[41] We are arguably observing something similar with forgery. Forged charters do not simply speak with the voice of the bishop or abbot; they also express (and respond to) the concerns of the community. The cathedral chapter takes on particular significance in this connection. The ninth century saw important efforts to separate episcopal and canonical lands, establishing chapters as distinct legal and institutional entities. Yet as with so much else, these Carolingian seeds first truly took root in the post-Carolingian age. In Italy, it is only in the tenth and eleventh centuries that chapter houses start coming into sharper focus, not least at Vercelli; much the same is true east of the Rhine and south of the Loire. Even in the northern Frankish heartlands, developments were patchy, frequently stretching into the tenth and eleventh centuries.[42] Nor were these developments restricted to bishoprics. In monasteries, the analogous distinction between abbatial and fraternal holdings was frequently a product of these years—indeed, their separation was a concern of many reformers.[43] This was, therefore, an important moment for the crystallization of various types of identity within the church, a time when many ninth-century initiatives started bearing fruit. We should not imagine these developments in too irenic terms. Just as the emergence of the nation state—and its attendant myths of origin—was accompanied by much vigorous debate and violent disagreement in the nineteenth century, so

40. Patzold, *Episcopus*; Reuter, 'Europe of Bishops' (a study first published in German in 2001). See also Reuter, 'Reading the Tenth Century', 20–21; C. Leyser, 'Episcopal Office'; Mazel, *L'évêque et le territoire*, 237–306.

41. Riches, 'Changing Political Horizons'. Cf. Anderson, *Imagined Communities*.

42. Kurdziel, 'Au prisme des faux'; Schieffer, *Entstehung von Domkapiteln*, 255–60, 264–83; Mazel, *L'évêque et le territoire*, 242–43, 339–40; Bates, *Normandy*, 215–16.

43. Bernhardt, *Itinerant Kingship*, 85–135.

the articulation of new corporate identities within the tenth-century church was fraught with tension, both within and between religious houses.[44] Here forgery did not just express new visions of past and present; it also defended existing ones against critics.

Loosely associated with these developments was a more general stabilization of church structures and hierarchies. In the Frankish heartlands, the introduction of formal metropolitan structures in the eighth and ninth centuries had spelt the end of tinkering with ecclesiastical jurisdiction for centuries to come (the anomalous foundation of Arras in 1095 notwithstanding). And if elsewhere greater fluidity remained, the trend was certainly towards stability.[45] In newly conquered Saxony, bishoprics had been established by the early to mid-tenth century; the only remaining questions concerned the Slavic frontier.[46] England, likewise, saw its last major diocesan changes before the Conquest, in 909; while in northern Italy, we see a few adjustments in the 960s, then little thereafter (barring the elevation of Bobbio in 1014). As part of this process, diocesan boundaries started to be drawn more precisely, sometimes for the first time.

This slowly closing window had a dual effect. On the one hand, those bishops with the opportunities to expand their sees and provinces scrabbled to make the most of these while they still could; on the other, those who did not were forced to exploit local resources more intensively. Prelates also now turned to new titles and honorifics as a means of competing with their neighbours and rivals, particularly those who had profited from these prospects. This is why the concept of primacy, first articulated among the forged decretals of Pseudo-Isidore, now came into its own (especially in Germany); it was joined by that of the papal vicar.[47] Neither office was particularly well defined, but that was part of the appeal—their holders and claimants might hope to mould them into something more tangible. Such jockeying is especially clear at Passau, where Pilgrim sought to carve out a missionary field for himself and his successors. But traces of similar strategies can be observed elsewhere. In Italy, where the language of primacy carried less weight, one-upmanship focused more on episcopal founders. Here Leo's interest in Eusebius was anything but innocent. Eusebius was northern Italy's oldest episcopal founder— older even than Ambrose, the proto-bishop of Milan. To focus on his legacy was to draw attention to Vercelli's proud pedigree. In the atomized sociopolitical world of France, primacy and antiquity frequently came second to

44. Cf. G. Cubitt, *History and Memory*, 206–14.

45. Reuter, 'Europe of Bishops', esp. 23–27. See further Patzold, 'Eine Hierarchie im Wandel'; Pangerl, *Metropolitanverfassung*.

46. Rembold, *Conquest and Christianization*, 143–87; W. Hartmann, 'Neues zur Entstehung'.

47. Roberts, 'Construire', 17–19, 21–24, and *Flodoard*, 63–70; Beumann, *Theutonum nova metropolis*. Cf. Fuhrmann, 'Studien'.

local power politics. Still, they were not entirely ignored. Reims harboured primatial ambitions, closely tied to the legacy of its founder, the saintly Remigius (Saint Remi), while Abbo's privilege and its forged derivatives claim a similar brand of abbatial primacy for Fleury, in terms which may reflect the abbot's Rémois connections. An equally important corollary to these developments was the increasingly territorialized nature of the bishopric. As Florian Mazel has shown, it was in these years that bishops began extending their authority beyond their urban seats, trends evident in Abbo's Orléanais, Anno's Middle Rhine and Leo's Piedmont. Bishops were inscribing their control of the countryside in new (and often controversial) manners.[48]

A final factor is changes to the wider socio-political order. Here we must tread softly. Much important work over the last three decades has been dedicated to demonstrating that there was *not* a dramatic shift in social and political structures around the year 1000, as Georges Duby and others once held.[49] Nevertheless, change was in the air. And if Duby's critics are right to urge caution about models of sudden rupture and revolution, there is an equal danger of downplaying developments. Recent archaeological evidence suggests significant shifts in patterns of farming, fishing and consumption around the turn of the millennium. These may be placed alongside new arguments which place the origins of globalization in these years, a process driven by an expansion in trade and production both within and beyond Eurasia.[50] Such changes may often have been slow and incremental, but they were also steady and cumulative, leaving a socio-political landscape almost unrecognizable from that of the eighth and ninth centuries. Or as R. I. Moore put it, 'as new straws were added the camel's back was beginning to creak, and . . . while one straw is indeed very much like another, their accumulation does produce a point at which merely quantitative change becomes rather painfully qualitative, at least from the point of view of the camel'.[51] The later years of the tenth century may not have been the tipping point in all places, but they were in some; and where they were not, they saw important steps in this direction. A common response was to seek solace and security in the past. Forgery helped compensate for recent losses and update records in the face of new challenges.

The spread and development of forgery also points to more fundamental changes. The fact that older records were no longer deemed sufficient, and new documentary forms evolved to take their place, indicates that something significant was afoot. An older generation of Francophone scholars identified

48. Mazel, *L'évêque et le territoire*, 234–35, 237–306.
49. Bibliography on the subject is immense. The best point of departure is now Barthélemy, *The Serf, the Knight*. For subsequent discussion, see West, *Reframing*; Mazel, *Féodalités*; Wickham, '"Feudal Revolution"', and *Medieval Europe*, 99–120; Buc, 'What is Order?'; Kohl, *Streit, Erzählung und Epoche*.
50. McClain and Sykes, 'Archaeologies', 92–97; Hansen, *The Year 1000*.
51. Moore, 'Birth of Popular Heresy', 25. Cf. Moore, *First European Revolution*.

significant (indeed revolutionary) changes in these years, not least in the relationship between land, lordship and political authority. While our findings fall short of endorsing the old *mutationiste* paradigm in full, they suggest that there is something to this.[52] At all of the centres examined, we can observe important developments in relations between institutions and individuals, be it in the form of Anno's territorial immunities, Passau's would-be papal vicariate, Abingdon's liberty, Fleury's exemption or Leo's comital offices. Nor were these developments limited to the ecclesiastical sphere. Anno and Leo claimed immunity and comital rights in response to threats from local office-holders; Abbo secured exemption to guard against castellans such as Arnulf of Yèvre, as well as to fend off the local bishop of Orléans; Abingdon's problems began with the interference of Ealdorman Ælfric of Hampshire; and Pilgrim's ongoing rivalry with Frederick of Salzburg was as much a local aristocratic family tiff as an intra-ecclesiastical contest. The common denominator here is that institutional rights were being challenged and redefined. We may be observing hints, in the process, of new attitudes and approaches to lordship and power, developments so evocatively sketched by Thomas Bisson. Lords were demanding more exclusive (and extensive) rights, whether they were associated with new fortifications or longstanding local offices.[53] And behind all this may lie wider processes of socio-political reification, identified by Charles West: offices and regelian rights (such as counties) were taking on the characteristics of property, being divided and distributed among churchmen and secular magnates alike.[54] It is, therefore, no coincidence that immunity, exemption and liberty should loom so large in our records. Not only were these the weapons of choice for ecclesiastics dealing with unruly neighbours; they also take us to the heart of the socio-political order. At a time when the demands of lords were increasing, what lay beyond their control—where the royal or lordly writ stopped—was an essential (and sometimes existential) question.[55]

To assert this is not to return to old models of sudden, abrupt and revolutionary change. The shifts we have been tracing began long before the tenth century and continued well into the twelfth. In some places, the turn of the millennium witnessed a distinct quickening in this regard; in others, developments remained gradual, though no less important for this fact. These continuities are significant. In recent years, scholars have tended to place greater emphasis on the eleventh century—and in particular its second half—as the moment of transition between the early and central Middle Ages, underlining

52. The classic remains Duby, *La société*. See also Poly and Bournazel, *Feudal Transformation*; Bonnassie, *Slavery to Feudalism*; Bisson, '"Feudal Revolution"'.

53. Bisson, *Crisis of the Twelfth Century*. See also Bisson, 'Medieval Lordship'.

54. West, *Reframing*, 171–227. See also Roach, 'Leiheformen und -praktiken'.

55. Moore, 'Treasures'. See also Mehu, *Paix et communautés*, 59–86, 133–93; Mazel, *L'évêque et le territoire*, 287–89.

the central role of church (and especially papal) reform in the process.[56] Yet for all their explanatory power, these models rarely explain how reform itself emerged. It is here that the tenth and early eleventh centuries come back into the picture. The first generation of papal reformers was fostered by Emperor Henry III (1039–56), who behaved much like (and often modelled himself on) his Ottonian forebears. And the movement's leading spokesmen were Lotharingian churchmen—the products, at only one or two removes, of the same circles as Anno of Worms.

We therefore underestimate the developments of the later tenth and early eleventh centuries at our peril. Revisionist scholarship has fruitfully problematized the relationship between written record and social reality here, noting that these years may simply have witnessed a 'documentary revelation' ('révélation documentaire'). Thanks to changes in our source base, we now see more clearly practices and phenomena which had long prevailed.[57] This is doubtless often so. But we must not lose sight of the fact that the documents we have been examining—charters both forged and authentic—are not disengaged witnesses. They played an active and essential part in later tenth-century society, as their frequent falsification attests. When they change in form and nature, this points towards—and potentially occasions—important developments elsewhere. There is little need for new and updated records when the sociopolitical order is stable.

In the end, this creative engagement with the past bore its own fruit. As David Lowenthal notes, just as we remake the past, so it remakes us.[58] The forgery complexes we have been examining are a case in point: these do not simply reflect change, but were active participants in it. Here the differences between our cases reveal as much as the similarities. The later tenth century may have seen some of the first steps towards the formation of a common European culture, but it also saw the Latin West become more localized and compartmentalized than ever before.[59] We must, therefore, be wary of simplification and generalization, of ironing out what Reuter called the 'lumpiness' of the past; the same forces were not at work everywhere, nor did they have the same effects where present.[60] Questions of rank and status may have been important across the board, but they were much more so in episcopal circles; and even here, they were felt more acutely on Pilgrim's Danube than in Anno's

56. Mazel, *L'évêque et le territoire*. See also Weinfurter, *Canossa*; Barthelémy, 'Mutation de l'an 1100'; Kohl, *Streit, Erzählung und Epoche*. For a stronger emphasis on continuous developments out of the tenth century, see Hamilton, *Church and People*; Bisson, *Crisis of the Twelfth Century*.

57. Barthélemy, *The Serf, the Knight*, 12–36. See also Barthélemy, *La société*, 19–83.

58. Lowenthal, *Past is a Foreign Country*, xxv.

59. For different (complementary) perspectives: Bartlett, *Making of Europe*; Wickham, 'Making Europes'; Borgolte, *Europa entdeckt seine Vielfalt*.

60. Cf. Reuter, 'Assembly Politics', 193.

Rhineland or Leo's Vercelli. Changing judicial structures can similarly be observed in all localities, but left a greater mark at Worms, Vercelli and Fleury than at Passau or Abingdon. And while institutional independence was valued everywhere, it was a particular concern at the monastic houses of Abingdon and Fleury. Yet even here, the problems were not the same: at Abbo's Fleury—as at William of Volpiano's Fruttuaria—it was local bishops who posed the threat; at Wulfgar's Abingdon, it was the king.

If in the end this diversity defies simple summary, it is to be all the more welcomed for this fact. There was not one change between the early and central Middle Ages, but many, playing out differently at different times and in different places. This does not invalidate broader models of change and transition, but it does mean that the devil is, as ever, firmly in the detail. It is in this sense that I hope my case studies are representative: not because they cover all the Latin West, nor because they encompass the full range of experience there, but because they shine a light on the concrete hopes and dreams, conflicts and concerns, of individual monks and clerics of these years. Marc Bloch memorably compared the historian to the fairy-tale ogre (or giant), stalking the scent of human flesh.[61] Well, here there is flesh aplenty. Through these documents, we can appreciate the appeal of tolls and immunity to a bishop of Worms in the 960s; we can understand the importance of the pallium to a prelate of Passau in the 970s; we can recognize the relevance of liberty to an abbot of Abingdon in the 990s; we can fathom the fragility of exemption in Fleury in the mid-eleventh century; and we can perceive the pertinence of the precedent of Charles the Fat to a bishop of Vercelli at the turn of the millennium. These texts are the snapshots of a bygone age: faded, perhaps, and certainly worn, but still capable of transporting us across the centuries at the most dizzying speed. All that remains is to sit back and enjoy the ride.

61. M. Bloch, *Historian's Craft*, 22.

Manuscripts

Bamberg, StA, Bamberger Urkunden 8
Bamberg, Staatsbibliothek, Msc. Can. 1
Bamberg, Staatsbibliothek, Msc. Hist. 5
Bern, Burgerbibliothek, Cod. 49
Bologna, AS, S. Cristina, Camaldolesi, 15/2876
Bordeaux, Archives départmentales de la Gironde, La Réole II, 6
BL, Add. 56488
BL, Cotton Augustus ii. 6
BL, Cotton Augustus ii. 23
BL, Cotton Augustus ii. 33
BL, Cotton Augustus ii. 38
BL, Cotton Augustus ii. 39
BL, Cotton Augustus ii. 40
BL, Cotton Augustus ii. 41
BL, Cotton Augustus ii. 43
BL, Cotton Charters vi. 4
BL, Cotton Charters viii. 6
BL, Cotton Charters viii. 11
BL, Cotton Charters viii. 17
BL, Cotton Charters viii. 22
BL, Cotton Charters viii. 33
BL, Cotton Claudius ii. 38
BL, Cotton Claudius B.vi
BL, Cotton Claudius C.ix
BL, Cotton Vespasian A.viii
BL, Stowe Charter 35
BnF lat. 5 (II)
BnF lat. 2278
BnF lat. 2400
BnF lat. 6114
BnF lat. 11674
CCCC 111
Darmstadt, HStA, A2 251/1
Darmstadt, HStA, A2 255/1
Darmstadt, HStA, A2 255/3
Darmstadt, HStA, A2 255/4
Darmstadt, HStA, A2 255/5
Dorchester, Dorset Record Office, D 124, 1
Einsiedeln, Klosterarchiv, KAE A.BI.5
Exeter, D.C., 2070
Exeter, Devon Heritage Centre, W1258M/D84/1–10
Halle, Universitäts- und Landesbibliothek Sachsen-Anhalt, Morbio VIII, 3
Hanover, Niedersächsische Landesbibliothek, HS XVIII 1020

Ivrea, BC, Cod. LXXXVII (54)
Karlsruhe, GLA, A 46a
Karlsruhe, GLA, A 47
Leiden, University Library, Voss. lat. Q 15
Leiden, University Library, Voss. lat. F 96 I
Longleat, Marquess of Bath, Muniment 10564
Lucca, AS, 22-08-1002—S. Giustina
Magdeburg, LA Sachsen-Anhalt, U 1, I 23
Magdeburg, LA Sachsen-Anhalt, U 1, I 34b
Magdeburg, LA Sachsen-Anhalt, U 1, I 44
Masino, Archivio Storico Castello di Masino, mazzo 43, 703
Milan, AS, Museo diplomatico, cart. 6, prot. 57/196
Milan, AS, Museo diplomatico, cart. 10, prot. 186/314
Milan, AS, Museo diplomatico, cart. 10, prot. 188/316
Milan, AS, Museo diplomatico, cart. 10, prot. 193/320
Milan, AS, Museo diplomatico, cart. 10, prot. 214/340
Milan, AS, Museo diplomatico, cart. 11, prot. 3/346½
Milan, AS, Museo diplomatico, cart. 11, prot. 8/351
Milan, AS, Museo diplomatico, cart. 11, prot. 20/363
Milan, AS, Museo diplomatico, cart. 14, prot. 150/488
Milan, Biblioteca Ambrosiana, O 55 sup.
Modena, AS, Casa e Stato, Membranacei, cassetta 1 n. 21
Munich, BayHStA, DU Passau 1
Munich, BayHStA, HL Passau 2
Munich, BayHStA, HL Passau 3
Munich, BayHStA, HL Passau 7
Munich, BayHStA, HU Passau 1
Munich, BayHStA, HU Passau 2/1
Munich, BayHStA, HU Passau 2/2
Munich, BayHStA, HU Passau 6
Munich, BayHStA, HU Passau 11
Munich, BayHStA, HU Passau 13
Munich, BayHStA, HU Passau 14
Munich, BayHStA, HU Passau 15
Munich, BayHStA, HU Passau 16
Munich, BayHStA, HU Passau 17/1
Munich, BayHStA, HU Passau 17/2
Munich, BayHStA, HU Passau 18
Munich, BayHStA, HU Passau 19
Munich, BayHStA, HU Passau 20
Munich, BayHStA, HU Passau 21
Munich, BayHStA, HU Passau 22
Munich, BayHStA, EU Salzburg 2
Orléans, Archives départementales du Loiret, H 29
Orléans, Archives départementales du Loiret, H 37
Oxford, Bodleian Library, Eng. hist. a. 2, no. vi
Oxford, Bodleian Library, Eng. hist. a. 2, no. vii
Oxford, Christ Church, MS 341
Rheda, Fürstliches Archiv, H 2
Stafford, William Salt Library, 84/4/41
Stafford, William Salt Library, 84/5/41

Speyer, LA, F 7, 2
Taunton, Somerset Record Office, DD/SAS PR 502
Trier, Stadtarchiv, Urk. D 4
Turin, AS, Materie ecclesiastiche, Abbazia di S. Benigno, mazzo 1, 1
Turin, AS, Materie ecclesiastiche, Abbazia di S. Benigno, mazzo 1, 6
Turin, AS, Materie politiche per rapporto all'estero, Diplomi imperiali, mazzo 1.1, 5.2
Turin, AS, Museo storico I, 1
Vatican, BAV, Reg. lat. 566
Vatican, BAV, Reg. lat. 592
Vatican, BAV, Reg. lat. 596
Vatican, BAV, Reg. lat. 598
Vatican, BAV, Vat. lat. 4322
Vercelli, BC, Cod. XV
Vercelli, BC, Cod. XXXVIII
Vercelli, BC, Cod. LXII
Vercelli, BC, Cod. CII
Vercelli, BC, Cod. CXXXIV
Vercelli, AC, Diplomi, I Cartella, 6
Vercelli, AC, Diplomi, I Cartella, 8
Vercelli, AC, Diplomi, I Cartella, 9
Vercelli, AC, Diplomi, II Cartella, 1
Vercelli, AC, Diplomi, II Cartella, 2
Vercelli, AC, Diplomi, II Cartella, 4
Vercelli, AC, Diplomi, II Cartella, 6
Vercelli, AC, Diplomi, II Cartella, 7
Vercelli, AC, Diplomi, II Cartella, 8
Vercelli, AC, Diplomi, II Cartella, 9
Vercelli, AC, Diplomi, II Cartella, 10
Vercelli, AC, Diplomi, III Cartella, 1
Vercelli, AC, Diplomi, III Cartella, 3
Vercelli, AC, Diplomi, III Cartella, 7
Vercelli, AC, Diplomi, III Cartella, 8
Vercelli, Archivio del Comune, *Biscioni* I
Vienna, HHStA, UR AUR 7
Vienna, HHStA, UR AUR 15
Vienna, HHStA, UR AUR 18
Vienna, HHStA, UR AUR 45
Vienna, HHStA, UR AUR 47

Sources and Registers

Abbo of Fleury, *Collectio canonum*, PL 139, cols 473–508
——, *Epistolae*, PL 139, cols 419–62
——, *Epitome de XCI Romanorum pontificum vitiis*, PL 139, cols 535–70
——, *Liber apologeticus*, PL 139, cols 461–72
——, *Passio S. Eadmundi*, ed. M. Winterbottom, *Three Lives of English Saints* (Toronto, 1972), 67–87
Actus pontificum Cenomannis, ed. M. Weidemann, *Geschichte des Bistums Le Mans von der Spätantike bis zur Karolingerzeit*, 3 pts (Mainz, 2002), 31–114
Adalbero of Laon, *Carmen ad Robertem regem*, ed. C. Carozzi, *Adalbéron de Laon, Poème au roi Robert* (Paris, 1979)

Adémar of Chabannes, *Chronicon*, ed. P. Bourgain with R. Landes and G. Pon, CCCM 129 (Turnhout, 1999)

Aimoin, *Gesta Francorum*, PL 139, cols 627–798

——, *Vita Abbonis*, ed. R.-H. Bautier and G. Labory, *L'abbaye de Fleury en l'an mil* (Paris, 2004), 9–143

Andrew of Fleury, *Vita Gauzlini*, ed. R.-H. Bautier and G. Labory (Paris, 1969)

Ælfric's Letter to the Monks at Eynsham, ed. C. A. Jones (Cambridge, 1999)

Die angelsächsischen Prosabearbeitungen der Benediktinerregel, ed. A. Schröer, Bibliothek der angelsächsischen Prosa 2 (Kassel, 1885–88)

The Anglo-Saxon Chronicle MS C, ed. K. O'Brien O'Keeffe (Cambridge, 2001)

Annales Hildesheimenses, ed. G. Waitz, MGH: SS rer. Germ. 8 (Hanover, 1878)

Annales regni Francorum, ed. F. Kurze, MGH: SS rer. Germ. 6 (Hanover, 1895)

Annales Sangallenses maiores, ed. R. Zingg, *Die St. Galler Annalistik* (Sigmaringen, 2019)

Annalista Saxo, *Chronicon*, ed. K. Naß, MGH: SS 37 (Hanover, 2006)

Arnulf, *Gesta episcoporum Mediolanensium*, ed. L. C. Bethmann and W. Wattenbach, MGH: SS 8 (Hanover, 1848), 1–31

Atto of Vercelli, *Epistolae*, PL 134, cols 95–124

——, *Sermones*, PL 134, cols 833–60

Bath and Wells, 1061–1205, ed. F. M. R. Ramsey, English Episcopal Acta 10 (Oxford, 1995)

Bede, *Historia ecclesiastica gentis Anglorum*, ed. B. Colgrave and R. H. S. Mynors (Oxford, 1969)

Bern of Reichenau(?), *Ratio generalis de initio adventus Domini*, ed. H. Parkes, *Berno Augiensis: Tractatus Liturgici*, CCCM 297 (Turnhout, 2020), 159–63

Böhmer, J. F., *Regesta Imperii*, i.1, *Die Regesten des Kaiserreiches unter den Karolingern 751–918*, 2nd edn, ed. E. Mühlbacher with J. Lechner (Innsbruck, 1908)

——, *Regesta imperii*, ii.2, *Die Regesten des Kaiserreiches unter Otto II. 955 (973)–983*, rev. H. L. Mikoletzky (Vienna, 1950)

——, *Regesta Imperii*, xi, *Die Urkunden Kaiser Sigmunds 1410–1437*, ed. W. von Altmann, 2 vols (Innsbruck, 1896–1900)

Boshof, E., *Die Regesten der Bischöfe von Passau*, i, *731–1206* (Munich, 1992)

Le carte dello Archivio Capitolare di Vercelli, i, ed. D. Arnoldi et al., BSSS 70 (Pinerolo, 1912)

Le carte dello Archivio Capitolare di Santa Maria di Novara, i, *739–1034*, ed. F. Gabotto et al., BSSS 78 (Turin, 1913)

Cartulaire de l'abbaye de Saint-Vaast d'Arras, ed. E. van Drival (Arras, 1875)

Cartularium Saxonicum: A Collection of Charters Relating to Anglo-Saxon History, ed. W. de G. Birch, 3 vols (London, 1885–93)

Charters of Abingdon Abbey, ed. S. E. Kelly, 2 pts, AS Charters 7–8 (Oxford, 2000–2001)

Charters of Barking Abbey, ed. S. E. Kelly, AS Charters (Oxford, forthcoming)

Charters of Burton Abbey, ed. P. H. Sawyer, AS Charters 2 (Oxford, 1979)

Charters of Christ Church, Canterbury, ed. N. Brooks and S. E. Kelly, 2 pts, AS Charters 17–18 (Oxford, 2013)

Charters of Glastonbury, ed. S. E. Kelly, AS Charters 15 (Oxford, 2012)

Charters of Malmesbury Abbey, ed. S. E. Kelly, AS Charters 11 (Oxford, 2005)

Charters of the New Minster, Winchester, ed. S. Miller, AS Charters 9 (Oxford, 2001)

Charters of the Northern Houses, ed. D. A. Woodman, AS Charters 16 (Oxford, 2012)

Charters of Peterborough Abbey, ed. S. E. Kelly, AS Charters 14 (Oxford, 2009)

Charters of Rochester, ed. A. Campbell, AS Charters 1 (Oxford, 1973)

Charters of Selsey, ed. S. E. Kelly, AS Charters 6 (Oxford, 1998)

Charters of Shaftesbury Abbey, ed. S. E. Kelly, AS Charters 5 (Oxford, 1995)

Charters of Sherborne, ed. M. A. O'Donovan, AS Charters 3 (Oxford, 1988)

Charters of St Albans, ed. J. Crick, AS Charters 12 (Oxford, 2007)

Codex Diplomaticus Aevi Saxonici, ed. J. M. Kemble, 6 vols (London, 1839–48)

Codice diplomatico longobardo, iii.1, *I diploma dei re longobardi*, ed. C. Brühl, FSI 64 (Rome, 1973)

Codice diplomatico parmense, i, *Secolo VIIII*, ed. U. Benassi (Parma, 1910)

Concilios visigóticos e hispano-romanos, ed. J. Vives (Barcelona, 1963)

Constituiones et acta publica imperatorum et regum, ed. L. Weiland, MGH: Const. 1 (Hanover, 1893)

Constitutum Constantini, ed. H. Fuhrmann, MGH: Fontes iuris 10 (Hanover, 1968)

Consuetudines Fructuarienses-Sanblasianae, ed. L. G. Spatling and P. Dinter, 2 vols (Siegburg, 1985–87)

Il conte Umberto I (Biancamano) e il re Aroino. Ricerche e documenti, ed. D. Carutti, 2nd edn (Rome, 1884)

Conversio Bagoarium et Carantanorum, ed. F. Lošek, MGH: Studien und Texte 15 (Hanover, 1997)

Councils and Synods with Other Documents Relating to the English Church, i, AD 871–1204, ed. D. Whitelock (Oxford, 1981)

The Crawford Collection of Early Charters and Documents, ed. A. S. Napier and W. H. Stevenson (Oxford, 1895)

I diplomi di Berengario I, ed. L. Schiaparelli, FSI 25 (Rome, 1903)

I diplomi di Ugo e di Lotario, di Berengario II e di Adalberto, ed. L. Schiaparelli, FSI 38 (Rome, 1924)

Eugippius, *Vita Severini*, ed. P. Regerat, SC 374 (Paris, 1991)

Facsimiles of Anglo-Saxon Charters, ed. S. Keynes, AS Charters: Supplementary Series 1 (London, 1991)

Facsimiles of Anglo-Saxon Manuscripts, ed. W. B. Saunders, 3 vols, Ordnance Survey (Southampton, 1878–84)

Flodoard, *Annales*, ed. P. Lauer (Paris, 1905)

——, *Historia Remensis ecclesiae*, ed. M. Stratmann, MGH: SS 36 (Hanover, 1998)

Fulbert of Chartres, *Epistolae*, ed. F. Behrends (Oxford, 1976)

Gerbert of Aurillac, *Epistolae*, ed. P. Riché and J.-P. Callu, 2 pts (Paris, 2008)

Gesta Aldrici, ed. M. Weidemann, *Geschichte des Bistums Le Mans von der Spätantike bis zur Karolingerzeit*, 3 pts (Mainz, 2002), 115–79

Die Gesetze der Angelsachsen, ed. F. Liebermann, 3 vols (Halle, 1903–16)

Great Domesday Book: Library Edition, ed. A. Williams and R. W. H. Erskine, 6 vols (London, 1986–92)

Gregory the Great, *Registrum epistularum*, ed. D. Norberg, CCSL 140, 2 pts (Turnhout, 1982)

Helgaud of Fleury, *Epitoma vite Robertii pii*, ed. R.-H. Bautier and G. Labory (Paris, 1965)

Historia ecclesie Abbendonensis, ed. J. Hudson, 2 vols (Oxford, 2002–7)

HMC, *Calendar of the Manuscripts of the Dean and Chapter of Wells*, ed. W. H. B. Bird, 2 vols (London, 1907–14)

John the Deacon, *Istoria Veneticorum*, ed. L. A. Berto (Bologna, 1999)

John of Salerno, *Vita S. Odonis*, PL 133, cols 43–86

Kaiserurkunden in Abbildungen, ed. H. von Sybel and T. Sickel, 12 vols (Berlin, 1880–91)

Die Konzilien Deutschlands und Reichsitaliens 916–1001, ed. E.-D. Hehl, 2 pts, MGH: Concilia 6 (Hanover, 1987–2007)

Die Konzilien der karolingischen Teilreiche 875–911, ed. W. Hartmann, I. Schröder and G. Schmitz, MGH: Concilia 5 (Hanover, 2012)

Die lateinischen Dichter des deutschen Mittelalters, v.1–2, *Die Ottonenzeit*, ed. K. Strecker and N. Fickermann, 2 pts, MGH: Poetae 5.i–ii (Leipzig, 1937–39)

Leo of Synada, *Correspondence*, ed. M. P. Vinson (Washington, D.C., 1985)

Leo of Vercelli, *Epistolae*, ed. H. Bloch, 'Beiträge zur Geschichte des Bischofs Leo von Vercelli und seiner Zeit', *NA* 22 (1897), 11–136, at 16–23

Liber diurnus Romanorum pontificum, ed. H. Foerster (Bern, 1958)

Miracula S. Benedicti, ed. E. de Certain (Paris, 1858)

Monumenta Novaliciensia Vetustiora, ed. C. Cipolla, FSI 31 (Rome, 1898)

Mosbacher Urkundenbuch. Stadt und Stift im Mittelalter, ed. K. Krimm (Elztal-Dallau, 1986)

Papsturkunden 896–1046, ed. H. Zimmermann, 2 pts rev. ed. (Vienna, 1988)

Papsturkunden in Frankreich, n.s. vi, *Orléanais*, ed. J. Ramackers (Göttingen, 1958)

Passio S. Floriani, ed. B. Krusch, MGH: SS rer. Merov. 3 (Hanover, 1896), 65–71

Le pergamene degli archivi di Bergamo, i, *a. 740–1000*, ed. M. Cortesi and A. Pretesi (Bergamo, 1988)

I Placiti del "Regnum Italiae", ed. C. Manaresi, 3 vols, FSI 92, 96–97 (Rome, 1955–60)

Property and Piety in Early Medieval Winchester: Documents Relating to the Topography of the Anglo-Saxon and Norman City and its Minsters, ed. A. Rumble (Oxford, 2002)

Raoul Glaber, *Vita Willelmi abbatis*, ed. N. Bulst, *Rodulfus Glaber: Opera* (Oxford, 1989), 254–98

Recueil des actes de Charles III le Simple, roi de France, 893–923, ed. F. Lot and P. Lauer (Paris, 1949)

Recueil des actes de Lothaire et Louis V, rois de France, 954–987, ed. L. Halphen with F. Lot (Paris, 1908)

Recueil des actes de Philippe Iᵉʳ, roi de France (1059–1108), ed. M. Prou (Paris, 1908)

Recueil des chartes de l'abbey de Saint-Benoît-sur-Loire, ed. M. Prou and A. Vidier, 2 vols (Paris, 1900–1907)

Regesta Pontificum Romanorum ab condita ecclesia ad annum post Christum natum 1198, ed. P. Jaffé, rev. S. Loewenfeld, F. Kaltenbrunner and P. Ewald, 2 pts (Leipzig, 1885–88)

Registrum Gregorii: Libri VIII–XIV, ed. L. M. Hartmann, MGH: Epp. 2 (Berlin, 1893)

Regula Benedicti, ed. J. Neufville with A. de Vogüé, 4 pts, SC 181–86 (Paris, 1972)

Regularis concordia, ed. T. Symons and S. Spath, CCM 7.iii (Siegburg, 1984)

Richer of Saint-Remi, *Historiae*, ed. H. Hoffmann, MGH: SS 38 (Hanover, 2000)

Salvian of Marseille, *Epistolae*, ed. G. Lagarrigue, *Salvien de Marseille: Oeuvres*, i, *Les lettres, les livres de Timothée à l'Église*, SC 176 (Paris, 1971)

Salzburger Urkundenbuch, 4 vols, ed. W. Hauthaler and F. Martin (Salzburg, 1910–33)

San Siro primo vescovo e patrona della città e diocese di Pavia, ii, *Documenti*, ed. C. Prelini (Pavia, 1890)

Sawyer, P. H., *Anglo-Saxon Charters: An Annotated List and Bibliography*, rev. S. E. Kelly and R. Rushforth (https://esawyer.lib.cam.ac.uk)

Thietmar of Merseburg, *Chronicon*, ed. R. Holtzmann, MGH: SRG n.s. 9 (Berlin, 1935)

Two Cartularies of Abingdon Abbey, ed. C. F. Slade and G. Lambrick (Oxford, 1990–92)

Two Cartularies of the Benedictine Abbeys of Muchelney and Athelney in the County of Somerset, ed. E. H. Bates (London, 1899)

Die Urkunden Arnolfs, ed. P. Kehr, MGH: DD regum Germaniae ex stirpe Karolinorum 3 (Berlin, 1940)

Die Urkunden Heinrichs II. und Arduins, ed. H. Bresslau, MGH: Dip. regum 3 (Hanover, 1900–1903)

Die Urkunden Heinrichs III., ed. H. Bresslau and P. Kehr, MGH: Dip. regum 5 (Berlin, 1931)

Die Urkunden Heinrichs IV., ed. D. von Gladiss and A. Gawlik, MGH: Dip. regum 6 (Berlin/Weimar/Hanover, 1941–78)

Die Urkunden Karls III., ed. P. Kehr, MGH: DD regum Germaniae ex stirpe Karolinorum 2 (Berlin, 1937)

Die Urkunden Konrads I., Heinrichs I. und Ottos I., ed. T. Sickel, MGH: Dip. regum 1 (Hanover, 1879–84)

Die Urkunden Konrads II., ed. H. Bresslau, MGH: Dip. regum 4 (Hanover, 1909)

Die Urkunden Lothars I. und Lothars II., ed. T. Schieffer, MGH: DD Kar. 3 (Berlin, 1966)

Die Urkunden Ludwigs des Deutschen, Karlmanns und Ludwigs des Jüngeren, ed. P. Kehr, MGH: DD regum Germaniae ex stirpe Karolinorum 1 (Berlin, 1934)

Die Urkunden Ludwigs des Frommen, ed. T. Kölzer, 3 pts, MGH: DD Kar. 2 (Hanover, 2016)

Die Urkunden der Merowinger, ed. T. Kölzer., 2 pts, MGH: DD Mer (Hanover, 2001)

Die Urkunden Otto des II., ed. T. Sickel, MGH: Dip. regum 2.i (Hanover, 1888)

Die Urkunden Otto des III., ed. T. Sickel, MGH: Dip. regum 2.ii (Hanover, 1893)

Die Urkunden Zwentibolds und Ludwigs des Kindes, ed. T. Schieffer, MGH: DD regum Germaniae ex stirpe Karolinorum 4 (Berlin, 1960)

Vita Burchardi, ed. H. Boos, Quellen zur Geschichte der Stadt Worms 3 (Berlin, 1893)

Vita S. Bononii, ed. G. Schwartz and A. Hofmeister, MGH: SS 30 (Hanover, 1934), 1023–33

Widukind of Corey, *Res gestae Saxonicae*, ed. H.-E. Lohmann and P. Husch, MGH: SS rer. Germ. 60 (Hanover, 1935)

William of Malmesbury, *De antiquitate Glastonie ecclesie*, ed. J. Scott (Woodbridge, 1981)

——, *Vita S. Dunstani*, ed. M. Winterbottom and R. M. Thomson, *William of Malmesbury: Saints' Lives* (Oxford, 2002), 8–302

Wolfhere, *Vita Godehardi (prior)*, ed. G. H. Pertz, MGH: SS 11 (Hanover, 1854), 167–96

Wulfstan Cantor, *Vita S. Æthelwoldi*, ed. M. Lapidge and M. Winterbottom (Oxford, 1991)

Literature

Abels, R., *Aethelred the Unready: The Failed King* (London, 2018)

Adam, H., *Das Zollwesen im Fränkischen Reich und das spätkarolingische Wirtschaftsleben. Ein Überblick über Zoll, Handel und Verkehr im 9. Jahrhundert* (Stuttgart, 1996)

Adrizio, G., 'Le origini dell'incastellamento nel Vercellese storico: fonti scritte ed evidenze archeologiche', in *Prima dei castelli medievali: materiali e luoghi nell'arco alpino orientale*, ed. B. Maurina and C. A. Postinger (Rovereto, 2015), 101–30

Airlie, S., 'True Teachers and Pious Kings: Salzburg, Louis the German, and Christian Order', in *Belief and Culture in the Middle Ages. Studies Presented to Henry Mayr-Harting*, ed. R. Gameson and H. Leyser (Oxford 2001), 89–105

Albert, P. P., 'Die ältesten Nachrichten über Stift und Stadt Mosbach', *ZGO* 23 (1908), 593–639

——, 'Noch einmal die Wormser Kaiserurkunde über Mosbach vom 15. November 976', *ZGO* 25 (1910), 355–57

Alberzoni, M. P., 'Vercelli e il papato', in *Vercelli nel secolo XII. Atti del quarto Congresso storico vercellese* (Vercelli, 2005), 79–136

Althoff, G., '*Causa scribendi* und Darstellungsabsicht: Die Lebensbeschreibungen der Königin Mathilde und andere Beispiele' (1988), repr. in his *Inszenierte Herrschaft. Geschichtsschreibung und politisches Handeln im Mittelalter* (Darmstadt, 2003), 78–104

——, *Spielregeln der Politik im Mittelalter. Kommunikation in Frieden und Fehde* (Darmstadt, 1996)

——, 'Magdeburg, Halberstadt, Merseburg. Bischöfliche Repräsentation und Interessenvertretung im ottonischen Sachsen', in *Herrschaftsrepräsentation im ottonischen Sachsen*, ed. G. Althoff and E. Schubert (Sigmaringen, 1998), 267–93

——, *Die Ottonen. Königsherrschaft ohne Staat*, rev. edn (Stuttgart, 2005)

Alvermann, D., *Königsherrschaft und Reichsintegration. Eine Untersuchung zur politischen Struktur von regna und imperium zur Zeit Kaiser Ottos II. (967) 973–983* (Berlin, 1995)

Andenna, G., 'Grandi patrimoni, funzioni pubbliche e famiglie su di un territorio: il "comitatus plumbiensis" e i suoi conti dal IX all'XI secolo', in *Formazione e strutture dei ceti dominanti nel medioevo. Marchesi, conti e visconti nel Regno italico secc. IX–XII. Atti del primo Convegno (Pisa, 10–11 maggio 1983)* (Rome, 1988), 201–28

Anderson, B., *Imagined Communities: Reflections on the Origin and Spread of Nationalism*, rev. edn (London, 1991)

Arnaldi, G., 'Arduino, re d'Italia', in *DBI*, iv (Rome, 1962), 53–60

Arnold, B., 'Episcopal Authority Authenticated and Fabricated: Form and Function in Medieval German Bishops' Catalogues', in *Warriors and Churchmen in the High Middle Ages: Essays Presented to Karl Leyser*, ed. T. Reuter (London, 1992), 63–78

Assmann, A., *Cultural Memory and Western Civilization: Functions, Media, Archives* (Cambridge, 2011)

Assmann, J., *Das kulturelle Gedächtnis. Schrift, Erinnerung und politische Identität in frühen Hochkulturen* (Munich, 1992)

——, *Religion and Cultural Memory: Ten Studies*, trans. R. Livingstone (Stanford, CA, 2005)

——, *Cultural Memory and Early Civilization: Writing, Remembrance, and Political Imagination* (Cambridge, 2011)

Atherton, M., *The Making of England: A New History of the Anglo-Saxon World* (London, 2017)

Atsma, H., and J. Vézin, 'Les faux sur papyrus de l'abbaye de Saint-Denis', in *Finances, pouvoirs et mémoire. Mélanges offerts à Jean Favier*, ed. J. Kerhervé and A. Rigaudière (Paris, 1999), 674–99

——, 'Originaux et copies: La reproduction des élements graphiques des actes des Xe et XIe siècles dans le cartulaire de Cluny', in *Charters, Cartularies, and Archives: The Preservation and Transmission of Documents in the Medieval West*, ed. A. J. Kosto and A. Winroth (Toronto, 2002), 113–26

Auer, L., 'Der Kriegsdienst des Klerus unter den sächsischen Kaisern', *MIÖG* 79 (1971), 316–407; 80 (1972), 48–70

Bachrach, D. S., 'The Written Word in Carolingian-Style Fiscal Administration under King Henry I, 919–936', *German History* 28 (2010), 399–423

——, 'Immunities as Tools of Royal Military Policy under the Carolingian and Ottonian Kings', *ZRG: GA* 130 (2013), 1–36

Baronio, C., *Annales Ecclesiastici*, x (Rome, 1602)

Barrett, G., 'The Written and the World in Early Medieval Iberia' (DPhil thesis, University of Oxford, 2015)

Barron, C., 'Latin Inscriptions and the Eighteenth-Century Art Market', in *Animo Decipiendi? Rethinking Fakes and Authorship in Classical, Late Antique, and Early Christian Works*, ed. A. Guzmán and J. Martínez (Groningen, 2018), 265–84

Barrow, J., 'The Ideology of the Tenth-Century English Benedictine "Reform"', in *Challenging the Boundaries of Medieval History: The Legacy of Timothy Reuter*, ed. P. Skinner (Turnhout, 2009), 141–54

——, *The Clergy in the Medieval World: Secular Clerics, their Families and Careers in North-Western Europe, c. 800–c. 1200* (Cambridge, 2015)

——, 'The Bishop in the Latin West 600–1100', in *Celibate and Childless Men in Power: Ruling Eunuchs and Bishops in the Pre-Modern World*, ed. A. Höfert et al. (Abingdon, 2018), 43–64

Barthélemy, D., *La société dans le comté de Vendôme, de l'an mil au XIVe siècle* (Paris, 1993)

——, *Chevaliers et miracles. La violence et le sacré dans la société féodale* (Paris, 2004)

——, 'La mutation de l'an 1100', *Journal des Savants* (2005), 3–28

——, *The Serf, the Knight and the Historian*, trans. G. R. Edwards (Ithaca, NY, 2009)

Bartlett, R., *The Making of Europe: Conquest, Colonization and Cultural Change 950–1350* (London, 1993)

Bates, D., *Normandy before 1066* (London, 1982)

Bautier, R.-H., 'Leçon d'ouverture du cours de diplomatique à l'École des chartes', *BEC* 119 (1961), 194–225

——, 'L'hérésie d'Orléans et le mouvement intellectuel au début du XIe siècle: documents et hypothèses' (1975), repr. in his *Recherches sur l'histoire de la France médiévale: des Mérovingiens aux premiers Capétiens* (Aldershot, 1991), no. viii

——, 'La chancellerie et les actes royaux dans les royaumes carolingiens', *BEC* 142 (1984), 5–80

——, 'De Robert le Fort à Louis VI le Gros: Orléans et la région d'entre Seine et Loire dans la politique des Robertiens et des premiers Capétiens', *Bulletin de la Société archéologique et historique de l'Orléanais* 10 (1988), 26–44

——, 'L'avènement d'Hughes Capet et le sacre de Robert le Pieux', in *Le roi de France et son royaume, autour de l'an Mil*, ed. M. Parisse et X. Barral I Altet (Paris, 1992), 27–37

Beach, A. I., *The Trauma of Monastic Reform: Community and Conflict in Twelfth-Century Germany* (Cambridge, 2017)

Bedina, A., 'Leone', *DBI*, liv (Rome, 2005), 478–482

Bellarbre, J., 'Adémar de Chabannes et le prétendu "corpus de Fleury"', in *L'écrit monastique dans l'espace ligérien (X^e–XIIIe siècle): Singularités, interférences et transferts documentaires*, ed. C. Senséby (Rennes, 2018), 231–43

Bennette, R. A., *Fighting for the Soul of Germany: The Catholic Struggle for Inclusion after Unification* (Cambridge, MA, 2012)

Berenbeim, J., *Art of Documentation: Documents and Visual Culture in Medieval England* (Toronto, 2015)

Berend, N., *At the Gate of Christendom: Jews, Muslims and 'Pagans' in Medieval Hungary c. 1000–c. 1300* (Cambridge, 2001)

Berkhofer, R. F. III, *Day of Reckoning: Power and Accountability in Medieval France* (Philadelphia, PA, 2004)

——, 'The Canterbury Forgeries Revisited', *HSJ* 18 (2006), 36–50

——, 'Guerno the Forger and his Confession', *ANS* 36 (2014), 53–68

Berland, J.-M., 'La place du monastère de La Réole parmi les prieurés de Fleury', in *Actes du colloque du millénaire de la fondation du prieuré de La Réole* (Bordeaux, 1980), 13–48

Bernhardt, J. W., *Itinerant Kingship and Royal Monasteries in Early Medieval Germany c. 936–1075* (Cambridge, 1993)

Bertrand, P., *Documenting the Everyday in Medieval Europe: The Social Dimensions of a Writing Revolution, 1250–1350*, trans. G. R. Edwards (Turnhout, 2019)

Beumann, H., 'Laurentius und Mauritius. Zu den missionspolitischen Folgen des Ungarnsieges Ottos des Großen' (1974), repr. in his *Ausgewählte Aufsätze aus den Jahren 1966–1986* (Sigmaringen, 1986), 139–76

——, 'Entschädigungen von Halberstadt und Mainz bei der Gründung des Erzbistums Magdeburg' (1991), repr. in his *Kirche und Reich. Beiträge zur früh- und hochmittelalterlichen Kloster-, Bistums- und Missionsgeschichte* (Goldbach, 2004), 291–306

——, *Theutonum nova metropolis. Studien zur Geschichte des Erzbistums Magdeburg in ottonischer Zeit* (Cologne, 2000)

Billett, J. D., 'The "Old Books of Glastonbury" and the Muchelney Breviary Fragment: London, British Library, Additional 56488, fols i, 1–5', *ASE* 47 (2018), 307–50

Bishop, T. A. M., *English Caroline Minuscule* (Oxford, 1971)

Bisson, T. N., 'The "Feudal Revolution"', *Past & Present* 142 (1994), 6–42

——, 'Medieval Lordship', *Speculum* 70 (1995), 743–59

——, *The Crisis of the Twelfth Century: Power, Lordship, and the Origins of European Government* (Princeton, NJ, 2009)

Bloch, H., 'Beiträge zur Geschichte des Bischofs Leo von Vercelli und seiner Zeit', *NA* 22 (1897), 11–136

Bloch, H., *Monte Cassino in the Middle Ages*, 3 pts (Rome, 1986)

Bloch, M., *The Historian's Craft*, trans. P. Putnam with a preface by P. Burke (Manchester, 1992)

Blumberg, F., 'Die Lorcher Fälschungen', *Archiv für Österreichische Geschichte* 46 (1871), 235–95

Blume, D., *Bern von Reichenau (1008–48). Abt, Gelehrter, Biograph* (Ostfildern, 2008)

Bonnassie, P., *From Slavery to Feudalism in South-Western Europe*, trans. J. Birrell (Cambridge, 1991)

Bönnen, G., 'Die Blütezeit des hohen Mittelalters. Von Bischof Burchard zum Rheinischen Bund (1000–1254)', in *Geschichte der Stadt Worms*, ed. G. Bönnen, 2nd edn (Darmstadt, 2015), 133–79

Borchers, H., 'Untersuchungen zur Handels- und Verkehrsgeschichte am Mittel- und Oberrhein bis zum Ende des 12. Jahrhunderts' (PhD diss., Universität Marburg, 1952)

Borgolte, M., *Europa entdeckt seine Vielfalt 1050–1250* (Stuttgart, 2002)

Bornscheuer, L., *Miseriae regum. Untersuchungen zum Krisen- und Todesgedanken in den herschaftstheologischen Vorstellungen der ottonisch-salischen Zeit* (Berlin, 1968)

Boshof, E., 'Köln, Mainz, Trier—Die Auseinandersetzung um die Spitzenstellung im deutschen Episkopat in ottonisch-salischer Zeit', *Jahrbuch des Kölnischen Geschichtsvereins* 49 (1978), 19–48

——, 'Die Reorganisation des Bistums Passau nach den Ungarnstürmen' (1994), repr. in his *Königtum, Kirche und Mission im Südosten des Reiches* (Passau, 2012), 61–82

Boüard, A. de, *Manuel de diplomatique française et pontificale*, i, *Diplomatique générale* (Paris, 1929)

——, *Manuel de diplomatique française et pontificale*, ii, *L'acte privé* (Paris, 1948)

Bouchard, C. B., 'Forging Papal Authority: Charters from the Monastery of Montier-en-Der', *Church History* 69 (2000), 1–17

——, *Rewriting Saints and Ancestors: Memory and Forgetting in France, 500–1200* (Philadelphia, PA, 2015)

Bougard, F., *La justice dans le royaume d'Italie de la fin du VIIIe siècle au début du XIe siècle* (Rome, 1995)

——, '"*Falsum falsorum iudicum consilium*": l'écrit et la justice en Italie centro-septentrionale au XIe siècle', *BEC* 155 (1997), 299–314

——, 'Actes privés et transfers patrimoniaux en Italie centro-septionale (VIIIe–Xe siècle)', *Mélanges de l'École française de Rome: Moyen Âge* 111.ii (1999), 539–62

——, 'Rationalité et irrationalité des procédures autour de l'an mil: le duel judiciaire en Italie', in *La justice en l'an mil*, ed. C. Gauvard (Paris, 2003), 93–122

——, 'Diplômes et notices de plaid: dialogue et convergence', in *Europäische Herrscher und die Toskana im Spiegel der urkundlichen Überlieferung (800–1100)*, ed. A. Ghignoli et al. (Leipzig, 2015), 15–22

——, 'Jugement divin, excommunication, anathème et malédiction: la sanction spirituelle dans les sources diplomatiques', in *Exclure de la communauté chrétienne: sens et pratiques sociales de l'anathème et de l'excommunication, IVe–XIIe siècle*, ed. G. Bührer-Thierry and S. Gioanni (Turnhout, 2015), 215–38

Bougard, F., and L. Morelle, 'Prévention, appréciation et sanction du faux documentaire, VIe–XIIe siècle', in *Juger le faux (Moyen Âge–Temps modernes)*, ed. O. Poncet (Paris, 2011), 19–57

Bowlus, C. R., *Franks, Moravians, and Magyars: The Struggle for the Middle Danube, 788–907* (Philadelphia, PA, 1995)

Bowman, J. A., *Shifting Landmarks: Property, Proof, and Dispute in Catalonia around the Year 1000* (Ithaca, NY, 2004)

Boynton, S., *Shaping a Monastic Identity: Liturgy and History at the Imperial Abbey of Farfa, 1000–1125* (Ithaca, NY, 2006)

Breay, C., and J. Story, eds, *Anglo-Saxon Kingdoms: Art, Word, War* (London, 2018)

Bresslau, H., Review of Lechner, 'Königsurkunden', *NA* 27 (1902), 545–47

——, 'Exkurse zu den Diplomen Konrads II.', *NA* 34 (1909), 67–123, 383–426

——, *Handbuch der Urkundenlehre für Deutschland und Italien*, 2 vols, 2nd edn (Berlin, 1912–31)

Brooke, C. N. L., 'Approaches to Medieval Forgery' (1968), repr. in his *Medieval Church and Society: Collected Essays* (London, 1971), 100–120

Brooks, N., *The Early History of the Church of Canterbury: Christ Church from 597 to 1066* (Leicester, 1984)

Browett, R., 'The Cult of St Æthelwold and its Context, *c.* 984–*c.* 1400' (PhD thesis, University of London, 2016)

Brown, E. A. R., '*Falsitas pia sive reprehensibilis*: Medieval Forgers and their Intentions', in *Fälschungen im Mittelalter*, 6 vols (Hanover, 1988), i, 101–19

Brown, P., *Through the Eye of a Needle: Wealth, the Fall of Rome, and the Making of Christianity in the West, 350–550 AD* (Princeton, NJ, 2012)

Brown, T. J., 'The Detection of Faked Literary Manuscripts', in his *A Palaeographer's View: The Selected Writings of Julian Brown* (London, 1993), 253–62

Brown, W., 'Charters as Weapons: On the Role Played by Early Medieval Dispute Records in the Disputes they Record', *JMH* 28 (2002), 227–48

Brühl, C., 'Zum Hauptstadtproblem im frühen Mittelalter' (1963), repr. in his *Aus Mittelalter und Diplomatik*, 3 vols (Hildesheim, 1989–97), i, 89–114

——, *Fodrum, Gistum, Servitium regis. Studien zu den wirtschaftlichen Grundlagen des Königtums im Frankenreich und in den fränkischen Nachfolgestaaten Deutschland, Frankreich und Italien vom 6. bis zur Mitte des 14. Jahrhunderts*, 2 vols (Cologne, 1968)

——, *Studien zu den langobardischen Königsurkunden* (Tübingen, 1970)

——, 'Der ehrbare Fälscher' (1979), repr. in his *Aus Mittelalter und Diplomatik*, 3 vols (Hildesheim, 1989–97), ii, 767–76

——, 'Die Entwicklung der diplomatischen Methode im Zusammenhang mit dem Erkennen von Fälschungen' (1988), repr. in his *Aus Mittelalter und Diplomatik*, 3 vols (Hildesheim, 1989–97), iii, 209–25

——, *Palatium und civitas. Studien zur Profantopographie spätantiker Civitates vom 3. bis zum 13. Jahrhundert*, ii.1, *Belgica I, beide Germanien und Raetia II* (Cologne, 1990)

——, *Deutschland—Frankreich. Die Geburt zweier Völker*, rev. edn (Cologne, 1995)

——, 'Die merowingische Immunität' (1995), repr. in his *Aus Mittelalter und Diplomatik*, 3 vols (Hildesheim, 1989–97), iii, 148–65

——, 'Clovis chez les faussaires', *BEC* 154 (1996), 219–40

——, *Studien zu den merowingischen Königsurkunden* (Cologne, 1998)

Brunhofer, U., *Arduin von Ivrea und seine Anhänger. Untersuchungen zum letzten italienischen Königtum des Mittelalters* (Augsburg, 1999)

Brunner, K., *Herzogtümer und Marken. Vom Ungarnsturm bis ins 12. Jahrhundert* (Vienna, 1994)

Buc, P., 'What is Order? In the Aftermath of the "Feudal Transformation" Debates', *Francia* 46 (2019), 281–300

Bucchi de Giuli, E., 'Le carte del vescovo di Pavia (secoli VIII–CII)' (*Tesi di laurea* [degree thesis], Università degli studi di Pavia, 2001–2)

Bude, T., *König und Bischof in ottonischer Zeit. Herschaftspraxis—Handlungsspielräume—Interaktionen* (Husum, 2015)

Bührer-Thierry, G., *Évêques et pouvoir dans le royaume de Germanie. Les églises de Bavière et de Souabe (876–973)* (Paris, 1997)

Bulst, N., *Untersuchungen zu den Klosterreformen Wilhelms von Dijon, 962–1031* (Bonn, 1973)

——, *Ricerche sulle riforme monastiche di Guglielmo da Volpiano (962–1031)* (Foglizzo, 2014)

Bur, M., 'Adalbéron, archevêque de Reims, reconsidéré', in *Le roi de France et son royaume, autour de l'an Mil*, ed. M. Parisse and X. Barral I Altet (Paris, 1992), 55–63

Burke, P., *The Renaissance Sense of the Past* (London, 1969)

Büttner, H., 'Ladenburg am Neckar und das Bistum Worms bis zum Ende des 12. Jahr-hunderts', *Archiv für hessische Geschichte und Alterthumskunde* n.s. 28 (1963), 83–98

——, 'Erzbischof Willigis von Mainz und das Papsttum bei der Bistumserrichtung in Böh-men und Mähren im 10. Jh.', *Rheinische Vierteljahrsblätter* 30 (1965), 1–22

Calco, T., *Mediolanensis historiae patriae libri viginti* (Milan, 1627)

Cancian, P., *L'abbazia di S. Genuario di Lucedio e le sue pergamene* (Turin, 1975)

Cappelletti, G., *Le chiese d'Italia dalla loro origine sino ai nostri giorni*, xii (Venice, 1857)

Caspar, E., *Petrus Diaconus und die Monte Cassineser Fälschungen* (Berlin, 1909)

Castagnetti, A., 'La feudalizzazione degli uffici pubblici', *Settimane* 47 (2000), 723–819

Chaplais, P., 'The Original Charters of Herbert and Gervase Abbots of Westminster (1121–1157)' (1962), repr. in his *Essays in Medieval Diplomacy and Administration* (London, 1981), no. xvii

Chaplais, P., 'The Royal Anglo-Saxon "Chancery" of the Tenth Century Revisited', in *Studies in Medieval History Presented to R. H. C. Davies*, ed. H. Mayr-Harting and R. I. Moore (London, 1985), 41–51

Ciccopiedi, C., *Diocesi e riforme nel Medioevo. Orientamenti ecclesiastici e religiosi dei vescovi nel Piemonte dei secoli X e XI* (Turin, 2012)

Cipolla, C., 'Di un diploma perduto di Carlo III (il Grosso) in favore della chiesa di Vercelli', *Atti della R. Accademia delle Scienze di Torino* 26 (1890–91), 670–84

Clanchy, M. T., 'Remembering the Past and the Good Old Law', *History* 55 (1970), 165–76

——, *From Memory to Written Record: England, 1066–1307*, 3rd edn (Chichester, 2013)

Clark, E. A., 'The Chronicle of Novalese: Translation, Text and Literary Analysis' (PhD diss., University of North Carolina at Chapel Hill, 2017)

Clark, F., 'Forgery, Misattribution, and a Case of Secondary Pseudonymity: Aethicus Ister's *Cosmographia* and its Early Modern Multiplications', in *Literary Forgery in Early Mod-ern Europe, 1450–1800*, ed. W. Stephens and E. A. Havens (Baltimore, MD, 2018), 73–98

Classen, P., 'Bemerkungen zur Pfalzenforschung am Mittelrhein' (1963), repr. in his *Aus-gewählte Aufsätze* (Sigmaringen, 1983), 475–501

Clayton, M., *The Cult of the Virgin Mary in Anglo-Saxon England* (Cambridge, 1990)

Constable, G., *Monastic Tithes from their Origins to the Twelfth Century* (Cambridge, 1964)

——, 'Forgery and Plagiarism in the Middle Ages' (1983), repr. in his *Culture and Spiritual-ity in Medieval Europe* (Aldershot, 1996), no. i

Costambeys, M., 'Disputes and Documents in Early Medieval Italy', in *Making Early Medi-eval Societies: Conflict and Belonging in the Latin West, 300–1200*, ed. K. Cooper and C. Leyser (Cambridge, 2016), 125–54

——, 'Archives and Social Change in Italy, *c.* 900–1100: The Evidence of Dispute Notices', in *Italy and Medieval Europe: Papers for Chris Wickham*, ed. R. Balzaretti, J. Barrow and P. Skinner (Oxford, 2018), 261–73

Coué, S., *Hagiographie im Kontext. Schreibanlaß und Funktion von Bischofsviten aus dem 11. und vom Anfang des 12. Jahrhunderts* (Berlin, 1997)

Cowdrey, H. E. J., *The Cluniacs and the Gregorian Reform* (Oxford, 1970)

——, *Lanfranc: Scholar, Monk, and Archbishop* (Oxford, 2003)

Crick, J., 'St Albans, Westminster and Some Twelfth-Century Views of the Anglo-Saxon Past', *ANS* 25 (2002), 65–83

——, 'Pristina *libertas*: Liberty and the Anglo-Saxons Revisited', *TRHS* 6th ser. 14 (2004), 47–71

——, 'Insular History? Forgery and the English Past in the Tenth Century', in *England and the Continent in the Tenth Century: Studies in Honour of Wilhelm Levison (1876–1947)*, ed. D. Rollason, C. Leyser and H. Williams (Turnhout, 2010), 515–44

——, 'Script and the Sense of the Past in Anglo-Saxon England', in *Anglo-Saxon Traces*, ed. J. Roberts and L. Webster (Tempe, AZ, 2011), 1–29

——, 'Historical Literacy in the Archive: Post-Conquest Imitative Copies of Pre-Conquest Charters and Some French Comparanda', in *The Long Twelfth-Century View of the Anglo-Saxon Past*, ed. D. A. Woodman and M. Brett (Aldershot, 2015), 159–90

Cubitt, C., 'The Tenth-Century Benedictine Reform in England', *EME* 6 (1997), 77–94

——, 'Bishops and Councils in Late Saxon England: The Intersection of Secular and Ecclesiastical Law', in *Recht und Gericht in Kirche und Welt um 900*, ed. W. Hartmann (Munich, 2007), 151–67

——, 'The Politics of Remorse: Penance and Royal Piety in the Reign of Æthelred the Unready', *Historical Research* 85 (2012), 179–92

Cubitt, G., *History and Memory* (Manchester, 2007)

Dachowski, E., 'The English Roots of Abbo of Fleury's Political Thought', *RB* 110 (2000), 95–105

——, *First among Abbots: The Career of Abbo of Fleury* (Washington, D.C., 2008)

D'Acunto, N., *Nostrum Italicum regnum. Aspetti della politica italiana di Ottone III* (Milan, 2002)

Dasler, C., *Forst und Wildbann im frühen deutschen Reich. Die königlichen Privilegien für die Reichskirche vom 9. bis zum 12. Jahrhundert* (Cologne, 2001)

Davies, W., *Windows on Justice in Northern Iberia, 800–1000* (Abingdon, 2016)

Davis, K., 'Caves of Dispute: Patterns of Correspondence and Suspicion in the Post-2002 "Dead Sea Scrolls" Fragments', *Dead Sea Discoveries* 24 (2017), 229–70

d'Avray, D. L., *Medieval Religious Rationalities: A Weberian Analysis* (Cambridge, 2010)

De Angelis, G., 'La tradizione in copia dei diplomi regi e imperiali per la chiesa vescovile di Bergamo (secoli IX–XI)', in *Originale—Fälschungen—Kopien. Kaiser- und Königsurkunden für Empfänger in Deutschland und Italien (9.-11. Jahrhundert) und ihre Nachwirkungen im Hoch- und Spätmittelalter (bis ca. 1500)*, ed. N. D'Acunto et al. (Leipzig, 2018), 175–93

de Jong, M., 'Carolingian Monasticism: The Power of Prayer', in *The New Cambridge Medieval History*, ii, c. 700–c. 900, ed. R. McKitterick (Cambridge, 1995), 622–53

Declerq, G., 'Originals and Cartularies: The Organization of Archival Memory (Ninth–Eleventh Centuries)', in *Charters and the Use of the Written Word in Medieval Society*, ed. K. Heidekker (Turnhout, 2000), 147–70

Della Chiesa, F. A., *S. R. E. cardinalium, archiepiscoporum, episcoporum et abbatum Pedemontanae regionis . . .* (Turin, 1645)

Demacopoulos, D. E., *The Invention of Peter: Apostolic Discourse and Papal Authority in Late Antiquity* (Philadelphia, PA, 2013)

Dendorfer, J., 'Roncaglia: Der Beginn eines lehnrechtlichen Umbaus des Reiches?', in *Staufisches Kaisertum im 12. Jahrhundert. Konzepte—Netzwerke—Politische Praxis*, ed. S. Burkhardt et al. (Regensburg, 2010), 111–32

Depreux, P., 'Saint Remi et la royauté carolingienne', *Revue historique* 285 (1991), 235–60

——, 'Investitures et rapports de pouvoirs: réflexions sur les symboles de la querelle en Empire', *Revue d'histoire de l'église de France* 96 (2010), 43–69

Deshman, R., '*Benedictus Monarcha et Monachus*: Early Ruler Theology and the Anglo-Saxon Realm' (1988), repr. in his *Eye and Mind*, ed. A. S. Cohen (Kalamazoo, MI, 2010), 104–36

Dessì, R. M., 'La double conversion d'Arduin d'Ivrée: pénitence et conversion autour de l'An Mil', in *Guerriers et moines. Conversion et sainteté aristocratiques dans l'Occident médiéval (IXᵉ-XIIᵉ siècle)*, ed. M. Lauwers (Turnhout, 2002), 317–48

Donnat, L., 'Recherches sur l'influence de Fleury au Xᵉ siècle', in *Études ligériennes d'histoire et d'archéologie médiévales*, ed. L. René (Paris, 1975), 165–74

Dormeier, H., 'Un vescovo in Italia alle soglie del Mille: Leone di Vercelli "episcopus Imperii, servus sancti Eusebii"', *BSV* 53 (1999), 37–74

——, 'Capitolo del duomo, vescovi e memoria a Vercelli (secc. X–XIII)', *BSV* 65 (2005), 19–59

Duby, G., *La société aux XIe et XIIe siècles dans la région mâconnaise*, rev. edn (Paris, 1971)

Dufour, J., 'État et comparaison des actes faux ou falsifiés intitulés au nom des Carolingiens français (840–987)', in *Fälschungen im Mittelalter*, 6 vols (Hanover, 1988), iv, 167–210

Dümmler, E. L., *Pilgrim von Passau und das Erzbisthum Lorch* (Leipzig, 1854)

——, 'Aus Handschriften X.', *NA* 5 (1880), 621–36

——, 'Über die Entstehung der Lorcher Fälschungen', *SB Berlin* 47 (1898), 758–75

——, 'Nachruf Paul Scheffer-Boichhorst', *NA* 27 (1902), 768–70

Dumville, D. N., 'Beowulf Come Lately: Some Notes on the Palaeography of the Nowell Codex' (1988), repr. in his *Britons and Anglo-Saxons in the Early Middle Ages* (Aldershot, 1993), no. vii

Edwards, H., *The Charters of the Early West Saxon Kingdom* (Oxford, 1988)

Eggers, M., '"Moravia" oder "Großmähren"?', *Bohemia* 39 (1998), 351–70

——, 'Die Slawenmission Passaus, Bischof Pilgrim und die "Lorcher Fälschungen"', *Südost-Forschungen* 57 (1998), 13–36

Ehrman, B. D., *Lost Christianities: The Battles for Scripture and the Faiths we Never Knew* (Oxford, 2003)

——, *Forgery and Counterforgery: The Use of Literary Deceit in Early Christian Polemics* (Oxford, 2013)

Eldevik, J., *Episcopal Power and Ecclesiastical Reform in the German Empire: Tithes, Lordship, and Community, 950–1150* (Cambridge, 2012)

England, J., 'The Crown-Wearing Abbeys of Westminster, Winchester, and Gloucester in Text and Written Record, *c.* 1100–1170' (PhD thesis, University of York, 2019)

Eisenlohr, E., 'Von ligierten zu symbolischen Invokations- und Rekognitionszeichen in frühmittelalterlichen Urkunden', in *Graphische Symbole in mittelalterlichen Urkunden. Beiträge zur diplomatischen Semiotik*, ed. P. Rück (Sigmaringen, 1996), 167–262

Eisenstein, E. L., *The Printing Revolution in Early Modern Europe* (Cambridge, 1983)

Erben, W., *Die Kaiser- und Königsurkunden des Mittelalters in Deutschland, Frankreich und Italien* (Munich, 1907)

——, *Rombilder auf kaiserlichen und päpstlichen Siegeln des Mittelalters* (Graz, 1931)

Erkens, F.-R., 'Die ältesten Passauer Bischofsurkunden', *Zeitschrift für Bayerische Landesgeschichte* 46 (1983), 469–514

——, 'Ludwig des Frommen Urkunde vom 28. Juni 23 für Passau (BM² 778)', *DA* 42 (1986), 86–117

——, 'Die Rezeption der Lorcher Tradition im hohen Mittelalter', *Ostbairische Grenzmarken* 28 (1986), 195–206

——, 'Die Ursprünge der Lorcher Tradition im Lichte archäologischer, historiographischer und urkundlicher Zeugnisse', in *Das Christentum im bairischen Raum. Von den Anfängen bis ins 11. Jahrhundert*, ed. E. Boshof and H. Wolff (Cologne, 1994), 423–59

——, 'Geschichtsbild und Rechtsstreit: Das Nachwirken der Fälschungen Pilgrims von Passau', *Passauer Jahrbuch* 47 (2005), 57–68

——, *Die Fälschungen Pilgrims von Passau* (Munich, 2011)

——, 'Vom Handwerk des Urkundenfälschers und seinen Schwierigkeiten: Das Beispiel der Pilgrimischen Fälschungen', *MIÖG* 126 (2018), 341–53

Everett, N., *Literacy in Lombard Italy, c. 568–774* (Cambridge, 2003)

——, 'Narrating the Life of Eusebius of Vercelli', in *Narrative and History in the Early Medieval West*, ed. E. M. Tyler and R. Balzaretti (Turnhout, 2006), 133–66

Ewald, W., *Siegelkunde* (Munich, 1914)

Ewig, E., 'Die Kathedralpatrozinien im römischen und im fränkischen Gallien' (1960), repr. in his *Spätantikes und fränkisches Gallien*, 2 vols (Munich, 1976–79), ii, 260–317

Falkenstein, L., *La papauté et les abbayes françaises aux XIe et XIIe siècles. Exemption et protection apostolique* (Paris, 1997)

——, 'Weitere Fälschungen unter den päpstlichen Privilegien für die Abtei Montier-en-Der?', *Francia* 33.i (2006), 101–18

Fagioli Vercellone, G. G., 'Gabotto, Ferdinando', in *DBI*, li (Rome, 1998), 28–30

Farmer, S., *Communities of Saint Martin: Legend and Ritual in Medieval Tours* (Ithaca, NY, 1991)

Fentress, J., and C. Wickham, *Social Memory: New Perspectives on the Past* (Oxford, 1992)

Ferrari, M., 'Libri e testi prima del Mille', in *Storia della Chiesa di Ivrea, dalle origini al XV secolo*, ed. G. Cracco (Rome, 1998), 511–33

Ferraris, G., 'La vita comune nelle canoniche di S. Eusebio e di S. Maria di Vercelli nel secolo XII', *Rivista di storia della Chiesa in Italia* 17 (1963), 365–94

——, *Le chiese 'stazionali' delle rogazioni minori a Vercelli dal sec. X al sec. XIV*, rev. edn (Vercelli, 1995)

——, 'Il "cerchio magico" dei privilegi imperiali per la chiesa di Vercelli', in *DCCCCXC-VIIII-1999. Per un millennio: da 'Trebledo' a Casalborgone*, ed. A. A. Cigna and A. A. Settia (Chivasso, 2000), 15–48

Fichtenau, H., 'Rhetorische Elemente in der ottonisch-salischen Herrscherurkunde' (1960), repr. in his *Beiträge zur Mediävistik. Ausgewählte Aufsätze*, 3 vols (Stuttgart, 1975–86), ii, 126–56

——, 'Zu den Urkundenfälschungen Pilgrims von Passau' (1964), rev. and repr. in his *Beiträge zur Mediävistik. Ausgewählte Aufsätze*, 3 vols (Stuttgart, 1975–86), ii, 157–78

——, *Das Urkundenwesen in Österreich vom 8. bis zum frühen 13. Jahrhundert* (Vienna, 1971)

——, *Lebensordnungen des 10. Jahrhunderts. Studien über Denkart und Existenz im einstigen Karolingerreich*, 2 pts (Stuttgart, 1984)

——, 'Forschungen über Urkundenformeln', *MIÖG* 94 (1986), 285–340

——, *Living in the Tenth Century: Mentalities and Social Orders*, trans. P. J. Geary (Chicago, IL, 1991)

Ficker, J., *Beiträge zur Urkundenlehre*, 2 vols (Innsbruck, 1877–78)

Fiechter, J.-J., *Egyptian Fakes: Masterpieces that Duped the Art World and the Experts Who Uncovered Them* (Paris, 2009)

Finberg, H.P.R., *Early Charters of Wessex* (Leicester, 1964)

Fissore, G. G., 'Antiche falsificazioni del capitolo cattedrale di Asti', *Bollettino Storico-Bibliografico Subalpino* 69 (1971), 5–86

Fleckenstein, J., 'Königshof und Bischofsschule unter Otto dem Großen' (1968), repr. in his *Ordnungen und formende Kräfte des Mittelalters. Ausgewählte Beiträge* (Göttingen, 1989), 168–92

Fletcher, R., *The Conversion of Europe: From Paganism to Christianity, 371–1386 AD* (London, 1997)

Foot, S., 'Reading Anglo-Saxon Charters: Memory, Record, or Story?', in *Narrative and History in the Early Medieval West*, ed. E. M. Tyler and R. Balzaretti (Turnhout, 2006), 39–65

Fouracre, P., 'Why Were so Many Bishops Killed in Merovingian Francia?', in *Bischofsmord im Mittelalter*, ed. N. M. Fryde and D. Reitz (Göttingen, 2003), 13–35

——, 'Forgetting and Remembering Dagobert II: The English Connection', in *Frankland: The Franks and the World of the Early Middle Ages*, ed. P. Fouracre and D. Ganz (Manchester, 2008), 70–89

Frank, H., *Die Klosterbischöfe des Frankenreiches* (Münster, 1932)

Fried, J., *Der Weg in die Geschichte. Die Ursprünge Deutschlands bis 1024* (Berlin, 1994)

Friedmann, A. U., *Die Beziehungen der Bistümer Worms und Speyer zu den ottonischen und salischen Königen* (Mainz, 1994)

Fuhrmann, H., 'Studien zur Geschichte mittelalterlicher Patriarchate II.', *ZRG: KA* 40 (1954), 1–84

——, 'Konstantinische Schenkung und abendländisches Kaisertum. Ein Beitrag zur Über-lieferungsgeschichte des Constitutum Constantini', *DA* 22 (1966), 63–178

——, *Einfluß und Verbreitung der pseudoisidorischen Fälschungen. Von ihrem Auftauchen bis in die neuere Zeit*, 3 pts (Hanover, 1972–74)

——, 'Fälschungen im Dienste der Wahrheit', in his *Überall ist Mittelalter. Vor der Gegen-wart einer vergangenen Zeit* (Munich, 1996), 48–62

Fryde, N. M., and D. Reitz, ed., *Bischofsmord im Mittelalter* (Göttingen, 2003)

Gabotto, F., 'Intorno ai diplomi regi ed imperiali della chiesa di Vercelli', *Archivio storico italiano* 5th ser. 21 (1898), 1–53, 255–96

——, 'Un millennio di storia eporediese (356–1357)', in *Eporediensia* (Pinerolo, 1900), 1–262

——, 'Un contrasto dei vescovi di Novara e di Vercelli per l'abazia di Lucedio sul principio del secolo X', *Bollettino storico per la provincia di Novara* 7 (1913), 1–9

Gandino, G., 'Orizzonti politici ed esperienze culturali dei vescovi di Vercelli tra i secoli IX e XI' (1998), repr. in his *Contemplare l'ordine. Intellettuali e potenti nell'alto medioevo* (Naples, 2004), 65–81

——, 'Ruolo dei linguaggi e linguaggio dei ruoli. Ottone III, Silvestro II e un episodio delle relazioni tra impero e papato' (1999), repr. with an addendum his *Contemplare l'ordine. Intellettuali e potenti nell'alto medioevo* (Naples, 2004), 141–88

Gänser, G., 'Das Diplom König Ludwigs des Deutschen von 851 für Erzbischof Liupram von Salzburg', *Zeitschrift des historischen Vereins für Steiermark* 80 (1989), 5–38

Gasnault, P., 'Étude sur les chartes de Saint-Martin de Tours des origines aux milieu de XIIᵉ siècle', *Positions des Thèses: École nationale des chartes* (1953), 36–40

Gavinelli, S., 'Leone di Vercelli postillatore di codici', *Aevum* 75 (2001), 233–62

——, Review of *Leone di Vercelli, Metrum Leonis, Aevum* 77 (2003), 487–89

Geary, P. J., *Living with the Dead in the Middle Ages* (Ithaca, NY, 1994)

——, *Phantoms of Remembrance: Memory and Oblivion at the End of the First Millen-nium* (Princeton, NJ, 1994)

Geldner, F., 'Geburtsort, Geburtsjahr und Jugendzeit Kaiser Heinrichs II.', *DA* 34 (1978), 520–38

Genser, K., *Der österreichische Donaulimes in der Römerzeit* (Vienna, 1986)

Ghignoli, A., 'La definizione dei principi e le metodologie diplomatistiche: innovazioni ed eredità', *Annali della Facoltà di Lettere e Filosofia dell'Università di Siena* 12 (1991), 39–53

——, '"Die Geschichte jeder Urkunde". Diplomi in originale, diplomi in copia negli archivi di destinatari della Toscana orientale', in *Originale—Fälschungen—Kopien. Kaiser- und Königsurkunden für Empfänger in Deutschland und Italien (9.–11. Jahrhundert) und ihre Nachwirkungen im Hoch- und Spätmittelalter (bis ca. 1500)*, ed. N. D'Acunto et al. (Leipzig, 2018), 81–104

Gilsdorf, S., *The Favor of Friends: Intercession and Aristocratic Politics in Carolingian and Ottonian Europe* (Leiden, 2014)

Ginzburg, C., *History, Rhetoric, and Proof* (Hanover, NH, 1999)

Giry, A., *Manuel de diplomatique*, rev. edn (Paris, 1925)

Glenn, J., *Politics and History in the Tenth Century: The Work and World of Richer of Reims* (Cambridge, 2004)

Goffart, W., *The Le Mans Forgeries: A Chapter from the History of Church Property in the Ninth Century* (Cambridge, MA, 1966)

Goldberg, E. J., *Struggle for Empire: Kingship and Conflict under Louis the German, 817–876* (Ithaca, NY, 2006)

Goodson, C. J., and J. L. Nelson, 'The Roman Contexts of the "Donation of Constantine"', *EME* 18 (2010), 446–67

Görich, K., *Otto III. Romanus Saxonicus et Italicus. Kaiserliche Rompolitik und säschische Historiographie* (Sigmaringen, 1993)

——, 'Mathilde—Edgith—Adelheid. Ottonische Herrscherinnen als Fürsprecherinnen', in *Ottonische Neuanfänge*, ed. B. Schneidmüller and S. Weinfurter (Mainz, 2001), 251–91

Goetz, H.-W., 'Der letzte "Karolinger"? Die Regierung Konrads I. im Spiegel seiner Urkunden', *AfD* 26 (1980), 56–125

——, 'Die Gegenwart der Vergangenheit im früh- und hochmittelalterlichen Geschichtsbewußtsein', *HZ* 255 (1992), 61–98

Grafton, A., *Defenders of the Text: The Traditions of Scholarship in an Age of Science, 1450–1800* (Cambridge, MA, 1991)

——, *What Was History? The Art of History in Early Modern Europe* (Cambridge, 2007)

——, *Forgers and Critics: Creativity and Duplicity in Western Scholarship*, rev. edn (Princeton, NJ, 2019)

Greer, S., A. Hicklin and S. Esders, eds, *Using and Not Using the Past after the Carolingian Empire, c. 900–c. 1050* (London, 2019)

Gretsch, M., 'Æthelwold's Translation of the *Regula Sancti Benedicti* and its Latin Exemplar', *ASE* 3 (1974), 125–51

——, *The Intellectual Foundations of the English Benedictine Reform* (Cambridge, 1999)

——, 'Cambridge, Corpus Christi College 57: A Witness to the Early Stages of the Benedictine Reform in England?', *ASE* 32 (2003), 111–46

Gransden, A., *Historical Writing in England*, i, c. *550–c. 1307* (London, 1974)

——, 'Abbo of Fleury's "Passio sancti Eadmundi"', *RB* 105 (1995), 20–78

Grant, L., *Abbot Suger of St-Denis: Church and State in Early Twelfth-Century France* (London, 1998)

Grillo, P., 'Il comune di Vercelli nel secolo XII: dalle origini alla lega lombarda', in *Vercelli nel secolo XII. Atti del quarto Congresso storico vercellese* (Vercelli, 2005), 161–88

Große, R., 'Frühe Papsturkunden und Exemtion des Klosters Saint-Denis (7.–12. Jh.)', in *Hundert Jahre Papsturkundenforschung. Bilanz—Methoden—Perspektiven*, ed. R. Hiestand (Göttingen, 2003), 167–88

——, '*Ubi papa, ibi Roma*. Papstreisen nach Frankreich im 11. und 12. Jahrhundert', in *Päpstliche Herrschaft im Mittelalter. Funktionsweisen—Strategien—Darstellungsformen*, ed. S. Weinfurter (Ostfildern, 2012), 313–34

Grünewald, M., 'Die Salier und ihre Burg zu Worms', in *Burgen der Salierzeit*, ed. H. W. Böhme, 2 vols (Sigmaringen, 1991), ii, 113–23

——, 'Worms von der vorgeschichtlichen Epoche bis in die Karolingerzeit', in *Geschichte der Stadt Worms*, ed. G. Bönnen, 2nd edn (Darmstadt, 2015), 44–101

Guyotjeannin, O., 'De la surinterprétation des sources diplomatiques médiévales. Quelques exemples français des alentours de l'an mil', *Enquête* 3 (1996), 153–62

——, 'Diplôme de Hugues Capet pour l'abbaye de Fleury', in *Autor de Gerbert d'Aurillac. Le pape de l'an mil*, ed. O. Guyotjeannin and E. Poulle (Paris, 1996), 111–18

——, '"*Penuria scriptorum*". Le mythe de l'anarchie documentaire dans la France du Nord (Xe–première moitié du XIe siècle)', *BEC* 155 (1997), 11–44

——, 'Les pouvoirs publics de l'évêque de Parme au miroir des diplômes royaux et impériaux (fin IXe–début XIe siècle)', in *Liber Largitorius. Études d'histoire médiévale offertes à Pierre Toubert par ses élèves*, ed. D. Barthélemy and J.-M. Martin (Geneva, 2003), 15–34

Guyotjeannin, O., J. Pycke and B.-M. Tock, *Diplomatique médiévale*, 3rd edn (Turnhout, 2006)

Hacke, C.-B., 'Die Palliumverleihungen bis 1143. Eine diplomatisch-historische Untersuchung' (PhD diss., Universität Göttingen, 1898)

Hägermann, D., 'Die Urkundenfälschungen auf Karl den Großen', in *Fälschungen im Mittelalter*, 6 vols (Munich, 1988), iii, 433–43

Hamilton, S., 'A New Model for Royal Penance? Helgaud of Fleury's *Life of Robert the Pious*', *EME* 6 (1997), 189–200

——, *The Practice of Penance, 900–1050* (Woodbridge, 2001)

——, 'Inquiring into Adultery and Other Wicked Deeds: Episcopal Justice in Tenth- and Early Eleventh-Century Italy', *Viator* 41.ii (2010), 21–43

——, *Church and People in the Medieval West, 900–1200* (Harlow, 2013)

——, 'Interpreting Diversity: Excommunication Rites in the Tenth and Eleventh Centuries', in *Understanding Medieval Liturgy: Essays in Interpretation*, ed. S. Hamilton and H. Gittos (Aldershot, 2015), 125–58

Hampe, K., 'Zum Streite Hincmars von Reims mit seinem Vorgänger Ebo und dessen Anhängern', *NA* 23 (1898), 180–95

Han, B.-C., *Shanzai: Deconstructon in Chinese*, trans. P. Hurd (Boston, MA, 2017)

Hansen, V., *The Year 1000: When Explorers Connected the World—and Globalization Began* (London, 2020)

Hart, C., and A. Syme, 'The Earliest Suffolk Charter' (1987), repr. in C. Hart, *The Danelaw* (London, 1992), 467–85

Härtel, R., 'Fälschungen im Mittelalter: geglaubt, verworfen, vertuscht', in *Fälschungen im Mittelalter*, 6 vols (Hanover, 1988), iii, 29–51

Hartmann, L. M., *Geschichte Italiens im Mittelalter*, iv.1, *Die ottonische Herrschaft* (Gotha, 1915)

Hartmann, W., 'Fälschungsverdacht und Fälschungsnachweis im früheren Mittelalter', in *Fälschungen im Mittelalter*, 6 vols (Hanover, 1988), ii, 111–27

——, 'Neues zur Entstehung der sächsischen Bistümer', *AfD* 63 (2017), 27–46

Hauck, A., *Kirchengeschichte Deutschlands*, iii, rev. edn (Leipzig, 1906)

Hausmann, F., *Die Reichskanzlei und Hofkapelle unter Heinrich V. und Konrad III.* (Hanover, 1956)

Head, T., *Hagiography and the Cult of Saints: The Diocese of Orleans, 800–1200* (Cambridge, 1990)

Hehl, E.-D., 'Merseburg—eine Bistumsgründung unter Vorbehalt. Gelübte, Kirchenrecht und politischer Spielraum im 10. Jahrhundert', *FMSt* 31 (1997), 96–119

Heideicker, K., '30 June 1047: The End of Charters as Legal Proof in France?', in *Strategies of Writing: Studies on Text and Trust in the Middle Ages*, ed. P. Schulte et al. (Turnhout, 2008), 85–94

Hen, Y., and M. Innes, eds, *The Uses of the Past in the Early Middle Ages* (Cambridge, 2000)

Herkommer, L., *Untersuchungen zur Abtsnachfolge unter den Ottonen im südwestdetuschen Raum* (Stuttgart, 1973)

Heß, W., *Kleine Wormser Münzgeschichte* (Worms, 1963)

Hiatt, A., *The Making of Medieval Forgeries: False Documents in Fifteenth-Century England* (London, 2004)

Hildebrandt, L. H., 'Der Umfang der Grafschaften und Vogteien der Grafen von Lauffen', in *Die Grafen von Lauffen am mittleren und unteren Neckar*, ed. C. Burkhart and J. Kreutz (Heidelberg, 2015), 75–110

Higbie, C., *Collectors, Scholars, and Forgers in the Ancient World: Object Lessons* (Oxford, 2017)

Hirsch, S., H. Pabst and H. Bresslau, *Jahrbücher des Deutschen Reichs unter Heinrich II.*, 3 vols (Leipzig, 1862–75)

Hobsbawm, E., and T. Ranger, eds, *The Invention of Tradition* (Cambridge, 1983)

Hoffmann, H., 'Chronik und Urkunde in Montecassino', *QFIAB* 51 (1971), 93–206

——, *Mönchskönig und rex idiota. Studien zur Kirchenpolitik Heinrichs II. und Konrads II.* (Hanover, 1993)

——, 'Die Historien Richers von Saint-Remi', *DA* 54 (1998), 445–532

——, 'Notare, Kanzler und Bischöfe am ottonischen Hof', *DA* 61 (2005), 435–80

——, 'Das Briefbuch Wibalds von Stablos', *DA* 63 (2007), 41–69

Hoffmann, H., and R. Pokorny, *Das Dekret des Bischofs Burchard von Worms. Textstufen— Frühe Verbreitung—Vorlagen* (Munich, 1991)

Hölbl, G., *A History of the Ptolemaic Empire*, trans. T. Saavedra (London, 2001)

Holdsworth, C., 'Tavistock Abbey in its Late Tenth Century Context', *Report and Transactions of the Devonshire Association for the Advancement of Science* 135 (2003), 31–58

Holmes, C., *Basil II and the Governance of Empire (976–1025)* (Oxford, 2005)

Holtzmann, R., 'Die Urkunden König Arduins', *NA* 25 (1900), 453–79

Holzfurtner, L., 'Destructio monasteriorum. Untersuchungen zum Niedergang der bayerischen Klöster im zehnten Jahrhundert', *Studien und Mitteilungen zur Geschichte des Benediktinerordens* 96 (1985), 65–86

Houghton, R., 'Reconsidering Donizone's *Vita Mathildis*: Boniface of Canossa and Emperor Henry II', *JMH* 41 (2015), 1–21

——, 'The Vocabulary of Groups in Eleventh-Century Mantua', *EME* 24 (2016), 448–77

——, 'Hugh, Lothar and Berengar: The Balance of Power in Italy 945–50', *JMH* 46 (2020), 50–76

Hudson, A., 'Æthelwold's Circle, Saints' Cults, and Monastic Reform, *c.* 956–1006' (DPhil thesis, University of Oxford, 2014)

Hudson, J., 'The Abbey of Abingdon, its Chronicle, and the Norman Conquest', *ANS* 19 (1996), 181–202

Huschner, W., 'Piacenza—Como—Mainz—Bamberg. Die Erzkanzler für Italien in den Regierungszeiten Ottos III. und Heinrichs II. (983–1024)', *Annali dell'Istituto storico italo-germanico in Trento* 26 (2000), 15–52

——, 'Original, Abschrift oder Fälschung? Imitative Kopien von ottonischen und salischen Diplomen in italienischen Archiven', in *Turbata per aequora mundi. Dankesgabe an Eckhard Müller-Mertens*, ed. O. B. Rader (Hanover, 2001), 49–66

——, 'Erzbischof Johannes von Ravenna (983–998), Otto II. und Theophanu', *QFIAB* 83 (2003), 1–40

——, *Transalpine Kommunikation im Mittelalter. Diplomatische, kulturelle und politische Wechselwirkungen zwischen Italien und dem nordalpinen Reich (9.-11. Jahrhundert)*, 3 pts (Hanover, 2003)

——, 'Die ottonische Kanzlei in neuem Licht', *AfD* 52 (2006), 353–70

——, 'Hoch- und spätmittelalterliche Fälschungen und Kopien ottonischer und salischer Diplome für Empfänger in Merseburg, Meißen und Naumburg', in *Originale— Fälschungen—Kopien. Kaiser- und Königsurkunden für Empfänger in Deutschland und Italien (9.-11. Jahrhundert) und ihre Nachwirkungen im Hoch- und Spätmittelalter (bis ca. 1500)*, ed. N. D'Acunto et al. (Leipzig, 2018), 117–43

——, 'Echt, gefälscht oder verloren? Die Verzeichnung von Urkunden in Thietmars Chronik', in *Thietmars Welt. Ein Merseburger Bischof schreibt Geschichte*, ed. M. Cottin and L. Merkel (Petersberg, 2018), 130–47

——, 'Originale, imitierende Kopien, Fälschungen. Die Nutzung und Sicherung mittelalterlicher Herrscherurkunden durch geistliche Empfänger Italiens (10.-12. Jahrhundert)', in *Die Urkunde. Text—Bild—Objekt*, ed. A. Stieldorf (Berlin, 2019), 363–82

Hussong, U., 'Studien zur Geschichte der Reichsabtei Fulda bis zur Jahrtausendwende II.', *AfD* 32 (1986), 129–304

Huth, V., 'Erzbischof Arnulf von Reims und der Kampf um das Königtum im Westfrankenreich', *Francia* 21.i (1994), 85–124

Igl, R., *Die Basilika St. Laurentius in Enns. Aufnahme und Neuinterpretation der Grabungsbefunde* (Vienna, 2008)

Immonen, T., 'A Saint as a Mediator between a Bishop and his Flock: The Cult of Saint Bononius in the Diocese of Vercelli under Bishop Arderic (1026/7–1044)', *Viator* 39 (2008), 65–92

Innes, M., *State and Society in the Early Middle Ages: The Middle Rhine Valley, 400–1000* (Cambridge, 2000)

Insley, C., 'Where did All the Charters Go? Anglo-Saxon Charters and the New Politics of the Eleventh Century', *ANS* 24 (2002), 109–27

——, 'Remembering Communities Past: Exeter Cathedral in the Eleventh Century', in *Cathedrals, Communities and Conflict in the Anglo-Norman World*, ed. P. Dalton et al. (Woodbridge, 2011), 41–60

——, 'Archives and Lay Documentary Practice in the Anglo-Saxon World', in *Documentary Culture and the Laity in the Early Middle Ages*, ed. W. Brown et al. (Cambridge, 2012), 336–62

Iogna-Prat, D., 'Entre anges et hommes: les moines "doctrinaires" de l'an Mil', in *La France de l'an Mil*, ed. D. Iogna-Prat and R. Delort (Paris, 1990), 245–63

Jaeger, C. S., *Envy of Angels: Cathedral Schools and Social Ideals in Medieval Europe, 950–1200* (Philadelphia, PA, 1994)

Jakobs, H., 'Zu den Fuldaer Papsturkunden des Frühmittelalters', *Blätter für deutsche Landesgeschichte* 128 (1992), 31–84

——, 'Sammlung für eine Urkundenfälscherkartei (Alt-)Sachsen', in *Vielfalt und Aktualität des Mittelalters. Festschrift für Wolfgang Petke zum 65. Geburtstag*, ed. S. Arend and D. Berger (Bielefeld, 2006), 591–614

Jarrett, J., 'Archbishop Ató of Osona: False Metropolitans on the Marca Hispanica', *AfD* 56 (2010), 1–42

Jestice, P. G., *Imperial Ladies of the Ottonian Dynasty: Women and Rule in Tenth-Century Germany* (London, 2018)

Johrendt, J., *Papsttum und Landeskirchen im Spiegel der päpstlichen Urkunden (896–1046)* (Hanover, 2004)

John, E., 'The Return of the Vikings', in *The Anglo-Saxons*, ed. J. Campbell (London, 1982), 192–213

Kaiser, R., 'Münzprivilegien und bischöfliche Münzprägung in Frankreich, Deutschland und Burgund im 9.–12. Jahrhundert', *Vierteljahrschrift für Sozial- und Wirtschaftsgeschichte* 63 (1976), 289–339

——, '"Mord im Dom". Von der Vertreibung zur Ermordung des Bischofs im frühen und hohen Mittelalter', *ZRG: KA* 79 (1993), 95–134

Kaldellis, A., *Streams of Gold, Rivers of Blood: The Rise and Fall of Byzantium, 955 AD to the First Crusade* (Oxford, 2017)

Kaminsky, H. H., 'Zur Gründung von Fruttuaria durch den Abt Wilhelm von Dijon', *Zeitschrift für Kirchengeschichte* 77 (1966), 238–67

Keats, J., *Forged: Why Fakes are the Great Art of Our Age* (Oxford, 2013)

Kehr, P., *Die Urkunden Otto III.* (Innsbruck, 1890)

Keller, H., *Adelsherrschaft und städische Gesellschaft in Oberitalien (9.–12. Jahrhundert)* (Tübingen, 1979)

——, 'Reichsstruktur und Herrschaftsauffassung in ottonisch-frühsalischer Zeit' (1982), repr. in his *Ottonische Königsherrschaft. Organisation königlicher Macht* (Darmstadt, 2002), 51–90, 213–37

——, 'Die Idee der Gerechtigkeit und die Praxis königlicher Rechtswahrung im Reich der Ottonen' (1997), repr. in his *Ottonische Königsherrschaft. Organisation und Legitimation königlicher Macht* (Darmstadt, 2002), 34–50, 204–13

——, 'Zu den Siegeln der Karolinger und der Ottonen. Urkunden als Hoheitszeichen in der Kommunikation des Herrschers mit seinen Getreuen', *FMSt* 32 (1998), 400–41

——, 'Entscheidungssituationen und Lernprozesse in den "Anfängen der deutschen Geschichte". Die "Italien- und Kaiserpolitik" Ottos des Großen', *FMSt* 33 (1999), 20–48

——, 'Das Edictum de beneficiis Konrads II. und die Entwicklung des Lehnswesens in der ersten Hälfte des 11. Jahrhunderts', *Settimane* 47 (2000), 227–57

——, 'Hulderweis durch Privilegien: Symbolische Kommunikation innerhalb und jenseits des Textes', *FMSt* 38 (2004), 309–21

Keller, H., and S. Ast, '*Ostensio cartae*. Italienische Gerichtsurkunden des 10. Jahrhunderts zwischen Schriftlichkeit und Performanz', *AfD* 53 (2007), 99–122

Kempshall, M., *Rhetoric and the Writing of History, 400–1500* (Manchester, 2011)

Kern, F., 'Recht und Verfassung im Mittelalter', *HZ* 120 (1919), 1–79

Keygnaert, F., 'L'excommunication collective du diocèse de Laon par l'évêque Hincmar (869): une "nouvelle" sanction en vue de la défense de l'autorité épiscopale aux temps carolingiens', in *Exclure de la communauté chrétienne: sens et pratiques sociales de l'anathème et de l'excommunication, IVᵉ-XIIᵉ siècle*, ed. G. Bührer-Thierry and S. Gioanni (Turnhout, 2015), 59–86

Keynes, S., *The Diplomas of King Æthelred 'the Unready', 978–1016: A Study in their Use as Historical Evidence* (Cambridge, 1980)

——, 'Royal Government and the Written Word in Late Anglo-Saxon England', in *The Uses of Literacy in Early Mediaeval Europe*, ed. R. McKitterick (Cambridge, 1990), 226–57

——, 'The West Saxon Charters of King Æthelwulf and His Sons', *EHR* 109 (1994), 1009–49

——, 'The Reconstruction of a Burnt Cottonian Manuscript: The Case of Cotton MS Otho A I', *The British Library Journal* 22 (1996), 113–60

——, 'Giso, Bishop of Wells (1061–88)', *ANS* 19 (1997), 203–70

——, *An Atlas of Attestations in Anglo-Saxon Charters, c. 670–1066*, rev. edn (Cambridge, 2002)

——, 'Conspectus of the Charters of King Edgar', in *Edgar, King of the English 959–975: New Interpretations*, ed. D. Scragg (Woodbridge, 2008), 60–80

——, 'Edgar, *rex admirabilis*', in *Edgar, King of the English 959–75: New Interpretations*, ed. D. Scragg (Woodbridge, 2008), 1–58

——, 'King Æthelred's Charter for Eynsham Abbey (1005)', in *Early Medieval Studies in Memory of Patrick Wormald*, ed. S. Baxter et al. (Farnham, 2009), 451–73

——, 'Church Councils, Royal Assemblies, and Anglo-Saxon Royal Diplomas', in *Kingship, Legislation and Power in Anglo-Saxon England*, ed. G. R. Owen-Crocker and B. W. Schneider (Woodbridge, 2013), 17–182

——, 'King Æthelred the Unready and the Church of Rochester', in *Textus Roffensis: Law, Language, and Libraries in Early Medieval England*, ed. B. O'Brien and B. Bombi (Turnhout, 2015), 315–62

Klebel, E., 'Die Ostgrenze des karolingischen Reiches', *Jahrbuch für Landeskunde von Niederösterreich* n.s. 21 (1928), 348–80

Klewitz, H.-W., 'Cancellaria. Ein Beitrag zur Geschichte des geistlichen Hofdienstes', *DA* 1 (1937), 44–79

Klimm, A., 'Ottonische Diplome im Bestand des Landesarchivs Sachsen-Anhalt. Originale, Falsifikate und kopiale Überlieferungen', in *Originale—Fälschungen—Kopien. Kaiser- und Königsurkunden für Empfänger in Deutschland und Italien (9.-11. Jahrhundert) und ihre Nachwirkungen im Hoch- und Spätmittelalter (bis ca. 1500)*, ed. N. D'Acunto et al. (Leipzig, 2018), 243–61

Knibbs, E., *Ansgar, Rimbert and the Forged Foundations of Hamburg-Bremen* (London, 2011)

——, 'Ebo of Reims, Pseudo-Isidore, and the Date of the False Decretals', *Speculum* 92 (2017), 144–83

Knowles, D., 'Essays in Monastic History, IV: The Growth of Exemption', *Downside Review* 50 (1932), 201–31, 396–436

Kohl, T., 'Religious Exemption, Justice, and Territories around the Year 1000: The Forgeries of Worms', *Medieval Worlds* 6 (2017), 217–30

———, *Streit, Erzählung und Epoche. Deutschland und Frankreich um 1100* (Stuttgart, 2019)

Kohl, T., and F. J. Felten, 'Worms—Stadt und Region im frühen Mittelalter von 600–1000', in *Geschichte der Stadt Worms*, ed. G. Bönnen, 2nd edn (Darmstadt, 2015), 102–32

Koller, H., 'König Arnolfs großes Privileg für Salzburg', *Mitteilungen der Gesellschaft für Salzburger Landeskunde* 109 (1969), 65–76

Kölzer, T., *Studien zu den Urkundenfälschungen St. Maximin vor Trier (10–12. Jahrhundert)* (Sigmaringen, 1989)

———, 'Die ottonisch-salische Herrscherurkunde', in *Typologie der Königsurkunden*, ed. J. Bistrický (Olomouc, 1998), 127–42

———, *Merowingerstudien*, 2 vols (Hanover, 1998–99)

———, Review of Resmini, *Benediktinerabtei*, *Rheinische Vierteljahrsblätter* 81 (2017), 460–64

———, *'Cui bono?* Beobachtungen zur Wirksamkeit von Urkundenfälschungen', in *Originale—Fälschungen—Kopien. Kaiser- und Königsurkunden für Empfänger in Deutschland und Italien (9.-11. Jahrhundert) und ihre Nachwirkungen im Hoch- und Spätmittelalter (bis ca. 1500)*, ed. N. D'Acunto et al. (Leipzig, 2018), 15–30

Kölzer, T., and D. Ludwig, 'Das Diplom Ottos III. für Meißen', in *Europas Mitte um 1000*, ed. A. Wieczorek and H. Hinz, 2 pts (Stuttgart, 2000), 764–66

Kortüm, H.-H., *Zur päpstlichen Urkundensprache im frühen Mittelalter. Die päpstlichen Privilegien 896–1046* (Sigmaringen, 1995)

———, '*Gerbertus qui et Silvester*. Papsttum um die Jahrtausendwende', *DA* 55 (1999), 29–62

Kosto, A. J., *Making Agreements in Medieval Catalonia: Power, Order and the Written Word 1000–1200* (Cambridge, 2001)

Koziol, G., *The Politics of Memory and Identity in Carolingian Royal Diplomas: The West Frankish Kingdom (840–987)* (Turnhout, 2012)

———, 'The Conquest of Burgundy, the Peace of God, and the Diplomas of Robert the Pious', *French Historical Studies* 37 (2014), 173–214

———, 'The Future of History after Empire', in *Using and Not Using the Past after the Carolingian Empire*, c. 900–c. 1050, ed. S. Greer et al. (London, 2019), 15–35

Kluge, B., *Deutsche Münzgeschichte von der späten Karolingerzeit bis zum Ende der Salier (ca. 900–1125)* (Sigmaringen, 1991)

Kramer, R., 'Monasticism, Reform, and Authority in the Carolingian Era', in *The Cambridge History of Medieval Monasticism in the Latin West*, ed. A. I. Beach and I. Cochelin, 2 pts (Cambridge, 2020), 432–49

Kurdziel, E., 'Au prisme des faux. Clergé, compétition pour les ressources et falsification en Italie du Nord et du Centre (XIᵉ–XIIᵉ siècles)', in *Acquérir, prélever, contrôler: les ressources en compétition (400–1100)*, ed. V. Loré et al. (Turnhout, 2017), 249–79

Kwakkel, E., 'Biting, Kissing and the Treatment of Feet: The Transitional Script of the Long Twelfth Century', in *Turning Over a New Leaf: Change and Development in the Medieval Book*, ed. E. Kwakkel, R. McKitterick and R. Thomson (Leiden, 2012), 78–126

Lake, J., *Richer of Saint-Rémi: The Methods and Mentality of a Tenth-Century Historian* (Washington, D.C., 2013)

———, 'Authorial Intention in Medieval Historiography', *History Compass* 12 (2014), 344–60

———, 'Rewriting Merovingian History in the Tenth Century: Aimoin of Fleury's *Gesta Francorum*', *EME* 25 (2017), 489–525

———, 'Arnulf of Orléans and the *De Cartillagine*', *Journal of Medieval Latin* 31 (forthcoming, 2021)

Lambert, T., *Law and Order in Anglo-Saxon England* (Oxford, 2017)

Lambrick, G., 'Abingdon Abbey Administration', *Journal of Ecclesiastical History* 17 (1966), 159–83

Landau, P., *Officium und Libertas christiana* (Munich, 1991)

Landes, R., *Relics, Apocalypse, and the Deceits of History: Ademar of Chabannes, 989–1034* (Cambridge, MA, 1998)

Lapidge, M., 'The Hermeneutic Style in Tenth-Century Anglo-Latin Literature' (1975), repr. in his *Anglo-Latin Literature 900–1066* (London, 1993), 105–49

——, 'Æthelwold as Scholar and Teacher' (1988), repr. in his *Anglo-Latin Literature 900–1066* (London, 1993), 183–211

Lebecq, S., *Marchands et navigateurs frisons du haut Moyen Âge*, 2 vols (Lille, 1983)

Lechner, J., 'Schwäbische Urkundenfälschungen des 10. und 12. Jahrhunderts', *MIÖG* 21 (1900), 28–106

——, 'Die älteren Königsurkunden für das Bistum Worms und die Begründung der bischöflichen Fürstenmacht', *MIÖG* 22 (1901), 361–419, 529–74

——, 'Zur Beurteilung der Wormser Diplome', *MIÖG* 25 (1904), 91–111

——, 'Die Wormser Kaiserurkunde Ottos III. über die Abtei Mosbach', *ZGO* 25 (1910), 151–57

Leesch, W., *Die deutschen Archivare, 1500–1945*, ii, *Biographisches Lexikon* (Munich, 1992)

Lehr, W., 'Pilgrim, Bischof von Passau, und die Lorcher Fälschungen' (PhD diss., Berlin, 1909)

Lemarignier, J.-F., 'L'exemption monastique et les origines de la réforme grégorienne' (1950), repr. in his *Structures politiques et religieuses dans la France du haut Moyen Âge* (Rouen, 1995), 285–337

——, 'De l'immunité à la seigneurie ecclésiastique' (1965), repr. in his *Structures politiques et religieuses dans la France du haut Moyen Âge* (Rouen, 1995), 273–84

——, 'Autour de la date du sacre d'Hugues Capet (1er juin ou 3 juillet 987?)' (1967), repr. in his *Structures politiques et religieuses dans la France du haut Moyen Âge* (Rouen, 1995), 233–43

Lemay, E., 'Diplomatic Mischief, Institutionalized Deception: Two Undated Merovingian Wills on Papyrus', *Viator* 47.ii (2016), 57–66

Lenain, T., *Art Forgery: The History of a Modern Obsession* (London, 2011)

Levillain, L., 'Études sur l'abbaye de Saint-Denis à l'époque mérovingienne, iii: *Privilegium* et *immunitates* ou Saint-Denis dans l'Église et dans l'État', *BEC* 87 (1926), 20–97, 245–356

Levison, W., 'Die Politik in Jenseitsvisionen des frühen Mittelalters' (1921), repr. in his *Aus rheinischer und fränkischer Frühzeit. Ausgewählte Aufsätze* (Düsseldorf, 1948), 229–46

Leyser, C., *Authority and Asceticism from Augustine to Gregory the Great* (Oxford, 2000)

——, 'Episcopal Office in the Italy of Liudprand of Cremona, c. 890–c. 970', *EHR* 125 (2010), 795–817

Leyser, K. J., 'The Tenth-Century Condition', in his *Medieval Germany and its Neighbours, 900–1250* (London, 1982), 1–10

——, 'The Ascent of Latin Europe' (1986), repr. in his *Communications and Power in Medieval Europe*, ed. T. Reuter, 2 vols (London, 1994), i, 215–32

——, '987: The Ottonian Connection', in his *Communications and Power in Medieval Europe*, ed. T. Reuter, 2 vols (London, 1994), i, 165–79

——, 'Ritual, Ceremony, Gesture: Ottonian Germany', in his *Communications and Power in Medieval Europe*, ed. T. Reuter, 2 vols (London, 1994), i, 189–213

Lhotsky, A., *Geschichte des Instituts für Österreichische Geschichtsforschung 1854–1954* (Graz, 1954)

——, *Quellenkunde zur mittelalterlichen Geschichte Österreichs* (Graz, 1963)

Lieftinck, G. I., *Manuscrits datés conservés dans les Pays-Bas*, i, *Les manuscrits d'origine étrangère (816–c. 1550)*, 2 pts (Amsterdam, 1964)

Lippelt, H., *Thietmar von Merseburg* (Cologne, 1973)

Lot, F., *Les derniers Carolingiens. Lothaire, Louis V, Charles de Lorraine (954–991)* (Paris, 1891)

——, *Études sur le règne de Hugues Capet et la fin du Xe siècle* (Paris, 1903)

Lowe, K. A., 'Lay Literacy in Anglo-Saxon England and the Development of the Chirograph', in *Anglo-Saxon Manuscripts and their Heritage*, ed. P. Pulsiano and E. M. Treharne (Basingstoke, 1998), 161–204

Lowenthal, D., *The Past is a Foreign Country* (Cambridge, 1985)

——, *The Past is a Foreign Country—Revisited* (Cambridge, 2015)

Lucioni, A., 'Arona e gli esordi del monastero dei SS. Felino e Gratiniano (secoli X–XII)', in *Arona, porta da entrare in Lombardia*, ed. P. Frigerio (Verbania, 1998), 19–78

——, 'Da Warmondo a Ogerio', in *Storia della Chiesa di Ivrea, dalle origini al XV secolo*, ed. G. Cracco (Rome, 1998), 119–89

——, 'L'abbazia di S. Benigno, l'episcopato, il papato e la formazione della rete monastica fruttuariense nel secolo XI', in *Il monachesimo italiano del secolo XI nell'Italia nordoccidentale*, ed. A. Lucioni (Cesena, 2010), 237–308

——, 'Re Arduino e il contesto religioso: monachesimo e vescovi fra inimicizie e protezioni', in *Arduino fra storia e mito*, ed. G. Sergi (Bologna, 2018), 25–84

Mabillon, J., *De re diplomatica libri VI*, rev. edn (Paris, 1709)

MacLean, S., *Kingship and Politics in the Late Ninth Century: Charles the Fat and the End of the Carolingian Empire* (Cambridge, 2003)

——, 'Shadow Kingdom: Lotharingia and the Frankish World, *c.* 850–*c.* 1050', *History Compass* 11 (2013), 443–57

——, *Ottonian Queenship* (Oxford, 2017)

Manaresi, C., 'Le tre donazioni della corte di Caresana alla canonica di Vercelli e la teoria della "ostensio cartae"', *Rendiconti del Reale istituto lombardo di scienze e lettere* 74 (1940–41), 39–55

——, 'Alle origini del potere dei vescovi sul territorio esterno delle città', *Bullettino dell'Istituto storico italiano per il medio evo* 57 (1944), 221–334

Manganaro, S., 'Forme e lessico dell'immunità nei diplomi di Ottone I. La mediazione cancelleresca tra Regno ed enti religiosi attraverso il privilegio scritto', *Studi medievali* 3rd ser. 51 (2010), 1–94

——, 'Protezione regia. I mundeburdi degli Ottoni per S. Maria di Farfa (secc. X–XI)', *Annali dell'Istituto italiano per gli studi storici* 27 (2012/13), 73–144

——, *Stabilitas regni. Percezione del tempo e durata dell'azione politica nell'età degli Ottoni (936–1024)* (Naples, 2018)

Marckhgott, G., 'Bischof Pilgrim (971–991): Realpolitik und "Lorcher Legende"', in *Kirche in Oberösterreich. 200 Jahre Bistum Linz*, ed. R. Zinnhobler (Linz, 1985), 51–62

Maskarinec, M., 'Why Remember Ratchis? Medieval Monastic Memory and the Lombard Past', *Archivio Storico Italiano* 177 (2019), 3–57

Mayer, T., *Fürsten und Staat. Studien zur Verfassungsgeschichte des deutschen Mittelalters* (Weimar, 1950)

Mayr-Harting, H., *Ottonian Book Illumination: An Historical Study*, 2 vols, rev. edn (London, 1999)

Mazel, F., *Féodalités, 888–1180* (Paris, 2010)

——, *L'évêque et le territoire. L'invention médiévale de l'espace (V^e–XIIIe siècle)* (Paris, 2016)

McClain, A., and N. Sykes, 'New Archaeologies of the Norman Conquest', *ANS* 41 (2019), 83–102

McCormick, M., *Origins of the European Economy: Communications and Commerce, AD 300–900* (Cambridge, 2001)

McHaffie, M. W., 'Law and Violence in Eleventh-Century France', *Past & Present* 238 (2018), 3–41

McKitterick, R., *History and Memory in the Carolingian World* (Cambridge, 2004)

McNair, F., 'A Post-Carolingian Voice of Dissent: The *Historia Francorum Senonensis*', *Journal of Medieval Latin* 28 (2018), 15–47

Meens, R., 'In the Mirror of Eusebius: The Episcopal Identity of Atto of Vercelli', in *Ego Trouble: Authors and Their Identities in the Early Middle Ages*, ed. R. Corradini et al. (Vienna, 2010), 243–48

——, *Penance in Medieval Europe, 600–1200* (Cambridge, 2014)

Mehu, D., *Paix et communautés de l'abbaye de Cluny (X^e–XVe siècle)* (Lyon, 2001)

Menant, F., 'Pour une histoire médiévale de l'entreprise minière en Lombardie', *Annales* 42 (1987), 779–96

——, *Campagnes lombardes du Moyen Âge. L'économie et la société rurales dans la région de Bergame, de Crémone et de Brescia du Xe au XIIIe siècle* (Rome, 1993)

Mersiowsky, M., '*Carta edita, causa finita?* Zur Diplomatik Kaiser Arnolfs', in *Kaiser Arnolf. Das ostfränkische Reich am Ende des 9. Jahrhunderts*, ed. F. Fuchs (Munich, 2002), 271–374

——, *Die Urkunde der Karolingerzeit. Originale, Urkundenpraxis und politische Kommunikation*, 2 pts (Wiesbaden, 2015)

——, 'Früh- bis spätmittelalterliche Kopien karolingischer Diplome für "deutsche" und "österreichische" Empfänger', in *Originale—Fälschungen—Kopien. Kaiser- und Königsurkunden für Empfänger in Deutschland und Italien (9.–11. Jahrhundert) und ihre Nachwirkungen im Hoch- und Spätmittelalter (bis ca. 1500)*, ed. N. D'Acunto et al. (Leipzig, 2018), 105–16

Merta, B., Review of Huschner, *Transalpine Kommunikation*, *MIÖG* 113 (2005), 403–9

Michałowski, R., *The Gniezno Summit: The Religious Premises of the Founding of the Archbishopric of Gniezno*, trans. A. Kijak (Leiden, 2016)

Mihm, S., *A Nation of Counterfeiters: Capitalists, Con Men, and the Making of the United States* (Cambridge, MA, 2007)

Miller, M. C., *The Bishop's Palace: Architecture and Authority in Medieval Italy* (Ithaca, NY, 2000)

Minghetti Rondoni, L., 'L'espansione territoriale del monastero di S. Ambrogio di Milano nella zona pedemontana', in *Il monastero di S. Ambrogio nel Medioevo*, ed. G. Picasso (Milan, 1988), 429–40

——, 'Il rinnovamento spirituale e nuove espressioni di vita monastica e canonicale nella diocesi eusebiana: il vescovo Gisulfo (1131–1151)', *BSV* 48 (1997), 5–20

Mittermüller, R., 'War Bischof Piligrim von Passau (971–991) ein Urkundenfälscher?', *Der Katholik* 2nd ser. 17 (1867), 337–62

Moehs, T. A., *Gregorius V, 996–999: A Biographical Study* (Stuttgart, 1972)

Molyneaux, G., *The Formation of the English Kingdom in the Tenth Century* (Oxford, 2015)

Moore, R. I., 'The Birth of Popular Heresy: A Millennial Phenomenon?', *Journal of Religious History* 24 (2000), 8–25

——, *The First European Revolution, c. 970–1215* (Oxford, 2000)

——, 'Treasures in Heaven: Defining the Eurasian Old Regime?', *Medieval Worlds* 6 (2017), 7–19

Morelle, L., 'Moines de Corbie sous influence sandionysienne? Les préparatifs corbéiens du synode romain de 1065', in *L'église de France et la papauté (X^e–XIIIe siècle)*, ed. R. Große (Bonn, 1993), 197–218

——, 'Histoire et archives vers l'an mil: une nouvelle "mutation"?', *Histoire et archives* 3 (1998), 119–41

——, 'La main du roi et le nom de Dieu: la validation de l'acte royal selon Hincmar, d'après un passage de son *De divortio*', in *Foi chrétienne et églises dans la société politique de l'Occident du Haut Moyen Âge, IVᵉ-XIIᵉ siècle*, ed. J. Hoareau-Dodinau and P. Texier (Limoges, 2004), 287–318

——, 'Suger et les archives: en relisant deux passages du *De administratione*', in *Suger en question: regards croisés sur Saint-Denis*, ed. R. Große (Munich, 2004), 117–39

——, 'Que peut-on savoir du temporel de Fleury à l'époque d'Abbon?', in *Abbon, un abbé de l'an mil*, ed. A. Dufour-Malbezin (Turnhout, 2008), 101–50

——, 'Diplomatic Culture and History Writing: Folcuin's Cartulary-Chronicle of Saint-Bertin', in *Representing History, 900–1300: Art, Music, History*, ed. R. A. Maxwell (University Park, PA, 2010), 53–65, 221–24

Mostert, M., 'Le séjour d'Abbon de Fleury à Ramsey', *BEC* 144 (1986), 199–208

——, *The Political Theology of Abbo of Fleury: A Study of the Ideas about Society and Law of the Tenth-Century Monastic Reform Movement* (Hilversum, 1987)

——, 'Die Urkundenfälschungen Abbos von Fleury', in *Fälschungen im Mittelalter*, 6 vols (Munich, 1988), iv, 287–318

——, *The Library of Fleury: A Provisional List of Manuscripts* (Hilversum, 1989)

——, 'Forgery and Trust', in *Strategies of Writing: Studies on Text and Trust in the Middle Ages*, ed. P. Schulte et al. (Turnhout, 2008), 37–59

Mühlbacher, E., 'Zwei weitere Passauer Fälschungen', *MIÖG* 24 (1903), 424–32

Müller-Mertens, E., *Die Reichsstruktur im Spiegel der Herrschaftspraxis Ottos des Großen* (Berlin, 1980)

Murnane, W. J., 'The Organization of Government under Amenhotep III', in *Amenhotep III: Perspectives on his Reign*, ed. D. O'Connor and E. H. Cline (Ann Arbor, MI, 1998), 173–221

Murray, A. C., 'Merovingian Immunity Revisited', *History Compass* 8 (2010), 913–28

Naß, K., *Die Reichschronik des Annalista Saxo und die sächsische Geschichtsschreibung im 12. Jahrhundert* (Hannover, 1996)

Nelson, J. L., 'England and the Continent in the Ninth Century: III, Rights and Rituals', *TRHS* 6th ser. 14 (2004), 1–24

Nienhaus, H., 'Das Schapbacher Schlössle. Ein herrschaftlicher Landsitz mit reicher und wechselvoller Geschichte', *Die Ortenau* 91 (2011), 433–52

Nightingale, J., 'Oswald, Fleury and Continental Reform', in *St Oswald of Worcester: Life and Influence*, ed. N. Brooks and C. Cubitt (London, 1996), 23–45

——, *Monasteries and Patrons in the Gorze Reform: Lotharingia c. 850–1000* (Oxford, 2001)

Noble, T. F. X., 'The Monastic Ideal as a Model for Empire: The Case of Louis the Pious', *RB* 86 (1976), 235–50

O'Brien, B., 'Forgery and the Literacy of the Early Common Law', *Albion* 27 (1995), 1–18

Olds, K. B., *Forging the Past: Invented Histories in Counter-Reformation Spain* (New Haven, CT, 2015)

Panero, F., *Una signoria vescovile nel cuore dell'impero: funzioni pubbliche, diritti signorili e proprietà della Chiesa di Vercelli dall'età tardocarolingia all'età sveva* (Vercelli, 2004)

——, 'Il consolidamento della signoria territoriale dei Vescovi di Vercelli fra XI e XII secolo', in *Vercelli nel secolo XII. Atti del quarto Congresso storico vercellese* (Vercelli, 2005), 411–49

Pangerl, D. C., *Die Metropolitanverfassung des karolingischen Frankenreiches* (Hanover, 2011)

Parisse, M., 'Écriture et réécriture des chartes: les pancartes aux XIᵉ et XIIᵉ siècles', *BEC* 155 (1997), 247–65

Parkes, H., *The Making of Liturgy in the Ottonian Church: Books, Music and Ritual in Mainz, 950-1050* (Cambridge, 2015)

Patzold, S., *Konflikte im Kloster. Studien zu Auseinandersetzungen in monastischen Gemeinschaften des ottonisch-salischen Reichs* (Husum, 2000)

——, 'Konsens und Konkurrenz. Überlegungen zu einem aktuellen Forschungskonzept der Mediävistik', *FMSt* 41 (2007), 75-103

——, 'Eine Hierarchie im Wandel: Die Ausbildung einer Metropolitanordnung im Frankenreich des 8. und 9. Jahrhunderts', in *Hiérarchie et stratification sociale dans l'Occident médiéval (400-1100)*, ed. F. Bougard et al. (Turnout, 2008), 161-84

——, *Episcopus. Wissen über Bischöfe im Frankenreich des späten 8. bis frühen 10. Jahrhunderts* (Ostfildern, 2008)

——, 'Capitularies in the Ottonian Realm', *EME* 27 (2019), 112-32

Pauler, R., *Das Regnum Italiae in ottonischer Zeit. Markgrafen, Grafen und Bischöfe als politische Kräfte* (Tübingen, 1982)

Paxton, F. S., '*Abbas* and *rex*: Power and Authority in the Literature of Fleury, 987-1044', in *The Experience of Power in Europe, 950-1350*, ed. R. F. Berkhofer III et al. (Aldershot, 2005), 197-212

Peirano, R., *The Rhetoric of the Roman Fake: Latin Pseudepigrapha in Context* (Cambridge, 2012)

Penco, G., 'Le "Consuetudines Fructuarienses"', in *Monasteri in alta Italia dopo le invasioni saracene e magiare (sec. X-XII)* (Turin, 1966), 137-56

Pfeiffer, G., 'Die Bamberg-Urkunde Ottos II. für den Herzog von Bayern', *Bericht des Historischen Vereins Bamberg* 109 (1973), 15-32

Pfister, C., *Études sur le règne de Robert le Pieux, 996-1031* (Paris, 1885)

Pivano, S., *Stato e chiesa da Berengario I ad Arduino, 888-1015* (Turin, 1908)

Pohl, B., *Dudo of Saint-Quentin's* Historia Normannorum*: Tradition, Innovation and Memory* (Woodbridge, 2015)

——, 'The Problem of Cluniac Exemption', in *A Companion to Cluny in the Middle Ages*, ed. S. Bruce and S. Vanderputten (Leiden, forthcoming 2021)

Pohl, B., and S. Vanderputten, 'Fécamp, Cluny, and the Invention of Traditions in the Later Eleventh Century', *Journal of Medieval Monastic Studies* 5 (2016), 1-41

Pohl, W., 'History in Fragments: Montecassino's Politics of Memory', *EME* 10 (2001), 343-74

——, *Werkstätte der Erinnerung. Montecassino und die Gestaltung der langobardischen Vergangenheit* (Vienna, 2001)

——, *The Avars: A Steppe Empire in Central Europe, 567-822*, trans. W. Sayers (Ithaca, NY, 2018)

Poly, J.-P., and E. Bournazel, *The Feudal Transformation, 900-1200*, trans. C. Higgitt (New York, 1991)

Pösinger, B., 'Die Rechtsstellung des Klosters Kremsmünster 777-1325', *Archiv für die Geschichte der Diözese Linz* 3 (1906), 13-133

Poupardin, R., *Le royaume de Bourgogne (888-1038)* (Paris, 1907)

Rabikauskas, P., *Die römische Kuriale in der päpstlichen Kanzlei* (Rome, 1958)

Rabotti, G., 'Dai vertici dei poteri medievali: Ravenna e la sua chiesa fra diritto e politica dal X al XIII secolo', in *Storia di Ravenna*, iii, *Dal mille alla fine della Signoria Polentana*, ed. A. Vasina (Venice, 1993), 129-68

Ramsey, F. M. R., 'Savaric (d. 1205)', in *ODNB*, xlix, 92-93

Rathsack, M., *Die Fuldaer Fälschungen*, 2 pts (Stuttgart, 1989)

Ratzinger, G., 'Lorch und Passau. Neue Forschungen', *Der Katholik* 2nd ser. 27 (1872), 570-603

——, 'Lorch und Passau', *Der Katholik* 3rd ser. 13 (1896), 167-83, 264-70, 358-67

Redlich, O., 'Johan Lechner', *MIÖG* 44 (1930), 399–400

Rembold, I., *Conquest and Christianization: Saxony and the Carolingian World, 772–888* (Cambridge, 2017)

——, 'History and (Selective) Memory: Articulating Community and Division in Folcuin's *Gesta abbatum Lobiensium*', in *Writing the Early Medieval West*, ed. E. Screen and C. West (Cambridge, 2018), 64–79

Remensnyder, A., *Remembering Kings Past: Monastic Foundation Legends in Medieval Southern France* (Ithaca, NY, 1995)

Rennie, K. R., '*Quam sit necessarium*. Monastic Exemption and the Privilege(d) Tradition', *ZGR: KA* 103 (2017), 323–39

——, *Freedom and Protection: Monastic Exemption in France, c. 590–c. 1100* (Manchester, 2018)

Resl, B., 'Ethnic History and Ecclesiastical Identity: The Example of Passau', in *Integration und Herrschaft im Frühmittelalter*, ed. W. Pohl and M. Diesenberger (Vienna, 2001), 91–103

——, 'Was bleibt, ist der Text—Passau und die Überlieferung der Vita Severini', in *Eugippius und Severin. Der Autor, der Text und der Heilige*, ed. W. Pohl and M. Diesenberger (Vienna, 2001), 123–37

Resmini, B., *Die Benediktinerabtei St. Maximin vor Trier*, Germania Sacra 3rd ser. 11, 2 pts (Berlin, 2016)

Reuter, T., *Germany in the Early Middle Ages, c. 800–1056* (London, 1991)

——, 'Reading the Tenth Century', in *The New Cambridge Medieval History*, iii, c. *900–c. 1024*, ed. T. Reuter (Cambridge, 1999), 1–24

——, 'Assembly Politics in Western Europe from the Eighth Century to the Twelfth' (2001), repr. in his *Medieval Polities and Modern Mentalities*, ed. J. L. Nelson (Cambridge, 2006), 193–216

——, 'Mandate, Privilege, Court Judgement: Techniques of Rulership in the Age of Frederick Barbarossa', in his *Medieval Polities and Modern Mentalities*, ed. J. L. Nelson (Cambridge, 2006), 413–31

——, 'A Europe of Bishops', in *Patterns of Episcopal Power: Bishops in Tenth and Eleventh Century Western Europe*, ed. L. Körntgen and D. Waßenhoven (Berlin, 2011), 17–38

Riché, P., *Gerbert d'Aurillac. Le pape de l'an mil* (Paris, 1987)

——, 'Arnoul, évêque d'Orléans en l'an mille', *Bulletin de la Société archéologique et historique de l'Orléanais* 10 (1988), 18–25

——, *Abbon de Fleury. Un moine savant et combatif (vers 950–1004)* (Turnhout, 2004)

Riches, T., 'The Changing Political Horizons of *gesta episcoporum* from the Ninth to Eleventh Centuries', in *Patterns of Episcopal Power: Bishops in Tenth and Eleventh Century Western Europe*, ed. L. Körntgen and D. Waßenhoven (Berlin, 2011), 51–62

Rieckenberg, H. J., 'Königsstraße und Königsgut in liudolfingischer und frühsalischer Zeit (919–1056)', *AfU* 17 (1941), 32–154

Riedel, C., 'Praising God Together: Monastic Reformers and Laypeople in Tenth-Century Winchester', *Catholic Historical Review* 102 (2016), 283–317

Rio, A., *Legal Practice and the Written Word in the Early Middle Ages: Frankish Formulae, c. 500–1000* (Cambridge, 2009)

——, *Slavery after Rome, 500–1100* (Oxford, 2016)

Roach, L., *Kingship and Consent in Anglo-Saxon England, 871–978: Assemblies and the State in the Early Middle Ages* (Cambridge, 2013)

——, *Æthelred the Unready* (New Haven, CT, 2016)

——, 'A Tale of Two Charters: Diploma Production and Political Performance in Æthelredian England', in *Writing Kingship and Power in Anglo-Saxon England*, ed. R. Naismith and D. A. Woodman (Cambridge, 2017), 234–56

——, 'The Ottonians and Italy', *Germany History* 36 (2018), 349–64

——, 'The Privilege of Liberty in Later Anglo-Saxon England', in *Magna Carta: New Approaches*, ed. S. T. Ambler and N. Vincent (Woodbridge, forthcoming)

——, 'Leiheformen und -praktiken in der Reichshistoriographie der Spätsalier- und Frühstauferzeit', in *Tenere et habere—Praktiken und Konzepte der Leihe (9.-13. Jahrhundert)*, ed. J. Dendorfer and S. Patzold (Sigmaringen, forthcoming)

Roberts, E., 'Flodoard, the Will of St Remigius and the See of Reims in the Tenth Century', *EME* 22 (2014), 201–30

——, 'Construire une hiérarchie épiscopale: Flodoard de Reims et la correspondance de l'archevêque Foulques (vers 850–vers 950)', *Cahiers de Civilisation Médiévale* 60 (2018), 11–26

——, 'Bishops on the Move: Rather of Verona, Pseudo-Isidore, and Episcopal Translation', *Medieval Low Countries* 6 (2019), 117–38

——, *Flodoard of Rheims and the Writing of History in the Tenth Century* (Cambridge, 2019)

——, 'Perceptions and Narratives of Reform in the Histories of Flodoard of Rheims' (forthcoming)

Roberts, E., and F. Tinti, 'Signalling Language Choice in Anglo-Saxon and Frankish Charters, *c.* 700–*c.* 900', in *The Languages of Early Medieval Charters: Latin, Germanic Vernaculars, and the Written Word*, ed. R. Gallagher et al. (Leiden, forthcoming)

Rolker, C., 'The Collection in Seventy-Four Titles: A Monastic Canon Law Collection from Eleventh-Century France', in *Readers, Texts, and Compilers in the Earlier Middle Ages: Studies in Medieval Canon Law in Honour of Linda Fowler-Magerl*, ed. M. Brett and K. G. Cushing (Aldershot, 2008), 59–72

——, 'Monastic Canon Law in the Tenth, Eleventh, and Twelfth Centuries', in *The Cambridge History of Medieval Monasticism in the Latin West*, ed. A. I. Beach and I. Cochelin, 2 pts (Cambridge, 2020), 618–30

Rollston, C. A., 'Non-Provenanced Epigraphs I–II', *Maarav* 10 (2003), 135–93; 11 (2004), 57–79

——, 'Forging History: From Antiquity to the Modern Period', in *Archaeologies of Text: Archaeology, Technology, and Ethics*, ed. M. T. Rutz and M. M. Kersel (Oxford, 2014), 176–97

Rosé, I., 'Un cas problématique de succession au Xe siècle. Le multi-abbatiat d'Odon de Cluny (vers 879–942)', in *Making and Breaking the Rules: Succession in Medieval Europe, c. 1000–c. 1600*, ed. F. Lachaud and M. Penman (Turnhout, 2007), 201–20

——, *Construire une société seigneuriale. Itinéraire et ecclésiologie de l'abbé Odon de Cluny (fin du IXe-milieu du Xe siècle)* (Turnhout, 2008)

——, 'Odon de Cluny, précurseur d'Abbon? La réforme de Fleury et l'ecclésiologie monastique d'Odon de Cluny († 942)', in *Abbon, un abbé de l'an mil*, ed. A. Dufour-Malbezin (Turnhout, 2008), 241–72

——, 'Judas, Dathan, Abiron, Simon et les autres. Les figures bibliques-repoussoirs dans les clauses comminatoires des actes originaux français', *AfD* 62 (2016), 59–106

——, 'Interactions between Monks and the Lay Nobility (from the Carolingian Era through the Eleventh Century)', in *The Cambridge History of Medieval Monasticism in the Latin West*, ed. A. I. Beach and I. Cochelin, 2 pts (Cambridge, 2020), 579–98

Rosenwein, B. H., *Negotiating Space: Power, Restraint, and Privileges of Immunity in Early Medieval Europe* (Ithaca, NY, 1999)

Rossi, G. (Hieronymus Rubeus), *Historiarvm Ravennatvm libri decem*, rev. edn (Venice, 1589)

Rößling, W., and H. Scharzmaier, *Unverrückbar für alle Zeiten. Tausendjährige Schriftzeugnisse in Baden-Württemberg* (Karlsruhe, 1992)

Roumy, F., 'Remarques sur l'œuvre canonique d'Abbon de Fleury', in *Abbon, un abbé de l'an mil*, ed. A. Dufour-Malbezin (Turnhout, 2008), 311–41

Rowland, I. D., *The Scarith of Scornello: A Tale of Renaissance Forgery* (Chicago, IL, 2004)

Rück, P., *Bildberichte vom König. Kanzlerzeichen, königliche Monogramme und das Signet der salischen Dynastie* (Marburg, 1996)

Rust, L. D., 'A guerra como sacramento: bispos e violência antes das cruzadas (850–1050)', *Locus: Revista de História* 22 (2016), 207–30

Saenger, P., *Space between Words: The Origins of Silent Reading* (Stanford, CA, 1997)

Sassier, Y., *Hugues Capet. Naissaince d'une dynastie* (Paris, 1987)

Savill, B., 'Prelude to Forgery: Baldwin of Bury meets Pope Alexander II', *EHR* 132 (2017), 795–822

Schaab, M., 'Ladenburg als wormische Bischofsresidenz', in *Südwestdeutsche Bischofsresidenzen außerhalb der Kathedralstädte*, ed. V. Press (Stuttgart, 1992), 83–97

Scharer, A., 'Bishops in Ottonian Bavaria', in his *Changing Perspectives on England and the Continent in the Early Middle Ages* (Farnham, 2014), no. xv

Scharzmaier, H., *Von Speyer nach Rom. Wegstationen und Lebensspuren der Salier* (Sigmaringen, 1991)

Schiaparelli, L., 'I diplomi dei re d'Italia. Ricerche storico-diplomatiche, 1: I diplomi di Berengario I', *Bullettino dell'Istituto storico italiano* 23 (1902), 1–167

——, 'I diplomi dei re d'Italia. Ricerche storico-diplomatiche, 5: I diplomi di Ugo e di Lotario', *Bullettino dell'Istituto storico italiano* 34 (1914), 7–255

Schieffer, R., *Die Entstehung von Domkapiteln in Deutschland* (Bonn, 1976)

——, *Die Entstehung des päpstlichen Investiturverbotes für den deutschen König* (Stuttgart, 1981)

——, 'Kanoniker', in *Lexikon des Mittelalters*, v (Munich, 1991), cols 903–4

——, 'Otto II. und sein Vater', *FMSt* 36 (2002), 255–70

Schmid, K., 'Unerforschte Quellen aus quellenarmer Zeit I. Zur amicitia zwischen Heinrich I. und dem westfränkischen König Robert im Jahre 923', *Francia* 12 (1984), 119–48

Schneider, O., *Erzbischof Hinkmar und die Folgen. Der vierhundertjährige Weg historischer Erinnerungsbilder von Reims nach Trier* (Berlin, 2008)

Schneidmüller, B., *Karolingische Tradition und frühes französisches Königtum. Untersuchungen zur Herrschaftslegitimation der westfränkisch-französischen Monarchie im 10. Jahrhundert* (Wiesbaden, 1979)

——, 'Die einzigartig geliebte Stadt. Heinrich II. und Bamberg', in *Kaiser Heinrich II. 1002–1024*, ed. J. Kirmeier et al. (Augsburg, 2002), 30–51

Schoenig, S. A., *Bonds of Wool: The Pallium and Papal Power in the Middle Ages* (Washington, D.C., 2016)

Scholz, S., *Politik—Selbstverständnis—Selbstdarstellung. Die Päpste in karolingischer und ottonischer Zeit* (Mainz, 2006)

Schramm, P. E., *Kaiser, Rom und renovatio. Studien zur Geschichte des römischen Erneuerungsgedankens vom Ende des karolingischen Reiches bis zum Investiturstreit*, 2 vols (Leipzig, 1929)

Schütte, B., 'Einige Bemerkungen zur Neuausgabe der Fälschungen Pilgrims von Passau', *Zeitschrift für bayerische Kirchengeschichte* 82 (2013), 53–61

Sennis, A., 'Documentary Practices, Archives and Laypeople in Central Italy, mid Ninth to Eleventh Centuries', in *Documentary Culture and the Laity in the Early Middle Ages*, ed. W. Brown et al. (Cambridge, 2012), 321–35

Sergi, G., *I confini del potere. Marche e signorie tra due regni medievali* (Turin, 1995)

——, 'The Kingdom of Italy', in *The New Cambridge Medieval History*, iii, c. *900–c. 1024*, ed. T. Reuter (Cambridge 1999), 346–71

——, 'Poteri temporali del vescovo: il problema storiografico', in *Vescovo e città nell'alto Medioevo*, ed. G. Francesconi (Pistoia, 2001), 1–16

——, 'Arduino marchese conservatore e re rivoluzionario', in *Arduino mille anni dopo. Un re tra mito e storia*, ed. L. L. Momigliano (Turin, 2002), 11–25

Settia, A. A., 'Assetto del popolamento rurale e coppie toponimiche nell'Italia padana (secoli IX–XIV)', *Studi Storici* 36 (1995), 243–66

——, 'Nelle foreste del re: le corti "Auriola", "Gardina" e "Sulcia" dal IX al XII secolo', in *Vercelli nel secolo XII. Atti del quarto Congresso storico vercellese* (Vercelli, 2005), 353–409

Sharpe, R., 'The Use of Writs in the Eleventh Century', *ASE* 32 (2003), 247–91

Sickel, T., 'Beiträge zur Diplomatik I.', *SB Wien* 39 (1861), 329–402

——, 'Beiträge zur Diplomatik VI.', *SB Wien* 85 (1877), 351–457

——, *Über Kaiserurkunden in der Schweiz* (Zürich, 1877)

——, 'Beiträge zur Diplomatik VIII.', *SB Wien* 101 (1882), 131–84

——, 'Erläuterungen zu den Diplomen Ottos II.', *MIÖG: Ergänzungsband* 2 (1888), 77–190

Snook, B., *The Anglo-Saxon Chancery: The History, Language and Production of Anglo-Saxon Charters from Alfred to Edgar* (Woodbridge, 2015)

Sot, M., *Gesta episcoporum, gesta abbatum* (Turnhout, 1981)

——, 'Pratique et usages de l'histoire chez Abbon de Fleury', in *Abbon, un abbé de l'an mil*, ed. A. Dufour-Malbezin (Turnhout, 2008), 205–23

Southern, R. W., 'Aspects of the European Tradition of Historical Writing: 4. The Sense of the Past', *TRHS* 5th ser. 23 (1973), 243–63

Speyer, W., *Die literarische Fälschung im heidnischen und christlichen Altertum. Ein Versuch ihrer Deutung* (Munich, 1971)

Stafford, P., 'Royal Government in the Reign of Æthelred II, AD 979–1016' (DPhil thesis, University of Oxford, 1973)

Staub, J., 'Domschulen am Mittelrhein um und nach 1000', in *Bischof Burchard von Worms 1000–1025*, ed. W. Hartmann (Mainz, 2000), 279–309

Stengel, E. E., *Die Immunität in Deutschland bis zum Ende des 11. Jahrhunderts*, i, *Diplomatik der deutschen Immunitäts-Privilegien* (Innsbruck, 1910)

Stengel, E. E., and O. Semmelmann, 'Fuldensia, IV. Untersuchungen zur Frühgeschichte des Fuldaer Klosterarchivs', *AfD* 4 (1958), 120–82

Stephens, W., and E. A. Havens, ed., *Literary Forgery in Early Modern Europe, 1450–1800* (Baltimore, MD, 2018)

Stieldorf, A., 'Die Magie der Urkunden', *AfD* 55 (2009), 1–32

Stock, B., *The Implications of Literacy: Written Language and Models of Interpretation in the Eleventh and Twelfth Centuries* (Princeton, NJ, 1983)

Stokes, P. A., 'King Edgar's Charter for Pershore (AD 972)', *ASE* 27 (2008), 31–78

Stone, R., 'Spiritual Heirs and Families: Episcopal Relatives in Early Medieval Francia', in *Celibate and Childless Men in Power: Ruling Eunuchs and Bishops in the Pre-Modern World*, ed. A. Höfert et al. (Abingdon, 2018), 129–48

Störmer, W., 'Die Herkunft Bischof Pilgrims von Passau (971–991) und die Nibelungen-Überlieferung', *Ostbairische Grenzmarken* 16 (1974), 62–67

Studtmann, J., 'Die Pönformel der mittelalterlichen Urkunden', *AfU* 12 (1932), 251–374

Stump, E., 'Della Chiesa, Francesco Agostino', in *DBI*, xxxvi (Rome, 1988), 748–51

Tellenbach, G., *Libertas. Kirche und Weltordnung im Zeitalter des Investiturstreites* (Stuttgart, 1936)

Tessier, G., 'Leçon d'ouverture du cours de diplomatique à l'École des chartes', *BEC* 91 (1930), 241–63

——, 'Originaux et pseudo-originaux carolingiens du chartrier de Saint-Denis', *BEC* 106 (1945/6), 35–69

——, Review of Ramackers, *Papsturkunden in Frankreich*, n.s. vi, *Orléanais*, *BEC* 117 (1959), 297–300

——, *Diplomatique royale française* (Paris, 1962)

Thacker, A., 'Æthelwold and Abingdon', in *Bishop Æthelwold: His Career and Influence*, ed. B. Yorke (Woodbridge, 1988), 43–64

Theis, L., *Robert le Pieux. Le roi de l'an mil* (Paris, 1999)

Thomas, H., 'Die Deutschen und die Rezeption ihres Volksnamens', in *Nord und Süd in der deutschen Geschichte des Mittelalters*, ed. W. Paravicini (Sigmaringen, 1990), 19–50

Thompson, S. D., *Anglo-Saxon Royal Diplomas: A Palaeography* (Woodbridge, 2006)

Tinti, F., *Sustaining Belief: The Church of Worcester from c. 870 to c. 1100* (Farnham, 2010)

——, 'Benedictine Reform and Pastoral Care in Late Anglo-Saxon England', *EME* 23 (2015), 229–51

Tout, T. F., 'Mediæval Forgers and Forgery', *Journal of the John Rylands Library* 5 (1919), 208–34

Trautz, F., *Das untere Neckarland im früheren Mittelalter* (Heidelberg, 1953)

Trumbore Jones, A., 'Discovering the Aquitanian Church in the Corpus of Ademar of Chabannes', *HSJ* 19 (2007), 82–98

——, 'The Power of an Absent Pope: Privileges, Forgery, and Papal Authority in Aquitaine, 877–1050', in *Canon Law, Religion, and Politics*: Liber amicorum *Robert Somerville*, ed. U.-R. Blumenthal et al. (Washington, D.C., 2012), 118–35

Ubl, K., *Inzestverbot und Gesetzgebung. Die Konstruktion eines Verbrechens (300–1100)* (Berlin, 2008)

Ubl, K., and D. Ziemann, eds, *Fälschung als Mittel der Politik? Pseudoisidor im Licht der neuen Forschung* (Wiesbaden, 2015)

Ugé, K., *Creating the Monastic Past in Medieval Flanders* (Woodbridge, 2005)

Uhlirz, K., 'Die Urkundenfälschung zu Passau im zehnten Jahrhundert', *MIÖG* 3 (1882), 177–229

——, *Die Geschichte des Erzbistums Magdeburg unter den Kaisern aus sächsischem Hause* (Magdeburg, 1887)

——, 'Excurse zu Ottonischen Diplomen IX.', *MIÖG: Ergänzungsband* 2 (1888), 548–50

——, *Jahrbücher des Deutschen Reiches unter Otto II. und Otto III.*, i, *Otto II. 973–83* (Leipzig, 1902)

Uhlirz, M., *Jahrbücher des Deutschen Reiches unter Otto II. und Otto III.*, ii, *Otto III. 983–1002* (Berlin, 1954)

——, 'Rechtsfragen in den Urkunden Ottos III.', *Settimane* 2 (1956), 220–44

Vallerani, M., 'Scritture e schemi rituali nella giustizia altomedievale', *Settimane* 59 (2012), 97–150

Vanderputten, S., *Reform as Process: Realities and Representations in Medieval Flanders, 900–1100* (Ithaca, NY, 2013)

——, 'Monastic Reform from the Tenth to the Early Twelfth Century', in *The Cambridge History of Medieval Monasticism in the Latin West*, ed. A. I. Beach and I. Cochelin, 2 pts (Cambridge, 2020), 599–617

Vezin, J., 'Écritures imitées dans les livres et les documents du haut Moyen Âge (VIIe–XIe siècle)', *BEC* 106 (2007), 47–66

——, 'Les manuscrits témoins des relations entre Fleury et Saint-Martial de Limoges, IXe–XIe siècles', in *Abbon, un abbé de l'an Mil*, ed. A. Dufour and G. Labory (Turnhout, 2008), 405–14

Vignodelli, G., *Il filo a piombo. Il Perpendiculum di Attone di Vercelli e la storia politica del regno italico* (Spoleto, 2011)

——, 'I palinsesti del codice CLXXI della Biblioteca Capitolare Eusebiana', *BSV* 86 (2016), 5–35

——, 'Politics, Prophecy and Satire: Atto of Vercelli's *Polipticum quod appellatur Perpendiculum*', *EME* 24 (2016), 209–35

——, 'La competizione per i beni fiscali: Ugo di Arles e le aristocrazie del regno italico (926–945)', in *Acquérir, prélever, contrôler: les ressources en compétition (400–1100)*, ed. V. Loré et al. (Turnhout, 2017), 151–70

——, 'Prima di Leone. Originali e copie di diplomi regi e imperiali nell'Archivio Capitolare di Vercelli', in *Originale—Fälschungen—Kopien. Kaiser- und Königsurkunden für Empfänger in Deutschland und Italien (9.–11. Jahrhundert) und ihre Nachwirkungen im Hoch- und Spätmittelalter (bis ca. 1500)*, ed. N. D'Acunto et al. (Leipzig, 2018), 53–81

Vincent, N., 'The Charters of King Henry II: The Introduction of the Royal Inspeximus Revisited', in *Dating Undated Medieval Charters*, ed. M. Gervers (Woodbridge, 2000), 97–120

——, *The Holy Blood: King Henry III and the Westminster Blood Relic* (Cambridge, 2001)

——, *Magna Carta: Origins and Legacy* (Oxford, 2015)

——, 'The Use and Abuse of Anglo-Saxon Charters by the Kings of England, 1100–1300', in *The Long Twelfth-Century View of the Anglo-Saxon Past*, ed. M. Brett and D. A. Woodman (Farnham, 2015), 290–327

Violante, C., 'Marchesi, conti e visconti tra circoscrizioni d'ufficio signorie e feudi nel Regno Italico (secc. IX–XII)', in *Formazione e strutture dei ceti dominanti nel medioevo. Marchesi, conti e visconti nel Regno Italico (secc. IX–XII)* (Rome, 1996), 1–19

Vogtherr, T., *Die Reichsabteien der Benediktiner und das Königtum im hohem Mittelalter* (Sigmaringen, 2000)

Volpini, R., 'Placiti del Regnum Italiae (secc. IX–XI). Primi contributi per un nuovo censimento', *Contributi dell'Istituto di storia medioevale* 3 (1975), 245–520

Wagner, W., 'Das Gebetsgedenken der Liudolfinger im Spiegel der Königs- und Kaiserurkunden von Heinrich I. bis zu Otto III.', *AfD* 40 (1994), 1–78

Walsham, A., 'Migrations of the Holy: Religious Change in Medieval and Early Modern Europe', *Journal of Medieval and Early Modern Studies* 44 (2014), 241–80

Wehrli, C., *Mittelalterliche Überlieferungen von Dagobert I.* (Berlin, 1982)

Weinert, H., 'Die offizielle Titulatur der Herrscher und die Bezeichnungen für das Reich in der Zeit von 911 bis 973' (PhD diss., Universität Heidelberg, 1953)

Weinfurter, S., 'Herrschaftslegitimation und Königsautorität im Wandel: Die Salier und ihr Dom zu Speyer', in *Die Salier und das Reich*, 3 vols, ed. S. Weinfurter et al. (Sigmaringen, 1991), i, 55–96

——, 'Kaiser Heinrich II. (1002–1024). Ein Herrscher aus Bayern', *Oberbayerisches Archiv* 122 (1998), 31–55

——, *Heinrich II. Herrscher am Ende der Zeiten* (Regensburg, 1999)

——, *Canossa. Die Entzauberung der Welt* (Munich, 2006)

Welton, M., and S. Greer, 'Establishing Just Rule: The Diplomatic Negotiations of the *Dominae Imperiales* in the Ottonian Succession Crisis of 983–5' *FMSt* (forthcoming)

Werle, H., 'Titelherzogtum und Herzogsherrschaft', *ZRG: GA* 73 (1956), 225–99

Werner, J., *Papsturkunden vom 9. bis ins 11. Jahrhundert. Untersuchungen zum Empfängereinfluss auf die äußere Urkundengestalt* (Berlin, 2017)

Werner, K.-F., 'Heeresorganisation und Kriegführung im deutschen Königreich des 10. und 11. Jahrhunderts', *Settimane* 15 (1968), 791–844

——, 'Die literarischen Vorbilder des Aimoin von Fleury und die Entstehung seiner *Gesta Francorum*' (1960), repr. in his *Einheit der Geschichte. Studien zur Historiographie* (Sigmaringen, 1998), 192–226

Wertsch, J. V., *Voices of Collective Remembering* (Cambridge, 2002)

West, C., *Reframing the Feudal Revolution: Political and Social Transformation between Marne and Moselle, c. 800–c. 1100* (Cambridge, 2013)

White, S. D., *Feuding and Peace-Making in Eleventh-Century France* (Aldershot, 2005)

Wickham, C., 'Making Europes', *New Left Review* 208 (1994), 133–43

——, 'Justice in the Kingdom of Italy in the Eleventh Century', *Settimane* 44 (1997), 179–250

——, *Framing the Early Middle Ages: Europe and the Mediterranean, 400–800* (Oxford, 2005)

——, 'The "Feudal Revolution" and the Origins of Italian City Communes', *TRHS* 6th ser. 24 (2014), 29–55

——, *Sleepwalking into a New World: The Emergence of Italian City Communes in the Twelfth Century* (Princeton, NJ, 2015)

——, *Medieval Europe* (New Haven, CT, 2016)

Widemann, J., 'Zur Lorcher Frage', *Verhandlungen des Historischen Vereins für Niederbayern* 32 (1896), 159–214

Wildung, D., *Egyptian Saints: Deification in Pharaonic Egypt* (New York, 1977)

Winandy, J., 'Äbte und Bischöfe im Kampf um die monastische Exemtion im Spiegel hagiographischer Quellen aus Fleury', in *Jenseits des Königshofs. Bischöfe und ihre Diözesen im nachkarolingischen ostfränkisch-deutschen Reich (850–1100)*, ed. A. Bihrer and S. Bruhn (Berlin, 2019), 337–58

Winckler, K., *Die Alpen im Frühmittelalter. Die Geschichte eines Raumes in den Jahren 500 bis 800* (Vienna, 2012)

Wisplinghoff, E., Review of Kölzer, *Studien*, *Blätter für deutschen Landesgeschichte* 127 (1991), 651–58

Witt, R. G., *The Two Latin Cultures and the Foundation of Renaissance Humanism in Medieval Italy* (Cambridge, 2012)

Wolfram, H., 'Einleitung oder Lügen mit der Wahrheit: Ein historiographisches Dilemma', in *Historiographie im frühen Mittelalter*, ed. A. Scharer and G. Scheibelreiter (Vienna, 1994), 11–25

——, *Salzburg, Bayern, Österreich. Die Conversio Bagoariorum et Carantanorum und die Quellen ihrer Zeit* (Vienna, 1995)

——, 'Bavaria in the Tenth and Early Eleventh Centuries', *The New Cambridge Medieval History*, iii, c. *900–c. 1024*, ed. T. Reuter (Cambridge, 1999), 293–309

——, *Conrad II, 990–1039: Emperor of Three Kingdoms*, trans. D. A. Kaiser (University Park, PA, 2006)

Wolter, H., *Die Synoden im Reichsgebiet und in Reichsitalien von 916 bis 1056* (Paderborn, 1988)

Wood, C. S., *Forgery, Replica, Fiction: Temporalities of German Renaissance Art* (Chicago, IL, 2008)

Wood, I. N., *The Missionary Life: Saints and the Evangelisation of Europe, 400–1050* (London, 2001)

——, 'Entrusting Western Europe to the Church, 400–750', *TRHS* 6th ser. 23 (2013), 37–73

Wood, S., *The Proprietary Church in the Medieval West* (Oxford, 2006)

Woodman, D. A., '"Æthelstan A" and the Rhetoric of Rule', *ASE* 42 (2013), 217–48

Wormald, P., 'Charters, Law and the Settlement of Disputes in Anglo-Saxon England' (1986), repr. in his *Legal Culture in the Early Medieval West: Law as Text, Image and Experience* (London, 1999), 289–311

——, 'Æthelwold and his Continental Counterparts: Contact, Comparison, Contrast' (1988), repr. in his *Times of Bede: Studies in Early English Christian Society and its Historian* (Oxford, 2006), 169–206

Zibermayr, I., *Noricum, Baiern und Österreich. Lorch als Haupstadt und die Einführung des Christentums*, rev. edn (Horn, 1956)

Zimmermann, M., *Écrire et lire en Catalogne (IXᵉ-XIIᵉ siècle)*, 2 pts (Madrid, 2003)

Zotz, T., 'Adelsherrschaften am Mittelrhein um 1000', in *Bischof Burchard von Worms 1000–1025*, ed. W. Hartmann (Mainz, 2000), 349–69

Aachen, 168, 236, 246
'Aachen rule', 217, 219
abbey(s), royal/imperial, 22–23, 49, 153, 158, 160, 163, 192, 199, 234, 237
Abbo of Fleury, 153–54, 156, 158–77, 180, 182–92, 210, 234, 266, 269–70, 272; *Collectio canonum* of, 166–67, 189–90; Italian trips of, 169–72, 180–81; *Liber apologeticus* of, 165–67, 183; *Quaestiones grammaticales* of, 180; sojourn in England of, 159, 188–89; youth and education of, 159
Abingdon, xxviii–xxix, 19, 113–48, 151–52, 160, 188, 256, 264, 266, 270, 272; cartulary-chronicle of, 127–31, 141–44
Abū l-Qāsim, emir of Sicily, 196–97
Actus Silvestri, 13
Adalbero, archbishop of Reims, 154–58
Adalbero, archbishop of Laon, 157, 191
Adalbert, bishop of Bergamo, 254
Adalbert, bishop of Passau, 71–72, 96
Adalbert, bishop of Vercelli, 203
Adalbert I, margrave of Ivrea, 194
Adalbert II, son and co-ruler of Berengar II, 195–97, 212–13, 221, 227
Adalwin, archbishop of Salzburg, 77
Adam, first man 114–15, 125
Adelheid, empress, 26, 66, 106, 195–96, 212–15
Adémar of Chabannes, 190
Adrevald of Fleury, 160, 191–92
Advent, 165–66
advocate, legal, 214–16
Ælfgar, son of Ælfric of Hampshire, 120, 148
Ælfric, ealdorman of Hampshire, 114–15, 119–20, 148, 150, 270
Ælfstan, bishop of Rochester, 147, 189
Ælfthryth, queen, 113, 116, 118–19, 137
Ælfwine, charter recipient, 128
Ælfwold, despoiler of Glastonbury, 150
Ælfwold, bishop of Crediton, 134
Ælfwold, bishop of Sherborne, 134

Æthelbald, Mercian ruler, 130–31, 142, 144–45
Æthelmær, founder of Eynsham, 136
Æthelred II ('the Unready'), English ruler, 113–21, 123–24, 126–27, 130, 133, 135–38, 140, 146–48, 150–51, 188, 256
Æthelsige, Kentish magnate, 147
Æthelstan, English ruler, 130–31, 138, 144, 147, 150
Æthelstan C, draftsman-scribe, 130
Æthelwold, bishop of Winchester, 113–21, 123, 131, 137, 140–42, 146, 148, 152, 160, 188, 229; *Life* of, 119
Æthelwulf, West Saxon ruler, 126
Agapit II, pope, 73, 78–80, 93, 107, 108, 142
Aimo, count (?of Lomello), 196, 221, 227
Aimoin of Fleury, 160–61, 169, 171–74, 178, 183–84, 189–91; *Gesta Francorum* of, 179, 192
Alberic, judge, 215
Alberic of Gassino, 245
Albert, Peter, 49
Albert of Vermandois, count, 156
Alderic, bishop of Le Mans, 263
Aleram, Italian margrave, 194–95
Alexander II, pope, 175, 177, 183–85
Alexandria, 196
Alice, 196, 221
'Alliterative Charters', 130 n. 46
Allstedt, 97
alpha-omega, 114, 136, 138–39. *See also* chrismon
Alps, 66–67, 91, 107, 168, 194–95, 197, 236, 238, 240, 243, 247–48. *See also* Great St Bernard pass; Little St Bernard pass; Mont Cenis pass
Alric, bishop of Asti, 254
Altötting, 89
Amandus, bishop of Maastricht, 41
Amandus, bishop of Worms, 32, 41
Amenhotep III, pharaoh, 1, 256
Amesbury, 136

anathema, 173, 201. *See also* excommunication

Ancien Régime, 16

Andorno, 221, 227–28

Andrew, bishop of Lodi, 242

Andrew of Fleury, 184–85, 191

Annalista Saxo, 72

Anno, bishop of Worms, xxviii–xxix, 21–60, 68, 112, 153–54, 181, 256–57, 261, 266–67, 269–72

Anscar, margrave of Ivrea, 194

Anscarid(s), 194–95, 197–98

Anselmo dedicata, 227

'anti-monastic reaction', 120, 146, 151

anachronism, 2, 8, 12, 33, 77, 138, 142, 152, 257, 260, 264

Ananias, 79

Annunciation, 242

Ansgar, bishop of Bremen, 263

antiquarianism, 15, 55–56, 152, 261, 264

antiquities, 2–3

antiquity, Classical, 2

apocrypha, biblical, 1

archaism, 35–7, 48, 55, 163. *See also* hyperarchaism

archchancellor, 204, 238, 241–42

archdeacon, 203–4, 215, 240, 243, 246

Archembald, abbot of Fleury, 160

Archembald, archbishop of Tours, 172

archive, papal, 79

archpriest, 204, 215–16, 238

Arderic, bishop of Vercelli, 218–19, 225–26, 228, 230

Ardicin, son of Arduin of Ivrea, 207–8, 236

Ardon, river, 156

Arduin Glaber, margrave of Turin, 194–95

Arduin of Ivrea, margrave of Ivrea and Italian ruler, 195–208, 211–13, 215–17, 221, 223–24, 227, 229, 235–50, 253–54; consecration of, 237; excommunication of, 200, 235; penance of, 202; retirement to Fruttuaria of, 246, 248

Arian heresy, 115, 205

Aripert II, Lombard ruler, 211, 225–26

Arles, 73

Armbruster, J. V., 28–29, 56

Arno, archbishop of Salzburg, 79

Arnulf, archbishop of Reims, 156–58, 170–71, 200

Arnulf, bishop of Metz, 41

Arnulf, bishop of Orléans, 153–54, 156–63, 166–68, 173–74, 184, 189

Arnulf (II), archbishop of Milan, 246

Arnulf of Carinthia, East Frankish ruler, 32–33, 35, 37, 52, 54–55, 57, 60, 68–69, 83, 89–93, 99, 112, 256

Arnulf of Milan, 242

Arnulf of Yèvre, castellan, 163–64, 168, 175, 189, 270

Arona, 227

Arras, 268

art, medieval, 13

Aruna, 227, 229

Ascension, 198, 230, 232

Assmann, Aleida, 16–17, 60

Assmann, Jan, 16–17, 57, 60, 266

Asti, 254

Athelney, 134

Atto, bishop of Vercelli, 196, 205, 210, 217–19, 221

Augsburg, 24

Augustine, archbishop of Canterbury, 73, 78

Austria, 63; Lower, 94; Upper, 104

authenticity, 13

Auxerre, 158, 160

Avaria, 75–76, 81

Avars, 71, 75–76, 79, 86

Aventine Hill, 168

Baden-Württemberg, 22

Baldred, south-west Midlands ruler, 146, 150

Bamberg, 95, 240, 248

baptism, 77, 79

Bartholomew, abbot of Marmoutier, 172

bastard, 157

Bath, 134

Bavaria, xxvii, 27, 61–66, 69–72, 79, 82, 84, 89, 94–95, 99, 108, 261; Hungarian frontier of, 66

Bazas, 187

Beddington, 148

Bede, 73–74, 78, 80, 171

Bedwyn, 131

Benedict III, pope, 263

Benedict VI, pope, 72–73, 80–81, 108

Benedict VII, pope, xxviii, 72–73, 80–81, 108, 177, 186–87, 189

Benedict VIII, pope, 247

Benedictine Rule, 23–24, 116–18, 121, 134, 137, 150, 174

Benedict of Nursia, 23–24, 116–17, 119, 121, 159, 161, 165, 173, 184, 187, 190–92, 266; feast day of (11 July), 184; feast of the reburial of (4 December), 165. *See also* Benedictine Rule

bene val(ete), 107, 128

bishop: diocesan, 12, 23, 114, 134, 159, 168, 188, 242; auxiliary, 78. *See also* office: episcopal

Berengar I, Italian ruler, 193–94, 218 n. 59, 223, 225

Berengar of Ivrea (alias Berengar II), Italian ruler, 194–97, 212–13, 221, 227

Berkhofer, Robert F. III, 17

Berkshire, historic county of, 127, 131, 141, 143–44

Berlin, 61–62

Baronio, Cesare, 15–16

Bergamo, 213, 254, 261

Bertha, wife of Robert the Pious, 167, 170–71

Bessels Leigh, 123, 141–42

Biella, 221–22, 223 n. 71

Biscioni cartulary. See *Liber Biscioni*

Bisson, Thomas, 270

Blankett, 95, 99, 102, 106 n. 105

Blessed Virgin. *See* Mary, Virgin

blessing-sanction, 206–7

Bloch, Marc, 272

blood relic, 24, 68

Bobbio, 199–200, 210, 234–35, 268

Bohemia, 70, 72, 104

Bologna, 213

Boniface, saint, 70, 76–77

Bononio, saint, 197, 214, 226; *Life* of, 197, 226

bookland, 121–22, 136, 143–44

Bosonid(s), 194

Bouchard, Constance, 17

boundary clause(s), 128–29, 135, 138, 147

Brandenburg, 70

Bratislava, battle of (907), 69

Breme, 223, 247

Bremen, 262–63

Britain, 57, 142

British Library, 114

British Museum, 1

Brixen, 69, 77, 94

Bromley, 147–48, 152

Brooke, Christopher, 5

Brown, Peter, 260

Bruning, son-in-law of Liuprand, 217

Brunner, Karl, 110

Bruno, archbishop of Cologne, 26

Bruno of Carinthia. *See* Gregory V

Brusasco, 224

Buonconvento, 57

Burchard, bishop of Passau, 89

Burchard, bishop of Worms, 26–27, 59

Burgundy, 194, 235

Burton, 124

Bush, George (Sr), 16

Büttner, Heinrich, 110

Cambrai, 187

Canava, 222, 227

canon law, 166, 175, 183, 186, 189, 227, 234, 262

Canterbury, 146, 151–52

Capetian dynasty, 18, 155, 160

capitularies, 264–65

Capo Colonna, battle of (982). *See* Crotone, battle of (982)

Caresana, 197–98, 212–20, 223, 226, 238, 245

Carinthia, 27, 31, 59; march of, 66–67

Carinthians, 71, 86

Carloman of Bavaria, East Frankish ruler, 89

Caroline minuscule, 179

Carolingian dynasty, xxviii, 26, 33, 63, 84, 153–55, 157, 161, 193, 264

Carolingian empire, 18–19

cartulary, 97, 149. *See also* Codex Lonsdorfianus; Eynsham: cartulary of; *Liber Biscioni*; Muchelney: cartulary of; Worms: cartulary of

cartulary-chronicle, genre, 127–28, 258. *See also* Abingdon: cartulary-chronicle of; Folcuin of Saint-Bertin

Casanova, 229

Catalonia, 265

Catholicism, 61–62, 261

Cavaglià, 196, 221, 227–28

Cenwahl, West Saxon ruler, 149

Cerreto, 229

Cervo, river, 221, 230

chancellor, 7, 11, 31, 206, 216, 238
chancery: royal/imperial, 7–8, 31, 51;
  papal, 107, 168, 172
chapel, royal, 65
chapter, cathedral, 217–19, 267–68
Charlemagne, Frankish ruler, 3, 6, 13,
  21, 32–33, 37, 41, 42, 57, 82–86, 112,
  181–82, 258, 261
Charles of Lotharingia (Lorraine), 154–58,
  166–67
Charles the Bald, West Frankish ruler,
  154, 168, 173, 181–82, 191
Charles the Fat, Frankish ruler, 84, 91, 98,
  192, 204–5, 211, 223–24, 226–29, 233,
  247, 254, 256, 272
Charles the Simple, West Frankish ruler,
  155
charters: criticism of, 3–6; constituent
  parts of, 8–11; copies of, 13–14, 56–57;
  folding of, 56; imitative copies of, 14,
  35, 231; judicial value of, 54, 66, 146,
  152, 230, 255, 257–58; narrative
  qualities of, 258–59; 'private', 20, 120,
  207, 241; production of, 6–8, 51,
  210; royal/imperial, 6–13; scribes of,
  7–8; sealing of, 8, 11; survival rates
  of, 56, 124. See also corroboration
  (clause); dating clause; diplomatic;
  endorsement; eschatocol; foundation
  charter; invocation; pancartes(s);
  preamble; prohibition clause; protocol; pseudo-original(s); publication
  (clause); recognition (clause); seal(s);
  witness-list(s)
Chiemgau, 63
Chiemsee, abbey of, 68
Chiemsee, Lake, 63
Chilcomb, 148–49
chorepiscopi. See bishop: auxillary
chrism, 77
chrismon, 8, 36, 47, 50, 83, 114, 136, 138,
  233, 245. See also alpha-omega
Christ, 118
Christian, bishop of Passau, 91, 111
Christmas, 156, 165, 236
Chronicle of Novalesa, 223, 247
Chy valley, 223
Cipolla, Carlo, 4
Cisidola, 222–23
Clanchy, Michael, 152

clerics, secular, 117–18
Clinton, Bill, 16
Clofesho, council of (747), 143–44
Cluny, 119, 159, 168, 175, 177, 182, 191, 245
Codex Lonsdorfianus, 97, 108, 111
Coenwald, bishop of Worcester, 130 n. 46
Coenwulf, Mercian ruler, 116, 123, 130–31,
  140–44, 152
Coggiola, 222
Collection in 74 Titles, 186
Cologne, 69, 76, 78, 206
Como, 240–41, 248, 252
Compiègne, 154
completion stroke, 91–92, 97, 99, 222 n. 70
Conquest, Norman, 151, 260
Conrad I, East Frankish ruler, 46
Conrad II, emperor, 59, 155, 177, 208–9,
  223, 230, 242, 247 n. 141, 253
Conrad the Red, duke of Lotharingia, 24,
  26–28
consanguinity, 171. See also incest
consecration: abbatial, 182–83, 185–86,
  243; episcopal, 77, 108; royal, 154–57;
  sacerdotal, 77, 174, 186
Constable, Giles, 5
Constantine, abbot of Micy, 167
Constantine, emperor, 13–14. See also
  Donation of Constantine
Constantinople, 198; court of, 237
Constantius, bishop (?of Lorch), xxvii,
  71, 74
Conversio Bagoariorum et Carantanorum,
  71, 73, 109–10
conversion, monastic, 236
Corbie, 172–73, 187, 262
Corrado Conone, margrave of Ivrea,
  195–98, 212–15, 227
corroboration (clause), 11, 99, 101, 103,
  105, 205, 209
Cortereggio, 223
Cossila, 223 n. 71
count. See office: comital
Cremona, 253–54
Crescentius (alias Crescenzio), Roman
  city prefect, 198–99
Crick, Julia, 129, 152, 264
Crotone, battle of (982), 196
Cruciform Monument, 1–2, 256
Culham, 141
Cuma, abbot of Abingdon, 131

Cumnor, 131, 141, 143–45
Cunibert, archpriest of Vercelli, 204,
    215–16, 238, 245
curial script, 107, 172
customary, monastic, 121
Czech Republic, 76

Dado, father of Arduin of Ivrea, 195, 204
Dagobert I, Frankish ruler, 3, 32–33,
    40–41, 42, 52, 56–57, 60, 261
Dagobert III, Frankish ruler, 41
Daniel, Book of, 1
Danube, river, 19, 61, 86, 93, 94, 271
dating clause, 11, 37–39, 84, 95, 97, 99,
    103, 138, 172, 231, 241–42, 245, 251
deacon, 145, 223, 239
Dead Sea Scrolls, 3
Della Chiesa, Francesco Agostino, 246
Denchworth, 141, 144–45
Déols, 175
De re diplomatica, 4. See also Mabillon,
    Jean
Desana, 238
Deutschlandsberg, 67
Dexter, Flavius, 261
diocesan boundaries, 268
diplomas. See charters: royal/imperial
diplomatic, 4–5, 7
diplomatic minuscule, 66, 83, 163, 231,
    245
display script, 114, 128–31, 143–44, 231.
    See also rustic capitals; square capi-
    tals; uncial(s)
Dissolution (of the Monasteries), 150
districtus, 203–4, 206–7, 210, 229, 236,
    238, 254
Djoser, pharaoh, 2
Domesday Book, 143–44
Donation of Constantine, 13–14
Downton, 148–50, 152
Dry Sandford, 141
Duby, Georges, 269
Dümmler, Ernst, 61–62, 72, 81–82, 107
Dunstan, archbishop of Canterbury, 152,
    188–89

Eadred, English ruler, 116, 119, 123, 131,
    138, 142–43, 145, 147–48
Eadwig, English ruler, 116, 123–24, 127–28,
    131, 138, 142–45

Eadwine, abbot of Abingdon, 114–16,
    119–20, 148
Ealdred, bishop of Cornwall, 136
Easter, 147, 200–201, 202–3, 235
East Francia, 72, 80, 154. See also Germany
Eaton, 141, 143, 146
Ebabar temple (at Sippar), 1
Ebbesborne, 148
Ebbo, archbishop of Reims, 263
Eberhard, bishop of Como, 240–42
Eberhard, duke of Bavaria, 78
Ecgberht, West Saxon ruler, 145–46, 149
Eden, 114–15
Edingen, 41
Edgar, English ruler, 114, 116–24, 127,
    130–31, 135, 140, 142–47, 159, 188
Edgar A, draftsman-scribe, 130, 142–43
Edmund of East Anglia, king and martyr,
    189, 191
Edward the Confessor, English ruler, 3
Edward the Elder, English ruler, 146, 148
Edward the Martyr, English ruler, 116,
    145–6
Egilolf, (arch)bishop of Salzburg, 72, 77–78
Egypt, 196–97
Egyptomania, 3
Elbe, river, 24, 30, 58
Elbe Slavs, 68, 70
election, abbatial, 12, 23–24, 121, 134–37,
    150, 173, 182–83
Elephantine, 2
elongated letters/script. See litterae
    elongatae
Elsenzgau, 45
Emilia, 254
emphyteusis, 199
endorsement, 55–56, 147–48, 165
England, 17–19, 116, 258, 260, 268
Enlightenment, 261
Enns, river, 71, 104
Ennsburg, 104
enrolement, 135
epigraphy, 261
erasure, 43, 99, 103, 138, 201, 219
Erembert, bishop of Worms, 32, 33–34
Erfurt, 96, 97
Ermentheus, bishop of Orléans, 153
eschatocol, 8, 10–11, 34, 36, 42–43 n. 54,
    45–48, 66, 78 n. 46, 85, 96, 102, 231,
    233, 245, 250

Esztergom, 111

Etterzhausen, 104–5

Eugenius II, pope, 72, 74–77

Euphrates, river, 1

Eurasia, 269

Europe, 120, 199, 261, 265; 'of bishops', 266–67; continental/mainland, 57, 116, 121; early modern, 15, 260; western, 161, 256

Eusebius, bishop of Vercelli, 205–7, 218, 226, 231, 268; *Life* of, 205

exchequer, 135

excommunication, 141, 163, 174, 186–87, 200–202, 235, 248–50

exemption: from duties of hospitality, 141; ecclesiastical, 11–12, 14, 153–54, 167–68, 171–72, 185, 187, 192, 242–43, 246–47, 259, 265–66, 270, 272; military, 28–30, 34, 51–52

Eynsham, 136–37; cartulary of, 130 n. 48

Fall of Man, 114–15, 118

Famine Stele, 2, 256

Farfa, 199, 203, 208, 243

Fater, abbot of Kremsmünster, 82

Fatimid dynasty, 197

Fawkham, 148

Fécamp, 186, 188

'Feudal Revolution', 164, 269–71

Fichtenau, Heinrich, 18, 53, 62, 65, 89, 100, 108–9, 112

fictio, rhetorical, 259

Fleury (Saint-Benoît-sur-Loire), xxviii–xxix, 19, 121, 153, 158–92, 243, 261, 264, 266, 269–70, 272; sack of (1562), 165

Flodoard of Reims, 258

Florence, 19

Florentine calendar, 242

Florian, saint, 72

Folcuin of Saint-Bertin, 258

Folwich, bishop of Worms, 32

forgery, *passim*; and antiquarianism, 15; definition of, 13–14. *See also* anachronism; antiquarianism; hyperarchaism

Formigliana, 226–27

foundation charter, 16, 136, 146, 151, 240, 265

France, 15–18, 153, 155, 159, 173–74, 190, 193, 206, 243, 262, 264–65, 268–69

Francia, region in France, 155

Frankfurt, 212

freda, 40, 52

Frederick, archbishop of Ravenna, 237

Frederick, archbishop of Salzburg, 63, 65–66, 68, 100–102, 103, 108, 267, 270

Frederick Barbarossa, emperor, 29, 254

Freising, 69

Fried, Johannes, 53

Fruttuaria, 185, 223, 235–36, 240–41, 242–48, 272

Fuhrmann, Horst, 5

Fulbert of Chartres, 184

Fulda, 22, 79, 80

Fulgentius, saint, 161

Fulk, bishop of Orléans, 184–85, 191

Gabotto, Ferdinando, 208, 247

Galen, 1

Gaul, 80, 173

Gauzbert, abbot of Saint-Julien, 166

Gauzlin, abbot of Fleury, 179–80, 184, 187, 191; *Life* of, 184

Geary, Patrick, 15–17

Gerbert of Aurillac, 157–59, 167–71, 184, 199–200, 202, 234–35, 238. *See also* Sylvester II

Gerhard, (arch)bishop of Lorch/Passau, 72–73, 77–80

German, 66

Germanus, abbot of Ramsey, 188

Germany, 17–18, 22, 70, 76, 80, 154–55, 193, 206, 219, 248, 264–65, 268. *See also* East Francia

gesta episcoporum, genre, 15, 263–64, 267

Gezo, bishop of Turin, 246

Ginge, 123, 131, 141–45

Giovanni Nanni (alias Annius of Viterbo), 261

Giry, Arthur, 4

Gisela, wife of Adalbert I of Ivrea, 194

Giselbert, archdeacon of Vercelli, 203–4, 215–17, 229

Giselbert, duke of Lotharingia, 24

Giselher, bishop of Merseburg and archbishop of Magdeburg, 24, 58

Giso, bishop of Wells, 134

Gisulf, bishop of Vercelli, 219–20, 230, 254

Glastonbury, 120, 134, 146, 150, 188, 261

Godehard, bishop of Hildesheim, 63–65, 266; *Life* of, 63–65

Godfrey, brother of William of Volpiano, 236, 246
gold mining, 208, 210–11
gold rush, American, 112
Goosey, 123, 131, 141–42, 144
Gotefred, chancellor of Arduin, 245
Graecomania, 3
Gran, 111
Grand Tour, 2
Grafton, Anthony, xxviii
Great St Bernard pass, 194
Greece, ancient, 1, 2
Gregory II, pope, 172
Gregory IV, pope, 173, 177, 179–83, 185–87, 189, 191, 263
Gregory V, pope, 59, 153, 167, 169–74, 177, 180–84, 186, 192, 197–202, 234
Gregory of Tours, 63
Gregory the Great (I), pope, 78, 80, 168, 170, 173–4, 183, 187, 189, 198; *Register* of, 183
Guibert, brother of Arduin of Ivrea, 235
Gumbert, Rhineland magnate, 46–48, 51
Gunthard, archdeacon of Turin, 246
Guy, bishop of Pavia, 246
Guy, margrave of Ivrea, 195–96, 213
Guy of Spoleto, Italian ruler, 194

Hadamar, abbot of Fulda, 79, 80
Hadwig, wife of Hugh the Great, 155
Halberstadt, 70
half-uncial, 148
Hamburg-Bremen, archbishopric of, 78, 94. *See also* Bremen
Hatto, bishop of Worms, 32, 35
Havelberg, 70
Helgaud of Fleury, 171, 179, 184, 192. *See also* Robert the Pious: *Life* of
Henry I, East Frankish ruler, 24, 170
Henry II (alias Henry IV of Bavaria), emperor, 59, 91, 95, 155, 212, 217, 223–24, 230, 241–42, 245–54; first Italian expedition of, 240–41; imperial coronation of, 211–12, 248; royal consecration of at Mainz, 237; royal consecration of at Pavia, 240–41; second Italian expedition of, 247–48
Henry III, emperor, 177–79, 218, 228, 230
Henry IV, emperor, 229, 254
Henry VII, emperor, 57

Henry I of Bavaria, duke, 69, 80, 96
Henry II ('the Quarrelsome') of Bavaria, duke, 66, 80, 94–98, 102, 104, 106
heresy, 115, 166, 206. *See also* Arian heresy; Sabellian heresy
Heribert, archbishop of Cologne, 206
'hermeneutic style', 135
Herold, archbishop of Salzburg, 79–80
Herveus, treasurer of Saint-Martin, 172
Hiatt, Alfred, 17
Higuera, Jerónimo Román de la, 261
Hildibald, bishop of Worms, 30–31, 40, 48, 53, 59
Hildibald B, draftsman-scribe, 31–53, 55–57, 58, 60, 68, 86, 210, 232: hand of, 39, 47–50; identity of, 53; preferred abbreviation sign of, 39, 48, 50
Hincmar of Laon, 63, 109
Hincmar of Reims, 5, 167, 262–63
history: institutional, 15–16, 263–64, 267; narrative, 16, 20, 257–59. *See also* memory
Hobsbawm, Eric, 16
Holy Spirit, 79, 113, 166
Hraban Maur, 219
Hubert 'the Red', count (?of Pombia), 212, 229, 248–50
Hugh, abbot of Farfa, 234
Hugh, archbishop of Reims, 160
Hugh, margrave of Tuscany, 206, 212, 214, 218–19
Hugh Capet, West Frankish/French ruler, 153–58, 160–61, 163–64, 166–69, 171, 191
Hugh of Arles (alias Hugh of Provence), Italian ruler, 23, 194–96, 214, 217, 221–22, 230
Hugh of Fleury, 187
Hugh of S. Lorenzo, papal legate, 230
Hugh the Great, duke of Francia, 157, 160
Humanists, Renaissance, 2
Hungarian frontier. *See* Bavaria: Hungarian frontier of
Hungarians, 63–65, 69, 71, 79, 80–81, 104, 193, 211
Hungary, 70–72, 75, 86, 93, 109
Hunibert, bishop of Cologne, 41
Huns, 76, 79
hunting, 154, 194
Huschner, Wolfgang, 53
hyperarchaism, 12–13, 91

Iberia, 20. *See also* Catalonia; Spain
Île-de-France, 157
Ilminster, 135
Ilvesheim, 41
Imhotep, adviser to Djoser, 2, 3
imitative script. *See* script imitation
immunity, 11–12, 14, 24–25, 27–30, 33–35,
    37–38, 40, 42, 45–46, 51–56, 59–60,
    91–93, 98–99, 105–6, 109, 121–22, 125,
    153–54, 158, 160, 173, 181, 242–43,
    246–47, 256, 259, 266, 270; 'ban'/
    territorial, 45–46, 54–55, 265. *See also*
    protection: royal
incastellamento, 210
incest, 167, 171–72
Indiculus loricatorum, 69
Ingelheim, 24, 71, 94, 168
Ingo, bishop of Vercelli, 196, 207, 221
ink, colour of, 38, 43, 114, 216
Innocent III, pope, 5
Inns, river, 89
inspection (of charters), 56–57, 135
inspeximus. *See* inspection (of charters)
Institute for Austrian Historical
    Research, 62
Insular minuscule, 148
interdict, 174–75, 186–87, 190
Investiture Contest, 243, 254
invocation, 8–9, 36, 206
Ireland, 57
Isidore of Seville, 171, 250; *Etymologies*
    of, 250
Isigrim, bishop of Regensburg, 72–73, 77
Italian C, draftsman-scribe, 66, 97
Italy, 13, 18, 23, 42, 44, 57, 65–69, 94–95,
    108, 170, 183, 193–94, 198, 205, 215,
    240–41, 255, 257, 260, 265, 267–68;
    kingdom of, 23, 193, 240, 248, 254;
    Lombard, 14
Itter, river, 45
Ivrea, 193–94, 196, 198–202, 206–7, 221,
    223, 236, 240, 243; local clergy of,
    239–40; march of, 194–97, 203, 213,
    215, 235–36, 238, 254

John, archbishop of Ravenna, 235, 237
John, bishop of Belluno, 197
John VIII, pope, 168, 174, 181–82, 186,
    191
John XV, pope, 150, 169–70, 173, 197

John XVIII, pope, 184
John XIX, pope, 182, 247 n. 141
John of Auxerre, scholar, 158
John Philagathos, (anti)pope, 198, 234
John the Baptist, saint, 204, 227
Justinian, emperor, 2

Kalbid dynasty, 196
Karloff, Boris, 2
Karlsruhe, Generallandesarchiv, 49
Kehr, Paul Fridolin, 90–91
Keller, Hagen, 15
Kelly, Susan, 122–23, 133, 141
Kempshall, Matthew, 259
Kent, 147, 262
Khnum, god of the Nile, 2
Kohl, Thomas, 54
Kölzer, Theo, 28
Konzept, 37
Koziol, Geoffrey, 15, 109, 263
Kremsmünster, 82–86, 89, 91, 93–94,
    97–99, 111–12, 170
Kulturkampf, 61–62

Ladenburg, 24, 27, 32–34, 37, 40–42, 45–46,
    49, 52, 54, 59; Roman ruins at, 57
Lanfranc, archbishop of Canterbury,
    185
Lantbert, bishop of Freising, 73, 77
Laon, 156–57
La Réole, 177, 186–87
Latin, 135, 204, 208, 238
Latin West, 18, 19, 262, 271–72
Laurence, (anti)pope, 74
Laurence, saint, 71, 77, 94–95, 97–99, 103,
    106
Lechfeld, battle of (955), 80, 95
Lechner, Johann, 30–32, 35, 37, 42–44,
    46, 48–53
Leckhamstead, 141
Lehr, Waldemar, 82
Leitha, 86
Le Mans, 160; forgeries of, 262–64
Lent, 248
Leo, abbot of SS Bonifacio ed Alessio,
    168–72, 203 n. 25, 234–35
Leo, archbishop of Ravenna (=Leo of SS
    Bonifacio ed Alessio?), 234
Leo, bishop of Vercelli, xxviii–xxix, 196–97,
    200, 202–55, 256, 261, 266–72;

appointment of, 203; hand of, 250–51; Latin style of, 205–6, 208, 238–39, 252, 259; *Versus de Gregorio papa et Ottone augusto* of, 234; *Versus de Ottone et Heinrico* of, 238

Leo III, pope, 75, 116, 123, 140

Leo VII, pope, 72–73, 77–79, 174, 177

Leo IX, pope, 172–73, 185

Leotheric, archbishop of Sens, 184–85

Leyser, Karl, 14–15, 19–20

libellus, 199

Liber Biscioni, 231, 233

Liber diurnus, 73–74, 168

Liber pontificalis, 74, 177, 191–92

liberty, ecclesiastical, 11–12, 14, 54, 114, 116–23, 125–26, 132–38, 150–51, 168, 242–43, 259, 265–66, 270, 272

Liguria, 194

Lincoln, 150

Lincoln, Abraham, 16–17

Linz, 94

Litaha, 86–87

literacy, 2, 66, 152, 205, 210, 229, 255, 264–65

litterae elongatae, 11, 25, 35, 42, 47, 49, 163, 231, 245

Little St Bernard pass, 194

Liudolf, son of Otto I, 23, 24, 27, 80

Liudolf F, draftsman-scribe, 66

Liudolf H, draftsman-scribe, 44, 53

Liudolf I, draftsman-scribe, 58

Liudolf K, draftsman-scribe, 53

Liudolfings. *See* Ottonian (Liudolfing) dynasty

Liupram, archbishop of Salzburg, 77

Liuprand, judge and advocate, 216–17

Liutgard, daughter of Otto I, 26, 28

Liutprand, Lombard ruler, 204

Liutward, bishop of Vercelli, 204–5

Lobdengau, 32, 40–45, 59

Locarno, 240

Loire, river, 19, 155, 159–60, 267

Lombard League, 254

Lombard rulers (of Italy), 3, 14, 262. *See also* Italy: Lombard

Lombardy, 68, 254

Lomellina, 247

London, 113, 148

Longworth, 123, 131, 141, 143

Lorch, xxvii–xxviii, 71–82, 85, 87–89, 93–94, 97–99, 103–7, 110–11; late antique remains at, 72

Lorsch, 22–23, 41–45, 59, 68, 257

Lot, Ferdinand, 175

Lothar I, Frankish ruler, 34–35, 37, 39, 40–41, 45, 55, 205, 225

Lothar II, Italian ruler, 23, 194–96, 213–14, 217, 221–22, 230

Lothar III, West Frankish ruler, 154–55, 157, 160

Lotharingia, 26, 80, 155–56, 190; Lower, 154, 157, 246; Upper, 155

Louis IV, West Frankish ruler, 156–57

Louis V, West Frankish ruler, 154–55, 160

Louis the Blind, Italian ruler, 193–94, 222

Louis the Child, East Frankish ruler, 63, 68–69, 89–90, 94

Louis the German, East Frankish ruler, 32–35, 37–38, 42, 45–46, 52, 54–55, 57, 60, 86–87, 91, 98

Louis the Pious, Frankish ruler, 28–30, 32–35, 37, 39, 40–42, 45, 51–52, 55–57, 60, 83, 86–89, 112, 181–82, 191, 256, 258, 261, 263

Lowenthal, David, 271

Lucedio, 197, 204–5, 207–8, 224–27, 235

Luitpold, duke of Bavaria, 69

Luitpoldings, Bavarian ducal family, 69

Mabillon, Jean, 4, 6

Madalwin, auxiliary bishop, 71

Magdeburg, 21, 24, 30, 42–44, 53, 58, 67–68, 70–71, 78, 95, 107–8, 261, 266

Maggiore, Lake, 227

Magna Carta, 114

Mainz, 22–24, 58, 69–70, 76, 78, 237

Maiolus, abbot of Cluny, 243–45

Maldon, 120

Malmesbury, 135

Manaresi, Cesare, 208–11, 225

Manfred, son of Count Aimo, 221, 227

manicule, 218

Maništušu, Akkadian ruler, 1–2

Mantua, 68

Marcham, 145

Marinianus, bishop of Ravenna, 189

Marmoutier, 172, 186

marriage, 77–78; clerical, 219

Martial, 1

Martin of Tours, 119
martyrdom, 75
martyrology, 219, 238. *See also* Vercelli:
    martyrology-necrology of
Mary, Virgin, 114–15, 118, 128, 131, 141–42
Mathilda, East Frankish queen, 170
Mattsee, 91
Maurice, saint, 71, 95
Maurus, saint, 161
Meißen, 70
memory: collective, 16; communicative,
    16–17; cultural, 16–17, 57, 59–60; insti-
    tutional, 15–16, 259–60, 263–64; local,
    15, 258–60; social, 16
mentalities, literate. *See* literacy
merchants, Frisian, 35, 37
Merovingian dynasty, 3, 4, 16, 262
Merseburg, 22, 58, 70, 95
Methodius, Greek missionary saint, 76
Methodius 'of Speculiiuliensi', 76
Metz, 22
Meuse, river, 155
microhistory, 19–20
Middle Rhine, 24, 26–27, 30, 57, 112
Milan, 195, 205, 227, 253–54
Miracles of Saint Benedict, 160, 191–92
Modena, 213
modius regis, 34–35, 38
Moimir, Moravian leader, 76
Molinaria, 221
monastery, royal. *See* abbey(s), royal/
    imperial
monogram, royal/imperial, 11, 13, 28,
    37–38, 40, 47, 83–84, 86, 89–90, 97,
    99–100, 128, 231–33, 250
Monroe, James, 16
Mont Cenis pass, 194
Monte, 222–23
Monte Casino, 4–5, 23–24, 116, 159, 259,
    266
Montier-en-Der, 188
Moore, R. I., 269
Moravia, 70, 75–76, 80–81, 109
Mosbach, 49–50, 51
Mostert, Marco, 172, 175–77, 180–83, 186
Mount Cisidola. *See* Cisidola
Mouzon, 169
Michałowski, Roman, 75
Micy, 161, 187–89
Middle East, 1

mint(ing), rights of, 34–35, 38, 54
mission, eastern, 65, 70–71, 75–81, 86–88,
    93–95, 97–98, 106, 111, 256
money laundering, 246
Monumenta Germaniae Historica, 62
Morelle, Laurent, 187
Muchelney, 133–35; cartulary of, 134–35
Mühlbacher, Engelbert, 30
Mummy, The, 2
murrain, 115
mutation féodale. See 'Feudal Revolution'

Neckar, river, 24, 32, 45, 49
Neckarhausen, 41
necrology, 219. *See also* Vercelli:
    martyrology-necrology of
Neuhausen, 46
Neunkirchen, 24
New Minster, Winchester, 117–18; refoun-
    dation charter of, 117–18, 121
Niblelungenlied, 61
Nicholas I, pope, 263
Nidrinhof, 66
Niederaltaich, 63–65, 70, 89, 266
Niedernburg, 99–103, 109
Nierstein, 94–95
Nile, river, 1, 2, 196
Nithard, brother of William of Volpiano,
    236, 246
Nordgau, 95
Nonantola, 234–35
Noricum, xxvii, 71, 75, 79, 108
notaries, communal, 230–31
notice(s): judicial, 214, 226, 241, 265;
    tradition, 70; transaction, 163, 265
Notitia Galliarum, 190
Novara, 194, 196, 206, 225–27, 236, 248
Noyon, 154, 156
Nunna, South Saxon ruler, 146

Oda, archbishop of Canterbury, 127
Odelric, bishop of Cremona, 242
Odenwald, 32–33, 39, 40–46, 51–53, 59
Odilo, abbot of Cluny, 245
Odilo, Bavarian duke, 63, 93, 99
Odo, abbot of Cluny, 159–60, 168, 175,
    182–83, 186, 192
Odo, bishop of Chartres, 163
Odolric, bishop of Orléans, 185
Odo of Blois, count, 156, 163, 167

Odo of Paris, West Frankish ruler, 155

Offa, Mercian ruler, 146, 150–51

office: comital, 30, 34, 45, 270; episcopal, 266–67

Oise, river, 155–56

Olderic-Manfred, margrave of Turin, 248, 254

Old Minster, Winchester, 116–20, 124, 136, 146–51

Old Testament, 1

Orco, estate (alias Regio), 218 n. 59, 223–24, 226–27, 229, 239, 247

Orco, river, 222, 236, 240, 247

ordination, 77. *See also* consecration: sacerdotal

Orléanais, 153, 159–61, 167

Orléans, 153, 156–61, 165, 174, 184–85, 188, 192, 270; canons of, 165–66

Orthodoxorum charters, 122–27, 131–33, 135–43, 145, 209–10, 256

Osbert de Clare, 259

Osgar, abbot of Abingdon, 119, 160, 188

Ossola, 194, 206

ostensio cartae, 214–15, 265. *See also* notice(s): judicial

Oswald, archbishop of York (and Worcester), 123, 152, 160, 188

Otbert, Italian margrave, 194–95

Ötting, 89–91

Otto I, emperor, 21, 26, 31–33, 35–37, 39–40, 42, 46–48, 50, 55, 63, 66, 80, 94–95, 107–8, 155, 213, 222; conquest of Italy of, 23, 194–96, 213, 221; missionary plans of, 67–68, 70

Otto II, emperor, 23, 26, 31–32, 35, 37–40, 50, 55, 69, 80, 83, 94–106, 108, 200, 213, 232; death of, 195; marriage of, 236; royal and imperial coronations of, 236; southern Italian campaign of (982), 69, 196

Otto III, emperor, 37, 59, 155, 170, 195–96, 197–200, 202–3, 213, 215, 219, 221, 230–35, 237–39, 266; death of, 223, 235–36; diplomas in favour of Vercelli of, 203–12; imperial consecration of, 198, 231–32; minority/regency of, 106, 195, 197, 212–13; royal consecration of, 236–37

Otto (I), duke of Swabia and Bavaria, 99, 102

Ottonian (Liudolfing) dynasty, 26, 63, 69, 80, 264–65, 271

Otto of Worms, duke of Carinthia, 27–31, 45, 58, 197, 240

Otto-William, count of Burgundy, 223–4

Oxfordshire, 141, 143–44

Oylbold, abbot of Fleury, 159, 161

pallium, 72–81, 108, 110, 272

pancartes(s), 140–41, 231

Panero, Francesco, 209, 228–29

Pannonia, 75–76, 79, 81, 108

Papebroch, Daniel, 4, 6

papyrus, 107

Paris, 16, 156, 159–60, 165, 188

Parma, 254

Paschasius, Roman deacon, 74

Passau, xxvii–xxviii, 19, 61–112, 121, 145–46, 250, 264, 266–68; canons of, 111

past, sense of the, xxviii–xxix, 256–61

Patzold, Steffen, 266

Pavia, 44, 199, 201, 207, 212, 229, 240–41, 248, 253

penance, 77; public, 202

Pennard, 150

Pentecost, 68, 113, 248

Perrecy, 186

Pershore, 123–24, 138–40, 151

Peter, advocate of Empress Adelheid, 214

Peter, bishop of Asti, 242

Peter, bishop of Como, 238–42, 245

Peter, bishop of Novara, 236, 238, 248, 251–52, 255

Peter, bishop of Vercelli, 193, 196–200, 202–4, 215, 217, 219–20, 226, 235, 243, 250, 253–55

Peter, papal legate, 184

Peter, saint, 26, 118, 130, 141–42, 170, 192

Peter the Deacon, 258–59, 261

Pfister, Christian, 173

Philae, 2

Piedmont, 19, 194–95, 197, 199–200, 208, 222, 236, 238, 241–42, 246–48, 254

Pilgrim, bishop of Passau, xxvii–xxix, 53, 61–112, 142, 170, 190, 210, 232, 250, 256, 266–68, 270–72; background and early education of, 63–68; knowledge of Salzburg sources of, xxviii, 65, 75–81

pious fraud (*pia fraus*), 5

Pippin I (alias Pippin III), Frankish ruler, 32–35, 37, 41, 52, 57
Pippin (I), mayor of the palace, 41
Pirmin, saint, 65, 70, 71
Pisa, Archivio storico diocesano, 57
plague, 120
Po, river, 194, 208, 212, 221–22, 224, 237–38, 240
Pombia, 195
Prague, 70
prayer clauses, 25, 116
preaching, 77
preamble, 11, 25–26, 33–35, 40, 84, 99, 114–15, 118, 125–27, 144–45, 163–64, 181–82, 205–6
prebend, 135
Preßburg, battle of (907). See Bratislava, battle of (907)
primacy, 175, 184, 190–91, 268–69
print, advent of, 3–4
priories, rights of, 187
private charters. See charters: 'private'
prohibition (immunity) clause, 11, 33–34, 41, 206
protection: papal, 153, 168, 185, 192; royal, 11, 54, 121, 192, 246–47
Protestantism, 61–62
protocol, 8–9, 11, 34, 42–43 n. 54, 45–46, 78 n. 46, 181, 231
protogothic minuscule, 128, 179
Prou, Maurice, 175, 177, 186
Prussia, 61–62
Prussian Academy of Sciences (Berlin), 61–62
Pseudo-Isidore, 166, 190, 262–63, 268
pseudo-original(s), 56–57, 82, 89, 91, 93, 145, 147, 150
publication (clause), 39, 84, 206

'Quadradula', 205, 224
Quattrocento, 19, 260
Quellenkritik, 61

Radulf, archbishop of Tours, 172
Raginfred, bishop of Bergamo, 203, 215, 254
Rainier, abbot (?of Fleury), 180
Ramackers, Johannes, 175–76
Ramsey, 159–60, 188
Ranger, Terrence, 16

Ranke, Leopold von, 61
Raoul Glaber, 235
Raoul of Burgundy, West Frankish ruler, 157
Rathsack, Mogens, 175–77
Ravenna, 42, 67, 197, 200, 208–9, 234, 237
recognition (clause), 11, 35, 49, 91, 99, 101, 105, 245
recognition sign, 11, 25, 35, 48, 84
referendarius, 107
reform: ecclesiastical, 233–34, 260; monastic, 23–25, 64–65, 113–14, 116–20, 137, 146, 152, 159–60, 265, 266; papal, 270–71
Regensburg, 69–70, 73, 77, 91, 96, 98, 100, 104, 247
Reggio, 213
Reginhard, bishop of Passau, 87
Regio. See Orco, estate
Regularis concordia, 121–22, 134, 137, 150, 188
Reichenau, 4–5, 29–30, 260
Reims, 22, 154–60, 168–69, 171–73, 175, 185, 189–90, 263, 268
Remensnyder, Amy, 16–17
Remigius, saint, 259
Reut, 91
Reuter, Timothy, 266–67, 271
Rheinland-Pfalz (Rhineland-Palatinate), 22
rhetor, antique, 259
Rhine, river, 19, 21–22, 26, 32, 76, 94, 154, 190–91, 264, 266
Rhineland, 26, 35, 76, 271–72
Rhine-Main-District, 22–23
Richard, bishop of Passau, 69
Richard, count (?of Ossola), 212
Riché, Pierre, 169
Richer of Saint-Remi, 154–55
Riches, Theo, 15, 267
Richgowo, bishop of Worms, 32
Rimbert, (arch)bishop of (Hamburg-) Bremen, 262–63
Ring cycle, 61
Robert I, West Frankish ruler, 155
Robertians, 154–58, 160. See also Capetian dynasty
Robert of Volpiano, 235
Robert the Pious (II), West Frankish/ French ruler, 156–58, 160, 166–72, 175,

179, 184, 191–92, 258; *Life* of, 171, 179, 184, 192

Rochester, 116, 124, 146–48, 151–52, 189; canons of, 147, 151, 189

Romagnano, 227–28

Romance speech, 66

Roman Empire, 21; Western, xxvii; Fall of, xxviii, 71

Rome, 13, 67, 80, 126, 153, 158, 167–70, 172–74, 182, 185, 192, 197–200, 202–3, 207, 209, 234, 240, 248; ancient, 1, 2, 121

Romnulf, abbot (?of Senones), 158

Romsey, 123–24, 138

Rosenberg, Marc, 49

rota(e), papal, 128–29

rotulus, 110

Rovasenda, 207

Rozala (Susana), wife of Robert the Pious, 167

Rozo, bishop of Treviso, 197

rubrication, 128, 135

Rudolf, count of Rimini, 197

Rudolf I, Burgundian ruler, 193–94

Rumble, Alex, 149

Rupert, bishop of Salzburg, 70

rustic capitals, 114, 128

Sabellian heresy, 115

Säben(-Brixen). *See* Brixen

Sabina, 234

Sacierges, 186

Saint-Aignan, 184

Saint-Basle-de-Verzy, council of (991), 156–59, 165–66, 168, 184, 190–91

Saint-Bénigne, Dijon, 246

Saint-Benoît-sur-Loire. *See* Fleury

Saint-Calais, 263

Saint-Denis, 4–5, 16, 107, 165, 167, 188, 261–62; council of (993/4), 167, 174, 184, 191; forgeries of, 107, 186, 188, 190–91

Saint-Martial, Limoges, 190

Saint-Martin, Tours, 161, 172

Saint-Maur-des-Fossés, 262

Saint-Remi, 154, 160, 190

Saint-Vaast, 187, 189, 191

Salian dynasty, 23, 26–27, 58–59, 170; castle of the (in Worms), 26–27, 59

Salvian of Marseilles, 5–6

Salzach, river, xxviii, 109

Salzburg, xxvii, 63, 65, 68–72, 74–81, 86–87, 91, 94, 98, 100, 102, 105–11, 264; forgeries of, 68, 105–6, 109, 264

Samuel, bishop of Worms, 32–33, 45

sanction, 11, 79, 88, 91, 125–26, 141–43, 145, 205–7; spiritual, 88; secular, 91. *See also* blessing-sanction

Santhià, 196, 204, 207, 210, 230, 233, 248, 249 n. 150; county of 206–7, 208–11, 231

Sapphira, 79

Savaric, bishop of Bath, 134–35

Saxony, 97, 250, 268; East, 22, 70

Schiaparelli, Luigi, 225–26

Schieffer, Theodor, 89

schoolmaster, 159

script imitation, xxviii–xxix, 13, 129, 147–48, 150, 152, 264. *See also* charters: imitative copies of

seal(s), 11, 13, 25, 28, 40, 47, 49, 86, 95, 99, 102, 222 n. 70, 230–31; false/forged, 84, 87, 89. *See also* charters: sealing of

'Second Decimation' charters, 126

Seguin, archbishop of Sens, 156–57, 161–62

Sehel Island, 1

Seine, river, 155–57, 261

Selsey, 146

Senlis, 154, 156

Sens, 156

Sesia, river, 19, 198, 212, 221, 230

Severin, saint, xvii, 71, 74; *Life* of, xxvii, 71, 74

Shaftesbury, 124

Shakespeare, 14

Shapbach, 49

shell company, 246

Sherborne, 134, 136

Sickel, Theodor, 4, 7, 30–32, 35, 37, 42, 46, 48, 50–51, 62

Sigehard, count of the Chiemgau, 63

Sigehardinger clan, 63

Sigismund, emperor, 56–57

simony, 115, 242

sin, 114–15, 118

sinthama charters, 149–50

Sippar, 1

Slavic (language), 66, 76. *See also* Elbe Slavs

Slovakia, 76
Snodland, 147, 151
Sohlingen, 250
Southern, Richard, 151, 261
Spain, 261, 265
Sparone, 247
Speyer, 22
Spoleto, 171
square capitals, 130, 231
square minuscule, 138
S. Ambrogio, 210, 222–23
S. Benigno Canavese. *See* Fruttuaria
S. Diogini, Milan, 242
S. Eusebio, Vercelli, 193, 202, 204, 218–19,
    224, 230, 236
S. Evasio, Casale Monferrato, 229
S. Maria, Pomposa, 237
S. Maria Maggiore, Vercelli, 218–19, 230
S. Maria del Senatore, Pavia, 221, 227
S. Michele, Pavia, 237, 240
S. Michele di Lucedio. *See* Lucedio
S. Michele in Marturi, 214
S. Pietro in Ciel d'Oro, 199–200, 210, 234;
    ordinances of, 199–200, 234
S. Salvatore, Lucca, 248
S. Salvatore, Pavia, 237–38, 248
S. Siro, Pavia, 241
SS Bonifacio ed Alessio, 168, 235. *See also*
    Leo, abbot of SS Bonifacio ed Alessio
St Albans, 124, 150–51, 261
St Florian, 98
St Gall, 196; *Annals* of, 196–97
St Germans, 124–25, 130, 137–38
St Maurice, Magdeburg. *See* Magdeburg
St Maximin, Trier, 23–25, 58, 261, 266
St Peter's, Ghent, 121
St Pölten, 98
staff, abbatial, 243
Starzer, Albert, 183
Stephen, saint, 77, 89, 94, 103, 111
Stephen I, Hungarian ruler, 111
Stephen II, pope, 187
subdeacon, 204
subscription: papal, 128; royal/imperial,
    11, 13, 36, 48–49, 84, 86, 91, 99, 101,
    105, 145, 232, 245
Suger of Saint-Denis, 258, 261
Sunningwell, 141
Susana, wife of Robert the Pious. *See* Rozala
    (Susana), wife of Robert the Pious

Swabia, 23, 29, 99
Switzerland, 240
Sylvester I, pope, 13
Sylvester II, pope, 202–3, 206, 209–10,
    234. *See also* Gerbert of Aurillac
Symmachus, pope, xxviii, 72–75, 77, 80
Syrus, bishop of Pavia, 251–52

Talbot, Robert, 128, 130 n. 46, 144
Tassilo (III), Bavarian duke, 82–83, 93, 99
Taunton, 150
Tavistock, 133, 135–36, 151
Tedevert, deacon of Ivrea, 223–24, 239–40,
    247
Tell Abu Habbah, 1
territorialisation, 54. *See also* immunity:
    'ban'/territorial
Thames, river, 19, 147
Thebes, 1
theodiscus, 67. *See also* German
Theodore, archbishop of Lorch, 72, 74
Theodore of Tarsus, archbishop of Can-
    terbury, 74
Theodoric, bishop of Metz, 94–95
Theodosius II, emperor, 2
Theodulf, bishop of Orléans, 161
Theophanu, empress, 106, 195, 236
Thierry of Amorbach, 165 n. 25
Thietmar of Merseburg, 248, 258
three orders, the, 166
Thurstan, abbot of Glastonbury, 134
Tigris, river, 1
Timothy, apostle, 5–6
tithes, 165–66
toll(s), 33–42, 45–46, 51–56, 59–60, 102–3,
    203, 272; comital third of, 34, 40, 55
Tours, 160
Tout, T. F., 5
trade, 21–22, 34
tradition: invention of, 16; missionary, 70;
    oral, 16
Trecate, 227, 229
Trier, 25, 58, 76, 78, 190, 261
tudun, Avar office, 76
Turin, 224, 238, 240, 243
'Tutund', 76
Tyburn, 146

Uhlirz, Karl, 31–32, 43–44, 62, 82, 89
uncial(s), 227, 231

United States, 16–17
Urolf, (arch)bishop of Lorch, 72, 75–76, 89

Vajk I, Hungarian ruler, 111
Van Buren, Martin, 17
vassals, episcopal, 253
Veneto, 197
Venice, 197
Vercellese, 248
Vercelli, xxviii–xxix, 19, 193–255, 264,
    266–68; Archivio Capitolare in, 215;
    canons of, 197–98, 203, 210, 214–21,
    226, 230, 238; cathedral chapter of,
    217–18, 254–55; cathedral library of,
    240; Commune of, 231, 233, 254;
    martyrology-necrology of, 219–20,
    238; sack of by the Hungarians (899),
    211
Verona, 248
Vesle, river, 155
Viale Giacomo Matteotti, 199
vicar, papal, 76–79, 108, 110, 268, 270
Vidier, Alexandre, 175, 177, 185
vidimus. See inspection (of charters)
Vienna, 62, 86, 94
Vignodelli, Giacomo, 215–16
vikings, 115, 120, 135, 155
violence, 164
Virgin Mary. See Mary, Virgin
Vittorio Emanuele II, Italian king, 247
Vivulo, bishop of Passau, 93
Vollziehungsstrich. See completion
    stroke
Volpiano: brothers, 236, 240, 246, 250;
    estate, 236
Vosloo, Arnold, 2
Vulpara/Vuplaria, 229

Wachau, 94, 98
Wagner, Richard, 61
Walderich, bishop of Passau, 82–83, 85
Walsham, Alexandra, 260
Walter, archbishop of Sens, 156
Warmund, bishop of Ivrea, 200, 235–36,
    238, 243, 246–48
Wars of Religion, French, 165
Washington, George, 16–17
Watchet, 120
Watling Street, 261
Wattenbach, Wilhelm, 61

Weingarteiba, 59
Weißenburg, 22
Werner, Karl Ferdinand, 171
Wessex, 116
West, Charles, 270
West Francia, 26, 153–54, 262. See also
    France
Westminster, 146, 150, 259
Wherwell, 136
Whitsun. See Pentecost
Wibald of Stavelot, 53
Wiching, bishop of Passau, 93
Widukind of Corvey, 26–27
Willa, wife of Berengar of Ivrea, 194
William, abbot of Fleury, 185, 189–90
William of Malmesbury, 135, 150
William of Volpiano, 226, 235–36, 240,
    243–47, 272; Life of, 226. See also
    Volpiano: brothers
William the Conqueror, 138
Willigis, archbishop of Mainz, 76–77
Willigis C, draftsman-scribe, 53, 62, 65,
    83–84, 89–91, 106
Wiltshire, 131
Wimpfen, 27, 32–33, 37, 42, 45–46, 49,
    52, 54, 59
Winchester, 113–14, 120; council of (c.
    960), 114, 121; council of (Pentecost
    993), 113–16. See also New Minster,
    Winchester; Old Minster, Winchester
wine, 21
Wisund, bishop of (Säben-)Brixen, 73, 77
witness-list(s), 8, 114, 120, 125–31, 134 n.
    57, 135, 138, 142, 144–45, 147–48
Wolfhere of Hildesheim, 63–65
Wolfram, Herwig, 112
Worcester, 123–24, 130 n. 46, 138, 146, 150
Worms, xxviii–xxix, 19, 21–60, 62, 68–70,
    82, 95, 107, 111–12, 121, 145–46, 170, 211,
    264, 266–67; canons of, 59; cartulary
    of, 35, 40, 41–42, 46, 49, 56; dissolution
    of bishopric of (1803), 56; mint at,
    34–35; Roman ruins at, 58; royal/
    imperial palace at, 21, 26; sack of
    (1689), 56
Wormsgau, 46
Wulfgar, abbot of Abingdon, 113–14, 116,
    140–41, 145, 261, 272
Wulfgar, bishop of Ramsbury, 114–15
Wulfhere, Mercian ruler, 146

Wulfred, archbishop of Canterbury, 262
Wulfric Cufing, Berkshire magnate, 144
Würzburg, 22

Yèvre-la-Châtel, 163
Yèvre-la-Ville, 163, 167–68, 185

Yonne, river, 156
York, 113

Zeiselmauer, 86–87, 89, 94, 98
Zeitz, 70
Zimmermann, Harald, 1975

INDEX OF ROYAL AND PAPAL CHARTERS

(INCLUDING JUDICIAL NOTICES)

CDL, iii.1, ed. Brühl, no. 8	211, 225–26
D Ard 1	237
D Ard 2	238–39
D Ard 3	238–39
D Ard 4	238–39
D Ard 6	238
D Ard 7	245n138
D Ard 8	223–24, 245n138
D Ard 9	241–45
D Ard 10	241–42, 245
D Arn 157	46
D Arn 161	89
D Arn 166	32, 35
D Arn 184	68
D Arn 192	33, 46, 52, 57, 60
D Ber 64	225
D Ber 87	218n59, 223, 226n81
D BerAd 3	222
D H II 20	59
D H II 74	240–41 (with 242n131)
D H II 75	241 (with 242n131)
D H II 95	223
D H II 120	246–47
D H II 132	223–24, 226n81, 247
D H II 226	59
D H II 227	59
D H II 305	247n141
D H II 306	248
D H II 319	59
D H II 320	227, 248, 251–52
D H II 321	211–12, 229, 248, 251–52
D H II 322	211–12, 217, 235, 250–52
D H II 336	248n147, 252
D H II 337	248n147, 252
D H II 494	247
D H III 317	222
D H III 328	220n64, 228
D H IV 320	229
D HuLo 64	222
D HuLo 73	218
D HuLo 81	210, 218, 221
D K I 37	46
D K II 58	242 (with 243n133)
D K II 70	247n141
D K II 84	228
D K II 147	223, 228
D K III 54	211, 226–27
D K III 134	98
D K III 135	91
D Kar 20	32, 33–34
D Kar 169	82–83, 111–12
D Kar 247	82–86
D Kar 257	32
D L D 7	86n67
D L D 9	87
D L D 22	86–87, 91, 98
D L D 74a	32, 34–35, 46, 52
D L D 74b	33, 42
D L D 179	33, 45–46, 57
D L Fr 25	28–30, 34, 51–53
D L Fr 31	182n68
D L Fr 142	182
D L Fr 225 (II)	86–89
D L Fr 282	32, 41–42
D L K 84	89
D L K 85	68
D Lo 41	225
D Mer 30	32, 34n34
D O I 84	32, 35–37, 39–40
D O I 138	222
D O I 151	27–28
D O I 161	24, 42
D O I 251	196, 221
D O I 260	213
D O I 272	213
D O I 310	9–10, 24–26, 29, 42
D O I 330	46–49
D O I 331	48–49
D O I 332	48–49
D O I 388b	42–45
D O I 389	65–67
D O I 392	33, 42–45
D O I 423	94–95
D O I 431	96n85
D O II 27	94–95
D O II 44	95–96

D O II 46	32, 37–40	D O III 389	209, 234
D O II 55	49n69	D O III 416	237 (with 237–38n119)
D O II 59	96–97	D O III 419	237 (with 237–38n119)
D O II 111a	83, 97–98	JE 2328	187
D O II 111b	83, 97–98	JE 2495	77–78
D O II 123	49n69	JE 2498	75
D O II 134	49n69, 100–1	JE 2503	77–78, 80
D O II 135	49n69, 98–99, 101	JE 2558	74–75
D O II 136a	99–101	JE 2570	177–86
D O II 136b	101–2, 103	JE 2580	77
D O II 137	102–3	JE 2566	72, 75–77
D O II 138	103	JE 2681	77
D O II 140	49n69	JE 3182	168
D O II 142	49n69	JK 767	72, 73–75
D O II 143	49–50	JL 3602	72, 77
D O II 165	68n18, 105–6	JL 3606	168, 190
D O II 167a	104–6	JL 3614	72–73, 77–78
D O II 167b	104–6	JL 3644	73
D O II 199	40, 55	JL 3690	78
D O II 279	27	JL 3752	150
D O III 50	221	JL 3767	108
D O III 112	91	JL 3771	73, 80–81
D O III 115	91	JL 3784	76–77
D O III 194	197	JL 3803	177, 186–87
D O III 201	198	JL 3872	173–75, 180–83, 185, 190
D O III 236	222	JL 3896	182
D O III 237	234	JL 3950	243, 247n141
D O III 264	203, 215, 218n59	JL 3958	184
D O III 266	222 (with n70)	JL 3989	184
D O III 276	234	JL 3960	184
D O III 277	234	JL 3961	184
D O III 281	199–200, 234	JL 4007	243n134
D O III 282	234	JL 4065	182
D O III 303	199–200, 234–35	JL 4083a	247n141
D O III 323	203–6, 211–12, 217, 223	JL 4212	172–73
D O III 324	206–7	JL 4708	175
D O III 329	234	*Placiti*, ed. Manaresi, no. II	226
D O III 330	209, 235		
D O III 331	234	*Placiti*, ed. Manaresi, no. 226	212, 214, 215
D O III 332	234		
D O III 340	234	*Placiti*, ed. Manaresi, no. 230*	212, 215–17
D O III 341	209n44, 235		
D O III 374	236	*Placiti*, ed. Manaresi, no. 236	203, 234
D O III 375	237		
D O III 376	236	*Placiti*, ed. Manaresi, no. 254	234
D O III 383	196, 207–8		
D O III 384	208, 223	*Placiti*, ed. Manaresi, no. 263	237
D O III 388	209		

* Now best consulted in the new critical edition in Vignodelli, 'Prima di Leone', 74–77.

Placiti, ed. Manaresi,		S 732	144–45
no. 266	235	S 733	144–45
Placiti, ed. Manaresi,		S 734	144–45
no. 269	241	S 736	138
Recueil Fleury,		S 745	117–18
no. 69	160	S 757	143–44
Recueil Fleury,		S 758	143–44
no. 70	163–64, 165	S 759	143–44
Recueil Lothaire et Louis V,		S 760	143–44
no. 27	160	S 778	145
Recueil Lothaire et Louis V,		S 786	123, 138–40
no. 28	160	S 788	123, 138
Recueil Lothaire et Louis V,		S 812	123, 138
no. 34	160	S 825	150
Recueil Lothaire et Louis V,		S 829	145
no. 70	160	S 838	135–36
Recueil Philippe Ier,		S 856	151n115
no. 55	160n19	S 860	151n115
S 93	142	S 861	151n115
S 136	150–51	S 872	151n115
S 136a	150–51	S 876	114–16, 123, 125, 130,
S 166	141–42		138, 143n84
S 183	141–42	S 878	130
S 229	149	S 880	124, 125, 130, 136, 138
S 236	150	S 881	151n115
S 275	149	S 883	151n115
S 278	145	S 884	134
S 376	148	S 891	124, 151n115
S 409	144	S 892	125
S 443	149–50	S 893	124, 147
S 447	130n45	S 895	136
S 449	130n45	S 896	151n115
S 540	148–49	S 899	124
S 544	130n46	S 901	151n115
S 550	130n46	S 902	151n115
S 567	142–43	S 904	134n58, 136
S 583	143	S 905	130
S 605	142–43	S 906	124
S 654	143	S 911	130n48, 134n58, 136–37
S 658	123	S 912	124
S 671	147–48	S 916	130, 151
S 673	123	S 918	140
S 687	127	S 922	130
S 690	125, 142n83	S 926	151n115
S 703	125	S 927	151n115
S 729	134–35	S 937	124, 140, 151n115

A NOTE ON THE TYPE

THIS BOOK has been composed in Miller, a Scotch Roman typeface designed by Matthew Carter and first released by Font Bureau in 1997. It resembles Monticello, the typeface developed for The Papers of Thomas Jefferson in the 1940s by C. H. Griffith and P. J. Conkwright and reinterpreted in digital form by Carter in 2003.

Pleasant Jefferson ("P. J.") Conkwright (1905–1986) was Typographer at Princeton University Press from 1939 to 1970. He was an acclaimed book designer and AIGA Medalist.

The ornament used throughout this book was designed by Pierre Simon Fournier (1712–1768) and was a favorite of Conkwright's, used in his design of the *Princeton University Library Chronicle*.